The Coriolis Group, LLC • 14455 North Hayden Road, Suite 220 • Scottsdale, Arizona 85260

A Note from Coriolis

Coriolis Technology Press was founded to create a very elite group of books: the ones you keep closest to your machine. In the real world, you have to choose the books you rely on every day *very* carefully, and we understand that.

To win a place for our books on that coveted shelf beside your PC, we guarantee several important qualities in every book we publish. These qualities are:

- *Technical accuracy*—It's no good if it doesn't work. Every Coriolis Technology Press book is reviewed by technical experts in the topic field, and is sent through several editing and proofreading passes in order to create the piece of work you now hold in your hands.

- *Innovative editorial design*—We've put years of research and refinement into the ways we present information in our books. Our books' editorial approach is uniquely designed to reflect the way people learn new technologies and search for solutions to technology problems.

- *Practical focus*—We put only pertinent information into our books and avoid any fluff. Every fact included between these two covers must serve the mission of the book as a whole.

- *Accessibility*—The information in a book is worthless unless you can find it quickly when you need it. We put a lot of effort into our indexes, and heavily cross-reference our chapters, to make it easy for you to move right to the information you need.

Here at The Coriolis Group we have been publishing and packaging books, technical journals, and training materials since 1989. We have put a lot of thought into our books; please write to us at **ctp@coriolis.com** and let us know what you think. We hope that you're happy with the book in your hands, and that in the future, when you reach for software development and networking information, you'll turn to one of our books first.

Coriolis Technology Press
The Coriolis Group
14455 N. Hayden Road, Suite 220
Scottsdale, Arizona
85260

Email: ctp@coriolis.com
Phone: (480) 483-0192
Toll free: (800) 410-0192

Look for these related books from The Coriolis Group:

Visual Basic .NET Programming with Peter Aiken
By Peter Aiken and Bonnie Biafore

Visual Studio .NET: The .NET Framework Black Book
By Julian Templeman and David Vitter

C# Core Language Little Black Book
By Bill Wagner

Also Recently Published by Coriolis Technology Press:

Windows XP Professional—The Ultimate User's Guide
By Joli Ballew

Windows 2000 System Administrator's Black Book, Second Edition
By Deborah Haralson, Stu Sjouwerman, Barry Shilmover, and James Michael Stewart

Mac OS X Version 10.1 Black Book
By Mark R. Bell and Debrah Suggs

C# Black Book
By Matthew Telles

To Nancy, of course, with thanks for seven wonderful years, and with anticipation for the next seventy.

About the Author

Steven Holzner is an award-winning author and master programmer who's been writing about Visual Basic even before version 1.0 went public. He's written 68 books on computing, and is a former contributing editor to *PC Magazine*, but Visual Basic is his favorite topic. His books have been translated into 16 languages around the world and sold over a million and a half copies. Holzner gives corporate seminars and training on programming around the country, and has his own Internet software company.

Steven graduated from MIT and received his PhD from Cornell. He's also been on the faculty of both MIT and Cornell. Steven loves to travel, and has been to more than 30 countries from Afghanistan to India, from Borneo to Iran, from Sweden to Thailand, with more to come. He and Nancy live in a small, picturesque town on the New England coast.

Acknowledgments

The book you are holding is the result of many people's dedication. I would especially like to thank Sean Tape, Managing Editor, who did such a great job of bringing this project together and shepherding it along, as well as Kim Eoff, Production Manager, Wendy Littley, Production Supervisor, and Meg Turecek, Production Coordinator, who kept things on track; Mary Swistara, the copyeditor who waded though everything and got it into such good shape; Jennifer Ashley, who proofread the book and helped polish the final product. Special thanks to Kourosh Ardestani for the terrific tech edit. Thanks to all: great job

Contents at a Glance

Table of Contents

Chapter 3
The Visual Basic Language: Procedures, Scope, and Exception Handling 109

In Depth

Immediate Solutions

Chapter 6
Windows Forms: Buttons, Checkboxes, Radio Buttons, Panels, and Group Boxes

Chapter 8
Windows Forms: Scroll Bars, Splitters, Track Bars, Pickers, Notify Icons, Tool Tips, and Timers

Chapter 10
Windows Forms: Image Lists, Tree and List Views, Toolbars, Status and Progress Bars, and Tab Controls 427

Chapter 11
Object-Oriented Programming 479

In Depth

Chapter 21
Binding Controls to Databases 885

Chapter 25
Creating Windows Services, Web Services, and Deploying Applications 1057

Introduction

Welcome to your Visual Basic .NET support package. That's what this book has been written to be: your complete Visual Basic .NET support package. It has been designed to be the one you turn to first, the one that gives you more of what you want than any other.

I've crammed as much Visual Basic .NET into this book as possible, broken down into hundreds of easily-accessible topics, each short and to the point, and each with an example. The format here is like no other computer book series, and it's designed to give you exactly what you want, when you want it.

And that's not an easy job, because the subject of this book, Visual Basic .NET, is huge. I've used and written about Visual Basic even before version 1.0 came out and in those 10 years, Visual Basic has grown in power and complexity enormously. The changes in Visual Basic .NET are immense, and this book has been entirely rewritten from its predecessor, the *Visual Basic 6 Black Book*.

That book was a bestseller, but this, the entirely new edition, is far better. (At least in my opinion, and I wrote both books.) There's much more material here, in greater depth, and there are many more of the programming "nuggets" that programmers want to see.

This book has been designed to give you the Visual Basic .NET coverage you just won't find in any other book. Other books often omit not only the larger topics, like deploying your program after you've created it, but also the smaller ones like covering just about every Windows and Web control that comes with Visual Basic .NET in depth—from the text box control to three-state checkboxes, from date-time pickers to hot tracking tab controls, and from Web page validation controls to ad rotators. And the advanced topics are here too, like creating your own Windows and Web controls, writing Windows and Web services, distributed data applications, multithreading, deploying applications, and more.

How This Book Works

The task-based format we use in this book is the one many programmers appreciate, because programming is a task-based business. Rather than reading about subjects in the order I might think best, you can go directly to your topic of interest and find the bite-sized nugget of information you need.

And best of all, there's a working example in code for almost every programming topic in the book. The actual process of programming is not abstract; it's very applied, and so instead of vague generalities, we get down to the specifics—all the specifics—that give you everything you need to understand and use Visual Basic .NET.

In the old days, programming books used to be very top-down, with chapters on subjects like "Conditional Branching," "Loop Structures," "Variable Declarations," and so forth. But who sits down to program by saying, "I'm about to create a conditional program flow branch"?

Instead, programmers are more interested in performing useful tasks, like adding buttons, menus, list boxes, or toolbars to a window; creating graphics animation; creating dialog boxes; creating setup programs; working with files; linking to Web pages; multi-threading; supporting online help; and so on. And this book is written for programmers.

Because this book is written for programmers, each chapter is broken up into dozens of practical programming tasks. After selecting the chapter you want, you can turn to the Table of Contents, the Index, or the first page in that chapter to find the task you're interested in. Hundreds of tasks are covered in this book, chosen to be the ones that programmers want to see.

In addition, this book is filled with examples—nearly *eight hundred* examples—covering nearly every Visual Basic .NET programming area there is. These examples are bite-sized and to the point, so you don't have to wade through a dozen files trying to understand one simple topic. And they're as comprehensive as I could make them, covering every programming area in the book.

What's in This Book

Just about everything we could write about Visual Basic .NET is in this book, and that's a lot of ground to cover. From a complete language reference to ADO.NET database programming, from creating Web applications to dragging and dropping data adapters onto forms, and from creating Windows and Web controls to setup programs, it's all here (or almost all of it anyway!).

Here's some of what we'll see in this book:

- The Visual Basic Integrated Development Environment (IDE)
- The Complete Visual Basic Syntax
- Using Structured Exception Handling
- Exception Filtering in the Catch Block
- Throwing Exceptions

- Creating Windows Applications
- Creating Web Applications
- Showing and Hiding Controls and Forms
- Working with Multiple Forms
- Creating Multiple Document Interface (MDI) Applications
- Creating Dialog Boxes
- Creating Owned Forms
- Anchoring and Docking Controls
- Adding and Removing Controls at Run Time
- Creating Always-on-Top Forms
- Sending Keystrokes to Other Programs
- Setting the Mouse Pointer
- Using nearly every Windows and Web control available, from text boxes to file dialog boxes, from list boxes to three-state checkboxes, from toggle buttons to splitters, and from ad rotators to validation controls
- Creating Menus
- Creating Submenus
- Creating Menu Access Keys
- Changing a Menu Item's Caption at Run Time
- Drawing Menu Items Yourself
- Merging MDI Menus
- Creating Context Menus
- Printing
- Creating Tree Views
- Creating List Views
- Creating Toolbars
- Hot Tracking Tabs
- Object-Oriented Programming (OOP)
- Creating Classes, Objects, OOP Structures, Modules, and Constructors
- Creating Data Members, Methods, Properties, and Events
- Overloading Methods
- Creating Class Libraries
- Inheriting from a Base Class

- Creating User Controls
- Creating Web User Controls
- Creating Multithreaded Applications
- Starting, Suspending, Resuming, Stopping, and Sleeping Threads
- Synchronizing Threads
- Joining Threads
- Creating a Windows Service
- Creating a Windows Service Installer
- Creating a Web Service
- Deploying Applications

In addition, the CD that accompanies this book holds the code for all the major projects we develop—to see how to use those projects, take a look at the readme.txt file on the CD. All the examples in this book have been tested by at least two people on two different machines, and each example has been carefully verified to work as it should. (Here's an important note—in the past, Microsoft has changed Visual Basic without changing major or minor version number, and these unannounced changes have meant that people with the new Visual Basic can't get some examples in the book to work—see the readme.txt file on the CD for more details. I try my best to keep up with these unannounced changes, but you should know that all the examples in the book have been fully tested—if you get compilation errors with an example, one thing to check is if Visual Basic itself has been changed. If you suspect it has, please send me email via Coriolis at once so I can get a fix up on the book's Web site quickly for everyone else.)

That's just some of what's coming up—Visual Basic .NET is a big topic, and the topics we'll cover number in the hundreds. And if you have suggestions for more, please send them in!

Conventions

There are a few conventions in this book that you should know about. For example, when some code is new and should be especially pointed out, it'll appear shaded. And when there's more code that I'm not showing to save space, you'll see three dots arranged vertically like at the end of this example:

```
Public Class Form1
    Inherits System.Windows.Forms.Form

#Region " Windows Form Designer generated code "
```

```
Public Sub New()
    MyBase.New()
    .
    .
    .
```

Also, when we discuss the in-depth syntax of Visual Basic statements, there are a few conventions and terms you should be aware of. In the formal definition of each statement, you use brackets, [and], for optional items, and curly braces, { and }, to indicate that you select one of the enclosed items, like this for the **Dim** statement:

```
[{ Public | Protected | Friend | Protected Friend | Private | Static }] [
Shared ] [ Shadows ] [ ReadOnly ] Dim [ WithEvents ] name[ (boundlist) ]
[ As [ New ] type ] [ = initexpr ]
```

And I use the standard syntax for menu items—for example, the File|New item refers to the New item in the File menu. You'll also see many tips throughout the book, which are meant to give you something more—more insight and more be-hind-the-scenes data. Tips look like this one from Chapter 23:

TIP: *Needing a server roundtrip to access your data can slow things down considerably. The Internet Explorer actually does have a number of data source objects that you can use to work with recordsets directly with scripting languages in the browser. One of the data source objects built into the Internet Explorer, the Remote Data Service (RDS), even lets you use connection strings, SQL, and so on, to fill a recordset object. For an example that uses the Internet Explorer XML data source object, which lets you read database files written in XML, see "Using XML-Format Databases Directly in the Internet Explorer" in this chapter.*

And you'll also see notes, which are designed to give you some additional infor-mation, like this note in Chapter 1:

NOTE: *In Visual Basic 6.0, coordinates for forms and controls were expressed in twips; in Visual Basic .NET, coordinates are expressed in pixels (and only pixels).*

What You'll Need

To use this book, you'll need Visual Basic .NET. In addition, if you want to create Web applications and services, you'll also need a Web server running the Microsoft Internet Information Server (IIS), as detailed in Chapter 14. IIS can be running on your local machine, and it comes with some Windows versions, such as Windows 2000. (Note that although comes on the Windows 2000 CDs, it may not have been installed on your machine by your computer's manufacturer.)

To work with databases, you'll need to use a data provider, as discussed in Chapter 20. I use SQL Server here, but you can use other providers. (However, note that most database examples that use a connection to a data provider use the pubs example database that comes with SQL Server.) Knowing some SQL will be a good idea to work with data applications. (You'll find an SQL primer in Chapter 20—see "Using Basic SQL" in that chapter.)

Also, now that Visual Basic works with browsers as easily as with Windows itself, knowing HTML becomes an issue. I've written an entire HTML 4.01 reference, htmlref.html, which you'll find on this book's CD, but if that's not enough, take a look at a good book on HTML, such as the Coriolis *HTML Black Book*.

At times, we'll make a small amount of use of regular expressions for text pattern matching, and JavaScript for client-side code in Web applications. You don't need to know either to read this book, but if you want more depth, take a look at the Coriolis *Perl Black Book* for all the details on regular expressions, and the Coriolis *HTML Black Book* for several chapters on JavaScript.

Resources

Where can you go for additional Visual Basic support? You can find Visual Basic user groups all over, and more are appearing every day. Although the content varies in accuracy, there are many usenet groups dedicated to Visual Basic as well, but be careful what you read there—there's no guarantee it's accurate. About three dozen of those groups are hosted by Microsoft, including the following:

- microsoft.public.dotnet.languages.vb
- microsoft.public.dotnet.languages.vb.upgrade
- microsoft.public.vb.bugs
- microsoft.public.vb.addins
- microsoft.public.vb.controls
- microsoft.public.vb.database
- microsoft.public.vb.installation
- microsoft.public.vb.syntax

Other, non-Microsoft groups include some of these usenet forums:

- comp.lang.basic.visual
- comp.lang.basic.visual.3rdparty
- comp.lang.basic.visual.announce
- comp.lang.basic.visual.database
- comp.lang.basic.visual.misc

And, of course, there are plenty of Web pages out there on Visual Basic. Here are a few starter pages from Microsoft:

- **http://msdn.microsoft.com/vbasic/** The main Visual Basic page
- **http://msdn.microsoft.com/vbasic/technical/articles.asp** The tech page for Visual Basic
- **www.microsoft.com/net/default.asp** The home page for the .NET initiative

And that it; that's all the introduction we need—it's time to start digging into Visual Basic .NET now. As I said, this book has been designed to be your complete support package for Visual Basic .NET, so if you see something that should be covered and isn't—let me know. In the meantime, happy programming!

Chapter 1

Essential Visual Basic

Welcome to our big book on Visual Basic. It's no secret that Visual Basic is the most popular programming tool available today. And it's also no secret that there have been massive changes in the latest version, Visual Basic .NET. If you've read previous editions of this book, you'll find a lot that's new here—in fact, just about *everything* is new. Almost this entire book has been rewritten.

Why the big change? The reason is Visual Basic itself, which has now become Visual Basic .NET (also called VB .NET). The difference between Visual Basic .NET and the previous version, Visual Basic 6.0, is revolutionary and far reaching. Visual Basic .NET has been almost three years in the making, and it represents entirely new directions for Visual Basic. Besides the biggest change—integrated support for Web development—the very syntax of Visual Basic has undergone tremendous changes. A great number of techniques that you've probably learned carefully are now completely different, such as data handling, and many controls, project types, and other aspects of Visual Basic 6.0 are no longer available at all. All of which means that there's a terrific amount of material we need to cover—so I'm going to pack as much Visual Basic .NET into this book as will fit.

Our coverage of the new Visual Basic is not going to be like some other books that hold their topic at an arm's length and just give you dry documentation. This book is written from the programmer's point of view, for programmers, and I'm going to try to give you as much of the good stuff as I can. I use Visual Basic .NET a lot myself, and I know that to master this subject, nothing is better than an in-depth treatment with many examples and tips that will save you a lot of time.

Visual Basic has a long and, so far, glorious history. When it first appeared, it created a revolution in Windows programming. Visual Basic introduced unheard-of ease to Windows programming—just build the program you want, right before your eyes, and then run it. In so doing, it changed programming from a chore to something very like fun.

In time, Visual Basic has gotten more complex, as well as more powerful. Today, it's more complex than ever, and if you've used Visual Basic 6.0, you may be surprised at all the new additions. In this book, you'll see how to use Visual Basic in a task-oriented way, which is the best way to write about programming. Instead of superimposing some abstract structure on the material in this book, I'll organize it the way programmers want it—task by task.

I'll start with an overview of Visual Basic, taking a look at topics common to the material in the rest of the book. In this chapter, we'll create the foundation we'll rely on later as we take a look at the basics of Visual Basic. This includes learning how to create Visual Basic projects, seeing what's in such projects, seeing what's new in Visual Basic .NET, getting an overview of essential Visual Basic .NET concepts such as Windows and Web forms, controls, events, properties, methods, and so on. Note, however, that I'll assume you have at least a little experience with Visual Basic and programming in this chapter.

I'll also give you a guided tour of the Visual Basic Integrated Development Environment—the IDE—that we'll be using continuously throughout this book. The IDE is what you see when you start Visual Basic, and it's where you develop your applications and debug them. Understanding the IDE and how to use it—and mastering some fundamental Visual Basic concepts—will give us the foundation we need for the rest of the book.

Many Visual Basic programmers do not have formal programming training, so they have to learn a lot of this material the hard way. As programming has matured, programmers have learned more about what are called "best practices"— the programming techniques that make robust, easily debugged programs. We'll take a look at those practices in this chapter, because they are becoming more essential for programmers in commercial environments these days, especially those programmers who work in teams. And we'll look at those practices from the viewpoint of programmers who program for a living, because frequently there's a gap between the way best practices are taught by academics and how they are actually needed by programmers facing the prospect of writing a 20,000 line program as part of a programming team.

Before we start covering all the details in Visual Basic in depth, let's take a look at an example first. Rather than getting lost in the details, let's see Visual Basic at work immediately. Because there are so many details one has to master, it's easy to forget that Visual Basic is there to make things as easy as possible for you. In fact, as stated earlier, programming in Visual Basic can be as close to *fun* as programming gets.

Putting Visual Basic to Work

Start Visual Basic now. You'll see the Visual Basic Integrated Development Environment appear, as in Figure 1.1. I'm not going to go into the details here, because we'll cover them later in this chapter—right now, let's just have a little fun.

Generally speaking, there are three types of applications in Visual Basic—those based on Windows forms (such applications are usually local to your machine), Web forms (that come to you across the Internet), and console applications (that run in a DOS window). I'll take a look at Windows forms here first, as those will be the most familiar to Visual Basic 6.0 programmers.

Creating a Windows Application

To create an application based on Windows forms, select the New item in the File menu, then select the Project item in the submenu that appears. This brings up the New Project dialog box you see in Figure 1.2.

Select the folder labeled Visual Basic Projects in the Project Types box, as shown in Figure 1.2, and select the Windows Application project type in the Templates box. You also can name the new project—I'll name it WinHello—and specify where

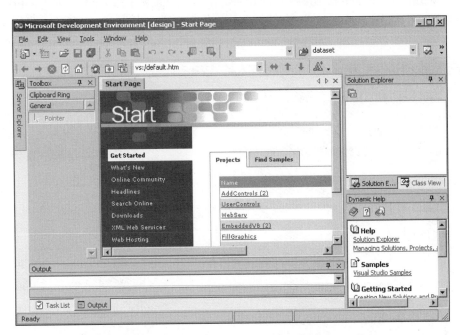

Figure 1.1   The Visual Basic Integrated Development Environment.

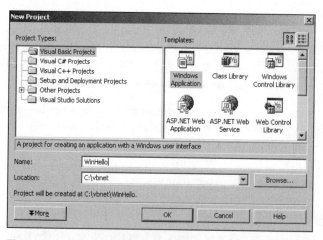

Figure 1.2   The Visual Basic New Project dialog box.

to store it—I'll store it in the c:\vbnet folder, as you see in Figure 1.2. Now click the OK button to create this new Visual Basic project. Visual Basic creates a new Windows project and gives you the result you see in Figure 1.3.

The window you see at the center of Figure 1.3, labeled **Form1**, is the window that will become our new Windows application; in Visual Basic, as you most likely know, these windows are called *forms*. The genius of Visual Basic has always

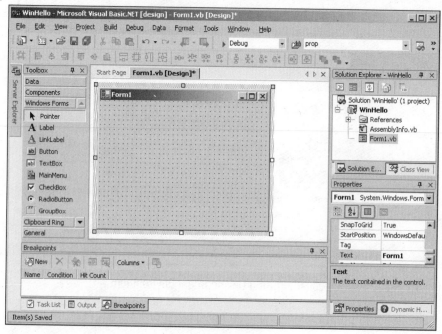

Figure 1.3   Designing a new Windows application.

been that it's *visual*, of course, which means that you can design your applications visually. In this case, I'll just add two Windows *controls* to this form—a text box and a button. When you click the button, the application will display the text "Hello from Visual Basic" in the text box.

Controls, of course, are user-interface elements that you see in Windows all the time, such as list boxes, scroll bars, button, menus, and so on. To add a text box to Form1, first make sure that the Visual Basic *toolbox* is open. You can see the toolbox to the left of Form1 in Figure 1.3; if you don't see the toolbox, select the View|Toolbox menu item to display it. Now click the Windows Forms item in the toolbox so the toolbox displays the possible controls you can use in Windows forms, such as text boxes, buttons, labels, link labels, and so on.

In a move that's very familiar to Visual Basic programmers, you can now simply *drag* a text box from the toolbox to Form1, or just double-click the TextBox entry in the toolbox. This adds a text box to Form1; position and stretch it with the mouse until it appears roughly as you see in Figure 1.4. (The boxes you see around the text box are *sizing handles*, and if you've used Visual Basic at all, you know you can use them to change the shape of the text box.)

Next, add a button to Form1 in the same manner, as illustrated in Figure 1.5. Visual Basic 6.0 programmers can already see many differences here—including

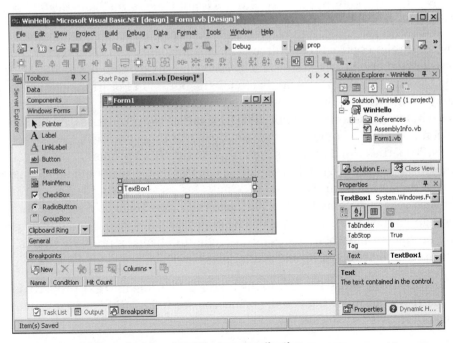

Figure 1.4   Adding a text box to a Windows application.

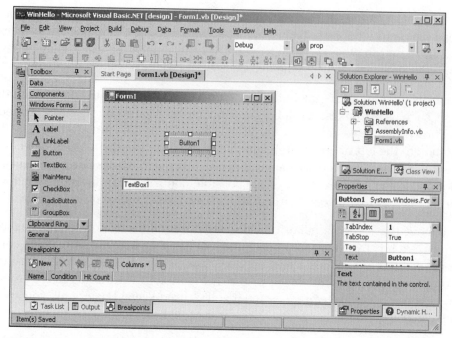

Figure 1.5   Adding a button to a Windows application.

the fact that the button is labeled **Button1**, not **Command1**, and the text box is labeled **TextBox1**, not **Text1**.

These are the controls that will appear in our application. The next step is to customize them; in this case, start by changing the caption of the button from "Button1" to "Click Me." To do that, click the button in Form1 to select it so the fuzzy outline you see in Figure 1.5 appears around it. Next, move to the Properties window at the lower right of the IDE; this lists the properties of the currently selected control or object (if you can't see the Properties window, select the View|Properties Window menu item). Click the **Text** property (no longer the **Caption** property of Visual Basic 6.0) in the Properties window, and change the text of the button from "Button1" to "Click Me," as you see in Figure 1.6. You set *properties* of objects such as this button to customize them, and we'll be doing so throughout the book. The Properties window lists properties like the **Text** property on the left and their values on the right; to change a property's value, you only have to edit its setting and press Enter.

In the same way, erase the text in the text box by using its **Text** property in the Properties window, giving you the result you see in Figure 1.7, where the text in both controls is as we want it.

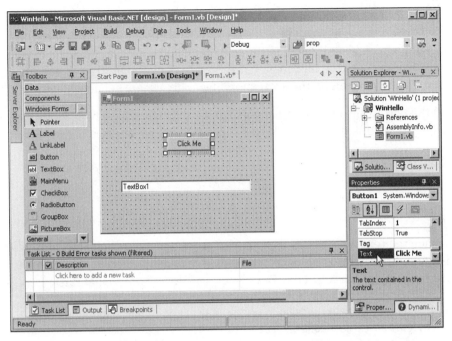

Figure 1.6   Customizing button text.

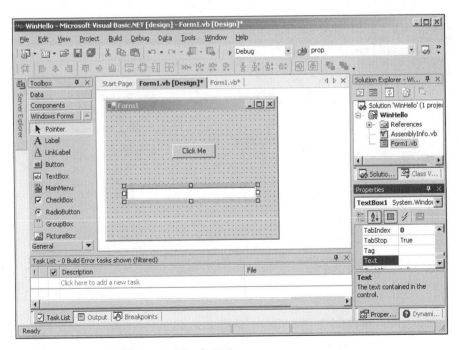

Figure 1.7   Customizing a text box's text.

Visual Basic has done a lot of programming for us to get us to this point, but it can't do everything; in particular, it's up to us to add some code to place the message "Hello from Visual Basic" in the text box when the user clicks the button. To associate code with the button, you just double-click the button, as you would in Visual Basic 6.0, opening the corresponding code, as you see in Figure 1.8.

Find the part of the code that handles clicks of the button, which looks like this (this will also look different to Visual Basic 6.0 programmers):

```
Private Sub Button1_Click(ByVal sender As System.Object, ByVal e As _
    System.EventArgs) Handles Button1.Click

End Sub
```

To place the text we want in the text box when the user clicks the button, type this code directly into the code window, as you see in Figure 1.8; this sets the **Text** property of our text box, **TextBox1**, to "Hello from Visual Basic":

```
Private Sub Button1_Click(ByVal sender As System.Object, ByVal e As _
    System.EventArgs) Handles Button1.Click
    TextBox1.Text = "Hello from Visual Basic"
End Sub
```

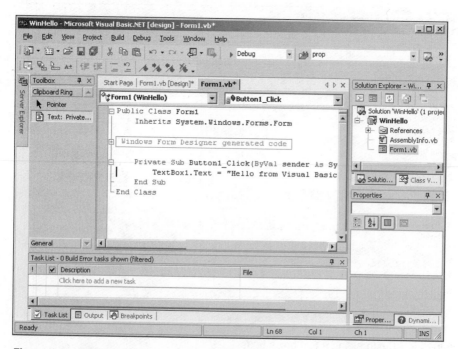

Figure 1.8   Editing code in a Windows application.

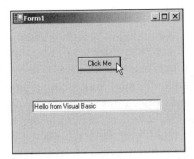

Figure 1.9   Running a Windows application.

And that's all it takes—now run the program by selecting the Debug|Start menu item, or by pressing F5. The application starts, as you see in Figure 1.9, and when you click the Click Me button, the message "Hello from Visual Basic" appears in the text box, as Figure 1.9 also shows. That's it—our first program is a success. To close the application, click the X button at upper right, as you would with any Windows application.

This is the magic of Visual Basic—with one line of code, we've created a functioning application. In the early days of Windows, it would have taken a minimum of five pages of dense C or C++ code to have done the same thing. That's our first Visual Basic application, already up and running. Make sure you save the WinHello application (Visual Basic will save all files when it runs an application, but you also can use the File|Save All menu item) before moving on.

TIP: *As Visual Basic programmers know, Visual Basic has a handy way of letting you know when a file has been changed and has not yet been saved—an asterisk (*) will appear after the name of the file. If you look in the IDE's title bar and in the tabs above the code window in Figure 1.8, you can see this asterisk for the file Form1.vb, which is where the code for Form1 is stored, because we've modified that file without saving it yet.*

In fact, all this is pretty familiar to Visual Basic 6.0 programmers—so let's do something that's new: create a Web application. This application will do the same as the Windows application we've just seen, but it'll run on a Web server and appear in a browser.

Creating a Web Application

To create a new Web application in Visual Basic, you select the File|New|Project menu item opening the New Project dialog box as before. Select the Visual Basic Projects folder in the Project Types box, also as before, but this time, select ASP.NET Web Application in the Templates box.

Give this new application the name WebHello, as you see in Figure 1.10—and now comes the tricky part. To create a Web application, you need a Web server that uses the Microsoft Internet Information Server (IIS) version 5.0 or later (with FrontPage extensions installed), and that server must be running. You can enter the location of your server in the Location box in the New Projects dialog box; if you have IIS running on your local machine, Visual Basic will find it and use that server by default, as you see in Figure 1.10, where Visual Basic has selected http://STEVE, my local IIS server (IIS comes with operating systems like Windows 2000 Server; it also comes with Windows 2000 Professional, although you have to install it from the Windows 2000 CDs). When you click the OK button, Visual Basic will create the new Web application, as you see in Figure 1.11.

As you also can see in Figure 1.11, designing Web applications looks much like designing Windows applications. You can see a note in the Web form under design—called a page—at the center of the IDE that says that we're using the *Grid layout mode*. In this mode, controls will stay where you position them, just as they did when we created our Windows application. The other layout mode is the *Flow layout mode*; in this mode, the controls in your application will move around, as they would in a standard Web page, depending on where the browser wants to put them. (If your Web application happens to start in Flow layout mode, click the Web form itself, then set the **pageLayout** property in the Pproperties window at lower right to **GridLayout**—if you've used Visual Basic before, you're already familiar with the properties window; it's also covered in detail later in this chapter.)

Now we can design our new Web application just as we did the Windows application—click the Web forms item in the toolbox, and add both a text box and a button to the Web form, as you see in Figure 1.12.

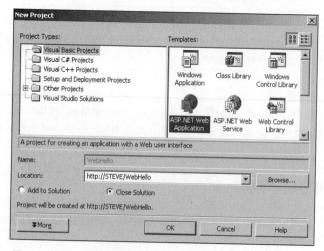

Figure 1.10   Creating a Web application.

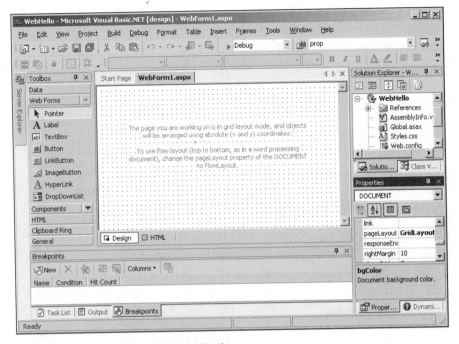

Figure 1.11   Designing a Web application.

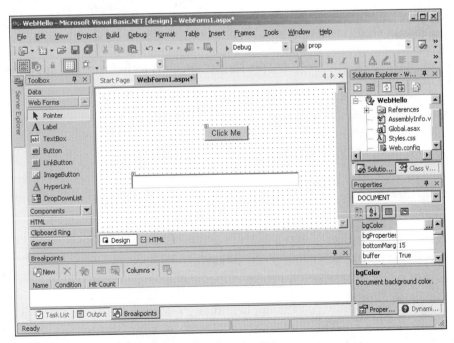

Figure 1.12   Adding controls to a Web application.

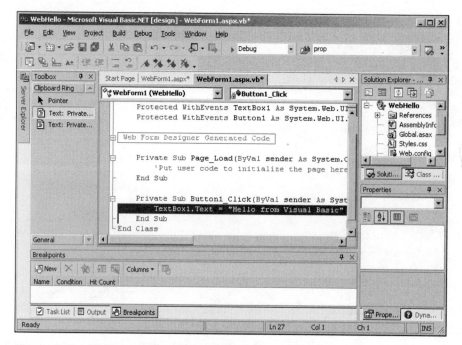

Figure 1.13   Adding code to a Web application.

And, as before, we can double-click the button to open its associated code, as you see in Figure 1.13.

We can add the same code to handle the button click as before; find this code in the code window:

```
Private Sub Button1_Click(ByVal sender As System.Object, ByVal e As _
    System.EventArgs) Handles Button1.Click

End Sub
```

and add this code:

```
Private Sub Button1_Click(ByVal sender As System.Object, ByVal e As _
    System.EventArgs) Handles Button1.Click
    TextBox1.Text = "Hello from Visual Basic"
End Sub
```

That's all it takes—now run the application by selecting the Debug|Start menu item, or pressing F5. The application comes up in your browser, as shown in Figure 1.14, and when you click the button, the message "Hello from Visual Basic" appears in the text box, just as it did in our Windows application.

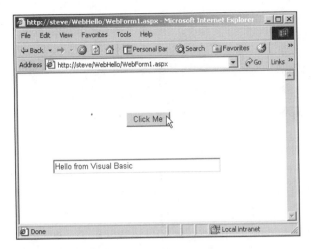

Figure 1.14   Running a Web application.

That's our first Web application—to close the application, just close the browser window. As you can see, this Web application is remarkably similar to our Windows application, and that's the primary inspiration behind VB .NET—bringing Visual Basic to the Internet. Web applications such as this one use HTML to display their controls in a Web page, so there are more limitations on those controls than on Windows controls, but as you can see, the design process is very similar. Behind the scenes, Visual Basic .NET has been storing the application's files on the Web server automatically—no special uploading needed. Anyone with a browser can look at the application on the Internet, simply by navigating to its URL (in this case, that's **http://steve/WebHello/WebForm1.aspx**, as you see the browser's title bar in Figure 1.14). If you're like me, the first time you create and run a Web application, you'll feel a lot like saying *Wow*. Web applications like this will make Web development a great deal easier and more popular on IIS platforms.

Creating a Console Application

There's another new type of Visual Basic application in VB .NET—console applications. These applications are command-line based and run in DOS windows. This gives one the feeling once again that VB .NET is following the lead of Java, because Java applications run in DOS windows in Windows (before this, Visual Basic itself hasn't interacted with DOS for years—not since the ancient and ill-fated VB DOS version). However, the change is a welcome one, because it provides us with an option for very simple programming, without worrying about user interface implementation and issues.

To see how console applications work, use the File|New|Project menu item to open the New Project menu item, and select Console Application in the Tem-

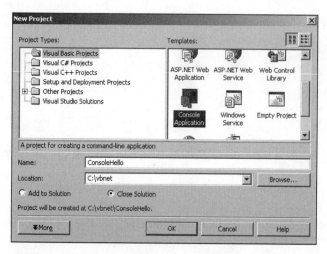

Figure 1.15   Creating a Console application.

plates box, as shown in Figure 1.15. Name this new project ConsoleHello, as also shown in Figure 1.15. Then click OK to create the new project.

When you create this new project, you see the result in Figure 1.16; note that in this case, because there is no user interface, Visual Basic opens the project directly to a code window.

The code here looks like this:

```
Module Module1

    Sub Main()

    End Sub

End Module
```

Console applications are based on Visual Basic *modules* that are specifically designed to hold code that is not attached to any form or other such class. Notice also the **Sub Main()** procedure here. As we'll see in more depth in Chapter 3, a **Sub** procedure is a series of Visual Basic statements enclosed by the **Sub** and **End Sub** statements. When the console application is run, those statements are run automatically.

We can display our "Hello from Visual Basic" message in this console application using the **WriteLine** method, a prewritten procedure available to us in Visual Basic. This method is part of the **System.Console** class, which in turn is part of the **System** *namespace*. The **System.Console** class is part of the .NET framework class library, along with thousands of other classes. To organize all those

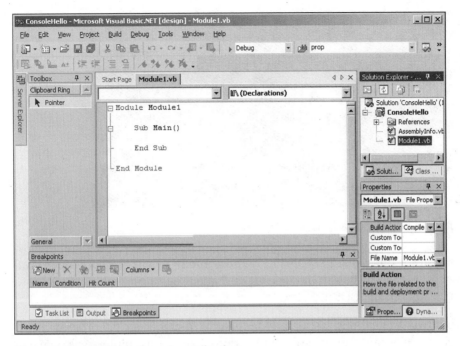

Figure 1.16 Coding a Console application.

classes, .NET uses namespaces. This gives classes their own space and stops conflicts between the various names in such classes; for example, if two classes defined a **WriteLine** method, you could keep them from conflicting by placing them in different namespaces so Visual Basic knows which one you mean. We'll become more familiar with namespaces starting in Chapter 2; for now, we can use **WriteLine** to display our message, like this:

```
Module Module1

    Sub Main()
        System.Console.WriteLine("Hello from Visual Basic")
    End Sub

End Module
```

You can run this program now by selecting the Debug|Start menu item; when the program runs, it displays both our message and the prompt about the Enter key, like this:

```
Hello from Visual Basic
Press any key to continue
```

Figure 1.17   Running a Console application.

You can see this result in Figure 1.17. There, the DOS window stays open until the user is ready to dismiss it by pressing the Enter key, or by clicking the X button at upper right in the DOS window.

Windows applications are already familiar to Visual Basic 6.0 programmers, but Web applications and console applications like the examples we've developed are new. In fact, there's a great deal that's new in VB .NET; I'll take a look at what's new in overview now.

What's New in VB .NET?

Rather than asking what's new, it would almost be easier to ask what's *not* new in VB .NET. The changes are extensive. We can't cover all the changes from Visual Basic 6.0 in a single chapter, but it's worth taking a look at them in overview here, in one place, so you get an idea of how things are different. We'll note the details of these changes throughout the book.

Be warned: if you are relatively new to Visual Basic, you might just want to skip this section, because there will be a number of advanced topics here that you've probably never seen before—you might want to refer back to this section as these topics become more clear. However, it might prove useful to at least simply skim this section, because besides giving you an outline of what's changed from VB6, it also gives you an outline of the kind of programming we'll see in this book, and what's possible.

Version 4.0 of Visual Basic was a big change, unsettling many programmers, but the change from VB6 to VB .NET is far bigger. Not only has how you design applications and what types of projects you can create changed, but the very syntax of the language has changed a great deal too. Some programmers have complained that Microsoft is trying to turn Visual Basic into Java; if you know Java, you'll see what that means throughout the book in dozens of places, as what was standard in Java has become standard in Visual Basic. One longstanding complaint about Visual Basic has been that it didn't offer a serious programming syntax, and programmers coming from C++ sometimes looked down on VB programmers. Now, however, Microsoft has changed all that, giving the Visual Basic language the same rigor as any other programming language.

This change will take some time for many accomplished VB programmers to come to terms with; for example, everything in Visual Basic is object-oriented now, as it is in Java, and you must declare your variables, as you do in Java, and the built-in VB functionality is encapsulated in a namespace called System, as it is in Java, and so on.

As we've also seen, aside from Windows development, you can also create Web applications in VB .NET. In fact, there's a third alternative now—in addition to Windows applications and Web applications, you can create *console applications*, as you can in Java. Console applications, as we'll see in this chapter, are command-line oriented applications that run in DOS windows. Those are the three application types with user interfaces: Windows applications, Web applications, and console applications. There's also an additional new type of application— one that doesn't have a built-in user interface: *Web services*. Web services are applications that run on Web servers and that communicate with other programs, and we'll see them later in this book.

One of the biggest changes in VB .NET is that now everything is object oriented. All items, even variables, are now objects, and we'll see what that means starting in Chapter 2. All aspects of object-oriented programming (OOP) have been implemented in VB .NET, including inheritance, overloading, and polymorphism. Like Java, VB .NET does not support multiple inheritance, but it does support interfaces. We'll get a good look at the OOP issues like these in Chapters 11 and 12.

You can also create *multithreaded* applications in VB .NET now. A threaded application can do a number of different things at the same time, running different execution threads. These threads can communicate with each other, pass data back and forth, and so on. This means, for example, that when your program is doing something heavily computation-intensive, your program's user interface, running in a different thread, can still respond to the user.

One of the biggest hurdles that VB6 programmers will have to overcome is the great change in Visual Basic syntax. Not only has the fundamental structure of Visual Basic projects like Windows applications become different, but there are a thousand other issues as well—for example, you now have to declare all variables and objects, you must always use parentheses when calling procedures, many keywords are either gone or renamed, there are restrictions on declaring arrays, many old controls are gone and new ones have appeared, strict data typing is now enforced, and so on. All this takes a great deal of effort to get used to, but VB .NET itself will usually tell you what you're doing wrong, and often will explain how to make it right.

In fact, the very data types you can use have changed in VB .NET, because these types have to be the same as you use in other languages like Visual C++ and Microsoft's C#. The reason for this, as we'll see in this chapter, is that the .NET framework that underlies VB .NET uses a *Common Language Runtime* (CLR) module that applications written in these languages all use.

As you can see, there are plenty of changes in VB .NET. I'll list them in overview in more detail here, starting with Web Development Changes.

Changes in Web Development

The big change in Web development is that you can do it at all. Previous versions of Visual Basic had support for DHTML applications, and other half-hearted attempts, but they never caught on. As you can see, however, Web development is now an integral part of VB .NET. The two major types of Web applications are Web forms and Web services, and we'll cover them both in this book. Here's an overview:

- Web forms let you create Web-based applications with user interfaces. These applications are based on ASP.NET (ASP stands for Active Server Pages, Microsoft's Web server technology). You can view these applications in any browser—the application will tailor itself to the browser's capabilities.

- You can build Web applications that use standard HTML controls, or new Server controls, that are handled on the Web server. Server controls are displayed using HTML, but execute code on the server.

- Web services are made up of code that can be called by other components on the Internet or applications that use Internet protocols. Using Web services, you can send and process data using HTTP and XML messaging standards on the Internet. Web services may be used, for example, as the middle tier of distributed database applications on the Internet.

- You can also now check the data a user enters into a Web form using validation controls, which you can add to a Web form while designing it.

- You can bind the controls on a Web form to all kinds of different data sources, simply by dragging those sources onto Web forms and setting a few properties.

- There are two ways to create your own Web server controls: you can create user controls—Web form pages that are then embedded in other Web form pages. Or, you can create custom server controls using a Software Development Kit (SDK) provided with the .NET Framework.

Changes in Data Handling

There have been many ways of handling data in previous versions of Visual Basic, starting with the simple DAO protocol, then RDO, followed by ADO (ActiveX Data Objects). Things have changed again; now you handle data with ADO.NET.

ADO.NET is a new data-handling model that makes it easy to handle data on the Internet. It's also what VB .NET uses on your local machine to communicate with local databases. At the heart of ADO.NET is XML; all data is represented in XML format and exchanged that way. VB .NET can use XML schema to make sure your data is checked for validity before use. This means that much of what you know about ADO, if you're a VB6 programmer, has to be replaced with the corresponding ADO.NET versions (although, for compatibility's sake, you can still use ADO if you need to). For example, you no longer use record sets, but rather *datasets*. A dataset is a collection of one or more tables or record sets as well as the relationships between those tables or record sets.

Note that ADO is no longer built into Visual Basic; ADO was based on COM protocols, and COM (as well as DCOM) is no longer built into Visual Basic either. Instead, ADO.NET uses XML to exchange data. Both COM and distributed COM (DCOM) technology has been replaced by the .NET framework, although you still have access to COM through what VB .NET calls *COM interoperability*, if you take special steps to implement it. Here is an overview of what's new in data handling:

- Data is handled through ADO.NET, which facilitates development of Web applications.

- ADO.NET is built on a disconnected data model that uses *snapshots* of data that are isolated from the data source. This means you can use and create disconnected, local datasets.

- Datasets are based on XML schema, so they can be strongly typed.

- There are many new tools and a wizard for handling data in VB .NET, including tools to generate datasets from data connections. You can use the connection wizard or the server explorer to drag and drop whole tables from data sources, as well as creating data adapters, connection objects, and more.

- You can now bind any control property to data from a data source.

- You can use the data classes provided in the .NET Framework to create and manipulate datasets in code.

- You can still work with ADO using the COM interoperability supported in the .NET Framework.

Changes in the Visual Basic Language

As mentioned earlier, there are many changes to the Visual Basic language itself. VB .NET now supports such OOP features as inheritance, interfaces, and overloading that make it a strong OOP language. You can now create multithreaded applications, and make use of structured exception handling, custom attributes, and more.

Probably the biggest single change is that everything is object oriented now. Generally speaking, a language is object oriented if it supports the following (more on this in Chapters 11 and 12):

- *Abstraction*—The ability to create an abstract representation of a concept in code (as an object named **employee** is an abstraction of a real employee).

- *Encapsulation*—This has to do with the separation between implementation and interface; that is, when you encapsulate an object, you make its code internal and not accessible to the outside except through a well-defined interface.

- *Polymorphism*—Broadly speaking, this is the ability to create procedures that can operate on objects of different types. For example, if both **person** and **employee** objects have a **last_name** property, a polymorphic procedure can use that property of both objects. Visual Basic handles polymorphism with late binding and multiple interfaces, both of which we'll cover in this book.

- *Inheritance*—Inheritance is the process by which you can derive new classes from other classes. Chapter 12 is all about inheritance in Visual Basic; the idea here is that if you were to create, for example, a class for a specific Visual Basic form and then derive a new type of form from that class, the derived class will inherit all the base's class's functionality, even before you start to customize the derived class by adding new functionality.

VB .NET now supports all these key OOP essentials, and it's become a true OOP language. VB .NET now uses *namespaces* to prevent naming conflicts by organizing classes, interfaces, and methods into hierarchies, much as Java does. You can *import* various namespaces to gain access to its classes, interfaces, and methods, and we'll see more on this later in this chapter. For example, the **Microsoft.VisualBasic** namespace gives you access to common Visual Basic keywords like **Asc**, **Beep**, **Chr**, and so on. The **Microsoft.VisualBasic.ControlChars** namespace gives you access to common Visual Basic constants like **Cr**, **CrLf**, and so on. The **Microsoft. VisualBasic.Compatibility.VB6** namespace gives you access to obsolete VB6 keywords such as **Open**, **Close**, **CreateObject**, and so on. The biggest namespace comes from the .NET framework itself, and is called **System**. For example, the class that supports Windows forms is **System.Windows.Forms.Form**.

The data types you can use are now restricted to those in the Microsoft Common Language Specification (CLS) as we'll see in the next chapter. On the one hand, that restricts what you can use for data types in Visual Basic, but on the other hand, it also means that any language that is CLS-compliant can use the classes, objects, and components you create in Visual Basic. And you can use classes, components, and objects from other CLS-compliant programming languages. Many new concepts have been added to Visual Basic programming as well, such as assemblies, namespaces, delegates, and attributes, as we'll see in this chapter and in Chapter 2.

Here's an overview of some of the changes to the language—there are too many to list them all here, but we'll see them throughout the book, especially in Chapters 11 and 12, where we cover OOP in VB .NET in depth:

- It's all OOP now. All data items are objects now, based on the **System.Object** class. Even integers and other primitive data types are based on this class. And all code has to be enclosed in a class.

- You can now create classes that serve as the base class for derived classes. As mentioned above, this is called *inheritance*. Derived classes inherit, and can extend, the properties and methods of the base class.

- You can now overload properties, methods, and procedures. Overloading means you can define properties, methods, or procedures that have the same name but use different data types. For example, overloaded procedures allow you to provide as many implementations as necessary to handle different kinds of data while giving the appearance of a single procedure.

- Visual Basic now supports structured exception handling, using an enhanced version of the **Try...Catch...Finally** syntax supported by other languages (such as C++).

- VB .NET now supports multithreaded applications.

- VB .NET now supports constructors and destructors for use when initializing an object of a specific class.

- There are three new data types in VB .NET: The **Char** data type is an unsigned 16-bit type used to store Unicode characters. The **Short** data type is a signed 16-bit integer (named **Integer** in earlier Visual Basic versions). Finally, the **Decimal** data type is a 96-bit signed integer (only available as **Variants** in earlier versions of Visual Basic).

- The **Variant** type no longer exists; instead, the **Object** type is the catch-all type. Also, the **Currency** data type has been replaced by the **Decimal** type.

- VB .NET is now strongly typed; this means you must declare all variables by default, and you can't usually assign one data type to another. You use the

CType statement to convert between types. There are also changes in the way you declare variables.

- Arrays can no longer be 1-based in VB .NET. That is, the **Option Base** statement no longer exists.

- User-defined types are no longer defined with the **Type** keyword, but rather with the **Structure** keyword.

- In Visual Basic 6.0, collections were part of the language itself; in VB .NET, they come from the **Systems.Collections** namespace, so we have to use the ones available in that namespace instead.

- There are a number of new compound arithmetic operators, such as **+=**, **-=**, **•=**, **/=**, **\=**, **^=**, and **&=**. These operators combine two operations in one, as in Java. For example, **y += 5** adds 5 to the value in y and assigns the result to y.

- **If...Then** statements are now short-circuited, as in Java, so Visual Basic will evaluate only the operands it needs to determine the result of the statement (see Chapter 2 for more information).

- The **And**, **Or**, **Not**, and **Xor** operators have changed from being bitwise operators to being Boolean operators, which only work on true/false values. The bitwise versions are **BitAnd**, **BitOr**, **BitNot**, and **BitXor**.

- You no longer need to use the **Set** statement to assign objects to variables.

- The syntax for use with procedures has changed—for example, you now always need to use parentheses to enclose the arguments you're passing to a procedure. There are other changes as well; for example, optional parameters now require default values.

- In VB6 most parameters were passed by reference; in Visual Basic .NET, the default is passing by value. More on this in Chapter 3.

- The syntax for writing property procedures has changed (including the fact that **Get** and **Let** have become **Get** and **Set**).

- Structured exception handling, including **Try...Catch...Finally** blocks, is now supported.

- In VB6, objects had a default property; for example, the default property of a TextBox control was the **Text** property; you could type **TextBox1** = "Hello from Visual Basic" instead of **TextBox1.Text** = "Hello from Visual Basic". In VB .NET, however, default properties are no longer supported.

- Event-handling procedures have changed; now event handlers are passed only two parameters.

- The **Gosub** keyword has been removed.

- The **DefType** keyword has been removed.

Many functions, keywords, and collections from VB6 are now obsolete. Here's a partial list, along with replacements:

- **Collection** has been replaced by **System.Collections**.

- **QBColor**, **RGB** have been replaced by **System.Drawing.Color**.

- **DateAdd**, **DateDiff**, **DatePart**, **DateSerial**, **DateValue**, **TimeSerial**, **TimeValue** have been replaced by elements in **System.DateTime**.

- **Close**, **EOF**, **FileAttr**, **Get**, **Put**, **FreeFile**, **Input**, **Line Input**, **Loc**, **Lock**, **LOF**, **Open**, **Print**, **Print Line**, **Rename**, **Reset**, **Seek**, **SPC**, **TAB**, **Unlock**, **Width**, **Write**, **WriteLine** have been replaced by elements in **System.IO**.

The way programs handle COM components has also changed. In VB6, COM components (such as ActiveX controls and documents) were very big. That's all changed now, and some people think that VB .NET is the end of COM, although that's not necessarily so. Although VB .NET does not use COM components internally, it integrates with COM components well. COM components can be treated as .NET components by .NET components, because the .NET framework encloses COM components in a .NET wrapper that .NET components can work with. And, using COM interoperability, COM components also can use .NET components.

As you can see, there are a great many changes going on in VB .NET. Microsoft is aware that the sheer magnitude of all these differences can present a serious obstacle to the adoption of VB .NET (as they say in the documentation, "Visual Basic .NET represents a major departure from previous versions of Visual Basic in several ways."), and has made some efforts to make upgrading from VB6 easier.

Upgrading from Visual Basic 6.0

The difference between VB6 and VB .NET is great, and to help you upgrade VB6 projects to VB .NET projects, Microsoft created the Visual Basic Upgrade Wizard. This Wizard is automatically invoked when you try to open a VB6 project, and you can see it in Figure 1.18.

This Wizard attempts to convert VB6 projects to VB .NET projects, but in all but the simplest cases, I've found it inadequate, because the differences are too great. When you do upgrade a VB6 project of any complexity, you'll usually find the resulting code filled with Visual Basic comments—lines of text that begin with an apostrophe (') to indicate to Visual Basic that they contain comments intended to be read by a person, not code to execute like this:

```
If blnDrawFlag Then
    'UPGRADE_ISSUE: Graphics statements can't be migrated.
    'Click for more: ms-help://MS.MSDNVS/vbcon/html/vbup2034.htm
    Line(X,Y)
End If
```

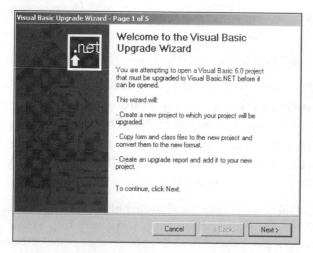

Figure 1.18   The Visual Basic Upgrade Wizard.

In the majority of cases, the differences between VB6 and VB .NET are simply too many for the Upgrade Wizard to overcome. However, give it a try if you'd like; it can convert some of your application's code and perhaps save you a little time.

TIP: *If you're truly stuck, you might try importing the* **Microsoft.VisualBasic.Compatibility.VB6** *namespace (we'll see how importing works in Chapter 2) into your application, which gives you access to obsolete VB6 keywords like* **Open**, **Close**, **CreateObject**, *and so on.*

Unfortunately, for any but the simplest project, I suggest recoding by hand. It can be a tedious process, but there's no alternative.

We've completed an overview of the differences between Visual Basic 6.0 and VB .NET, and now it's time to get cracking with VB .NET itself. The first aspect to examine is the .NET part of VB .NET, and I'll do that now.

The .NET Framework and the Common Language Runtime

VB .NET is only one component of a revolution in Windows—the .NET framework. This framework provides the new support for software development and operating system support in Windows, and it's more extensive than anything we've seen in Windows before. The .NET framework wraps the operating system with its own code, and your VB .NET programs actually deal with .NET code instead of dealing with the operating system itself. And it is specially designed to make working with the Internet easy.

At the base of the .NET framework is the Common Language Runtime (CLR). The CLR is the module that actually runs your VB .NET applications. When you create a VB .NET application, what really happens is that your code is *compiled* into the CLR's *Intermediate Language* (named MSIL, or IL for short), much like bytecodes in Java. When you run the application, that IL code is translated into the binary code your computer can understand by some special *compilers* built into the CLR. Compilers translate your code into something that your machine's hardware, or other software, can deal with directly. In this way, Microsoft can one day create a CLR for operating systems other than Windows, and your VB .NET applications, compiled into IL, will run on them.

The .NET Framework class library is the second major part of the .NET framework. The class library holds an immense amount of prewritten code that all the applications you create with Visual Basic, Visual C++, C#, and other Visual Studio languages build on. The class library gives your program the support it needs—for example, your program may create several forms, and as there is a class for forms in the class library, your program doesn't have to perform all the details of creating those forms from scratch. All your code has to do is declare a new form, and the CLR compilers can get the actual code that supports forms from the .NET Framework class library. In this way, your programs can be very small compared to earlier Windows applications; because you can rely on the millions of lines of code already written in the class library, not everything has to be in your application's executable (EXE) file.

All this assumes that you're working on a machine that has the .NET framework, and therefore the CLR and the .NET Framework class library, installed. The code for all elements we use in a VB .NET application—forms, buttons, menus, and all the rest—all comes from the class library. And other Visual Studio applications use the same class library, making it easy to mix languages in your programming, even in the same application. Also, distributing applications is easier, because all the support you need is already on the machine you're installing your application to.

As mentioned, the .NET framework organizes its classes into namespaces. For example, the .NET framework includes the namespaces **Microsoft.VisualBasic**, **Microsoft.JScript**, **Microsoft.CSharp**, and **Microsoft.Win32**. In fact, these namespaces contain relatively few classes; the real way we'll interact with the .NET framework class library in this book is through the **System** namespace.

The System Namespaces

You can't build a VB .NET application without using classes from the .NET **System** namespace, as we'll see over and over again in this book. When you want to use a Windows form, for example, you must use the **System.Windows.Forms.**

Form class. A button in a Windows form comes from the **System.Windows.Forms.Button** class, and so on. There are many such classes, organized into various namespaces like **System.Windows.Forms**. Here's an overview of some of those namespaces:

- *System*—Includes essential classes and base classes that define commonly-used data types, events and event handlers, interfaces, attributes, exceptions, and so on.

- *System.Collections*—Includes interfaces and classes that define various collections of objects, including such collections as lists, queues, arrays, hash tables, and dictionaries.

- *System.Data*—Includes classes that make up ADO.NET. ADO.NET lets you build data-handling components that manage data from multiple distributed data sources.

- *System.Data.OleDb*—Includes classes that support the OLE DB .NET data provider.

- *System.Data.SqlClient*—Includes classes that support the SQL Server .NET data provider.

- *System.Diagnostics*—Includes classes that allow you to debug your application and to step through your code. Also includes code to start system processes, read and write to event logs, and monitor system performance.

- *System.Drawing*—Provides access to the GDI+ graphics packages that give you access to drawing methods.

- *System.Drawing.Drawing2D*—Includes classes that support advanced two-dimensional and vector graphics.

- *System.Drawing.Imaging*—Includes classes that support advanced GDI+ imaging.

- *System.Drawing.Printing*—Includes classes that allow you to customize and perform printing.

- *System.Drawing.Text*—Includes classes that support advanced GDI+ typography operations. The classes in this namespace allow users to create and use collections of fonts.

- *System.Globalization*—Includes classes that specify culture-related information, including the language, the country/region, calendars, the format patterns for dates, currency and numbers, the sort order for strings, and so on.

- *System.IO*—Includes types that support synchronous and asynchronous reading from and writing to both data streams and files.

- *System.Net*—Provides an interface to many of the protocols used on the Internet.

- *System.Net.Sockets*—Includes classes that support the Windows Sockets interface. If you've worked with the Winsock API, you should be able to develop applications using the **Socket** class.

- *System.Reflection*—Includes classes and interfaces that return information about types, methods, and fields, and also have the ability to dynamically create and invoke types.

- *System.Security*—Includes classes that support the structure of the common language runtime security system.

- *System.Threading*—Includes classes and interfaces that enable multithreaded programming.

- *System.Web*—Includes classes and interfaces that support browser/server communication. Included in this namespace are the **HTTPRequest** class that provides information about HTTP requests, the **HTTPResponse** class that manages HTTP output to the client, and the **HTTPServerUtility** class that provides access to server-side utilities and processes. You can also use cookies, support file transfer, and more with these classes.

- *System.Web.Security*—Includes classes that are used to implement ASP.NET security in Web server applications.

- *System.Web.Services*—Includes classes that let you build and use Web services, programmable entities on Web Server that code can communicate with using standard Internet protocols.

- *System.Windows.Forms*—Includes classes for creating Windows-based forms that make use of the user interface controls and other features available in the Windows operating system.

- *System.Xml*—Includes classes that support processing of XML.

These, along with the many other **System** classes, form the foundation on which VB .NET applications rest. It's time now to start taking a look at how to build those applications.

Building VB .NET Applications

To build applications in VB .NET, we have to get some terminology under our belts, because the .NET framework requires a new structure for applications. In particular, *assemblies* are now the building blocks of the .NET Framework; they form the fundamental unit of deployment, version control, reuse, security permissions, and more. An assembly provides the CLR with the information and compiled code it needs to know how to run your code, much as EXE files did for Windows in VB6.

Assemblies

You combine assemblies to form .NET applications, and although we won't deal with them directly very often, we need to get the terminology down. An *assembly* holds the Intermediate Language modules for your application. When you create an application in VB .NET and run it, VB .NET creates one or more assemblies, which are run by the CLR. That is, assemblies are how your applications interact with the .NET framework instead of the EXE or DLL files of VB6.

Here's what's in a .NET assembly: first is the *manifest*—similar to a table of contents—giving the name and version of the assembly. The manifest also lists the other assemblies needed to support this one, and explains how to handle security issues. The actual meat of the assembly is made up of *modules*, which are internal files of IL code, ready to run. That's how VB .NET stores the IL it creates, in modules inside assemblies. Each module, in turn, contains *types*—the classes and interfaces that your code has defined, and that the assembly has to know about to let the various modules interact with each other.

We won't deal with assemblies directly much, because all that's needed happens behind the scenes with the CLR and the .NET framework—but we do have to know the terminology, because you'll hear these terms frequently when using VB .NET. For example, to set the version of a Visual Basic project, you edit its AssemblyInfo.vb file in the Visual Basic IDE.

Solutions and Projects

When you created applications in Visual Basic 6.0, you created *projects*. Each project held the code and data for an application, ActiveX control, or whatever else you wanted to build. If you wanted to combine projects together, you created a *project group*. In VB .NET, however, project groups have become far more integral to the development process, and now they're called *solutions*.

By default, when you create a new project in VB .NET, Visual Basic will create a new solution first, and then add a project to that solution. For example, look at the Solution Explorer window, at right in Figure 1.8, above the Properties window. In that case, we've created our Visual Basic project called WinHello, and you can see that project in the Solutions Explorer—but note that Visual Basic has also placed that project inside a solution with the same name, WinHello. If we were to add new projects to the current solution (which you can do with the New Project dialog box), those new projects would appear in the Solution Explorer as part of the current solution. This is a change from VB6, where you created projects by default, not project groups. It's also worth noting that Microsoft calls the files in each project, such as the files for a form, *items*. So the terminology here is that solutions contain projects, and these in turn contain items.

File Extensions Used in VB .NET

When you save a solution, it's given the file extension .sln (such as WinHello.sln), and all the projects in the solution are saved with the extension .vbproj. Here's a list of the types of file extensions you'll see in files in VB .NET, and the kinds of files they correspond to; the most popular file extension is .vb. This is a useful list, because if VB .NET has added files to your solution that you haven't expected, you often can figure them out by their file extension:

- *.vb*—Can be a basic Windows form, a code file, a module file for storing functions, a user control, a data form, a custom control, an inherited form, a Web custom control, an inherited user control, a Windows service, a custom setup file, an image file for creating a custom icon, or an AssemblyInfo file (used to store assembly information such as versioning and assembly name).

- *.xsd*—An XML schema provided to create typed datasets.

- *.xml*—An XML document file.

- *.htm*—An HTML document.

- *.txt*—A text file.

- *.xslt*—An XSLT stylesheet file, used to transform XML documents and XML schemas.

- *.css*—A cascading stylesheet file.

- *.rpt*—A Crystal Report.

- *.bmp*—A bitmap file.

- *.js*—A JScript file (Microsoft's version of JavaScript).

- *.vbs*—A VBScript file.

- *.wsf*—A Windows scripting file.

- *.aspx*—A Web form.

- *.asp*—An active server page.

- *.asmx*—A Web service class.

- *.vsdisco*—A dynamic discovery project; .vsdisco provides a means to enumerate all Web Services and all schemas in a Web project.

- *.web*—A Web configuration file, .web configures Web settings for a Web project.

- *.asax*—A global application class, used to handle global ASP.NET application-level events.

- *.resx*—A resource file used to store resource information.

Debug and Release Versions

Note that so far we've started our programs from the Debug menu's Start item. This causes Visual Basic to launch the program while staying in the background; if there's a problem, Visual Basic will reappear to let you debug the program's code. That's useful for development, of course, but when your program is ready to go and to be used by others, you hardly want them to have to launch your program from Visual Basic.

That's where the difference between *debug* and *release* versions of your program comes in. In a debug version of your program, Visual Basic stores a great deal of data needed to interface with the debugger in your program when it runs, and this not only makes the corresponding assembly larger, but also slower. In the release version of your program, the program doesn't have all that added data, and can run as a stand-alone program, without needing to be launched from Visual Basic (although it still needs the .NET Framework, of course).

When you create a new solution, Visual Basic creates it in debug mode, meaning that you launch it from the Debug menu as we've been doing. However, you can switch to release mode in several ways (like many things in VB .NET, there's more than one way to do it):

- Select the Configuration Manager item in the Build menu, then select Release in the Active Solution Configuration list box and click OK.

- Select the solution you want to set the mode for by clicking it in the Solution Explorer, and find its **Active Config** property in the properties window. When you click the right-hand column in the properties window next to this property, a drop-down list box will appear; select Release in that list box.

- Select the solution you want to set the mode for by clicking it in the Solution Explorer, and select the Properties item in the Project menu, opening the solution's property pages. Select the Configuration Properties folder in the box at left, and the Configuration item in that folder. Then select Release from the drop-down list box in the configuration column of the table that appears, and click OK.

- Probably the easiest way to set the solution mode to release or debug is simply to use the drop-down list box that appears in the Visual Basic .NET standard toolbar, at the top of the IDE. When you create a new solution or project, this list box displays the word Debug, and all you need to do to switch to release mode is to select Release instead.

When you've set the mode for a solution to Release, you build it using the Build menu's Build item (the Build menu item causes Visual Basic to compile only items it thinks have been newly changed; to force it to compile all items in the solution, choose the Rebuild All item instead of Build). This builds the solution in a way that others can use it, and you can deploy your program this way (usually with the help of a deployment project that you build in Visual Basic, as we'll do later in the book).

Now we have the background we need on VB .NET solutions and projects as we head into the following chapters, where we'll assume this knowledge and put it to work. We'll also take for granted that you know your way around Visual Basic .NET itself, so in this introductory chapter, I'll also take a look at the Visual Basic Integrated Development Environment—the VB IDE.

The Visual Basic Integrated Development Environment

The IDE, shown in Figure 1.19, has become more complex than in previous versions of Visual Basic, and being able to use it, or at least knowing what the various parts are called, is a skill we'll need in the coming chapters. Part of the reasons it's become more complex is that the same IDE is now shared by all Visual Studio languages, such as VB and C# (something Microsoft has promised for many years, but only implemented now). We've already seen the IDE at work, of course, but now it's time to take a more systematic look.

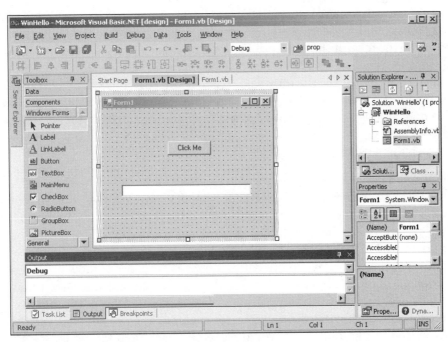

Figure 1.19   The Visual Basic Integrated Development Environment.

There are so many independent windows in the IDE that it's easy to misplace or rearrange them inadvertently. The IDE windows are docking windows, which means you can use the mouse to move windows around as you like; when the windows are near an edge, they'll "dock"—adhere—to that edge, so you can reconfigure the IDE windows as you like. If you move IDE windows inadvertently, don't panic; just use the mouse to move them back.

TIP: *You also can restore the default window layout by selecting the Tools|Options item, then selecting the General item in the Environment folder, and clicking the Reset Window Layout button. That's really good to know, because sooner or later, Visual Basic will dock some window you didn't want to dock, such as the Edit|Replace window, to the IDE, rearranging all your other windows, and it can take a long time to try to fix that manually.*

Also note that the windows in the IDE come with an X button at upper left, which means you can close them. I don't know about you, but I sometimes click these when I don't mean to, and a window I wanted disappears. It's easy to panic: The toolbox is gone! I'll have to reinstall everything! In fact, all you have to do is to find that window in the View menu again (such as View|Toolbox) to make it reappear. (Note that some windows are hidden in the View|Other Windows menu item, which opens a submenu of additional windows—there are simply too many windows to fit them all into one menu without needing to use a submenu.)

There's so much packed into the IDE that Microsoft has started to make windows share space, and you can keep them separate using tabs such as those you can see above the form at the center of Figure 1.19. If you click the Form1.vb[Design] tab, you see the form itself as it'll appear when the program runs; if you click the Form1.vb tab, you'll see the form's code, and if you click the Start Page tab, you'll see the Start page, which lets you select from among recent solutions to open. Also note at lower right that the Properties window and the Dynamic Help window—a new VB .NET feature—are sharing the same space, and you can select between them using tabs.

The IDE is a very crowded place, and in an effort to unclutter the cluttered IDE a little, VB .NET adds a new button in dockable IDE windows—a little thumbtack button at upper right as you see in various windows in Figure 1.19, next to the X close button. This is the "auto-hide" feature, which lets you reduce a window to a tab connected to the edge it's docked on. For example, in Figure 1.19, the Server Explorer (which lets you explore data sources on servers) window is hidden and has become a tab at upper left in the IDE. If I let the mouse move over that tab, the full Sever Explorer window will glide open, covering most of the toolbox. You can auto-hide most windows like this; for example, if I were to click the thumbtack button in the toolbox, it would close and become a tab under the Server Explorer tab in the IDE. To restore a window to stay-open status, just click the thumbtack again.

And, of course, you can customize the IDE as well. For example, to customize IDE options such as the fonts and colors used to display code, you select the Tools|Options menu item and use the various items in the Environment folder. To customize menus and toolbars, such as specifying the toolbars to display (How many are there to choose from? Twenty-seven.), or what buttons go on what toolbars, use the Tools|Customize menu item.

That's it for general discussion—it's time to get to the IDE itself, starting with the Start page.

The Start Page

We've already seen the Start page, which is what you see when you first start Visual Basic, and which appears outlined in Figure 1.20. You can use the Start page to select from recent projects; by default, the Get Started item is selected in the Start page at upper left. You can also create a new project here by clicking the New Project button.

The Start page has other useful aspects as well: for example, because you use the same IDE for all Visual Studio languages, it'll also search through all those languages when you search the help files. To make it search only pertinent help files, you can select the My Profile item in the Start page, and select either Visual Basic

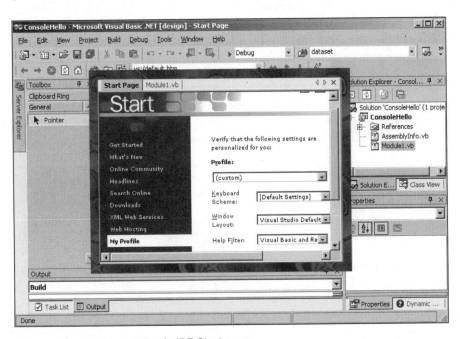

Figure 1.20   The Visual Basic IDE Start page.

or Visual Basic and Related (which is my preference) in the Help Filter drop-down list box.

TIP: *The Start page is actually being displayed in a browser. Its URL is **vs:/default.htm**, as you can see in a drop-down list box above the Start page. Entering a new URL in that drop-down list box and pressing Enter navigates to that new URL, replacing the Start page. And if you have an URL in your code (a quoted string that begins with "http://"), VB .NET will turn that text into a hyperlink, underline it, and allow you to click that URL to bring up the corresponding Web page in place of the Start page.*

The Menu System

After you've started Visual Basic and have seen the Start page, you often turn to the menu system to proceed, as when you want to create a new project and use the File|New|Project menu item to bring up the New Project dialog box (you can do the same thing by clicking the New Project button in the Start page).

The IDE menu system is very involved, with many items to choose from—and you don't even see it all at once. The menu system changes as you make selections in the rest of the IDE—for example, the Project menu will display 16 items if you first select a project in the Solution Explorer, but only 4 items if you have selected a solution, not a project. In fact, there are even more dramatic changes; for example, try clicking a form under design and you'll see a Data menu in the menu bar, used to generate datasets. If you then select not the form but the form's code, however (for example, double-click the form to open the code window), the Data menu disappears.

There are hundreds of menu items here, and many useful ones that will quickly become favorites, such as File|New|Project that you use to create a new project, or the most recently used (MRU) list of files and projects that you can access from the Recent Files or Recent Projects items near the bottom of the File menu.

TIP: *You can set the number of items that appear in MRU lists by selecting the Tools|Options menu item, clicking the Environment folder and selecting the General item, and entering a value in the "most recently used lists" text box.*

The menu system also allows you to switch from debug to release modes if you use the Build|Configuration Manager item, lets you configure the IDE with the Tools|Options and Tools|Customize items, and so on. I'll introduce more and more menu items throughout the book as appropriate.

Toolbars

The toolbars feature is another handy aspect of the IDE. These appear near the top of the IDE, as shown in Figure 1.21. There are plenty of toolbars to choose

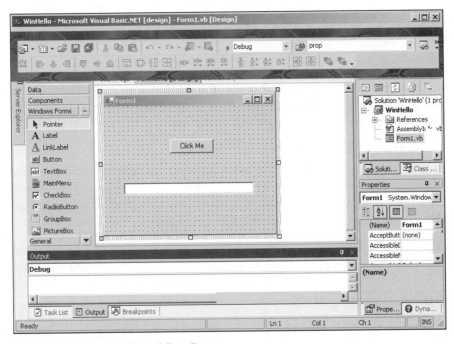

Figure 1.21   Visual Basic IDE toolbars.

from, and sometimes VB .NET will choose for you, as when it displays the Debug toolbar when you've launched a program with the Start item in the Debug menu.

Because the IDE displays tool tips (those small yellow windows with explanatory text that appear when you let the mouse rest over controls such as buttons in a toolbar), it's easy to get to know what the buttons in the toolbars do. As mentioned, you can also customize the toolbars in the IDE, selecting which toolbars to display or customizing which buttons appear in which toolbars with the Tools|Customize menu item, or you can right-click a toolbar itself to get a menu of the possible toolbars to display (the bottom item in this popup menu is Customize, which lets you customize which buttons go where), or you can open the Toolbars submenu in the View menu to do the same thing (as is often the case in VB, there's more than one way to do it).

Toolbars provide a quick way to select menu items, and although I personally usually stick to using the menu system, there's no doubt that toolbar buttons can be quicker; for example, to save the file you're currently working on, you only need to click the diskette button in the standard toolbar (as you see in Figure 1.21), or the stacked diskettes button to save all the files in the solution.

The New Project Dialog Box

When you want to create a new project, you turn to the New Project dialog box. We've already used this quite a bit, and you can see it in Figure 1.22.

In addition to letting you select from all the possible types of projects you can create in Visual Basic, you can also set the name of the project, and its location; for Windows projects, the location is a folder on disk, but for Web projects, you specify a server running IIS.

Note also that you can add projects to the current solution using the New Project dialog box; just click the Add to Solution radio button instead of the Close Solution one (the default). If your project is entirely new, VB .NET will create an enclosing solution for the new project if there isn't already one.

Finally, note the Setup and Deployment Projects folder, which you use to create projects for deploying your program as we'll do near the end of the book.

Graphical Designers

When you're working on a project that has user interface elements—such as forms, VB .NET can display what those elements will look like at run time, and, of course, that's what makes Visual Basic *visual*. For example, when you're looking at a Windows form, you're actually looking at a *Windows form designer*, as you see in Figure 1.23, and you can manipulate the form, as well as add controls to it and so on.

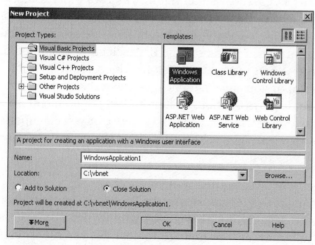

Figure 1.22 The New Project dialog box.

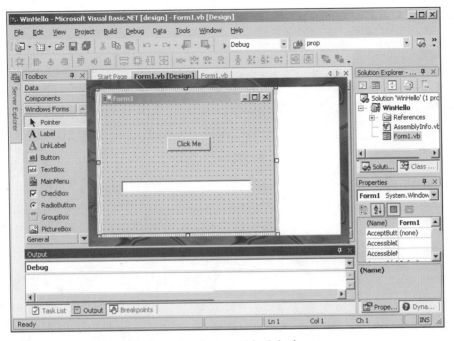

Figure 1.23   A Visual Basic application graphical designer.

There are several different types of graphical designers, including:

- Windows form designers
- Web form designers
- Component designers
- XML designers

You may have noticed—or may already know from VB6—that Windows forms display a grid of dots, which you can see in Figure 1.23. To set the grid spacing, and specify whether or not controls should "snap" to the grid (that is, position their corners on grid points), you can use the Tools|Options menu item to open the Options dialog box, and select the Windows Form Designer folder, displaying the possible options for you to set.

NOTE: *In Visual Basic 6.0, coordinates for forms and controls were expressed in twips; in Visual Basic .NET, coordinates are expressed in pixels (and only pixels).*

Code Designers

Unlike graphical designers, code designers let you edit the code for a component, and you can see a code designer in Figure 1.24. You can use the tabs at the top

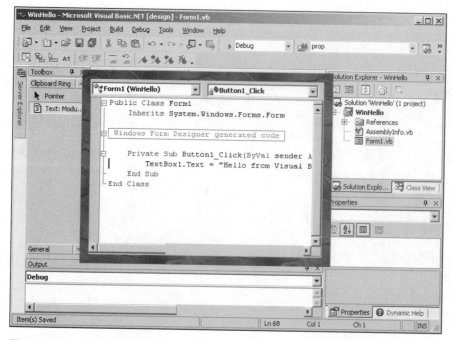

Figure 1.24   A code designer.

center of the IDE to switch between graphical designers (such as the tabs Form1.vb[Design], which displays a graphical designer, and the Form1.vb tab, which displays the corresponding code designer). You can also switch between graphical and code designers using the Designer and Code items in the View menu, or you can use the top two buttons at left in the Solution Explorer.

Note the two drop-down list boxes at the top of the code designer; the one on the left lets you select what object's code you're working with, and the one on the right lets you select the part of the code that you want to work on, letting you select between the declarations area, functions, Sub procedures, and methods (all of which we'll see starting in Chapter 2). The declarations area, which you select by selecting the (Declarations) item in the right-hand list box, is where you can put declarations of module-level objects, as we'll discover in Chapter 3 (see "Understanding Scope" in that chapter).

TIP: *When you double-click a control in a graphical designer, its code designer will open and Visual Basic creates an event handler (see "Handling Events" in Chapter 4) for its default event (such as the **Click** event for buttons), which is a procedure that is called when the event occurs, as we'll see in Chapter 4. To add code to a different event handler, select the object you want to work with in the left-hand drop-down list box in the code designer, and select the event you want to add code to in the right-hand drop-down list box; Visual Basic will create an event handler for that event.*

Also note the + and - boxes in the code designer's text area, at left. Those are new in VB .NET, and were introduced because VB .NET now writes a great deal of code for your forms and components automatically. You can use the + and - buttons to show or hide that code. For example, here's what that code looks like for a typical Windows form:

```
#Region " Windows Form Designer generated code "

    Public Sub New()
        MyBase.New()

        'This call is required by the Windows Form Designer.
        InitializeComponent()

        'Add any initialization after the InitializeComponent() call

    End Sub

    'Form overrides dispose to clean up the component list.
    Protected Overloads Overrides Sub Dispose(ByVal disposing As Boolean)
        If disposing Then
            If Not (components Is Nothing) Then
                components.Dispose()
            End If
        End If
        MyBase.Dispose(disposing)
    End Sub
    Friend WithEvents TextBox1 As System.Windows.Forms.TextBox
    Friend WithEvents Button1 As System.Windows.Forms.Button

    'Required by the Windows Form Designer
    Private components As System.ComponentModel.Container

    'NOTE: The following procedure is required by the Windows Form Designer
    'It can be modified using the Windows Form Designer.
    'Do not modify it using the code editor.
    <System.Diagnostics.DebuggerStepThrough()> Private Sub _
        InitializeComponent()
        Me.TextBox1 = New System.Windows.Forms.TextBox()
        Me.Button1 = New System.Windows.Forms.Button()
        Me.SuspendLayout()
        '
        'TextBox1
        '
        Me.TextBox1.Location = New System.Drawing.Point(32, 128)
        Me.TextBox1.Name = "TextBox1"
```

```
            Me.TextBox1.Size = New System.Drawing.Size(224, 20)
            Me.TextBox1.TabIndex = 0
            Me.TextBox1.Text = ""
            '
            'Button1
            '
            Me.Button1.Location = New System.Drawing.Point(112, 56)
            Me.Button1.Name = "Button1"
            Me.Button1.TabIndex = 1
            Me.Button1.Text = "Click Me"
            '
            'Form1
            '
            Me.AutoScaleBaseSize = New System.Drawing.Size(5, 13)
            Me.ClientSize = New System.Drawing.Size(292, 213)
            Me.Controls.AddRange(New System.Windows.Forms.Control() _
                {Me.Button1, Me.TextBox1})
            Me.Name = "Form1"
            Me.Text = "Form1"
            Me.ResumeLayout(False)

        End Sub

#End Region
```

We'll dissect what this code means when we start working with Windows applications in depth in Chapter 4; for now, note the **#Region** and **#End Region** directives at top and bottom of this code—those are how the code designer knows that this region of code can be collapsed or expanded with a + or - button. Visual Basic also automatically adds those + or - buttons for other programming constructions like procedures, enumerations, and so on, allowing you to hide the parts of your code you don't want to see. The IDE is cluttered enough, and this helps a little in uncluttering it.

TIP: You can use the **#Region** and **#End Region** directives in your own code as well, allowing you to expand and contract whole sections of code at once.

As with the rest of the IDE, there are features upon features packed into code designers—for example, right-clicking a symbol lets you go to its definition, or its declaration, and so on.

IntelliSense

One useful feature of VB .NET code designers is Microsoft's *IntelliSense*. IntelliSense is what's responsible for those boxes that open as you write your code, listing all the possible options and even completing your typing for you. IntelliSense is one of

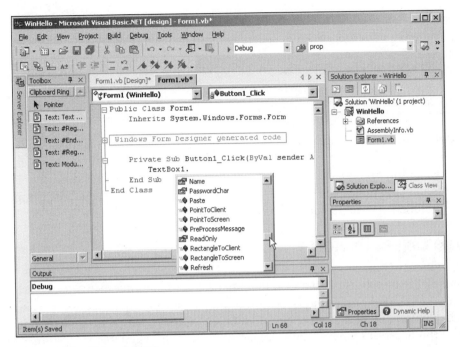

Figure 1.25   Using IntelliSense.

the first things you encounter when you use VB .NET, and you can see an example in Figure 1.25, where I'm looking at all the members of a text box object.

TIP: *If you enter some code that VB .NET considers a syntax error, it will underline the error with a wavy red line. You can rest the mouse over the underlined text to see a tool tip explaining what VB .NET thinks is wrong. That's not part of the IntelliSense package, although it also is useful.*

IntelliSense is made up of a number of options, including:

- *List Members*—Lists the members of an object.
- *Parameter Info*—Lists the arguments of procedure calls.
- *Quick Info*—Displays information in tool tips as the mouse rests on elements in your code.
- *Complete Word*—Completes typed words.
- *Automatic Brace Matching*—Adds parentheses or braces as needed.

There's also a Visual Basic-specific IntelliSense, which offers syntax tips that display the syntax of the statement you're typing. That's great if you know what statement you want to use but don't recall its exact syntax, because its syntax is automatically displayed.

TIP: *IntelliSense is particularly useful when you can't remember what arguments a built-in Visual Basic procedure accepts (if these terms are not familiar to you, note that they're coming up in the next chapter), because it'll display those arguments as you type in the call to the procedure. Such procedures also can be overloaded, which means they have several forms that take different arguments—in such cases, IntelliSense will display an up and down arrow in its tool tip with the text "1 of n" where n is the number of overloaded forms, and you can use the arrows to select the overloaded form of the procedure you want prompts for.*

IntelliSense is something you quickly get used to, and come to rely on. However, you can turn various parts of IntelliSense off if you want; just select the Tools|Options menu item, then select the Text Editor folder, then the Basic subfolder, and finally the General item in the Basic subfolder. You'll see a number of IntelliSense options you can turn on and off with check boxes.

The Object Explorer

IntelliSense is useful because it tells you what syntax is correct automatically, or lists all the members of an object that are available. Another useful tool that's too often overlooked by Visual Basic programmers is the Object Explorer. This tool lets you look at all the members of an object at once, which is invaluable to pry into the heart of objects you've added to your code. The Object Explorer helps open up any mysterious objects that Visual Basic has added to your code so you can see what's going on inside.

To open the Object Explorer, select View|Other Windows|Object Explorer (see Figure 1.26.)

The Object Explorer shows all the objects in your program and gives you access to what's going on in all of them. For example, in Figure 1.26, I'm looking at a Windows form, Form1, and all its internal members—and the parameters they require—are made visible. To close the Object Explorer, just click the X button at its upper right.

The Toolbox

The toolbox is something that all veteran Visual Basic developers are familiar with, and you can see it in Figure 1.27.

Microsoft has crammed more into the toolbox with each successive version of Visual Basic, and now the toolbox uses tabs to divide its contents into categories; you can see these tabs, marked Data, Components, Windows Forms, and General, in Figure 1.27. The tabs available, as you might surmise, depend on the type of project you're working on—and even what type of designer you're working with. The Data, Components, Windows Forms, and General tabs appear when you're working with a Windows form in a Windows form designer, but when you switch to a code designer in the same project, all you'll see are General and Clipboard Ring (which

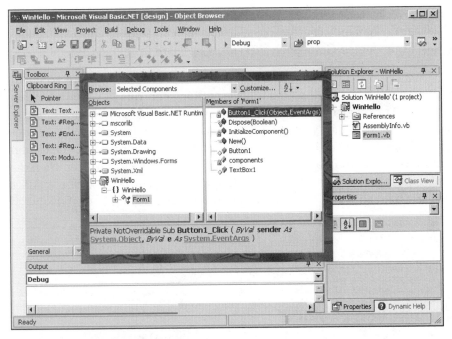

Figure 1.26   The Object Explorer.

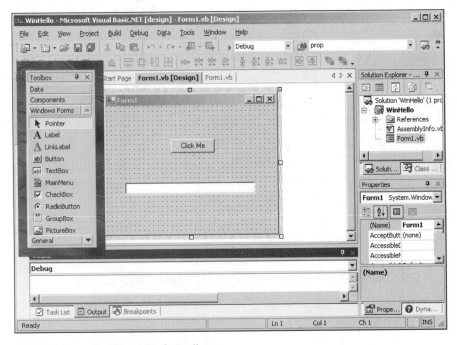

Figure 1.27   The Visual Basic toolbox.

displays recent items stored in the clipboard, and allows you to select from among them) in the toolbox. When you're working on a Web form, you'll see Data, Web Forms, Components, Components, HTML, Clipboard Ring, and General, and so on.

The Data tab displays tools for creating datasets and making data connections, the Windows Forms tab displays tools for adding controls to Windows forms, the Web Forms tab displays tools for adding server controls to Web forms, and so on. The General tab is empty by default, and is a place to store general components, controls, and fragments of code in. (You can even add more tabs to the toolbox by right-clicking the toolbox and selecting the Add Tab item.) In fact, there are so many controls that even when you click a tab in the toolbox, you'll still most likely get a list that you have to scroll to see everything that's available.

TIP: *When you're adding controls to forms using the toolbox, note that you can use the items in the Format menu and the Layout toolbar to align, make the same size, and set the spacing for controls. You can also select multiple controls and move and resize them all at once.*

The Solution Explorer

We've already discussed the Solution Explorer quite a bit; this window gives you an overview of the solution you're working with, including all the projects in it, and the items in those projects. (You can see the Solution Explorer in Figure 1.28.) This

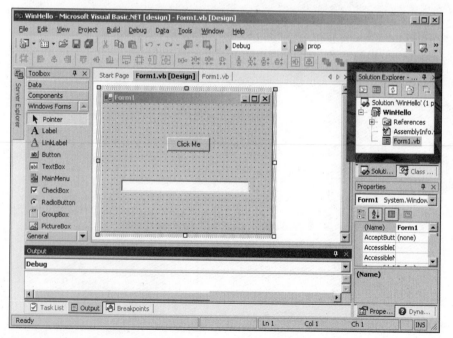

Figure 1.28   The Solution Explorer.

tool displays a hierarchy—with the solution at the top of the hierarchy, the projects one step down in the hierarchy, and the items in each project as the next step down.

You can set the properties of various items in a project by selecting them in the Solution Explorer and then setting their properties in the properties window. And you can set properties of solutions and projects by right-clicking them and selecting the Properties item in the menu that appears, or you can select an item and click the properties button, which is the right-most button at the top of the Solutions Explorer.

If you're working on an object that has both a user interface and code, you can switch between graphical and code designers by using the buttons that appear at top left in the Solution Explorer when that object has been selected. You can right-click a solution and add a new project to it by selecting the Add|New Project menu item in the popup menu that appears. And you can specify which of multiple projects runs first—that is, is the startup project or projects—by right-clicking the project and selecting the Set As Startup Object item, or by right-clicking the solution and selecting the Set Startup Projects item.

Much of what goes on in the VB .NET IDE depends on which solution or project is the current one, and you set that by selecting it in the Solution Explorer. For example, you can specify what icon you want an application to use in Windows if you don't like the plain default one; to do that, you select its project in the Solution Explorer, select Properties in the Project menu, then open the Common Properties|Build folder, browse to the .ico (icon) file you want, and click OK.

The Solution Explorer tracks the items in your projects; to add new items, you can use the menu items in the Project menu, such as Add Windows Form and Add User Control. To add new empty modules and classes to a project (we'll see what these terms mean in detail in the next chapter), you can use the Project|Add New Items menu item.

The Solution Explorer sees things in terms of files, as you can see in Figure 1.28. There, the References folder holds the currently referenced items (such as namespaces) in a project, AssemblyInfo.vb is the file that holds information about the assembly you're creating, and Form1.vb is the file that holds the code for the form under design. However, there's another way of looking at object-oriented programs—in terms of classes—and the Class View Window does that.

TIP: *The data in AssemblyInfo.vb gives all kinds of information about the assembly, such as its version number. To set the version number of the assembly you're creating, open AssemblyInfo.vb and edit the line **<Assembly: AssemblyVersion("1.0.*")>** according to the directions you'll find directly above this line. Windows will be able to display this version number to the user in Windows tools such as the Windows Explorer.*

The Class View Window

If you click the Class View tab under the Solution Explorer, you'll see the Class View window, as shown in Figure 1.29. This view presents solutions and projects in terms of the classes they contain, and the members of these classes.

Using the Class View window gives you an easy way of jumping to a member of class that you want to access quickly—just find it in the Class View window, and double-click it to bring it up in a code designer.

The Properties Window

The Properties window is another old favorite in Visual Basic, although now it shares its space with the Dynamic Help window. The Properties window appears in Figure 1.30.

You set properties of various objects in Visual Basic to customize them; for example, we've set the **Text** property of a button in the WinHello project to "Click Me" to make that text appear in the button. To set an object's properties when you're designing your program in Visual Basic—called *design time* (as opposed to run time)—you select that object (by clicking a control or form, or a project, or a solution), and then set the new property values you want in the Properties window.

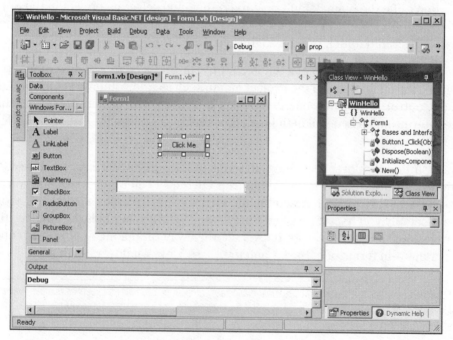

Figure 1.29   The Class View window.

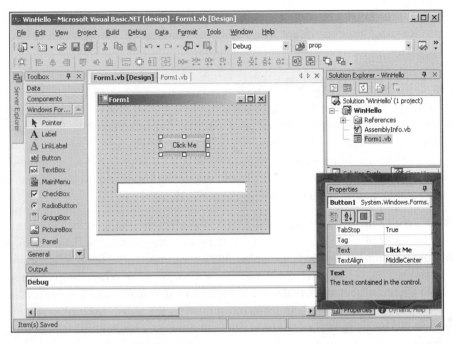

Figure 1.30   The Properties window.

The Properties window is divided into two columns of text, with the properties on the left, and their settings on the right. The object you're setting properties for appears in the drop-down list box at the top of the Properties window, and you can select from all the available objects using that list box. When you select a property, Visual Basic will give you an explanation of the property in the panel at the bottom of the Properties window, as you see in Figure 1.30. And you can display the properties alphabetically by clicking the second button from the left at the top of the Properties window, or in categories by clicking the left-most button.

To change a property's setting, you only have to click the right-hand column next to the name of the property, and enter the new setting. Often properties can have only a few specific values, in which case Visual Basic will display a drop-down list box next to the property's name when you click the right-hand column, and you can select values from that list. Sometimes, Visual Basic requires more information, as when you create data connections, and instead of a list box, a button with an ellipsis ("...") appears; when you click that button, Visual Basic will usually walk you through the steps it needs to get that information. Note also that, as usual with properties and methods in Visual Basic, not all properties of a form or control will be available at design time in the Properties window when you're designing your code—some will be available only at run time.

In fact, there aren't many changes in the Properties window from VB6 (something VB6 programmers might be pleased to hear), so if you've used it before, you're all set.

The Dynamic Help Window

The window that shares the Properties window's space, however, is quite new—the Dynamic Help window. Visual Basic .NET includes the usual Help menu with Contents, Index, and Search items, of course, but it also now supports dynamic help, which looks things up for you automatically. You can see the Dynamic Help window by clicking the Dynamic Help tab under the Properties window, and you can see the Dynamic Help window in Figure 1.31.

VB .NET looks up all kinds of help topics on the element you've selected automatically; for example, in Figure 1.31, I've selected a button on a Windows form, and dynamic help has responded by displaying all kinds of helpful links to information on buttons. This is more helpful than simply searching the whole help system for the word "button", because dynamic help will typically select introductory and overview help topics, not all the hundreds of topics with the word "button" in their text. If you click a help link in the Dynamic Help window, the corresponding help topic is opened in the central space of the IDE where the designers appear (and you can switch between designers and help topics using tabs).

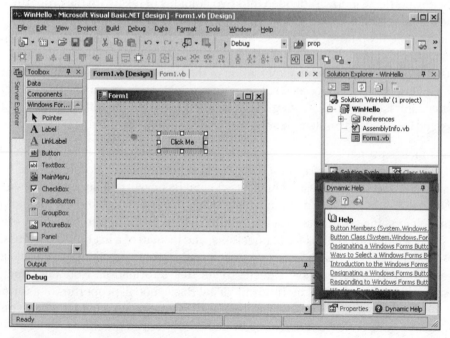

Figure 1.31   The Dynamic Help window.

Component Trays

In VB6, when you added a component to a form, and that component wasn't visible at run time—such as a timer control—the timer would still appear on the form at design time. That's changed in VB .NET; now, when you add components that are invisible at run time, they'll appear in a *component tray*, which will appear automatically in the designer, as you see in Figure 1.32.

The Server Explorer

You use the Server Explorer, which appears in Figure 1.33, to explore what's going on in a server, and it's a great tool to help make distant severs feel less distant, because you can see everything you need in an easy graphical environment.

You can do more than just look using the Server Explorer too—you can drag and drop whole items onto Windows forms or Web forms from the Server Explorer. For example, if you dragged a database table onto a form, VB .NET would create the connection and command objects you need to access that table from code.

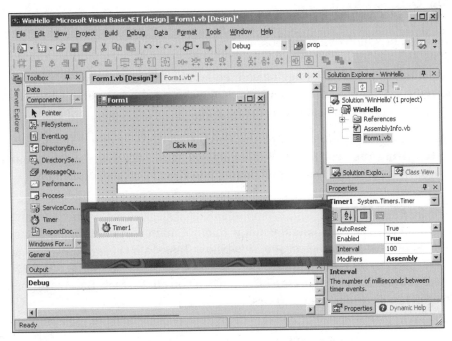

Figure 1.32   Adding a timer to an application in a component tray.

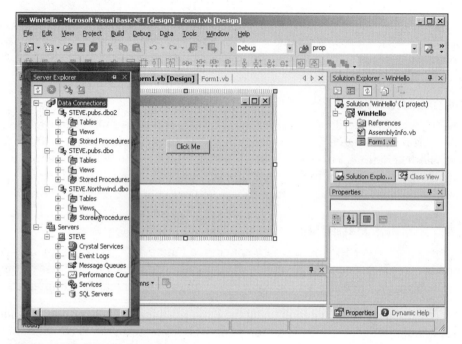

Figure 1.33   The Server Explorer.

The Output Window

If you look at the bottom of the IDE, you'll see two tabs for the Output and Breakpoints windows. We'll look at the Breakpoints window when we discuss debugging, because it lets you manage the breakpoints at which program execution halts when you're debugging your code. The Output window, which you see in Figure 1.34, on the other hand, gives you the results of building and running programs, as you can also see in Figure 1.34.

You can also send messages to the Output window yourself if you use the **System.Diagnostics.Debug.Write** method like this: **System.Diagnostics. Debug.Write("Hello from the Output window!")**.

The Task List

The Task List is another useful window that not many Visual Basic programmers know about. To see it, select the View|Show Tasks|All; this window appears in Figure 1.35. As its name implies, the Task List displays tasks that VB .NET assumes you still have to take care of, and when you click a task, the corresponding location in a code designer appears.

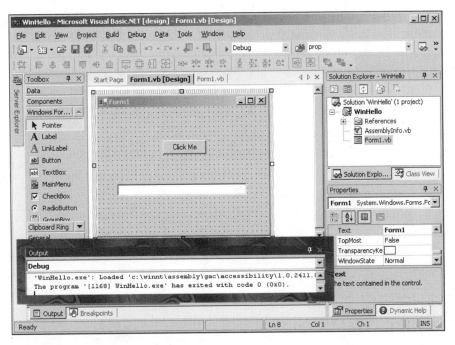

Figure 1.34 The Output window.

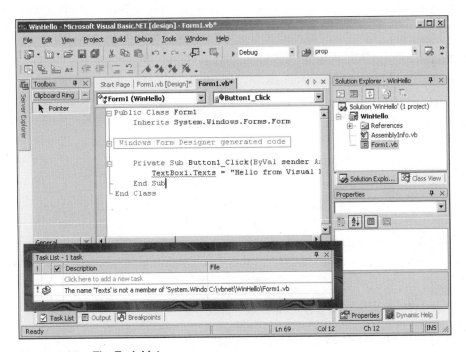

Figure 1.35 The Task List.

There are a number of such tasks; for example, if VB .NET has detected a syntax error, underlined with a wavy line as shown in Figure 1.35, that error will appear in the task list. If you've used a wizard, such as the Upgrade Wizard where VB .NET still wants you to take care of certain issues, it'll put a TODO comment into the code, as we saw earlier:

```
If blnDrawFlag Then
    'UPGRADE_ISSUE: Graphics statements can't be migrated.
    'Click for more: ms-help://MS.MSDNVS/vbcon/html/vbup2034.htm
    Line(X,Y)
End If
```

TODO comments like this will appear in the Task List.

TIP: *In fact, you can create your own custom comments that the Task List will track. To do so, select the Tools|Options menu item then select the Task List item in the Environment folder, and enter the name of your custom comments in the Comment Token area. For example, if I entered STEVE there, then any comments beginning with 'STEVE will be tracked in the Task List.*

The Command Window

Plenty of other windows are available. For example, selecting View|Other Windows|Command Window opens the Command window, as you see in Figure 1.36.

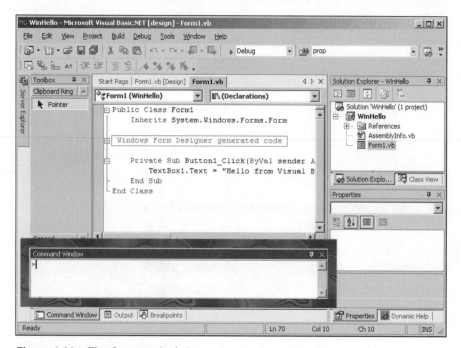

Figure 1.36   The Command window.

This window is a little like the Immediate window in VB6, because you can enter commands like **File.AddNewProject** here and VB .NET will display the Add New Project dialog box. However, this window is not exactly like the Immediate window, because you can't enter Visual Basic code and have it executed.

And there are other windows that we'll see as needed, such as when we're discussing debugging programs where we'll introduce the Call Stack window, the Breakpoints window, Watch and Value display windows, Autos and Locals windows, and so on.

There's another new aspect of the IDE that bears mention—macros. You can use macros to execute a series of commands in the Visual Studio environment. If you want to give macros a try, take a look at the Macros submenu in the Tools menu.

There's more to the IDE than we've been able to cover here, but now we've gotten the foundation we'll need in the coming chapters. I'll end this chapter by taking a look at coding practices in VB .NET; if you're not thoroughly familiar with Visual Basic yet, some of this might not make sense, so treat it as a section to refer back to later.

Coding to Get the Most from Visual Basic

In this section, we'll discuss some of the best coding practices for Visual Basic. All of these practices come from professional programmers, but whether you implement them or not is up to you, of course. Here we go.

Avoid "magic numbers" when you can. A magic number is a number (excluding 0 or 1) that's hardwired right into your code like this:

```
Function blnCheckSize(dblParameter As Double) As Boolean

    If dblParameter > 1024 Then
        blnCheckSize = True

    Else
        blnCheckSize = False

    End If
End Function
```

Here, 1024 is a magic number. It's better to declare such numbers as constants, especially if you have several of them. When it's time to change your code, you just have to change the constant declaration in one place, instead of trying to find all the magic numbers scattered around your code.

Be modular. Putting code and data together into modules and classes hides it from the rest of the program, makes it easier to debug, makes it easier to work with conceptually, and even makes load-time of procedures in the same module quicker. Being modular, also called information-hiding or encapsulation in OOP, is the backbone of working with larger programs. Divide and conquer is the idea here.

Program defensively. For example, check data passed to you in a procedure before using it. This can save a bug from propagating throughout your program, and also help pinpoint its source. Make no assumptions.

Visual Basic procedures should have only one purpose, ideally. This is also an aid in larger programs when things start to get complex. Certainly if a procedure has two distinct tasks, consider breaking it up.

Avoid deep nesting of conditionals or loops, because debugging them visually is very, very inefficient. If you need to, place some of the inner loops or conditionals in new procedures and call them. Three levels of nesting should be about the maximum.

Use property procedures to protect sensitive data (this is part of programming defensively). Property procedures are called by the rest of the program when you want to work with sensitive data, and provide an interface to that data.

Ideally, variables should always be defined with the smallest scope possible. Global variables can create enormously complex conditions.

Do not pass global variables to procedures; if you do, the procedure you pass that variable to might give it one name (as a passed parameter) and also reference it as a global variable, which can lead to some serious bugs, because now the procedure has two different names for the variable.

When you create a long string, use the underscore line-continuation character to create multiple lines of code so that you can read or debug the string easily. For example:

```
Dim Msg As String
Msg = "Well, there is a problem " _
& "with your program. I am not sure " _
& "what the problem is, but there is " _
& "definitely something wrong."
```

Microsoft recommends that you indent your code with 4 spaces (believe it or not, there have been serious studies undertaken here, and 2–4 spaces was found to be best). But at least be consistent.

If you work in teams, use version control. There are several well-known utilities that help programmers work in teams, and you can integrate such utilities into VB .NET. The enterprise edition of Visual Basic comes with Visual SourceSafe, which is perfect for this purpose.

And that's enough overview—it's time to start creating Visual Basic programs and seeing what goes into the process. Let's get to some working programs now in Chapter 2.

Chapter 2

The Visual Basic Language: Operators, Conditionals, and Loops

In Depth

This chapter and the chapters that follow are all about the glue that holds the various parts of a Visual Basic program together: the Visual Basic language itself. In this chapter, we'll take a look at the elements of the Visual Basic language: how to declare variables and arrays, and how to use those elements. We'll see how to use strings, conditionals, operators, loops, and math techniques. We'll also see how to handle special Visual Basic formats like dates and financial data. And we'll see some items that programmers like but don't often see in programming books, like how to use **Switch** and **Choose**.

We'll cover tasks that involve some complexity and whose syntax is hard to remember in this chapter. In this way, this chapter also acts as a reference for easy lookup of those hard-to-remember items—and can save you from reinventing the wheel.

We'll see a lot of code in this chapter and throughout the book. To keep things simple, I'll use console applications, because they're the simplest to code and will keep extraneous details from getting in the way. Here's the console application we developed in the previous chapter that displayed the words "Hello from Visual Basic" in a DOS window:

```
Module Module1
    Sub Main()
        System.Console.WriteLine("Hello from Visual Basic")
    End Sub
End Module
```

Here, we're creating a Visual Basic *module*, and modules are designed to hold code. **Sub Main** indicates the entry point of our program—the part that will be executed first. And we're using the **WriteLine** *method* of the **System.Console** class to write to the console (that is, DOS window). Methods are procedures that are built into classes—note the syntax here; to call a method, you specify the class or object the method is part of, followed by a dot (.) and the method name. This tells Visual Basic where to look to find the method you want to use. We'll become familiar with syntax like this in this chapter and Chapter 3. As you can see, there are all kinds of terms here that have special meaning in Visual Basic, such as **Sub**, **Module**, **End**, and so on; those are Visual Basic *keywords*.

The Visual Basic Keywords

As with all programming languages, Visual Basic is built using keywords. You'll find these keywords in Table 2.1. These keywords are reserved for use by Visual Basic, and you use them to build your programs.

Table 2.1   The Visual Basic keywords.

#Const	#If...Then...#Else	&	&=	*
*=	/	/=	\	\=
^^=	+	+=	=	-=
Add	AddHandler	AddressOf	Alias	And
AndAlso	Ansi	AppActivate	As	Asc
AscW	Assembly	Auto	Beep	Boolean
ByRef	Byte	ByVal	Call	CallByName
Case	Catch	CBool	CByte	CChar
CDate	CDbl	CDec	Char	ChDir
ChDrive	Choose	Chr	CInt	Class
Clear	CLng	Close	CObj	Command
Const	Count	CreateObject	CShort	CSng
CStr	CType	CurDir	Date	DateAdd
DateDiff	DatePart	DateSerial	DateString	DateValue
Day	DDB	Decimal	Declare	Default
Delegate	DeleteSetting	Description	Dim	Dir
Do	Double	Each	Else	ElseIf
End	Enum	Environ	EOF	Erase
Erl	Err	Error	ErrorToString	Event
Exit	ExternalSource	False	FileAttr	FileCopy
FileDateTime	FileGet	FileLen	FileOpen	FilePut
FileWidth	Filter	Finally	Fix	For
FormatCurrency	FormatDateTime	FormatNumber	FormatPercent	FreeFile
Friend	Function	FV	Get	GetAllSettings
GetAttr	GetChar	GetException	GetObject	GetSetting
GetType	GoTo	Handles	HelpContext	HelpFile
Hex	Hour	If	IIf	Implements
Imports	In	Inherits	Input	InputBox
InputString	InStr	InStrRev	Int	Integer
Interface	IPmt	IRR	Is	IsArray
IsDate	IsDBNull	IsError	IsNothing	IsNumeric
IsReference	Item	Join	Kill	LastDllError
LBound	LCase	Left	Len	Let
Lib	Like	LineInput	Loc	Lock
LOF	Long	Loop	LSet	LTrim
Me	Mid	Minute	MIRR	MkDir
Mod	Module	Month	MonthName	MsgBox

(continued)

Table 2.1   The Visual Basic keywords *(continued)*.

MustInherit	MustOverride	MyBase	MyClass	Namespace
New	Next	Not	Nothing	NotInheritable
NotOverridable	Now	NPer	NPV	Number
Object	Oct	On	Option	Optional
Or	OrElse	Overloads	Overridable	Overrides
ParamArray	Partition	Pmt	PPmt	Preserve
Print	PrintLine	Private	Property	Protected
Public	PV	QBColor	Raise	RaiseEvent
Randomize	Rate	ReadOnly	ReDim	Region
Rem	Remove	RemoveHandler	Rename	Replace
Reset	Resume	Return	RGB	RmDir
Rnd	RSet	RTrim	SaveSetting	Seek
ScriptEngine BuildVersion	ScriptEngine MajorVersion	ScriptEngine MinorVersion	ScriptEngine Select	Second Set
SetAttr	Shadows	Shared	Shell	Short
Single	SLN	Source	Space	Spc
Split	Static	Step	Stop	Str
StrComp	StrConv	StrDup	String	StrReverse
Structure	Sub	Switch	SYD	SyncLock
SystemTypeName	Tab	Then	Throw	TimeOfDay
Timer	TimeSerial	TimeString	TimeValue	To
Today	Trim	True	Try	TypeName
TypeOf	UBound	UCase	Unicode	Unlock
Until	Val	Variant	VarType	VbTypeName
WeekDay	WeekDayName	When	While	With
WithEvents	Write	WriteLine	WriteOnly	Xor
Year				

TIP: *Although the keywords in Table 2.1 are reserved for use by VB .NET, it turns out you can use them for your own use if you surround them with brackets, [and]. For example, if you wanted to name a text string* **Error***, you could actually use the term* **[Error]** *as a variable.*

There are also quite a few keywords and phrases in VB6 that are now obsolete, which you can see in Table 2.2.

In general, Visual Basic programs are made up line by line of code, and these lines of code are called *statements*.

Table 2.2   Visual Basic 6 keywords and phrases now obsolete.

As Any	Atn	Calendar	Circle	Currency
Date$	Debug.Assert	Debug.Print	Deftype	DoEvents
Empty	Eqv	GoSub	Imp	Initialize
Instancing	IsEmpty	IsMissing	IsNull	IsObject
Let	Line	LSet	MsgBox	Now
Null	On...GoSub	On...GoTo	Option Base	Option
Private	Module	Property Get,	PSet	Rnd
Round	RSet	Property Let, and	Scale	Set
Sgn	Sqr	Property Set	Terminate	Time
Time$	Type	Varian	VarType	Wend

Visual Basic Statements

A Visual Basic statement is a complete instruction. It can contain:

- *keywords*—Words reserved for Visual Basic's use.

- *operators*—Symbols used to perform operations, like **+**, which performs addition operations; **-**, which performs subtraction operations; and so on.

- *variables*—Symbolic names given to values stored in memory and declared with the **Dim** keyword. For example, if you've declared a variable named **temperature** as an Integer type, you can store integer values like **72** or **83** in it.

- *literal values*—Simple values, like **5** or "**Hello**."

- *constants*—The same as variables, except that constants are assigned a value that cannot then be altered.

- *expressions*—Combinations of terms and/or keywords that yield a value. For example, if the variable **temperature** holds the value **72**, then the expression **temperature + 3** yields the value **75**.

Each statement is one of the following:

- A declaration statement, which can name and create a variable, constant, or procedure and can also specify a *data type*. The data type can be **Boolean**, **Byte**, **Char**, **Date**, **Decimal**, **Double**, **Integer**, **Long**, **Object**, **Short**, **Single**, or **String**; or the name of an enumeration (a series of constants defined at the same time), structure, class, or interface.

- An executable statement, which can perform an action. These statements can execute a method or function, or they can loop through code using one of the Visual Basic *loops* we'll see in this chapter, which execute a series of statements repetitively, or they can be an *assignment statement*, which assign a value or expression to a variable or constant such as this: **temperature = 72**, and so on.

Besides having single statements in your code, statements can also be grouped into *blocks*, as we'll see when we discuss conditions like the **If** statement, which might look like this, where I'm testing the value in the variable **BankBalance** to see if it's less than 0:

```
Module Module1

    Sub Main()
        Dim BankBalance As Single = 500.01
        If (BankBalance < 0) Then
            Dim strError As String
            strError = "Hey, your bank balance is negative!"
            System.Console.WriteLine(strError)
        End If
    End Sub

End Module
```

In this case, I've surrounded three statements inside an **If** statement, which starts with **If (BankBalance < 0) Then** and ends with **End If**, creating a block of statements. The statement that uses the **Dim** keyword is a declaration statement that creates the variable **BankBalance** and gives it the value **500.01**. When you create a variable like this you can also set its *data type*, selecting **Boolean**, **Byte**, **Char**, **Date**, **Decimal**, **Double**, **Integer**, **Long**, **Object**, **Short**, **Single**, or **String**, or the name of an enumeration, structure, class, or interface—more on these options later in this chapter.

Statements like **System.Console.WriteLine("Press Enter to continue...")** are execution statements that perform actions. Note also the statement **strError = "Hey, your bank balance is negative!"**—this is an *assignment statement* (a type of execution statement) that I'm using to assign the text "Hey, your bank balance is negative!" to the variable **strError**. To be able to handle text strings this way, I've declared **strError** as a variable of type **String**. After I've declared **strError**, I can assign strings to this variable using the = *assignment operator*.

You also can have multiple statements on the same line in VB .NET, if you separate them with a colon (:), as I'm doing here, where I'm declaring a variable named **temperature** (you need to declare variables before using them) and giving it a value of **72**:

```
Dim temperature As Integer : temperature = 72
```

Conversely, you can also break long statements up over several lines if you want, as long as you use an underscore (_) at the end of each line, like this, where I'm assigning a value to the **temperature** variable:

```
Dim temperature As Integer
temperature = 1 + 2 + 3 _
+ 4 + 5 + 6 _
+ 7 + 8 + 9 + 10
```

You have to be careful about strings of text, which are enclosed in quotation marks in Visual Basic. If you want to break a statement in the middle of a string, you must divide the string into two or more strings, using the **&** *string concatenation operator* (**+** can also function as a concatenation operator) to tell Visual Basic that you want multiple strings joined together into one, like this:

```
System.Console.WriteLine("This is a very long sentence that I " _
& "want to display to the user")
```

All About Statement Syntax

Each statement has its own syntax, and there are a few conventions and terms you should be aware of before getting started: In the formal definition of each statement, you use brackets, [and], for optional items, and curly braces, { and }, to indicate that you select one of the enclosed items, like this for the **Dim** statement:

```
[ <attrlist> ] [{ Public | Protected | Friend | Protected Friend |
Private | Static }] [ Shared ] [ Shadows ] [ ReadOnly ] Dim [ WithEvents ]
name[ (boundlist) ] [ As [ New ] type ] [ = initexpr ]
```

Here, all the items in square brackets are optional, and you only choose one of the items in curly braces if you want to use the keyword **Public**, **Protected**, **Friend**, **Protected Friend**, **Private**, or **Static**. I'll explain the keywords used in each statement; note that keywords like **Public**, **Protected**, **Friend**, **Protected Friend**, and **Private** will only really make sense when you've mastered object-oriented programming, which we'll discuss later in the book:

- *attrlist*—A list of attributes that apply to the variables you're declaring in this statement. You separate multiple attributes with commas.

- **Public**—Gives variables public access, which means there are no restrictions on their accessibility. You can use **Public** only at module, namespace, or file level (which means you can't use it inside a procedure). Note that if you specify **Public**, you can omit the **Dim** keyword if you want to.

- **Protected**—Gives variables protected access, which means they are accessible only from within their own class or from a class derived from that class. You can use **Protected** only at class level (which means you can't use it inside a procedure), because you use it to declare members of a class. Note that if you specify **Protected**, you can omit the **Dim** keyword if you want to.

- **Friend**—Gives variables friend access, which means they are accessible from within the program that contains their declaration, as well as anywhere else in the same assembly. You can use **Friend** only at module, namespace, or file level (which means you can't use it inside a procedure). Note that if you specify **Friend**, you can omit the **Dim** keyword if you want to.

- **Protected Friend**—Gives variables both protected and friend access, which means they can be used by code in the same assembly, as well as by code in derived classes.

- **Private**—Gives variables private access, which means they are accessible only from within their declaration context (usually a class), including any nested procedures. You can use **Private** only at module, namespace, or file level (which means you can't use it inside a procedure). Note that if you specify **Private**, you can omit the **Dim** keyword if you want to.

- **Static**—Makes variables static, which means they'll retain their values, even after the procedure in which they're declared ends. You can declare static variables inside a procedure or a block within a procedure, but not at class or module level. Note that if you specify **Static**, you can omit the **Dim** keyword if you want to, but you cannot use either **Shadows** or **Shared**.

- **Shared**—Declares a shared variable, which means it is not associated with a specific instance of a class or structure, but can be shared across many instances. You access a shared variable by referring to it either with its class or structure name, or with the variable name of an instance of the class or structure. You can use **Shared** only at module, namespace, or file level (but not at the procedure level). Note that if you specify **Shared**, you can omit the **Dim** keyword if you want to.

- **Shadows**—Makes this variable a shadow of an identically named programming element in a base class. A shadowed element is unavailable in the derived class that shadows it. You can use **Shadows** only at module, namespace, or file level (but not inside a procedure). This means you can declare shadowing variables in a source file or inside a module, class, or structure, but not inside a procedure. Note that if you specify **Shadows**, you can omit the **Dim** keyword if you want to.

- **ReadOnly**—Means this variable only can be read and not written. This can be useful for creating constant members of reference types, such as an object variable with preset data members. You can use **ReadOnly** only at module, namespace, or file level (but not inside procedures). Note that if you specify **ReadOnly**, you can omit the **Dim** keyword if you want to.

- **WithEvents**—Specifies that this variable is used to respond to events caused by the instance that was assigned to the variable. Note that you cannot specify both **WithEvents** and **New** in the same variable declaration.

- *name*—The name of the variable. You separate multiple variables by commas. If you specify multiple variables, each variable is declared of the data type given in the first **As** clause encountered after its *name* part.

- *boundlist*—Used to declare arrays; gives the upper bounds of the dimensions of an array variable. Multiple upper bounds are separated by commas. An array can have up to 60 dimensions.

- **New**—Means you want to create a new object immediately. If you use **New** when declaring an object variable, a new instance of the object is created. Note that you cannot use both **WithEvents** and **New** in the same declaration.

- *type*—The data type of the variable. Can be **Boolean**, **Byte**, **Char**, **Date**, **Decimal**, **Double**, **Integer**, **Long**, **Object**, **Short**, **Single**, or **String**; or the name of an enumeration, structure, class, or interface. To specify the type, you use a separate **As** clause for each variable, or you can declare a number of variables of the same type by using common **As** clauses. If you do not specify *type*, the variable takes the data type of *initexpr*. Note that if you don't specify either *type* or *initexpr*, the data type is set to **Object**.

- *initexpr*—An initialization expression that is evaluated and the result is assigned to the variable when it is created. Note that if you declare more than one variable with the same **As** clause, you cannot supply *initexpr* for those variables.

Overview: Procedures, Classes, Modules, Methods, and More

Note the terms like *module* and *class* above; they are important in the definition of the **Dim** statement. If you've programmed in Visual Basic before, you're familiar with terms like these. However, if these terms are unfamiliar to you, they can present a barrier in your study of Visual Basic, because—as with so many aspects of Visual Basic .NET—you need some preliminary understanding of terms like these to get anywhere at all. Here's an overview of like terms that will come up a great deal; if you're already familiar with Visual Basic programming, feel free to skip this list, and if some of these are unfamiliar to you, don't worry, we'll see them all in detail in this book:

- *block*—As we've seen, a block of statements is made up of a number of statements, enclosed inside another statement designed for that purpose.

- *file*—Refers to code in the same file.

- *variable*—A named memory location of a specific data type (such as **Integer**) that stores data. You can assign data to a variable with the assignment operator; for example, if you have a variable named **temperature**, you can assign it a value of **72** like this: **temperature = 72**.

- *procedure*—A callable series of statements that may or may not return a value. You may pass data to the procedure in the form of *parameters* in a procedure call like this **addem(2, 3)**, where **2** and **3** are parameters I'm passing to a procedure named **addem**. When the series of statements terminates, control returns to the statement that called the procedure.

- *sub procedure*—A procedure that does not return a value.

- *function*—A procedure that returns a value.

- *method*—A procedure that is built into a class.

- *constructor*—A special method that is automatically called when you create an object from a class. Used to initialize and customize the object. You can pass data to constructor methods just like other methods.

- *module*—Visual Basic modules are designed to hold code—that is, to separate the code in them from other, possibly conflicting, code. Their main purpose is to make your code more modular, and if your program is a long one, you should consider breaking it up into modules.

- *class*—This is an OOP class, which can contain both code and data; you use classes to create objects. A class can have *members*, which are elements that can be accessible from outside the class if you so specify. Data members are called *fields*, procedure members are called *methods*.

- *object*—This is an *instance* of a class, much like a variable is an instance of a data type.

- *shared or static members and instance members*—Fields and methods that apply to a class and are invoked with the class name are called *shared* or *static* fields and methods; the fields and methods that apply to objects created from the class are called *instance* fields and methods.

- *structure*—Also an OOP element, just like a class but with some additional restrictions. In VB6 and earlier, you used structures to create user-defined types; now they are another form of OOP classes.

Note also the term *attrlist* in the description of the parts of the **Dim** statement above. This term corresponds to a list of attributes; attributes are new to VB .NET, and I'll take a look at them here.

Understanding Attributes

Attributes are items that let you specify information about the items you're using in VB .NET. You enclose attributes in angle brackets, < and >, and you use them when VB .NET needs to know more than standard syntax can specify. For example, if you want to call one of the functions that make up the Windows Application Programming Interface (API), you have to specify the Windows Dynamic Link Libraries (DLLs) that the function you're calling resides in, which you can do with the **DllImport** attribute, like this:

```
Public Shared Function <DllImport("user32.dll")> MessageBox(ByVal Hwnd...
```

As we need to use various attributes, I'll discuss how they work. You can use an attribute like this: **<theAttribute>**, or pass its values as parameters as you do to a procedure, like this: **<theAttribute("Watch out!")>**. Some attributes require the use of named parameters, which you must list specifically when you assign a value to them with the **:=** operator like this: **<theAttribute(Warning := "Watch out!")>**. We won't be using attributes in these early chapters.

The Option and Imports Statements

Two additional statements that are very important to know about when constructing programs are the **Option** and **Imports** statements. The **Option** statement sets a number of options for the rest of your code, and the **Imports** statement imports namespaces into your code, making them more readily available.

Option Statements

You use **Option** statements to set the "ground rules" for your code, helping prevent syntax and logic errors. Here are the possibilities:

- **Option Explicit**—Set to **On** or **Off**. **On** is the default. Requires declaration of all variables before they are used (this is the default).

- **Option Compare**—Set to **Binary** or **Text**. This specifies if strings are compared using binary or text comparison operations.

- **Option Strict**—Set to **On** or **Off**. **Off** is the default. When you assign a value of one type to a variable of another type Visual Basic will consider that an error if this option is on and there is any possibility of data loss, as when you're trying to assign the value in a variable to a variable of less precise data storage capacity. In that case, you must use explicit conversion functions of the kind we'll see in this chapter, like **CLng**.

You use **Option** statements first thing in code, like this one in which I'm turning **Option Strict** off:

```
Option Strict Off
Module Module1
    Sub Main()
        System.Console.WriteLine("Hello from Visual Basic")
    End Sub

End Module
```

Imports Statements

You use **Imports** statements to import a namespace so you don't have to qualify items in that namespace by listing the entire namespace when you refer to them. For example, here's what our code might look like; the **WriteLine** procedure is built into the **System.Console** namespace, so it is a method of that namespace, and to use it, I qualify its name with the namespace it belongs to:

```
Option Strict Off
Module Module1

    Sub Main()
        System.Console.WriteLine("Hello from Visual Basic")
    End Sub

End Module
```

On the other hand, if we import the **System.Console** namespace, that makes that namespace immediately available, so we don't have to qualify the **WriteLine** method name anymore (note that **Option** statements, if there are any, must still come first):

```
Option Strict Off
Imports System.Console
Module Module1

    Sub Main()
        WriteLine("Hello from Visual Basic")
    End Sub

End Module
```

TIP: *Each project has its own root namespace, and by default, Visual Basic uses the name of the project for the root namespace. If you prefer, you can set another namespace—just right-click the project in the Solutions Explorer, select the Properties menu item, open the Common Properties folder, select the General item, and enter the new namespace name in the Root Namespace box.*

And that's it—that completes the introductory material we need. It's time to turn to the Immediate Solutions to the Visual Basic Language.

Immediate Solutions

Declaring Constants

You've filled your code with numeric values—and now it's time to change them all as you start work on the new version of the software! What a pain to have to track down and change all the numeric values throughout all the code. Isn't there a better way?

There is. Use constants and declare them all in one place. Then refer to the constants by name throughout the code instead of hardwiring numeric values in the code. When it's time to change those values, you just change the constants, all in one well-defined part of the code.

How do you use constants? You declare constants in Visual Basic with the **Const** statement, which you can use at the module, class, structure, procedure, or block level to declare constants for use in place of literal values:

```
[ <attrlist> ] [{ Public | Protected | Friend | Protected Friend |
Private }] [ Shadows ] Const name [ As type ] = initexpr
```

Here are the various parts of this statement:

- *attrlist*—A list of attributes that apply to the constants you're declaring in this statement. You separate multiple attributes with commas.

- **Public**—Gives constants public access, which means there are no restrictions on their accessibility. You can use **Public** only at module, namespace, or file level (which means you can't use it inside a procedure). Note that if you specify **Public**, you can omit the **Dim** keyword if you want to.

- **Protected**—Gives constants protected access, which means they are accessible only from within their own class or from a class derived from that class. You can use **Protected** only at class level (which means you can't use it inside a procedure), because you use it to declare members of a class. Note that if you specify **Protected**, you can omit the **Dim** keyword if you want to.

- **Friend**—Gives constants friend access, which means they are accessible from within the program that contains their declaration, as well as anywhere else in the same assembly. You can use **Friend** only at module, namespace, or file level (which means you can't use it inside a procedure). Note that if you specify **Friend**, you can omit the **Dim** keyword if you want to.

- **Protected Friend**—Gives constants both protected and friend access, which means they can be used by code in the same assembly, as well as by code in derived classes.

- **Private**—Gives constants private access, which means they are accessible only from within their declaration context (usually a class), including any nested procedures. You can use **Private** only at module, namespace, or file level (which means you can't use it inside a procedure). Note that if you specify **Private**, you can omit the **Dim** keyword if you want to.

- **Shadows**—Makes this constant a shadow of an identically named programming element in a base class. A shadowed element is unavailable in the derived class that shadows it. You can use **Shadows** only at module, namespace, or file level (but not inside a procedure). This means you can declare shadowing variables in a source file or inside a module, class, or structure, but not inside a procedure. Note that if you specify **Shadows**, you can omit the **Dim** keyword if you want to.

- *name*—The name of the constant. You can declare as many constants as you like in the same declaration statement, specifying the *name* and *initexpr* parts for each one. You separate multiple constants with commas.

- *type*—The data type of the constant. Can be **Boolean**, **Byte**, **Char**, **Date**, **Decimal**, **Double**, **Integer**, **Long**, **Object**, **Short**, **Single**, **String**, or the name of an enumeration. Note that you must use a separate **As** clause for each constant being defined. Note also that if *type* is **Object**, *initexpr* must be **Nothing**.

- *initexpr*—An initialization expression. Can consist of a literal, another constant, a member of an enumeration, or any combination of literals, constants, and enumeration members.

Each attribute in the *attrlist* list must use this syntax:

```
<attrname [({ attrargs | attrinit })]>
```

Here are the parts of the *attrlist* list:

- *attrname*—Name of the attribute.

- *attrargs*—List of arguments for this attribute. Separate multiple arguments with commas.

- *attrinit*—List of field or property initializers for this attribute. Separate multiple arguments with commas.

Here's an example showing how to declare and use a constant; in this case, I'm creating a constant named **Pi**, as well as **Area** and **Radius** variables, using the * (multiplication) operator to find the area of a circle, then converting that area from a number to a string with the Visual Basic **Str** function, and displaying the result:

```
Imports System.Console
Module Module1

    Sub Main()
        Const Pi = 3.14159
        Dim Radius, Area As Single
        Radius = 1
        Area = Pi * Radius * Radius
        WriteLine("Area = " & Str(Area))
    End Sub

End Module
```

Creating Enumerations

You've got a hundred constants to declare, and you would like to break them up into functional groups—isn't there an easy way to handle this? There is—you can create an *enumeration*, which is a related set of constants. You create enumerations with the **Enum** statement at module, class, structure, procedure, or block level:

```
[ <attrlist> ] [{ Public | Protected | Friend | Protected Friend |
Private }] [ Shadows ] Enum name [ As type ]
   [<attrlist1>] membname1 [ = initexpr1 ]
   [<attrlist2>] membname2 [ = initexpr2 ]
       .
       .
       .
   [<attrlistn>] membnamen [ = initexprn ]
End Enum
```

The parts of this statement are the same as for constants (see the previous Solution). Here's an example that shows how this works; in this case, I'm setting up an enumeration that assigns a constant to every day of the week:

```
Module Module1
    Enum Days
        Sunday = 1
        Monday = 2
```

```
        Tuesday = 3
        Wednesday = 4
        Thursday = 5
        Friday = 6
        Saturday = 7
    End Enum

    Sub Main()
        System.Console.WriteLine("Friday is day " & Days.Friday)
    End Sub

End Module
```

To use a constant in the enumeration, you refer to it like this: **Days.Friday**, **Days.Monday**, and so on. Here's the result of this code:

```
Friday is day 6
Press any key to continue
```

Declaring Variables

You need to store some data in your program—so you need to declare some variables. How does that work? Unlike VB6 and earlier versions of Visual Basic, you must declare all variables before using them by default in VB .NET, and you can do that with the **Dim** statement (which originally stood for dimension, as when you set the dimensions of an array); this statement is used at module, class, structure, procedure, or block level:

```
[ <attrlist> ] [{ Public | Protected | Friend | Protected Friend |
Private | Static }] [ Shared ] [ Shadows ] [ ReadOnly ] Dim [ WithEvents ]
name[ (boundlist) ] [ As [ New ] type ] [ = initexpr ]
```

Here are the parts of this statement:

- *attrlist*—A list of attributes that apply to the variables you're declaring in this statement. You separate multiple attributes with commas.

- **Public**—Gives variables public access, which means there are no restrictions on their accessibility. You can use **Public** only at module, namespace, or file level (which means you can't use it inside a procedure). Note that if you specify **Public**, you can omit the **Dim** keyword if you want to.

- **Protected**—Gives variables protected access, which means they are accessible only from within their own class or from a class derived from that class. You can use **Protected** only at class level (which means you can't use it inside a procedure), because you use it to declare members of a class. Note that if you specify **Protected**, you can omit the **Dim** keyword if you want to.

- **Friend**—Gives variables friend access, which means they are accessible from within the program that contains their declaration, as well as from anywhere else in the same assembly. You can use **Friend** only at module, namespace, or file level (which means you can't use it inside a procedure). Note that if you specify **Friend**, you can omit the **Dim** keyword if you want to.

- **Protected Friend**—Gives variables both protected and friend access, which means they can be used by code in the same assembly, as well as by code in derived classes.

- **Private**—Gives variables private access, which means they are accessible only from within their declaration context (usually a class), including any nested procedures. You can use **Private** only at module, namespace, or file level (which means you can't use it inside a procedure). Note that if you specify **Private**, you can omit the **Dim** keyword if you want to.

- **Static**—Makes variables static, which means they'll retain their values, even after the procedure in which they're declared ends. You can declare static variables inside a procedure or a block within a procedure, but not at class or module level. Note that if you specify **Static**, you can omit the **Dim** keyword if you want to, but you cannot use either **Shadows** or **Shared**.

- **Shared**—Declares a shared variable, which means it is not associated with a specific instance of a class or structure, but can be shared across many instances. You access a shared variable by referring to it either with its class or structure name, or with the variable name of an instance of the class or structure. You can use **Shared** only at module, namespace, or file level (but not at the procedure level). Note that if you specify **Shared**, you can omit the **Dim** keyword if you want to.

- **Shadows**—Makes this variable a shadow of an identically named programming element in a base class. A shadowed element is unavailable in the derived class that shadows it. You can use **Shadows** only at module, namespace, or file level (but not inside a procedure). This means you can declare shadowing variables in a source file or inside a module, class, or structure, but not inside a procedure. Note that if you specify **Shadows**, you can omit the **Dim** keyword if you want to.

- **ReadOnly**—Means this variable only can be read and not written. This can be useful for creating constant members of reference types, such as an object variable with preset data members. You can use **ReadOnly** only at module, namespace, or file level (but not inside procedures). Note that if you specify **Shadows**, you can omit the **ReadOnly** keyword if you want to.

- **WithEvents**—Specifies that this variable is used to respond to events caused by the instance that was assigned to the variable. Note that you cannot specify both **WithEvents** and **New** in the same variable declaration.

- *name*—The name of the variable. You separate multiple variables by commas. If you specify multiple variables, each variable is declared of the data type given in the first **As** clause encountered after its *name* part.

- *boundlist*—Used to declare arrays; gives the upper bounds of the dimensions of an array variable. Multiple upper bounds are separated by commas. An array can have up to 60 dimensions.

- **New**—Means you want to create a new object immediately. If you use **New** when declaring an object variable, a new instance of the object is created. Note that you cannot use both **WithEvents** and **New** in the same declaration.

- *type*—The data type of the variable. Can be **Boolean**, **Byte**, **Char**, **Date**, **Decimal**, **Double**, **Integer**, **Long**, **Object**, **Short**, **Single**, or **String**; or the name of an enumeration, structure, class, or interface. To specify the type, you use a separate **As** clause for each variable, or you can declare a number of variables of the same type by using common **As** clauses. If you do not specify *type*, the variable takes the data type of *initexpr*. Note that if you don't specify either *type* or *initexpr*, the data type is set to **Object**.

- *initexpr*—An initialization expression that is evaluated and the result is assigned to the variable when it is created. Note that if you declare more than one variable with the same **As** clause, you cannot supply *initexpr* for those variables.

Each attribute in the *attrlist* list must use this syntax:

```
<attrname [({ attrargs | attrinit })]>
```

Here are the parts of the *attrlist* list:

- *attrname*—Name of the attribute.

- *attrargs*—List of arguments for this attribute. Separate multiple arguments with commas.

- *attrinit*—List of field or property initializers for this attribute. Separate multiple arguments with commas.

Here are a few examples where I'm declaring variables—note in particular that you can initialize the value in a variable when you declare it by using the = sign and assigning it a value, as here, where I'm initializing the first variable to the value **1**, and the second one to **"Bob Owens"**:

```
Dim EmployeeID As Integer = 1
Dim EmployeeName As String = "Bob Owens"
Dim EmployeeAddress As String
```

The default data type if you do not specify one is **Object** (not **Variant**, as in VB6, because **Variant** no longer exists). Note also that if you do not specify an initialization value for a variable, Visual Basic will initialize it to a default value for its data type:

- **0** for all numeric types (including **Byte**).

- Binary **0** for **Char**.

- **Nothing** for all reference types (including **Object**, **String**, and all arrays). **Nothing** means there is no object associated with the reference.

- **False** for **Boolean**.

- **12:00 AM of January 1 of the year 1** for **Date**.

To create a new object, you use the **New** keyword, as in this case, where I'm creating a new VB .NET **LinkLabel** control (which we'll see in Chapter 5):

```
Dim LinkLabel1 As New LinkLabel
```

Note that you do not have to create a new object using **New** when you declare it—you can create it later using **New**, after it's been declared:

```
Dim LinkLabel1 As LinkLabel
     .
     .
     .
```

```
LinkLabel1 = New LinkLabel()
```

In VB6, you could also declare an object with the **New** keyword to create that object—but although it seemed that that would create the new object immediately, the object wasn't actually created until used in code, resulting in some hard-to-find bugs. This has been fixed in VB .NET, where the new object is created immediately if you declare it with the **New** keyword.

Also in Visual Basic 6.0, you could declare variables of different types in the same statement, but you had to specify the data type of each variable or it defaulted to **Variant** (which no longer exists). Here's an example:

```
Dim count1, count2 As Integer    'count1 is a Variant, count2 is an Integer.
```

In Visual Basic .NET, on the other hand, you can declare multiple variables of the same data type without having to repeat the type keyword:

```
Dim count1, count2 As Integer    'count1 is an Integer, count2 is an
    Integer.
```

Some people think that variable names should be prefixed to indicate their data type. Table 2.3 lists the some of the prefixes that have become conventional for the Visual Basic data types (for more on these types, see the next topic). This use is optional.

For example, here are some prefixed variable names:

```
blnTrueFalse         'Boolean
intCounter 'Integer
sngDividend 'Single
```

Using variable prefixes this way provides some clue as to the variable's type, and that can be extraordinarily helpful if someone else will be reading your code.

Table 2.3   Variable prefixes.

Data type	Prefix
Boolean	bln
Byte	byt
Collection object	col
Date (Time)	dtm
Double	dbl
Error	err
Integer	int
Long	lng
Object	obj
Single	sng
String	str
User-defined type	udt

What Data Types Are Available?

It's time to create a new variable—but what type should you use? For that matter, exactly what kinds of variable types are there and what do they do? Even if you remember what types there are, you probably won't remember the range of possible values a particular variable type allows.

There is a wide range of data types. The Visual Basic variable types appear in Table 2.4 for reference, making selecting the right type a little easier. Note that the **Single** and **Double** types handle floating point values, which the Integer types (such as **Short**, **Integer**, and **Long**) do not; these names are short for *single precision floating point* and *double precision floating point*. You might also notice that there are some new types in VB .NET that weren't in VB6, like **Char**, and that

Table 2.4   Visual Basic data types.

Type	Storage size	Value range
Boolean	2 bytes	True or False
Byte	1 byte	0 to 255 (unsigned)
Char	2 bytes	0 to 65535 (unsigned)
Date	8 bytes	January 1, 0001 to December 31, 9999
Decimal	16 bytes	+/-79,228,162,514,264,337,593,543,950,335 with no decimal point; +/-7.92281625142643 37593543950335 with 28 places to the right of the decimal; smallest non-zero number is +/-0.00000 00000000000000000001
Double	8 bytes	-1.79769313486231E+308 to -4.94065645841247E-324 for negative values; 4.94065645841247E-324 to 1.79769313486231E+308 for positive values
Integer	4 bytes	-2,147,483,648 to 2,147,483,647
Long	8 bytes	-9,223,372,036,854,775,808 to 9,223,372,036,854,775,807
Object	4 bytes	Any type can be stored in a variable of type Object
Short	2 bytes	-32,768 to 32,767
Single	4 bytes	-3.402823E+38 to -1.401298E-45 for negative values; 1.401298E-45 to 3.402823E+38 for positive values
String	Depends on implementing platform	0 to approximately 2 billion Unicode characters
User-Defined Type (structure)	Sum of the sizes of its members. Each member of the structure has a range determined by its data type and independent of the ranges of the other members	

some other types, like **Currency** or **Variant**, are gone. Note in particular the **Boolean** data type, which takes values like **True** or **False** only—also called *logical* values.

TIP: *To see an example using the **Date** data type, see the topic "Handling Dates and Times" in this chapter.*

Converting between Data Types

Take a look at this code:

```
Option Strict On
Module Module1
    Sub Main()
        Dim dblData As Double
        Dim intData As Integer
        dblData = 3.14159
        intData = dblData
        System.Console.WriteLine("intData = " & Str(intData))
    End Sub

End Module
```

TIP: *Note how I'm using **WriteLine** to display text and the value in a variable by passing it the expression **"intData = " & Str(intData)**. You can also embed codes like **{0}**, **{1}**, and so on into a text string, which will then be replaced by successive values passed to **WriteLine**. For example, this code: **System.Console.WriteLine("The time is: {0} hours {1} minutes", 10, 2)** displays the text "The time is: 10 hours 2 minutes".*

In this case, I've turned **Option Strict** on, which means that Visual Basic will not automatically convert data types when you assign a value of one type to a variable of another, so it'll have problems with the statement highlighted above, where I assign a double precision floating point variable to an integer variable. To fix this problem, I have to do a specific type conversion. I do this with the **CInt** function, which converts its argument to type **Integer**:

```
Option Strict On
Module Module1
    Sub Main()
        Dim dblData As Double
        Dim intData As Integer
        dblData = 3.14159
```

```
        intData = CInt(dblData)
        System.Console.WriteLine("intData = " & Str(intData))
    End Sub

End Module
```

When I run this code, I get this result—notice that the decimal places have been removed to make the value of **pi** into an integer:

```
intData = 3
Press any key to continue
```

Here's the list of conversion functions you can use:

- **CBool**—Convert to **Bool** data type.
- **CByte**—Convert to **Byte** data type.
- **CChar**—Convert to **Char** data type.
- **CDate**—Convert to **Date** data type.
- **CDbl**—Convert to **Double** data type.
- **CDec**—Convert to **Decimal** data type.
- **CInt**—Convert to **Int** data type.
- **CLng**—Convert to **Long** data type.
- **CObj**—Convert to **Object** type.
- **CShort**—Convert to **Short** data type.
- **CSng**—Convert to **Single** data type.
- **CStr**—Convert to **String** type.

If you can't remember the name of a particular conversion function, you also can use the **CType** function, which lets you specify a type to convert to. (This is useful if you're converting to a type that is not one of the simple types in the list above.):

```
Option Strict On
Module Module1
    Sub Main()
        Dim dblData As Double
        Dim intData As Integer
        dblData = 3.14159
```

```
        intData = CType(dblData, Integer)
        System.Console.WriteLine("intData = " & Str(intData))
    End Sub
End Module
```

TIP: CType *is compiled in-line, meaning the conversion code is part of the code that evaluates the expression. Execution is faster because there is no call to a procedure to perform the conversion.*

Visual Basic supports a number of ways of converting from one type of variable to another—in fact, that's one of the strengths of the language. You can also use the conversion statements and procedures that appear in Table 2.5.

Table 2.5   Visual Basic data conversion functions.

To convert	Use this
Character code to character	**Chr**
String to lowercase or uppercase	**Format, LCase, UCase, String.ToUpper, String.ToLower, String.Format**
Date to a number	**DateSerial, DateValue**
Decimal number to other bases	**Hex, Oct**
Number to string	**Format, Str**
One data type to another	**CBool, CByte, CDate, CDbl, CDec, CInt, CLng, CObj, CSng, CShort, CStr, Fix, Int**
Character to character code	**Asc**
String to number	**Val**
Time to serial number	**TimeSerial, TimeValue**

Checking Data Types

Visual Basic has a number of data verification functions, which appear in Table 2.6, and you can use these functions to interrogate objects and determine their types.

TIP: *You can also use the* **TypeOf** *keyword to get the type of an object like this:* **If (TypeOf Err.GetException() Is OverflowException) Then....** *See "Making Decisions with* **If...Else** *Statements" in this chapter for more details.*

Table 2.6   Type checking functions.

Function	Does this
IsArray()	Returns **True** if passed an array
IsDate()	Returns **True** if passed a date
IsDBNull()	Returns **True** if passed a database **NULL** value; that is, a **System.DBNull** value
IsError()	Returns **True** if passed an error value
IsNumeric()	Returns **True** if passed an numeric value
IsReference()	Returns **True** if passed an **Object** variable that has no object assigned to it; otherwise, returns **False**

Declaring Arrays and Dynamic Arrays

It's time to start coding that database program. But wait a moment—how are you going to handle the data? It's just a simple program, so you don't want to start tangling with the full database techniques. An array would be perfect; how do you set one up?

Arrays are programming constructs that let you access your data by numeric index. To dimension arrays, you can use **Dim** (standard arrays), **ReDim** (dynamic arrays), **Static** (arrays that don't change when between calls to the procedure they're in), **Private** (arrays private to the form or module they're declared in), **Protected** (arrays restricted to a class or classes derived from that class), **Public** (arrays global to the whole program), and more as discussed in the topic "Declaring Variables." I'll start with standard arrays.

Standard Arrays

You usually use the **Dim** statement to declare a standard array; here are a few examples of standard array declarations:

```
Dim Data(30)
Dim Strings(10) As String
Dim TwoDArray(20, 40) As Integer
Dim Bounds(10, 100)
```

The **Data** array now has 30 elements, starting from **Data(0)**, which is how you refer to the first element, up to **Data(29)**. 0 is the *lower bound* of this array, and 19 is the *upper bound* (following the lead of Java, in VB .NET, the lower bound of every array index is 0, and you can no longer use the **Option Base** statement or **To** keyword that used to be available to set custom lower bounds). The **Bounds** array has two indices, one of which runs from 0 to 9, and the other of which runs from 0 to 99.

I can treat an array as a set of variables accessible with the array index, as here, where I'm storing a string in **Strings(3)** (that is, the fourth element in the array) and then displaying that string on the console:

```
Dim Data(30)
Dim Strings(10) As String
Dim TwoDArray(20, 40) As Integer
Dim Bounds(10, 100)
Strings(3) = "Here's a string!"
System.Console.WriteLine(Strings(3))
```

You can also initialize the data in an array if you don't give an array an explicit size; here's the syntax to use, where I'm initializing an array with the values **10**, **3**, and **2**:

```
Dim Data() = {10, 3, 2}
```

Dynamic Arrays

You can use the **Dim** statement to declare an array with empty parentheses to declare a *dynamic array*. Dynamic arrays can be dimensioned or redimensioned as you need them with the **ReDim** statement (which you must also do the first time you want to use a dynamic array). Here's how you use **ReDim**:

```
ReDim [Preserve] varname(subscripts)
```

You use the **Preserve** keyword to preserve the data in an existing array when you change the size of the last dimension. The *varname* argument holds the name of the array to (re)dimension. The *subscripts* term specifies the new dimension of the array.

This is one of those topics that is made easier with an example, so here's an example using dynamic arrays, in which we declare an array, dimension it, and then redimension it:

```
Dim DynaStrings() As String
ReDim DynaStrings(10)
DynaStrings(0) = "String 0"
'Need more data space!
ReDim DynaStrings(100)
DynaStrings(50) = "String 50"
```

TIP: You can find the upper bound of an array with the **UBound** function, which makes it easy to loop over all the elements in an array using a **For** loop (see "Using the **For** Loop" in this chapter) like this: **For intLoopIndex = 0 To UBound(intArray)...**

Handling Strings

You've decided to lead the way into the future by letting your users type in sentences as commands to your program. Unfortunately, this means that you have to *parse* (i.e., break down to individual words) what they type. So what was that string function that lets you break a string into smaller strings again? We'll get an overview of string handling in this topic. Strings are supported by the .NET **String** class in Visual Basic. You declare a string this way:

```
Dim strText As String
```

As with other types of variables, you can also initialize a string when you declare it, like this:

```
Dim myString As String = "Welcome to Visual Basic"
```

A string can contain up to approximately 2 billion Unicode characters, and it can grow or shrink to match the data you place in it. There are quite a number of string-handling functions built into Visual Basic.NET. For example, you use **Left**, **Mid**, and **Right** to divide a string into substrings, you find the length of a string with **Len**, and so on.

Besides the string-handling functions that are built into VB .NET, many .NET framework functions are built into the **String** class that VB .NET uses. For example, the Visual Basic **UCase** function will convert strings to upper case, and so will the **String** class's **ToUpper** method. That means that I can convert a text string to uppercase either by using the VB .NET **UCase** function, or the **String** class's **ToUpper** method:

```
Option Strict On
Module Module1
    Sub Main()
        Dim strText1 As String = "welcome to visual basic"
        Dim strText2 As String
        Dim strText3 As String
        strText2 = UCase(strText1)
        strText3 = strText1.ToUpper
        System.Console.WriteLine(strText2)
        System.Console.WriteLine(strText3)
    End Sub

End Module
```

In this example, I'm changing some text to upper case, and you can see the result in Figure 2.1.

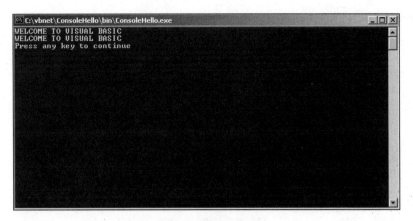

Figure 2.1   Working with strings in Visual Basic.

Here's another example—I can use the **Mid** function to get a substring from the middle of another string if I pass it that string, the location to start extracting the substring from (starting a position 1), and the length of the substring. I can do the same thing with the **String** class's **Substring** method, if I pass it the location to start extracting the substring from (starting a position 0 this time), and the length of the substring. In this case, I'll extract "look" from "Hey, look here!":

```
Module Module1
    Sub Main()
        Dim strText1 As String = "Hey, look here!"
        Dim strText2 As String
        Dim strText3 As String
        strText2 = Mid(strText1, 6, 4)
        strText3 = strText1.Substring(5, 4)
        System.Console.WriteLine(strText2)
        System.Console.WriteLine(strText3)
    End Sub
End Module
```

Here's what you see when you execute this example:

```
look
look
Press any key to continue
```

For reference, the popular Visual Basic string-handling functions and methods appear in Table 2.7, organized by task (new in VB .NET: note that you now cannot use **LSet** and **RSet** to assign one data type to another). Note in particular the string-trimming functions, which are very handy and can trim leading or trailing spaces or other characters.

Table 2.7   String-handling functions and methods.

To do this	Use this
Concatenate two strings	**&, +, String.Concat, String.Join**
Compare two strings	**StrComp, String.Compare, String.Equals, String.CompareTo**
Convert strings	**StrConv, CStr, String.ToString**
Copying strings	**=, String.Copy**
Convert to lowercase or uppercase	**Format, Lcase, Ucase, String.Format, String.ToUpper, String.ToLower**
Convert to and from numbers	**Str, Val.Format, String.Format**
Create string of a repeating character	**Space, String, String.String**
Create an array of strings from one string	**String.Split**
Find length of a string	**Len, String.Length**
Format a string	**Format, String.Format**
Get a substring	Mid, String.SubString
Insert a substring	**String.Insert**
Justify a string with padding	**LSet, Rset, String.PadLeft, String.PadRight**
Manipulate strings	**InStr, Left, LTrim, Mid, Right, RTrim, Trim, String.Trim, String.TrimEnd, String.TrimStart**
Remove text	**Mid, String.Remove**
Replace text	**Mid, String.Replace**
Set string comparison rules	Option Compare
Search strings	**InStr, String.Chars, String.IndexOf, String.IndexOfAny, String.LastIndexOf , String.LastIndexOf Any**
Trim leading or trailing spaces	**LTrim, RTrim, Trim, String.Trim, String.TrimEnd, String.TrimStart**
Work with character codes	**Asc, AscW, Chr**

Here's another point you should know—to concatenate (join) strings together, you can use the **&** or **+** operators, or the **String** class's **Concat** method. Here's an example we saw in Chapter 1, breaking up a long string over several lines:

```
Dim Msg As String
Msg = "Well, there is a problem " _
& "with your program. I am not sure " _
& "what the problem is, but there is " _
& "definitely something wrong."
```

Fixed-Length Strings

VB6 and earlier supported fixed-length strings, where you can specify a non-changing length for a string, but that's changed in VB .NET to match the .NET Framework. However, there is a special class in VB .NET—**VB6.FixedLengthString**,—that supports fixed-length strings; for example, this declaration in VB6, which declares a string of 1000 characters:

```
Dim strString1 As String * 1000
```

now becomes:

```
Dim strString1 As New VB6.FixedLengthString(1000)
```

TIP: If you're going to use fixed-length strings in structures (that is, user-defined types), you should know that the fixed-length string is not automatically created when the structure is created. As we'll see in Chapter 13, you must initialize the fixed-length string before referencing the structure in code.

---

*TIP: You also can create strings of spaces with the **SPC** function, or insert tabs into strings with the **TAB** function.*

Converting Strings to Numbers and Back Again

You're all set to write your calculator program, *SuperDuperDeluxeCalc*, in Visual Basic—but suddenly you realize that the user will be entering numbers in text form, not in numeric form! How can you translate text into numbers—and then numbers into text—to display your results?

It's common in Visual Basic to have to convert values from numbers to strings or from strings to numbers, and it's easy to do. You can use the **Str** to return a string representation of a number, and you use **Val** to convert a string to a number. That's all there is to it, but it's easy to forget those two functions, so I'm including them here for reference. Here's an example that converts a string into a number and then back into a string:

```
Module Module1
    Sub Main()
        Dim strText1 As String = "1234"
        Dim intValue1 As Integer
        intValue1 = Val(strText1)
```

```
        strText1 = Str(intValue1)
        System.Console.WriteLine(strText1)
    End Sub
End Module
```

Besides **Str** and **Val**, you can also use **Format** and **String.Format**, which let you format expressions and convert them to string form.

Converting between Characters and Character Codes

The characters a program stores internally are stored using Unicode character codes; for example, the character code 65 stands for "A". How can you convert back and forth between characters and character codes? You can use the **Asc** and **Chr** functions:

- **Asc**—Takes a character and returns its character code. For example, **Asc("A")** returns 65.

- **Chr**—Takes a character code and returns the corresponding character. For example, **Chr(65)** returns "A".

Using Visual Basic Operators

You've seen all kinds of ways of setting up variables and strings, but what about doing something with that data? Visual Basic comes with plenty of built-in operators, which let you manipulate your data. For example, here I'm adding the values in **intVariable1** and **intVariable2** with the addition operator, **+**, and storing the result in **intVariable3** with the assignment operator, **=**:

```
Module Module1
    Sub Main()
        Dim intVariable1 As Integer = 1234
        Dim intVariable2 As Integer = 2345
        Dim intVariable3 As Integer
        intVariable3 = intVariable1 + intVariable2
        System.Console.WriteLine(intVariable3)
    End Sub
End Module
```

This code prints out the result of adding **1234** and **2345**, which is 3579. An operator works on *operands*; for example, in the expression 5 + 4, **5** is *operand1*, **+** is the **operator**, and **4** is *operand2*. Some operators in Visual Basic take two operands, and some take one.

There are various types of operators in Visual Basic, and I'll go over them all here. Here are the Arithmetic operators (for example, the expression 5 + 4 yields a value of **9**):

- ^ Exponentiation
- * Multiplication
- / Division
- \ Integer division
- **Mod** Modulus
- + Addition
- - Subtraction

These are the Assignment operators (for example, **temperature = 72** stores the value **72** in the variable **temperature**):

- = Assignment
- ^= Exponentiation followed by assignment
- *= Multiplication followed by assignment
- /= Division followed by assignment
- \= Integer division followed by assignment
- += Addition followed by assignment
- -= Subtraction followed by assignment
- &= Concatenation followed by assignment

Here are the Comparison operators, which we'll use later in this chapter—see the topic "Using **If...Else** Statements" (these values yield true or false values—for example, **5 > 4** yields a value of **True**):

- < (Less than)—**True** if *operand1* is less than *operand2*
- <= (Less than or equal to)—**True** if *operand1* is less than or equal to *operand2*
- > (Greater than)—**True** if *operand1* is greater than *operand2*
- >= (Greater than or equal to)—**True** if *operand1* is greater than or equal to *operand2*

- **=** (Equal to)—**True** if *operand1* equals *operand2*

- **<>** (Not equal to)—**True** if *operand1* is not equal to *operand2*

- **Is**—**True** if two object references refer to the same object

- **Like**—Performs string pattern matching

These are the String Concatenation operators (for example, "**Hi**" **&** "**there**" yields the string "Hi there".):

- **&** String concatenation

- **+** String concatenation

These are the Logical/Bitwise operators, where *bitwise* means working bit by bit with numerical values. These types of operators can work on logical values (for example, if **blnValue1** is set to **True** and **blnValue2** is set to **False**, then **blnValue1 Or blnValue2** returns a value of **True**) or numbers for bitwise operations, which work on their operands bit by bit (for example, if **intValue1** is set to 2 and **intValue2** is set to 1, then **intValue1 Or intValue2** yields 3):

- **And**—Performs an **And** operation (for logical operations: **True** if both operands are **True**, **False** otherwise; the same for bit-by-bit operations where you treat **0** as **False** and **1** as **True**).

- **Not**—Reverses the logical value of its operand, from **True** to **False** and **False** to **True**, for bitwise operations, turns **0** into **1** and **1** into **0**.

- **Or**—Operator performs an **Or** operation (for logical operations: **True** if either operand is **True**, **False** otherwise; the same for bit-by-bit operations where you treat **0** as **False** and **1** as **True**).

- **Xor**—Operator performs an **exclusive-Or** operation (for logical operations: **True** if either operand, but not both, is **True**, and **False** otherwise; the same for bit-by-bit operations where you treat **0** as **False** and **1** as **True**).

- **AndAlso**—Operator **A** "short circuited" **And** operator; if the first operand is **False**, the second operand is not tested.

- **OrElse**—Operator **A** "short circuited" **Or** operator, if the first operand is **True**, the second is not tested.

And here are two other miscellaneous operators:

- **AddressOf**—Gets the address of a procedure.

- **GetType**—Gets information about a type.

VB6 programmers will note a whole new set of assignment operators, such as **+=**, **-=**, and so on. Following the lead of languages like Java, VB .NET now supports these *combination operators*. For example, **+=** is a combination of **+** and **=**, which means that you can write **intValue1 = intValue1 + 1** as **intValue1 += 1**. In a similar way, you can write **intValue1 = intValue1 * 5** as **intValue1 *= 5**, providing an easy shortcut.

Also, in Visual Basic .NET, if the first operand of an **And** operator evaluates to **False**, the remainder of the logical expression is not evaluated. Similarly, if the first operand of an **Or** operator evaluates to **True**, the remainder of the logical expression is not evaluated. This is called *short-circuiting*.

Understanding Visual Basic Operator Precedence

You've done well in your computer class—so well that the instructor has asked you to calculate the average grade on the final. Nothing could be easier, you think, and you put together the following program:

```
Module Module1
    Sub Main()
        Dim intGrade1, intGrade2, intGrade3, intNumberStudents As Integer
        intGrade1 = 60
        intGrade2 = 70
        intGrade3 = 80
        intNumberStudents = 3
        System.Console.WriteLine("Average grade = " & _
        Str(intGrade1 + intGrade2 + intGrade3 / intNumberStudents))
    End Sub
End Module
```

But when you run the program, it calmly informs you that the average score is 156.66666667. That doesn't look so good—what's wrong? The problem lies in this line:

```
Module Module1
    Sub Main()
        Dim intGrade1, intGrade2, intGrade3, intNumberStudents As Integer
        intGrade1 = 60
        intGrade2 = 70
        intGrade3 = 80
        intNumberStudents = 3
        System.Console.WriteLine("Average grade = " & _
```

```
            Str(intGrade1 + intGrade2 + intGrade3 / intNumberStudents))
        End Sub
End Module
```

Visual Basic evaluates the expression in parentheses from left to right, using pairs of operands and their associated operator, so it adds the first two grades together first. Instead of adding the final grade, however, it first divides that grade by **NumberStudents**, because the division operation has higher precedence than addition, so the result is $60 + 70 + (80/3) = 156.66666667$.

The solution here is to *group* the values to add together this way using parentheses:

```
Module Module1
    Sub Main()
        Dim intGrade1, intGrade2, intGrade3, intNumberStudents As Integer
        intGrade1 = 60
        intGrade2 = 70
        intGrade3 = 80
        intNumberStudents = 3
        System.Console.WriteLine("Average grade = " & _
            Str((intGrade1 + intGrade2 + intGrade3) / intNumberStudents))
    End Sub
End Module
```

Running this new code gives us an average of 70, as it should. This example points out the need to understand how Visual Basic evaluates expressions involving operators. In general, such expressions are evaluated left to right, and when it comes to a contest between two operators (such as **+** and **/** in the last term of our original program above), the operator with the higher precedence is used first. When several operations occur in an expression, each part is evaluated and re-solved in a predetermined order called *operator precedence*.

When expressions contain operators from more than one category, they are evaluated according to the following rules. The arithmetic and concatenation operators have an order of precedence that is described below, and all have higher precedence than the comparison and logical operators. Comparison operators have higher precedence than the logical operators, but lower precedence than the arithmetic and concatenation operators. All comparison operators have equal precedence; that is, they are evaluated in the order, left to right, in which they appear.

The Arithmetic operators have the highest precedence and are arranged this way, from highest precedence to lowest:

- Exponentiation (^)

- Negation (–) (for example, **-intValue** reverses the sign of the value in **intValue**)

- Multiplication and division (*****, **/**)
- Integer division (****)
- Modulus arithmetic (**Mod**)
- Addition and subtraction (**+**, **−**)

Next come the Concatenation operators:

- String concatenation (**+**)
- String concatenation (**&**)

Next come the Comparison operators, which all have the same precedence and are evaluated from left to right as Visual Basic encounters them:

- Equality (**=**)
- Inequality (**<>**)
- Less than, greater than (**<**, **>**)
- Greater than or equal to (**>=**)
- Less than or equal to (**<=**)
- **Like**
- **Is**

Finally come the Logical/Bitwise operators, which have this precedence order, from highest to lowest:

- Negation—(**Not**)
- Conjunction—(**And**, **AndAlso**)
- Disjunction—(**Or**, **OrElse**, **Xor**)

Commenting Your Code

In general, you should add comments to your code when you can to make what's going on clearer. Comments in Visual Basic start with an apostrophe (') and make Visual Basic ignore whatever follows the apostrophe on the line. Here's an example in which I'm adding comments to code to make the code easier to read:

```
Module Module1
    Sub Main()
        'Declare the variables we will use
        Dim intGrade1, intGrade2, intGrade3, NumberStudents As Integer
        'Fill the variables with data
```

```
        intGrade1 = 60
        intGrade2 = 70
        intGrade3 = 80
        NumberStudents = 3        'Three students
        'Display the average value
        System.Console.WriteLine("Average grade = " & _
        Str((intGrade1 + intGrade2 + intGrade3) / NumberStudents))
    End Sub
End Module
```

TIP: *The Edit toolbar has a button that will automatically comment out any lines of code that are selected when you click it. And here's a little-known Visual Basic fact left over from Visual Basic's early days: instead of an apostrophe, you can use the term* **REM** *in your code to create a comment.*

Related Solution:	Found on page:
Commenting Your Procedures	126

Making Decisions with **If...Else** Statements

How can you make choices in your code, deciding what to do next depending on the values in your variables? You can use the **If** statement, which is the bread-and-butter of Visual Basic conditionals, and which lets you evaluate your data and execute appropriate code. Here's how this statement works:

```
If condition Then
    [statements]
[ElseIf condition-n Then
    [elseifstatements] ...]
[Else
    [elsestatements]]
End If
```

You use comparison operators in the condition here to generate a logical result that's true or false; for example, if *condition* is **intVariable > 5**, then *condition* will be true if the value in **intVariable** is greater than 5.

If *condition* is **True**, the statements immediately following the **Then** keyword in the body of the **If** statement will be executed, and the **If** statement will terminate before the code in any **ElseIf** or **Else** statement is executed. If *condition* is **False**, the following **ElseIf** statements are evaluated, if there are any; this statement lets you test additional conditions, and if any are **True**, the corresponding code (*elseifstatements* above) is executed and the **If** statement terminates. If there are no **ElseIf** statements, or if none of their conditions are **True**, the code in the **Else** statement (*elsestatements* above), if there is one, is executed automatically.

Here's an example to show you how to use the various parts of this popular statement. In this case, I'm reading an integer that the user types at the console—using the **System.Console.ReadLine** method—and checking it against various values:

```
Module Module1
    Sub Main()
        Dim intInput As Integer
        System.Console.WriteLine("Enter an integer...")
        intInput = Val(System.Console.ReadLine())
        If intInput = 1 Then
            System.Console.WriteLine("Thank you.")
        ElseIf intInput = 2 Then
            System.Console.WriteLine("That's fine.")
        ElseIf intInput = 3 Then
            System.Console.WriteLine("Too big.")
        Else
            System.Console.WriteLine("Not a number I know.")
        End If
    End Sub
End Module
```

Note that when you compare strings, not numbers, in *condition*, the string expressions are evaluated on the basis of their alphabetical sort order by default. The sort order for strings is evaluated based upon the **Option Compare** setting (see the In Depth section "The Option and Imports Statements" of this chapter). You can also use the **String.Compare** method to compare strings.

Also note that you can also use the **TypeOf** and **Is** keywords to check the type of an object in an **If** statement, like this:

```
If (TypeOf Err.GetException() Is OverflowException) Then
    System.Console.WriteLine("Overflow error!")
End If
```

Using Select Case

You have to get a value from the user and respond in several different ways, but you're not looking forward to a long and tangled series of **If...Then...Else** statements. What can you do?

If your program can handle multiple values of a particular variable and you don't want to stack up a lot of **If Else** statements to handle them, you should consider **Select Case**. You use **Select Case** to test an expression, determine which of several *cases* it matches, and execute the corresponding code. Here's the syntax:

```
Select Case testexpression
[Case expressionlist-n
    [statements-n]] ...
[Case Else
    [elsestatements]]
End Select
```

You use multiple **Case** statements in a **Select** statement, each specifying a different value to test against *textexpression*, and the code in the **Case** statement that matches is executed.

Here's an example using **Select Case**. In this example, I'm modifying the code from the previous topic to use **Select Case** instead of **If...Then**. Note that I'm also using the **Select Is** keyword, which you can use like this: **Case Is** *condition*, allowing you to test *testexpression* against some condition (such as **Case Is > 7**). You can also test *testexpression* against a range of values with the **To** keyword (such as **Case 4 To 7**). And **Case Else** can handle values we don't explicitly provide code for—it's just like the **Else** statement in an **If...Then** statement, because the code in it is executed if no other case matches. Here's the code:

```
Module Module1
    Sub Main()
        Dim intInput As Integer
        System.Console.WriteLine("Enter an integer...")
        intInput = Val(System.Console.ReadLine())
        Select Case intInput
            Case 1
                System.Console.WriteLine("Thank you.")
            Case 2
                System.Console.WriteLine("That's fine.")
            Case 3
                System.Console.WriteLine("OK.")
            Case 4 To 7
```

```
                    System.Console.WriteLine("In the range 4 to 7.")
            Case Is > 7
                    System.Console.WriteLine("Definitely too big.")
            Case Else
                    System.Console.WriteLine("Not a number I know.")
        End Select
    End Sub
End Module
```

Making Selections with **Switch** and **Choose**

For some reason, few books on Visual Basic cover the **Switch** and **Choose** functions, but they certainly have their uses and we'll take a look at them here.

The Switch Function

The **Switch** function evaluates a list of expressions and returns an **Object** value or an expression associated with the first expression in the list that is true. Here's the syntax:

```
Switch(expr-1, value-1[, expr-2, value-2 … [, expr-n, value-n]])
```

In this case, *expr-1* is the first expression to evaluate; if true, **Switch** returns *value-1*. If *expr-1* is not true but *expr-2* is, **Switch** returns *value-2* and so on. Here's an example showing how to use **Switch**. In this case, I'm using **Switch** to calculate the absolute value of the value in the variable **intValue** (having temporarily forgotten how to use the built-in Visual Basic absolute value function, **Abs**):

```
intAbsValue = Switch(intValue < 0, -1 * intValue, intValue >= 0, intValue)
```

TIP: *Using the negation operator, -, you can write **-1 * intValue** simply as **-intValue**.*

The Choose Function

You use the **Choose** function to return one of a number of choices based on an index. Here's the syntax:

```
Choose(index, choice-1[, choice-2, ... [, choice-n]])
```

If the index value is **1**, the first choice is returned, if index equals **2**, the second choice is returned, and so on. Here's an example using **Choose**. In this case, we have three employees, Bob, Denise, and Ted, with employee IDs 1, 2, and 3. This code uses an ID value to assign the corresponding employee name to **strEmployName**:

```
strEmployeeName = Choose(intID, "Bob", "Denise", "Ted")
```

Looping to Execute Statements Repetitively

You use *loops* to execute a series of statements repeatedly. Of course, that doesn't mean you perform one identical task repeatedly; you might be operating on different data items each time through the loop. Loops are one thing that computers are great at—providing you with a way of executing repetitive code quickly. You can also have *nested* loops, where one loop encloses another—any of the Visual Basic loops can be nested with other loops of the same or other types.

Many programmers have a love/hate relationship with looping, based primarily on syntax. Programmers often have to switch back and forth these days between languages, and can find themselves writing, for example, a C++ loop in the middle of a Visual Basic program, and being taken by surprise when the compiler objects.

To make it easier, we'll include examples here of all the Visual Basic loops, starting with the **Do** loop.

Using the **Do** Loop

The **Do** loop keeps executing its enclosed statements while or until (depending on which keyword you use, **While** or **Until**) *condition* is true. You can also terminate a **Do** loop at any time with an **Exit Do** statement. The **Do** loop has two versions; you can either evaluate a condition at the beginning:

```
Do [{While | Until} condition]
    [statements]
    [Exit Do]
    [statements]
Loop
```

or at the end:

```
Do
```

```
    [statements]
    [Exit Do]
    [statements]
Loop [{While | Until} condition]
```

Here's an example where the code keeps displaying the message "What should I do?" until the user types "Stop" (note that I'm using **UCase** to uppercase what the user types and comparing it to "STOP" to let them use any combination of case when they type "Stop"):

```
Module Module1
    Sub Main()
        Dim strInput As String
        Do Until UCase(strInput) = "STOP"
            System.Console.WriteLine("What should I do?")
            strInput = System.Console.ReadLine()
        Loop
    End Sub
End Module
```

TIP: *The second form of the **Do** loop insures that the body of the loop is executed at least once.*

Using the **For** Loop

The **For** loop is probably the most popular of all Visual Basic loops. The **Do** loop doesn't need a *loop index*, but the **For** loop does; a loop index counts the number of loop iterations as the loop executes. Here's the syntax for the **For** loop—note that you can terminate a **For** loop at any time with **Exit For**:

```
For index = start To end [Step step]
    [statements]
    [Exit For]
    [statements]
Next [index]
```

The *index* variable is originally set to *start* automatically when the loop begins. Each time through the loop, *index* is incremented by *step* (*step* is set to a default of **1** if you don't specify a value) and when *index* equals end, the loop ends.

Here's how to put this loop to work; in this case, I'm displaying "Hello from Visual Basic" four times (that is, **intLoopIndex** will hold 0 the first time; 1, the next; followed by 2; and then 3, at which point the loop terminates):

```
Module Module1
    Sub Main()
        Dim intLoopIndex As Integer
        For intLoopIndex = 0 To 3
            System.Console.WriteLine("Hello from Visual Basic")
        Next intLoopIndex
    End Sub
End Module
```

Here's what you see when you run this code:

```
Hello from Visual Basic
Hello from Visual Basic
Hello from Visual Basic
Hello from Visual Basic
Press any key to continue
```

If I were to use a **step** size of 2:

```
For intLoopIndex = 0 To 3 Step 2
    System.Console.WriteLine("Hello from Visual Basic")
Next intLoopIndex
```

I'd see this result:

```
Hello from Visual Basic
Hello from Visual Basic
Press any key to continue
```

TIP: *Although it's been common practice to use a loop index after a loop completes (to see how many loop iterations were executed), that practice is now discouraged by people who make it their business to write about good and bad programming practices.*

We'll see **For** loops throughout the book.

Using the **For Each...Next** Loop

You use the **For Each...Next** loop to loop over elements in an array or a Visual Basic collection. This loop is great, because it automatically loops over all the elements in the array or collection—you don't have to worry about getting the loop indices just right to make sure you get all elements, as you do with a **For** loop. Here's the syntax of this loop:

```
For Each element In group
    [statements]
    [Exit For]
    [statements]
Next [element]
```

You can get a look at this loop in action with an example like this, in which I'm displaying all the elements of an array:

```
Module Module1
    Sub Main()
        Dim intIDArray(3), intArrayItem As Integer
        intIDArray(0) = 0
        intIDArray(1) = 1
        intIDArray(2) = 2
        intIDArray(3) = 3

        For Each intArrayItem In intIDArray
            System.Console.WriteLine(intArrayItem)
        Next intArrayItem
    End Sub
End Module
```

And here's the result of this code:

```
0
1
2
3
Press any key to continue
```

Using the **While** Loop

While loops keep looping while the condition they test remains true, so you use a **While** loop if you have a condition that will become false when you want to stop looping. Here's the **While** loop's syntax (note that you used to end this loop with **Wend** in VB6 and before—that's changed to **End While** now):

```
While condition
    [statements]
End While
```

And here's an example putting **While** to work:

```
Sub CheckWhile()
    Dim intCounter As Integer = 0
    Dim intNumber As Integer = 10
    While intNumber > 6
        intNumber -= 1
        intCounter += 1
    End While
    MsgBox("The loop ran " & intCounter & " times.")
End Sub
```

And here's what you see when you run this code:

```
The loop ran 4 times.
Press any key to continue
```

TIP: Many Visual Basic functions, like **EOF**—which is true when you've reached the end of a file while reading from it— are explicitly constructed to return values of **True** or **False** so that you can use them to control loops such as **Do** and **While** loops.

The **With** Statement

The **With** statement is not a loop, properly speaking, but it can be as useful as a loop—and in fact, many programmers actually think of it as a loop. You use the **With** statement to execute statements using a particular object. Here's the syntax:

```
With object
    [statements]
End With
```

Here's an example showing how to put **With** to work. Here, I'm use a text box, **Text1**, in a Windows form program, and setting its **Height**, **Width**, and **Text** properties in the **With** statement:

```
With TextBox1
    .Height = 1000
    .Width = 3000
    .Text = "Welcome to Visual Basic"
End With
```

Handling Higher Math

Well, it may have been a mistake taking on that programming job from the astrophysics department. How do you calculate a hyperbolic cosecant anyway? Can Visual Basic do it? Yes, although not directly. The built-in Visual Basic math functions appear in Table 2.8—note that the old VB6 functions like **Atn** and **Abs** have been replaced by methods of the **System.Math** namespace.

To use these functions without qualification, import the **System.Math** namespace into your project. Here's an example that uses the **Atan** method:

Table 2.8   Math methods.

Old	New Visual Basic .NET method	Description
Abs	**System.Math.Abs**	Yields the absolute value of a given number.
Atn	**System.Math.Atan**	Yields a Double value containing the angle whose tangent is the given number.
Cos	**System.Math.Cos**	Yields a Double value containing the cosine of the given angle.
Exp	**System.Math.Exp**	Yields a Double value containing *e* (the base of natural logarithms) raised to the given power.
Log	**System.Math.Log**	Yields a Double value containing the logarithm of a given number.
Round	**System.Math.Round**	Yields a Double value containing the number nearest the given value.
Sgn	**System.Math.Sign**	Yields an Integer value indicating the sign of a number.
Sin	**System.Math.Sin**	Yields a Double value specifying the sine of an angle.
Sqr	**System.Math.Sqrt**	Yields a Double value specifying the square root of a number.
Tan	**System.Math.Tan**	Yields a Double value containing the tangent of an angle.

```
Imports System.Math
Module Module1
    Sub Main()
        System.Console.WriteLine("Pi =" & 4 * Atan(1))
    End Sub
End Module
```

And here's the result:

```
Pi =3.14159265358979
Press any key to continue
```

If what you want, like hyperbolic cosecant, is not in Table 2.8, try Table 2.9, which shows you how to calculate other results using the built-in Visual Basic functions. There's enough math power in Table 2.9 to keep most astrophysicists happy.

Table 2.9   Calculated math functions.

Function	Calculate this way
Secant	$Sec(X) = 1 / Cos(X)$
Cosecant	$Cosec(X) = 1 / Sin(X)$
Cotangent	$Cotan(X) = 1 / Tan(X)$
Inverse Sine	$Arcsin(X) = Atn(X / Sqr(-X * X + 1))$
Inverse Cosine	$Arccos(X) = Atn(-X / Sqr(-X * X + 1)) + 2 * Atn(1)$
Inverse Secant	$Arcsec(X) = Atn(X / Sqr(X * X - 1)) + Sgn((X) - 1) * (2 * Atn(1))$
Inverse Cosecant	$Arccosec(X) = Atn(X / Sqr(X * X - 1)) + (Sgn(X) - 1) * (2 * Atn(1))$
Inverse Cotangent	$Arccotan(X) = Atn(X) + 2 * Atn(1)$
Hyperbolic Sine	$HSin(X) = (Exp(X) - Exp(-X)) / 2$
Hyperbolic Cosine	$HCos(X) = (Exp(X) + Exp(-X)) / 2$
Hyperbolic Tangent	$HTan(X) = (Exp(X) - Exp(-X)) / (Exp(X) + Exp(-X))$
Hyperbolic Secant	$HSec(X) = 2 / (Exp(X) + Exp(-X))$
Hyperbolic Cosecant	$HCosec(X) = 2 / (Exp(X) - Exp(-X))$
Hyperbolic Cotangent	$HCotan(X) = (Exp(X) + Exp(-X)) / (Exp(X) - Exp(-X))$
Inverse Hyperbolic Sine	$HArcsin(X) = Log(X + Sqr(X * X + 1))$
Inverse Hyperbolic Cosine	$HArccos(X) = Log(X + Sqr(X * X - 1))$
Inverse Hyperbolic Tangent	$HArctan(X) = Log((1 + X) / (1 - X)) / 2$
Inverse Hyperbolic Secant	$HArcsec(X) = Log((Sqr(-X * X + 1) + 1) / X)$

(continued)

Table 2.9 Calculated math functions *(continued)*.

Function	Calculate this way
Inverse Hyperbolic Cosecant	$HArccosec(X) = Log((Sgn(X) * Sqr(X * X + 1) + 1) / X)$
Inverse Hyperbolic Cotangent	$HArccotan(X) = Log((X + 1) / (X - 1)) / 2$
Logarithm to base N	$LogN(X) = Log(X) / Log(N)$

Handling Dates and Times

One of the biggest headaches a programmer can have is working with dates. Handling hours, minutes, and seconds can be as bad as working with shillings, pence, and pounds. Fortunately, Visual Basic has a number of date and time handling functions, which appear in Table 2.10—you can even add or subtract dates using those functions. VB6 programmers will notice a number of new properties in this table.

Here's an example in which I'm adding 22 months to 12/31/2001 using **DateAdd**—you might note in particular that you can assign dates of the format 12/31/2001 to variables of the **Date** type if you enclose them inside # symbols:

```
Imports System.Math
Module Module1
    Sub Main()
        Dim FirstDate As Date
        FirstDate = #12/31/2001#
        System.Console.WriteLine("New date: " & DateAdd_
        (DateInterval.Month, 22, FirstDate))
    End Sub
End Module
```

Here's what you see when you run this code:

```
New date: 10/31/2003
Press any key to continue
```

There's something else you should know—the **Format** function makes it easy to format dates into strings, including times. For easy reference, see Table 2.11, which shows some ways to display the date and time in a string—note how many ways there are to do this.

You can also compare dates and times directly. For example, here's how you loop until the current time (returned as a string by **TimeString**) exceeds a certain time; when the time is up, the code beeps using the Visual Basic **Beep** function:

```
While TimeString < "15:45:00"
End While
Beep()
```

> **TIP:** *Don't use the above code snippet for more than an example of how to compare times! The eternal looping while waiting for something to happen is a bad idea in Windows, because your program monopolizes a lot of resources that way. Instead, set up a Visual Basic Timer and have a procedure called, say, every second.*

Table 2.10   Visual Basic date and time properties.

To do this	Use this
Get the current date or time	**Today, Now, TimeofDay, DateString, TimeString**
Perform date calculations	**DateAdd, DateDiff, DatePart**
Return a date	**DateSerial, DateValue**
Return a time	**TimeSerial, TimeValue**
Set the date or time	**Today, TimeofDay**
Time a process	**Timer**

Table 2.11   Using Format to display dates and times.

Format Expression	Yields this
Format(Now, "M-d-yy")	"1-1-03"
Format(Now, "M/d/yy")	"1/1/03"
Format(Now, "MM - dd - yy")	"01 /01 / 03"
Format(Now, "ddd, MMMM d, yyy")	"Friday, January 1, 2003"
Format(Now, "d MMM, yyy")	"1 Jan, 2003"
Format(Now, "hh:mm:ss MM/dd/yy")	"01:00:00 01/01/03"
Format(Now, "hh:mm:ss tt MM-dd-yy")	"01:00:00 AM 01-01-03"

Handling Financial Data

You finally landed that big programming job at MegaMegaBank—congratulations!
But now there's some trouble—just what is an "internal rate of return" anyway?
Visual Basic to the rescue—there are 13 Visual Basic functions devoted entirely
to financial work, and they appear in Table 2.12.

Table 2.12   The Visual Basic financial functions.

To do this	Use this
Calculate depreciation	**DDB, SLN, SYD**
Calculate future value	**FV**
Calculate interest rate	**Rate**
Calculate internal rate of return	**IRR, MIRR**
Calculate number of periods	**NPer**
Calculate payments	**IPmt, Pmt, PPmt**
Calculate present value	**NPV, PV**

Ending a Program at Any Time

Our last topic in this chapter will be about ending programs. There are times
when you want to end a program without further ado—for example, to make an
Exit menu item active. How do you do that?

You use the **End** statement. This statement stops execution of your program;
here's an example in which I end the program when the user types "Stop" (or
"stop" or "STOP" and so on):

```
Module Module1
    Sub Main()
        Dim strInput As String
        Do Until UCase(strInput) = "STOP"
            System.Console.WriteLine("What should I do?")
            strInput = System.Console.ReadLine()
        Loop
        End
    End Sub
End Module
```

*TIP: The **Stop** statement is similar to **End**, except that it puts the program in a break state. Executing a **Stop** statement,
therefore, will make the Visual Basic debugger come up.*

Chapter 3

The Visual Basic Language: Procedures, Scope, and Exception Handling

In Depth

In this chapter, we'll take a look at three crucial aspects of the Visual Basic language: procedures, scope, and exception handling. Dividing your code into *procedures* allows you to break it up into more modular units. As your programs become longer, that's invaluable as it stops everything from becoming too cluttered. In Visual Basic, all executable code must be in procedures. There are two types of procedures: *Sub procedures* and *functions*. In Visual Basic, Sub procedures do not return values when they terminate, but functions do.

As your code gets longer, it also becomes more important to know what parts of your code are accessible from other parts of your code; this issue is known as *scope*. Now that Visual Basic is laying a heavier emphasis on OOP, scope becomes a more important issue, as we'll see in this chapter and when we discuss OOP in detail in Chapter 11.

Finally, we'll take a look at *exception handling* in this chapter, because that's also something that's been given considerable emphasis in VB .NET. Exception handling is really runtime error handling in VB .NET (although other languages make a distinction between exceptions and errors). There are two ways to handle such exceptions: *structured* and *unstructured* exception handling. Structured exception handling uses the same **Try...Catch...Finally** type of construct that Java does; unstructured exception handling is really the traditional Visual Basic error handling that uses the **On Error GoTo** statement. We'll see both in this chapter.

Sub Procedures and Functions

Procedures are made up of series of Visual Basic statements that, when called, are executed. After the call is finished, control returns to the statement that called the procedure. In this way, procedures make it simple for you to package your code into discrete units. Ideally, each Visual Basic procedure should handle one—and only one—task, to make this easy to remember. You can pass data to procedures and the code in the procedure can work on that data. As mentioned above, there are two types of procedures in Visual Basic .NET: Sub procedures and functions. Sub procedures do not return a value, while functions do.

Let's take a look at creating a Sub procedure first. We've already placed all our executable code in the Sub procedure named **Main** in the previous chapter, so this will be easy to do:

```
Module Module1
    Sub Main()
        System.Console.WriteLine("Hello from Visual Basic")
    End Sub
End Module
```

When this console application starts, control is transferred to the **Main** Sub procedure automatically, and the code in it runs. However, we can create our own Sub procedures as well, as below where I'm creating a Sub procedure named **DisplayMessage** to display the same message the above code does:

```
Module Module1
    Sub Main()
    End Sub

    Sub DisplayMessage()
        System.Console.WriteLine("Hello from Visual Basic")
    End Sub
End Module
```

To execute the code in **DisplayMessage**, you must call that Sub procedure, which looks like this:

```
Module Module1
    Sub Main()
        DisplayMessage()
    End Sub

    Sub DisplayMessage()
        System.Console.WriteLine("Hello from Visual Basic")
    End Sub
End Module
```

TIP: *Optionally, you also can use the **Call** statement to call a Sub procedure like this: **Call DisplayMessage.** Although this usage is considered old-fashioned, it can make your code more readable.*

This produces the same results as before, displaying the message "Hello from Visual Basic"; when you call **DisplayMessage**, the code in that Sub procedure is executed. Note the parentheses following **DisplayMessage** above; you use these to enclose data you pass to the procedure, which are called *arguments*. For example, to pass to **DisplayMessage** the text string we want to display, you can indicate that it accepts a text-string argument, like this:

```
Module Module1
    Sub Main()
    End Sub

    Sub DisplayMessage(ByVal strText As String)
            .
            .
            .
    End Sub
End Module
```

Here, the keyword **ByVal** indicates that the text string is passed *by value*, which means a copy of the string is passed. This is the default in VB .NET. The other possibility is **ByRef**, which means that the argument will be passed *by reference*. When you pass a variable by reference (which was the default in VB6 and earlier), the *location* of the variable is passed to the procedure, which means you have direct access to that variable back in the calling code. Changing the value in that variable (as by assigning it a new value like this: **intArgument1 = 5**) actually changes its value back in the code that called the procedure. In this way, if you pass variables by reference (but not by value) to a procedure, the code in that procedure can change the value in those variables.

Now that I've given the argument passed to **DisplayMessage** a name (**strText**), I can refer to that argument by name in the body of **DisplayMessage**:

```
Module Module1
    Sub Main()
    End Sub

    Sub DisplayMessage(ByVal strText As String)
        System.Console.WriteLine(strText)
    End Sub
End Module
```

And I can pass data to **DisplayMessage** when I call it (this string, "Hello from Visual Basic", will be stored in **strText** in **DisplayMessage**):

```
Module Module1
    Sub Main()
        DisplayMessage("Hello from Visual Basic")
    End Sub

    Sub DisplayMessage(ByVal strText As String)
        System.Console.WriteLine(strText)
    End Sub
End Module
```

This code displays our message as before.

TIP: *In VB6 and earlier versions, using parentheses to enclose the arguments you're passing to a procedure was optional under certain circumstances (as when you called Sub procedures). In VB .NET, that's no longer true; you must always use parentheses now, unless you're not passing any arguments to the procedure, in which case you can either use empty parentheses or omit them altogether.*

You can also create functions, which return values. For example, I might create a function named **Addem** that accepts two integer arguments and returns their sum. Declaring a function is much like declaring a Sub procedure, except that you use the keyword **Function** instead of **Sub**, and specify the return type of the function like this (note that you separate multiple arguments in the declaration of a procedure with commas):

```
Module Module1
    Sub Main()
    End Sub

    Function Addem(ByVal int1 As Integer, ByVal int2 As Integer) As Long
        Return int1 + int2
    End Function
End Module
```

You return a value from a function with the **Return** statement, as I have here, where I'm returning the sum of the two arguments passed to us. You also can avoid using the **Return** statement if you simply assign a value to the name of a function, as in this example, where the **Always5** function always returns a value of **5**:

```
Private Sub Form1_Load(ByVal sender As System.Object, _
    ByVal e As System.EventArgs) Handles MyBase.Load
    MsgBox(Always5())
End Sub

Private Function Always5() As Integer
    Always5 = 5
End Function
```

> **TIP:** In Visual Basic 6.0, you could use the **Return** statement only to branch back to the code following a **GoSub** statement. In Visual Basic .NET, the **GoSub** statement is not supported, and you can use the **Return** statement to return control to the calling program from a **Function** or **Sub** procedure.

When you call a function by using its name and an argument list enclosed in parentheses, that name is replaced by the value returned by the function. For example, the call **Addem(2, 2)** is replaced by the value **4**, as in this code:

```
Module Module1
    Sub Main()
        Dim intValue As Integer = 2
        System.Console.WriteLine("{0}+{1}={2}", _
            intValue, intValue, Addem(intValue, intValue))
    End Sub

    Function Addem(ByVal int1 As Integer, ByVal int2 As Integer) As Long
        Return int1 + int2
    End Function
End Module
```

> **TIP:** Note that I'm using syntax in **WriteLine** that we've seen in the previous chapter, passing it a text string with terms like **{0}**, **{1}**; **{0}** will be replaced with the first argument following the text string, **{1}** with the second, and so on.

When you run this code, you see this result:

```
2+2=4
```

Understanding Scope

The *scope* of an element in your code is all the code that can refer to it without qualifying its name (or making it available through an **Imports** statement). In other words, an element's scope is its *accessibility* in your code. As we write larger programs, scope will become more important, because we'll be dividing code into classes, modules, procedures, and so on. You can make the elements in those programming constructs private, which means they are tightly restricted in scope.

In VB .NET, *where you declare an element determines its scope,* and an element can have scope at one of the following levels:

- *Block scope*—available only within the code block in which it is declared
- *Procedure scope*—available only within the procedure in which it is declared
- *Module scope*—available to all code within the module, class, or structure in which it is declared
- *Namespace scope*—available to all code in the namespace

For example, if you declare a variable in a module outside of any procedure, it has module scope, as in this case, where I'm declaring and creating a **LinkLabel** control that has module scope:

```
Dim LinkLabel1 As LinkLabel
```

```
Private Sub Button1_Click(ByVal sender As System.Object, _
    ByVal e As System.EventArgs) Handles Button1.Click
    LinkLabel1 = New LinkLabel()
    LinkLabel1.AutoSize = True
    LinkLabel1.Location = New Point(15, 15)
    .
    .
    .
```

TIP: When you want to declare module-level variables, you can place the declaration outside any procedure in the module. You also can select the module in the left-hand drop-down list box in the code designer and the (**Declarations**) item in the right-hand drop-down box, which will take you to a location at the very beginning of the module, outside any procedure.

Declaring a variable in a procedure gives it procedure scope, and so on. Inside these levels of scope, you can also specify the scope of an element when you declare it. Here are the possibilities in VB .NET, which we'll become familiar with throughout the book:

- **Public**—The **Public** statement declares elements to be accessible from anywhere within the same project, from other projects that reference the project, and from an assembly built from the project. You can use **Public** only at module, namespace, or file level. This means you can declare a **Public** element in a source file or inside a module, class, or structure, but not within a procedure.

- **Protected**—The **Protected** statement declares elements to be accessible only from within the same class, or from a class derived from this class. You can use **Protected** only at class level, and only when declaring a member of a class.

- **Friend**—The **Friend** statement declares elements to be accessible from within the same project, but not from outside the project. You can use **Friend** only at module, namespace, or file level. This means you can declare a **Friend** element in a source file or inside a module, class, or structure, but not within a procedure.

- **Protected Friend**—The **Protected** statement with the **Friend** keyword declares elements to be accessible either from derived classes or from within the same project, or both. You can use **Protected Friend** only at class level, and only when declaring a member of a class.

- **Private**—The **Private** statement declares elements to be accessible only from within the same module, class, or structure. You can use **Private** only at module, namespace, or file level. This means you can declare a **Private** element in a source file or inside a module, class, or structure, but not within a procedure.

Let's take a look at an example. Here's what block scope looks like—in this case, I'll declare a variable, **strText** in an **If** statement. That variable can be used *inside* the **If** statement's block, but not *outside* (VB .NET will tag the second use here as a syntax error):

```
Module Module1
    Sub Main()
        Dim intValue As Integer = 1
        If intValue = 1 Then
            Dim strText As String = "No worries."
            System.Console.WriteLine(strText)
        End If
        System.Console.WriteLine(strText)        'Will not work!
    End Sub
End Module
```

Here's another example. In this case, I've created a second module, **Module2**, and defined a function, **Function1**, in that module. To make it clear that I want to be able to access **Function1** outside **Module2** (as when I call it as **Module2. Function1** in the **Main** procedure), I declare **Function1** public:

```
Module Module1
    Sub Main()
        System.Console.WriteLine(Module2.Function1())
    End Sub
End Module

Module Module2
    Public Function Function1() As String 'OK
        Return "Hello from Visual Basic"
    End Function
End Module
```

TIP: *Note that in this case, I've put **Module2** into the same file as **Module1**. You can also create a new file for **Module2** if you prefer—just select Project|Add New Item and then select Module in the Templates box of the Add New Item dialog that opens.*

However, if I declared **Function1** as private to **Module2**, it's inaccessible in **Module1** (and VB .NET will tag **Module2.Function1** below as a syntax error):

```
Module Module1
    Sub Main()
        System.Console.WriteLine(Module2.Function1())    'Will not work!
    End Sub
End Module

Module Module2
    Private Function Function1() As String
        Return "Hello from Visual Basic"
    End Function
End Module
```

Besides procedures, you also can make other elements—such as variables—public or private. Here, I'm declaring **strData** as public in **Module2** to make it clear that I want to access it outside the module, which I can do in **Module1**, referring to **strData** as **Module2.strData**:

```
Module Module1
    Sub Main()
        System.Console.WriteLine(Module2.strData)
    End Sub
End Module
```

```
Module Module2
    Public strData As String = "Hello from Visual Basic"
End Module
```

In fact, when you declare elements like **strData** public throughout the program, you need not qualify their names in other code, so I can refer to **strData** in **Module1** as well:

```
Module Module1
    Sub Main()
        System.Console.WriteLine(strData)
    End Sub
End Module

Module Module2
    Public strData As String = "Hello from Visual Basic"
End Module
```

Now that VB .NET is object-oriented, understanding scope is more important. In object-oriented programming, scope becomes a major issue, because when you create objects, you often want keep the data and code in those objects private from the rest of the program. Scope also becomes an issue when you derive one OOP class from another—we'll see a great deal more on this issue in Chapters 11 and 12.

Handling Exceptions

As mentioned earlier, there are two ways of handling errors that occur at run time in VB .NET—with structured and unstructured exception handling. What's an exception? Exceptions are just runtime errors; in Visual Basic (unlike some other languages), the terms *exception handling* and *error handling* have become interchangeable. Exceptions occur when a program is running (as opposed to syntax errors, which will prevent VB .NET from running your program at all). You can trap such exceptions and recover from them, rather than letting them bring your program to an inglorious end.

Unstructured Exception Handling

The old error-handling mechanism in VB6 and before is now called unstructured exception handling, and it revolves around the **On Error Goto** statement. You use this statement to tell VB .NET where to transfer control to in case there's been an exception, as in this case, where I'm telling Visual Basic to jump to the label "Handler" if there's been an exception. You create labels in your code with the label name followed by a colon, and the exception-handling code will follow that label (note that I've added an **Exit Sub** statement to make sure the code in the exception handler is not executed by mistake as part of normal program execution):

```
Module Module1
    Sub Main()
        On Error Goto Handler
            .
            .
            .
        Exit Sub
Handler:
            .
            .
            .
    End Sub
End Module
```

Now I can execute some code that may cause an exception, as here, where the code performs a division by zero, which causes an exception. When the exception occurs, control will jump to the exception handler, where I'll display a message and then use the **Resume Next** statement to transfer control back to the statement immediately after the statement that caused the exception:

```
Module Module1
    Sub Main()
        Dim int1 = 0, int2 = 1, int3 As Integer
        On Error Goto Handler
        int3 = int2 / int1
        System.Console.WriteLine("The answer is {0}", int3)
Handler:
        System.Console.WriteLine("Divide by zero error")
        Resume Next
    End Sub
End Module
```

When you run this code, you see this message:

```
Divide by zero error
```

Structured Exception Handling

Visual Basic also supports structured exception handling. In particular, Visual Basic uses an enhanced version of the **Try...Catch...Finally** syntax already supported by other languages, such as Java. Here's an example that follows our previous example handling a division by zero exception; I start by creating a **Try** block—you put the exception-prone code in the **Try** section and the exception-handling code in the **Catch** section:

```
Module Module1
    Sub Main()
        Try
            .
            .
            .
        Catch e As Exception
            .
            .
        End Try
    End Sub
End Module
```

Note the syntax of the **Catch** statement, which catches an *Exception* object that I'm naming **e**. When the code in the **Try** block causes an exception, I can use the **e.ToString** method to display a message:

```
Module Module1
    Sub Main()
        Dim int1 = 0, int2 = 1, int3 As Integer
        Try
            int3 = int2 / int1
            System.Console.WriteLine("The answer is {0}", int3)
        Catch e As Exception
            System.Console.WriteLine(e.ToString)
        End Try
    End Sub
End Module
```

Here's what you see when you run this code:

```
System.OverflowException: Exception of type System.OverflowException was
thrown.
```

```
at Microsoft.VisualBasic.Helpers.IntegerType.FromObject(Object Value)
at ConsoleHello.Module1.Main() in
C:\vbnet\ConsoleHello\Module1.vb:line 5
```

Besides using the **e.ToString** method, you can also use the **e.message** field, which contains this message:

```
Exception of type System.OverflowException was thrown.
```

And now it's time to turn to the Immediate Solutions section to see the details on creating procedures, setting scope, and handling exceptions.

Immediate Solutions

Creating Sub Procedures

We know all about Sub procedures: They're the handy blocks of code that can organize your code into single-purpose sections to make programming easier. Unlike functions, Sub procedures do not return values, but like functions, you can pass values to Sub procedures in an argument list.

You declare Sub procedures with the **Sub** statement:

```
[ <attrlist> ] [{ Overloads | Overrides | Overridable | NotOverridable |
MustOverride | Shadows | Shared }]
[{ Public | Protected | Friend | Protected Friend | Private }]
Sub name [(arglist)]
    [ statements ]
    [ Exit Sub ]
    [ statements ]
End Sub
```

Here are the parts of this statement:

- *attrlist*—List of attributes for this procedure. You separate multiple attributes with commas.

- **Overloads**—Specifies that this Sub procedure overloads one (or more) procedures defined with the same name in a base class. In this case, the argument list must be different from the argument list of every procedure that is to be overloaded (that is, the lists must differ in the number of arguments, their data types, or both). You cannot specify both **Overloads** and **Shadows** in the same procedure declaration.

- **Overrides**—Specifies that this Sub procedure overrides a procedure with the same name in a base class. Note that the number and data types of the arguments must match those of the procedure in the base class.

- **Overridable**—Specifies that this Sub procedure can be overridden by a procedure with the same name in a derived class.

- **NotOverridable**—Specifies that this Sub procedure may not be overridden in a derived class.

- **MustOverride**—Specifies that this Sub procedure is not implemented. Instead, this procedure must be implemented in a derived class. If it is not, that class will not be creatable.

- **Shadows**—Makes this Sub procedure a shadow of an identically named programming element in a base class. A shadowed element is unavailable in the derived class that shadows it. You can use **Shadows** only at module, namespace, or file level (but not inside a procedure). This means you can declare shadowing variables in a source file or inside a module, class, or structure, but not inside a procedure. Note that you cannot specify both **Overloads** and **Shadows** in the same procedure declaration.

- **Shared**—Specifies that this Sub procedure is a shared procedure. As a shared procedure, it is not associated with a specific instance of a class or structure, and you can call it by qualifying it either with the class or structure name, or with the variable name of a specific instance of the class or structure.

- **Public**—Procedures declared **Public** have public access. There are no restrictions on the accessibility of public procedures.

- **Protected**—Procedures declared **Protected** have protected access. They are accessible only from within their own class or from a derived class. Protected access can be specified only on members of classes.

- **Friend**—Procedures declared **Friend** have friend access. They are accessible from within the program that contains their declaration and from anywhere else in the same assembly.

- **Protected Friend**—Procedures declared **Protected Friend** have both protected and friend accessibility. They can be used by code in the same assembly, as well as by code in derived classes.

- **Private**—Procedures declared **Private** have private access. They are accessible only within their declaration context, including from any nested procedures.

- *name*—Name of the Sub procedure.

- *arglist*—List of expressions (which can be single variables or simple values) representing arguments that are passed to the Sub procedure when it is called. Multiple arguments are separated by commas. Note that in VB .NET, if you supply an argument list, you must enclose it in parentheses.

- *statements*—The block of statements to be executed within the Sub procedure.

Each argument in the *arglist* part has the following syntax and parts:

```
[ <attrlist> ] [ Optional ] [{ ByVal | ByRef }] [ ParamArray ] argname[( )]
[ As argtype ] [ = defaultvalue ]
```

Here are the parts of the *arglist*:

- ***attrlist***—List of attributes that apply to this argument. Multiple attributes are separated by commas.

- **Optional**—Specifies that this argument is not required when the procedure is called. Note that if you use this keyword, all following arguments in *arglist* must also be optional and be declared using the **Optional** keyword. Every optional argument declaration must supply a *defaultvalue*. Also, **Optional** cannot be used for any argument if you also use **ParamArray**.

- **ByVal**—Specifies passing by value. In this case, the procedure cannot replace or reassign the underlying variable element in the calling code (unless the argument is a reference type). **ByVal** is the default in Visual Basic.

- **ByRef**—Specifies passing by reference. In this case, the procedure can modify the underlying variable in the calling code the same way the calling code itself can.

- **ParamArray**—Used as the last argument in *arglist* to indicate that the final argument is an optional array of elements of the specified type. The **ParamArray** keyword allows you to pass an arbitrary number of arguments to the procedure. A **ParamArray** argument is always passed **ByVal**.

- ***argname***—Name of the variable representing the argument.

- ***argtype***—This part is optional unless **Option Strict** is set to **On**, and holds the data type of the argument passed to the procedure. Can be **Boolean**, **Byte**, **Char**, **Date**, **Decimal**, **Double**, **Integer**, **Long**, **Object**, **Short**, **Single**, or **String**; or the name of an enumeration, structure, class, or interface.

- ***defaultvalue***—Required for **Optional** arguments. Any constant or constant expression that evaluates to the data type of the argument. Note that if the type is **Object**, or a class, interface, array, or structure, the default value can be only **Nothing**.

Each attribute in the *attrlist* part has the following syntax and parts:

```
<attrname [({ attrargs | attrinit })]>
```

Here are the parts of *attrlist*:

- ***attrname***—Name of the attribute.

- ***attrargs***—List of positional arguments for this attribute. Multiple arguments are separated by commas.

- ***attrinit***—List of field or property initializers for this attribute. Multiple initializers are separated by commas.

TIP: *When you use **ByVal** (the default in VB .NET), you pass a copy of a variable to a procedure; when you use **ByRef**, you pass a reference to the variable, and if you make changes to that reference, the original variable is changed.*

You call a Sub procedure using the procedure name followed by the argument list. The **Exit Sub** keywords cause an immediate exit from a Sub procedure. Finally, **End Sub** ends the procedure definition. Here's an example we saw in the In Depth section of this chapter, where I'm passing a text string, "Hello from Visual Basic", to the **DisplayMessage** Sub procedure, which displays that message in a console application:

```
Module Module1
    Sub Main()
        DisplayMessage("Hello from Visual Basic")
    End Sub

    Sub DisplayMessage(ByVal strText As String)
        System.Console.WriteLine(strText)
    End Sub
End Module
```

Creating Functions

Unlike Sub procedures (see the previous topic), functions can return values, as discussed in the In Depth section of this chapter. You use the **Function** statement to create a function:

```
[ <attrlist> ] [{ Overloads | Overrides | Overridable | NotOverridable |
MustOverride | Shadows | Shared }]
[{ Public | Protected | Friend | Protected Friend | Private }] Function
name[(arglist)] [ As type ]
    [ statements ]
    [ Exit Function ]
    [ statements ]
End Function
```

TIP: *When you use **ByVal** (the default in VB .NET), you pass a copy of a variable to a procedure; when you use **ByRef**, you pass a reference to the variable, and if you make changes to that reference, the original variable is changed.*

The various parts of this statement are the same as for Sub procedures (see the previous topic) except for the **As** *type* clause, which specifies the type of the return value from the function; here's how to set the *type* item:

- *type*—This is optional unless **Option Strict** is **On**. Data type of the value returned by the **Function** procedure can be **Boolean**, **Byte**, **Char**, **Date**, **Decimal**, **Double**, **Integer**, **Long**, **Object**, **Short**, **Single**, or **String**; or the name of an enumeration, structure, class, or interface.

TIP: *If you use* **Exit Function** *without assigning a value to* name, *the function returns the default value appropriate to* argtype. *This is* **0** *for* **Byte**, **Char**, **Decimal**, **Double**, **Integer**, **Long**, **Short**, *and* **Single**; **Nothing for Object**, **String**, *and all arrays;* **False** *for* **Boolean**; *and* **#1/1/0001 12:00 AM#** *for* **Date**.

The **Return** statement simultaneously assigns the return value and exits the function; any number of **Return** statements can appear anywhere in the procedure. (You also can mix **Exit Function** and **Return** statements.) Here's an example function—**Addem**—we saw in the In Depth section of this chapter, which adds two integer values passed to it:

```
Module Module1
    Sub Main()
        Dim intValue As Integer = 2
        System.Console.WriteLine("{0}+{1}={2}", _
            intValue, intValue, Addem(intValue, intValue))
    End Sub

    Function Addem(ByVal int1 As Integer, ByVal int2 As Integer) As Long
        Return int1 + int2
    End Function
End Module
```

Commenting Your Procedures

In general, you should add a new comment when you declare a new and important variable, or if you wish to make clear some implementation method. Ideally, procedures should only have one purpose, and they should be named clearly enough so that excessive comments are not needed.

In addition, procedures should begin with a comment describing what the procedure does, and that comment should be broken up into various sections. The Microsoft recommendations for those sections appears in Table 3.1.

Table 3.1 Procedure starting comment block sections.

Section heading	Comment description
Purpose	What the procedure does.
Assumptions	List of each external variable, control, open file, or other element that is not obvious.
Effects	List of each affected external variable, control, or file and the effect it has (only if this is not obvious).
Inputs	Each argument that may not be obvious. Arguments are on a separate line with inline comments.
Returns	Explanation of the values returned by functions.

Here's an example, showing how to set up a comment preceding a function named **dblSquare( )**:

```
'*******************************************************
' dblSquare()
' Purpose: Squares a number
' Inputs: sngSquareMe, the value to be squared
' Returns: The input value squared
'*******************************************************
Function dblSquare() (sngSquareMe As Integer) As Double
    dblSquare = sngSquareMe * sngSquareMe    'Use *, not ^2, for speed
End Function
```

Related solution:	Found on page:
Commenting Your Code	93

Passing a Variable Number of Arguments

Usually, you cannot call a procedure with more arguments than the procedure declaration specifies. When you need an indefinite number of arguments, you can declare a *parameter array*, which allows a procedure to accept an array of values for an argument. You do not have to know the number of elements in the parameter array when you define the procedure. The array size is determined by each call to the procedure.

NOTE: *In Visual Basic .NET,* **ParamArray** *arguments are always passed using* **ByVal**. *All of the arguments in the array must be of the data type of the* **ParamArray** *argument.*

Here's an example; in this case, I'll pass different numbers of arguments to a Sub procedure, **DisplayMessage**. As you can see in the way **DisplayMessage** is declared, all arguments after the first one go into the parameter array, and I can loop over the parameter array to get all arguments passed to us (note that I use the **UBound** function, which we first saw in the previous chapter, to determine the upper bound of the array—and notice also that I'm passing a compete array of text strings to **DisplayMessage** with no problem):

```
Module Module1
    Sub Main()
        DisplayMessage("First message:", "Hi")
        DisplayMessage("Second message:", "Hello", "there")
        Dim TextArray() As String = {"Hello", "from", "Visual", _
            "Basic"}
        DisplayMessage("Third message:", TextArray)
        Resume Next
    End Sub


    Sub DisplayMessage(ByVal Title As String, ByVal ParamArray _
        MessageText() As String)
        Dim intLoopIndex As Integer
        System.Console.WriteLine(Title)
        For intLoopIndex = 0 To UBound(MessageText)
            System.Console.WriteLine(MessageText(intLoopIndex))
        Next intLoopIndex
    End Sub
End Module
```

Here's what you see when this code runs:

```
First message:
Hi
Second message:
Hello
there
Third message:
Hello
from
Visual
Basic
```

Specifying Optional Procedure Arguments

You also can make arguments *optional* in VB .NET procedures if you use the **Optional** keyword when declaring those arguments. Note that if you make one argument optional, all the following arguments must also be optional, and you have to specify a *default value* for each optional argument (although you can set them to the keyword **Nothing** if you wish). You specify a default value with **= default_value** in the procedure's argument list. Here's an example where I'm making the string argument you pass to a Sub procedure named **DisplayMessage** optional, and giving that argument the default value "**Hello from Visual Basic**":

```
Module Module1
    Sub Main()
        DisplayMessage()
    End Sub

    Sub DisplayMessage(Optional ByVal strText As String = _
        "Hello from Visual Basic")
        System.Console.WriteLine(strText)
    End Sub
End Module
```

Now when I call **DisplayMessage** with no arguments, as in the code above, the default value is used and this code displays:

```
Hello from Visual Basic
```

TIP: *VB6 had a function named **IsMissing** that would test if an optional argument had been given a value or not, but now that all optional arguments have default values, **IsMissing** has been removed. You can, however, use the **IsNothing** function to check if an argument has been set to **Nothing**.*

Preserving a Variable's Values between Procedure Calls

You've written a function named **Counter** to keep track of the number of times the user clicks a particular button. Each time through a loop, you call the **Counter** function to increment the count, but when the program ends, it just displays 0 counts. Why? Let's look at the code:

```
Module Module1
    Sub Main()
```

```
            Dim intLoopIndex As Integer, intValue = 0
            For intLoopIndex = 0 To 4
                intValue = Counter()
            Next intLoopIndex
            System.Console.WriteLine(intValue)
        End Sub

    Function Counter() As Integer
        Dim intCountValue As Integer
        intCountValue += 1
        Return intCountValue
    End Function
End Module
```

The problem here is that the counter variable, **intCountValue**, in the **Counter** function is reinitialized each time the **Counter** function is called (because a new copy of all the variables local to procedures is allocated each time you call that procedure). The solution is to declare **intCountValue** as *static*. This means it will retain its value between calls to the **Counter** function. Here's the working code:

```
Module Module1
    Sub Main()
        Dim intLoopIndex As Integer, intValue = 0
        For intLoopIndex = 0 To 4
            intValue = Counter()
        Next intLoopIndex
        System.Console.WriteLine(intValue)
    End Sub

    Function Counter() As Integer
        Static intCountValue As Integer
        intCountValue += 1
        Return intCountValue
    End Function
End Module
```

Running this code displays a value of **5**, as it should.

TIP: *You can also make **intCountValue** preserve its value between procedure calls by making it a module-level variable—just declare it outside any procedure. But note that you should restrict the scope of your variables as much as possible (to avoid inadvertent conflicts with variables of the same name), so making this variable a static variable in a procedure is probably a better choice.*

NOTE: *You were able to declare a whole function static in VB6, which meant that all the variables in it would be static, but you can't do that in VB .NET.*

Creating Procedure Delegates

Sometimes, it's useful to be able to pass the *location* of a procedure to other procedures. That location is the address of the procedure in memory, and it's used in VB .NET to create the callback procedures we'll see later in the book. To work with the address of procedures, you use delegates in VB .NET.

Here's an example; in this case, I'll create a delegate for a Sub procedure named **DisplayMessage**:

```
Module Module1
    Sub Main()
        .
        .
        .
    End Sub

    Sub DisplayMessage(ByVal strText As String)
        System.Console.WriteLine(strText)
    End Sub
End Module
```

I start by declaring the delegate type, which I'll call **SubDelegate1**, and creating a delegate called **Messager**:

```
Module Module1
    Delegate Sub SubDelegate1(ByVal strText As String)

    Sub Main()
        Dim Messager As SubDelegate1
        .
        .
        .
    End Sub

    Sub DisplayMessage(ByVal strText As String)
        System.Console.WriteLine(strText)
    End Sub
End Module
```

Now I use the **AddressOf** operator to assign the address of **DisplayMessage** to **Messager**, and then use **Messager**'s **Invoke** method to call **DisplayMessage** and display a message:

```
Module Module1
    Delegate Sub SubDelegate1(ByVal strText As String)

    Sub Main()
        Dim Messager As SubDelegate1
        Messager = AddressOf DisplayMessage
        Messager.Invoke("Hello from Visual Basic")
    End Sub

    Sub DisplayMessage(ByVal strText As String)
        System.Console.WriteLine(strText)
    End Sub
End Module
```

And that's all it takes—this code will display the message "Hello from Visual Basic", as it should.

Creating Properties

Visual Basic objects can have methods, fields, and *properties*. If you've worked with Visual Basic before, you're familiar with properties, which you use to set configuration data for objects, such as the text in a text box or the width of a list box. Using properties provides you with an interface to set or get the value of data internal to an object. You declare properties using **Get** and **Set** procedures in a **Property** statement (and, as you might expect, the syntax has changed from VB6):

```
[ <attrlist> ] [ Default ] [ Public | Private | Protected | Friend |
Protected Friend ] [ ReadOnly | WriteOnly ] [Overloads | Overrides ]
[Overridable | NotOverridable] | MustOverride | Shadows | Shared] Property
varname([ parameter list ]) [ As typename ] [ Implements interfacemember ]
    [ <attrlist> ] Get
        [ block ]
    End Get
    [ <attrlist> ] Set(ByVal Value As typename )
        [ block ]
    End Set
End Property
```

Here are the parts of this statement that are different from the keywords used in the Sub statement. (See the Immediate Solution "Creating Sub Procedures"):

- **Default**—Makes this a default property. **Default** properties can be set and retrieved without specifying the property name, and must accept parameters.

- **ReadOnly**—Specifies that a properties value can be retrieved, but it cannot be the modified. **ReadOnly** properties contain **Get** blocks but no **Set** blocks.

- **WriteOnly**—Specifies that a property can be set but its value cannot be retrieved. **WriteOnly** properties contain **Set** blocks but no **Get** blocks.

- *varname*—A name that identifies the Property.

- *parameter list*—The parameters you use with the property. The list default is **ByVal**.

- *typename*—The type of the property. If you don't specify a data type, the default type is **Object**.

- *interfacemember*—When a property is part of a class that implements an interface, this is the name of the property being implemented.

- **Get**—Starts a **Get** property procedure used to return the value of a property. **Get** blocks are optional unless the property is **ReadOnly**.

- **End Get**—Ends a **Get** property procedure.

- **Set**—Starts a **Set** property procedure used to set the value of a property. **Set** blocks are optional unless the property is **WriteOnly**. Note that the new value of the property is passed to the **Set** property procedure in a parameter named **Value** when the value of the property changes.

- **End Set**—Ends a **Set** property procedure.

Visual Basic passes a parameter named **Value** to the **Set** block during property assignments, and the **Value** parameter contains the value that was assigned to the property when the **Set** block was called. Here's an example where I'm creating a read/write property named **Prop1** in **Module2**, and storing the property's value in a private text string named **PropertyValue** in **Module2**:

```
Module Module1
    Sub Main()
        .
        .
        .
    End Sub
End Module

Module Module2
    Private PropertyValue As String
```

```
        Public Property Prop1() As String
            Get
                Return PropertyValue
            End Get
            Set(ByVal Value As String)
                PropertyValue = Value
            End Set
        End Property
End Module
```

TIP: *When you type the first line of a property procedure, as* **Public Property Prop1( ) As String** *here, VB .NET will add a skeleton for the* **Get** *and* **Set** *procedures automatically.*

Now I can refer to **Prop1** of **Module2**, setting it and reading its value, like this:

```
Module Module1
    Sub Main()
        Module2.Prop1 = 2
        System.Console.WriteLine("Prop1 = " & Module2.Prop1)
        System.Console.WriteLine("Press Enter to continue...")
    End Sub
End Module

Module Module2
    Private PropertyValue As String
    Public Property Prop1() As String
        Get
            Return PropertyValue
        End Get
        Set(ByVal Value As String)
            PropertyValue = Value
        End Set
    End Property
End Module
```

This console application displays this text in a DOS window:

```
Prop1 = 2
Press Enter to continue...
```

You also can index properties by passing an index value when referring to a property. Here's an example; in this case, I'm creating a property array by adding an index value that you must specify each time you use the property:

```
Public Module Module1
    Private Data(200) As Integer

    Public Property Property1(ByVal Index As Integer) As Integer
        Get
            Return Data(Index)
        End Get
        Set(ByVal Value As Integer)
            Data(Index) = Value
        End Set
    End Property
End Module
```

Now instead of referring to the property simply as **Property1**, I must use an index value, such as **Property1(5)**, which refers to a particular element in the property array:

```
Private Sub Form1_Load(ByVal sender As System.Object, _
    ByVal e As System.EventArgs) Handles MyBase.Load
    Module1.Property1(5) = 1
    MsgBox(Module1.Property1(5))
End Sub
```

Want to see how to create write-only and read-only properties? Take a look at "Creating Properties" in Chapter 11.

Related solutions:	Found on page:
Creating Properties	508
Creating Class (Shared) Properties	509

Understanding Scope

The *scope* of a variable or constant is the set of all code that can refer to it without qualifying its name. A variable's scope is determined by where the variable is declared. It's usually a good idea to make the scope of variables or constants as narrow as possible (block scope is the narrowest). This helps conserve memory and minimizes the chances of your code referring to the wrong item. I'll take a look at the different kinds of scope in VB .NET here.

Block Scope

As discussed in the In Depth section of this chapter, a block is a series of statements terminated by an **End**, **Else**, **Loop**, or **Next** statement, and an element declared within a block can be used only within that block. Here's what block scope looks like in an example from the In Depth section of this chapter. In this case, I'll declare a variable, **strText** in an **If** statement. That variable can be used *inside* the **If** statement's block, but not *outside* (VB .NET will tag the second use here as a syntax error):

```
Module Module1
    Sub Main()
        Dim intValue As Integer = 1
        If intValue = 1 Then
            Dim strText As String = "No worries."
            System.Console.WriteLine(strText)
        End If
        System.Console.WriteLine(strText)           'Will not work!
    End Sub
End Module
```

Procedure Scope

An element declared within a procedure is not available outside that procedure, and only the procedure that contains the declaration can use it. Elements at this level are also called *local* elements, and you declare them with the **Dim** or **Static** statement.

Note also that if an element is declared inside a procedure but outside any block within that procedure, the element can be thought of as having block scope, where the block is the entire procedure.

Module Scope

When discussing scope, Visual Basic uses the term *module level* to apply equally to modules, classes, and structures. You can declare elements at this level by placing the declaration statement outside of any procedure or block within the module, class, or structure.

When you make a declaration at the module level, the accessibility you choose determines the scope. The namespace that contains the module, class, or structure also affects the scope.

Elements for which you declare **Private** accessibility are available for reference to every procedure in that module, but not to any code in a different module. The **Dim** statement at module level defaults to **Private** accessibility, so it is equivalent to using the **Private** statement. However, you can make the scope and accessibility more obvious by using **Private**. In this example from the In Depth section of this chapter, I've declared **Function1** as private to **Module2**, so it's inaccessible in **Module1** (VB .NET will tag **Module2.Function1** below as a syntax error):

```
Module Module1
    Sub Main()
        System.Console.WriteLine(Module2.Function1())    'Will not work!
    End Sub
End Module

Module Module2
    Private Function Function1() As String
        Return "Hello from Visual Basic"
    End Function

End Module
```

Namespace Scope

If you declare an element at module level using the **Friend** or **Public** statement, it becomes available to all procedures throughout the entire namespace in which it is declared. Note that an element accessible in a namespace is also accessible from inside any namespace nested inside that namespace.

NOTE: *If your project does not contain any **namespace** statements, everything in the project is in the same namespace. In this case, namespace scope can be thought of as procedure scope.*

Using Unstructured Exception Handling

As discussed in the In Depth section of this chapter, there are now two ways of handling runtime errors in Visual Basic—you can use structured or unstructured exception handling (exceptions are runtime errors). Unstructured exception handling revolves around the **On Error GoTo** statement, and structured exception handling uses the **Try...Catch...Finally** statement. Without an **On Error GoTo** or **Try...Catch...Finally** statement, any exception that occurs is fatal and your program will stop.

I'll take a look at the **On Error GoTo** statement first in this and the next few topics. Although one gets the impression that Microsoft would far rather you use

Try...Catch...Finally, there are simply some things you can do with **On Error GoTo** that you can't do with **Try...Catch...Finally**, such as resume execution with a **Resume** statement.

The **On Error GoTo** statement enables exception handling and specifies the location of the exception-handling code within a procedure. Here's how the **On Error GoTo** statement works:

```
On Error { GoTo [ line | 0 | -1 ] | Resume Next }
```

Here are the parts of this statement:

- **GoTo *line***—Enables the exception-handling code that starts at the line specified in the required *line* argument. The *line* argument is any line label or line number. If an exception occurs, program execution goes to the given location. (Note that the specified line must be in the same procedure as the **On Error** statement.)

- **GoTo 0**—Disables enabled exception handler in the current procedure and resets it to **Nothing**.

- **GoTo -1**—Same as **GoTo 0**.

- **Resume Next**—Specifies that when an exception occurs, execution skips over the statement that caused the problem and goes to the statement immediately following. Execution continues from that point.

NOTE: *If a trappable exception occurs in a procedure, you can handle that exception in an exception handler. But what if you call another procedure, and an exception occurs before control returns from that procedure? If the called procedure has an exception handler, the code in that exception handler will be executed. However, if the called procedure does not have an exception handler, control will return to the exception handler in the calling procedure. In this way, control moves back up the calling chain to the closest exception handler.*

Here's an example showing how to use the **On Error GoTo** statement that uses a division by zero to create an overflow exception. In this case, I'm directing execution to the label "Handler", which you create by placing this label on a line of its own, followed by a colon—note that I also place an **Exit Sub** statement before the exception handler so the exception-handling code isn't executed inadvertently during normal program execution:

```
Module Module1
    Sub Main()
        Dim int1 = 0, int2 = 1, int3 As Integer
        On Error Goto Handler
```

```
        int3 = int2 / int1
        Exit Sub
Handler:
        .
        .
        .

    End Sub
End Module
```

And I can add exception-handling code in the exception handler like this:

```
Module Module1
    Sub Main()
        Dim int1 = 0, int2 = 1, int3 As Integer
        On Error Goto Handler
        int3 = int2 / int1
        Exit Sub
Handler:
        System.Console.WriteLine("Overflow error!")
    End Sub
End Module
```

Now when this console application runs, you'll see "Overflow error!". You can also handle specific exceptions in different ways depending which exception occurred by checking the **Err** object's **Number** property, which holds the exception's number. Here, I'm handling only arithmetic overflow exceptions, which are exception number 6:

```
Module Module1
    Sub Main()
        Dim int1 = 0, int2 = 1, int3 As Integer
        On Error Goto Handler
        int3 = int2 / int1
        Exit Sub
Handler:
        If (Err.Number = 6) Then
            System.Console.WriteLine("Overflow error!")
        End If
    End Sub
End Module
```

The **Err** object also has a new **GetException** method that returns an exception object. For more on these objects, see the topic "Using Structured Exception Handling" in this chapter. Using the **TypeOf** and **Is** keywords in an **If** statement, you can handle exception objects such as **OverflowException** like this:

```
Module Module1
    Sub Main()
        Dim int1 = 0, int2 = 1, int3 As Integer
        On Error Goto Handler
        int3 = int2 / int1
        Exit Sub
Handler:
        If (TypeOf Err.GetException() Is OverflowException) Then
            System.Console.WriteLine("Overflow error!")
        End If
    End Sub
End Module
```

Now that structured exception handling has been added to Visual Basic, the real attraction of unstructured exception handling is the **Resume** statement—see the next topic.

TIP: *System errors during calls to Windows dynamic-link libraries (DLL) do not throw exceptions which means they can't be trapped with Visual Basic exception trapping. When calling DLL functions, you should check each return value for success or failure, and in case of failure, check the value in the **Err** object's **LastDLLError** property.*

Using **Resume Next** and **Resume** *Line*

One of the most useful aspects of unstructured exception handling is the **Resume** statement, which lets you resume program execution even after an exception has occurred. You can use **Resume** to resume execution with the statement that caused the exception, **Resume Next** to resume execution with the statement after the one that caused the exception, and **Resume** *line*, where *line* is a line number or label that specifies where to resume execution. Here's an example using **Resume Next**, which lets you skip over the line that caused the problem:

```
Module Module1
    Sub Main()
        Dim int1 = 0, int2 = 1, int3 As Integer
        On Error Goto Handler
```

```
        int3 = int2 / int1
        System.Console.WriteLine("Program completed...")
        Exit Sub
Handler:
        If (TypeOf Err.GetException() Is OverflowException) Then
            System.Console.WriteLine("Overflow error!")
            Resume Next
        End If
    End Sub
End Module
```

Here's what you see when you run this console application:

```
Overflow error!
Program completed...
```

And here's an example using the **Resume *line*** form:

```
Module Module1
    Sub Main()
        Dim int1 = 0, int2 = 1, int3 As Integer
        On Error Goto Handler
        int3 = int2 / int1
Nextline:
        System.Console.WriteLine("Program completed...")
        Exit Sub
Handler:
        If (TypeOf Err.GetException() Is OverflowException) Then
            System.Console.WriteLine("Overflow error!")
            Resume Nextline
        End If
    End Sub
End Module
```

You can also use an **On Error Resume Next** or **On Error Resume *line*** statement to make Visual Basic continue program execution after an exception has occurred. This form is sometimes preferable to the **On Error GoTo** form if you don't want to write an explicit exception handler:

```
Module Module1
    Sub Main()
        Dim int1 = 0, int2 = 1, int3 As Integer
        On Error Resume Next
```

```
        int3 = int2 / int1
        .
        .
        .
```

Using **On Error GoTo 0**

To turn off unstructured exception handling, you can use the **On Error GoTo 0** or **On Error GoTo -1** statements. Here's an example:

```
Module Module1
    Sub Main()
        Dim int1 = 0, int2 = 1, int3 As Integer
        On Error Goto Handler
        int3 = int2 / int1
        On Error Goto 0  'Turn error handling off
        System.Console.WriteLine("Program completed...")
Handler:
        If (TypeOf Err.GetException() Is OverflowException) Then
            System.Console.WriteLine("Overflow error!")
            Resume Next
        End If
    End Sub
End Module
```

Getting an Exception's Number and Description

For more information on exceptions, you can use the **Err** object's **Number** and **Description** properties, like this:

```
Module Module1
    Sub Main()
        Dim int1 = 0, int2 = 1, int3 As Integer
        On Error Goto Handler
        int3 = int2 / int1
        System.Console.WriteLine("Program completed...")
Handler:
```

```
        System.Console.WriteLine("Error number {0} occurred: {1}", _
            Err.Number, Err.Description)
    End Sub
End Module
```

Here's what you see when you run this console application:

```
Error number 6 occurred: Exception of type System.OverflowException was
thrown.
```

TIP: *You can determine the object that caused the exception using the Visual Basic **Err** object's **Source** property. This property holds the name of the object or application that caused the exception. For example, if you connect to Microsoft Excel and it generates an exception, Excel sets **Err.Number** to its error code for that exception, and it sets **Err.Source** to "Excel.Application".*

Raising an Exception Intentionally

There are cases in programs where you might want to create an exception because, although no Visual Basic trappable exception has occurred, some situation may have occurred that's incompatible with your program's logic. You can create an exception intentionally, called *raising* an exception, with the Visual Basic **Err** object's **Raise** method, which is declared this way internally in VB .NET:

```
Raise(ByVal Number As Integer, Optional ByVal Source As Object = Nothing,
Optional ByVal Description As Object = Nothing, Optional ByVal HelpFile As
Object = Nothing, Optional ByVal HelpContext As Object = Nothing)
```

Here are the arguments for the **Raise** method:

- *Number*—Long integer that identifies the nature of the exception.

- *Source*—String expression naming the object or application that generated the exception; use the form project.class. (If source is not specified, the name of the current Visual Basic project is used.)

- *Description*—String expression describing the exception.

- *Helpfile*—The path to the Help file in which help on this exception can be found.

- **Helpcontext**—A context ID identifying a topic within **helpfile** that provides help for the exception.

When setting the exception number for a custom exception, note that Visual Basic reserves a certain range of exceptions for itself. To make sure your custom exception doesn't conflict with that range, add the value **vbObjectError** to your exception number, then subtract it when you handle the exception to recover your original exception number. Let's see an example. Here, I'll generate our own exception, exception number 51:

```
Module Module1
    Sub Main()
        On Error Goto Handler
        Err.Raise(vbObjectError + 51)
        System.Console.WriteLine("Program completed...")
Handler:
        System.Console.WriteLine("Error number {0} occurred: {1}", _
            Err.Number - vbObjectError, Err.Description)
    End Sub
End Module
```

You can handle these custom exceptions in the way that makes sense for your application. Here's what you see when you run this console application:

```
Error number 51 occurred: Application-defined or object-defined error.
```

TIP: You can also use the Visual Basic **Error** statement to raise an error like this: **Error errnumber**. However, the **Error** function is considered obsolete now, replaced by the **Raise** method of the **Err** object.

Using Structured Exception Handling

Microsoft has added structured exception handling to Visual Basic, and as you might expect, it's now considered the recommended method of exception handling. In fact, it is appropriate to call the **On Error GoTo** method of exception handling unstructured, because using this statement just sets the internal exception handler in Visual Basic; it certainly doesn't add any structure to your code, and if your code extends over procedures and blocks, it can be hard to figure out what exception handler is working when.

Structured exception handling is based on a particular statement, the **Try...Catch...Finally** statement, which is divided into a **Try** block, optional **Catch** blocks, and an optional **Finally** block. The **Try** block contains code where exceptions can occur, the **Catch** block contains code to handle the exceptions that occur. If an exception occurs in the **Try** block, the code *throws* the exception—actually an object based on the Visual Basic **Exception** class—so it can be caught and handled by the appropriate **Catch** statement. After the rest of the statement finishes, execution is always passed to the **Finally** block, if there is one. Here's what the **Try...Catch...Finally** statement looks like in general:

```
Try
    [ tryStatements ]
    [Catch [ exception1 [ As type1 ] ] [ When expression1 ]
        catchStatements1
        [Exit Try] ]
    [Catch [ exception2 [ As type2 ] ] [When expression2 ]
        catchStatements2
        [ Exit Try ] ]

        .

        .

        .

    [Catch [ exceptionn [ As typen ] ] [ When expressionn ]
        catchStatementsn ]
        [ Exit Try ] ]
    [ Finally
        [ finallyStatements ] ]
End Try
```

Here are the parts of this statement:

- **Try**—Begins the **Try** block for structured exception handling.

- *tryStatements*—Sensitive statements where you expect exceptions.

- **Catch**—If an exception happens in the **Try** block, the exception is thrown and each **Catch** statement is examined in order to determine if it will handle the exception.

- *exception*—A variable name you give the exception. The value of *exception* is the value of the thrown exception.

- *type*—Specifies the type of the exception you're catching in a **Catch** statement.

- **When**—A **Catch** clause with a **When** clause will only catch exceptions when *expression* evaluates to **True**.

- ***expression***—An expression used to select exceptions to handle; must be convertible to a **Boolean** value. Often used to filter exceptions by number.

- ***catchStatements***—Statements to handle exceptions occurring in the **Try** block.

- **Exit Try**—Statement that breaks out of the **Try...Catch...Finally** structure. Execution is transferred to the code immediately following the **End Try** statement. Note that **Exit Try** is not allowed in **Finally** blocks.

- **Finally**—A **Finally** block is always executed when execution leaves any part of the **Try** statement.

- ***finallyStatements***—Statements that are executed after all other exception processing has occurred.

NOTE: *If a **Try** statement does not contain any **Catch** blocks, it must contain a **Finally** block.*

TIP: *Bear in mind that if exceptions occur that the code does not specifically handle, Visual Basic will default to its normal exception message.*

If you supply the optional **Finally** statement, the corresponding statement block is always the last code to be executed just before control leaves **Try...Catch... Finally**. This is true even if an unhandled exception occurs, or if you execute an **Exit Try** statement. And note that you can have any number of **Catch** statements (however, you must have at least one **Catch** statement or a **Finally** statement).

Here's an example; in this case, the exception-prone code executes a division by zero, which generates an arithmetic overflow exception. Note that I place the sensitive code in the **Try** block, and the exception-handling code in the **Catch** block:

```
Module Module1
    Sub Main()
        Dim int1 = 0, int2 = 1, int3 As Integer
        Try
            int3 = int2 / int1
            System.Console.WriteLine("The answer is {0}", int3)
        Catch
            System.Console.WriteLine("Exception: Arithmetic overflow!")
        End Try
    End Sub
End Module
```

When you run this console application, you'll see:

```
Exception: Arithmetic overflow!
```

You also can get more information about the exception by getting an exception object; I'll do that here by catching any exception based on the **Exception** class—which means all exceptions—and using the exception object's **ToString** method to display information about the exception:

```
Module Module1
    Sub Main()
        Dim int1 = 0, int2 = 1, int3 As Integer
        Try
            int3 = int2 / int1
            System.Console.WriteLine("The answer is {0}", int3)
        Catch e As Exception
            System.Console.WriteLine(e.ToString)
        End Try
    End Sub
End Module
```

Here's what you see when you run this code:

```
System.OverflowException: Exception of type System.OverflowException was
thrown.

   at Microsoft.VisualBasic.Helpers.IntegerType.FromObject(Object Value)
   at ConsoleApp.Module1.Main() in C:\vbnet\ConsoleApp\Module1.vb:line 5
```

This kind of information is more useful to the programmer than to the user. For the user, you might display the message in the exception object's message property (that is, use **e.message** instead), which gives you this:

```
Exception of type System.OverflowException was thrown.
```

That's a little better, but of course, it's best to catch individual exceptions yourself and to customize the messages you display to your application. Take a look at the next topic for the details.

Exception Filtering in the **Catch** Block

When you're handling exceptions, you usually want to handle different types of exceptions differently, according to the nature of the exception that occurred. This process is called *filtering*. There are actually two ways to filter exceptions with **Catch** blocks. First, you can filter on specific classes of exceptions, which means you have to prepare for the various exceptions you want to handle.

Exceptions are based on the Visual Basic **Exception** class (which, like all other objects in Visual Basic, is based on the **Object** class). In general, when you use Visual Basic statements that are capable of throwing exceptions, the Visual Basic documentation will tell you what possible exceptions each statement may throw. However, that won't help in tracking down exceptions that occur when you're just using the general syntax of the language, such as when you divide two numbers and an overflow exception occurs. To track down what class such an exception corresponds to, you could take a look at the Visual Basic documentation for the Exception class, which lists the classes derived from it:

```
Object
    Exception
        ApplicationException
        CodeDomSerializerException
        InvalidPrinterException
        IOException
        IsolatedStorageException
        PathTooLongException
        CookieException
        ProtocolViolationException
        WebException
        MissingManifestResourceException
        SUDSGeneratorException
        SUDSParserException
        SystemException
        UriFormatException
        SoapException
```

Each derived class itself has many derived classes, and if you keep searching (each class above is a hyperlink in the documentation, so you just keep clicking), you'll eventually find the **OverflowException** class, which is based on the **ArithmeticException** class, which is based on the **SystemException** class, which is based on the **Exception** class:

```
Object
    Exception
        SystemException
            ArithmeticException
                OverflowException
```

There is an easier way to do this if you can generate the exception you're antici-pating—just use the **Exception** class's **getType** method (such as **e.getType**) to get the type of the exception as a string. Here's an example where I'm providing code to explicitly handle overflow exceptions:

```
Module Module1
    Sub Main()
        Dim int1 = 0, int2 = 1, int3 As Integer
        Try
            int3 = int2 / int1
            System.Console.WriteLine("The answer is {0}", int3)
        Catch e As OverflowException
            System.Console.WriteLine("Exception: Arithmetic overflow!")
        End Try
    End Sub
End Module
```

The second exception-filtering option lets you use the **Catch** statement to filter on any conditional expression, using the **When** keyword. This option is often used to filter by exception number, which you can check with the **Err** object's **Number** property. Here's an example that filters overflow exceptions by number (which is exception number 6 in Visual Basic .NET):

```
Module Module1
    Sub Main()
        Dim int1 = 0, int2 = 1, int3 As Integer
        Try
            int3 = int2 / int1
            System.Console.WriteLine("The answer is {0}", int3)
        Catch When Err.Number = 6
            System.Console.WriteLine("Exception: Arithmetic overflow!")
        End Try
    End Sub
End Module
```

Using Multiple **Catch** Statements

You also can use multiple **Catch** statements when you filter exceptions. Here's an example that specifically handles overflow, invalid argument, and argument out of range exceptions:

```
Module Module1
    Sub Main()
        Dim int1 = 0, int2 = 1, int3 As Integer
        Try
            int3 = int2 / int1
            System.Console.WriteLine("The answer is {0}", int3)
        Catch e As System.OverflowException
            System.Console.WriteLine("Exception: Arithmetic overflow!")
        Catch e As System.ArgumentException
            System.Console.WriteLine("Exception: Invalid argument value!")
        Catch e As System.ArgumentOutOfRangeException
            System.Console.WriteLine("Exception: Argument out of range!")
        End Try
    End Sub
End Module
```

If you want to add a general exception handler to catch any exceptions not filtered, you can add a **Catch** block for the **Exception** class at the end of the other **Catch** blocks:

```
Module Module1
    Sub Main()
        Dim int1 = 0, int2 = 1, int3 As Integer
        Try
            int3 = int2 / int1
            System.Console.WriteLine("The answer is {0}", int3)
        Catch e As System.ArgumentOutOfRangeException
            System.Console.WriteLine("Exception: Argument out of range!")
        Catch e As System.ArgumentException
            System.Console.WriteLine("Exception: Invalid argument value!")
        Catch e As Exception
            System.Console.WriteLine("Exception occurred!")
        End Try
    End Sub
End Module
```

Using **Finally**

The code in the **Finally** block, if there is one, is always executed in a **Try...Catch...Finally** statement, even if there was no exception, and even if you execute an **Exit Try** statement. This allows you to deallocate resources and so on; here's an example with a **Finally** block:

```
Module Module1
    Sub Main()
        Dim int1 = 0, int2 = 1, int3 As Integer
        Try
            int3 = int2 / int1
            System.Console.WriteLine("The answer is {0}", int3)
        Catch e As System.OverflowException
            System.Console.WriteLine("Exception: Arithmetic overflow!")
        Catch e As System.ArgumentException
            System.Console.WriteLine("Exception: Invalid argument value!")
        Catch e As System.ArgumentOutOfRangeException
            System.Console.WriteLine("Exception: Argument out of range!")
        Finally
            System.Console.WriteLine("Execution of sensitive code " & _
                "is complete")
        End Try
    End Sub
End Module
```

And here's what you see when you execute this console application:

```
Exception: Arithmetic overflow!
Execution of sensitive code is complete
```

Throwing an Exception

You can throw an exception using the **Throw** statement, and you can also rethrow a caught exception using the **Throw** statement. Here's an example where I'm explicitly throwing an overflow exception:

```
Module Module1
    Sub Main()
        Try
```

```
                Throw New OverflowException()
        Catch e As Exception
                System.Console.WriteLine(e.Message)
        End Try
    End Sub
End Module
```

TIP: *In fact, it's even possible to mix structured and unstructured exception handling to some extent—if you're using unstructured exception handling, you can get an exception object with the **Err** object's **GetException** method and throw that exception in a **Try** block.*

Throwing a Custom Exception

You can customize the exceptions you throw by creating a new exception object based on the **ApplicationException** object. Here's an example where I'm creating a new **ApplicationException** object with the text "This is a new exception", and then throwing and catching that exception:

```
Module Module1
    Sub Main()
        Try
            Throw New ApplicationException("This is a new exception")
        Catch e As Exception
            System.Console.WriteLine(e.Message)
        End Try
    End Sub
End Module
```

Here's what you see when you run this console application:

```
This is a new exception
```

Chapter 4

Windows Forms

In Depth

In this chapter, we start to get visual. As you know, there are two types of forms in Visual Basic .NET—Windows forms and Web forms. This chapter is all about working with Windows forms.

There's a great deal to see about Windows forms in Visual Basic; we'll take a look at it here. We'll see how to customize forms; how to work with multiple forms; how to support the Multiple Document Interface (MDI); how to handle MDI child forms; how to use **MsgBox**, **MessageBox**, and **InputBox** to create message boxes and input boxes; how to create, hide, and show forms in code; how to add controls at run time; and much more. We'll begin the chapter with an overview of Visual Basic Windows forms.

All About Windows Forms

Technically speaking, forms are what you work with in forms designers; they represent the windows that will appear in your application. However, it's become common to refer to both the windows under design and the windows in your running application as forms in Visual Basic applications.

The whole power of Visual Basic has been that you can develop forms visually, adding controls and other items from the toolbox. In VB .NET, the support for Windows forms is in the **System.Windows.Forms** namespace, and the form class is **System.Windows.Forms.Form**. The **Form** class itself is based on the **Control** class, which means that forms share a lot of the properties and methods that controls do. Here's what the class hierarchy looks like for the **Form** class; every level is derived from the one above it (note that all classes are derived from the **Object** class):

```
Object
    MarshalByRefObject
        Component
            Control
                ScrollableControl
                    ContainerControl
                        Form
```

You can see a form in a form designer in the Visual Basic Integrated Development Environment (IDE) in Figure 4.1, which shows several aspects of forms. At the

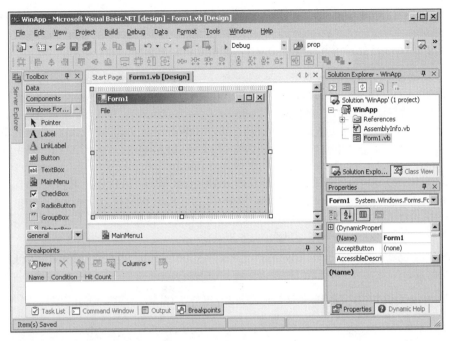

Figure 4.1 A form under design.

top of the form is the *title bar*, which displays the form's title; here that's just Form1. At right in the title bar is the *control box*, including the minimizing/maximizing buttons and the close button. These are controls the user takes for granted in most windows, although we'll see that they are inappropriate in others, such as dialog boxes.

Under the title bar comes the *menu bar*, if there is one. In Figure 4.1, the form has one menu—the File menu. (We'll see how to work with menus in the next chapter). Under the menu bar, forms can have *toolbars*, as you see in the IDE itself.

The main area of a form—the area where everything takes place—is called the *client area*. In general, Visual Basic code works with controls in the client area and leaves the rest of the form to Visual Basic. (In fact, the client area is itself a window.) In Figure 4.1, I've added a control—a command button—to the form.

Finally, the whole form is surrounded by a *border*. There are several types of borders that you can use, as we'll see when working with dialog boxes and using the fixed, non-resizable borders appropriate to them.

The important class for Windows forms is the **Form** class in the **System.Windows. Forms** namespace. Each form in this namespace is an instance (that is, an object) of that class. As mentioned in Chapter 2, objects are instances of classes, much as an integer variable is an instance of the **Integer** type. (You can think of a class as a type you create objects from.) As we also know, classes can have *members—fields* (data items), *methods* (built-in procedures), and *properties* (data items accessed through an interface based on methods).

As I mentioned in Chapter 2, it's important to realize—now that we're actually starting to work with classes such as the **Form** class—that there are *two* kinds of class members. First, there are those members inherent to the *class* itself (accessed through the class), such as **Form.ActiveForm**, or just **ActiveForm**. For these members—called Static, Shared, or class members—you don't need an object. Then there are those members, called instance or object members, that are built into *objects*, such as **MyForm1.BackColor**. With this type, **MyForm1** is an instance of the **Form** class, where you do need an object. In other words, the difference is that to use class members, you don't need an object of that class to work with, and with object members, you do:

- *Static/Shared members* are *class members*, accessed directly using the class like this: *classname.membername*. No object needed.

- *Instance members* are *object members*, accessed by using an instance of a class (an object) like this: *objectname.membername*.

I prefer the terms "class members" and "object members," because that makes clear what kinds of members they are, but the VB .NET documentation often uses the terms "Static (Shared) members" and "Instance members." With all that under our belts, we can talk about the members of the **Form** class. For more information on this topic, see "Class Vs Object Members" in the In Depth section of Chapter 11—in that chapter, we see how to create both class and object members from scratch.

The **Form** class only has one class property, **ActiveForm**, which holds the currently active form for the entire application. If you want to determine what window has the focus (that is, is the target of keystrokes), use the **ActiveForm** property. However, the **Form** class does have many object properties. Some of these object properties are public, some private to the object, and some protected (that is, only accessible to objects of the **Form** class or objects of classes derived from **Form**). When working with forms, one usually uses the public object members (that is, the public properties, methods, and events of **Form** objects); you'll find an overview of the most interesting **Form** public object properties in Table 4.1, and the most interesting **Form** public object methods (recall that methods are the procedures built into a class) in Table 4.2. Note that—as is usual with properties and methods in Visual Basic—not all these properties and methods will be available at the time you're designing your code—some only will be available at run time. It's worth scanning through these tables to familiarize yourself with what's available—such as the **Icon** property, which sets the icon for the form in Windows, or the **BackColor** property, which sets the background color of the form, and so on.

Table 4.1 Windows forms public object properties.

Property	Description
AcceptButton	Gets or sets the button on the form that is pressed when the user uses the Enter key.
ActiveControl	Gets or sets the active control (the one with the focus).
ActiveMdiChild	Gets the currently active multiple document interface (MDI) child window.
AllowDrop	Indicates if the form can accept data that the user drags and drops into it.
AutoScale	Indicates if the form adjusts its size to fit the height of the font used on the form and scales its controls.
AutoScroll	Indicates if the form implements autoscrolling.
BackColor	Gets or sets the background color for this form.
BackgroundImage	Gets or sets the background image in the form.
Bottom	Gets the location of the bottom of the form.
Bounds	Gets or sets the bounding rectangle for the form.
CancelButton	Indicates the button control that is pressed when the user presses the ESC key.
CanFocus	Indicates if the form can receive focus.
Capture	Specifies if the form has captured the mouse, or captures the mouse.
ClientRectangle	Returns the rectangle that represents the client area.
ClientSize	Gets or sets the size of the client area.
ContainsFocus	Indicates if the form, or a child control, has the input focus.
ContextMenu	Gets or sets the shortcut menu for this form.
ControlBox	Gets or sets a value indicating if a control box is displayed.
Controls	Gets or sets the collection of controls contained within the form.
Cursor	Gets or sets the cursor that is displayed when the user moves the mouse pointer over this form.
DesktopBounds	Gets or sets the size and location of the form on the Windows desktop.
DesktopLocation	Gets or sets the location of the form on the Windows desktop.
DialogResult	Gets or sets the dialog result for the form.
Enabled	Gets or sets a value indicating if the form is enabled.
Focused	Indicates if the form has input focus.
ForeColor	Gets or sets the foreground color of the form.
FormBorderStyle	Gets or sets the border style of the form.
Height	Gets or sets the height of the form.
Icon	Gets or sets the icon for the form.
IsMdiChild	Indicates if the form is an MDI child form.
IsMdiContainer	Gets or sets a value indicating if the form is a container for MDI child forms.

(continued)

Table 4.1   Windows forms public object properties *(continued)*.

Property	Description
Left	Gets or sets the x-coordinate of a form's left edge in pixels.
Location	Gets or sets the coordinates of the upper-left corner of the form relative to the upper-left corner of its container.
MaximizeBox	Gets or sets a value indicating if the maximize button is displayed in the caption bar of the form.
MaximumSize	Returns the maximum size the form can be resized to.
MdiChildren	Returns an array of forms of the MDI child forms that are parented to this form.
MdiParent	Gets or sets the current MDI parent form of this form.
Menu	Gets or sets the MainMenu that is displayed in the form.
MinimizeBox	Gets or sets a value indicating if the minimize button is displayed in the caption bar of the form.
MinimumSize	Gets the minimum size the form can be resized to.
Modal	Gets a value indicating if this form is displayed modally.
Name	Gets or sets the name of the form.
OwnedForms	Gets an array of **Form** objects of all forms that are owned by this form.
Owner	Gets or sets the form that owns this form.
Parent	Gets or sets the parent container of this form.
ParentForm	Gets or sets the form that the container form is assigned to.
Right	Gets the distance between the right edge of the form and the left edge of its container.
ShowInTaskbar	Gets or sets a value indicating if the form is displayed in the Windows taskbar.
Size	Gets or sets the size of the form.
StartPosition	Gets or sets the starting position of the form at run time.
TabStop	Gets or sets a value indicating if the user can give the focus to this form using the Tab key.
Tag	Gets or sets the object that contains data about the form.
Text	Gets or sets the text associated with this form.
Top	Gets or sets the top coordinate of the form.
TopLevel	Gets or sets a value indicating if the form should be displayed as a top-level window.
TopMost	Gets or sets a value indicating if the form should be displayed as the topmost form of your application.
Visible	Gets or sets a value indicating if the form is visible.
Width	Gets or sets the width of the form.
WindowState	Gets or sets the form's window state.

Table 4.2   Windows forms public object methods.

Method	Description
Activate	Activates the form (gives it focus and makes it active).
AddOwnedForm	Adds an owned form to this form.
BringToFront	Brings the form to the front of the stacking order.
Close	Closes the form.
Contains	Indicates if the specified control is a child of this form.
Dispose	Releases the resources used by the form.
DoDragDrop	Begins a drag-and-drop operation.
Focus	Gives the form the focus.
GetChildAtPoint	Gets the child control that is located at the specified coordinates.
GetNextControl	Gets the next control in the tab order of child controls.
Hide	Hides the form.
LayoutMdi	Arranges the MDI child forms within the MDI parent form.
PointToClient	Finds the location of the specified screen point to client coordinates.
PointToScreen	Finds the location of the specified client point to screen coordinates.
RectangleToClient	Finds the location of the specified screen rectangle to client coordinates.
RectangleToScreen	Finds the location of the specified client rectangle to screen coordinates.
Refresh	Forces the form to repaint (redraw) itself and any child controls.
Select	Selects this form.
SendToBack	Sends the form to the back of the stacking order.
SetBounds	Sets the bounds of the form.
SetDesktopBounds	Sets the bounds of the form in desktop coordinates.
SetDesktopLocation	Sets the location of the form in desktop coordinates.
Show	Makes the form display by setting the visible property to true.
ShowDialog	Displays the form as a modal dialog box.

Windows forms also support *events*, which we've discussed as far back as Chapter 1. Events let you know that something's happened with a form; for example, when you click a form, a **Click** event occurs, and when the form is closed, a **Closed** event occurs. You'll find an overview of the more interesting public object events for Windows forms in Table 4.3.

4. Windows Forms

Table 4.3   Windows forms public object events.

Event	Description
Activated	Occurs when the form is activated in code or by the user.
Click	Occurs when the form is clicked.
Closed	Occurs when the form is closed.
Closing	Occurs when the form is closing.
ControlAdded	Occurs when a new control is added.
ControlRemoved	Occurs when a control is removed.
CursorChanged	Occurs when the cursor property value has changed.
Deactivate	Occurs when the form loses focus and is not the active form.
DoubleClick	Occurs when the form is double-clicked.
DragDrop	Occurs when a drag-and-drop operation is completed.
DragEnter	Occurs when an object is dragged into the form's bounds.
DragLeave	Occurs when an object has been dragged into and out of the form's bounds.
DragOver	Occurs when an object has been dragged over the form's bounds.
Enter	Occurs when the form is entered.
ForeColorChanged	Occurs when the **ForeColor** property value has changed.
GotFocus	Occurs when the form receives focus.
KeyDown	Occurs when a key is pressed down while the form has focus.
KeyPress	Occurs when a key is pressed while the form has focus.
KeyUp	Occurs when a key is released while the form has focus.
Layout	Occurs when a form has to lay out its child controls.
Load	Occurs before a form is displayed for the first time.
LocationChanged	Occurs when the **Location** property value has changed.
LostFocus	Occurs when the form loses focus.
MdiChildActivate	Occurs when an MDI child form is activated or closed within an MDI application.
MouseDown	Occurs when the mouse pointer is over the form and a mouse button is pressed.
MouseEnter	Occurs when the mouse pointer enters the form.
MouseHover	Occurs when the mouse pointer hovers over the form.
MouseLeave	Occurs when the mouse pointer leaves the form.
MouseMove	Occurs when the mouse pointer is moved over the form.
MouseUp	Occurs when the mouse pointer is over the form and a mouse button is released.
MouseWheel	Occurs when the mouse wheel moves while the form has focus.
Move	Occurs when the form is moved.

(continued)

Table 4.3 **Windows forms public object events** *(continued).*

Event	Description
Paint	Occurs when the form is redrawn.
Resize	Occurs when the form is resized.
SizeChanged	Occurs when the **Size** property value has changed.
TextChanged	Occurs when the **Text** property value has changed.

All About Windows MDI Forms

Besides standard forms, Visual Basic also supports Multiple Document Interface (MDI) forms. An MDI form appears in Figure 4.2.

You can see that an MDI form closely resembles a standard form, with one major difference—the client area of an MDI form acts as a kind of corral for other forms. That is, an MDI form, also called an MDI parent form, can display MDI children in it, which is how the multiple document interface works. In Figure 4.2, we have five documents open in the MDI form. (We'll create this application later in this chapter.)

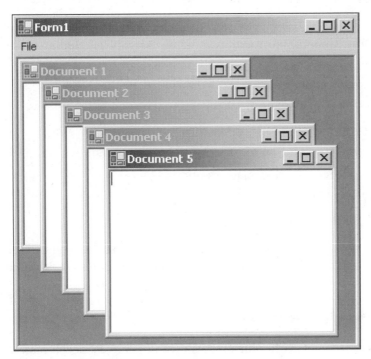

Figure 4.2   An MDI form.

That's the third type of form you can have in Visual Basic—MDI child forms. These forms appear in MDI child windows, but otherwise are very similar to standard forms. In fact, MDI forms and MDI child forms are both based on the standard **System.Windows.Forms** namespace like other Windows forms—you make forms into MDI parents and children by setting the **IsMdiContainer** and **MdiParent** properties, as we'll see in this chapter.

Those, then, are the three types of Windows forms available to us in Visual Basic: standard forms, MDI forms, and MDI child forms. We'll work with all of them here.

Creating Windows Applications

We've already created Windows applications in Chapter 1. Doing so is easy—you just open the New Project dialog with the New Project button in the Start page, or the New|Project menu item in the File menu. Then you select the Visual Basic Projects folder in the Project Types box at right in this dialog, select the Windows Application icon in the Templates box, give a new Name (I'll call this project WinHello) and Location to the application in the boxes of the same names, and click OK. This creates a Windows project and solution as you see in Figure 4.1; these are the files created, and what they mean:

- *WindowsApp.vbproj*—A Visual Basic project.
- *AssemblyInfo.vb*—General Information about an assembly, including version information.
- *Form1.vb*—A form's code file.
- *Form1.resx .NET*—An XML-based resource template.
- *WindowsApp.vbproj.user*—Stores project user options.
- *WindowsApp.sln*—The solution file, storing the solution's configuration.
- *WindowsApp.suo*—Stores solution user options.
- *bin*—Directory for binary executables.
- *obj*—Directory for debugging binaries.

All these files are created for us automatically by Visual Basic. As you can see in Figure 4.1, however, there's not much happening in this program yet. It's time to add some *controls*.

Adding Controls to Forms

In Windows, users interact with your program using controls: scroll bars, buttons, text boxes, menus, and so on—all the user interface elements Windows users are accustomed to. In VB .NET, you use the toolbox, introduced in Chapter 1, to add controls to a form.

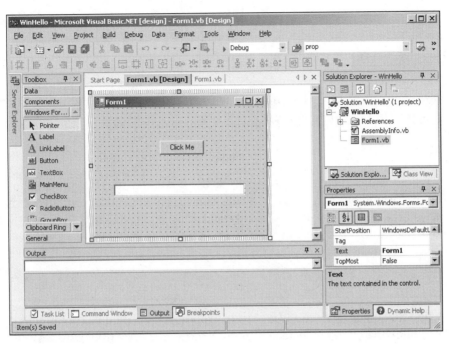

Figure 4.3   Adding controls to a form.

To make this more concrete, add a button and a text box to the new Windows application we just created, as you see in Figure 4.3. Visual Basic gives these controls new names automatically—**Button1** and **TextBox1**.

In this example, we'll have the application display text in the text box when the user clicks the button, so change the **Text** property of the button to "Click Me", as you see in Figure 4.3, using the Properties window. Then, delete the text in the text box, so it appears empty. This creates the user interface of our application—and VB6 programmers will already note a difference from control handling in VB6, where you set the button's **Caption** property, not the **Text** property.

Changes in Controls from VB6

In fact, the **Caption** property no longer exists; it's been replaced by the **Text** property. There are other changes in controls from VB6 as well—and plenty of them, as we'll see in the upcoming chapters. (Also see "What's New in VB .NET" in Chapter 1.) I'll take a look at a number of general points here to start us off.

There are no more control arrays. In VB6 and before, you could assemble controls into arrays, and handle events from all those controls in one place. But in an effort to standardize the way event-handling procedures work, VB .NET has removed support for control arrays (however, see "Imitating Control Arrays" in Chapter 6).

Also, in Visual Basic 6.0, coordinates for forms and controls were expressed in twips (1/1440ths of an inch); in Visual Basic .NET, coordinates are expressed in pixels—and only pixels, you can't change to other scales.

Default properties for controls are no longer supported for objects, which includes controls, in VB .NET (unless those properties take arguments). For example, in VB6, you could write:

```
Text1 = "Hello from Visual Basic"
```

This would assign the text "Hello from Visual Basic" to the **Text** property of the text box **Text1**, because **Text** was this control's default property. In VB .NET, however, the default name for this control would be **TextBox1**, and if you want to assign a value to its **Text** property, you must do so explicitly:

```
TextBox1.Text = "Hello from Visual Basic"
```

There are also changes to help internationalize Visual Basic; for example, you'll now find that controls have an **ImeMode** property, which stands for Input Method Editor, allowing controls to accept input in various international modes, such as Katakana.

The default names for controls have changed—for example, in VB6, the default name for a text box was **Text1**, in VB .NET, it's **TextBox1**; **List1** has become **ListBox1**, **Command1** has become **Button1**, **Option1** has become **RadioButton1**, and so on.

You'll also find changes in the names of many events (**DblClick** is now **DoubleClick**, for example), properties (**selText** is now **SelectedText**, for example), and in the arguments passed to event handlers. You also can now *anchor* and *dock* controls (see "Anchoring and Docking Controls" in the Immediate Solutions section in this chapter for more details). We'll see other changes on a control-by-control basis, but these are some to keep in mind.

Handling Events

Although we've added two controls to our program, a button and a text box, they don't actually do anything when the program runs. We want to display a message when the user clicks the button, so double-click the button now to open the form's code designer to this Sub procedure:

```
Private Sub Button1_Click(ByVal sender As System.Object, _
    ByVal e As System.EventArgs) Handles Button1.Click


End Sub
```

This is the event handler for the button's **Click** event, and it's called when the button is clicked. This Sub procedure is passed the object that caused the event (the button object itself) and an **EventArgs** object that has more information about the event. Note also the **Handles Button1.Click** part at the end, which indicates that this Sub procedure handles the **Click** event of **Button1**. In VB6, event handlers such as this could have different numbers of arguments depending on the event, but in VB .NET, event handlers are written to take two—and only two—arguments. To place text in **TextBox1** when the button is clicked, all we have to do is to add this code:

```
Private Sub Button1_Click(ByVal sender As System.Object, _
    ByVal e As System.EventArgs) Handles Button1.Click
    TextBox1.Text = "Welcome to Visual Basic"
End Sub
```

Now you can run the application, as you see in Figure 4.4; when you click the button, the message appears in the text box, as you also see in that figure.

In this way, you can add code to an object's default event handler. To add code to a different event handler, select the object in the left-hand drop-down list box in a code designer, and select the event you want to add code to in the right-hand drop-down list box. Visual Basic will add an event handler for that event.

Windows user interface programming is event-driven in general; rather than long blocks of code executing by themselves, you normally place your code in event-handling procedures that react to the user's actions. Forms support many events (as you see in Table 4.3), such as the **Load** event, which occurs when the form is first loaded and about to be displayed. This is where you can place initialization code to customize the form when it loads (such as displaying other forms you want to make visible when the program starts). Controls support many events as well, as we'll see in the upcoming chapters.

Figure 4.4 shows how this Windows form appears—now let's take it apart in code, piece by piece.

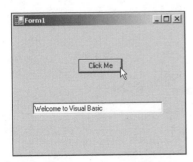

Figure 4.4   Running a Windows application.

A Windows Form in Code

When you take a look at the code for this form, **Form1** in our application (which you'll find in its code designer), the first thing you'll see is that **Form1** is a public class, and that it inherits its functionality (inheritance was discussed in Chapter 1) from **System.Windows.Forms.Form**—that is, the **Form1** class is derived from the **Form** class:

```
Public Class Form1
    Inherits System.Windows.Forms.Form

#Region " Windows Form Designer generated code "

    Public Sub New()
        MyBase.New()
        .
        .
        .
```

Next is the Windows form designer code added by Visual Basic (which, as discussed in Chapter 1, you expand and collapse with the +/- buttons at left in the code designer). The first thing you find in this code is the class's **New** method. This method is the first one run when you create an object from a class (as Visual Basic does automatically when you run this application). It is the form's *constructor* (constructors were mentioned in Chapter 2), which is a special method of a class automatically run when you create an object from the class and which is used to customize that object. Constructors can take arguments or not—in this case, the **New** method does not take any arguments. In the **New** Sub procedure, the code calls a procedure named **InitializeComponent**, which adds and arranges the controls in the form:

```
Public Class Form1
    Inherits System.Windows.Forms.Form

#Region " Windows Form Designer generated code "

    Public Sub New()
        MyBase.New()

        'This call is required by the Windows Form Designer.
        InitializeComponent()

        'Add any initialization after the InitializeComponent() call

    End Sub
```

```
'Form overrides dispose to clean up the component list.
Protected Overloads Overrides Sub Dispose(ByVal disposing As Boolean)
    If disposing Then
        If Not (components Is Nothing) Then
            components.Dispose()
        End If
    End If
    MyBase.Dispose(disposing)
End Sub
Friend WithEvents TextBox1 As System.Windows.Forms.TextBox
Friend WithEvents Button1 As System.Windows.Forms.Button
    .
    .
    .
```

Note that at the end of the above code, the actual text box, **TextBox1**, and button, **Button1**, are declared as objects of the **System.Windows.Forms.TextBox** and **System.Windows.Forms.Button** classes. As we'll see when we discuss object-oriented programming (OOP) in more detail, declaring them as **Friend** gives those objects access to the code in the form, and the **WithEvents** keyword enables event handling. Now that we have objects corresponding to the button and the text box, the code can initialize and position them in the **InitializeComponent** method; note that our event handler for button clicks appears at the very end of the code:

```
Public Class Form1
    Inherits System.Windows.Forms.Form

#Region " Windows Form Designer generated code "

    Public Sub New()
        MyBase.New()

        'This call is required by the Windows Form Designer.
        InitializeComponent()

        'Add any initialization after the InitializeComponent() call

    End Sub

    'Form overrides dispose to clean up the component list.
    Protected Overloads Overrides Sub Dispose(ByVal disposing As Boolean)
        If disposing Then
            If Not (components Is Nothing) Then
                components.Dispose()
            End If
```

```
        End If
        MyBase.Dispose(disposing)
    End Sub
    Friend WithEvents TextBox1 As System.Windows.Forms.TextBox
    Friend WithEvents Button1 As System.Windows.Forms.Button

    'Required by the Windows Form Designer
    Private components As System.ComponentModel.Container

    'NOTE: The following procedure is required by the Windows Form Designer
    'It can be modified using the Windows Form Designer.
    'Do not modify it using the code editor.
    <System.Diagnostics.DebuggerStepThrough()> Private Sub _
        InitializeComponent()
        Me.TextBox1 = New System.Windows.Forms.TextBox()
        Me.Button1 = New System.Windows.Forms.Button()
        Me.SuspendLayout()
        '
        'TextBox1
        '
        Me.TextBox1.Location = New System.Drawing.Point(32, 128)
        Me.TextBox1.Name = "TextBox1"
        Me.TextBox1.Size = New System.Drawing.Size(224, 20)
        Me.TextBox1.TabIndex = 0
        Me.TextBox1.Text = ""
        '
        'Button1
        '
        Me.Button1.Location = New System.Drawing.Point(112, 56)
        Me.Button1.Name = "Button1"
        Me.Button1.TabIndex = 1
        Me.Button1.Text = "Click Me"
        '
        'Form1
        '
        Me.AutoScaleBaseSize = New System.Drawing.Size(5, 13)
        Me.ClientSize = New System.Drawing.Size(292, 213)
        Me.Controls.AddRange(New System.Windows.Forms.Control() _
            {Me.Button1, Me.TextBox1})
        Me.Name = "Form1"
        Me.Text = "Form1"
        Me.ResumeLayout(False)

    End Sub

#End Region
```

```
Private Sub Button1_Click(ByVal sender As System.Object, ByVal e As _
    System.EventArgs) Handles Button1.Click
    TextBox1.Text = "Welcome to Visual Basic"
End Sub
End Class
```

TIP: *There's a lot of code here for such a simple application—far more than you would have seen in VB6. However, the automatically generated code is restricted to a region that's collapsed by default in the code designer, so it's out of the way. And you have access to that code, which is what Visual Basic uses to set up the form. In VB6 and before, all the details of the form were stored in .frm files as data, but now you have direct access to the code that sets your form up. Microsoft recommends that you don't edit that code directly, but, of course, you can—and when you know what you're doing, you've gained a lot of power as compared with the VB6 days. Here's another tip: because the placement of controls is now set in code, you can duplicate projects easily just by copying all the code in one project and overwriting all the code in another—not only will the new code appear in the second project, but all the controls also will appear.*

You also might note the **Me** keyword in the above code; you use that keyword to refer to the current object, which in this case is the current form. For example, to set the **Name** property for a form, you can execute code like this:

```
Me.Name = "Form1"
```

Actually, you don't need the **Me** keyword here, because the properties of the current object are used by default in the code for that object, so this code will perform the same task:

```
Name = "Form1"
```

The Visual Basic code above that uses **Me** does so to make it explicit that it's referring to the current form. (Normally, you only use **Me** when you need some way of indicating the current form, as when you want to pass the current form to a procedure.)

That completes our survey of the code of this Windows application—we'll become more familiar with the structure of applications such as this in time, but this gives us enough of an overview to start. We've seen forms at work, and we've seen them in code. Now it's time to start handling detailed issues in the Immediate Solutions section.

Immediate Solutions

Setting Title Bar Text

You've submitted your project to the user testing stage and feel smug. What could go wrong? Suddenly the phone rings—it seems they don't like the title in the program's title bar: "Form1". How can you change it?

Setting the text in the title bar of a form couldn't be easier. At design time, you just change the form's **Text** (formerly **Caption**) property. You also can set the **Text** property at run time in code like this (technically, one should use **Me.Text** in this case, but the current form is the default in this code):

```
Private Sub Button1_Click(ByVal sender As System.Object, _
    ByVal e As System.EventArgs) Handles Button1.Click
        Text = "Welcome to my Application"
End Sub
```

Adding/Removing Min/Max Buttons and Setting a Form's Border

Forms usually come with minimizing and maximizing buttons, as well as a close box at upper right. However, that's not appropriate in all cases, as we'll see when we design dialog boxes later in this chapter. To remove these buttons, you can set the form's **ControlBox** property to **False**. You can also remove the minimizing and maximizing buttons independently, with the **MaximizeBox** and **MinimizeBox** properties.

TIP: If you are thinking of designing a dialog box, take a look at our dialog box material later in this chapter—besides removing the control box, you should also set the dialog's border correctly, add OK and Cancel buttons, and take care of a few more considerations.

You also can set what buttons are in a form by setting its border type—for example, if you set the border style to a fixed type, the minimizing and maximizing buttons will disappear.

Setting a Form's Border

You set a form's border style with its **FormBorderStyle** property; here are the possible values for that property:

- **Fixed3D**—A fixed, three-dimensional border.

- **FixedDialog**—A thick, fixed dialog-style border.

- **FixedSingle**—A fixed, single-line border.

- **FixedToolWindow**—A tool window border that is not resizable.

- **None**—No border.

- **Sizable**—A resizable border.

- **SizableToolWindow**—A resizable tool window border.

We'll see more about using the **FormBorderStyle** property when we work with dialog boxes later in this chapter.

Setting Control Tab Order

Another call from the testing department. They've been going over your program with a fine-tooth comb and are asking about the keyboard interface. What does that mean? you ask. They explain that theoretically, according to Microsoft, users should be able to run all Windows programs with the keyboard alone. But that was archaic years ago, you say. Add it to your program, they say.

In Visual Basic, you can make controls accessible to the keyboard by setting their *tab order*. The user can move from control to control, highlighting the currently selected control, using the Tab key. But it's up to you to set the order in which control moves from control to control, and even whether or not a control can be reached with the Tab key.

To set the tab order of the controls in your program, follow these steps:

1. Select a control whose tab order you want to set.

2. Next, make sure the control's **TabStop** property is set to **True**. If this property is **False**, the user cannot reach the control using the Tab key.

3. Now set the control's position in the tab order by setting its **TabIndex** property. The first control in the **Tab** order has a **TabIndex** of 0, the next a **TabIndex** of 1, and so on.

4. When you run the program, the first control is highlighted; when the user presses the Tab key, the focus moves to the second control in the tab order, when they press Tab again, the focus moves to the third control, and so on.

That's all it takes—now you've given your program a keyboard interface.

Setting Forms' Initial Positions

Your application looks great—but it's not starting off right. The displayed windows are just not where you want them. How can you fix this? You can use a form's **StartPosition** property to specify its initial position on the screen. You assign this property values from the **FormStartPosition** enumeration. Here are the possible values:

- **CenterParent**—The form is centered within the bounds of its parent form.

- **CenterScreen**—The form is centered on the current display and has the dimensions specified in the form's size.

- **Manual**—The **Location** and **Size** properties of the form will determine its starting position.

- **WindowsDefaultBounds**—The form is positioned at the Windows default location and has the bounds determined by Windows default.

- **WindowsDefaultLocation**—The form is positioned at the Windows default location and has the dimensions specified in the form's size.

Here's how you can set a form's **StartPosition** property from code:

```
Form1.StartPosition = FormStartPosition.CenterScreen
```

Moving and Sizing Forms and Controls in Code

In Visual Basic 6.0 and earlier, you could use the **Move** method to move forms and controls (and optionally set their dimensions), and the **Height** and **Width** methods to set their dimensions. In VB .NET, you use the **SetBounds** method to move forms and controls (and optionally set their dimensions), and the **Size** and **Location** properties to set their dimensions.

You set the **Size** property to a new **Size** object, and the **Location** property to a new **Point** object. The dimensions you set in **Size** and **Point** objects are measured in pixels, as are all measurements in Visual Basic; you create these objects by passing x and y dimensions to their class's constructors, like this: **Size(x_dimension, y_dimension)** and **Point(x_location, y_location)**. (Note that in the Visual Basic screen coordinate system, the upper left of the screen is the origin (0, 0) and that positive x values increase downwards, and positive y values increase to the right.)

Here's an example. Suppose you wanted to change the size and location of both a form and a button in the form when the user clicks a button. You can do that like this (the origin of coordinates for the form is the upper left of the screen and the origin for the button contained in the form is the upper left of the form's client area):

```
Private Sub Button1_Click(ByVal sender As System.Object, _
    ByVal e As System.EventArgs) Handles Button1.Click
        Size = New Size(100, 100)
        Location = New Point(0, 0)
        Button1.Size = New Size(100, 50)
        Button1.Location = New Point(0, 0)
End Sub
```

You can also use the **SetBounds** method to do the same thing:

```
Overloads Public Sub SetBounds(ByVal x As Integer, ByVal y As Integer, _
    ByVal width As Integer, ByVal height As Integer)
```

Here are the arguments you pass to **SetBounds**:

- *x*—The new **Left** property value of the control.
- *y*—The new **Right** property value of the control.
- *width*—The new **Width** property value of the control.
- *height*—The new **Height** property value of the control.

As you see with the **Overloads** keyword above, **SetBounds** is *overloaded*, which means there is more than one form of this method. Here is the other form (Visual Basic will know which one you want to use depending on how many arguments you pass):

```
Overloads Public Sub SetBounds( ByVal x As Integer, ByVal y As Integer, _
    ByVal width As Integer, ByVal height As Integer, _
    ByVal specified As BoundsSpecified)
```

This form has a new argument, specified, which is a combination of values from the **BoundsSpecified** enumeration; here are the possible values (to use the **X** item, use **BoundsSpecified.X**, and so on):

- **All**—Specifies that both Location and Size property values are indicated.
- **Height**—Specifies that the height of the control is indicated.
- **Location**—Specifies that both x and y coordinates of the control are indicated.
- **None**—Specifies that no bounds are indicated.
- **Size**—Specifies that both **Width** and **Height** property values of the control are indicated.

4. Windows Forms

- **Width**—Specifies that the width of the control is indicated.

- **X**—Specifies that the left edge of the control is indicated.

- **Y**—Specifies that the top edge of the control is indicated.

To use **SetBounds** to do the same thing as in the code at the beginning of this topic, you can do this:

```
Private Sub Button1_Click(ByVal sender As System.Object, _
    ByVal e As System.EventArgs) Handles Button1.Click
        SetBounds(0, 0, 100, 100)
        Button1.SetBounds(0, 0, 100, 50)
End Sub
```

---

*TIP: One way of creating simple animation is to use a picture box control to display an image and use the **SetBounds** method to move it around a form.*

Showing and Hiding Controls and Forms

The testing department is on the phone again—does your program really *need* 120 buttons in the main form? After all, that's exactly what menus were designed for: to hide controls not needed, getting them out of the user's way. (In fact, that's usually a good way to determine if a control item should be in a menu or on the main form: you use menus to make options available to the user at all times, while keeping them out of the way.)

However, let's say you really don't want to put your control items into menus—you can still use buttons if you hide the ones that don't apply at a particular time, showing them when appropriate. Hiding and showing controls in a form as needed can produce dramatic effects at times.

Showing and hiding controls and forms is easy: just use the control's or form's **Visible** property. Setting this property to **True** displays the control or form; setting it to **False** hides it. Here's an example where we make a button disappear (probably much to the user's surprise) when the user clicks it:

```
Private Sub Button1_Click(ByVal sender As System.Object, _
    ByVal e As System.EventArgs) Handles Button1.Click
        Button1.Visible = False
End Sub
```

You can also use the **Show** and **Hide** methods of controls and forms to show and hide them. For example, when the user clicks **Button1**, we can hide **Form2** and show **Form3** this way:

```
Private Sub Button1_Click(ByVal sender As System.Object, _
    ByVal e As System.EventArgs) Handles Button1.Click
    Form2.Hide()
    Form3.Show()
End Sub
```

Using the **MsgBox** Function

Later in this chapter, we'll start discussing multiform applications, but there's an easy way to add multiple forms already built into Visual Basic—you can use the **MsgBox** and **InputBox** functions. You can also use the **MessageBox** class built into the .NET Framework to display messages and accept input from the user. You'll find all of these at work in the MsgAndInputBoxes example on the CD-ROM—all you need to do is to click a button to use these various functions. I'll start with the **MsgBox** function in this topic:

```
Public Function MsgBox(Prompt As Object [, Buttons As MsgBoxStyle =
MsgBoxStyle.OKOnly [, Title As Object = Nothing]]) As MsgBoxResultArguments
```

Here are the arguments you pass to this function:

- *Prompt*—A string expression displayed as the message in the dialog box. The maximum length is about 1,024 characters (depending on the width of the characters used).

- *Buttons*—The sum of values specifying the number and type of buttons to display, the icon style to use, the identity of the default button, and the modality of the message box. If you omit *Buttons*, the default value is zero. See below.

- *Title*—String expression displayed in the title bar of the dialog box. Note that if you omit *Title*, the application name is placed in the title bar.

---

*TIP: If you want the message box prompt to be more than one line of text, you can force separate lines of text using a carriage return character (**Chr(13)**), a linefeed character (**Chr(10)**), or a carriage return/linefeed together (**Chr(13) & Chr(10)**) between each line.*

You can find the possible constants to use for the *Buttons* argument in Table 4.4.

Table 4.4   MsgBox constants.

Constant	Value	Description
OKOnly	0	Shows OK button only.
OKCancel	1	Shows OK and Cancel buttons.
AbortRetryIgnore	2	Shows Abort, Retry, and Ignore buttons.
YesNoCancel	3	Shows Yes, No, and Cancel buttons.
YesNo	4	Shows Yes and No buttons.
RetryCancel	5	Shows Retry and Cancel buttons.
Critical	16	Shows Critical Message icon.
Question	32	Shows Warning Query icon.
Exclamation	48	Shows Warning Message icon.
Information	64	Shows Information Message icon.
DefaultButton1	0	First button is default.
DefaultButton2	256	Second button is default.
DefaultButton3	512	Third button is default.
ApplicationModal	0	Application modal, which means the user must respond to the message box before continuing work in the current application.
SystemModal	4096	System modal, which means all applications are unavailable until the user dismisses the message box.
MsgBoxSetForeground	65536	Specifies the message box window as the foreground window.
MsgBoxRight	524288	Text will be right-aligned.
MsgBoxRtlReading	1048576	Specifies text should appear as right-to-left on RTL systems such as Hebrew and Arabic.

Note also that this function returns a value from the **MsgBoxResult** enumeration. Here are the possible **MsgBoxResult** values, indicating which button in the message box the user clicked:

- **OK**
- **Cancel**
- **Abort**
- **Retry**
- **Ignore**
- **Yes**
- **No**

For example, here's how we use **MsgBox** in the **MsgAndInput** example. In this case, I'm adding OK and Cancel buttons to the message box, adding an information icon, and making the message box *modal* (which means you have to dismiss it before doing anything else). And I also check to see if the user clicked the OK button, in which case I display the message "You clicked OK" in a text box:

```
Private Sub Button1_Click(ByVal sender As System.Object, _
    ByVal e As System.EventArgs) Handles Button1.Click
    Dim Result As Integer
    Result = MsgBox("This is a message box!", MsgBoxStyle.OKCancel +
        MsgBoxStyle.Information + MsgBoxStyle.SystemModal, "Message Box")
    If (Result = MsgBoxResult.OK) Then
        TextBox1.Text = "You clicked OK"
    End If
End Sub
```

You can see the results of this code in Figure 4.5.

Figure 4.5 A message box created with the **MsgBox** function.

Using the **MessageBox.Show** Method

In addition to the **MsgBox** function (see the previous topic), you can use the .NET framework's **MessageBox** class's **Show** method to display message boxes. This method has many overloaded forms; here's one of them:

```
Overloads Public Shared Function Show( ByVal text As String, _
    ByVal caption As String, ByVal buttons As MessageBoxButtons, _
    ByVal icon As MessageBoxIcon, ByVal defaultButton As _
    MessageBoxDefaultButton, ByVal options As MessageBoxOptions _)
As DialogResult
```

Here are the arguments you pass to this method:

- *text*—The text to display in the message box.

- *caption*—The text to display in the title bar of the message box.

- *buttons*—One of the **MessageBoxButtons** enumeration values that specifies which buttons to display in the message box. See below.

- *icon*—One of the **MessageBoxIcon** enumeration values that specifies which icon to display in the message box. See below.

- *defaultButton*—One of the **MessageBoxDefaultButton** enumeration values that specifies which is the default button for the message box. See below.

- *options*—One of the **MessageBoxOptions** enumeration values that specifies which display and association options will be used for the message box. See below.

Here are the **MessageBoxButtons** enumeration values:

- **AbortRetryIgnore**—The message box will show Abort, Retry, and Ignore buttons.

- **OK**—The message box will show an OK button.

- **OKCancel**—The message box will show OK and Cancel buttons.

- **RetryCancel**—The message box will show Retry and Cancel buttons.

- **YesNo**—The message box will show Yes and No buttons.

- **YesNoCancel**—The message box will show Yes, No, and Cancel buttons.

Here are the **MessageBoxIcon** enumeration values:

- **Asterisk**—Shows an icon displaying a lowercase letter i in a circle.

- **Error**—Shows an icon displaying a white X in a circle with a red background.

- **Exclamation**—Shows an icon displaying an exclamation point in a triangle with a yellow background.

- **Hand**—Shows an icon displaying a white X in a circle with a red background.

- **Information**—Shows an icon displaying a lowercase letter i in a circle.

- **None**—Shows no icons.

- **Question**—Shows an icon displaying a question mark in a circle.

- **Stop**—Shows an icon displaying white X in a circle with a red background.

- **Warning**—Shows an icon displaying an exclamation point in a triangle with a yellow background.

Here are the **MessageBoxDefaultButton** enumeration values:

- **Button1**—Makes the first button on the message box the default button.

- **Button2**—Makes the second button on the message box the default button.

- **Button3**—Makes the third button on the message box the default button.

Here are the **MessageBoxOptions** enumeration values:

- **DefaultDesktopOnly**—Displays the message box on the active desktop.

- **RightAlign**—The message box text is right-aligned.

- **RtlReading**—Specifies that the message box text is displayed with right to left reading order.

The result of the **Show** method is a value from the **DialogResult** enumeration, showing what button the user clicked:

- **Abort**—Returns Abort.

- **Cancel**—Returns Cancel.

- **Ignore**—Returns Ignore.

- **No**—Returns No.

- **None**—Nothing is returned from the dialog box. (Note that this means that a modal dialog continues running.)

- **OK**—Returns OK.

- **Retry**—Returns Retry.

- **Yes**—Returns Yes.

Here's an example putting this to work, from the MsgAndInputBoxes example on the CD-ROM. Note that I'm testing the returned result to see if the user clicked the OK button:

```
Private Sub Button2_Click(ByVal sender As System.Object, _
    ByVal e As System.EventArgs) Handles Button2.Click
    Dim Result As Integer
    Result = MessageBox.Show("This is a message box!", "Message Box", _
        MessageBoxButtons.OKCancel, MessageBoxIcon.Information, _
        MessageBoxDefaultButton.Button1, _
            MessageBoxOptions.DefaultDesktopOnly)
    If (Result = DialogResult.OK) Then
        TextBox1.Text = "You clicked OK"
    End If
End Sub
```

You can see the results of this code in Figure 4.6. Note that this message box looks just like the one created with the **MsgBox** function in the previous topic.

Figure 4.6   A message box created with the **MessageBox** class's **Show** method.

Using the **InputBox** Function

You can use the **InputBox** function to get a string of text from the user. Here's the syntax for this function:

```
Public Function InputBox(Prompt As String [, Title As _
String = "" [, DefaultResponse As String = "" [, _
XPos As Integer = -1 [, YPos As Integer = -1]]]]) As String
```

And here are the arguments for this function:

- **Prompt**—A string expression displayed as the message in the dialog box. The maximum length is about 1,024 characters (depending on the width of the characters used).

- **Title**—String expression displayed in the title bar of the dialog box. Note that if you omit **Title**, the application name is placed in the title bar.

- **DefaultResponse**—A string expression displayed in the text box as the default response if no other input is provided. Note that if you omit **DefaultResponse**, the displayed text box is empty.

- **XPos**—The distance in pixels of the left edge of the dialog box from the left edge of the screen. Note that if you omit **XPos**, the dialog box is centered horizontally.

- **YPos**—The distance in pixels of the upper edge of the dialog box from the top of the screen. Note that if you omit **YPos**, the dialog box is positioned vertically about one-third of the way down the screen.

Input boxes let you display a prompt and read a line of text typed by the user, and the InputBox function returns the string result. Here's an example from the MsgAndInputBoxes example on the CD-ROM:

```
Private Sub Button3_Click(ByVal sender As System.Object, _
    ByVal e As System.EventArgs) Handles Button3.Click
    Dim Result As String
    Result = InputBox("Enter your text!")
    TextBox1.Text = Result
End Sub
```

You can see the results of this code in Figure 4.7.

When the user enters text and clicks OK, the **InputBox** function returns that text, and the code displays it in the text box in the **MsgAndInput** example, as you see in Figure 4.8.

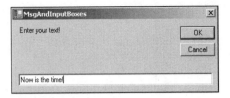

Figure 4.7   An input box.

Figure 4.8   Reading text using an input box.

Working with Multiple Forms

You've designed your program and it's a beauty: an introductory form to welcome the user, a data entry form to get data from the user, a summary form to display the data analysis results, and a logon form to connect to the Internet—it's all there.

Suddenly it occurs to you—aren't Visual Basic Windows projects organized into modules, classes, and forms? How does the code in one form reach the code in another—that is, how can the code in the analysis module read what the user has entered in the data entry form? It's time to take a look at working with multiple forms.

To see how to create multiple-form applications, and how to communicate between forms, create a new Windows application. I'll call this example Multiwindow, and you'll find it on the CD-ROM. When you create this application, it has one Windows form, **Form1**. To add another, select the Project|Add Windows Form item to open the Add New Item dialog you see in Figure 4.9; select the Windows Form icon in the Templates box and click Open. This adds a new form, **Form2**, to the project, as you see in the IDE in Figure 4.10.

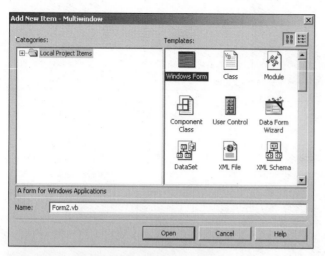

Figure 4.9   Adding a new Windows form.

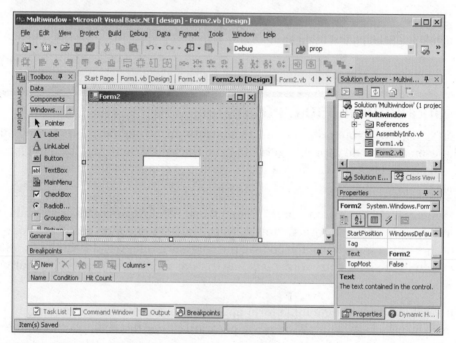

Figure 4.10   A new Windows form.

Here, I'll add a text box, **TextBox1**, to **Form2**, as you see in Figure 4.10. When the user clicks a button in **Form1**, I'll read the text in that text box and display it in a text box in **Form1**. In **Form1**, I start by creating a new object of **Form2** and calling it **OtherWindow**:

```
Dim OtherWindow As New Form2()
```

Place this declaration anywhere in the code for **Form1**, outside any procedure, like this:

```
Public Class Form1
    Inherits System.Windows.Forms.Form
    Dim OtherWindow As New Form2()

        .

        .

        .
```

(You can also select the (Declarations) item in the right-hand drop-down list box in the code designer to move to this area of your code automatically.) To display this new form as soon as the program starts and **Form1** is displayed, double-click **Form1** to bring up its **Load** event handler, which is called when **Form1** is about to be displayed. You can show the second form with its **Show** method:

```
Private Sub Form1_Load(ByVal sender As System.Object, _
    ByVal e As System.EventArgs) Handles MyBase.Load
    OtherWindow.Show()
End Sub
```

Now add a button, **Button1**, to **Form1**, give it the text "Read text", and also add a text box to **Form1**. When the user clicks this button, we want to read the text in the text box in **OtherWindow** and display it in the text box in **Form1**. To do that, we can access the text box in the **OtherWindow** object as **OtherWindow. TextBox1**, and the **Text** property of that text box as **OtherWindow.TextBox1. Text**. To display this text in the text box in **Form1**, I can use this code (note that I also hide the second window with the **OtherWindow** object's **Hide** method):

```
Private Sub Button1_Click(ByVal sender As System.Object, _
    ByVal e As System.EventArgs) Handles Button1.Click
    TextBox1.Text = OtherWindow.TextBox1.Text
    OtherWindow.Hide()
End Sub
```

Now when the user types something into the text box in the second window—as you see in Figure 4.11—and clicks the "Read text" button, the second window disappears and the text from its text box appears in the text box in **Form1** (see Figure 4.12). This example is a success.

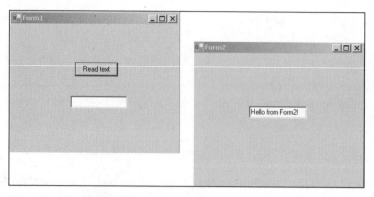

Figure 4.11 A multiwindow application.

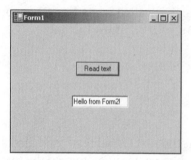

Figure 4.12   Accessing data between forms.

Using Properties to Communicate between Forms

Besides the direct approach in the previous topic, another way to communicate between forms is to use properties, which we first saw in Chapter 3. For example, I can modify the example in the previous topic by adding this code to create a property named **TextData** to **Form2**, which gets or sets the text **TextBox1**:

```
Property TextData() As String
    Get
        Return TextBox1.Text
    End Get
    Set(ByVal Value As String)
        TextBox1.Text = Value
    End Set
End Property
```

Then I can use that property to recover the text from the second window, like this:

```
Dim OtherWindow As New Form2()

Private Sub Form1_Load(ByVal sender As System.Object, _
    ByVal e As System.EventArgs) Handles MyBase.Load
    OtherWindow.Show()
End Sub

Private Sub Button1_Click(ByVal sender As System.Object, _
    ByVal e As System.EventArgs) Handles Button1.Click
    TextBox1.Text = OtherWindow.TextData
    OtherWindow.Hide()
End Sub
```

Using properties is a better way to communicate between forms than accessing another form's data directly, because it gives you a well-defined interface. Instead of reaching into the code for **Form2** and getting the text straight out of its text box, you use the **Get** and **Set** methods in the **TextData** property to get and set the text in the text box, which means you can test the data going into the text box, and return an error if you want to reject it.

Related solution:	Found on page:
Creating Properties	132

Setting the Startup Form

Well, the program is complete, and you've saved writing the best for last: the opening form in which you greet the user. Unfortunately, that greeting form is **Form249**, and when you actually test the program, Visual Basic pops **Form1**, the Import File dialog box, onto the screen first. How can you make the program start with **Form249**?

Just right-click your project in the Solutions Explorer, select Properties, then select the Common Properties folder and the General item in the box at left. Next, select Form249 from the Startup Object drop-down list on the right, click OK, and you're done. That's it—now the program will display the form you've selected first when the program runs.

Creating Multiple Document Interface (MDI) Applications

The new editor program you've written took a lot of work, and it's a great success. But then you start getting calls from the field-testing department: users want to open more than one document at a time. How do you do that?

You use Multiple Document Interface (MDI) forms. MDI frame windows can display multiple child windows inside them; in fact, the Visual Basic IDE itself is an MDI frame window. Here's an example—called MDI on the CD-ROM for this book. In this example, I'll let the user create new MDI windows, and arrange them just by selecting a menu item. We haven't created menus before, and in fact, we won't work with menu controls in a systematic way until Chapter 9, but MDI applications almost invariably use menus to create new windows and so on, so we'll get a foretaste of menu handling here.

To see how MDI applications work, create a new Windows application now, as shown in Figure 4.13. The main form, **Form1**, will be our MDI container or parent, containing MDI children, so set its **IsMdiContainer** property to **True**. This alters its appearance from a white client area to a gray one; next, drag a **MainMenu** control from the toolbox onto **Form1**. This causes a new control, **MainMenu1**, to appear in the new pane at the bottom of the form designer, as you see in Figure 4.13, and a new menu bar to appear in **Form1**, with the text "Type Here" in it. To create a File menu, type "File" in the "Type Here" box, as you also see in Figure 4.13.

When you create a new File menu, additional "Type Here" boxes appear for the next menu in the menu bar and the first item in the File menu, as you see in Figure 4.13. Add a New item to the File menu; when you do, another "Type Here" box appears beneath that item. Create a new Arrange menu item in that new box, as you see in Figure 4.14.

Now double-click the New item in the File menu to open the event handler for this menu item in code (as you see from this code, the New item is **MenuItem2**, not **MenuItem1**; the File menu itself is **MenuItem1**):

```
Public Class Form1
    Inherits System.Windows.Forms.Form

'Windows Form Designer generated code

    Private Sub MenuItem2_Click(ByVal sender As System.Object, _
        ByVal e As System.EventArgs) Handles MenuItem2.Click

    End Sub
        .
        .
        .
```

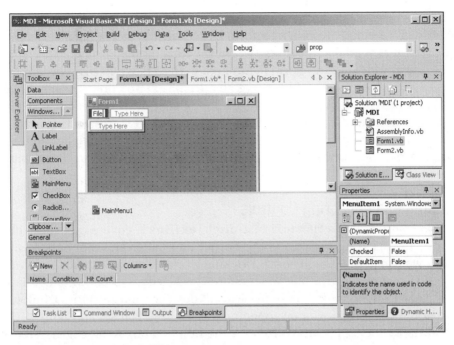

Figure 4.13   Creating an MDI parent.

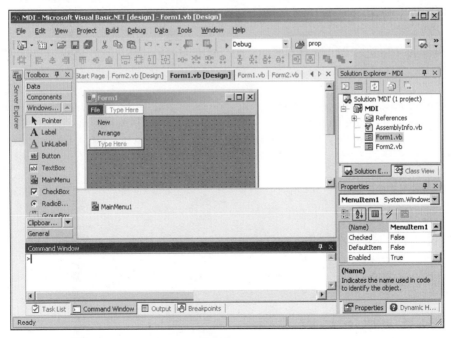

Figure 4.14   Creating an MDI parent menu system.

When the user clicks the New menu item, we want to display a new MDI child window. To do that, create a new form class, **Form2**, by adding a new form to the project, as we did in the topic "Working with Multiple Forms." (That is, with the Project|Add Windows Form menu item in the VB .NET IDE). We can make these child windows useful by dragging a **RichTextBox** control onto **Form2.** Rich text boxes, which we'll see in Chapter 5, support rich format (RTF) text, including all kinds of formatting, from italics to bold text to selecting fonts and colors. This allows you to create mini-word processors in your application. Make sure the rich text box's **Multiline** property is set to **True** so it can handle multiline text.

Docking and Anchoring Controls

To make sure that the rich text box, **RichTextBox1**, covers the whole client area of **Form2** (the area inside the border and under any tool bars or menu bars), we can *dock* and *anchor* it. Docking works as we've already seen in the IDE—when you dock a window, it adheres to the edges of its container. In this case, select the rich text box in the **Form2** designer and select its **Dock** property in the Properties window, opening the window you see in Figure 4.15 on top of the Properties window. To dock the rich text box to all edges of its container, click the button in the middle of Figure 4.15, which sets its **Dock** property to **Fill**. You can also do the same thing in code, like this: **richTextBox1.Dock = DockStyle.Fill**.

TIP: *You can also set the form's **DockPadding** property, which sets the padding used between docked controls and the form's edge.*

You also can anchor a control to the edges of its container with the **Anchor** property. Selecting this property opens the window you see in Figure 4.16 on top of the Properties window, and you can select what edge to anchor the control to.

Figure 4.15   Docking a control.

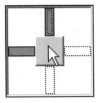

Figure 4.16   Anchoring a control.

Creating MDI Child Windows in Code

Now that we've created a new form class, **Form2**, for our MDI child windows, we can create and display a new object of that class each time the user clicks the File|New menu item in our program. To make that new form object a child window of our MDI parent, **Form1**, all we have to do is to set its **MdiParent** property to the main window (which also sets its **IsMdiChild** property to **True**). Because we'll be working with a number of child windows, I'll store them in an array of forms, incrementing the number of forms each time a new one is created, setting the text in its title bar to "Document1", "Document2", and so on, like this:

```
Public Class Form1
    Inherits System.Windows.Forms.Form
    Dim NumberForms As Integer = 0
    Dim Forms(10) As Form2

'Windows Form Designer generated code

    Private Sub MenuItem2_Click(ByVal sender As System.Object, _
        ByVal e As System.EventArgs) Handles MenuItem2.Click
        NumberForms += 1
        Forms(NumberForms) = New Form2()
        Forms(NumberForms).Text = "Document" & Str(NumberForms)
        Forms(NumberForms).MdiParent = Me
        Forms(NumberForms).Show()
    End Sub
End Class
```

TIP: *As it turns out, there's another way to access all your child MDI forms in an array—use the **MdiChildren** property of the MDI parent, which returns an array of its MDI child forms.*

Arranging MDI Child Windows

All that's left is to enable the File|Arrange menu item in our application. To automatically arrange MDI child windows, you can use the **LayoutMdi** method:

```
Public Sub LayoutMdi(ByVal value As MdiLayout)
```

This Sub procedure takes one argument, *value*, which is one of the **MdiLayout** enumeration values that defines the layout of MDI child forms:

- **ArrangeIcons**—All MDI child icons (which are displayed when you minimize an MDI child window) are arranged.

- **Cascade**—All MDI child windows are cascaded.

- **TileHorizontal**—All MDI child windows are tiled horizontally.

- **TileVertical**—All MDI child windows are tiled vertically.

In our example, I'll use the cascade layout, so I add this code to the Arrange menu item's event handler:

```
Private Sub MenuItem3_Click(ByVal sender As System.Object, _
    ByVal e As System.EventArgs) Handles MenuItem3.Click
    Me.LayoutMdi(MdiLayout.Cascade)
End Sub
```

And you can see the results in Figure 4.17—just select the File|New menu item to display a new MDI child, and the File|Arrange menu item to arrange the MDI children.

Now you're using MDI forms!

TIP: *In Visual Basic, you can use all kinds of forms—including different types in the same application—as MDI children in an MDI window, as long as their **MdiParent** property is set to the main MDI window. You can also use **Show** and **Hide** on those windows to manage them as you like.*

Figure 4.17   An MDI application.

Creating Dialog Boxes

Sometimes, nothing will do but to create your own dialog boxes. Visual Basic supports message boxes and input boxes, but they're very basic—in real applications, you'll need to create custom dialog boxes.

To see how this works, create a new Windows application now; I'll call this example Dialog on the CD-ROM. In this example, I'll let the user enter some text in a dialog box, and read the entered text when the dialog box is closed.

Creating a Dialog Box

To create the dialog box, add a new Windows form, **Form2**, to the project now, and add two buttons with the captions OK and Cancel to this form, as well as a text box, as you see in Figure 4.18. I've set the **Text** property of this form to "Enter your text" to set the text in the title bar, and added a *label* control above the text box with the prompt "Enter your text:". Label controls just display text like this prompt. (We'll see them in Chapter 5.) To create this label, just drag a **Label** control from the toolbox to **Form2** and set its **Text** property.

In addition, set the **FormBorderStyle** property of **Form2** to **FixedDialog**, giving it a dialog box border, and set the **ControlBox** property to **False** to remove the control box (the minimize, maximize, and close buttons at upper right). Also,

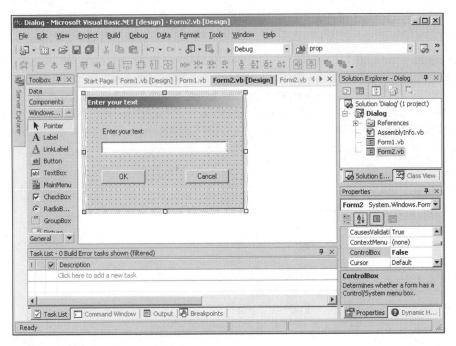

Figure 4.18   Creating a dialog box.

set the **ShowInTaskbar** property of **Form2** to **False**—this means that when this dialog box appears, it will not display an icon in the Windows task bar, which dialog boxes shouldn't.

Finally, set the **DialogResult** property of the OK button to **OK**, and the same property of the Cancel button to **Cancel**. This property returns a value of the **DialogResult** enumeration when the dialog box is closed, so you can determine which button the user has clicked. Here are the possible settings for this property:

- **OK**
- **Cancel**
- **Abort**
- **Retry**
- **Ignore**
- **Yes**
- **No**
- **None**

Displaying Reading Data from Dialog Boxes

We'll need some way of displaying our new dialog box from **Form1**, the form that appears when the application starts, so add a button, **Button1**, to **Form1** now, giving it the text "Enter your text". Also, we'll need a way of displaying the text we read from the dialog, so add a text box, **TextBox1**, to **Form1** now.

To display the dialog box when the user clicks the "Enter your text" button, I'll create a new object of the **Form2** dialog box class, **DialogBox**. To display this dialog box, I'll use the **ShowDialog** method, not the **Show** method, because **ShowDialog** will return a **DialogResult** value indicating what button the user clicked. If the user clicked the OK button, I'll display the text from the text box in the dialog box in the main form:

```
Public Class Form1
    Inherits System.Windows.Forms.Form
    Dim DialogBox As New Form2()

'Windows Form Designer generated code

    Private Sub Button1_Click(ByVal sender As System.Object, _
        ByVal e As System.EventArgs) Handles Button1.Click
        If DialogBox.ShowDialog = DialogResult.OK Then
            TextBox1.Text = DialogBox.TextBox1.Text
```

```
            End If
        End Sub
End Class
```

Creating Accept and Cancel Buttons

The last step is to add some code to the dialog box, **Form2**, to close the dialog box when the user clicks a button. Also, I'll set the dialog box's **AcceptButton** and **CancelButton** properties to indicate which button is the accept button and which the Cancel button; this allows the user to press Enter to select the accept (OK) button, and Esc to select the Cancel button:

```
Public Class Form2
    Inherits System.Windows.Forms.Form

'Windows Form Designer generated code

    Private Sub Form2_Load(ByVal sender As System.Object, _
        ByVal e As System.EventArgs) Handles MyBase.Load
        Me.AcceptButton = Button1
        Me.CancelButton = Button2
    End Sub

    Private Sub Button1_Click(ByVal sender As System.Object, _\
        ByVal e As System.EventArgs) Handles Button1.Click
        Me.Close()
    End Sub

    Private Sub Button2_Click(ByVal sender As System.Object, _
        ByVal e As System.EventArgs) Handles Button2.Click
        Me.Close()
    End Sub
End Class
```

And that completes the code—now run the application, as shown in Figure 4.19. The dialog box appears when you click the button in **Form1**, and you can enter text in it. When you click the OK button, the dialog box disappears and the text you entered appears in the text box in **Form1**, as you see in Figure 4.20. Everything works as we planned it.

TIP: *One good rule for constructing dialog boxes—always add a Cancel button so that if the user has opened the dialog box by mistake, they can close it without consequences.*

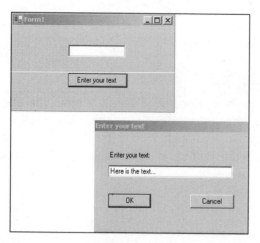

Figure 4.19   Displaying a newly created dialog box.

Figure 4.20   Recovering text from a created dialog box.

Creating Owned Forms

You can also create *owned forms* in Visual Basic. An owned form is tied to the form that owns it; if the user minimizes the owner form, the owned form will also be minimized, and so on. You can add an owned form with the **AddOwnedForm** method, and remove an owned form with the **RemoveOwnedForm** method. Here's an example called OwnedForms on the CD-ROM. In this case, I'll place a button in **Form1** that will make an object of the **Form2** class into an owned form and display it:

```
Public Class Form1
    Inherits System.Windows.Forms.Form
    Dim OwnedForm1 As New Form2()

'Windows Form Designer generated code

    Private Sub Button1_Click(ByVal sender As System.Object, _
        ByVal e As System.EventArgs) Handles Button1.Click
```

```
        Me.AddOwnedForm(OwnedForm1)
        OwnedForm1.Show()
    End Sub
End Class
```

You can see the results in Figure 4.21, where I've placed a label with the text "This is an owned form" in the owned form.

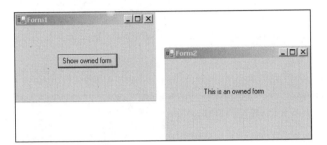

Figure 4.21   An owned form.

Passing Forms to Procedures

You can pass forms to procedures just as you would any object. Here, we've set up a Sub procedure, **ColorWindowRed**, to turn the background color of a form to red using the **Form BackColor** property:

```
Sub ColorWindowRed(ByVal FormToColor As Form)
    FormToColor.BackColor = System.Drawing.Color.Red
End Sub
```

This is a good technique to know if you want to coordinate between forms in a multiform application.

Minimizing/Maximizing and Enabling/Disabling Forms

To exert a little more control over the windows in your programs, you can set the **WindowState** property to maximize or minimize them. Here's how you set that property, and what those settings mean:

- **FormWindowState.Maximized**—Window is maximized.

- **FormWindowState.Minimized**—Window is minimized.

- **FormWindowState.Normal**—Window is set to normal state.

Here's an example in which we minimize a form when the user clicks a button:

```
Private Sub Button1_Click(ByVal sender As System.Object, _
    ByVal e As System.EventArgs) Handles Button1.Click
    Me.WindowState = FormWindowState.Normal
End Sub
```

You can also set the **Enabled** property to enable or disable a window. (When it's disabled, it will only beep if the user tries to give it the focus.) You set the **Enabled** property to **True** to enable a window and to **False** to disable it.

Anchoring and Docking Controls

You use the **Anchor** and **Dock** properties to anchor and dock controls, new in VB .NET. See "Creating Multiple Document Interface (MDI) Applications" earlier in this chapter for an example.

Adding and Removing Controls at Run Time

You can add or remove controls to your application at run time—all you need to do is to use the form's **Controls** *collection*'s **Add** or **Remove** methods. We'll see collections later in the book; they let you operate on a number of objects at once, as with the **Add** and **Remove** methods.

Here's an example (AddControls on the CD-ROM) that adds a new text box at run time—all you have to do is to create a new text box in code, give it a size and location, set its text, and use the **Add** method when the user clicks a button:

```
Private Sub Button1_Click(ByVal sender As System.Object, _
    ByVal e As System.EventArgs) Handles Button1.Click
    Dim NewTextBox As New TextBox()
    NewTextBox.Size = New Size(100, 20)
    NewTextBox.Location = New Point(100, 100)
    NewTextBox.Text = "Hello from Visual Basic"
    Me.Controls.Add(NewTextBox)
End Sub
```

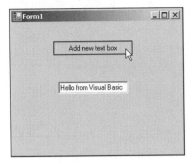

Figure 4.22   Adding controls at run time.

You can see the results in Figure 4.22; when the user clicks a button, a new text box appears in the form.

Related solutions:	Found on page:
Creating a **LinkLabel** in Code	244
Adding Controls to Group Boxes in Code	284

Creating Always-on-Top Forms

You can make sure a form stays on top of all others by setting its **TopMost** property to **True**. You can also change the stacking order of your forms at run time with the **BringToFront** and **SendToBack** methods.

Using Visual Inheritance between Forms

As you know, inheritance allows you to derive one class from another. Visual Basic even provides a visual way of deriving one form from another. To see how this works, create a new Windows application and add a button to **Form1**. Then select the Build|Build menu item to build the project; this makes **Form1** available for inheritance.

To derive a form from **Form1**—which will inherit all aspects of **Form1**, including the button—select the Project|Add Inherited Form menu item, then double-click the Inherited Form icon in the Templates box to open the Inheritance Picker, as you see in Figure 4.23.

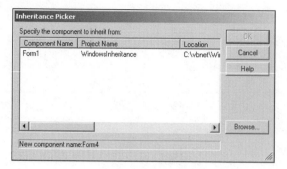

Figure 4.23   The Inheritance Picker.

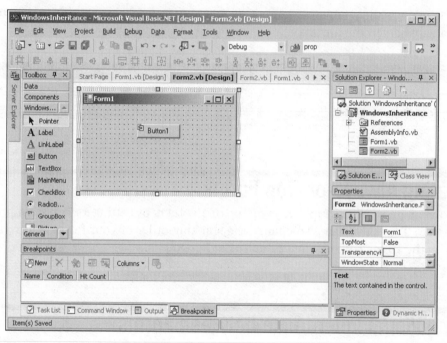

Figure 4.24   An inherited form.

Select **Form1** in the Inheritance Picker, and click OK, adding a new form, **Form2**, derived from **Form1**, as you see in Figure 4.24. Note that even the title text, "Form1", was copied from **Form1**, and that there's a special icon at upper left in the button in this new form to indicate that this button is locked—because it's been inherited from **Form1**, it cannot be removed.

Handling Mouse Events

You can handle mouse events—such as mouse movements—in forms and controls; here are the possible events for the **Control** class, which is a base class for controls and forms:

- **MouseDown**—Happens when the mouse pointer is over the control and a mouse button is pressed.

- **MouseEnter**—Happens when the mouse pointer enters the control.

- **MouseHover**—Happens when the mouse pointer hovers over the control.

- **MouseLeave**—Happens when the mouse pointer leaves the control.

- **MouseMove**—Happens when the mouse pointer is moved over the control.

- **MouseUp**—Happens when the mouse pointer is over the control and a mouse button is released.

- **MouseWheel**—Happens when the mouse wheel moves while the control has focus.

Here are the properties of the **MouseEventArgs** object passed to the mouse event handler (not all properties will be filled for all mouse events):

- **Button**—Indicates which mouse button was pressed (see below).

- **Clicks**—The number of times the mouse button was pressed and released.

- **Delta**—A signed count of the number of detents the mouse wheel has rotated. A *detent* is the rotation of the mouse wheel one notch.

- **X**—The x-coordinate of a mouse click.

- **Y**—The y-coordinate of a mouse click.

The **Buttons** property holds one of these members of the **MouseButtons** enumeration:

- **Left**—The left mouse button was pressed.

- **Middle**—The middle mouse button was pressed.

- **None**—No mouse button was pressed.

- **Right**—The right mouse button was pressed.

- **XButton1**—The first XButton was pressed (Microsoft IntelliMouse Explorer).

- **XButton2**—The second XButton was pressed (Microsoft IntelliMouse Explorer).

Here's an example (Mouser on the CD-ROM) that checks for all mouse events in a form (note that for those events that involve button presses, it checks only the left mouse button) and reports on them in a text box. If you play around with this example, you'll see that when you handle some mouse events they virtually cover up others; for example, if you handle mouse move events, you'll rarely see mouse hovering events:

```vb
Public Class Form1
    Inherits System.Windows.Forms.Form

    'Windows Form Designer generated code

    Private Sub Form1_MouseDown(ByVal sender As Object, _
    ByVal e As System.Windows.Forms.MouseEventArgs) _
    Handles MyBase.MouseDown
        If e.Button = MouseButtons.Left Then
            TextBox1.Text = "Mouse down at " + CStr(e.X) + ", " + CStr(e.Y)
        End If
    End Sub

    Private Sub Form1_MouseEnter(ByVal sender As Object, _
        ByVal e As System.EventArgs) Handles MyBase.MouseEnter
        TextBox1.Text = "Mouse entered."
    End Sub

    Private Sub Form1_MouseHover(ByVal sender As Object, _
        ByVal e As System.EventArgs) Handles MyBase.MouseHover
        TextBox1.Text = "Mouse is hovering."
    End Sub

    Private Sub Form1_MouseLeave(ByVal sender As Object, _
        ByVal e As System.EventArgs) Handles MyBase.MouseLeave
        TextBox1.Text = "Mouse left."
    End Sub

    Private Sub Form1_MouseMove(ByVal sender As Object, _
        ByVal e As System.Windows.Forms.MouseEventArgs) _
        Handles MyBase.MouseMove
        TextBox1.Text = "Mouse moved: " + CStr(e.X) + ", " + CStr(e.Y)
    End Sub

    Private Sub Form1_MouseUp(ByVal sender As Object, _
        ByVal e As System.Windows.Forms.MouseEventArgs) _
        Handles MyBase.MouseUp
        If e.Button = MouseButtons.Left Then
```

```
            TextBox1.Text = "Mouse up at " + CStr(e.X) + ", " + CStr(e.Y)
        End If
    End Sub

    Private Sub Form1_MouseWheel(ByVal sender As Object, _
        ByVal e As System.Windows.Forms.MouseEventArgs) _
        Handles MyBase.MouseWheel
            TextBox1.Text = "Mouse rotated " + CStr(e.Delta) + " detents"
    End Sub
End Class
```

You can see the Mouser example at work in Figure 4.25, where it's reporting a **MouseDown** event.

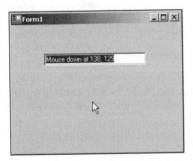

Figure 4.25   Handling mouse events.

Handling Keyboard Events

You can handle keyboard events in forms and many controls with these events:

- **KeyDown**—Happens when a key is pressed down while the control has focus.
- **KeyPress**—Happens when a key is pressed while the control has focus.
- **KeyUp**—Happens when a key is released while the control has focus.

For **KeyDown** and **KeyUp** events, the event handler receives an argument of type **KeyEventArgs** containing data related to this event, with these properties:

- **Alt**—Holds a value indicating whether the Alt key was pressed.
- **Control**—Holds a value indicating whether the Ctrl key was pressed.
- **Handled**—Holds or sets a value indicating whether the event was handled.
- **KeyCode**—Holds the keyboard code for a **KeyDown** or **KeyUp** event.
- **KeyData**—Holds the keyboard data for a **KeyDown** or **KeyUp** event.

- **KeyValue**—Holds the keyboard value for a **KeyDown** or **KeyUp** event.

- **Modifiers**—Holds the modifier flags for a **KeyDown** or **KeyUp** event. This indicates which modifier keys (Ctrl, Shift, and/or Alt) were pressed. These values can be ORed together (for more on the **OR** operator and how it works, see "Using Visual Basic Operators" in Chapter 2)—using the **Control**, **Shift**, and **Alt** properties is usually easier.

- **Shift**—Holds a value indicating whether the Shift key was pressed.

For **KeyPress** events, you get an argument of type **KeyPressEventArgs** containing the following **KeyPressEventArgs** properties:

- **Handled**—Gets or sets a value indicating whether the **KeyPress** event was handled. If you set this value to **True**, Visual Basic will not handle this key (so if you want to delete it, set **Handled** to **True** and do no further processing on it).

- **KeyChar**—Holds the character corresponding to the key pressed.

In the **KeyDown** and **KeyUp** events, you're responsible for determining which modifier key—Ctrl, Shift, or Alt—is down. Letter characters are passed to you as character codes as though they were in upper case, whether or not they should be. Here's an example where I check if Shift was actually on, and decipher the key code passed to us, displaying it in a message box in a **KeyDown** event handler (I'm only handling letter keys in this example):

```
Dim strText As String

Private Sub Form1_KeyDown(ByVal sender As Object, _
    ByVal e As System.Windows.Forms.KeyEventArgs) Handles MyBase.KeyDown
    If e.KeyCode >= Keys.A And e.KeyCode <= Keys.Z Then
        strText += Switch(e.Shift, Chr(e.KeyCode), Not e.Shift, _
            Char.ToLower(Chr(e.KeyCode)))
        MsgBox(strText)
    End If
End Sub
```

If you want to get the actual character typed without this kind of checking, use the **KeyPress** event, which passes you the character as a **Char** object directly, making handling that character much easier (**KeyPress** events occur after Visual Basic has had a chance to process and decipher the key itself):

```
Dim strText As String

Private Sub Form1_KeyPress(ByVal sender As Object, _
    ByVal e As System.Windows.Forms.KeyPressEventArgs) _
```

```
      Handles MyBase.KeyPress
        strText += e.KeyChar
        MsgBox(strText)
End Sub
```

For more on **KeyPress**, including an example showing how to discard typed input, see "Controlling Input in a Text Box" in Chapter 5.

Sending Keystrokes to Other Programs

This one isn't a part of form handling, but it's a part of **System.Windows.Forms**, and it's one of my absolutely favorite parts of Visual Basic—**SendKeys**, which you can use to send keystrokes to other applications. Say it's time to print out the 349 screen spreadsheets you've created in your new spreadsheet program to show the boss. Regrettably, there just doesn't seem to be any way to print them out except one at a time, using the File menu's Print item. Can Visual Basic help here?

Yes. You can use the **SendKeys** function to send keys to the program that currently has the Windows focus, just as if you typed in those keys yourself. Using Alt keys, you can reach the menu items in your spreadsheet's File menu. The day is saved, because now you can automate your printing job. If the keys you want to send are not simple text, just embed the codes you see in Table 4.5 in the text you send to **SendKeys**.

Table 4.5 SendKeys Key Codes.

Key	Code
Backspace	{BACKSPACE}, {BS}, or {BKSP}
Break	{BREAK}
Caps Locl	{CAPSLOCK}
Del or Delete	{DELETE} or {DEL}
Down Arrow	{DOWN}
End	{END}
Enter/Return	{ENTER}or ~
Esc	{ESC}
Help	{HELP}

(continued)

Table 4.5   SendKeys Key Codes *(continued)*.

Key	Code
Home	{HOME}
Ins or Insert	{INSERT} or {INS}
Left Arrow	{LEFT}
Numloick	{NUMLOCK}
Page Down	{PGDN}
Page Up	{PGUP}
Print Screen	{PRTSC}
Right Arrow	{RIGHT}
Scroll Lock	{SCROLLLOCK}
Tab	{TAB}
Up Arrow	{UP}
F1	{F1}
F2	{F2}
F3	{F3}
F4	{F4}
F5	{F5}
F6	{F6}
F7	{F7}
F8	{F8}
F9	{F9}
F10	{F10}
F11	{F11}
F12	{F12}
F13	{F13}
F14	{F14}
F15	{F15}
F16	{F16}
Shift	+
Ctrl	^
Alt	%

Here's an example showing how to use **SendKeys**. I'll give the Windows WordPad program the focus with the Visual Basic **AppActivate** function, passing it the title of that program (which appears in its title bar), and send the string "Hello from Visual Basic" to that program as follows:

```
Public Class Form1
    Inherits System.Windows.Forms.Form

'Windows Form Designer generated code

    Private Sub Button1_Click(ByVal sender As System.Object, _
        ByVal e As System.EventArgs) Handles Button1.Click
        AppActivate("Document - WordPad")
        System.Windows.Forms.SendKeys.Send("Hello from Visual Basic!")
    End Sub
End Class
```

The result appears in Figure 4.26—now we're able to send keystrokes to another program.

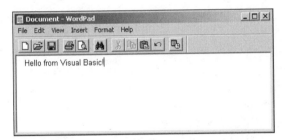

Figure 4.26   Sending keystrokes to Windows WordPad.

Beeping

Here's another one that, as with **SendKeys** (see the previous topic), doesn't really fit into a specific chapter, but is handy to know—the **Beep** function. You can use this function to make the computer emit a beep, as in this case when the user clicks a picture box control:

```
Private Sub PictureBox1_Click(ByVal sender As System.Object, _
    ByVal e As System.EventArgs) Handles PictureBox1.Click
    Beep()
End Sub
```

*TIP: **Beep** comes in handy as an ultra-quick debugging aid to see if code is being run—for example, if you embed a **Beep** call in the code and you get a beep when you run it, the code is indeed being called and run.*

Chapter 5

Windows Forms: Text Boxes, Rich Text Boxes, Labels, and Link Labels

(continued)

In Depth

This chapter starts our in-depth look at Windows forms controls. We'll begin with text boxes, rich text boxes, labels, and link labels; you can see these controls in Figure 5.1. All these controls are used to handle text. Text boxes and rich text boxes let the user enter text, labels and link labels display text, rich text boxes let you format text, and link labels let you support hyperlinks. These controls get a lot of use in Visual Basic programs, so there's a great deal of programming power coming up in this chapter.

Like all the Windows controls we'll be looking at in this and the next several chapters, these controls are based on the ***Control*** class. The many controls derived from this class inherit a lot of functionality from it, so their common base class, the **Control** class, is the first thing I'll take a look at here, providing us with a good foundation for this and the chapters to come.

The Control Class

The **Control** class is in the **System.Windows.Forms** namespace. It serves as a base class for the Windows controls we'll see—such as rich text boxes—which have this class hierarchy (that is, the **MarshalByRefObject** class is derived from the **Object** class, and the **Component** class is derived from the **MarshalByRef Object** class, and so on):

```
Object
    MarshalByRefObject
        Component
            Control
                TextBoxBase
                    RichTextBox
```

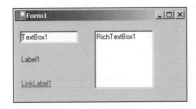

Figure 5.1   A text box, a rich text box, a label, and a link label.

Because Windows controls are based on the **Control** class, they inherit many properties, methods, and events from that class, so I'll list the more interesting ones here. (Keep in mind that the **Form** class is also derived from **Control**, so it also shares these properties, methods, and events). You can find noteworthy public properties of the **Control** class in Table 5.1, noteworthy methods in Table 5.2, and events in Table 5.3.

Table 5.1   Noteworthy public properties of Control objects.

Property	Means
AllowDrop	Sets/gets a value specifying if the control can accept data dropped into it.
Anchor	Sets/gets which edges of the control are anchored.
BackColor	Sets/gets the background color of this control.
BackgroundImage	Sets/gets the background image in the control.
Bottom	Gets the distance between the bottom of the control and the top of its container's client area.
Bounds	Sets/gets the control's bounding rectangle.
CanFocus	Returns a value specifying if the control can receive the focus.
CanSelect	Returns a value specifying if the control can be selected.
Capture	Sets/gets a value specifying if the control has captured the mouse.
CausesValidation	Sets/gets a value specifying if the control causes validation for all controls that require validation.
ContainsFocus	Returns a value specifying if the control has the input focus.
ContextMenu	Sets/gets the shortcut menu associated with this control.
Controls	Sets/gets the collection of controls contained within the control.
Cursor	Sets/gets the cursor displayed when the user moves the mouse pointer over this control.
DataBindings	Gets the data bindings for the control.
Dock	Sets/gets which edge of the parent a control is docked to.
Enabled	Sets/gets a value specifying if the control is enabled.
Focused	Returns a value specifying if the control has input focus.
Font	Sets/gets the current font for the control.
ForeColor	Sets/gets the foreground color of the control.
HasChildren	Returns a value specifying if the control contains child controls.
Height	Sets/gets the height of the control.
Left	Sets/gets the x-coordinate of a control's left edge in pixels.
Location	Sets/gets the coordinates of the upper-left corner of the control with respect to the upper-left corner of its container.

(continued)

Table 5.1   Noteworthy public properties of Control objects *(continued)*.

Property	Means
Name	Sets/gets the control's name.
Parent	Sets/gets the control's parent container.
Right	Returns the distance between the right edge of the control and the left edge of its container.
RightToLeft	Sets/gets a value indicating if the alignment of the control's elements is reversed to support right-to-left fonts.
Size	Sets/gets the height and width of the control.
TabIndex	Sets/gets the tab order of this control in its container.
TabStop	Sets/gets a value specifying if the user can tab to this control with the Tab key.
Tag	Sets/gets an object that contains data about the control.
Text	Sets/gets the text connected to this control.
Top	Sets/gets the top coordinate of the control.
Visible	Sets/gets a value specifying if the control is visible.
Width	Sets/gets the width of the control.

Table 5.2   Noteworthy public methods of Control objects.

Method	Means
BringToFront	Brings the control to the front of the stacking order.
Contains	Retrieves a value specifying if the control is a child of this control.
CreateGraphics	Creates a **Graphics** object for the control.
Dispose	Releases the resources used by the control.
DoDragDrop	Starts a drag-and-drop operation.
Equals	Indicates if two controls are equal.
FindForm	Retrieves the form that this control is on.
Focus	Gives the focus to the control.
GetChildAtPoint	Gets the child control at the specified coordinates.
GetNextControl	Retrieves the next control in the tab order of child controls.
GetType	Gets the type of the control.
Hide	Hides the control.
Invalidate	Invalidates a part of the control and sends a paint message to the control.
PointToClient	Translates the location of the specified screen point to client coordinates.
PointToScreen	Translates the location of the specified client point to screen coordinates.

(continued)

Table 5.2   Noteworthy public methods of Control objects (continued).

Method	Means
RectangleToClient	Translates the location of the specified screen rectangle to client coordinates.
RectangleToScreen	Translates the location of the specified client rectangle to screen coordinates.
Refresh	Forces the control to invalidate its client area and repaint itself (and any child controls).
Scale	Scales the control and any child controls.
Select	Activates this control.
SendToBack	Sends the control to the back of the stacking order.
SetBounds	Sets the bounds of the control.
Show	Displays the control (sets its visible property to **True**).
ToString	Returns a string that represents the current control.
Update	Forces the control to paint any currently invalid areas.

Table 5.3   Noteworthy public events of Control objects.

Event	Means
BackColorChanged	Occurs when the value of the **BackColor** property is changed.
BackgroundImageChanged	Occurs when the **BackgroundImage** property is changed.
Click	Occurs when the control is clicked.
ContextMenuChanged	Occurs when the **ContextMenu** property value is changed.
ControlAdded	Occurs when a new control is added.
ControlRemoved	Occurs when a control is removed.
CursorChanged	Occurs when the **Cursor** property value is changed.
Disposed	Represents the method which will handle the **Disposed** event of a **Component**.
DoubleClick	Occurs when the control is double-clicked.
DragDrop	Occurs when a drag-and-drop operation is completed.
DragEnter	Occurs when an object is dragged into the control's bounds.
DragLeave	Occurs when an object has been dragged into and out of the control's bounds.
DragOver	Occurs when an object has been dragged over the control's bounds.
EnabledChanged	Occurs when the **Enabled** property value is changed.
Enter	Occurs when the control is entered.
FontChanged	Occurs when the **Font** property value is changed.
ForeColorChanged	Occurs when the **ForeColor** property value is changed.
GotFocus	Occurs when the control receives focus.
Invalidated	Occurs when a control's display is updated.

(continued)

Table 5.3   Noteworthy public events of Control objects *(continued)*.

Event	Means
KeyDown	Occurs when a key is pressed down while the control has focus.
KeyPress	Occurs when a key is pressed while the control has focus.
KeyUp	Occurs when a key is released while the control has focus.
Layout	Occurs when a control has to lay out its child controls.
Leave	Occurs when the control is left.
LocationChanged	Occurs when the **Location** property value is changed.
LostFocus	Occurs when the control loses focus.
MouseDown	Occurs when the mouse pointer is over the control and a mouse button is pressed.
MouseEnter	Occurs when the mouse pointer enters the control.
MouseHover	Occurs when the mouse pointer hovers over the control.
MouseLeave	Occurs when the mouse pointer leaves the control.
MouseMove	Occurs when the mouse pointer is moved over the control.
MouseUp	Occurs when the mouse pointer is over the control and a mouse button is released.
MouseWheel	Occurs when the mouse wheel moves while the control has focus.
Move	Occurs when the control is moved.
Paint	Occurs when the control is redrawn.
ParentChanged	Occurs when the **Parent** property value is changed.
Resize	Occurs when the control is resized.
RightToLeftChanged	Occurs when the **Right-ToLeft** property value is changed.
Validated	Occurs when the control is done validating.
Validating	Occurs when the control is validating.
VisibleChanged	Occurs when the **Visible** property value is changed.

I've included Tables 5.1, 5.2, and 5.3 for reference sake, and it's really worth looking through these tables, finding out, for example, what properties to use to change the background color of a control (**BackColor**), what method makes a control invisible (**Hide**), what event handles mouse button press events (**MouseDown**), and so on. Note that when listing the noteworthy properties, methods, and events of Windows controls in similar tables in this and the next chapters, I'm going to *omit* those inherited from the **Control** class, because there simply isn't room to list them all. You'll find all those common **Control** properties, methods, and events in Tables 5.1, 5.2, and 5.3.

Text Boxes

Every Windows user is familiar with text boxes: they're exactly what their name implies: box-like controls in which you can enter text. Text boxes can be multiline, have scroll bars, be read-only, and have many other attributes, as we'll see in this chapter. (Not every Windows user is familiar with rich text boxes, on the other hand. Rich text boxes support not only plain text, but also rich text format [RTF] text.) The **TextBox** class is derived from the **TextBoxBase** class, which is based on **Control**:

```
Object
    MarshalByRefObject
        Component
            Control
                TextBoxBase
                    TextBox
```

NOTE: *In fact, most of the functionality of the text box control is simply inherited from the* **TextBoxBase** *class, which is also a base class for the rich text box control.*

Windows forms text boxes are used to get input from the user or to display text. The **TextBox** control is generally used for editable text, although it can also be made read-only. Text boxes can display multiple lines, wrap text to the size of the control, and add basic formatting, such as quotation marks and masking characters for passwords.

The text displayed by the control is contained in the **Text** property. By default, you can enter up to 2,048 characters in a text box. If you set the **MultiLine** property to **True** to make the control accept multiple lines of text, you can enter up to 32KB of text. The **Text** property can be set at design time with the Properties window, at run time in code, or by user input at run time. The current contents of a text box can be retrieved at run time by reading the **Text** property. We've seen how to do this already, as in this example, which inserts text into a text box:

```
Private Sub Button1_Click(ByVal sender As System.Object, _
    ByVal e As System.EventArgs) Handles Button1.Click
    TextBox1.Text = "Hello from Visual Basic"
End Sub
```

You can set or read text from text boxes at run time, and the user can enter and edit text in text boxes as well. You can limit the amount of text entered into a **TextBox** control by setting the **MaxLength** property to a specific number of characters. **TextBox** controls also can be used to accept passwords if you use the **PasswordChar** property to mask characters.

You also can restrict text from being entered in a **TextBox** control by creating an event handler for the **KeyDown** event, letting you validate each character entered in the control. And you can restrict any data entry in a **TextBox** control by setting the **ReadOnly** property to **True**.

Rich Text Boxes

The Windows forms **RichTextBox** control is used for displaying, entering, and manipulating rich text with formatting. The **RichTextBox** control does everything the **TextBox** control does, but in addition, it can display fonts, colors, and links; load text and embedded images from a file; undo and redo editing operations; and find specified characters.

Rich text format (RTF) text supports a variety of formats. For example, you can color text in a rich text box, underline it, bold it, or make it italic. You can select fonts and fonts sizes, as well as write the text out to disk or read it back in. Rich text boxes also can hold a great amount of data, unlike standard text boxes. Like standard text boxes, they're derived from the **TextBoxBase** class:

```
Object
    MarshalByRefObject
        Component
            Control
                TextBoxBase
                    RichTextBox
```

RTF text was designed to be a step beyond plain text, and because many word processors let you save text in the rich text format, it can provide a link between different types of word processors. Using rich text boxes, you also can create your own word processors. Rich text boxes are used to support text manipulation and display features similar to the big-time word processors such as Microsoft Word. Like the **TextBox** control, the **RichTextBox** control can display scroll bars.

As with the **TextBox** control, the text displayed is set by the **Text** property. The **RichTextBox** control has many properties to format text, and we'll explore them here. You can set font attributes, set indents, create hanging indents, create bulleted paragraphs, and more. To work with files, you can use the **LoadFile** and **SaveFile** methods. You can even use a **RichTextBox** for Web-style links by setting the **DetectUrls** property to **True** and writing code to handle the **LinkClicked** event. And you can undo and redo most edit operations by calling the **Undo** and **Redo** methods; the **CanRedo** method will let you know if the last operation the user has undone can be reapplied.

Although plenty of Visual Basic programmers know about the rich text control, very few of them actually know how to format text in these controls; we'll see how to do that in this chapter. (As you might expect, it's changed totally from the way you used to do it in VB6.)

TIP: To format text in a rich text box, you first select text, so here's a tip for VB6 programmers—selection properties that began with **Sel** now begin with **Selection**.

Labels

You use labels for just what they sound like—to label other parts of your application. Labels usually are used to display text that cannot be edited by the user. Your code can change the text displayed by a label. Labels are based directly on the **Control** class:

```
Object
    MarshalByRefObject
        Component
            Control
                Label
```

The caption for a label is stored in the **Text** property. Because you can change that caption in code, labels can act a little like non-editable text boxes, displaying text and messages to the user. The **TextAlign** (formerly **Alignment**) property allows you to set the alignment of the text within the label.

Here's another interesting aspect of labels—they cannot receive the focus (that is, become the selected target of keystrokes), but you can set up mnemonic characters for them with the **UseMnemonic** property; just specify a mnemonic character in their caption by preceding it with a & character. In that case, when the user presses Alt and the mnemonic character, the focus goes to the control after the label (that is, the control which the label is labeling), which lets you support keyboard navigation for the many controls that don't support mnemonic characters. (For more information, see "Using Labels to Give Access Keys to Controls without Captions" later in this chapter.) You also can support images in labels with the **Image** property, or the **Image** and **ImageList** properties together.

Link Labels

Link labels are new in VB .NET. They're based on the **Label** class, but also let you support Web-style hyperlinks to the Internet and other Windows forms. In other words, you can use a link label control for everything that you can use a label control for, and you can also make part of the text in this control a link to a Visual Basic object or Web page. Here's the class inheritance hierarchy of this control:

```
Object
    MarshalByRefObject
        Component
            Control
                Label
                    LinkLabel
```

Besides functioning as a full label control, you can display multiple hyperlinks in a single link label control, and use the **LinkColor**, **VisitedLinkColor**, and **ActiveLinkColor** properties to set the colors of the link, as you would in a Web page in a browser. The **LinkArea** property sets the area of the text that activates a link, and the **LinkClicked** event determines what happens when the link is clicked, as we'll see.

Each hyperlink is an object of the **LinkLabel.Link** class and is stored in a collection called **Links**. You can use the **Add** method of the **Links** collection to specify the hyperlinks in a link label and use a **LinkClicked** event handler to handle the link when it is clicked. We'll see how this works in detail later in this chapter.

And that's enough overview—it's time to start creating these controls, text boxes, rich text boxes, labels, and link labels in our Windows applications.

Immediate Solutions

Setting the Mouse Pointer in Controls

I'll start off this section by taking a look at a very useful property of the **Control** class—**Cursor**. You can use this property to set the mouse cursor type when the mouse moves over a control. (Keep in mind that Windows forms are also derived from the **Control** class so it works for forms, too.) Just set the **Cursor** (formerly **Mousepointer** in VB6 and before) property to one of the values in Table 5.4.

Table 5.4 Mouse cursor options.

Constant	Description
AppStarting	Cursor that is displayed when an application starts.
Arrow	Arrow cursor.
Cross	Crosshair cursor.
Default	Default cursor, usually an arrow cursor.
Hand	Hand cursor, usually used when hovering over a Web link.
Help	Help cursor, a combination of an arrow and a question mark.
HSplit	Cursor that appears when the mouse is positioned over a horizontal splitter bar.
IBeam	I-beam cursor, used to show where the text cursor appears when the mouse is clicked.
No	Cursor that indicates that a particular region is invalid for the current operation.
NoMove2D	Cursor for mouse wheel operations when the mouse is not moving, but the window can be scrolled in either a horizontal and vertical direction.
NoMoveHoriz	Cursor for mouse wheel operations when the mouse is not moving, but the window can be scrolled in a horizontal direction.
NoMoveVert	Cursor for mouse wheel operations when the mouse is not moving, but the window can be scrolled in a vertical direction.
PanEast	Cursor for mouse wheel operations when the mouse is moving and the window is scrolling horizontally to the right.
PanNE	Cursor for mouse wheel operations when the mouse is moving and the window is scrolling horizontally and vertically upward and to the right.
PanNorth	Cursor for mouse wheel operations when the mouse is moving and the window is scrolling vertically in an upward direction.

(continued)

Table 5.4   Mouse cursor options *(continued)*.

Constant	Description
PanNW	Cursor for mouse wheel operations when the mouse is moving and the window is scrolling horizontally and vertically upward and to the left.
PanSE	Cursor for mouse wheel operations when the mouse is moving and the window is scrolling horizontally and vertically downward and to the right.
PanSouth	Cursor for mouse wheel operations when the mouse is moving and the window is scrolling vertically in a downward direction.
PanSW	Cursor for mouse wheel operations when the mouse is moving and the window is scrolling horizontally and vertically downward and to the left.
PanWest	Cursor for mouse wheel operations when the mouse is moving and the window is scrolling horizontally to the left.
SizeAll	Four-headed sizing cursor.
SizeNESW	Two-headed diagonal (northeast/southwest) sizing cursor.
SizeNS	Two-headed vertical (north/south) sizing cursor.
SizeNWSE	Two-headed diagonal (northwest/southeast) sizing cursor.
SizeWE	Two-headed horizontal (west/east) sizing cursor.
UpArrow	Up-arrow cursor, usually used to identify an insertion point.
VSplit	Cursor that appears when the mouse is over a vertical splitter bar.
WaitCursor	Wait cursor, usually an hourglass shape.

Text Boxes

We've discussed text boxes in the In Depth section of this chapter and already put them to use throughout the book. Take a look at Tables 5.5, 5.6, and 5.7 to see the notable properties, methods, and events of the **TextBox** class. These tables do not include all the notable properties, methods, and events this class inherits from the **Control** class—you'll find them in Tables 5.1, 5.2, and 5.3.

Table 5.5   Noteworthy public properties of TextBox objects.

Property	Means
AutoSize	Sets/gets a value specifying if the height of the control automatically adjusts when the font in the control is changed.
BackColor	Sets/gets the background color of the control.
BorderStyle	Sets/gets the border type of the text box control.
CanUndo	Returns a value specifying if the user can undo the previous operation.

(continued)

219

Table 5.5   Noteworthy public properties of TextBox objects *(continued)*.

Property	Means
ForeColor	Sets/gets the foreground color.
HideSelection	Sets/gets a value specifying if the selected text in the text box control remains highlighted when the text box loses focus.
Lines	Sets/gets the lines of text.
MaxLength	Sets/gets the maximum number of characters the user can type into the text box.
Modified	Indicates if the text box control has been modified by the user since the control was created or its contents were last set.
Multiline	Sets/gets a value specifying if this is a multiline text box control.
PasswordChar	Sets/gets the character used to mask characters of a password in a single-line text box.
ReadOnly	Sets/gets a value specifying if text in the text box is read-only.
ScrollBars	Sets/gets what scroll bars should appear in a multiline text box.
SelectedText	Sets/gets a value specifying the currently selected text in the control.
SelectionLength	Sets/gets the number of characters selected in the text box.
SelectionStart	Sets/gets the starting point of text selected in the text box.
Text	Sets/gets the current text in the text box.
TextAlign	Sets/gets how text is aligned in a text box control.
TextLength	Gets the length of text in the control.
WordWrap	Indicates if a multiline text box control automatically wraps words.

Table 5.6   Noteworthy public methods of TextBox objects.

Methods	Means
AppendText	Appends text to the current text in the text box.
Clear	Clears all text from the text box.
ClearUndo	Clears information about the most recent operation of the text box.
Copy	Copies the selected text in the text box to the Clipboard.
Cut	Moves the selected text in the text box to the Clipboard.
Paste	Replaces the selected text in the text box with the contents of the Clipboard.
ScrollToCaret	Scrolls the text box to the caret position.
Select	Selects text in the text box.
SelectAll	Selects all text in the text box.
Undo	Undoes the last edit operation in the text box.

Table 5.7   Noteworthy public events of TextBox objects.

Event	Means
AutoSizeChanged	Occurs when the value of the **AutoSize** property is changed.
Click	Occurs when the text box is clicked.
ReadOnlyChanged	Occurs when the value of the **ReadOnly** property is changed.

Creating Multiline, Word-wrap Text Boxes

You've got a text box all set up for user feedback, and it can hold about 60 characters of text. Surely that's enough, you think. But when you start reading the users' comments, you find that they're all favorable, but truncated (e.g., "I loved your program! In fact, let me say that I never s"). Maybe it's worthwhile to allow the user to enter more text.

You can do that by setting the text box's **MultiLine** property to **True**, converting a text box into a multiline text box, complete with word wrap. The result appears in Figure 5.2. Now your program's users can type in line after line of text.

Note that you also can add scroll bars to multiline text boxes (see "Adding Scroll Bars to Text Boxes" later in this section).

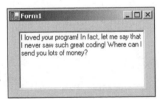

Figure 5.2   Creating a multiline text box.

Accessing Text in a Text Box

Java, C++, Visual Basic—a programmer has to switch between many languages these days. So, how do you set the text in a text box again? Is there a **SetText** method? No, you use the **Text** property, like this:

```
Private Sub Button1_Click_1(ByVal sender As System.Object, _
    ByVal e As System.EventArgs) Handles Button1.Click
    TextBox1.Text = "Hello from Visual Basic"
End Sub
```

When the user clicks the command button **Button1**, the text "Hello from Visual Basic" appears in the text box. And you can recover text from a text box in the same way:

```
Private Sub Button1_Click_1(ByVal sender As System.Object, _
    ByVal e As System.EventArgs) Handles Button1.Click
        Dim strText As String
        strText = TextBox1.Text
End Sub
```

Adding Scroll Bars to Text Boxes

Now that you're using multiline text boxes, it would be even better if you could add scroll bars to let the user enter even more text. If your program's users are going to be entering a lot of text into text boxes, you can avoid the need for huge text boxes by adding scroll bars.

Using the **ScrollBars** property, there are four ways to add scroll bars to a text box; here are the settings you use for **ScrollBars**, and the type of scroll bars each setting displays:

- 0: None

- 1: Horizontal

- 2: Vertical

- 3: Both

Note that in order for the scroll bars to actually appear, the text box's **MultiLine** property must be **True**. After you install scroll bars in a text box, the result appears as in Figure 5.3. Now the user can enter much more text simply by scrolling appropriately.

TIP: *Although multiline text boxes can hold up to 32KB characters, that may be too much for you to conveniently handle, and you may want to limit the maximum number of characters a text box can hold. You do that by setting the text box's* **MaxLength** *property to the maximum number of characters you want the user to be able to enter.*

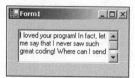

Figure 5.3   Using scroll bars in a text box.

Aligning Text in Text Boxes

The Aesthetic Design Department has sent you a memo. Your new program meets its requirements for design standards, except for one thing: All the text boxes in your program are stacked on top of one another, and the Aesthetic Design Department thinks it would be terrific if you display the text in those boxes as centered, not left-justified.

Well, you seem to remember that text boxes have an **TextAlign** property, so you set it to Centered (there are three possibilities: 0: left-justified, 1: right-justified, and 2: centered) at design time in all the text boxes. You can see the result in Figure 5.4.

*TIP: In VB6 and before, you needed to set a text box's **MultiLine** property to **True** before text alignment would work, but that's no longer true.*

Figure 5.4   Aligning text in a text box.

Making a Text Box Read-only

There are times when you want to make text boxes read-only. For example, you might have written a calculator program in which you let the user enter operands in text boxes and display the result in another text box. The result text box should be read-only, so that the user doesn't enter text there by mistake. You do this with the **ReadOnly** property.

Using the **ReadOnly** Property

In VB6 and before, you used the **Locked** property to "lock" a text box so it couldn't be edited, but now the **Locked** property is used to lock controls in position. Now you use the **ReadOnly** property to make a text box read-only. Setting this property to **True** means that the user cannot enter text into the text box (except under your program's control in code).

Disabling a Text Box

You also can disable a text box by setting its **Enabled** property to **False**. However, although this means the user can't enter text into the text box, it also means the text in the box appears grayed. Disabling is better done to indicate that the control is inaccessible.

Using Labels Instead of Text Boxes

Another alternative to using read-only text boxes is to display read-only text in label controls. You can change the text in a label control from code using the label's **Text** property.

Selecting and Replacing Text in a Text Box

To work with part of the text in a text box, you select the text you want using three properties:

- **SelectionLength**—Returns or sets the number of characters selected.
- **SelectionStart**—Returns or sets the starting point of text selected; indicates the position of the insertion point if no text is selected.
- **SelectedText**—Returns or sets the string containing the currently selected text; consists of a zero-length string ("") if no characters are selected.

For example, here's how we select all the text in a text box and replace it with "Hello from Visual Basic". Note the use of the **Len** function to get the length of the text currently in the text box:

```
Private Sub Button1_Click(ByVal sender As System.Object, _
    ByVal e As System.EventArgs) Handles Button1.Click
    TextBox1.SelectionStart = 0
    TextBox1.SelectionLength = Len(TextBox1.Text)
    TextBox1.SelectedText = "Hello from Visual Basic"
End Sub
```

That's how it works when you want to select some text—you specify the beginning of the selected text in **SelectionStart**, the end in **SelectionLength**, and refer to the text with the **SelectedText** property. Note that text selected under program control this way does *not* appear highlighted in the text box; when the user selects text, the text will appear highlighted, and these properties will be set automatically.

The **HideSelection** Property

While on the topic of text selection, we might note the **HideSelection** property, which, when **True**, turns off text selection highlighting when your program loses the focus.

Copying or Getting Selected Text to or from the Clipboard

After entering their new novels into your program, users were surprised that they couldn't copy them to the clipboard and so paste them into other applications. How can you support the clipboard with text in a text box? You can use the **Clipboard** object's **SetDataObject** and **GetDataObject** class methods. Here's an example, which is called Clipboard on the CD-ROM. In this case, I'm placing the selected text from one text box into the clipboard when the user clicks a button, and putting it into another text box when the user clicks another. The call to **SetDataObject** places the data in the clipboard; **GetDataObject** gets the data from the clipboard; you can check if it is text data with the **GetDataPresent** method and the **DataFormats** enumeration's **Text** item; and you get the actual data with **GetData**:

```
Public Class Form1
    Inherits System.Windows.Forms.Form

    'Windows Form Designer generated code

    Private Sub Button1_Click(ByVal sender As System.Object, _
        ByVal e As System.EventArgs) Handles Button1.Click
        System.Windows.Forms.Clipboard.SetDataObject_
            (TextBox1.SelectedText)
    End Sub

    Private Sub Button2_Click(ByVal sender As System.Object, _
        ByVal e As System.EventArgs) Handles Button2.Click
        Dim ClipboardData As System.Windows.Forms.IDataObject = _
            System.Windows.Forms.Clipboard.GetDataObject()
        If ClipboardData.GetDataPresent(DataFormats.Text) Then
            TextBox2.Text = ClipboardData.GetData(DataFormats.Text)
        End If
    End Sub
End Class
```

5. Windows Forms: Text Boxes, Rich Text Boxes, Labels, and Link Labels

You can see this example at work in Figure 5.5.

This example shows how to use the clipboard in a general way, but in fact, there's an easier way to do this with text boxes to handle selected text—you can use the **TextBox** class's **Copy**, **Cut**, and **Paste** methods.

TIP: *Text boxes already allow the user to use these shortcuts to work with the clipboard: Ctrl+C to copy selected text, Ctrl+V to paste text from the clipboard, and Ctrl+X to cut selected text.*

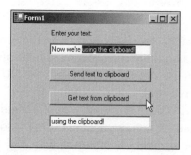

Figure 5.5   Using the clipboard.

Creating a Password Control

It's time to heighten security—users of your new *SuperSpecialDataBase* program are worried about the low security of your program, so you can add a little security with password controls. Visual Basic can help.

To convert a standard text box into a password box, you just assign some character (usually an asterisk, "*") to the text box's **PasswordChar** property. After that, your program can read the text in the text box, but only the password character will appear on the screen each time the user types a character, as shown in Figure 5.6.

TIP: *You may be concerned that someone can copy the text in a password control and paste it into a word processor to read it, but in fact, clipboard handling from the text box is disabled if you are using a password character.*

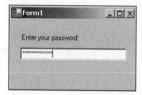

Figure 5.6   Creating a password control.

Controlling Input in a Text Box

The Testing department is on the phone—there's a bug in your program! The users are getting runtime errors! Don't panic, you say; you'll be right down. You ask the user to duplicate what caused the problem—and find that they're trying to add two numbers with your program: 15553 and 955Z. What's 955Z, you ask? A typo, they say. Is there any way you can restrict user input so this doesn't happen?

Yes, you can—just use the **KeyPress** event and check the key that was typed, which is passed to you as **e.KeyChar**. For example, to check if the user is typing single digits, you might use this code:

```
Private Sub TextBox1_KeyPress(ByVal sender As Object, _
    ByVal e As System.Windows.Forms.KeyPressEventArgs) _
    Handles TextBox1.KeyPress
    If (e.KeyChar < "0" Or e.KeyChar > "9") Then
        MsgBox("Please enter single digits")
    End If
End Sub
```

If you simply want to stop anything but digits appearing in the text box, you can set the **KeyPressEventArgs Handled** property to **True**, which indicates that we've handled the key (although we've actually discarded it):

```
Private Sub TextBox1_KeyPress(ByVal sender As Object, _
    ByVal e As System.Windows.Forms.KeyPressEventArgs) _
    Handles TextBox1.KeyPress
    If (e.KeyChar < "0" Or e.KeyChar > "9") Then
        e.Handled = True
    End If
End Sub
```

Besides the **KeyPress**, **KeyUp**, and **KeyDown** events, you also can use the text box's **TextChanged** (formerly **Change**) event, which occurs when there's a change in the text box's text. For example, each time the user types a key into **TextBox1**, you might want to echo what's in **TextBox1** to **TextBox2**. You can do that because you're passed the object that caused the **TextChanged** event, which is the text box itself, so this code will work:

```
Private Sub TextBox1_TextChanged(ByVal sender As System.Object, _
    ByVal e As System.EventArgs) Handles TextBox1.TextChanged
    TextBox2.Text = sender.Text
End Sub
```

Related solution:	Found on page:
Handling Keyboard Events	201

Creating a Text Box in Code

You also can create text boxes in code. Here's an example—CreateTextBox on the CD-ROM—that creates a text box when you click a button. In this case, I'm calling the **TextBox** class's constructor (**TextBox( )** in the code below—as discussed in Chapter 2, a constructor is a special method you call to create an object from a class) to create a new text box, then positioning it and adding it to the form's **Controls** collection, as we did in Chapter 4:

```
Private Sub Button1_Click(ByVal sender As System.Object, _
    ByVal e As System.EventArgs) Handles Button1.Click
    Dim TextBox1 As New TextBox()
    TextBox1.Size = New Size(150, 20)
    TextBox1.Location = New Point(80, 20)
    TextBox1.Text = "Hello from Visual Basic"
    Me.Controls.Add(TextBox1)
End Sub
```

You can see this code at work in Figure 5.7.

Related solution:	Found on page:
Adding and Removing Controls at Run Time	196

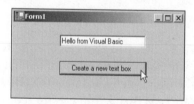

Figure 5.7   Creating a text box from code.

Rich Text Boxes

Want a full-fledged word processor in your application? Use a rich text box. Not only can you enter formatted text (selecting fonts, italics, bolding, and more) in a rich text box, you also can save that text in rich text format (RTF) files, and read

RTF files in it. Commercial word processors like Microsoft Word can read RTF files, allowing you to interface to those word processors fully. (In fact, many people prefer RTF files these days because they cannot harbor macro viruses.)

We've discussed rich text boxes in the In Depth section of this chapter. Take a look at Tables 5.8, 5.9, and 5.10 to see the notable properties, methods, and events of the **RichTextBox** class. These tables do not include all the notable properties, methods, and events this class inherits from the **Control** class—you'll find them in Tables 5.1, 5.2, and 5.3.

Table 5.8   Noteworthy public properties of RichTextBox objects.

Property	Means
AutoSize	Sets/gets a value specifying if the size of the rich text box automatically adjusts when the font changes.
AutoWordSelection	Sets/gets a value specifying if automatic word selection is enabled.
BorderStyle	Sets/gets the border type of the rich text box.
BulletIndent	Sets/gets the indentation used in the rich text box when the bullet style is applied to the text.
CanRedo	Indicates if there were actions in rich text box that can be reapplied.
CanUndo	Returns a value specifying if the user can undo the previous operation in the rich text box.
DetectUrls	Sets/gets a value specifying if the rich text box should detect URLs when typed into the **RichTextBox** control.
HideSelection	Sets/gets a value specifying if the selected text should stay highlighted when the **RichTextBox** control loses focus.
Lines	Sets/gets the lines of text in a **RichTextBox** control.
MaxLength	Sets/gets the maximum number of characters the user can type into the rich text box.
Modified	Sets/gets a value that indicates that the **RichTextBox** control has been modified by the user since the Control was created or its contents were last set.
Multiline	Sets/gets a value specifying if this is a multiline **RichTextBox** control.
PreferredHeight	Gets the preferred height for a single-line rich text box.
ReadOnly	Sets/gets a value specifying if text in the rich text box is read-only.
RightMargin	Sets/gets the size of a single line of text within the **RichTextBox** control.
Rtf	Sets/gets the text of the **RichTextBox** control, including all rich text format (RTF) codes.
ScrollBars	Sets/gets the kind of scroll bars to display in the **RichTextBox** control.

(continued)

5. Windows Forms: Text Boxes, Rich Text Boxes, Labels, and Link Labels

Table 5.8 Noteworthy public properties of **RichTextBox** objects *(continued)*.

Property	Means
SelectedRtf	Sets/gets the currently selected rich text format (RTF) formatted text in the control.
SelectedText	Sets/gets the selected text within the rich text box.
SelectionAlignment	Sets/gets the alignment to apply to the current selection or insertion point.
SelectionBullet	Sets/gets a value specifying if the bullet style is applied to the current selection or insertion point.
SelectionCharOffset	Sets/gets if text in the **RichTextBox** control appears on the baseline, as a superscript, or as a subscript.
SelectionColor	Sets/gets the text color of the current text selection or insertion point.
SelectionFont	Sets/gets the font of the current text selection or insertion point.
SelectionHangingIndent	Sets/gets the distance between the left edge of the first line of text in the selected paragraph and the left edge of the next lines in the same paragraph.
SelectionIndent	Sets/gets the distance in pixels between the left edge of the rich text box and the left edge of the current text selection or text added after the insertion point.
SelectionLength	Sets/gets the number of characters selected in control.
SelectionRightIndent	The distance in pixels between the right edge of the **RichTextBox** control and the right edge of the text that is selected.
SelectionStart	Sets/gets the starting point of text selected in the text box.
SelectionTabs	Sets/gets the absolute tab stop positions in a **RichTextBox** control.
Text	Sets/gets the current text in the rich text box.
TextLength	Gets the length of text in the **RichTextBox** control.
WordWrap	Indicates if a multiline **RichTextBox** control automatically wraps words.
ZoomFactor	Sets/gets the current zoom level of the rich text box.

Table 5.9 Noteworthy public methods of **RichTextBox** objects.

Method	Means
AppendText	Appends text to the current text of the rich text box.
CanPaste	Determines if you can paste information from the Clipboard.
Clear	Clears all text from the **RichTextBox** control.
ClearUndo	Clears information about the most recent operation from the undo buffer of the rich text box.
Copy	Copies the current selection in the rich text box to the Clipboard.
Cut	Moves the current selection in the rich text box to the Clipboard.
Find	Searches for text within the contents of the rich text box.

(continued)

Table 5.9   Noteworthy public methods of RichTextBox objects *(continued).*

Method	Means
GetLineFromCharIndex	Gets the line number from the specified character position within the text of the **RichTextBox** control.
GetPositionFromCharIndex	Gets the location within the control at the specified character index.
LoadFile	Loads the contents of a file into the **RichTextBox** control.
Paste	Pastes the contents of the Clipboard into the **RichTextBox** control.
Redo	Reapplies the last operation that was undone in the **RichTextBox** control.
SaveFile	Saves the contents of the rich text box to a file.
ScrollToCaret	Scrolls the contents of the **RichTextBox** control to the current caret position.
Select	Selects text within the **RichTextBox** control.
SelectAll	Selects all text in the rich text box.
Undo	Undoes the last edit operation in the rich text box.

Table 5.10   Noteworthy public events of RichTextBox objects.

Event	Means
Click	Occurs when the rich text box is clicked.
LinkClicked	Occurs when the user clicks on a link within the text of the **RichTextBox** control.
ModifiedChanged	Occurs when the value of the **Modified** property is changed.
ReadOnlyChanged	Occurs when the value of the **ReadOnly** property is changed.
SelectionChanged	Occurs when the selection of text within the **RichTextBox** control is changed.
VScroll	Occurs when the user clicks the vertical scroll bars of the **RichTextBox** control.

5. Windows Forms: Text Boxes, Rich Text Boxes, Labels, and Link Labels

*TIP: Now you can even use a **RichTextBox** for Web-style links by setting the **DetectUrls** property to **True** and writing code to handle the **LinkClicked** event.*

Accessing Text in a Rich Text Box

To access text in a rich text box, you can use two properties: **Text** and **Rtf**. As their names imply, **Text** holds the text in a rich text box in plain text format (like a text box), and **Rtf** holds the text in rich text format.

Here's an example where we read the text in **RichTextBox1** without any RTF codes and display that text as plain text in **RichTextBox2**:

```
Private Sub Button1_Click(ByVal sender As System.Object, _
    ByVal e As System.EventArgs) Handles Button1.Click
    RichTextBox2.Text = RichTextBox1.Text
End Sub
```

Here's the same operation where we transfer the text including all RTF codes—that is, here we're transferring rich text from one rich text box to another:

```
Private Sub Button1_Click(ByVal sender As System.Object, _
    ByVal e As System.EventArgs) Handles Button2.Click
    RichTextBox2.Rtf = RichTextBox1.Rtf
End Sub
```

Creating Bold, Italic, Underlined, and Strikeout Text

Plenty of programmers know about rich text boxes, but few know how to actually format text in them (partially because everything has changed here from VB6, too). To work with rich text boxes, see the RichTextBoxes example on the CD-ROM. This example displays three rich text boxes and several buttons, as you see in Figure 5.8.

Note the top right rich text box in Figure 5.8, which is displaying formatted text. How does it add formatting like that? First, you select the text you want to format, which I do with the **Find** method, setting the return value of that method to the **SelectionStart** property. That selects the text to format.

TIP: You also can use the text box and rich text box **Select** method to select text, passing it the start and end location of the text to select.

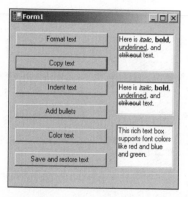

Figure 5.8   The RichTextBoxes example.

Next, you need to create a new **Font** object to assign to the rich text box's **SelectionFont** property (which sets the font of the selected text). You can use **Font** objects to set the typeface and size of text, and you also can set font style using members of the **FontStyle** enumeration—for example, italic text is **FontStyle.Italic**, bold text is **FontStyle.Bold**, and so on. To preserve the other aspects of the text in the rich text box, I'll get the current font used in that control from its **Font** property, then use the **Font** class's constructor to base a new font on the current font while also setting a new attribute, such as italics, bolding, and so on. That looks like this:

```
Private Sub Button1_Click(ByVal sender As System.Object, _
    ByVal e As System.EventArgs) Handles Button1.Click
    RichTextBox1.SelectionStart = RichTextBox1.Find("italic")
    Dim ItalicFont As New Font(RichTextBox1.Font, FontStyle.Italic)
    RichTextBox1.SelectionFont = ItalicFont

    RichTextBox1.SelectionStart = RichTextBox1.Find("bold")
    Dim BoldFont As New Font(RichTextBox1.Font, FontStyle.Bold)
    RichTextBox1.SelectionFont = BoldFont

    RichTextBox1.SelectionStart = RichTextBox1.Find("underlined")
    Dim UnderlineFont As New Font(RichTextBox1.Font, FontStyle.Underline)
    RichTextBox1.SelectionFont = UnderlineFont

    RichTextBox1.SelectionStart = RichTextBox1.Find("strikeout")
    Dim StrikeoutFont As New Font(RichTextBox1.Font, FontStyle.Strikeout)
    RichTextBox1.SelectionFont = StrikeoutFont
End Sub
```

The second button in the RichTextBoxes example copies this text with formatting intact to the middle rich text box (as you can see in Figure 5.8), using the kind of code discussed in the previous topic:

```
Private Sub Button2_Click(ByVal sender As System.Object, _
    ByVal e As System.EventArgs) Handles Button2.Click
    RichTextBox2.Rtf = RichTextBox1.Rtf
End Sub
```

Indenting Text in Rich Text Boxes

One of the aspects of word processors that users have gotten used to is the ability to indent text, and rich text boxes (which are designed to be RTF word processors in a control) have this capability.

To indent paragraph by paragraph, you use these properties (you set them to numeric values to indicate the indentation amount, using pixels):

- **SelectionIndent**—Indents first line of the paragraph
- **SelectionHangingIndent**—Indents all other lines of the paragraph with respect to **SelectionIndent**
- **SelectionRightIndent**—Sets the right indentation of the paragraph

To see this at work, take a look at the RichTextBoxes example on the CD-ROM and click the Indent text button as in Figure 5.9, which indents the text in the top rich text box this way (keep in mind all measurements are in pixels):

```
Private Sub Button3_Click(ByVal sender As System.Object, _
    ByVal e As System.EventArgs) Handles Button3.Click
    RichTextBox1.SelectionIndent = 20
    RichTextBox1.SelectionHangingIndent = -25
    RichTextBox1.SelectionRightIndent = 10
End Sub
```

> **TIP:** Besides working paragraph by paragraph, you can set the right margin for the whole rich text at once with the **RightMargin** property. Just assign this property the new value you want for the right margin and you're set.

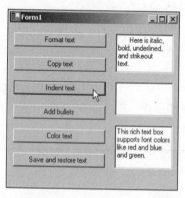

Figure 5.9   Indenting a paragraph of text.

Adding Bullets to Rich Text Boxes

Rich text boxes support *bullets*—those black dots that appear in lists of items that you want to set off in text. Putting a bullet in front of each item gives the list a snappy appearance and can be very effective visually.

To set bullets, you use the **SelectionBullet** and **BulletIndent** properties. The **SelectionBullet** property displays a bullet in front of the paragraph in which the current selection is, and the **BulletIndent** property indicates how much you want the bullet to be indented from the left. Here's an example from the RichTextBoxes example on the CD-ROM:

```
Private Sub Button4_Click(ByVal sender As System.Object, ByVal e As_
    System.EventArgs) Handles Button4.Click
    RichTextBox1.Text = "This rich text box shows how to use bullets " + _
        "and indent bulleted text."
    RichTextBox1.SelectionIndent = 20
    RichTextBox1.BulletIndent = 10
    RichTextBox1.SelectionBullet = True
End Sub
```

That's it—the result appears in Figure 5.10.

TIP: It's a good idea to set the bullet indentation, because if you don't, the bullet will appear right in front of the first character in the paragraph you're bulleting, which can look odd.

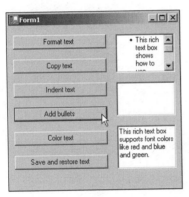

Figure 5.10   Adding a bullet to text in a rich text box.

Setting Text Color in RTF Boxes

Another call from the Testing Department—now the users want to use different text *colors* in your word processing program. Can you do that? Yes, you can, using the **SelectionColor** property.

To set colors in a rich text box, you can make a selection and set the rich text box's **SelectionColor** property. One way to set colors in VB .NET is with the **Colors** enumeration, using colors such as **Colors.Red**, **Colors.Green**, and so on.

The RichTextBoxes example on the CD-ROM is there to make this clearer. In it, I display the text "This rich text box supports font colors like red and blue and green" in a rich text box, and color the word "red" red, "blue" blue, and "green" green (although that'll be hard to see in the figure in this book, of course). Here's how that example looks in code:

```
Private Sub Button5_Click(ByVal sender As System.Object, _
    ByVal e As System.EventArgs) Handles Button5.Click
    RichTextBox3.SelectionStart = RichTextBox3.Find("red")
    RichTextBox3.SelectionColor = Color.Red

    RichTextBox3.SelectionStart = RichTextBox3.Find("green")
    RichTextBox3.SelectionColor = Color.Green

    RichTextBox3.SelectionStart = RichTextBox3.Find("blue")
    RichTextBox3.SelectionColor = Color.Blue
End Sub
```

This program produces the display you see in Figure 5.11.

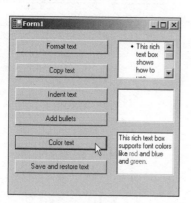

Figure 5.11   Coloring text in a rich text box.

Saving and Loading RTF Files from and to Rich Text Boxes

You've gotten feedback from a user of your word processor, *SuperDuperTextPro*, and it seems they've written a 600-page novel with the program and now find there's no way to save it to disk. Can you help? They will keep their computer on until they hear from you.

You use the **SaveFile** method to save the text in a rich text box to disk, and the **LoadFile** method to read it back. And doing so is easy. To see how this works, take a look at the RichTextBoxes example on the CD-ROM; when you click the "Save and restore text", the text in the bottom rich text box (**RichText3**) is written to a rich text file, text.rtf, then read back in and stored in the top rich text box (**RichText1**):

```
Private Sub Button6_Click(ByVal sender As System.Object, _
    ByVal e As System.EventArgs) Handles Button6.Click
    RichTextBox3.SaveFile("text.rtf")
    RichTextBox1.LoadFile("text.rtf")
End Sub
```

You can see this at work in Figure 5.12. That's all it takes—now we've written RTF to a file, and read it back in.

TIP: *Many word processors, such as Microsoft Word, support RTF files, so you can now write formatted text files that such word processors can read in and use.*

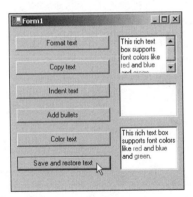

Figure 5.12   Saving rich text to a file and reading it back in.

Aligning Text in a Rich Text Box

You can set the alignment of text in a rich text box paragraph by paragraph using the **SelectionAlignment** property. You just select the paragraph you want to align—or place the insertion point in that paragraph—and set the **SelectionAlignment** property to one of the following values:

- **HorizontalAlignment.Left**—0 (the default)—The paragraph is aligned along the left margin.

- **HorizontalAlignment.Right**—1—The paragraph is aligned along the right margin.

- **HorizontalAlignment.Center**—2—The paragraph is centered between the left and right margins.

Being able to align text paragraph by paragraph like this is much more powerful than the simple **TextAlign** property of standard text box, which aligns all the text at the same time.

Creating Rich Text Boxes in Code

Creating rich text boxes in code works much like creating standard text boxes in code (see "Creating Text Boxes in Code" earlier in this chapter). Here's an example—CreateRichTextBox on the CD-ROM—that creates a new rich text box when the user clicks a button:

```
Private Sub Button1_Click(ByVal sender As System.Object, _
    ByVal e As System.EventArgs) Handles Button1.Click
    Dim RichTextBox1 As New RichTextBox()
    RichTextBox1.Size = New Size(150, 100)
    RichTextBox1.Location = New Point(70, 20)
    RichTextBox1.Text = "Hello from Visual Basic"
    Me.Controls.Add(RichTextBox1)
End Sub
```

You can see the results of this code in Figure 5.13.

Related solution:	Found on page:
Adding and Removing Controls at Run Time	196

Figure 5.13   Creating a rich text box.

Labels

We've discussed labels in the In Depth section of this chapter. Take a look at Table 5.11 to see the notable properties of the **Label** class. (There aren't any truly notable methods or events of this class that it doesn't inherit from the **Control** class.) This table does not include all the notable properties, methods, and events this class inherits from the **Control** class—you'll find them in Tables 5.1, 5.2, and 5.3.

Table 5.11   **Noteworthy public properties of Label objects.**

Property	Means
AutoSize	Sets/gets a value specifying if the control should be automatically resized to display all its contents.
BorderStyle	Sets/gets the border style for the control.
FlatStyle	Sets/gets the flat style appearance of the label control.
Image	Sets/gets the image that is displayed on a **Label**.
ImageAlign	Sets/gets the alignment of an image that is displayed in the control.
PreferredHeight	Gets the preferred height of the control.
PreferredWidth	Gets the preferred width of the control.
TextAlign	Sets/gets the alignment of text in the control.
UseMnemonic	Sets/gets a value specifying if the control treats an ampersand character (&) in the control's **Text** property to be an access key character.

Using Labels Instead of Text Boxes

There are several advantages to using labels instead of text boxes in a Visual Basic program. Labels display read-only text (although you *can* make text boxes read-only by setting their **ReadOnly** property to **True**), and they give the appearance of text directly on the form; this can look much better than a text box on occasion. For example, you might want to display the result of a calculation in a label instead of a text box, so the user can't edit that result.

In fact, you can make text boxes and labels resemble each other. To make a text box look like a label, set the text box's **BackColor** property to **Control** in the popup box that appears when you set this property in the properties window; its **ReadOnly** property to **True**; and its **BorderStyle** property to **None**. To make a label look like a text box, set its **BackColor** property to **Window** and its **BorderStyle** property to **Fixed3D**.

Formatting Text in Labels

When you add labels to a form, you can make the label match the text's size by setting the **AutoSize** property to **True**. You also can format the text in a label with the **Font** property, setting it to a **Font** object. (We first saw the **Font** class in the "Creating Bold, Italic, Underlined, and Strikeout Text" topic in this chapter.)

Keep in mind that you can use labels as a borderless read-only text box, so formatting the text can be a very useful thing to do.

Aligning Text in Labels

As with text boxes, you can align text in labels. To do that, you just set the label's **TextAlign** property at design time or run time. This property takes values from the **ContentAlignment** enumeration:

- **BottomCenter**—Vertically aligned at the bottom, and horizontally aligned at the center.

- **BottomLeft**—Vertically aligned at the bottom, and horizontally aligned on the left.

- **BottomRight**—Vertically aligned at the bottom, and horizontally aligned on the right.

- **MiddleCenter**—Vertically aligned in the middle, and horizontally aligned at the center.

- **MiddleLeft**—Vertically aligned in the middle, and horizontally aligned on the left.

- **MiddleRight**—Vertically aligned in the middle, and horizontally aligned on the right.

- **TopCenter**—Vertically aligned at the top, and horizontally aligned at the center.

- **TopLeft**—Vertically aligned at the top, and horizontally aligned on the left.

- **TopRight**—Vertically aligned at the top, and horizontally aligned on the right.

For example, if you're writing a calculator program and have a column of right-justified text boxes above a label that displays a running sum, you can also right justify the label to match the controls above it.

Handling Label Events

Here's something that even experienced Visual Basic programmers often don't know—labels have events like **Click** and **DoubleClick** (although they don't have any keystroke-handling events). Using these events can be a good thing if you're using a label control as more than just a label; for example, to reset a setting of some kind. Here's an example using the **DoubleClick** event to change the text in the label when the user double-clicks it:

```
Private Sub Label1_DoubleClick(ByVal sender As Object, _
    ByVal e As System.EventArgs) Handles Label1.DoubleClick
    Label1.Text = "Quit clicking me!"
End Sub
```

Using Labels to Give Access Keys to Controls without Captions

The Testing Department is calling again: the old thorny issue of keyboard access has resurfaced. Theoretically, they say, users should be able to use your program, *SuperDuperDataCrunch*, with just the keyboard. Fine, you say; we can add access keys to all the button captions, so the user can give the button the focus just by pressing Alt and the access key (just like menu items). Don't forget to do the same to all the text boxes, the Testing Department says, and hangs up. You think: how do you give an access key to a *text box*?

This is where a useful aspect of labels comes in handy. In fact, this aspect of the label control is built just to handle this problem: you can give access keys to controls with **Text** properties that display caption text for the control (like buttons) just by placing an ampersand (&) in the caption in front of the letter you want to make the access key. The access key appears underlined and the corresponding control is given the focus if the user presses Alt and the access key—but how can you do that if a control (like a text box) uses the **Text** property to store user-editable text?

Here's the way you do it: you give the access key to a label control, and then make sure the control you want to give the focus to with that access key is next in the tab order (i.e., has the next highest **TabIndex** property value). Because labels cannot accept the focus themselves, this is a neat feature; when the user presses Alt and the access key, the label passes the focus on to the next control. In this way, you can give even controls like text boxes access keys.

NOTE: *When you use access keys, make sure you set the label's **UseMnemonic** property to **True** (the default), or the access key won't be enabled.*

Link Labels

We've discussed link labels in the In Depth section of this chapter—they are those labels that support hyperlinks (the **LinkLabel** class is derived from the **Label** class). Take a look at Table 5.12 to see the notable properties of the **LinkLabel** class, and Table 5.13 to see its notable events. These tables do not include all the notable properties, methods, and events this class inherits from the **Control** class—you'll find them in Tables 5.1, 5.2, and 5.3; nor do they include all the notable properties it inherits from the **Label** class—see Table 5.11 for those.

TIP: *Now you can even use a **RichTextBox** for Web-style links by setting the **DetectUrls** property to **True** and writing code to handle the **LinkClicked** event.*

Table 5.12   Noteworthy public properties of LinkLabel objects.

Property	Means
ActiveLinkColor	Sets/gets the color for an active link.
DisabledLinkColor	Sets/gets the color for a disabled link.
LinkArea	Sets/gets the range in the text to treat as a link.
LinkBehavior	Sets/gets a value that represents the behavior of a link.
LinkColor	Sets/gets the color for a normal link.
Links	Gets the collection of links in the **LinkLabel** control.
LinkVisited	Sets/gets a value specifying if a link should be displayed as though it had been visited.
VisitedLinkColor	Sets/gets the color used for links that that have been visited.

Table 5.13   Noteworthy public events of LinkLabel objects.

Event	Means
LinkClicked	Occurs when a link is clicked inside the link label.

Creating a **LinkLabel**

You can create a link label just as you'd create a label, by dragging one onto a Windows form and entering text into its **Text** property. The difference here is that you also can add hyperlinks; you do that by clicking the **LinkArea** property in the properties window and clicking the ellipsis ("...") button that appears to open the LinkArea editor you see in Figure 5.14. Select the area you want to make into a hyperlink there, and click OK. You can also set the **LinkColor**, **VisitedLinkColor**, and **ActiveLinkColor** properties to set the colors of the hyperlink.

When that hyperlink is clicked, the link label raises a **LinkClicked** event. In the example on the CD-ROM, LinkLabels, I want to navigate to the Coriolis Web site, **www.coriolis.com**, when the user clicks the hyperlink in our link label. I can do that in the **LinkClicked** event handler using the **System.Diagnostics.Process. Start** method (note that I also set the color of the hyperlink to the visited hyperlink color by setting the **LinkVisited** property to true):

```
Private Sub LinkLabel1_LinkClicked(ByVal sender As System.Object, _
    ByVal e As System.Windows.Forms.LinkLabelLinkClickedEventArgs) _
    Handles LinkLabel1.LinkClicked
    LinkLabel1.LinkVisited = True
    System.Diagnostics.Process.Start("www.coriolis.com")
End Sub
```

You can see the results in Figure 5.15—when the user clicks the hyperlink, their default browser will appear and navigate to **www.coriolis.com**.

In addition, you can create link labels in code, support multiple links in one link label control, and navigate to other forms as well as URLs. See the next few topics for more information.

Figure 5.14   The LinkArea editor.

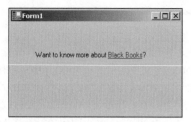

Figure 5.15   A Link Label.

Creating a **LinkLabel** in Code

I'll create a link label in code with multiple hyperlinks in it in this and the following two topics. You can see this in the CreateLinkLabel example on the CD-ROM; to create this example, I've added a button, **Button1**, to a form with the text "Create LinkLabel". When the user clicks that button, I create a new link label control, giving it the text "Interested in Black Books? Click here to see them all!" (note that I must declare the new link label **LinkLabel1** with the **WithEvents** keyword to indicate to Visual Basic that I want to let this object handle events):

```
Private WithEvents LinkLabel1 As LinkLabel

Private Sub Button1_Click(ByVal sender As System.Object, _
    ByVal e As System.EventArgs) Handles Button1.Click
    LinkLabel1 = New LinkLabel()
    LinkLabel1.AutoSize = True
    LinkLabel1.Location = New Point(15, 15)
    LinkLabel1.Size = New Size(135, 15)
    LinkLabel1.Text = _
        "Interested in Black Books? Click here to see them all!"
        .
        .
        .
```

The hyperlinks in the new link label control are stored in its **Links** collection, and I can use the **Add** method to add new hyperlinks. You pass this method the start location for the hyperlink in the control's text, the length of the link text, and some text to associate with the hyperlink. I can add two hyperlinks to this control, connecting them to the text "Black Books" and "here":

```
Private WithEvents LinkLabel1 As LinkLabel
```

```
Private Sub Button1_Click(ByVal sender As System.Object, _
    ByVal e As System.EventArgs) Handles Button1.Click
    LinkLabel1 = New LinkLabel()
    LinkLabel1.AutoSize = True
    LinkLabel1.Location = New Point(15, 15)
    LinkLabel1.Size = New Size(135, 15)
    LinkLabel1.Text = _
        "Interested in Black Books? Click here to see them all!"

    LinkLabel1.Links.Add(14, 11, "info")
    LinkLabel1.Links.Add(33, 4, "www.coriolis.com")
        .
        .
        .
```

We'll also need to connect an event handler to the new link label. I will connect an event handler named **LinkLabel1_LinkClicked** to the link label's **LinkClicked** event using the **AddHandler** method and the **AddressOf** operator (which returns the address the **LinkLabel1_LinkClicked** Sub procedure in this case), and then add the link label to the form's **Controls** collection to display it:

```
Private WithEvents LinkLabel1 As LinkLabel

Private Sub Button1_Click(ByVal sender As System.Object, _
    ByVal e As System.EventArgs) Handles Button1.Click
    LinkLabel1 = New LinkLabel()
    LinkLabel1.AutoSize = True
    LinkLabel1.Location = New Point(15, 15)
    LinkLabel1.Size = New Size(135, 15)
    LinkLabel1.Text = _
        "Interested in Black Books? Click here to see them all!"

    LinkLabel1.Links.Add(14, 11, "info")
    LinkLabel1.Links.Add(33, 4, "www.coriolis.com")

    AddHandler LinkLabel1.LinkClicked, AddressOf Me.LinkLabel1_LinkClicked
    Me.Controls.Add(LinkLabel1)
End Sub

Private Sub LinkLabel1_LinkClicked(ByVal sender As Object, _
    ByVal e As System.Windows.Forms.LinkLabelLinkClickedEventArgs)
        .
        .
        .

End Sub
```

The actual hyperlink is passed to us in the **LinkLabel1_LinkClicked** event handler's **e** argument as **e.Link**. I can set its **Visited** property to **True** to set its color to the color in the **VisitedLinkColor** property, like this:

```
Private Sub LinkLabel1_LinkClicked(ByVal sender As Object, _
    ByVal e As System.Windows.Forms.LinkLabelLinkClickedEventArgs)
    LinkLabel1.Links(LinkLabel1.Links.IndexOf(e.Link)).Visited = True
        .
        .
        .

End Sub
```

When you run this program and click the Create LinkLabel button, you'll see the link label with two hyperlinks in it, as in Figure 5.16.

This is fine as far as it goes, but nothing happens when you click the links. To make them active, see the following two topics.

Related solution:	*Found on page:*
Adding and Removing Controls at Run Time	196

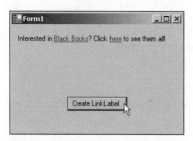

Figure 5.16   Creating a link label in code.

Linking to Another Form

When the user clicks the "Black Books" link in the CreateLinkLabel example on the CD-ROM from the previous topic, I'll have the code bring up a new form with the explanatory text "Black Books are designed to meet all your computing needs." How do we determine which link in the link label the user clicked? We can get the text associated with the link with the **e.Link.LinkData.ToString** method like this, displaying a new form if warranted:

```
Private Sub LinkLabel1_LinkClicked(ByVal sender As Object, _
    ByVal e As System.Windows.Forms.LinkLabelLinkClickedEventArgs)
    LinkLabel1.Links(LinkLabel1.Links.IndexOf(e.Link)).Visited = True
```

```
    If (e.Link.LinkData.ToString() = "info") Then
        Dim InfoWindow As New Form2()
        InfoWindow.Show()
    End If
End Sub
```

You can see this new link at work in Figure 5.17.

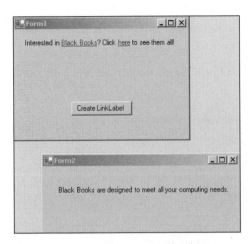

Figure 5.17   Linking to another form.

Linking to the Web

In the previous topic, we linked to a form in the CreateLinkLabel example on the CD-ROM; in this topic, I'll add support for the other hyperlink in that example, which links to **www.coriolis.com**. You can recover the text "www.coriolis.com" from the clicked hyperlink with the **e.Link.LinkData.ToString** method, so you open the user's default browser and navigate to that URL this way:

```
Private Sub LinkLabel1_LinkClicked(ByVal sender As Object, _
    ByVal e As System.Windows.Forms.LinkLabelLinkClickedEventArgs)
    LinkLabel1.Links(LinkLabel1.Links.IndexOf(e.Link)).Visited = True
    If (e.Link.LinkData.ToString() = "info") Then
        Dim InfoWindow As New Form2()
        InfoWindow.Show()
    Else
        System.Diagnostics.Process.Start(e.Link.LinkData.ToString())
    End If
End Sub
```

Now when the user clicks the "here" hyperlink you see in Figure 5.17, the user's default browser opens and navigates to the Coriolis Web site.

Chapter 6

Windows Forms: Buttons, Checkboxes, Radio Buttons, Panels, and Group Boxes

(continued)

In Depth

In this chapter, we're going to look at what are arguably the most popular controls in Visual Basic: buttons. This includes buttons, checkboxes, and radio buttons. I'll also take a look at two grouping controls—panels and group controls. You use panels and group controls to enclose other controls, and that's particularly important with controls such as radio buttons, which operate in groups. I'll start with an overview of buttons.

Buttons

There is no more popular control in Visual Basic than buttons, with the possible exception of text boxes. Buttons are the plain controls that you simply click and release, the buttons you see everywhere in Visual Basic applications—usually just rounded rectangular, gray buttons with a caption, as you see in the Buttons example on the CD-ROM and which you will see at work in Figure 6.1.

Buttons provide the most popular way of creating and handling an event in your code—every Visual Basic programmer is familiar with the button **Click** event. Buttons can be clicked with the mouse or with the Enter key if the button has the focus.

Besides using buttons in forms directly, they're very popular in dialog boxes. As we've seen in Chapter 4, you can set the **AcceptButton** or **CancelButton** property of a form to let users click a button by pressing the Enter or Esc keys—even if the button does not have focus. And when you display a form using the **ShowDialog** method, you can use the **DialogResult** property of a button to specify the return value of **ShowDialog**.

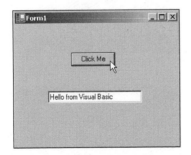

Figure 6.1   A button at work.

You also can change the button's appearance, giving it an image or aligning text and images in it as you like. You can evem-make it look flat for a "Web" look, setting the **FlatStyle** property to **FlatStyle.Flat**. Or, you can set the **FlatStyle** property to **FlatStyle.Popup**, which means it looks flat until the mouse pointer passes over it, when the button pops up to give it the standard Windows button appearance.

Checkboxes

Checkboxes are also familiar controls—you click a checkbox to select it, and click it again to deselect it. When you select a checkbox, a check appears in it, indicating that the box is indeed selected. You use a checkbox to give the user an option, such as true/false or yes/no. The checkbox control can display an image or text or both. You can see some checkboxes at work in Figure 6.2 and in the CheckBoxes example on the CD-ROM.

You can use the **Appearance** property to specify if the checkbox appears as a typical checkbox or as a button. And the **FlatStyle** property determines the style and appearance of the control. If the **FlatStyle** property is set to **FlatStyle.System**, the user's operating system sets the appearance of the control.

Also, the **ThreeState** property determines whether the control supports two or three states. For standard checkboxes, you use the **Checked** property to get or set the value of a checkbox control, but for three-state checkboxes, which support an "indeterminate" state, you use the **CheckState** property. The indeterminate state is sort of a middle state between checked and unchecked. For example, if you use a checkbox to specify that selected text in a text control of some type should be in italics, but have selected text that is partly normal and partly italic text, the checkbox can show the indeterminate state—in which a checkbox appears on a gray background—to show that neither the checked nor the unchecked states fully apply.

Figure 6.2   A checkbox at work.

Radio Buttons

Radio buttons, also called option buttons, are similar to checkboxes—the user can select and deselect them—except for two things: they are round where checkboxes are square, and you usually use radio buttons together in groups.

In fact, that's the functional difference between checkboxes and radio buttons—checkboxes can work independently, but radio buttons are intended to work in groups. When you select one radio button in a group, the others are automatically deselected. For example, although you might use checkboxes to select trimmings on a sandwich (of which there can be more than one), you would use radio buttons to let the user select one of a set of exclusive options, such as the current day of the week. You can see radio buttons at work in Figure 6.3 and in the RadioButtons example on the CD-ROM.

When the user selects one radio button in a group, the others clear automatically. All radio buttons in a given container, such as a form, make up a group. To create multiple groups on one form, you place each additional group in its own container, such as a group box or panel control.

Like checkboxes, you use the **Checked** property to get or set the state of a radio button. Radio buttons can display text, an image, or both. Also, a radio button's appearance may be altered to appear as a toggle-style button or as a standard radio button by setting the **Appearance** property.

Panels

You use panels to group other controls, usually to divide a form into regions by function. For example, you may have a menu form that lets the user select drinks in one panel and what they want on their sandwich in another.

You can use grouping controls such as panels and group controls to make it clear which controls are associated—and it makes it easier to handle groups of controls at

Figure 6.3   A radio button at work.

Figure 6.4   Panels at work.

design time too, because when you move a panel, all the controls it contains are moved as well. You can see a panel at work in Figure 6.4 and in the Panels example on the CD-ROM; here, I've set the panel's **BorderStyle** to **Fixed3D.** (By default, panels do not have borders; you can set **BorderStyle** to **None**, **FixedSingle**, or **Fixed3D**.) As you can see, the radio buttons groups in that figure can operate independently.

The **Panel** control is similar to the **GroupBox** control; however, only the **Panel** control can have scroll bars, and only the **GroupBox** control displays a caption. To display scroll bars, you set the **AutoScroll** property to **True**. Besides using the **BorderStyle** property to customize a panel, you also can use the **BackColor** and **BackgroundImage** properties.

Group Boxes

Like panels, group boxes are used to provide a grouping for other controls. Group boxes are similar to panels, but, as mentioned above, only group boxes display captions and only the panels can have scroll bars. Group boxes display frames around their contained controls and can display text in a caption, as you see in Figure 6.5, which shows the GroupBox example from the CD-ROM. You set the group box's caption with the **Text** property.

Figure 6.5   Group boxes at work.

The usual use for group boxes is to contain radio buttons, as you see in Figure 6.5. As with panel controls, when you group radio buttons using group boxes, each set of radio buttons can function independently, which means that one radio button in each set may be selected.

And that's enough overview—it's time to start putting these controls to work and addressing the finer points of each in the Immediate Solutions section.

Immediate Solutions

All About Buttons

Everyone who uses Windows knows about buttons. I presented an overview of buttons in the In Depth section of this chapter—now for more of the individual details. Like other Windows controls, the **Button** class is based on the **Control** class. In fact, the **Button** class is based directly on the **ButtonBase** class, which is also the base class for other types of buttons; here's the class hierarchy for **Button**:

```
Object
    MarshalByRefObject
        Component
            Control
                ButtonBase
                    Button
```

You can find the more notable public properties of the **Button** class in Table 6.1 and the more notable methods in Table 6.2, including those inherited from the **ButtonBase** class. Note that as with other Windows controls, I am not listing the notable properties, methods, and events **Button** inherits from the **Control** class, such as the **Click** event—you can see all that in Chapter 5, Tables 5.1, 5.2, and 5.3.

Table 6.1   Noteworthy public properties of Button objects.

Property	Means
DialogResult	Gets/sets the value returned to the parent form when the button is clicked. Often used when you're creating dialog boxes.
FlatStyle	Gets/sets a flat style appearance.
Image	Gets/sets an image displayed in a button.
ImageAlign	Gets/sets the alignment of the image in a button.
ImageIndex	Gets/sets the image list index value of the image displayed in the button.
ImageList	Gets/sets the **ImageList** that contains the images displayed in a button.
TextAlign	Gets/sets the alignment of the text in the button.

Table 6.2   Noteworthy public methods of Button objects.

Method	Means
PerformClick	Causes a **Click** event for a button.

Setting a Button's Caption

You use a button's **Text** property (formerly the **Caption** property in VB6 and before) to set its caption. This property is available at both design time and run time. After you add a button to a form, you set its caption by placing the appropriate text in the **Text** property in the properties window:

```
Private Sub Button1_Click(ByVal sender As System.Object, _
    ByVal e As System.EventArgs) Handles Button1.Click
    Button1.Text = "You clicked me!"
End Sub
```

TIP: *It's useful to be able to change the caption of buttons. For example, if a button's caption reads "Connect to Internet", then, when connected, you could change the button's caption to "Disconnect from Internet", and disconnect from the Internet when the button is clicked.*

Setting a Button's Foreground and Background Color

You've got your program running at last—but now the Aesthetic Design department is on the phone. The "emergency" window in your program is colored red—why not also the PANIC button in the middle of that window? So how do you do that?

You use the button's **Background** property. Here, I'm setting the background color of a button at design time, and three sets of colors are available: a set of standard Visual Basic System colors, Web colors, and a palette of custom colors, as shown in Figure 6.6.

You also can set the button's **Background** property at run time, setting it to a color value, such as those in the Visual Basic **Color** enumeration. Here, I'm setting a button's background to blue:

```
Private Sub Button1_Click(ByVal sender As System.Object, _
    ByVal e As System.EventArgs) Handles Button1.Click
    Button1.BackColor = Color.Blue
End Sub
```

6. Windows Forms: Buttons, Checkboxes, Radio Buttons, Panels...

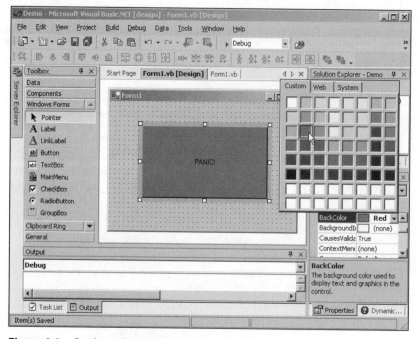

Figure 6.6   Setting a button's background color.

You can also set the foreground color of a button—the color of the caption's text. Much like the **BackColor** property, you can set a button's **ForeColor** property at design time, or at run time, like this:

```
Private Sub Button1_Click(ByVal sender As System.Object, _
    ByVal e As System.EventArgs) Handles Button1.Click
    Button1.ForeColor = Color.Red
End Sub
```

Setting Button Fonts

You've written an adventure-type game for your grandfather, but he's emailed to let you know he can't read the "tiny text" in the buttons; he likes to run his screen in super high resolution mode. Can you fix that?

Yes you can—all you have to do is to make the font size in the buttons' captions larger. To do that, you use the button's **Font** property. Selecting the **Font** item in the property window and then clicking the ellipsis ("...") button that appears opens the Font dialog shown in Figure 6.7. As that figure shows, you can see all kinds of fonts and settings for buttons' captions, and the Microsoft Sans Serif font goes up to 72 points, which should be big enough for grandfather.

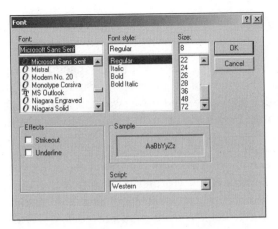

Figure 6.7   Selecting a font for a button.

You also can set the **Font** property of a button at run time. Here's an example, where I'm changing a button's caption to italic to give it a little more emphasis. First, I recover the current **Font** object in the button, then I use the **Font** class's constructor to base a new font on that original font, but making the new font italic:

```
Private Sub Button1_Click(ByVal sender As System.Object, _
    ByVal e As System.EventArgs) Handles Button1.Click
    Button1.Font = New Font(Button1.Font, FontStyle.Italic)
End Sub
```

Handling Button Clicks

We've covered this topic before, as far back as Chapter 1, but for completeness, I'll include it again here; you respond to button clicks with the button's **Click** event. To add a click event handler, just double-click the button at design time, adding a Sub procedure such as this one to your code:

```
Private Sub Button1_Click(ByVal sender As System.Object, _
    ByVal e As System.EventArgs) Handles Button1.Click


End Sub
```

Place the code you want to execute when the button is clicked in this Sub procedure; this code is from the Buttons example on the CD-ROM:

```
Private Sub Button1_Click(ByVal sender As System.Object, _
    ByVal e As System.EventArgs) Handles Button1.Click
```

```
        TextBox1.Text = "Hello from Visual Basic"
End Sub
```

Here, the **sender** argument is the button object itself that caused the event, and the **e** argument is a simple **EventArgs** object that doesn't contain any additional useful information, such as where the button was clicked. (For that kind of information, see the **MouseDown** event in "Handling Mouse Events" in Chapter 4.)

All types of buttons have a **Click** event—they wouldn't be much use otherwise—as well as a double-click event, **DoubleClick** (formerly **DblClick** in VB6 and before). Note that if you double-click a checkbox, you select and then deselect it (or deselect and then select it), so you're back to where you started. If you double-click a radio button, however, you select it, no matter what its original state, and cause a **DoubleClick** event.

Related solution:	*Found on page:*
Handling Mouse Events	199

Imitating Control Arrays

You've decided that your new game program really does need 144 buttons in the main form, arranged in a grid of 12×12. But what a pain it is to write 144 subroutines to handle the click event for each of them! Isn't there a better way?

There used to be. In VB6 and before, you could use a *control array* and one event-handler function. The control array index of the button that was clicked was passed to the event handler, so you could tell which button you needed to respond to. To create a control array, you just gave two controls of the same type the same name (in the **Name** property); when you did, Visual Basic would ask if you wanted to create a control array.

Control arrays don't exist in Visual Basic .NET—at least, they're not built in anymore. However, you can still create something very like a control array yourself, in code. The main feature of control arrays is that all the controls in it share the same event handler, and you can use the **AddHandler** method to assign the same event handler to multiple controls.

Here's an example, named ControlArray on the CD-ROM. In this example, I'll create three buttons in code and give them all the same click event handler, **Button_Click**. Because the actual button that caused the event is passed to the event handler, we can determine which button was clicked. Note that although I'm creating the buttons in code here, you do not need to create them at run time—you can create them at design time and use **AddHandler** at run time to connect them into a control array.

I start by declaring the new buttons we'll use, **Button1**, **Button2**, and **Button3**. To create the control array in the ControlArray example, do the following (note that I use the **WithEvents** keyword to indicate that these objects will handle events):

```
Public Class Form1
    Inherits System.Windows.Forms.Form
    Dim WithEvents Button1 As Button
    Dim WithEvents Button2 As Button
    Dim WithEvents Button3 As Button
        .
        .
        .
```

And I add another button to **Form1** at design time, which I call **Button4** and give the caption "Create control array". When the user clicks this button, I create the new button objects, set their sizes and locations, and add them to the form's **Controls** collection to add them to the form (see "Adding and Removing Controls at Run Time" in Chapter 4 for more information):

```
Private Sub Button4_Click(ByVal sender As System.Object, _
    ByVal e As System.EventArgs) Handles Button4.Click
    Button1 = New Button()
    Button2 = New Button()
    Button3 = New Button()

    Button1.Size = New Size(80, 30)
    Button1.Location = New Point(115, 20)
    Button1.Text = "Button 1"

    Button2.Size = New Size(80, 30)
    Button2.Location = New Point(115, 60)
    Button2.Text = "Button 2"

    Button3.Size = New Size(80, 30)
    Button3.Location = New Point(115, 100)
    Button3.Text = "Button 3"

    Controls.Add(Button1)
    Controls.Add(Button2)
    Controls.Add(Button3)
```

6. Windows Forms: Buttons, Checkboxes, Radio Buttons, Panels...

```
        .
        .
        .
    End Sub
```

To imitate a control array with the three new buttons, I use **AddHandler** to connect the same event handler, **Button_Click**, to all three button's **Click** events. To connect that event handler, you need to pass its memory address using the **AddressOf** operator to **AddHandler**:

```
Private Sub Button4_Click(ByVal sender As System.Object, _
    ByVal e As System.EventArgs) Handles Button4.Click
    Button1 = New Button()
    Button2 = New Button()
    Button3 = New Button()
    .

    .

    .

    AddHandler Button1.Click, AddressOf Button_Click
    AddHandler Button2.Click, AddressOf Button_Click
    AddHandler Button3.Click, AddressOf Button_Click
End Sub
```

Now in **Button_Click**, I can determine which button was clicked and display a corresponding message in a text box, **TextBox1**:

```
Private Sub Button_Click(ByVal sender As System.Object, _
    ByVal e As System.EventArgs)
    If sender Is Button1 Then
        TextBox1.Text = "You clicked button 1"
    End If
    If sender Is Button2 Then
        TextBox1.Text = "You clicked button 2"
    End If
    If sender Is Button3 Then
        TextBox1.Text = "You clicked button 3"
    End If
End Sub
```

And that's it—now all three buttons share the same event handler, just as they would have in a control array in earlier versions of Visual Basic. Here's the whole code:

```
Public Class Form1
    Inherits System.Windows.Forms.Form
    Dim WithEvents Button1 As Button
    Dim WithEvents Button2 As Button
```

```
Dim WithEvents Button3 As Button
Friend WithEvents Button4 As Button
Friend WithEvents TextBox1 As TextBox

'Windows Form Designer generated code

Private Sub Button4_Click(ByVal sender As System.Object, _
    ByVal e As System.EventArgs) Handles Button4.Click
    Button1 = New Button()
    Button2 = New Button()
    Button3 = New Button()

    Button1.Size = New Size(80, 30)
    Button1.Location = New Point(115, 20)
    Button1.Text = "Button 1"

    Button2.Size = New Size(80, 30)
    Button2.Location = New Point(115, 60)
    Button2.Text = "Button 2"

    Button3.Size = New Size(80, 30)
    Button3.Location = New Point(115, 100)
    Button3.Text = "Button 3"

    Controls.Add(Button1)
    Controls.Add(Button2)
    Controls.Add(Button3)

    AddHandler Button1.Click, AddressOf Button_Click
    AddHandler Button2.Click, AddressOf Button_Click
    AddHandler Button3.Click, AddressOf Button_Click
End Sub

Private Sub Button_Click(ByVal sender As System.Object, _
    ByVal e As System.EventArgs)
    If sender Is Button1 Then
        TextBox1.Text = "You clicked button 1"
    End If
    If sender Is Button2 Then
        TextBox1.Text = "You clicked button 2"
    End If
    If sender Is Button3 Then
        TextBox1.Text = "You clicked button 3"
    End If
End Sub

End Class
```

6. Windows Forms: Buttons, Checkboxes, Radio Buttons, Panels…

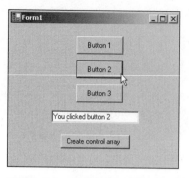

Figure 6.8   Creating a control array.

You can see the results in Figure 6.8—when you click the "Create control array" button, the three top buttons appear. Clicking one of those buttons displays a message in the text box indicating which button was clicked.

Related solution:	Found on page:
Adding and Removing Controls at Run Time	196

Resetting the Focus after a Button Click

When you click a button, the input focus is transferred to the button—and in some cases, you don't want that to happen. For example, say you've got a word processor program based on a rich text control, and that you have a button labeled "Search" in the program. When the user clicks the button, they can search for target text in the rich text box using that box's **Find** method, but the focus remains on the button the user clicked. When the user starts typing again, nothing appears in the rich text control, because the focus is still on the button. So how do you transfer the focus back to the rich text box?

You do that with the control's **Focus** method, and that's something you frequently do in real programs after button clicks. This is how it might look in code:

```
Private Sub Button1_Click(ByVal sender As System.Object, _
    ByVal e As System.EventArgs) Handles Button1.Click
    RichTextBox1.Find("Visual Basic")
    RichTextBox1.Focus()
End Sub
```

Now, when the user clicks the button and starts typing again, the focus will be back on the rich text box, as it should be.

Giving Buttons and Other Controls Access Characters

The Testing Department is on the phone again. Everyone loves your new program, *SuperDuperTextPro*, but as usual, there are "one or two little things." And, as usual, one of those things is *keyboard access*. Ideally, they say, the user should be able to use programs entirely from the keyboard, without the mouse at all. Well, you say, the button's tab order was set correctly (see the next topic). But, they say, what about giving your buttons *access characters*?

Can you do that? You know you can give menu items access characters—those underlined characters in a menu item that the user can reach with the Alt key. For example, if the File menu's access character is F, the user can open that menu by pressing Alt+F. Can you add access characters to buttons?

Yes you can; just place an ampersand (&) in front of the character in the button's caption. For example, placing & in front of the word Me in Click Me (i.e., Click &Me), makes M the access character for that button. (Be sure that the access character you choose is unique among all the access characters available at one time.)

Setting Button Tab Order

To make your buttons more accessible from the keyboard—especially if you've got a lot of them—you can use the **TabStop** and **TabIndex** properties. Here's what those properties do:

- **TabStop** indicates if this button can accept the focus when the user tabs to it.

- **TabIndex** is the index of the current button in the tab order (starts at 0).

When the user presses the Tab key, the focus moves from button to button, ascending through the tab order.

Disabling Buttons

Another problem from the Testing Department concerning your program, *SuperDuperTextPro*. It seems the users are sometimes clicking your "Connect to the Internet" button twice by mistake, confusing the program and causing crashes. Can you stop that from happening?

Yes, you can—you can disable the button by setting its **Enabled** property to **False** when it's inappropriate to use that button. For example, we've disabled all the buttons in Figure 6.9. When a button is disabled, it is inaccessible to the user (and it can't accept the focus).

You also can disable buttons at run time, of course, like this:

```
Private Sub Button1_Click(ByVal sender As System.Object, _
    ByVal e As System.EventArgs) Handles Button1.Click
    Button1.Enabled = False
End Sub
```

Figure 6.9   Disabling buttons in a form.

Showing and Hiding Buttons

In the last topic, we saw that we can disable buttons using the **Enabled** property. However, it's an inefficient use of space (and frustrating to the user) to display a lot of disabled buttons. If you have to disable several buttons, you should hide them.

To make a button disappear, just set its **Visible** property to **False**. To make it reappear, set the **Visible** property to **True**. You can set this property at either design time or run time. Here's how to make a button disappear when you click it (and probably startle the user):

```
Private Sub Button1_Click(ByVal sender As System.Object, _
    ByVal e As System.EventArgs) Handles Button1.Click
    Button1.Visible = False
End Sub
```

You can also use the **Control** class's **Show** and **Hide** methods to show and hide buttons.

TIP: *If your program shows and hides buttons, you can rearrange the visible buttons to hide any gaps using the buttons' **SetBounds** method.*

Resizing and Moving Buttons from Code

Your new April fool's program has an Exit button, but it moves around and resizes itself, making it a moving target for the user to try to hit. Your co-workers think it's hilarious, and they love it. Your boss hates it and asks to see you to discuss time management—immediately.

In Visual Basic 6.0 and earlier, you could use the **Move** method to move forms and controls (and optionally set their dimensions), and the **Height** and **Width** methods to set their dimensions. In VB .NET, you use the **SetBounds** method to move forms and controls (and optionally set their dimensions), and the **Size** and **Location** properties to set their dimensions.

You set the **Size** property to a new **Size** object, and the **Location** property to a new **Point** object. The dimensions you set in **Size** and **Point** objects are measured in pixels, as are all measurements in Visual Basic, and you create these objects by passing x and y dimensions to their class's constructors like this: **Size(x_dimension, y_dimension)** and **Point(x_location, y_location)**. Note that in the Visual Basic screen coordinate system, the upper left of the screen is the origin (0, 0) and that positive x values increase downward, and positive y values increase to the right.

Here's an example: Say that you wanted to change the size and location of a button in the form when the user clicks that button. You can do that like this (the origin of coordinates for the form is the upper left of the screen, and the origin for the button contained in the form is the upper left of the form's client area):

```
Private Sub Button1_Click(ByVal sender As System.Object, ByVal e As
System.EventArgs) Handles Button1.Click
        Button1.Size = New Size(100, 50)
        Button1.Location = New Point(0, 0)
End Sub
```

You also can use the **SetBounds** method to do the same thing; this method is overloaded and has several forms—here's a popular one:

```
Overloads Public Sub SetBounds(ByVal x As Integer, ByVal y As Integer, _
    ByVal width As Integer, ByVal height As Integer)
```

Here are the arguments you pass to **SetBounds**:

- *x*—The new **Left** property value of the control.
- *y*—The new **Right** property value of the control.
- *width*—The new **Width** property value of the control.
- *height*—The new **Height** property value of the control.

Adding a Picture to a Button

The Style department is calling again—how about souping up your program's user interface by adding a few images? But all you've got in your program are buttons, you say. No problem, they say, add images to them.

You can display images in buttons, as in the ImageButtons example on the CD-ROM. You can add images to buttons at design time and at run time. At design time, you only need to set the **Image** property in the Properties window to an image file. At run time, you can do the same thing if you use the **Image** class's **FromFile** class method and assign the resulting **Image** object to the button's **Image** property. In the ImageButtons example, I load a new image into a button when that button is clicked, and I use the **ImageAlign** property to set the alignment of the image, as well as setting the button's **FlatStyle** property to **FlatStyle.Flat** to make it appear flat:

```
Private Sub Button1_Click(ByVal sender As System.Object, _
    ByVal e As System.EventArgs) Handles Button1.Click
    Button1.Image = _
        Image.FromFile("C:\vbnet\ch06\imagebuttons\clicked.jpg")
    Button1.ImageAlign = ContentAlignment.TopLeft
    Button1.Text = ""
    Button1.FlatStyle = FlatStyle.Flat
    TextBox1.Text = "You clicked the button"
End Sub
```

You can see the results in Figure 6.10. When the program starts, it displays the image I loaded into it at design time, button.jpg (which is included in the ImageButtons folder on the CD-ROM).

Figure 6.10   Using an image in a button.

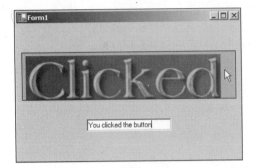

Figure 6.11   Setting an image in a button from code.

When you click the button in this example, the code above executes and the new image, clicked.jpg, appears in the button, as you see in Figure 6.11.

TIP: *In VB6 and earlier, you could use a number of image properties such as **DisabledImage** and **DownImage** to add images for various button states. In VB .NET, you do that yourself, although you can attach an **ImageList** control to a button and select the image in that control for display with the **ImageIndex** property.*

Adding Buttons at Run Time

Your new program lets the user add options to customize things, and you want to display a new button for each option. Is there a way to add buttons to a Visual Basic program at run time?

Yes, there is. In fact, we've already seen how to do that earlier in this chapter, in the topic "Imitating Control Arrays." We declared new buttons there and added them to an imitation control array. There, all the buttons used the same event handler, but we can modify that code so each new button has its own event handler, like this:

```
Public Class Form1
    Inherits System.Windows.Forms.Form
    Dim WithEvents Button1 As Button
    Dim WithEvents Button2 As Button
    Dim WithEvents Button3 As Button
    Friend WithEvents Button4 As Button
    Friend WithEvents TextBox1 As TextBox

    'Windows Form Designer generated code

    Private Sub Button4_Click(ByVal sender As System.Object, _
        ByVal e As System.EventArgs) Handles Button4.Click
        Button1 = New Button()
        Button2 = New Button()
        Button3 = New Button()

        Button1.Size = New Size(80, 30)
        Button1.Location = New Point(115, 20)
        Button1.Text = "Button 1"

        Button2.Size = New Size(80, 30)
        Button2.Location = New Point(115, 60)
        Button2.Text = "Button 2"

        Button3.Size = New Size(80, 30)
        Button3.Location = New Point(115, 100)
        Button3.Text = "Button 3"

        Controls.Add(Button1)
        Controls.Add(Button2)
        Controls.Add(Button3)

        AddHandler Button1.Click, AddressOf Button1_Click
        AddHandler Button2.Click, AddressOf Button2_Click
        AddHandler Button3.Click, AddressOf Button3_Click
    End Sub

    Private Sub Button1_Click(ByVal sender As System.Object, _
        ByVal e As System.EventArgs)
        TextBox1.Text = "You clicked button 1"
    End Sub
```

```
   Private Sub Button2_Click(ByVal sender As System.Object, _
       ByVal e As System.EventArgs)
       TextBox1.Text = "You clicked button 2"
   End Sub


   Private Sub Button3_Click(ByVal sender As System.Object, _
       ByVal e As System.EventArgs)
       TextBox1.Text = "You clicked button 3"
   End Sub

End Class
```

That's all it takes.

Passing Buttons to Procedures

You've got 200 buttons in your new program, and each one has to be initialized with a long series of code statements. Is there some easy way to organize this process? There is—you can pass the buttons to a procedure, and place the initialization code in that procedure.

Here's an example—we can set a button's caption by passing it to a Sub procedure named **SetCaption** like this:

```
Private Sub Button1_Click(ByVal sender As System.Object, _
    ByVal e As System.EventArgs) Handles Button1.Click
    SetCaption(Button1)
End Sub
```

In the **SetCaption** Sub procedure, I pass the button as an object of class **Button**, and I pass it by reference; passing it by reference makes it explicit that I want to be able to change the **Button** object:

```
Private Sub Button1_Click(ByVal sender As System.Object, _
    ByVal e As System.EventArgs) Handles Button1.Click
    SetCaption(Button1)
End Sub

Private Sub SetCaption(ByRef TargetButton As Button)
    .
    .
    .
End Sub
```

And in the **SetCaption** Sub procedure, I can change the **Text** property of the button, like this:

```
Private Sub Button1_Click(ByVal sender As System.Object, _
    ByVal e As System.EventArgs) Handles Button1.Click
    SetCaption(Button1)
End Sub

Private Sub SetCaption(ByRef TargetButton As Button)
    TargetButton.Text = "I've been clicked"
End Sub
```

The result appears in Figure 6.12; when you click the command button, the **SetCaption** Sub procedure changes its caption, as you see in that figure.

Figure 6.12   Passing a button to a procedure to change its caption.

Handling Button Releases

You can tell when a button has been pushed using its **Click** event, but can you tell when it's been released? Yes, by using the **MouseUp** event. In fact, buttons support the **MouseDown**, **MouseMove**, **MouseUp**, **KeyDown**, **KeyPress**, and **KeyUp** events.

To determine when a button has been released, you can just use its **MouseUp** event this way:

```
Private Sub Button1_MouseUp(ByVal sender As Object, _
    ByVal e As System.Windows.Forms.MouseEventArgs) _
    Handles Button1.MouseUp
    TextBox1.Text = "The button went up."
End Sub
```

This can be useful if you want the user to complete some action that has two parts. For example, you can use **MouseDown** to start a setting of some kind changing in real time—giving the user interactive visual feedback, and **MouseUp** to freeze the setting when the user releases the button.

Using the **Checkbox** Class

We've discussed checkboxes in the In Depth section of this chapter; they're based on the **CheckBox** class, which has this class hierarchy:

```
Object
   MarshalByRefObject
      Component
         Control
            ButtonBase
               CheckBox
```

You can find the more notable public properties of the **CheckBox** class in Table 6.3 and the more notable events in Table 6.4, including those inherited from the **ButtonBase** class. Note that as with other controls, I am not listing the notable properties, methods, and events **CheckBox** inherits from the **Control** class, such as the **Click** event—you can see all that in Tables 5.1, 5.2, and 5.3 in Chapter 5.

Table 6.3 Noteworthy public properties of **Checkbox** objects.

Property	Means
Appearance	Gets/sets the appearance of a checkbox.
AutoCheck	Specifies if the **Checked** or **CheckState** values and the checkbox's appearance are automatically changed when the checkbox is clicked.
CheckAlign	Gets/sets the horizontal and vertical alignment of a checkbox in a checkbox control.
Checked	Gets/sets a value indicating if the checkbox is in the checked state.
CheckState	Gets/sets the state of a three-state checkbox.
FlatStyle	Gets/sets the flat style appearance of the checkbox.
Image	Gets/sets the image that is displayed in a checkbox.
ImageAlign	Gets/sets the alignment of the image on the checkbox.
ImageIndex	Gets/sets the image list index value of the image displayed in the checkbox.
ImageList	Gets/sets the **ImageList** that contains the image displayed in a checkbox.
ThreeState	Specifies if the checkbox will allow three check states rather than two.

Table 6.4 Noteworthy public events of **Checkbox** objects.

Event	Means
AppearanceChanged	Occurs when the **Appearance** property changes.
CheckedChanged	Occurs when the **Checked** property changes.
CheckStateChanged	Occurs when the **CheckState** property changes.

Creating Checkboxes

We've already seen how to create checkboxes in the In Depth section of this chapter. You can handle checkbox **CheckChanged** events, which happen when the **Checked** property changes; here's some code from the CheckBoxes example on the CD-ROM:

```
Private Sub CheckBox1_CheckedChanged(ByVal sender As System.Object, _
    ByVal e As System.EventArgs) Handles CheckBox1.CheckedChanged
    TextBox1.Text = "You clicked check box 1"
End Sub
```

You can see the results of this code in Figure 6.2.

Getting a Checkbox's State

You've added all the checkboxes you need to your new program, *WinBigSuperCasino*, and you've connected those checkboxes to **Click** event handlers. But now there's a problem—when the user sets the current amount of money they want to bet, you need to check if they've exceeded the limit they've set for themselves. But they set their limit by clicking other checkboxes—how can you determine which one they've checked?

You can see if a checkbox is checked by examining its **Checked** property. This property can be set to either **True** or **False**. Here's an example; in this case, I will change a button's caption if a checkbox, **CheckBox1**, is checked, but not otherwise:

```
Private Sub Button1_Click(ByVal sender As System.Object, _
    ByVal e As System.EventArgs) Handles Button1.Click
    If CheckBox1.Checked Then
        Button1.Text = "The check mark is checked"
    End If
End Sub
```

Setting a Checkbox's State

Your new program, *SuperSandwichesToGoRightNow*, is just about ready, but there's one hitch. You use checkboxes to indicate what items are in a sandwich (Cheese, Lettuce, Tomato, and more) to let the user custom-build their sandwiches, but you also have a number of specialty sandwiches with preset ingredients. When the user selects one of those already-built sandwiches, how do you set the ingredients checkboxes to show what's in them?

You can set a checkbox's state by setting its **Checked** property to **True** or **False**, as in this code:

```
Private Sub Button1_Click(ByVal sender As System.Object, _
    ByVal e As System.EventArgs) Handles Button1.Click
    CheckBox1.Checked = True
End Sub
```

TIP: *How can you make a checkbox appear checked when your program first starts? Just set its **Checked** property to* ***True*** *at design time.*

Creating Three-State Checkboxes

In VB6 and before, you could set any checkbox to one of three states—now you need to set the checkbox's **ThreeState** property to **True** to indicate that you want it to support three states.

By default, checkboxes are two-state controls; you use the **Checked** property to get or set the value of a two-state checkbox. However, if you set the checkbox's **ThreeState** property to **True**, you make the checkbox into a three-state control.

You use the **CheckState** property to get or set the value of the three-state checkbox. The three states are:

- **Checked**—A check appears in the checkbox.
- **Unchecked**—No check appears in the checkbox.
- **Indeterminate**—A check appears in the checkbox on a gray background.

There's a discussion of these three states in the In Depth section of this chapter. You can see a checkbox in the indeterminate state in Figure 6.13.

TIP: *If the **ThreeState** property is set to **True**, the **Checked** property will return **True** for either a checked or indeterminate state.*

Figure 6.13 A checkbox in the indeterminate state.

If you've set the checkbox's **ThreeState** property to **True**, you can set its **CheckState** property to **CheckState.Indeterminate** at design time or run time to set the checkbox to the indeterminate state:

```
Private Sub CheckBox1_CheckedChanged(ByVal sender As System.Object, _
    ByVal e As System.EventArgs) Handles CheckBox1.CheckedChanged
    TextBox1.Text = "You clicked checkbox 1"
    CheckBox1.CheckState = CheckState.Indeterminate
End Sub
```

Using the **RadioButton** Class

As discussed in the In Depth section of this chapter, radio buttons are much like checkboxes, except that they're usually used in groups. Here is the class hierarchy of the **RadioButton** class:

```
Object
    MarshalByRefObject
        Component
            Control
                ButtonBase
                    RadioButton
```

You can find the more notable public properties of the **RadioButton** class in Table 6.5, the notable methods in Table 6.6, and the notable events in Table 6.7, including those inherited from the **ButtonBase** class. Note that as with other controls, I am not listing the notable properties, methods, and events **RadioButton** inherits from the **Control** class, such as the **Click** event—you can see all that in Chapter 5, Tables 5.1, 5.2, and 5.3.

Table 6.5   Noteworthy public properties of RadioButton objects.

Property	Means
Appearance	Gets/sets the value that determines the appearance of the radio button.
AutoCheck	Gets/sets a value indicating whether the **Checked** value and the appearance of the l control automatically change when the radio button is clicked.
Checked	Gets/sets a value indicating whether the radio button is checked.
FlatStyle	Gets/sets the flat style appearance of the radio button.
Image	Gets/sets the image that is displayed in a radio button.
ImageAlign	Gets/sets the alignment of the image in a radio button.
ImageIndex	Gets/sets the image list index value of the image displayed in a radio button.
ImageList	Gets/sets the **ImageList** that contains the image displayed in a radio button.
TextAlign	Gets/sets the alignment of the text in a radio button.

Table 6.6   Noteworthy public methods of RadioButton objects.

Method	Means
PerformClick	Generates a **Click** event for the radio button, simulating a click by a user.

Table 6.7   Noteworthy public events of RadioButton objects.

Event	Means
AppearanceChanged	Occurs when the **Appearance** property changes.
CheckedChanged	Occurs when the value of the **Checked** property changes.

Creating Radio Buttons

We've already seen how to create radio buttons in the In Depth section of this chapter. You can handle radio button **CheckChanged** events, which happen when the **Checked** property changes; here's some code from the RadioButtons example on the CD-ROM:

```
Private Sub RadioButton1_CheckedChanged(ByVal sender As System.Object, _
    ByVal e As System.EventArgs) Handles RadioButton1.CheckedChanged
    TextBox1.Text = "You clicked radio button 1"
End Sub
```

We saw the results of this code in Figure 6.3.

Getting a Radio Button's State

You can check if a radio button is selected or not with the **Checked** property (formerly the **Value** property in VB6 and earlier). Radio buttons' **Checked** property only has two settings: **True** if the button is selected, and **False** if not.

Here's an example showing how to determine whether a radio button is selected or not. In this case, we display a message in a message box that indicates if a radio button, **RadioButton1**, is selected or not:

```
Private Sub Button1_Click(ByVal sender As System.Object, _
    ByVal e As System.EventArgs) Handles Button1.Click
    If RadioButton1.Checked Then
        MsgBox ("The Radio Button is selected.")
    Else
        MsgBox ("The Radio Button is not selected.")
    End If
End Sub
```

And that's all there is to it.

Setting a Radio Button's State

Besides examining a radio button's state, you also can set it using the **Checked** property. The **Checked** property can take two values, **True** or **False**. Here's an example. In this case, we just set a radio button, **RadioButton1**, to its selected state by setting its **Checked** property to **True**:

```
Private Sub Button1_Click(ByVal sender As System.Object, _
    ByVal e As System.EventArgs) Handles Button1.Click
    RadioButton1.Checked = True
End Sub
```

And that's all it takes.

TIP: How can you make a radio button appear checked when your program first starts? Just set its **Checked** property to **True** at design time.

Creating Toggle Buttons

You can turn checkboxes or radio buttons into toggle buttons if you set their **Appearance** property to **Button** (the other option is **Normal**). Toggle buttons resemble standard buttons but act like the checkboxes or radio buttons they really are. When you click a checkbox button, for example, it stays clicked until you click it again.

You can see three radio buttons that have been made into toggle buttons in Figure 6.14.

Also, in the ToggleButtons example on the CD-ROM, you can click the "Create toggle buttons" button to change the appearance of radio buttons at run time. Here's the code that does the trick:

```
Private Sub Button1_Click(ByVal sender As System.Object, _
    ByVal e As System.EventArgs) Handles Button1.Click
    RadioButton1.Appearance = Appearance.Button
    RadioButton2.Appearance = Appearance.Button
    RadioButton3.Appearance = Appearance.Button
End Sub
```

Figure 6.14   Creating toggle buttons.

Using the **Panel** Class

As discussed in the In Depth section of this chapter, you can use panels to group controls together in a Windows form. Here is the class hierarchy of the **Panel** class:

```
Object
    MarshalByRefObject
        Component
            Control
                ScrollableControl
                    Panel
```

You can find the more notable public properties of the **Panel** class in Table 6.8. Note that as with other controls, I am not listing the notable properties, methods, and events **Panel** inherits from the **Control** class, such as the **Click** event—you can see all that in Tables 5.1, 5.2, and 5.3 in Chapter 5.

Table 6.8   Noteworthy public properties of **Panel** objects.

Property	Means
AutoScroll	Specifies if the panel will display scroll bars if needed.
AutoScrollMargin	Gets/sets the size of the auto-scroll margin.
AutoScrollMinSize	Gets/sets the minimum size of the auto-scroll.
AutoScrollPosition	Gets/sets the location of the auto-scroll position.
DockPadding	Gets the dock padding settings for all edges of the panel.

Creating Panels

When you add radio buttons to a form, they are automatically coordinated so that only one radio button can be selected at a time. If the user selects a new radio button, all the other options buttons are automatically deselected. But there are times when that's not convenient; for example, you may have two sets of options buttons: day of the week and day of the month. You want the user to be able to select one radio button in each list. How do you group radio buttons together into different groups on the same form?

You can use the panel or group box controls. Inside either of these controls, radio buttons will act as though they were in their own group, and the user can select one radio button in each group, as shown in Figure 6.4.

You can create panels at design time or run time; for example, I'm creating panels in Figure 6.15 at design time. Here, I've set the panels' **BorderStyle** property to **Fixed3D.** (The other possibilities are **None**, which is the default, and **Fixed Single**.)

Panels support scroll bars, which group boxes do not. To enable scroll bars in a panel, set its **AutoScroll** property to **True**. You also can customize the panel's scrolling behavior with the **AutoScrollMargin** and **AutoScrollMin Size** properties.

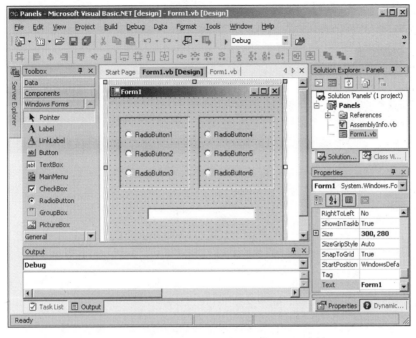

Figure 6.15 Grouping radio buttons together using panels.

After you've created a panel, you can add controls to it; at design time, the controls will then become part of the panel, and when you move the panel, the contained controls will move as well. For an example showing how to add controls to panels in code, see the next topic.

Adding Controls to Panels in Code

You can add controls to a panel at run time just as you can add controls to a form. When you add controls to a form, you use the form's **Controls** collection; when you add controls to a panel, you use the panel's **Controls** collection. Here's an example, AddControlsPanel on the CD-ROM, where I'm creating a panel, giving it a **Fixed3D** border, and adding a label and text box to the panel—note that you use the **Controls** collection's **Add** method to add the new controls to the panel:

```
Public Class Form1
    Inherits System.Windows.Forms.Form

    'Windows Form Designer generated code
```

```
Private Sub Button1_Click(ByVal sender As System.Object, _
    ByVal e As System.EventArgs) Handles Button1.Click
    Dim Panel1 As New Panel()
    Dim TextBox1 As New TextBox()
    Dim Label1 As New Label()

    Panel1.Location = New Point(60, 20)
    Panel1.Size = New Size(100, 150)
    Panel1.BorderStyle = System.Windows.Forms.BorderStyle.Fixed3D

    Label1.Location = New Point(16, 16)
    Label1.Text = "Enter text:"
    Label1.Size = New Size(60, 16)
    TextBox1.Location = New Point(16, 32)
    TextBox1.Text = ""
    TextBox1.Size = New Size(60, 20)

    Me.Controls.Add(Panel1)
    Panel1.Controls.Add(Label1)
    Panel1.Controls.Add(TextBox1)
End Sub
End Class
```

You can see this example at work in Figure 6.16; when the user clicks the button in this example, the new panel appears with its contained controls.

Related solution:	Found on page:
Adding and Removing Controls at Run Time	196

Figure 6.16   Creating a panel at run time.

Using the **GroupBox** Class

You can use group boxes to group controls together, much like panels. Unlike panels, however, group boxes can support captions, which you set with the **Text** property. However, group boxes cannot support scroll bars, which panels can.

You can see group boxes at work in Figure 6.5. Here is the class hierarchy of the **GroupBox** class:

```
Object
    MarshalByRefObject
        Component
            Control
                GroupBox
```

Creating Group Boxes

You can create group boxes at design time or run time. I've created two group boxes in the GroupBoxes example on the CD-ROM at design time, as you see in Figure 6.17. After you've created the group boxes, you can drag other controls into them. Note that although you can set the caption for group boxes with the

6. Windows Forms: Buttons, Checkboxes, Radio Buttons, Panels...

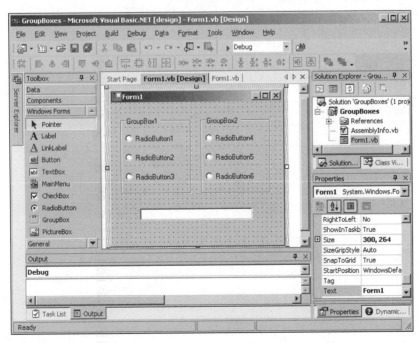

Figure 6.17   Creating a group box at design time.

Text property, group boxes do not have either a **BorderStyle** property, nor do they support scroll bars, as panels do.

You can see this example running in Figure 6.5. You also can create group boxes at run time—see the next topic for the details.

Adding Controls to Group Boxes in Code

Here's an example, AddControlsGroupBox on the CD-ROM, where I'm creating a group box at run time, placing three radio buttons into the group box, and adding an event handler for each radio button. Note that as when we added controls to a panel (see "Adding Controls to Panels in Code" earlier in this chapter), I use the group box's **Controls** collection's **Add** method to add controls to a group box. To connect the new radio buttons to event handlers, I use the **AddHandler** function:

```
Public Class Form1
    Inherits System.Windows.Forms.Form
    Dim GroupBox1 As New GroupBox()
    Dim WithEvents RadioButton1 As RadioButton
    Dim WithEvents RadioButton2 As RadioButton
    Dim WithEvents RadioButton3 As RadioButton

    'Windows Form Designer generated code

    Private Sub Button1_Click(ByVal sender As System.Object, _
        ByVal e As System.EventArgs) Handles Button1.Click

        RadioButton1 = New RadioButton()
        RadioButton2 = New RadioButton()
        RadioButton3 = New RadioButton()

        GroupBox1.Text = "GroupBox1"
        GroupBox1.Location = New Point(40, 40)
        GroupBox1.Size = New Size(200, 100)

        RadioButton1.Location = New Point(16, 16)
        RadioButton1.Text = "RadioButton1"
        RadioButton1.Size = New Size(120, 16)

        RadioButton2.Location = New Point(16, 32)
        RadioButton2.Text = "RadioButton2"
```

```
        RadioButton2.Size = New Size(120, 20)

        RadioButton3.Location = New Point(16, 48)
        RadioButton3.Text = "RadioButton3"
        RadioButton3.Size = New Size(120, 20)

        GroupBox1.Controls.Add(RadioButton1)
        GroupBox1.Controls.Add(RadioButton2)
        GroupBox1.Controls.Add(RadioButton3)

        Controls.Add(GroupBox1)

        AddHandler RadioButton1.CheckedChanged, AddressOf _
            RadioButton1_CheckedChanged
        AddHandler RadioButton2.CheckedChanged, AddressOf _
            RadioButton2_CheckedChanged
        AddHandler RadioButton3.CheckedChanged, AddressOf _
            RadioButton3_CheckedChanged
    End Sub

    Private Sub RadioButton1_CheckedChanged(ByVal sender As _
        System.Object, ByVal e As System.EventArgs) Handles _
        RadioButton1.CheckedChanged
        TextBox1.Text = "You clicked radio button 1"
    End Sub

    Private Sub RadioButton2_CheckedChanged(ByVal sender As _
        System.Object, ByVal e As System.EventArgs) Handles _
        RadioButton2.CheckedChanged
        TextBox1.Text = "You clicked radio button 2"
    End Sub

    Private Sub RadioButton3_CheckedChanged(ByVal sender As _
        System.Object, ByVal e As System.EventArgs) Handles _
        RadioButton3.CheckedChanged
        TextBox1.Text = "You clicked radio button 3"
    End Sub
End Class
```

You can see this example at work in Figure 6.18. When the user clicks the button in this example, it creates a new group box, adds three radio buttons to the group box, and adds an event handler to each radio button. As you can see in Figure 6.18, the user can now click radio buttons and the program indicates which radio button was clicked in the text box.

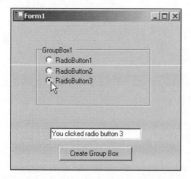

Figure 6.18   Creating a group box at run time.

Related solution:	Found on page:
Adding and Removing Controls at Run Time	196

Chapter 7

Windows Forms: List Boxes, Checked List Boxes, Combo Boxes, and Picture Boxes

(continued)

In Depth

In this chapter, we're going to take a look at four popular Visual Basic controls: list boxes, checked list boxes, combo boxes, and picture boxes. These controls are part of the core arsenal of every Visual Basic programmer.

List boxes, of course, do just what their name implies: display a list of items. The user can make a selection from that list, and we can handle such selections with event handlers. Because list boxes can use scroll bars if a list gets too long, these controls are very useful to present long lists of items in a way that doesn't take up too much space.

Checked list boxes are derived from list boxes, and also support a checkbox for each item in a list. In VB6 and before, you could add checkboxes to ordinary list boxes, but in VB .NET, checked list boxes are separate controls. These controls are useful when you've got a long list of checkable items and want to scroll that list. We'll see how to handle checkbox events in this control.

Combo boxes are list boxes combined with text boxes. With combo boxes, you can give the user the option of selecting from a list (usually a drop-down list activated when the user clicks the downward pointing arrow at right in a combo box) or typing their selection directly into the text box part of the combo box.

Picture boxes display images, as their name implies. In VB6 and before, picture boxes were powerhouses, not only displaying images, but also letting you edit them as well as reading images from disk and saving them too. And picture boxes were container controls, letting you insert other controls into them. (In fact, in Visual Basic's early days, you used to create toolbars with picture boxes which you filled with buttons.) All that's changed now, unfortunately, and picture boxes have been made much more like VB6's image controls, which only displayed images (image controls do not exist in VB .NET).

I'll take a look at all these controls in some detail here in the In Depth section.

List Boxes

As you know, list boxes display a list of items from which the user can select one or more. If there are too many items to display at once, a scroll bar automatically appears to let the user scroll through the list. In Visual Basic .NET, each item in a

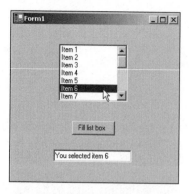

Figure 7.1   A list box control.

list box is itself an object. You can see a list box—this is the ListBoxes example on the CD-ROM—in Figure 7.1.

You also can scroll list boxes horizontally when you set the **MultiColumn** property to **True**. Alternatively, when the **ScrollAlwaysVisible** property is set to **True**, a scroll bar always appears.

How do you find out which item is selected in a list box? You can keep track of the selected item in a list box two ways—by numeric index (starting at 0) or by accessing the selected item's object directly. The **SelectedIndex** property returns an integer value that corresponds to the selected item. If the first item in the list is selected, then the **SelectedIndex** value is **0**. You can change the selected item by changing the **SelectedIndex** value in code; the corresponding item in the list will appear highlighted on the Windows form. If no item is selected, the **SelectedIndex** value is **-1**. You also can set which items are selected with the **SetSelected** method in code.

The **SelectedItem** property is similar to **SelectedIndex**, but returns the object corresponding to the item itself (which is usually a string value, but need not be—see "Storing Objects in a List Box or Combo Box" later in this chapter).

The items in list boxes are stored in the **Items** collection; the **Items.Count** property holds the number of items in the list. (The value of the **Items.Count** property is always one more than the largest possible **SelectedIndex** value because **SelectedIndex** is zero-based.) To add or delete items in a **ListBox** control, you can use the **Items.Add**, **Items.Insert**, **Items.Clear,** or **Items.Remove** methods. You also can add a number of objects to a list box at once with the **AddRange** method. Or you can add and remove items to the list by using the **Items** property at design time.

You also can use the **BeginUpdate** and **EndUpdate** methods. These enable you to add a large number of items to the **ListBox** without the list box being redrawn each time an item is added to the list. The **FindString** and **FindStringExact** methods enable you to search for an item in the list that contains a specific search string.

You also can support multiple selections in list boxes. The **SelectionMode** property determines how many list items can be selected at a time; you can set this property to **None**, **One**, **MultiSelect**, or **MultiExtended**:

- **MultiExtended**—Multiple items can be selected, and the user can use the Shift, Ctrl, and arrow keys to make selections.

- **MultiSimple**—Multiple items can be selected.

- **None**—No items may be selected.

- **One**—Only one item can be selected.

When you support multiple selections, you use the **Items** property to access the items in the list box, the **SelectedItems** property to access the selected items, and the **SelectedIndices** property to access the selected indices.

And in addition to all this, we'll also see how to handle list box events in this chapter.

Checked List Boxes

Windows forms checked list boxes are derived from standard list boxes, except that they also support a checkbox for each item, as you see in Figure 7.2—that's the CheckedListBoxes example on the CD-ROM.

As with standard list boxes, you can access the items in a checked list box using the **Items** property. To check an item, the user has to double-click a checkbox by default, unless you set the **CheckOnClick** property to **True**, in which case it only takes one click.

You can handle the checked items with the **CheckedItems** property and the **CheckedIndices** property. You also can use the **GetItemChecked** method to verify if an item is checked. And you can use the **ItemCheck** event to handle

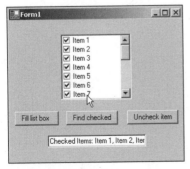

Figure 7.2   A checked list box control.

check events, and the **SetItemChecked** method to check or uncheck items. We'll do all that in this chapter.

Checked list boxes also can support three states with the **CheckState** enumeration: **Checked**, **Indeterminate**, and **Unchecked**. (Note that you must set the state of **Indeterminate** in the code because the user interface does not provide a way of doing so.) To use three-state checkboxes, you use the **GetItemCheckState** and **SetItemCheckState** methods instead of **GetItemChecked** and **SetItemChecked** methods.

Combo Boxes

The Windows forms combo box control is used to display data in a drop-down combo box. The combo box is made up of two parts: The top part is a text box that allows the user to type in all or part of a list item. The other part is a list box that displays a list of items from which the user can select one or more. You can allow the user to select an item from the list, or enter their own data. You can see a combo box from the ComboBoxes example on the CD-ROM in Figure 7.3.

You can set and access the text in a combo box's text box with its **Text** property. How can you tell which item is selected in a combo box? You can use the **SelectedIndex** property to get the selected list item. You can change the selected item by changing the **SelectedIndex** value in code, which will make the corresponding item appear in the text box portion of the combo box. As with list boxes, if no item is selected, the **SelectedIndex** value is **-1**. If the first item in the list is selected, then the **SelectedIndex** value is **0**.

In addition, you also can use the **SelectedItem** property, which is similar to **SelectedIndex**, but returns the item itself (often a string value). The **Items.Count** property reflects the number of items in the list (the value of the **Items.Count** property is always one more than the largest possible **SelectedIndex** value because **SelectedIndex** is zero-based).

Figure 7.3   A combo box control.

To add or delete items in a **ListBox** control, use the **Items.Add**, **Items.Insert**, **Items.Clear**, **Items.AddRange**, or **Items.Remove** method. Or you can add and remove items to the list by using the **Items** property at design time.

By default, a combo box displays a text box with a hidden drop-down list. The **DropDownStyle** property determines the style of combo box to display. You can set this property to make the combo box's list box a simple drop-down, where the list always displays; a drop-down list box, where the text portion is not editable and you must use an arrow to see the drop-down list box; or the default drop-down list box, where the text portion may be edited and the user must use the arrow key to view the list.

TIP: *To display a list that the user cannot edit, you should use a list box instead of a combo box. In VB6 and before, you used to be able to use the **Locked** property to make a combo box uneditable, but now you use the **Locked** property to indicate that a control may not be moved.*

You can add and remove items in combo boxes in the same ways as you can with list boxes. You also can use the **BeginUpdate** and **EndUpdate** methods to add a large number of items to the **ComboBox** without the control being redrawn each time an item is added to the list. And the **FindString** and **FindStringExact** methods let you to search for an item in the list that contains a particular search string. As with list boxes, you use the **SelectedIndex** property to get or set the current item, and the **SelectedItem** property to get or set a reference to the object. And you can also use the **Text** property to specify the string displayed in the text box part of the combo box.

Picture Boxes

Picture boxes are used to display graphics from a bitmap, icon, JPEG, GIF or other image file type. You can see a picture box—from the PictureBoxes example on the CD-ROM—at work in Figure 7.4.

To display an image in a picture box, you can set the **Image** property to the image you want to display, either at design time or at run time. You can clip and position an image with the **SizeMode** property, which you set to values from the **PictureBoxSizeMode** enumeration:

- **Normal**—Standard picture box behavior (the upper-left corner of the image is placed at upper left in the picture box).
- **StretchImage**—Allows you to stretch the image in code.
- **AutoSize**—Fits the picture box to the image.
- **CenterImage**—Centers the image in the picture box.

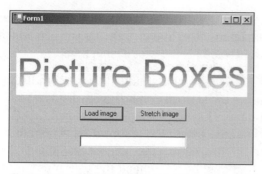

Figure 7.4   A picture box control.

You also can change the size of the image at run time with the **ClientSize** property, stretching an image as you want. By default, a **PictureBox** control is displayed without any borders, but you can add a standard or three-dimensional border using the **BorderStyle** property. And you can even handle events such as **Click** and **MouseDown** to convert an image into an image map, as we'll see later in this chapter.

For more details on all these controls, see the Immediate Solutions section, coming right up.

Immediate Solutions

Using the **ListBox** Class

Windows forms list boxes are based on the **Control** class, of course, but not directly—instead, they're based directly on the **ListControl** class, which also is used by other controls, such as checked list boxes. Here's the class hierarchy for the **ListBox** class:

```
Object
    MarshalByRefObject
        Component
            Control
                ListControl
                    ListBox
```

You can find the more notable public properties of the **ListBox** class in Table 7.1, the more notable methods in Table 7.2, and the more notable events in Table 7.3, including those members inherited from the **ListControl** class. Note that as with other Windows controls, I am not listing the notable properties, methods, and events **ListBox** inherits from the **Control** class, such as the **Click** event—you can see all that in Tables 5.1, 5.2, and 5.3 in Chapter 5.

Table 7.1   Noteworthy public properties of ListBox objects.

Property	Means
ColumnWidth	Gets/sets column width; use with multicolumn list boxes.
DisplayMember	Indicates which property of objects in a list box to show. If this property if empty, the object's **ToString** method is used.
DrawMode	Gets/sets the drawing mode for the list box.
HorizontalExtent	Gets/sets the width a list box can scroll horizontally.
HorizontalScrollbar	Gets/sets if a horizontal scroll bar is displayed in the list box.
IntegralHeight	Gets/sets if the list box should resize so it doesn't show partial items.
ItemHeight	Gets/sets an item's height in the list box.
Items	Returns a collection of the items of the list box.
MultiColumn	Gets/sets if the list box supports multiple columns.

(continued)

Table 7.1   Noteworthy public properties of ListBox objects (continued).

Property	Means
PreferredHeight	Returns the total height of all items in the list box.
ScrollAlwaysVisible	Gets/sets if a vertical scroll bar is always shown.
SelectedIndex	Gets/sets the index of the list box's currently selected item.
SelectedIndices	Gets a collection that contains the indices of all selected items in the list box.
SelectedItem	Gets/sets the selected item in the list box.
SelectedItems	Gets a collection containing the list box's selected items.
SelectionMode	Gets/sets the mode with which items are selected.
Sorted	Gets/sets if the items in the list box are sorted. The sort is alphabetical.
Text	Gets the text of the selected item in the list box.
TopIndex	Gets/sets the index of the first item that is visible in the list box.

Table 7.2   Noteworthy public methods of ListBox objects.

Methods	Means
BeginUpdate	Turns off visual updating of the list box until the **EndUpdate** method is called.
ClearSelected	Unselects all the items in a list box.
EndUpdate	Resumes visual updating of the list box.
FindString	Finds the first item in the list box that begins with the indicated string.
FindStringExact	Finds the first item in the list box that matches the indicated string exactly.
GetItemHeight	Returns the height of a list box item.
GetSelected	Returns **True** if the indicated item is selected.
IndexFromPoint	Returns the index of the item at the given coordinates.
SetSelected	Selects or deselects the indicated item in a list box.

Table 7.3   Noteworthy public events of ListBox objects.

Event	Means
SelectedIndexChanged	Occurs when the **SelectedIndex** property has changed.

Adding Items to a List Box

The Testing Department is calling again, and they're telling you to get rid of all the beautiful buttons that you've placed on the main form of your program. But, you say, it's a program that lets the user buy computer parts. We have to list what computer parts are available. That's just it, they say: A list should go in a list box.

So you've added your list box by dragging it from the toolbox, and now it's staring at you: a blank white box. How do you add items to the list box?

You can add items to a list box at either design time or at run time; the first item will have index 0, the next index 1, and so on in the list box. At design time, you can use the **Items** property, which is a very handy array of the items in the list box, and at run time, you can use both the **Items** property and the **Add** (formerly **AddItem**) method.

How do you keep track of the total number of items in a list box? You use the **Items.Count** property; that is, if you loop over the items in the control, you'll use **Items.Count** as the maximum value to loop to. You can access items individually in a list box by index using the **Items** property, like this: **strText = ListBox1.Items(5)**.

At design time, you can add items directly to your list box by typing them into the **Items** property in the Properties window. Selecting the **Items** property displays the String Collection Editor, which you can see in Figure 7.5, and you can type item after item into the list box that way.

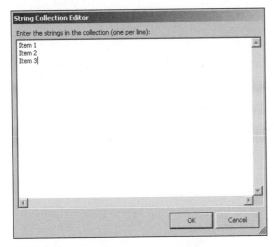

Figure 7.5   Adding items to a list box.

At run time, you either can use the indexed **Items** property as detailed above, or the Items property's **Add** or **Insert** methods this way. Here's an example from the ListBoxes example on the CD-ROM. In this case, I'm using the **Add** method to add items to a list box at run time. To see this code work, click the "Fill list box" button in the example:

```
Private Sub Button1_Click(ByVal sender As System.Object, _
    ByVal e As System.EventArgs) Handles Button1.Click
    ListBox1.BeginUpdate()
    Dim intLoopIndex As Integer
    For intLoopIndex = 1 To 20
        ListBox1.Items.Add("Item " & intLoopIndex.ToString())
    Next intLoopIndex
    ListBox1.EndUpdate()
End Sub
```

Running the above code gives us the list box in Figure 7.6.

Note that when you place items in a list box, they are stored by index, and you can refer to them by their index with the **List** property. When you use the Insert method, you can specify the index location at which to insert an item, like this: **ComboBox1.Items.Insert (3, "Item 3")**.

You also can use the **AddRange** method to add a collection of objects to a list box all at once; here's an example where I'm adding an array of strings to a list box all at once:

```
Private Sub Button2_Click(ByVal sender As System.Object, _
    ByVal e As System.EventArgs) Handles Button2.Click
    Dim DataArray(4) As String
    Dim intLoopIndex As Integer

    For intLoopIndex = 0 To 4
        DataArray(intLoopIndex) = New String("Item " & intLoopIndex)
    Next intLoopIndex

    ListBox1.Items.AddRange(DataArray)
End Sub
```

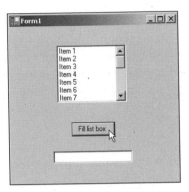

Figure 7.6   Placing items in a list box.

Referring to Items in a List Box by Index

When you add items to a list box, each item is given an *index*, and you can refer to the item in the list box with this index by using the **Items** property, like this: **ListBox1.Items(5)**. The first item added to a list box gets the index 0, the next index 1, and so on. You also can get the index of an object in a list box with the **IndexOf** method, like this: **ListBox1.Items.IndexOf(Object5)**.

When the user selects an item in a list box, you can get the selected item's index with the list box's **SelectedIndex** (formerly **ListIndex**) property. You also can get the selected item's corresponding object with the **SelectedItem** property. Here's an example where I display the index of an item the user has selected in the **SelectedIndexChanged** event of a list box:

```
Private Sub ListBox1_SelectedIndexChanged(ByVal sender As _
    System.Object, ByVal e As System.EventArgs) Handles _
    ListBox1.SelectedIndexChanged
    TextBox1.Text = "You selected item " & ListBox1.SelectedIndex + 1
End Sub
```

For more information, see "Determining Which List Box Items Are Selected" later in this chapter.

Responding to List Box Events

Now you've created your new list box, and it's a beauty. The boss is very pleased with it when you show your new program at the company's expo. The boss clicks the list box with the mouse—and nothing happens. The boss asks: Didn't you connect that list box to code? Oh, you think.

SelectedIndexChanged

You can use the **SelectedIndexChanged** event, which is the default event for list boxes, to handle the case where the selected item changes in a list box. In the ListBoxes example on the CD-ROM, I indicate which item was clicked in the list box using this event (adding one to the item's index, which is 0-based), like this:

```
Private Sub ListBox1_SelectedIndexChanged(ByVal sender As _
    System.Object, ByVal e As System.EventArgs) Handles _
    ListBox1.SelectedIndexChanged
        TextBox1.Text = "You selected item " & ListBox1.SelectedIndex + 1
End Sub
```

You can see the results in Figure 7.7; in that figure, I've clicked Item 6 in the list box, which the code reports in the text box as you see.

Click and DoubleClick

You also can use **Click** and **DoubleClick** with list boxes. How you actually use them is up to you, because different programs have different needs. For example, if a list box sets a new font which doesn't become active until a font chooser dialog box is closed, it's fine to respond to the **Click** event to display a sample of the font the user has selected in text box. On the other hand, if you display the names of programs to launch in a text box, you should probably launch a program only after a user double-clicks it in the list box to avoid mistakes.

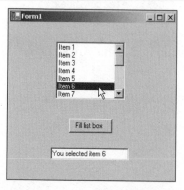

Figure 7.7   Handling list box events.

You can use the **Click** event just much as you'd use the **Click** event in a button, with a **Click** event handler. Here, I'll display the index of the item in the list box the user has clicked:

```
Private Sub ListBox1_Click(ByVal sender As Object, _
    ByVal e As System.EventArgs) Handles ListBox1.Click
    TextBox1.Text = ListBox1.SelectedIndex
End Sub
```

And it's the same for **DoubleClick**—you just add a **DoubleClick** handler with the code you want:

```
Private Sub ListBox1_DoubleClick(ByVal sender As Object, _
    ByVal e As System.EventArgs) Handles ListBox1.DoubleClick
    TextBox1.Text = ListBox1.SelectedIndex
End Sub
```

*TIP: A **DoubleClick** event also triggers the **Click** event, because to double-click an item, you must first click it.*

Removing Items from a List Box

The Testing Department is calling again—how about letting the users customize your program? You ask: what do you mean? Well, they say, let's give the user some way of removing the 50 fine French cooking tips from the list box.

You can use the **RemoveAt** method to delete items from a list box. To remove the item at index 5, you'd use this code:

```
ListBox1.Items.RemoveAt(5)
```

Here's how you'd remove the currently selected item with **RemoveAt**:

```
ListBox1.Items.RemoveAt(ListBox1.SelectedIndex)
```

You also can use the **Remove** method to remove a specific object from a list box. Here's how I'd remove the currently selected item with **Remove**:

```
ListBox1.Items.Remove(ListBox1.SelectedItem)
```

You also can remove items by passing the corresponding object to **Remove**. For example, if I've filled a list box with **String** objects, I can remove the item "Item 1" this way:

```
ListBox1.Items.Remove ("Item 1")
```

TIP: *You should note that removing an item from a list box changes the indices of the remaining items. After you remove item 1 in the above example, item 2 now gets index 1, and item 3 gets index 2, and so on.*

You also can use the **Items.Clear** method to remove all items from the list box.

Sorting a List Box

You're very proud of your new program's list box, which lists *all* the classical music recordings available for the last 40 years. But the Testing Department isn't so happy. They ask: Can't you *alphabetize* that list?

You can alphabetize the items in a list box by setting its **Sorted** property to **True** (it's **False** by default) at design time or run time. That's all it takes, just set its **Sorted** property to **True**. (In fact, I've known lazy programmers who sorted arrays of text by placing the text into a hidden list box and then reading it back to save writing the code for the string comparisons.)

TIP: *You should know, however, that sorting a list box can change the indices of the items in that list box (unless they were already in alphabetical order). After the sorting is finished, the first item in the newly sorted list has index 0, the next index 1, and so on.*

Determining How Many Items Are in a List Box

You want to loop over the items in your list box to find out if a particular item is in the list—but you need to know how many items are in the list box in order to set up the loop. How can you set up the loop?

You can use the **Items.Count** value to determine how many items are in a list box. Here's an example where I'm displaying each item in a list box in a message box, one by one in a loop:

```
Private Sub Button1_Click(ByVal sender As System.Object, _
    ByVal e As System.EventArgs) Handles Button1.Click
```

```
    Dim intLoopIndex As Integer

    For intLoopIndex = 0 To ListBox1.Items.Count - 1
        MsgBox(ListBox1.Items(intLoopIndex))
    Next
End Sub
```

Determining Which List Box Items Are Selected

The big point of list boxes is to let the user make selections, of course, and there are a number of properties to handle that process. Here's an overview.

If a list box supports only single selections, you can use the **SelectedIndex** property to get the index of the selected item, and the **SelectedItem** property to get the selected item itself. Here's how I can display a selected item's index:

```
Private Sub ListBox1_Click(ByVal sender As Object, _
    ByVal e As System.EventArgs) Handles ListBox1.Click
    TextBox1.Text = ListBox1.SelectedIndex
End Sub
```

I also can use the **SelectedItem** property to get the object corresponding to the selected item, and if that object supports a **ToString** method, I can display it like this:

```
Private Sub ListBox1_Click(ByVal sender As Object, _
    ByVal e As System.EventArgs) Handles ListBox1.Click
    TextBox1.Text = ListBox1.SelectedItem.ToString()
End Sub
```

You can see an example, ListBoxes on the CD-ROM, where I've selected and reported on an item in Figure 7.7. There's another, even easier, way to get the text of the selected item's text from a list box—just use the list box's **Text** property, like this:

```
Private Sub ListBox1_Click(ByVal sender As Object, _
    ByVal e As System.EventArgs) Handles ListBox1.Click
    TextBox1.Text = ListBox1.Text
End Sub
```

Note that list boxes can support multiple selections if you set their **MultiSelect** property to **True**, and the story is different for multiselect list boxes. For multiselect list boxes, you use the **SelectedItems** and **SelectedIndices** properties to get access to the selected items. For example, here's how I can use a **For Each** loop to loop over and display the selected items in a multiselect list box using the **SelectedItems** collection:

```
For Each Item In ListBox1.SelectedItems
    TextBox1.Text &= Item.ToString()
Next
```

And here's how I can do the same thing using the **SelectedIndices** collection, like this:

```
For Each Index In ListBox1.SelectedIndices
    TextBox2.Text &= ListBox1.Items(Index).ToString()
Next
```

For more information, see "Creating Multiselect List Boxes" later in this chapter.

Making List Boxes Scroll Horizontally (Multicolumn List Boxes)

It's a pity that there's so little vertical space for the list box in your new program's layout—the user can view only 4 of the more than 40 items in the list box at once. Can't you make a list box work horizontally instead of vertically?

You sure can, if you set the **MultiColumn** property of a list box to **True**, giving it multiple columns. Here's how that looks in code, where I'm creating a multicolumn list box:

```
Dim ListBox1 As ListBox

Private Sub Button1_Click(ByVal sender As System.Object, _
    ByVal e As System.EventArgs) Handles Button1.Click
    ListBox1 = New ListBox()
    ListBox1.Size = New System.Drawing.Size(270, 100)
    ListBox1.Location = New System.Drawing.Point(10, 40)
    Me.Controls.Add(ListBox1)
    ListBox1.MultiColumn = True

    ListBox1.BeginUpdate()
    Dim intLoopIndex As Integer
    For intLoopIndex = 1 To 20
```

```
        ListBox1.Items.Add("Item " & intLoopIndex.ToString())
    Next intLoopIndex
    ListBox1.EndUpdate()
End Sub
```

What does this list box look like? See the next topic, where I'm also making this list box support multiple selections.

Creating Multiselect List Boxes

Everyone's very pleased with your new program to sell classical music CDs—except for the Sales department. Why, they want to know, can the user buy only one CD at a time? Well, you explain, the program uses a list box to display the list of CDs, and when the user makes selection, the program orders that CD. They ask: How about using a multiselect list box? So what's that?

This example is called MultiselectListBoxes on the CD-ROM, and it lets you create a multicolumn, multiselect list box at run time. To make the list box a multiselect list box, I'll set its **SelectionMode** property to **MultiExtended**; here are the possible values:

• **MultiExtended**—Multiple items can be selected, and the user can use the Shift, Ctrl, and arrow keys to make selections.

• **MultiSimple**—Multiple items can be selected.

• **None**—No items may be selected.

• **One**—Only one item can be selected.

To indicate how multiple selections look, I'll also use the list box's **SetSelection** method, which you can use to set selections; here's what the code looks like:

```
Dim ListBox1 As ListBox

Private Sub Button1_Click(ByVal sender As System.Object, _
    ByVal e As System.EventArgs) Handles Button1.Click
    ListBox1 = New ListBox()
    ListBox1.Size = New System.Drawing.Size(270, 100)
    ListBox1.Location = New System.Drawing.Point(10, 40)
    AddHandler ListBox1.SelectedIndexChanged, AddressOf _
        ListBox1_SelectedIndexChanged
    Me.Controls.Add(ListBox1)
    ListBox1.MultiColumn = True
    ListBox1.SelectionMode = SelectionMode.MultiExtended
```

```
    ListBox1.BeginUpdate()
    Dim intLoopIndex As Integer
    For intLoopIndex = 1 To 20
        ListBox1.Items.Add("Item " & intLoopIndex.ToString())
    Next intLoopIndex
    ListBox1.EndUpdate()

    ListBox1.SetSelected(1, True)
    ListBox1.SetSelected(3, True)
    ListBox1.SetSelected(5, True)
End Sub
```

To handle multiple selections, you can use the list box's **SelectedItems** and **SelectedIndices** properties. I've added an event handler for the list box's **SelectedIndexChanged** event to this example, and loop over all items in those collections, reporting which items are selected in text boxes this way:

```
Private Sub ListBox1_SelectedIndexChanged(ByVal _
    sender As System.Object, ByVal e As System.EventArgs)
    Dim Item As String
    Dim Index As Integer

    TextBox1.Text = "Selected items: "
    For Each Item In ListBox1.SelectedItems
        TextBox1.Text &= Item.ToString() & " "
    Next

    TextBox2.Text = "Selected indices: "
    For Each Index In ListBox1.SelectedIndices
        TextBox2.Text &= Index.ToString() & " "
    Next
End Sub
```

You can see the results in Figure 7.8. As you see in that figure, the new list box is created when you click the "Create list box" button, and it supports multiple columns and selections. The new selections also are reported in the two text boxes at bottom; this program is a success.

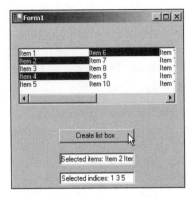

Figure 7.8　A multiselect, multicolumn list box.

Clearing a List Box

It's time to load new items into a list box—do you really have to clear the old items out one at a time with **Remove** or **RemoveAt**?

No, you can use the **Clear** method to clear a list box. Nothing could be easier (so be careful—there's no "undelete" function here): You just use **Clear**, like this: *ListBox*.**Clear( )**. Here's how that looks in code; in this case, I'm clearing a list box, **ListBox1**, when the user clicks a button:

```
Private Sub Button1_Click(ByVal sender As System.Object, _
    ByVal e As System.EventArgs) Handles Button1.Click
    ListBox1.Clear()
End Sub
```

Using the **CheckedListBox** Class

As discussed in the In Depth section of this chapter, checked list boxes support checkboxes for each item. The **CheckedListBox** class is derived from the **ListBox** class like this (note that that means you can use the **ListBox** members we've already covered in this chapter in **CheckListBox** controls):

```
Object
    MarshalByRefObject
        Component
            Control
                ListControl
                    ListBox
                        CheckedListBox
```

You can find the more notable public properties of the **ListBox** class in Table 7.4, the more notable methods in Table 7.5, and the more notable events in Table 7.6. Note that as with other Windows controls, I am not listing the notable properties, methods, and events **ListBox** inherits from the **Control** class, such as the **Click** event—you can see all that in Tables 5.1, 5.2, and 5.3 in Chapter 5.

Here's one property to note in particular—**CheckOnClick**. When you set this property to **True**, an item in a checked list box is checked or unchecked when you click it; otherwise, it takes a double-click. I'll set **CheckOnClick** to **True** for the **CheckedListBoxes** example in this chapter. (The default setting for this property is **False**.)

Table 7.4 Noteworthy public properties of CheckedListBox objects.

Property	Means
CheckedIndices	Holds the collection of checked indices in this checked list box.
CheckedItems	Holds the collection of checked items in this checked list box.
CheckOnClick	Gets/sets if the checkbox should be toggled when the corresponding item is selected.
ColumnWidth	Gets/sets the width of columns; use this only in multicolumn checked list boxes.
DisplayMember	Indicates which property of object in the list box to show. If empty, the checked list box uses the object's **ToString** method instead.
HorizontalScrollbar	Gets/sets if a the checked list box should display a horizontal scroll bar.
IntegralHeight	Gets/sets a value specifying if the checked list box should automatically resize so it doesn't partial items.
ItemHeight	Returns the height of an item.
Items	Returns a collection of items in this checked list box.
MultiColumn	Gets/sets if the checked list box allows multiple columns.
ScrollAlwaysVisible	Gets/sets if the checked list box always shows a vertical scroll bar.
SelectedIndex	Gets/sets the index of the selected item in a checked list box.
SelectedIndices	Gets a collection that contains the zero-based indices of all currently selected items in the checked list box.
SelectedItem	Gets/sets the selected item in the checked list box.
SelectedItems	Gets a collection containing the selected items in the checked list box.
SelectionMode	Gets/sets the current selection mode.
Sorted	Gets/sets if the items in the checked list box should be sorted. The sort is alphabetical.
Text	Gets the text of the selected item in a checked list box.
ThreeDCheckBoxes	Gets/sets if the checkboxes are displayed **Flat** or **Normal**.
TopIndex	Gets/sets the index of the first item that is visible in the checked list box.

Table 7.5   Noteworthy public methods of CheckedListBox objects.

Method	Means
BeginUpdate	Turns off visual updating of the list box until the **EndUpdate** method is called.
ClearSelected	Unselects all items in a checked list box.
EndUpdate	Resumes visual updating of the checked list box.
FindString	Finds the first item that begins with the indicated string in the checked list box.
FindStringExact	Finds the first item in the checked list box that matches the indicated string exactly.
GetItemChecked	Gets if the indicated item is checked or not.
GetItemCheckState	Gets the check state of the current item.
GetItemHeight	Gets the height of an item in the checked list box.
GetItemText	Gets an item's text.
GetSelected	Gets if the indicated item is selected.
IndexFromPoint	Returns the index of the item at the indicated coordinates.
SetItemChecked	Checks the item at the indicated index.
SetItemCheckState	Sets the indicated item's check state.
SetSelected	Selects or clears the selection for the indicated item in a checked list box.

Table 7.6   Noteworthy public events of CheckedListBox objects.

Event	Means
ItemCheck	Occurs when an item's checked state changes.
SelectedIndexChanged	Occurs when the **SelectedIndex** property has changed.

Adding Items to Checked List Boxes

You can add items to checked list boxes much the same way you add items to standard list boxes. However, you also can add another argument to the **Items.Add** method call when you add items to a checked list box in code. Here's how that looks in the CheckedListBoxes example on the CD-ROM—by passing an argument of **True**, I'm adding a check mark to all the new checkboxes:

```
Private Sub Button1_Click(ByVal sender As System.Object, _
    ByVal e As System.EventArgs) Handles Button1.Click
    CheckedListBox1.BeginUpdate()
    Dim intLoopIndex As Integer
    For intLoopIndex = 1 To 20
        CheckedListBox1.Items.Add("Item " & intLoopIndex.ToString(), True)
```

```
        Next intLoopIndex
        CheckedListBox1.EndUpdate()
End Sub
```

You can see the results of this code in the CheckedListBoxes example by clicking the "Fill list box" button, as shown in Figure 7.9.

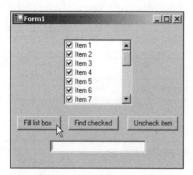

Figure 7.9　A checked list box.

Determining What Items Are Checked in Checked List Boxes

You can determine if an item displays a checkmark in a checked list box using the **GetItemChecked** method, which returns **True** if an item is checked. For example, in the CheckedListBox example, I can loop over all items in the checked list box and display those that are checked in a text box, like this:

```
Private Sub Button2_Click(ByVal sender As System.Object, _
    ByVal e As System.EventArgs) Handles Button2.Click
    Dim intLoopIndex As Integer
    Dim strText, strData As String
    strText = "Checked Items: "

    For intLoopIndex = 0 To (CheckedListBox1.Items.Count - 1)
        If CheckedListBox1.GetItemChecked(intLoopIndex) = True Then
            strText &= CheckedListBox1.Items(intLoopIndex).ToString & ", "
        End If
    Next

    TextBox1.Text = strText
End Sub
```

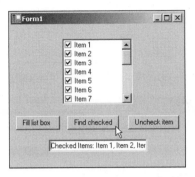

Figure 7.10 Determining what items are checked in a checked list box.

You can see the results in Figure 7.10, where the text box is displaying the checked items.

That was the hard way; there's an easier way—you can just loop through the collection returned by the **CheckedItems** property, which holds all the checked items:

```
Dim strText, strData As String

strText = "Checked Items: "

For Each strData In CheckedListBox1.CheckedItems
    strText &= strData & ", "
Next

TextBox1.Text = strText
```

Besides **CheckedItems**, there's also a **CheckedIndices** property, which returns a collection holding the indices of the checked items in the checked list box.

You also can use three-state checkboxes in checked list boxes, as discussed in the In Depth section of this chapter. In this case, you can use **GetItemCheckState** to determine the check *state* of an item. This method returns one of these values from the **CheckState** enumeration:

- **Checked**—The control is checked.

- **Indeterminate**—The control is indeterminate. An indeterminate control generally has a shaded appearance.

- **Unchecked**—The control is unchecked.

Here's an example:

```
Dim State As CheckState
State = CheckedListBox1.GetItemCheckState(0)
```

Related solution:	Found on page:
Creating Three-State Checkboxes	275

Checking or Unchecking Items in Checked List Boxes from Code

You can use a checked list box's **SetItemChecked** method to check or uncheck items in a checked list box by passing a value of **True** or **False**, respectively. Here's an example from the CheckedListBoxes example on the CD-ROM where I'm unchecking item 0 in the checked list box:

```
Private Sub Button3_Click(ByVal sender As System.Object, _
    ByVal e As System.EventArgs) Handles Button3.Click
    CheckedListBox1.SetItemChecked(0, False)
End Sub
```

You can see the results in Figure 7.11; in this case, I've clicked the "Uncheck item" button, which has removed the check mark in the checked list box in front of item 0.

You also can use the **SetItemCheckState** method to work with three-state checkboxes; you pass this method the index of the item to change and a value from the **CheckState** enumeration:

- **Checked**—The control is checked.

- **Indeterminate**—The control is indeterminate. An indeterminate control generally has a shaded appearance.

- **Unchecked**—The control is unchecked.

Here's an example: **CheckedListBox1.SetItemCheckState(0, CheckState. Unchecked)**.

Related solution:	Found on page:
Creating Three-State Checkboxes	275

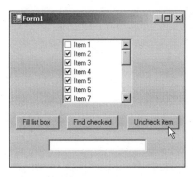

Figure 7.11   Unchecking an item in a checked list box.

Handling Item Check Events in Checked List Boxes

When the check in front of an item in checked list box changes, an **ItemCheck** event occurs. The **ItemCheckEventArgs** object passed to the associated event handler has an **Index** member that gives you the index of the item whose check mark has changed, and a **NewValue** member that gives you the new setting for the item (which will be a member of the **CheckState** ennumeration: **Checked**, **Indeterminate**, or **Unchecked**—note that the item does *not* yet have this setting when you're handling this event; it will be assigned to the item after the event handler terminates). Here's how I report if an item has just gotten checked or unchecked in the CheckedListBoxes example on the CD-ROM, using this event:

```
Private Sub CheckedListBox1_ItemCheck(ByVal sender As Object, _
    ByVal e As System.Windows.Forms.ItemCheckEventArgs) Handles _
    CheckedListBox1.ItemCheck
    Select Case e.NewValue
        Case CheckState.Checked
            TextBox1.Text = "Item " & e.Index + 1 & " is checked"
        Case CheckState.Unchecked
            TextBox1.Text = "Item " & e.Index + 1 & " is not checked"
    End Select
End Sub
```

You can see the results in Figure 7.12, where I've just unchecked item 4 in the checked list box, and the program reports that, as it should.

NOTE: *I've set **CheckOnClick** to **True** for the CheckedListBoxes example in this chapter (the default setting for this property is **False**), so all it takes is one click to generate an **ItemCheck** event. By default, however, a double-click would be needed.*

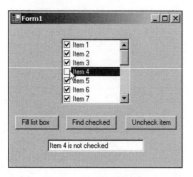

Figure 7.12   Responding to check events in a checked list box.

Using the **ComboBox** Class

As discussed in the In Depth section of this chapter, combo boxes combine a text box and a list box (which is why they're called combo boxes). In fact, combo boxes are derived from the **ListBox** class:

```
Object
    MarshalByRefObject
        Component
            Control
                ListControl
                    ComboBox
```

You can find the more notable public properties of the **ComboBox** class in Table 7.7, the more notable methods in Table 7.8, and the more notable events in Table 7.9. Note that as with other Windows forms controls, I am not listing the notable properties, methods, and events **ComboBox** inherits from the **Control** class, such as the **Click** event—you can see all that in Chapter 5, Tables 5.1, 5.2, and 5.3.

Table 7.7   Noteworthy public properties of **ComboBox** objects.

Property	Means
DisplayMember	Indicates which property of the objects in the combo box to show. If empty, the combo box uses the **ToString** method.
DropDownStyle	Gets/sets the style of the combo box.
DropDownWidth	Gets/sets a combo box's drop-down part's width.
DroppedDown	Gets/sets if the combo box is displaying its drop-down part.
Focused	Gets a value specifying if the combo box has the focus.
IntegralHeight	Gets/sets if the combo box should resize so it doesn't show partial items.

(continued)

Table 7.7   Noteworthy public properties of ComboBox objects (continued).

Property	Means
ItemHeight	Gets the height of an item in a combo box.
Items	Gets a collection of the items in this combo box.
MaxDropDownItems	Gets/sets the maximum number of items visible in the drop-down part of a combo box.
MaxLength	Gets/sets the maximum number of characters in the combo box's text box.
SelectedIndex	Gets/sets the index of the currently selected item.
SelectedItem	Gets/sets currently selected item in the combo box.
SelectedText	Gets/sets the selected text in the text box part of a combo box.
SelectionLength	Gets/sets the number of characters selected in the text box part of the combo box.
SelectionStart	Gets/sets the beginning index of selected text in the combo box.
Sorted	Gets/sets if the items in the combo box are sorted.

Table 7.8   Noteworthy public methods of ComboBox objects.

Method	Means
BeginUpdate	Turns off visual updating of the combo box until the **EndUpdate** method is called.
EndUpdate	Resumes visual updating of the combo box.
FindString	Finds the first item in the combo box that begins with the indicated string.
FindStringExact	Finds the item that matches the indicated string exactly.
GetItemText	Gets an item's text.
Select	Selects a range of text.
SelectAll	Selects all the text in the text box of the combo box.

Table 7.9   Noteworthy public events of ComboBox objects.

Event	Means
DropDown	Occurs when the drop-down portion of a combo box is shown.
DropDownStyleChanged	Occurs when the **DropDownStyle** property has changed.
SelectedIndexChanged	Occurs when the **SelectedIndex** property has changed.

7. Windows Forms: List Boxes, Check List Boxes, Combo Boxes

Creating Simple Combo Boxes, Drop-down Combo Boxes, and Drop-down List Combo Boxes

You might think there is only one kind of combo box, but there are really *three* types. You select which type you want with the combo box's **DropDownStyle** (formerly **Style**) property.

The default type of combo box is probably what you think of when you think of combo boxes, because it is made up of a text box and a drop-down list. However, you also can have combo boxes where the list doesn't drop down (the list is always open, and you have to make sure to provide space for it when you add the combo box to your form), and combo boxes where the user only can select from the list. Here are the settings for the combo box **DropDownStyle** property—these are members of the **ComboBoxStyle** enumeration:

- **DropDown** (the default)— Includes a drop-down list and a text box. The user can select from the list or type in the text box.

- **Simple**—Includes a text box and a list, which doesn't drop down. The user can select from the list or type in the text box. The size of a simple combo box includes both the edit and list portions. By default, a simple combo box is sized so that none of the list is displayed. Increase the **Height** property to display more of the list.

- **DropDownList**—This style allows selection only from the drop-down list. This is a good one to keep in mind when you want to restrict the user's input, but if you want to use this one, you also should consider simple list boxes.

You can see a drop-down combo box in the ComboBoxes example on the CD-ROM, and you can see that example at work in Figure 7.3.

Adding Items to a Combo Box

You've added a new combo box to your program, and it looks great, but when you run it, all you see is "ComboBox1" in it—how do you add items to your combo box?

A combo box is a combination of a text box and a list box, so at design time, you can change the text in the text box part by changing the **Text** property. You change the items in the list box part with the **Items** property (this item opens the String Collection Editor discussed for list boxes when you click it in the Properties window) at design time.

As with list boxes, you also can use the **Items.Insert**, **Items.Add**, and **Items.AddRange** methods to add items to the list part of a combo box. Here's some code from the ComboBoxes example on the CD-ROM where I'm adding some items to a combo box (note that I'm also adding text, "Select one...", to the text box in the combo box):

```
Private Sub Button1_Click(ByVal sender As System.Object, _
    ByVal e As System.EventArgs) Handles Button1.Click
    ComboBox1.BeginUpdate()
    Dim intLoopIndex As Integer
    For intLoopIndex = 0 To 20
        ComboBox1.Items.Add("Item " + intLoopIndex.ToString())
    Next
    ComboBox1.Text = "Select one..."
    ComboBox1.EndUpdate()
End Sub
```

You can see the results in the ComboBoxes example in Figure 7.3 when you click the "Fill combo box" button.

Responding to Combo Box Selections

So you've installed a new combo box in your program, *SuperDuperTextPro*, to let the user select new text font sizes, and the combo box is staring at you, just a blank box. How do you connect it to your code?

Combo boxes are combinations of text boxes and list boxes, and that combination means that there are two sets of input events: **TextChanged** events when the user types into the text box, and **SelectedIndexChanged**, **Click**, or **DoubleClick** when the user uses the list box part of the combo box. Note that, unlike standard list boxes, you cannot make multiple selections in a combo box's list box.

TextChanged Events

When the user changes the text in a combo box, a **TextChanged** event occurs, just as it does when the user types in a standard text box. You can read the new text in the text box with the **Text** property; for example, here's how we display the new text in the combo box every time the user changes that text by typing:

```
Private Sub ComboBox1_TextChanged(ByVal sender As Object, _
    ByVal e As System.EventArgs) Handles ComboBox1.TextChanged
    TextBox1.Text = ComboBox1.Text
End Sub
```

SelectedIndexChanged Events

When the selection changes in a combo box, a **SelectionChanged** event happens, and you can use the **SelectedIndex** and **SelectedItem** properties to get the index of the newly selected item and the item itself. Here's some code from the ComboBoxes example on the CD-ROM that reports the new selection when the user makes a new selection in the combo box:

```
Private Sub ComboBox1_SelectedIndexChanged(ByVal _
    sender As System.Object, ByVal e As System.EventArgs) _
    Handles ComboBox1.SelectedIndexChanged
    Dim SelectedIndex As Integer
    SelectedIndex = ComboBox1.SelectedIndex
    Dim SelectedItem As Object
    SelectedItem = ComboBox1.SelectedItem

    TextBox1.Text = "Selected item text: " & SelectedItem.ToString() & _
        " Selected index: " & SelectedIndex.ToString()
End Sub
```

You can see the results in Figure 7.13, where the code is responding to a **SelectedIndexChanged** event (see also "Getting the Current Selection in a Combo Box" in this chapter).

Click Events

You also can get **Click** events when the user makes a selection in the list box using the mouse. You can determine which item the user clicked using the combo's **SelectedIndex** property, which holds the index of the clicked item, or get that item directly using the **SelectedItem** property, because when you click an item, it is made the new selected item in the text box.

Figure 7.13   Responding to **SelectedIndexChanged** events in a combo box.

DoubleClick Events

You might expect that where there are **Click** events there are **DoubleClick** events, and that's true—but for simple combo boxes only (**DropDownStyle = ComboBoxStyle.Simple**). When you click an item in the list part of a combo box once, the list closes, so it's impossible to double-click an item—except in simple combo boxes, where the list stays open at all times.

Removing Items from a Combo Box

Just as with list boxes, you can remove items from combo boxes using the **Items.Remove** and **Items.RemoveAt** methods. You just pass the object to remove to **Items.Remove** of the index of the item you want to remove from the combo box's list to **Items.RemoveAt**.

Here's an example. In this case, I'll remove item 1 in the list this way:

```
Private Sub Button1_Click(ByVal sender As System.Object, _
    ByVal e As System.EventArgs)
    ComboBox1.Items.RemoveAt(1)
End Sub
```

TIP: *You should note that removing an item from a combo box changes the indices of the remaining items. After you remove item 1 in the above example, item 2 now gets index 1, and item 3 gets index 2.*

Getting the Current Selection in a Combo Box

When you make a selection in a combo box, that new selection appears in the combo box's text box, so it's easy to get the text of the current selection—you just use the combo box's **Text** property.

You also can use the **SelectedIndex** and **SelectedItem** properties to get the index of the selected item and the selected items itself. Here's how I display information about the currently selected item in a combo box in the ComboBoxes example when the user clicks the "Get selected" button:

```
Private Sub Button2_Click(ByVal sender As System.Object, _
    ByVal e As System.EventArgs) Handles Button2.Click
    Dim selectedIndex As Integer
```

```
selectedIndex = ComboBox1.SelectedIndex
Dim selectedItem As Object
selectedItem = ComboBox1.SelectedItem

TextBox1.Text = "Selected item text: " & selectedItem.ToString() & _
    " Selected index: " & selectedIndex.ToString()
End Sub
```

TIP: *If you want to restrict the user's input to items from the combo box's list, set the combo box's* **DropDownStyle** *property to* **DropDownList**. *In this style of combo boxes, the user cannot type into the text part of the control.*

Sorting a Combo Box

You've been newly commissioned to write the guidebook to the zoo with Visual Basic, and everything looks great—except for one thing. The program features a combo box with a list of animals that the user can select to learn more about, and it would be great if you could make that list appear in alphabetical order—but the zoo keeps adding and trading animals all the time. Still, it's no problem, because you can leave the work up to the combo box itself if you set its **Sorted** property to **True** (the default is **False**).

For example, say we set the **Sorted** property to **True** for a combo box, **ComboBox1**. Now it doesn't matter in what order you add items to that combo box:

```
Private Sub Form1_Load(ByVal sender As System.Object, _
    ByVal e As System.EventArgs) Handles MyBase.Load
    ComboBox1.Items.Add("zebra")
    ComboBox1.Items.Add("tiger")
    ComboBox1.Items.Add("hamster")
    ComboBox1.Items.Add("aardvark")
End Sub
```

The sorted combo box appears in Figure 7.14—now you'll be able to handle the animals from aardvark to zebra automatically and alphabetically.

TIP: *You should know, however, that sorting a combo box can change the indices of the items in that combo box (unless they were already in alphabetical order). After the sorting is finished, the first item in the newly sorted combo list has index 0, the next index 1, and so on.*

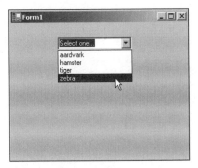

Figure 7.14   Sorting the items in a combo box.

Clearing a Combo Box

It's time to put new items into a combo box—but does that mean you have to delete all the current items there one by one with **Remove** or **RemoveAt**? No, you can clear a whole combo box at once with the **Items.Clear** method. Here's an example where I'm clearing a combo box when the user clicks a button:

```
Private Sub Button1_Click_1(ByVal sender As System.Object, _
    ByVal e As System.EventArgs) Handles Button1.Click
    ComboBox1.Items.Clear()
End Sub
```

Note that there is no "Unclear" method—once you remove the items from a combo box, they're gone until you expressly add them again.

*TIP: The **Clear** method does not clear the text in the combo box's **Text** property.*

Getting the Number of Items in a Combo Box

You're trying to bend over backwards to make your program user-friendly and have let the user add items to the main combo box. But now you need to see if they've added a particular item to the combo box—how do you find out how many items there are in the combo box currently so you can set up your loop?

No problem; you can get the number of items in a combo box with the **Items.Count** property like this:

```
Private Sub Button1_Click(ByVal sender As System.Object, _
    ByVal e As System.EventArgs) Handles Button1.Click
        MsgBox("The combo box contains " & ComboBox1.Items.Count & " items.")
End Sub
```

Storing Objects in a List Box or Combo Box

You've been asked to write the employee phone directory program and place a combo box with all the employee's names in the middle of a form. Now how do you connect phone numbers to the names?

In VB6 and before, each item in list boxes and combo boxes had an **ItemData** property, which allowed you to store text data for each item. Now, each item in a list box or combo box is itself an object, so I'll jump ahead a few chapters to Chapter 12, where we'll start creating our own classes and objects, to show how you can store additional data for each item in these controls. This example is named ComboBoxData on the CD-ROM.

To see how this works, I'll create a new class named **DataItem**, and each item in a combo box will be an object of this class. (To understand how to create classes, see Chapter 12.) This class will store both the name of each combo box item and some data. I'll let the **New** constructor store both the name and data for each item in private data members:

```
Public Class DataItem
    Private Data As Single
    Private Name As String

    Public Sub New(ByVal NameArgument As String, ByVal Value As Single)
        Name = NameArgument
        Data = Value
    End Sub
        .
        .
        .
```

I'll also add a **ToString** method, overriding the **Object** class's **ToString** method, because this method will be called when the combo box needs to display the name of each item, and I'll also add a **GetData** method that we can use to get the internal, private data from objects:

```
Public Class DataItem
    Private Data As Single
    Private Name As String

    Public Sub New(ByVal NameArgument As String, ByVal Value As Single)
        Name = NameArgument
        Data = Value
    End Sub

    Overrides Function ToString() As String
        Return CStr(Name)
    End Function

    Public Function GetData() As Single
        Return Data
    End Function
End Class
```

TIP: *If the list box contains objects that support properties, the **DisplayMember** property indicates which property of the object to show. If empty, this property is empty and the object's **ToString** method is used.*

When the form loads, we can create 20 objects of the **DataItem** class—item 5 will be named "Item 5" and store the internal value 5, for example—and place them in the combo box with the **Items.Add** method:

```
Private Sub Form1_Load(ByVal sender As System.Object, _
    ByVal e As System.EventArgs) Handles MyBase.Load
    Dim Objects(20) As DataItem

    ComboBox1.BeginUpdate()
    Dim intLoopIndex As Integer
    For intLoopIndex = 0 To 20
        Objects(intLoopIndex) = New DataItem("Item " & _
            intLoopIndex, CSng(intLoopIndex))
        ComboBox1.Items.Add(Objects(I))
    Next
    ComboBox1.Items.AddRange(Objects)
    ComboBox1.EndUpdate()
End Sub
```

Using **AddRange**

Because we've stored the **DataItem** objects in an array (named **Objects** here), there's another way of adding these items to a combo box or list box that's worth pointing out here—you can use the **AddRange** method like this to add all the objects in the **Objects** array to the combo box at once:

```
Private Sub Form1_Load(ByVal sender As System.Object, _
    ByVal e As System.EventArgs) Handles MyBase.Load
    Dim Objects(20) As DataItem

    ComboBox1.BeginUpdate()
    Dim intLoopIndex As Integer
    For intLoopIndex = 0 To 20
        Objects(intLoopIndex) = New DataItem("Item " & _
            intLoopIndex, CSng(intLoopIndex))
    Next
    ComboBox1.Items.AddRange(Objects)
    ComboBox1.EndUpdate()
End Sub
```

Now when the user selects an item in the combo box, I can use the **SelectedItem** property to get the selected object, and that object's **GetData** method to get the object's stored data (note that I must cast the item to an object of the **DataItem** class first, using **CType**), which I display in a message box. Here's the full code:

```
Public Class Form1
    Inherits System.Windows.Forms.Form

    'Windows Form Designer generated code

    Private Sub Form1_Load(ByVal sender As System.Object, _
        ByVal e As System.EventArgs) Handles MyBase.Load
        Dim Objects(20) As DataItem
        ComboBox1.BeginUpdate()
        Dim intLoopIndex As Integer
        For intLoopIndex = 0 To 20
            Objects(intLoopIndex) = New DataItem("Item " & intLoopIndex, _
            CSng(intLoopIndex))
        Next
        ComboBox1.Items.AddRange(Objects)
        ComboBox1.EndUpdate()
    End Sub
```

```
    Private Sub ComboBox1_SelectedIndexChanged(ByVal sender As _
        System.Object, ByVal e As System.EventArgs) Handles _
        ComboBox1.SelectedIndexChanged
        MsgBox("The data for the item you selected is: " & _
            CType(ComboBox1.SelectedItem, DataItem).GetData())
    End Sub
End Class

Public Class DataItem
    Private Data As Single
    Private Name As String
    Public Sub New(ByVal NameArgument As String, ByVal Value As Single)
        Name = NameArgument
        Data = Value
    End Sub

    Overrides Function ToString() As String
        Return CStr(Name)
    End Function

    Public Function GetData() As Single
        Return Data
    End Function
End Class
```

You can see this example, ComboBoxData, at work in Figure 7.15. Now we're storing objects in combo boxes, and using object methods to store and retrieve data in those objects.

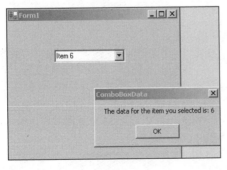

Figure 7.15   Recovering data from combo box items.

Using the **PictureBox** Class

As discussed in the In Depth section of this chapter, you use picture boxes to display images. In VB6 and before, picture boxes were powerhouses of image handling and editing, but now their capabilities are limited to displaying images and a little more, such as stretching those images. The **PictureBox** class is derived directly from the **Control** class:

```
Object
    MarshalByRefObject
        Component
            Control
                PictureBox
```

You can find the more notable public properties of the **PictureBox** class in Table 7.10, and the more notable events in Table 7.11. Note that as with other Windows forms controls, I am not listing the notable properties, methods, and events **PictureBox** inherits from the **Control** class, such as the **Click** event—you can see all that in Chapter 5, Tables 5.1, 5.2, and 5.3.

TIP: *Although picture boxes no longer have drawing methods built in, you can use a picture box's built-in* **Graphics** *object to do as much as picture boxes used to do and more—see "Scrolling Images" in Chapter 8 to get a sample, where we're scrolling an image in a picture box.*

Related solution:	Found on page:
Scrolling Images	349

Table 7.10   Noteworthy public properties of PictureBox objects.

Property	Means
BorderStyle	Gets/sets the border style for the picture box.
Image	Gets/sets the image that is in a picture box.

Table 7.11   Noteworthy public events of PictureBox objects.

Event	Means
Resize	Occurs when the picture box is resized.
SizeModeChanged	Occurs when **SizeMode** changes.

Setting or Getting the Image in a Picture Box

You've added a new picture box to your form, and it looks fine—except for one thing: it's completely blank. How do you add images to a picture box? You use the **Image** property. You set the **Image** property to an **Image** object, which you can create using the **Image** class's **FromFile** method. This method is versatile and can load images from bitmap (.bmp), icon (.ico) or metafile (.wmf), JPEG (.jpg), GIF (.gif) files, and other types of files.

At design time, you can click the **Image** property in the Properties window and click the button with an ellipsis ("...") in it to open a dialog box that lets you select an image file to load into a picture box. At run time, you can load an image into the **Image** property like this, where I'm loading image.jpg (which is on the CD-ROM):

```
Private Sub Button1_Click(ByVal sender As System.Object, _
    ByVal e As System.EventArgs) Handles Button1.Click
    PictureBox1.Image = _
        Image.FromFile("c:\vbnet\ch07\pictureboxes\image.jpg")
End Sub
```

You can see this code at work in the PictureBoxes example on the CD-ROM, as you see in Figure 7.16. When you click the "Load image" button, the image you see in the picture box is loaded.

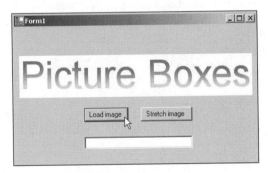

Figure 7.16   Loading an image into a picture box.

Adjusting Picture Box Size to Contents

You've displayed the image of the company's Illustrious Founder in a picture box in your new program—but the picture box was a little small, and you can only see most of the I.F.'s forehead. There's some email waiting for you from the president's office, and you think you know what it says. How can you make sure picture boxes readjust themselves to fit the picture they're displaying?

When you load a picture into a picture control, it does not readjust itself to fit the picture (although image controls do)—at least, not by default. Picture boxes will resize themselves to fit their contents if you set their **SizeMode** property; here are the possible values, which come from the **PictureBoxSizeMode** enumeration:

- **Normal**—Standard picture box behavior (the upper-left corner of the image is placed at upper left in the picture box).

- **StretchImage**—Allows you to stretch the image in code.

- **AutoSize**—Fits the picture box to the image.

- **CenterImage**—Centers the image in the picture box.

Here's an example from the PictureBoxes example on the CD-ROM; in this case, I set a picture box's **SizeMode** property to **StretchImage** and then give it a new size this way:

```
Private Sub Button2_Click(ByVal sender As System.Object, _
    ByVal e As System.EventArgs) Handles Button2.Click
    PictureBox1.SizeMode = PictureBoxSizeMode.StretchImage
    PictureBox1.ClientSize = New Size(300, 100)
End Sub
```

You can see the stretched image in Figure 7.17.

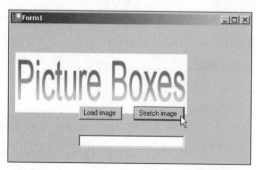

Figure 7.17   Stretching an image in a picture box.

Handling Picture Box Events (and Creating Image Maps)

The New Products Department is on the phone; they want you to design a program to welcome new employees to the company. The program should display a picture of the main plant, and when the new employee clicks part of that image, "it should sort of zoom in on it." Can you do that in Visual Basic?

You can if you handle mouse events for the picture box and respond accordingly. For example, the PictureBoxes example on the CD-ROM handles **MouseDown** events by displaying the location where the mouse went down in a text box:

```
Private Sub PictureBox1_MouseDown(ByVal sender As Object, _
    ByVal e As System.Windows.Forms.MouseEventArgs) Handles _
    PictureBox1.MouseDown
    TextBox1.Text = "You clicked at " & e.X & ", " & e.Y
End Sub
```

You can see the results of this code in Figure 7.18, where I've clicked the picture box.

Related solution:	Found on page:
Handling Mouse Events	199

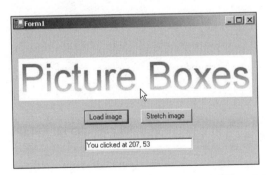

Figure 7.18   Creating an image map with a picture box.

Chapter 8

Windows Forms: Scroll Bars, Splitters, Track Bars, Pickers, Notify Icons, Tool Tips, and Timers

In Depth

We've got quite a number of Windows forms controls to cover in this chapter—scroll bars, splitters, track bars, pickers, notify icons, tool tips, and timers. Fortunately, they're all simple controls. Some of them—such as splitters and notify icons—are entirely new to Visual Basic .NET, and the others have all changed greatly from the VB6 days, as you might expect. I'll start by discussing each of these controls in some depth, including their useful properties, methods, and events.

Scroll Bars

Anyone familiar with Windows knows what scroll bars are—those vertical or horizontal controls that display a *scroll box* or *thumb* that you can manipulate, and when you drag it to a new position, the value of the scroll bar changes, causing a corresponding action in the program. You can see scroll bars in our ScrollBars example on the CD-ROM at work in Figure 8.1. In that figure, I've docked two scroll bars to the edges of a form, and am using them to move a label (which displays the text "I'm moving!") around the form. There's also a horizontal scroll bar in this example that displays its value (which ranges from 0 to 100) directly in a text box.

There are two types of scroll bar controls—horizontal and vertical. There are two primary events for scroll bars—the **Scroll** event, which happens continuously as the scroll bar is scrolled, and the **ValueChanged** event, which occurs every time the scroll bar's value changes by even one unit (which means it'll happen many times during a normal scroll operation).

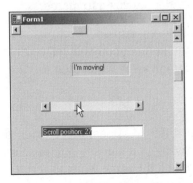

Figure 8.1   Scroll bars at work.

Most controls that typically use scroll bars come with them built in, such as multiline text boxes, list controls, or combo boxes. However, scroll bars still have their uses, as when you want to do some custom work, such as scrolling the image in a picture box (which does not come with built-in scroll bars—see "Scrolling Images" later in this chapter), or letting the user get visual feedback while setting numeric ranges, as when they're setting red, green, and blue values to select a color.

You use the **Minimum** and **Maximum** (formerly **Min** and **Max**) properties to set the range of values the user can select using the scroll bar. The **LargeChange** property sets the scroll increment that happens when the user clicks in the scroll bar but outside the scroll box. The **SmallChange** property sets the scroll increment when the user clicks the scroll arrows at each end of the scroll bar. The default values for the **Minimum**, **Maximum**, **SmallChange**, and **LargeChange** values are 0, 100, 1, and 10 respectively. You get the actual setting of a scroll bar with its **Value** property.

TIP: Actually, when setting the **Maximum** property for a scroll bar, you should keep in mind that the scroll bar can scroll up only to that maximum minus the width of the scroll box. For example, if you set the **Minimum** property to 0 and the **Maximum** property to 1,000, the actual maximum value the user can scroll to is 991.

Splitters

You can use splitters to let the user resize controls. Here's how it works: you add a control to a form, then dock it. Next, you add a splitter and dock it to the same side of the same container, which places the control just before the splitter in the docking order. When you run the program, the splitter is invisible until the mouse passes over it, when the splitter changes the mouse cursor, indicating that the control can be resized, as you see in Figure 8.2, which is the Splitters example on the CD-ROM. In that figure, I'm moving the splitter, and when I release it, the control I'm resizing (a text box in this case) is indeed resized to match.

That's about all there is to this control, but it can be a useful one, because space is always at a premium in Windows programs, and splitter controls let you resize controls, extending them as needed, or tucking them away when their job is over.

Track Bars

Track bars are very much like scroll bars but differ in appearance. Track bars look more like controls you might see on stereos—you can see one at work in Figure 8.3. As that figure shows, track bars do much the same work as scroll bars do—let the user specify numeric values from a continuous range.

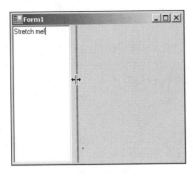

Figure 8.2   A splitter in action.

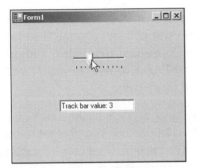

Figure 8.3   A track bar at work.

You can configure a track bar's range with the **Minimum** (default = 0) and **Maximum** (default = 10) properties. You can specify how much the **Value** property should be incremented when clicks occur to the sides of the slider by means of the **LargeChange** (default = 5) property, and how much when the user uses arrow keys when the control has the focus with the **SmallChange** property (default = 1). A track bar can be displayed horizontally or vertically—you set its orientation with the **Orientation** property.

You also can configure track bars with the **TickStyle** property, which lets you determine how ticks are displayed; this property can take values from the **TickStyle** enumeration:

- **Both**—Tick marks are located on both sides of the control.
- **BottomRight**—Tick marks are located on the bottom of a horizontal control or on the right side of a vertical control.
- **None**—No tick marks appear in the control.
- **TopLeft**—Tick marks are located on the top of a horizontal control or on the left of a vertical control.

You also can set the tick frequency, which sets the distance between ticks, with the **TickFrequency** property (the default is 1).

Pickers

There are two types of pickers—date-time pickers, and month calendar controls. You can see them in Figure 8.4; the date-time picker is the drop-down list box at the top, and the month calendar control appears beneath it.

Date-Time Pickers

You can set a date and time in a date-time picker just by editing the displayed values in the control; if you click the arrow in the date-time picker, it displays a month calendar, just as a combo box would display a drop-down list; you can make selections just by clicking the calendar.

You can limit the date and times that can be selected in a date-time picker by setting the **MinDate** and **MaxDate** properties. And you can change the look of the calendar part of the control by setting the **CalendarForeColor**, **Calendar Font**, **CalendarTitleBackColor**, **CalendarTitleForeColor**, **CalendarTrailing ForeColor**, and **CalendarMonthBackground** properties.

When the user makes a selection, the new selection appears in the text box part of the date-time picker, and a **ValueChanged** event occurs. You can get the new text in the text box part of the control with the **Text** property, or as a Visual Basic **DateTime** object with the **Value** property. **DateTime** objects are good to know about. (We'll use them in several places in this chapter.) You can find the static properties of this class (the class properties that you can use with the class alone, without needing to create a **DateTime** object) in Table 8.1, the public properties of **DateTime** objects in Table 8.2, and the public object methods in Table 8.3.

Figure 8.4   A date-time picker and a month calendar control.

Table 8.1 Noteworthy public shared (static) properties of the **DateTime** class.

Property	Means
Now	Holds a **DateTime** object holding the current local time.
Today	Holds a **DateTime** object holding the current date.
UtcNow	Holds a **DateTime** object holding the current local time in universal time (UTC).

Table 8.2 Noteworthy public properties of **DateTime** objects.

Property	Means
Date	Holds the date of this object.
Day	Holds the day of the month of this object.
DayOfWeek	Holds the day of the week of this object.
DayOfYear	Holds the day of the year of this object.
Hour	Holds the hour part of the date of this object.
Millisecond	Holds the milliseconds (thousandths of a second) part of the time represented by this object.
Minute	Holds the minutes of the time in this object.
Month	Holds the month part of the date in this object.
Second	Holds the seconds part of the date in this object.
Ticks	Holds the number of 100-nanosecond ticks that represent the date and time of this object.
TimeOfDay	Holds the time of day for this object.
Year	Holds the year part of the date in this object.

Table 8.3 Noteworthy public methods of **DateTime** objects.

Method	Means
Add	Adds a **TimeSpan** object to this object.
AddDays	Adds a number of days to this object.
AddHours	Adds a number of hours to this object.
AddMilliseconds	Adds a number of milliseconds to this object.
AddMinutes	Adds a number of minutes to this object.
AddMonths	Adds a number of months to this object.
AddSeconds	Adds a number of seconds to this object.
AddTicks	Adds a number of ticks to this object.
AddYears	Adds a number of years to this object.

(continued)

Table 8.3   Noteworthy public methods of **DateTime** objects *(continued).*

Method	Means
CompareTo	Compares this object to another object, returning a value indicating their relative values.
Equals	Indicates if an object is equal to another object.
Subtract	Subtracts a time from this object.
ToFileTime	Converts this object to local time format.
ToLocalTime	Converts coordinated universal time (UTC) to local time.
ToLongDateString	Converts this object to its equivalent long date **String** value.
ToLongTimeString	Converts this object to its equivalent long time **String** value.
ToShortDateString	Converts this object to its equivalent short date **String** value.
ToShortTimeString	Converts this object to its equivalent short time **String** value.
ToString	Converts this object to its equivalent **String** value.
ToUniversalTime	Converts the local time to universal time (UTC).

The **Format** property sets the **DateTimePickerFormat** property of the control. The default date **Format** is **DateTimePickerFormat.Long**. If the **Format** property is set to **DateTimePickerFormat.Custom**, you can create your own format style by setting the **CustomFormat** property and using a custom format string. The custom format string can be a combination of custom field characters and other literal characters; see "Setting Date-Time Picker Custom Formats" later in this chapter.

To use an up-down style control to adjust the date-time value, set the **ShowUpDown** property to **True**. In this case, the calendar control will not drop down when the control is selected—here, the date and time can be set by selecting each item individually and using the up and down buttons in the control.

Month Calendar Controls

The month calendar control allows the user to select a date and time visually, as you can see in Figure 8.4. You can limit the date and times that can be selected by setting the **MinDate** and **MaxDate** properties. When a new date is selected, a **DateSelected** event occurs, and when the date is changed, a **DateChanged** event occurs. Because the user can use the mouse to select a range of dates, you can use the month calendar control's **SelectionRange** property to determine which date or dates have been selected.

The **SelectionRange** property returns a **SelectionRange** object. This has two useful properties: **Start** and **End**, which return **DateTime** objects corresponding to the start and end of the selected date. If only one date has been selected, both **Start** and **End** will point to that date. For example, the currently selected starting day in a month calendar control would be **MonthCalendar1.Selection Range.Start.Day**.

You also can use the month calendar control's **SelectionStart** and **SelectionEnd** properties to directly access the start and end dates selected without using the **SelectionRange** properties at all. Both of these properties return **DateTime** objects as well. And note also that you can change the look of the calendar part of the control by setting the **ForeColor**, font, **TitleBackColor**, **TitleForeColor**, **TrailingForeColor**, and **BackColor** properties.

Notify Icons

This is a pretty cool one, new to Visual Basic .NET. Notify icons let you display an icon in the status notification area of the Windows taskbar (in the indented panel at extreme right in the taskbar) called the Windows system tray. You can see a notify icon in the Windows taskbar in Figure 8.5 from the NotifyIcons example on the CD-ROM. It's the one at right, next to the time. (I've created this icon myself; it's not something inherent in the notify icon control.)

To set the icon displayed for a control, you use the **Icon** property. You also can write code in the **DoubleClick** event handler so that something happens when the user double-clicks the icon. And you can make the icon appear and disappear by setting the control's **Visible** property.

This is a great one for processes that run in the background, and don't have their own windows, although they may be parts of applications that do display windows. Visual Basic .NET now lets you create *Windows services*, which run in the background and can display control panels (much like Microsoft SQL Server), and you can use notify icons to let the user open such control panels.

Tool Tips

All Windows users know what tool tips are—they're those small windows that appear with explanatory text when you let the mouse rest on a control or window. That's what tool tips are used for—to give quick help when the mouse rests on an item. You can see a tool tip at work in the ToolTips example from the CD-ROM in Figure 8.6, explaining the rather obvious fact that the mouse is resting on a button.

Figure 8.5   A notify icon in the Windows taskbar.

Figure 8.6   A tool tip at work.

In VB6 and before, controls themselves had a **ToolTip** property, but now tool tips are separate components. You can associate a tool tip with any other control. To connect a tool tip with a control, you use its **SetToolTip** method. For example, to connect the tool tip you see in Figure 8.6 to **Button1**, you can use this code:

```
ToolTip1.SetToolTip(Button1, "This is a button")
```

You also can use the **GetToolTip** method to get information about a tool tip object.

The important properties for tool tip controls are **Active**, which must be set to **True** for the tool tip to appear, and **AutomaticDelay**, which sets the length of time that the tool tip is shown, how long the user must point at the control for the tool tip to appear, and how long it takes for subsequent tool tip windows to appear.

Timers

Timers are also very useful controls, because they let you create periodic events. Strictly speaking, timers are no longer controls but components, and they do not appear in a window at run time. At design time, they appear in the component tray underneath the form you've added them to. There's a timer at work behind the scenes in the Timers example in Figure 8.7, which shows a clock (using a label control) and lets the user set an alarm setting—as soon as the current time matches the alarm setting, the program will start to beep until you click the "Alarm off" radio button.

Windows timers are designed for a single-threaded (as opposed to multithreaded) environment; you set how often you want the timer to generate **Tick** events by setting the **Interval** property (in milliseconds, one thousandths of a second). Each time a **Tick** event happens, you can execute code in a handler for this event, just as you would for any other event.

Figure 8.7   A timer at work.

TIP: *In VB6 and before, you could set a timer's **Interval** property to 0 to disable the timer, but the minimum possible value for this property is now 1—you now use the **Enabled** property to turn timers on and off. You also can use the new **Start** and **Stop** methods to start and stop a timer.*

This control is a useful one for, among other things, creating clocks like the one you see in Figure 8.7. However, you should use it with care. One of the guiding principles behind Windows programming is that the user should direct the action as much as possible; if you find yourself using a timer just to wrest control away from the user, think twice about what you're doing.

That's enough detail for the moment—it's time to get to the Immediate Solutions section to handle point-by-point issues.

Immediate Solutions

Using the **HScrollBar** and **VScrollBar** Classes

Well, the new company banner logo is 2,000 by 4,000 pixels, which is a little too large for most screens. What can you do? One thing you might consider is using scroll bars to scroll the image (see "Scrolling Images" later in this chapter). There are two types of scroll bars, horizontal ones (**HScrollBar**) and vertical ones (**VScrollBar**). Here are the class hierarchies for both:

```
Object
    MarshalByRefObject
        Component
            Control
                ScrollBar
                    HScrollBar

Object
    MarshalByRefObject
        Component
            Control
                ScrollBar
                    VScrollBar
```

You can find the more notable public properties of the **HScrollBar** and **VScrollBar** class in Table 8.4 and the more notable events in Table 8.5. Note that as with other Windows forms controls, I am not listing the notable properties, methods, and events **HScrollBar** and **VScrollBar** inherit from the **Control** class—you can see all that in Chapter 5, Tables 5.1, 5.2, and 5.3.

Table 8.4   Noteworthy public properties of HScrollBar and VScrollBar objects.

Property	Means
LargeChange	Gets/sets the value added to or subtracted from to the **Value** property when the scroll bar itself is clicked (outside the scroll box).
Maximum	Gets/sets the upper limit of the scrollable range.
Minimum	Gets/sets the lower limit of the scrollable range.
SmallChange	Gets/sets the value added to or subtracted from to the **Value** property when the user clicks an arrow button.
Value	Gets/sets a value corresponding to the current position of the scroll box.

Table 8.5   Noteworthy public events of HScrollBar and VScrollBar objects.

Event	Means
Scroll	Occurs when the scroll box is moved (either by the mouse or the keyboard).
ValueChanged	Occurs when the **Value** property has changed, either by a **Scroll** event or programmatically.

Setting Scroll Bars' Minimum and Maximum Values

The Testing Department is calling again. The Field Testing Unit loves the new program you've written to help them record in-the-field performance of the company's products, but there's just one problem: performance is measured on a scale of 1–10, and the scroll bars in your program seem to go from 0–100. It's been very hard for the users of your program to operate with only one-tenth of the whole scroll bar—can you rescale it?

Yes, you can. After you place a scroll bar in a program, the first thing to do is to set its range of possible values, which by default is 0–100. The minimum value a scroll bar can be set to is stored in its **Minimum** property, and the maximum value in the **Maximum** property. You can set the **Minimum** and **Maximum** properties for scroll bars at design time or at run time; here's how we change those properties in a horizontal scroll bar when a form loads:

```
Private Sub Form1_Load(ByVal sender As System.Object, _
    ByVal e As System.EventArgs) Handles MyBase.Load
    HScrollBar1.Minimum = 0
    HScrollBar1.Maximum = 10
End Sub
```

Setting Up Scroll Bar Clicks (Large Changes)

The Testing Department is calling again. The scroll bars you've added to your program, *SuperDuperTextPro*, look terrific. But why doesn't anything happen when the user clicks the scroll bar itself, in the area between the scroll box and an arrow button? You ask: Should something happen? They say: Yes.

When the user clicks the scroll bar itself, not the scroll box and not an arrow button, the scroll box should move in that direction by the amount set by the scroll bar's **LargeChange** property (see also the next topic, which deals with the **SmallChange** property). For example, if you've set the scroll bar's range to be 1–100, a reasonable **LargeChange** setting would be 10. You can set the **LargeChange** property at design time, or at run time.

Here's an example where we set the **LargeChange** property for two scroll bars, a horizontal one and a vertical one:

```
Private Sub Form1_Load(ByVal sender As System.Object, _
    ByVal e As System.EventArgs) Handles MyBase.Load
    HScrollBar1.Minimum = 0
    HScrollBar1.Maximum = 100
    HScrollBar1.LargeChange = 10
End Sub
```

Now, when the user clicks the scroll bar between the scroll box and arrow buttons, the scroll bar's value will increase or decrease by 10.

Note that on some occasions, you should change the **LargeChange** property while a program is running. For example, if you let the user scroll through a document with this property, setting it to 1, and the user loads in a 30,000-line document, it might be wise to change the value of this property.

TIP: *This is one of those values that you should test yourself, because it's part of your program's feel. I know of a graphics program that scrolls exactly one pixel at a time when you click the arrow buttons in the scroll bars next to an image. Such a thing is annoying and gives users the impression that your program is unresponsive and hard to use.*

Setting Up Scroll Bar Arrow Clicks (Small Changes)

As far as the user is concerned, there are three ways to change the setting of a scroll bar: to move the scroll box (also called the thumb), to click the area of the scroll bar between the scroll box and an arrow button, and to click an arrow button. When the user clicks an arrow button, the scroll box moves by an amount stored in the **SmallChange** property (see also the previous topic, which deals with the **LargeChange** property).

I know a programmer who thought the **SmallChange** property was a joke because its name can be interpreted humorously, but it certainly exists. When the user clicks a scroll bar's arrow, the setting of the scroll bar is incremented or decremented (depending on which arrow was clicked) by the value in the **SmallChange** property. You can set a scroll bar's **SmallChange** property at design time or at run time.

For example, here I'm setting the **SmallChange** property for two scroll bars, a horizontal one and a vertical one:

```
Private Sub Form1_Load(ByVal sender As System.Object, _
    ByVal e As System.EventArgs) Handles MyBase.Load
```

```
    HScrollBar1.Minimum = 0
    HScrollBar1.Maximum = 100
    HScrollBar1.LargeChange = 10
    HScrollBar1.SmallChange = 1
End Sub
```

Now when the user clicks the arrow buttons, the setting of the scroll bar will change by 1.

Note that on some occasions, you should change the **SmallChange** property while a program is running. For example, if you let the user scroll through a document with this property, setting it to 1, and the user loads in a 30,000-line document, it might be wise to change the value of this property.

TIP: *This is one of those values that you should test yourself, because it's part of your program's feel. I know of a graphics program that scrolls exactly one pixel at a time when you click the arrow buttons in the scroll bars next to an image. Such a thing is annoying and gives users the impression that your program is unresponsive and hard to use.*

Getting and Setting a Scroll Bar's Current Value

You've added the scroll bars you need to a program, and set their **Minimum**, **Maximum**, **SmallChange**, and **LargeChange** properties, but you'd like to add one more touch. When your program first displays the scroll bars, you'd like them to display a default value, which is right in the middle of their range. How do you set the setting of a scroll bar?

You use the **Value** property to set a scroll bar's setting. You can set this value at either design time or run time, to read a scroll bar's setting while the program is running. The **Value** property holds values that can be in the range spanned by the values in the **Minimum** and **Maximum** properties.

Here's an example. In this case, we're setting up two scroll bars, a horizontal one and a vertical one, and placing the scroll box of each scroll bar in the center of the range when the scroll bar first appears by setting the **Value** properties this way:

```
Private Sub Form1_Load(ByVal sender As System.Object, _
    ByVal e As System.EventArgs) Handles MyBase.Load
    HScrollBar1.Minimum = 0
    HScrollBar1.Maximum = 100
    HScrollBar1.LargeChange = 10
    HScrollBar1.SmallChange = 1
    HScrollBar1.Value = 20
End Sub
```

When the user makes a change in a scroll bar, you get the new setting from the **Value** property when the **Scroll** event is triggered (see the next topic).

Handling Scroll Bar Events

You've added the scroll bars the Testing Department wanted. You've set the scroll bars' **Minimum**, **Maximum**, **SmallChange**, and **LargeChange** properties. Now what—how do you respond to the scroll bars in your program's code?

There are two events you typically use in scroll bars: **Scroll**—which happens when the scroll box is moved either with the mouse or keyboard, and **ValueChanged**—which happens when the **Value** property changes, even by one unit, whether through the user's actions, or in code. In a normal scroll operation, many **ValueChanged** events occur—as, for example, the **Value** property changes from 42 to 43, then to 44, then to 45, and so on.

I usually use the **Scroll** event. When the user changes the setting in a scroll bar, a **Scroll** event occurs; you can react to those changes with an event handler attached to that event. For example, you may use scroll bars to move other controls around on the form (using those controls' **SetBounds** method), and when the user changes a scroll bar's setting, you'll be informed of the new value in the **Scroll** event handler.

Let's take a look at an example that does exactly that. In this case, I'll use two scroll bars docked to the top and right side of a form to move a label control around the form; this example is called ScrollBars on the CD-ROM.

I start by adding two scroll bars—a horizontal scroll bar, **HScrollBar1**, and a vertical scroll bar, **VScrollBar1**—to a form. Dock those two scroll bars to the edges of the form using their **Dock** properties, as you see in Figure 8.1. Next, add a label, **Label1**, to the form; this is the label we'll move around with the scroll bars.

When a scroll bar is scrolled, it triggers a **Scroll** event. You can determine the new setting of the scroll bar with its **Value** property. However, there's more information available to you here in the **ScrollEventArgs** object passed to you in the **Scroll** event handler. This object has two members, **NewValue**, which gives you the new setting of the scroll bar, and **Type**, which tells you the type of the scroll operation. The **Type** values come from the **ScrollEventType** enumeration:

- **EndScroll**—The scroll box has stopped moving.

- **First**—The scroll box was moved to the **Minimum** position.

- **LargeDecrement**—The user clicked the scroll bar to the left (horizontal scroll bars) or above (vertical scroll bars) the scroll box, or pressed the Page Up key.

- **LargeIncrement**—The user clicked the scroll bar to the right (horizontal scroll bars) or below (vertical scroll bars) the scroll box, or pressed the Page Down key.

- **Last**—The scroll box was moved to the **Maximum** position.

- **SmallDecrement**—The user clicked the left (horizontal scroll bars) or top (vertical scroll bars) scroll arrow or pressed the Up Arrow key.

- **SmallIncrement**—The user clicked the right (horizontal scroll bars) or bottom (vertical scroll bars) scroll arrow or pressed the Down Arrow key.

- **ThumbPosition**—The scroll box was moved.

- **ThumbTrack**—The scroll box is currently being moved.

We can move the label around using the scroll bars in our example if we know the present dimensions of the form, which we can get as **Me.Size.Width** and **Me.Size.Height**. Because, by default, the values returned by our scroll bars can go up to a maximum of 100, we can move the label like this, setting its text to "I'm moving!":

```
Private Sub HScrollBar1_Scroll(ByVal sender As System.Object, _
    ByVal e As System.Windows.Forms.ScrollEventArgs) Handles _
        HScrollBar1.Scroll
    Label1.Location = New Point(e.NewValue * Me.Size.Width / 100, _
        Label1.Location.Y)
    Label1.Text = "I'm moving!"
End Sub

Private Sub VScrollBar1_Scroll(ByVal sender As System.Object, _
    ByVal e As System.Windows.Forms.ScrollEventArgs) Handles _
        VScrollBar1.Scroll
    Label1.Location = New Point(Label1.Location.X, _
        e.NewValue * Me.Size.Height / 100)
    Label1.Text = "I'm moving!"
End Sub
```

There's also another scroll bar in this example—a horizontal one—that simply displays its current setting in a text box. Here's the code for that scroll bar:

```
Private Sub HScrollBar2_Scroll(ByVal sender As System.Object, _
    ByVal e As System.Windows.Forms.ScrollEventArgs) Handles _
        HScrollBar2.Scroll
```

8. Windows Forms: Scroll Bars, Splitters, Track Bars, Pickers

```
TextBox1.Text = "Scroll position: " & e.NewValue
End Sub
```

You can see the results in Figure 8.1—when you use the docked scroll bars at the edge of the form, the label moves to match. And you can use the undocked horizontal scroll bar to increment or decrement the value shown in the text box. That's all it takes—now we're handling scroll bar events.

Showing and Hiding Scroll Bars

Unlike other controls, there are well-defined times when scroll bars should disappear from your program. If the object you're scrolling can be entirely visible, there is no need for scroll bars, and you should remove them.

In general, you make a scroll bar disappear by setting its **Visible** property to **False**, and make it reappear by setting that property to **True**. (For an example of this, see "Scrolling Images" later in this chapter.) You also can use the **Show** and **Hide** methods.

TIP: Another option to disable scroll bars is by setting their **Enabled** property to **False**. Disabled scroll bars appear gray and don't display a scroll box.

Coordinating Scroll Bar Pairs

The Testing Department is calling again—the two scroll bars you've added to your *SuperDuperWinBigCasino* game look great, but there's one problem. A pair of scroll bars straddle the user's view of the roulette table in *SuperDuperWin BigCasino*, but when you scroll one, the other doesn't move to match it. Can you fix that?

It's common to have two scroll bars that perform the same scrolling action—one on either side of an image you're scrolling, for example. The user should be able to scroll either scroll bar and have the other one match.

It's easy to keep scroll bars coordinated. All you have to do is to make sure that when one scroll bar has a **Scroll** event, you update the other scroll bar's **Value** property. For example, if we have two vertical scroll bars, **VScrollBar1** and

VScrollBar2, that straddle an object they're in charge of scrolling, you can up-date **VScrollBar2** when **VScrollBar1** changes, this way:

```
Private Sub VScrollBar1_Scroll(ByVal sender As System.Object, _
    ByVal e As System.Windows.Forms.ScrollEventArgs) Handles _
        VScrollBar1.Scroll
    VScrollBar2.Value = e.NewValue
End Sub

Private Sub VScrollBar2_Scroll(ByVal sender As System.Object, _
    ByVal e As System.Windows.Forms.ScrollEventArgs) Handles _
        VScrollBar2.Scroll
    VScrollBar1.Value = e.NewValue
End Sub
```

That's all there is to it—now the scroll bars are coordinated.

TIP: *If appropriate for your code, another way of doing this is to give each scroll bar the same **Scroll** event handler. To see an example of this, take a look at "Scrolling Images" in this chapter.*

Scrolling Images

Well, you've got that company logo to display in a picture box, and it's 2,000×4,000 pixels, and the Big Boss refuses to let you make it smaller. That's too large for most screens, and picture boxes don't come with built-in scroll bars to let you scroll around the image. What can you do?

You can scroll the image yourself by adding scroll bars to the picture box manu-ally; we'll do that in the ScrollImage example on the CD-ROM. This is a useful technique to know, but note that I'll have to use a few methods we haven't seen yet, such as using **Graphics** objects, which we'll see later in this book.

To set up this project, add a picture box to a form (the one in the ScrollImage example is 200×96 pixels), and then add both a horizontal and a vertical scroll bar, positioned so they're *inside* the picture box, as shown in Figure 8.8. The reason they're inside the picture box is that we'll make these scroll bars appear only if the displayed image is too large for the picture box, and if we make the scroll bars appear, we don't want them to inadvertently overlap other controls in the program.

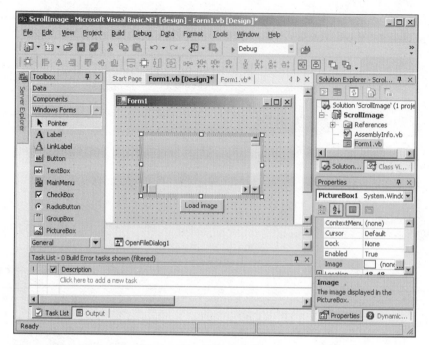

Figure 8.8   Adding scroll bars to a picture box.

Also, add a button with the text "Load image" as you see in Figure 8.8. When the user clicks this button, we'll load the image to display into the picture box. I'll let the user select which image to load (the image I'll use here, image.jpg, is included in the ScrollImage folder on the CD-ROM) by displaying a File Open dialog box using the **OpenFileDialog** control we'll see in the next chapter (see "Creating Open File Dialogs" in the next chapter for the details—we won't need to know much about File Open dialogs here). To make this work, add a new **OpenFile Dialog** control from the toolbox to our project, which makes that control appear in the component tray underneath the form, as shown in Figure 8.8.

When the user clicks the "Load image" button, I can use the **OpenFileDialog1** control's **ShowDialog** method to show an Open File dialog. If the return value of that method is not **DialogResult.Cancel** (which means the user clicked the Cancel button), the name of the image file to open that the user selected will be in the **OpenFileDialog1.FileName** property, so I pass that filename to the **Image.From File** method that we saw in the previous chapter. This creates an **Image** object I can assign to the picture box's **Image** property, and so display the image:

```
Private Sub Button1_Click(ByVal sender As System.Object, _
    ByVal e As System.EventArgs) Handles Button1.Click
```

```
        If OpenFileDialog1.ShowDialog() <> DialogResult.Cancel Then
            PictureBox1.Image = Image.FromFile(OpenFileDialog1.FileName)
            .
            .
            .
        End If
    End Sub
```

Next, I'll set the maximum for the scroll bars to be the amount that the image is wider or higher than the picture box; note that I can find the image's dimensions with the **PictureBox1.Image.Width** and **PictureBox1.Image.Height** properties:

```
    Private Sub Button1_Click(ByVal sender As System.Object, _
        ByVal e As System.EventArgs) Handles Button1.Click
        If OpenFileDialog1.ShowDialog() <> DialogResult.Cancel Then
            PictureBox1.Image = Image.FromFile(OpenFileDialog1.FileName)
            HScrollBar1.Maximum = PictureBox1.Image.Width - _
                PictureBox1.Width
            VScrollBar1.Maximum = PictureBox1.Image.Height - _
                PictureBox1.Height
            .
            .
            .
        End If
    End Sub
```

Finally, to determine if the scroll bars should actually be visible (i.e., if the image is larger than the picture box in one or both dimensions), I'll call a new Sub procedure, **ShowScrollBars**:

```
    Private Sub Button1_Click(ByVal sender As System.Object, _
        ByVal e As System.EventArgs) Handles Button1.Click
        If OpenFileDialog1.ShowDialog() <> DialogResult.Cancel Then
            PictureBox1.Image = Image.FromFile(OpenFileDialog1.FileName)
            HScrollBar1.Maximum = PictureBox1.Image.Width - _
                PictureBox1.Width
            VScrollBar1.Maximum = PictureBox1.Image.Height - _
                PictureBox1.Height
            ShowScrollBars()
        End If
    End Sub
```

In the **ShowScrollBars** Sub procedure, I'll check if either of the two scroll bars should be displayed by checking if the image doesn't fit in one or both dimensions of the picture box, like this:

```
Private Sub ShowScrollBars()
    VScrollBar1.Visible = True
    HScrollBar1.Visible = True

    If PictureBox1.Height > PictureBox1.Image.Height Then
        VScrollBar1.Visible = False
    End If

    If PictureBox1.Width > PictureBox1.Image.Width Then
        HScrollBar1.Visible = False
    End If
End Sub
```

Now the scroll bars will appear if they're needed. In this case, I'm going to give both scroll bars the same **Scroll** event handler, using the **AddHandler** function, to avoid duplicating code. The **Scroll** event handler will be named **ScrollBars_ Scroll**, so I'll connect the **Scroll** event of both scroll bars to that handler when the form loads:

```
Private Sub Form1_Load(ByVal sender As System.Object, _
    ByVal e As System.EventArgs) Handles MyBase.Load
    AddHandler HScrollBar1.Scroll, AddressOf ScrollBars_Scroll
    AddHandler VScrollBar1.Scroll, AddressOf ScrollBars_Scroll
End Sub
```

Now, when either scroll bars is actually scrolled, the **ScrollBars_Scroll** event handler will be called, so I'll model it after a standard **Scroll** event handler:

```
Public Sub ScrollBars_Scroll(ByVal sender As Object, _
    ByVal se As ScrollEventArgs)
        .
        .
        .
End Sub
```

This is where we'll scroll the image. That will actually happen with a **Graphics** object, where we draw a section of the image interactively, depending on the scroll bars' current values. We'll see more about **Graphics** objects later in this book; all we need to know now is that they let you work with the graphics drawing in a control, and that to use a **Graphics** object you should import the **System.Drawing** namespace. To get a **Graphics** object for the picture box, you can use the **CreateGraphics** method; in this case, I'll create a **Graphics** object named **graphics**:

```
Public Sub ScrollBars_Scroll(ByVal sender As Object, _
    ByVal se As ScrollEventArgs)
    Dim graphics As Graphics = PictureBox1.CreateGraphics()
    .
    .
    .

End Sub
```

To actually draw the "scrolled" image, we'll just draw a section of the whole image, as dictated by the current scroll bar settings. You can do that with the **DrawImage** method, which has numerous overloaded forms. In this case, we can pass this method the image to work on (which is **PictureBox1.Image**), the target rectangle to draw in (which is the picture box's main area minus the areas taken up by the scroll bars), the source rectangle to get the image section from (which is the section the user has scrolled to in the image), and the units of measurement we're using (which is **GraphicsUnit.Pixel** here to indicate that we're working in pixel measurements). Here's what that looks like in the **ScrollBars_Scroll** event handler:

```
Public Sub ScrollBars_Scroll(ByVal sender As Object, _
    ByVal se As ScrollEventArgs)
    Dim graphics As Graphics = PictureBox1.CreateGraphics()
    graphics.DrawImage(PictureBox1.Image, New Rectangle(0, 0, _
        PictureBox1.Width - HScrollBar1.Height, _
        PictureBox1.Height - VScrollBar1.Width), _
        New Rectangle(HScrollBar1.Value, VScrollBar1.Value, _
        PictureBox1.Width - HScrollBar1.Height, _
        PictureBox1.Height - VScrollBar1.Width), GraphicsUnit.Pixel)
End Sub
```

This code draws the section of the image that the user has scrolled to in the picture box, which is what we need. Here's the whole code for this example:

```
Imports System.Drawing
Public Class Form1
    Inherits System.Windows.Forms.Form

    'Windows Form Designer generated code

    Private Sub ShowScrollBars()
        VScrollBar1.Visible = True
```

```
                HScrollBar1.Visible = True

                If PictureBox1.Height > PictureBox1.Image.Height Then
                    VScrollBar1.Visible = False
                End If

                If PictureBox1.Width > PictureBox1.Image.Width Then
                    HScrollBar1.Visible = False
                End If
            End Sub

            Public Sub ScrollBars_Scroll(ByVal sender As Object, _
                ByVal se As ScrollEventArgs)
                Dim graphics As Graphics = PictureBox1.CreateGraphics()
                graphics.DrawImage(PictureBox1.Image, New Rectangle(0, 0, _
                    PictureBox1.Width - HScrollBar1.Height, _
                    PictureBox1.Height - VScrollBar1.Width), _
                    New Rectangle(HScrollBar1.Value, VScrollBar1.Value, _
                    PictureBox1.Width - HScrollBar1.Height, _
                    PictureBox1.Height - VScrollBar1.Width), GraphicsUnit.Pixel)
            End Sub

            Private Sub Form1_Load(ByVal sender As System.Object, _
                ByVal e As System.EventArgs) Handles MyBase.Load
                AddHandler HScrollBar1.Scroll, AddressOf ScrollBars_Scroll
                AddHandler VScrollBar1.Scroll, AddressOf ScrollBars_Scroll
            End Sub

            Private Sub Button1_Click(ByVal sender As System.Object, _
                ByVal e As System.EventArgs) Handles Button1.Click
                If OpenFileDialog1.ShowDialog() <> DialogResult.Cancel Then
                    PictureBox1.Image = Image.FromFile(OpenFileDialog1.FileName)
                    HScrollBar1.Maximum = PictureBox1.Image.Width - _
                        PictureBox1.Width
                    VScrollBar1.Maximum = PictureBox1.Image.Height - _
                        PictureBox1.Height
                    ShowScrollBars()
                End If
            End Sub
        End Class
```

You can see the results of this example, ScrollImage, in Figure 8.9, where I've loaded the image that comes with this example, image.jpg, into the picture box and am scrolling it around using the scroll bars. Now you're scrolling picture boxes.

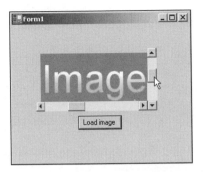

Figure 8.9   Scrolling an image.

Related solution:	Found on page:
Setting or Getting the Image in a Picture Box	327

Adding Scroll Bars to Text Boxes

How do you add scroll bars to text boxes? You use the text box's **ScrollBars** property instead of using actual scroll bar controls, but I'm including this topic here anyway because this is a natural chapter to turn to with this question.

First, make sure the text box's **MultiLine** property is set to **True**, because only multiline text boxes support scroll bars. Next, decide what kind of scroll bars you want on the text box: horizontal, vertical, or both, and set the **ScrollBars** property to match. That property can take these values from the **ScrollBars** enumeration:

- **None**—(the default) No scroll bars

- **Horizontal**

- **Vertical**

- **Both**

For example, I've added both horizontal and vertical scroll bars to the text box in Figure 8.10; note that the bottom scroll bar will appear only if you've set the **WordWrap** property to **False**.

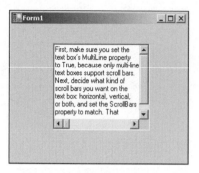

Figure 8.10   Adding scroll bars to a text box.

Using the **Splitter** Class

As discussed in the In Depth section of this chapter, you can use a splitter to resize a control at run time. Here is the class hierarchy for the **Splitter** class:

```
Object
    MarshalByRefObject
        Component
            Control
                Splitter
```

You can find the more notable public properties of the **Splitter** class in Table 8.6 and the more notable events in Table 8.7. Note that as with other Windows controls, I am not listing the notable properties, methods, and events **Splitter** inherits from the **Control** class, such as the **Click** event; you can see all that in Chapter 5 in Tables 5.1, 5.2, and 5.3.

Table 8.6   Noteworthy public properties of **Splitter** objects.

Property	Means
BorderStyle	Gets/sets the splitter's border type.
MinExtra	Gets/sets the minimum size of the container that does not display controls docked to the edge.
MinSize	Gets/sets the minimum size of the splitter's target.
SplitPosition	Gets/sets the current position of the splitter.

Table 8.7   Noteworthy public events of **Splitter** objects.

Event	Means
SplitterMoved	Occurs when the splitter has moved.
SplitterMoving	Occurs as the splitter is moving.

Creating Splitter Controls

As discussed in the In Depth section of this chapter, splitters are relatively simple controls; you use them to let the user resize controls at run time. You can see the Splitters example from the CD-ROM at work in Figure 8.2.

You can enable or disable the splitter with the **Enabled** property, set the cursor that appears with the splitter with the **Cursor** property (for vertical splitters, the default is **VSplit**, for horizontal splitters, it's **HSplit**; see "Setting the Mouse Pointer in Controls" in Chapter 5 for more information). You also can set the **BorderStyle** to **None** (the default), **Fixed**, or **Fixed3D**. Also, note that the **MinSize** property specifies the minimum size of the control you're resizing.

As discussed in the In Depth section of this chapter, you create a splitter at design time. First, you dock the control you want to use the splitter with to an edge of its container, then add the splitter and dock it the same way, as you see in Figure 8.11 (the splitter is the dotted double line in that figure). The splitter automatically works with the control that immediately precedes it in the docking order, which in this case is a text box (with its **MultiLine** property set to **True** so it can extend from the top of the form to the bottom).

When you run the Splitters example, you can use the splitter to resize the text box, as you see in Figure 8.2. Note the cursor in that figure, which is the **VSplit** cursor, indicates that you can resize the related control.

Of course, you may not want your control to extend from the top to the bottom of your form, in which case you can dock it in a container control. For example, take a look at Figure 8.12; here, I've docked a multiline text box and a splitter inside a borderless **Panel** control, which acts as a container.

Related solutions:	Found on page:
Setting the Mouse Pointer in Controls	218
Creating Panels	280

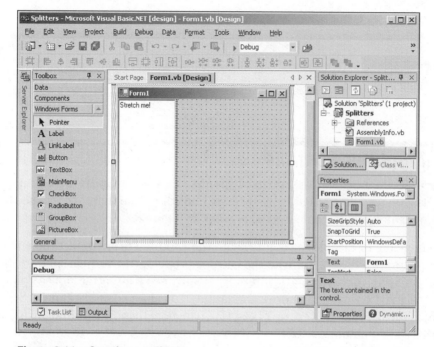

Figure 8.11 Creating a splitter.

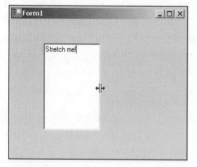

Figure 8.12 Using a splitter inside a **Panel** container.

Using the **TrackBar** Class

As discussed in the In Depth section of this chapter, track bars work much like scroll bars, but they have a different appearance, resembling the controls you'd find on a stereo. Like scroll bars, the **Value** property holds the track bar's current setting, and you can handle the **Scroll** and **ValueChanged** events to work with this control. Track bars also can display *ticks*, giving the user an idea of the scale used to set the control's value. Here is the class hierarchy for the **TrackBar** class:

```
Object
   MarshalByRefObject
      Component
         Control
            TrackBar
```

You can find the more notable public properties of the **TrackBar** class in Table 8.8, the more notable methods in Table 8.9, and the more notable events in Table 8.10. Note that as with other Windows controls, I am not listing the notable properties, methods, and events **TrackBar** inherits from the **Control** class, such as the **Click** event—you can see all that in Tables 5.1, 5.2, and 5.3 in Chapter 5.

Table 8.8   Noteworthy public properties of TrackBar objects.

Property	Means
AutoSize	Gets/sets if the track bar's height or width should be automatically sized.
ForeColor	Holds the foreground color of the track bar.
LargeChange	Gets/sets the value added to or subtracted from to the **Value** property when the scroll box moves a large distance.
Maximum	Holds the upper limit of the range of this track bar.
Minimum	Holds the lower limit of the range of this track bar.
Orientation	Gets/sets the horizontal or vertical orientation of the track bar.
SmallChange	Gets/sets a value which is added to or subtracted from the **Value** property when the scroll box moves a small distance.
TickFrequency	Gets/sets a value specifying the distance between ticks.
TickStyle	Gets/sets how to display the tick marks in the track bar.
Value	Gets/sets the current position of the slider in the track bar.

Table 8.9   Noteworthy public methods of TrackBar objects.

Method	Means
SetRange	Sets the **Minimum** and **Maximum** values for the track bar.

Table 8.10   Noteworthy public events of TrackBar objects.

Event	Means
Scroll	Occurs when the slider moves (either by mouse or keyboard action).
ValueChanged	Occurs when the **Value** property of a track bar changes (either by moving the slider or through code).

Handling Track Bar Events

As with scroll bars, track bars have two events—**Scroll** and **ValueChanged**. And—also as with scroll bars—you can get the current value of the track bar with the **Value** property. Here's how the TrackBars example, which you can see at work in Figure 8.3, works; all we do there is to display the current value of the track bar in a text box in a **Scroll** event handler:

```
Private Sub TrackBar1_Scroll(ByVal sender As System.Object, _
    ByVal e As System.EventArgs) Handles TrackBar1.Scroll
    TextBox1.Text = "Track bar value: " & TrackBar1.Value
End Sub
```

You can see the results of this code in Figure 8.3.

Setting Track Bar Ticks

You also can configure track bars with the **TickStyle** property, which lets you determine how ticks are displayed; this property can take values from the **TickStyle** enumeration:

- **Both**—Tick marks are located on both sides of the control.
- **BottomRight**—Tick marks are located on the bottom of a horizontal control or on the right side of a vertical control.
- **None**—No tick marks appear in the control.
- **TopLeft**—Tick marks are located on the top of a horizontal control or on the left of a vertical control.

You also can set the tick frequency—which sets the distance between ticks—with the **TickFrequency** property (default = 1).

For example, I've set the **TickStyle** of the track bar you see in Figure 8.13 to **TopLeft**, the **Maximum** property to 100, and the **TickFrequency** property to 5.

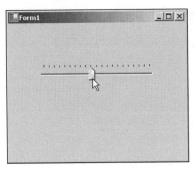

Figure 8.13   Setting tick style and frequency in a track bar.

Using the **DateTimePicker** Class

As discussed in the In Depth section of this chapter, date-time pickers let the user select dates and times. Here's the class hierarchy for the **DateTimePicker** class:

```
Object
    MarshalByRefObject
        Component
            Control
                DateTimePicker
```

You can find the more notable public shared (static) properties of the **DateTimePicker** class in Table 8.11, the more notable public object properties in Table 8.12, and the more notable events in Table 8.13. Note that as with other Windows forms controls, I am not listing the notable properties, methods, and events **DateTimePicker** inherits from the **Control** class, such as the **Click** event—you can see all that in Chapter 5, Tables 5.1, 5.2, and 5.3.

Table 8.11   Noteworthy public shared (static) properties of the **DateTimePicker** class.

Property	Means
MaxDateTime	Specifies the maximum date value of the date-time picker control. Note that this field is read-only.
MinDateTime	Specifies the minimum date value of the date-time picker control. Note that this field is read-only.

Table 8.12   Noteworthy public properties of DateTimePicker objects.

Property	Means
CalendarFont	Gets/sets the font style for the calendar.
CalendarForeColor	Gets/sets the foreground color of the calendar.
CalendarMonthBackground	Gets/sets the background color of the calendar month.
CalendarTitleBackColor	Gets/sets the background color of the calendar title.
CalendarTitleForeColor	Gets/sets the foreground color of the calendar title.
CalendarTrailingForeColor	Gets/sets the foreground color of the calendar trailing dates.
Checked	Gets/sets whether the **Value** property holds a valid date-time value.
CustomFormat	Gets/sets a custom date-time format string.
DropDownAlign	Gets/sets the alignment of the drop-down calendar on the date-time control.
Format	Gets/sets the format of dates and times.
MaxDate	Gets/sets the maximum selectable date and time.
MinDate	Gets/sets the minimum selectable date and time.
PreferredHeight	Holds the preferred height of the date-time picker control.
ShowCheckBox	Gets/sets if a check box should appear to the left of a selected date.
ShowUpDown	Gets/sets if an up-down control should be used to adjust date-time values.
Text	Gets/sets the text in this control.
Value	Gets/sets the date-time value.

Table 8.13   Noteworthy public events of DateTimePicker objects.

Event	Means
CloseUp	Occurs when the drop-down calendar disappears.
DropDown	Occurs when the drop-down calendar appears.
FormatChanged	Occurs when the **Format** property value has changed.
ValueChanged	Occurs when the **Value** property changes.

Handling Date-Time Picker Events

How do you set a date and time in a date-time picker? You simply edit the date and/or time displayed in the control, as you see in Figure 8.14. To make that easier, if the user clicks the down arrow in a date-time picker, a drop-down month calendar appears by default, and you can make date selections from that calendar.

Figure 8.14   Using a date-time picker.

When the date and/or time changes, a **ValueChanged** event occurs, which I handle in the Pickers example on the CD-ROM. You can get the new, selected date and time with the **Text** property of the control, or the **Value** property, which returns a **DateTime** object (see Tables 8.1–8.3 for more on **DateTime** objects). In the Pickers example, I copy the selected date to a text box, like this:

```
Private Sub DateTimePicker1_ValueChanged(ByVal sender As System.Object, _
    ByVal e As System.EventArgs) Handles DateTimePicker1.ValueChanged
    TextBox1.Text = "Date selected: " & DateTimePicker1.Text
End Sub
```

You can see the results of this code in Figure 8.15, where I've selected a new date.

This is all very well, but how do you set the format for the date and time displayed in the control? By default, date-time pickers don't even let the user edit the time, for example. You can set the format with these members of the **DateTimePicker Format** enumeration:

- **Custom**—The date-time control displays the date-time value in a custom format.

- **Long**—The date-time control displays the date-time value in the long date format set by the user's operating system.

- **Short**—The date-time control displays the date-time value in the short date format set by the user's operating system.

- **Time**—The date-time control displays the date-time value in the time format set by the user's operating system.

You also can customize the display of this control. For more on this subject, take a look at the next topic.

Figure 8.15   Handling date-time picker events.

Setting Date-Time Picker Custom Formats

You can set the format for the dates and times displayed in date-time pickers customizing that format as you like; for example, you can display (and so let the user set by editing) just dates, or just times, or both. To set a custom format, you set the date-time control's **Format** property to **DateTimePickerFormat.Custom**, then you assign a custom format string to the **CustomFormat** property.

You create a custom format string using these items:

- **d**—The one or two-digit day.

- **dd**—The two-digit day. Note that single-digit day values are preceded by a zero.

- **ddd**—The three-character day-of-week abbreviation.

- **dddd**—The full day-of-week name.

- **h**—The one- or two-digit hour in 12-hour format.

- **hh**—The two-digit hour in 12-hour format. Note that single-digit values are preceded by a zero.

- **H**—The one- or two-digit hour in 24-hour format.

- **HH**—The two-digit hour in 24-hour format. Note that single-digit values are preceded by a zero.

- **m**—The one- or two-digit minute.

- **mm**—The two-digit minute. Note that single-digit values are preceded by a zero.

- **M**—The one- or two-digit month number.

- **MM**—The two-digit month number. Note that single-digit values are preceded by a zero.

- **MMM**—The three-character month abbreviation.

- **MMMM**—The full month name.

- **s**—The one- or two-digit seconds.

- **ss**—The two-digit seconds. Note that single-digit values are preceded by a zero.

- **t**—The one-letter AM/PM abbreviation ("AM" is displayed as "A").

- **tt**—The two-letter AM/PM abbreviation ("AM" is displayed as "AM").

- **y**—The one-digit year (2002 is displayed as "2").

- **yy**—The last two digits of the year (2002 is displayed as "02").

- **yyyy**—The full year (2002 is displayed as "2002").

To display literals, such as : or /, you must *escape* them by surrounding them in single quotes. For example, to display the date and time in the format 12/01/2002 12:00 PM, the **CustomFormat** property should be set to **MM'/'dd'/'yyyy hh':'mm tt**.

Here's another example; in this case, I'm creating the display you see in Figure 8.14 in the date-time picker at the top of the form. This will display dates and times in the format "September 27 12:00:00 PM":

```
Private Sub Form1_Load(ByVal sender As System.Object, _
    ByVal e As System.EventArgs) Handles MyBase.Load
    DateTimePicker1.Format = DateTimePickerFormat.Custom
    DateTimePicker1.CustomFormat = "MMMM dd hh:mm:ss tt"
End Sub
```

Using the **MonthCalendar** Class

As discussed in the In Depth section of this chapter, you can use month calendar controls to let the user select days of the month; you can see an example in Figure 8.4. Here's the class hierarchy for this control:

```
Object
    MarshalByRefObject
        Component
            Control
                MonthCalendar
```

You can find the more notable public properties of the **MonthCalendar** class in Table 8.14, the more notable methods in Table 8.15, and the more notable events in Table 8.16. Note that as with other Windows forms controls, I am not listing the notable properties, methods, and events **MonthCalendar** inherits from the **Control** class, such as the **Click** event—you can see all that in Tables 5.1, 5.2, and 5.3, Chapter 5.

Table 8.14   Noteworthy public properties of MonthCalendar objects.

Property	Means
AnnuallyBoldedDates	Holds an array of **DateTime** objects specifying which days should be bold.
BoldedDates	Gets/sets an array of **DateTime** objects specifying which dates should be bold.
CalendarDimensions	Gets/sets the number of columns and rows.
FirstDayOfWeek	Gets/sets the first day of the week.
MaxDate	Gets/sets the maximum possible date.
MaxSelectionCount	Holds the maximum number of days that can be selected.
MinDate	Gets/sets the minimum possible date.
MonthlyBoldedDates	Holds the array of **DateTime** objects which specify which monthly days to display bold.
ScrollChange	Holds the scroll rate.
SelectionEnd	Gets/sets the end date of a selected range.
SelectionRange	Gets the selected range of dates for a month calendar control.
SelectionStart	Gets/sets the start date of a selected range of dates.
ShowToday	Gets/sets if today's date is shown at the bottom of the control.
ShowTodayCircle	Gets/sets if today's date should appear inside a circle.
ShowWeekNumbers	Gets/sets if the month calendar control should display week numbers.
SingleMonthSize	Returns the minimum size in which to display a month.
TitleBackColor	Gets/sets the back color of the calendar's title area.
TitleForeColor	Gets/sets the fore color of the calendar's title area.
TodayDate	Gets/sets today's date.
TodayDateSet	Indicates if the **DateTime** property has been set.

Table 8.15   Noteworthy public methods of MonthCalendar objects.

Method	Means
AddAnnuallyBoldedDate	Adds a day, displayed in bold annually.
AddBoldedDate	Adds a day that is displayed as bold.
AddMonthlyBoldedDate	Adds a day to be displayed in bold monthly in the calendar.
GetDisplayRange	Gets date information that specifies the range displayed dates.
RemoveAllAnnuallyBoldedDates	Removes all annually bolded dates.
RemoveAllBoldedDates	Removes all non-recurring bolded dates.
RemoveAllMonthlyBoldedDates	Removes all monthly bolded dates.

(continued)

Table 8.15   Noteworthy public methods of **MonthCalendar** objects *(continued)*.

Method	Means
RemoveAnnuallyBoldedDate	Removes indicated date from the calendar's internal list of annually bolded dates.
RemoveBoldedDate	Removes a date from the calendar's internal list of non-recurring dates to display in bold.
RemoveMonthlyBoldedDate	Removes a date from the calendar's internal list of monthly dates to display in bold.
SetCalendarDimensions	Sets the number of columns and rows.
SetDate	Sets the selected date.
SetSelectionRange	Sets the selected dates to the given range of dates.
UpdateBoldedDates	Redisplays the bolded dates.

Table 8.16   Noteworthy public events of **MonthCalendar** objects.

Event	Means
DateChanged	Occurs when the date in the calendar control changes.
DateSelected	Occurs when a date is selected in the calendar.

Handling Month Calendar Control Events

There are two main events in month calendar controls—**DateChanged** (the default event), which happens when the date in the control changes (either through user actions or in code); and **DateSelected**, which happens when the user selects a new date.

As discussed in the In Depth section of this chapter, you can select entire ranges of dates in month calendar controls. To handle such ranges, you can use the **SelectionStart**, **SelectionEnd**, **SelectionRange.Start**, and **SelectionRange. End** properties to get **DateTime** objects set to times that straddle the selected range. For example, here's how I indicate which day of the month the user has selected in the Pickers example:

```
Private Sub MonthCalendar1_DateSelected(ByVal sender As Object, _
    ByVal e As System.Windows.Forms.DateRangeEventArgs) Handles _
    MonthCalendar1.DateSelected
    TextBox1.Text = "Day of the month selected: " & _
        MonthCalendar1.SelectionRange.Start.Day
End Sub
```

8. Windows Forms: Scroll Bars, Splitters, Track Bars, Pickers

Figure 8.16   Handling month calendar control events.

You can see the result in Figure 8.16, where I've selected a date; the corresponding day of the month is reported in the text box at the bottom of the form.

Using the **NotifyIcon** Class

I've used notify icons for a while, but I still think they're cool. Notify icons display icons in the Windows system tray; you can handle events like **Click** and **DoubleClick** for these icons, displaying a control panel, for example. As mentioned in the In Depth section of this chapter, this is a great feature for processes that run in the background and don't have their own windows, although they may be parts of applications that do display windows. Visual Basic .NET now lets you create Windows services, which run in the background and can display control panels (much like Microsoft SQL Server). You can use notify icons to let the user open such control panels. You can see a notify icon right next to the time of day in Figure 8.5; here's the class hierarchy of the **NotifyIcon** class:

```
Object
    MarshalByRefObject
        Component
            NotifyIcon
```

You can find the more notable public properties of the **NotifyIcon** class in Table 8.17 and the more notable events in Table 8.18.

Table 8.17   Noteworthy public properties of NotifyIcon objects.

Property	Means
ContextMenu	Gets/sets the context menu for the tray icon.
Icon	Gets/sets the current icon.
Text	Gets/sets the ToolTip text which is to be displayed when the mouse hovers over a system tray icon.
Visible	Gets/sets if the icon is visible in the Windows System Tray.

Table 8.18   Noteworthy public events of NotifyIcon objects.

Event	Means
Click	Occurs when the user clicks the system tray icon.
DoubleClick	Occurs when the user double-clicks the system tray icon.
MouseDown	Occurs when the user presses the mouse button on the icon in the system tray.
MouseMove	Occurs when the user moves the mouse over the icon in the system tray.
MouseUp	Occurs when the user releases the mouse button over the icon in the system tray.

Creating Notify Icons and Using Icon Designers

To create a notify icon component, you need an icon file to assign to this control's **Icon** property. You can create new icons with an *icon designer*. I'll do that here as part of the NotifyIcons project on the CD-ROM.

To open an icon designer, just select Project|Add New Item to open the Add New Item dialog, then select Icon File in the Templates box and click Open. This will create a new icon and open it for design in an icon designer, as you see in Figure 8.17.

To design your icon, you can use the tools you see in the toolbar immediately above the icon. I've drawn a rudimentary icon here, and saved it as icon1.ico in the NotifyIcons folder.

TIP: *Many, many icons ready for you to use come with Visual Basic—take a look at the Common7\graphics\icons directory.*

The next step is to add a **NotifyIcon** component to the form in this project. When you do, this component will appear in the component tray beneath the form, because this is a component, not a control. Set the **Icon** property of this component to icon1.ico. In addition, the text you place in the notify icon's **Text** property becomes the tool tip text for the icon in the system tray.

Figure 8.17 Using an icon designer.

By default, the notify icon's **Visible** property is set to **True**, but in this case, I'll set it to **False** and let the user display the icon with a button:

```
Private Sub Button1_Click(ByVal sender As System.Object, _
    ByVal e As System.EventArgs) Handles Button1.Click
    NotifyIcon1.Visible = False
End Sub
```

And that's all it takes—now when the user clicks this button, the notify icon appears in the system tray, as you see in Figure 8.5. You also can handle events for the notify icon, as we'll see in the next topic.

Handling Notify Icon Events

As mentioned above, you can handle events for notify icons, such as **Click** and **DoubleClick.** In the NotifyIcons example on the CD-ROM, I handle the **DoubleClick** event by displaying a message box, like this:

```
Private Sub NotifyIcon1_DoubleClick(ByVal sender As Object, _
    ByVal e As System.EventArgs) Handles NotifyIcon1.DoubleClick
```

```
    MsgBox("You double-clicked the icon!")
End Sub
```

Being able to handle notify icon events lets you display control panels or bring background processes to the front as needed, which is very useful.

Using the **ToolTip** Class

As discussed in the In Depth section of this chapter, tool tips are those windows that display explanatory text when the mouse hovers over a control or form, as you see in Figure 8.6. Here is the class hierarchy of the **ToolTip** class:

```
Object
    MarshalByRefObject
        Component
            ToolTip
```

You can find the more notable public properties of the **ToolTip** class in Table 8.19 and the more notable methods in Table 8.20.

Table 8.19   Noteworthy public properties of ToolTip objects.

Event	Means
Active	Gets/sets if the tool tip control is active.
AutomaticDelay	Gets/sets the time (in milliseconds) before the tool tip appears.
InitialDelay	Gets/sets the starting delay for the tool tip.
ShowAlways	Gets/sets whether the tool tip should appear when its parent control is not active.

Table 8.20   Noteworthy public events of ToolTip objects.

Event	Means
GetToolTip	Returns the tool tip text.
SetToolTip	Connects tool tip text with the tool tip.

8. Windows Forms: Scroll Bars, Splitters, Track Bars, Pickers

Creating Tool Tips

Tool tips are components, not controls, so when you add them to a Windows forms project, they'll appear in a component tray beneath the form you're adding them to. You can associate them with controls with the **SetToolTip** method if you pass that method the control you want to associate the tool tip with (and remember that this works for forms, which are derived from the **Control** class, as well). Here's how that looks in the ToolTips example on the CD-ROM:

```
Private Sub Form1_Load(ByVal sender As System.Object, _
    ByVal e As System.EventArgs) Handles MyBase.Load
    ToolTip1.SetToolTip(Me, "This is a form.")
    ToolTip2.SetToolTip(Button1, "This is a button")
End Sub
```

You can see the result in Figure 8.6, where the tool tip attached to the button is displayed.

Using the **Timer** Class

As discussed in the In Depth section of this chapter, timers are components that cause periodic **Tick** events that you can use to execute code at specific intervals. Here is the class hierarchy of this component:

```
Object
    MarshalByRefObject
        Component
            Timer
```

You can find the more notable public properties of the **Timer** class in Table 8.21, the more notable methods in Table 8.22, and the more notable events in Table 8.23.

Table 8.21 . Noteworthy public properties of Timer objects.

Property	Means
Enabled	Gets/sets whether the timer is running.
Interval	Gets/sets the time (in milliseconds) between timer ticks.

Table 8.22   Noteworthy public methods of Timer objects.

Method	Means
Start	Starts the timer.
Stop	Stops the timer.

Table 8.23   Noteworthy public events of Timer objects.

Event	Means
Tick	Occurs when the timer interval has elapsed (and the timer is enabled).

Setting a Timer's Interval

Setting a timer's interval—the time between **Tick** events—is easy; just set the timer's **Interval** property. This property is measured in milliseconds, and the minimum setting is 1. For an example of timers at work, take a look at "Handling Timer Events—and Creating an Alarm Clock."

TIP: *In fact, **Timer** components use the computer's built-in clock interrupt, which only happens about 18 times a second in a PC, so you really can't get more frequent timer ticks than that, no matter what you set the **Interval** property to.*

Turning Timers On and Off

You can use a timer component's **Enabled** property to turn the timer on (which means **Tick** events will occur) or off (which means they won't). You can also use the **Start** and **Stop** methods to do the same thing. For an example of timers at work, take a look at the next solution "Handling Timer Events—and Creating an Alarm Clock."

Handling Timer Events—and Creating an Alarm Clock

To get an idea how timers work, I'll create an example alarm clock, called Timers on the CD-ROM. You can see this example at work in Figure 8.7. Here, the user can click the "Start clock" button to start the clock, which is displayed in a label control. (I've set the font of the label at design time to use a large font face, as shown in Figure 8.7.) The clock's display is updated once a second in the timer in this example, **Timer1**. I've set the timer's **Interval** property to 1000 milliseconds, or one second, which means its **Tick** event occurs every second. I update the label's text like this in the **Tick** event handler: **Label1.Text = TimeOfDay** (the **TimeOfDay** property returns a **DateTime** object with the current time).

The user also can enter a time for the alarm to go off in three text boxes (using 24-hour format; for example 13:00:00 for 1:00:00 P.M.), and click the "Alarm on" radio button to "arm" the alarm clock. When the current time equals or exceeds the alarm time, the clock will beep once a second until the user clicks the "Alarm off" radio button. (These two radio buttons, "Alarm on" and "Alarm off", actually set the state of an internal Boolean variable, **blnAlarm**, which is **True** when the alarm is armed and **False** otherwise.)

Here's the whole code. Note that I'm using three handy properties here— **TimeOfDay**, which returns a **DateTime** object holding the current time of day; **Today**, which returns a **DateTime** object holding today's date; and **Now**, which returns a **DateTime** object that holds both today's time and date:

```
Public Class Form1
    Inherits System.Windows.Forms.Form

    'Windows Form Designer generated code

    Dim blnAlarm As Boolean = False

    Private Sub Timer1_Tick(ByVal sender As System.Object, _
        ByVal e As System.EventArgs) Handles Timer1.Tick
        Label1.Text = TimeOfDay
        If TextBox1.Text <> "" And TextBox2.Text <> "" And _
            TextBox3.Text <> "" Then
            Dim AlarmTime = New DateTime(Today.Year, Today.Month, _
                Today.Day, CInt(TextBox1.Text), CInt(TextBox2.Text), _
                CInt(TextBox3.Text))
            If Now > AlarmTime And blnAlarm Then
                Beep()
            End If
        End If
    End Sub

    Private Sub Button1_Click(ByVal sender As System.Object, _
        ByVal e As System.EventArgs) Handles Button1.Click
        Timer1.Enabled = True
    End Sub

    Private Sub RadioButton1_CheckedChanged(ByVal sender As _
        System.Object, ByVal e As System.EventArgs) _
        Handles RadioButton1.CheckedChanged
        If RadioButton1.Checked Then
            blnAlarm = True
        End If
    End Sub
```

```
    Private Sub RadioButton2_CheckedChanged(ByVal sender As _
        System.Object, ByVal e As System.EventArgs) _
        Handles RadioButton2.CheckedChanged
        If RadioButton1.Checked Then
            blnAlarm = False
        End If
    End Sub
End Class
```

And that's all it takes—you can see the results in Figure 8.7. Now we've created a working alarm clock, using timers.

Chapter 9

Windows Forms: Menus, Built-in Dialog Boxes, and Printing

(continued)

In Dept

In this chapter, I'm going to take a look at some very popular topics—menus, Visual Basic's built-in dialog boxes, and printing. If you're familiar with Visual Basic 6.0, you'll find many differences here. Menus have their own control now, instead of a separate menu editor (giving menus their own control is actually more in line with the Visual Basic philosophy, so that's an improvement). Each of the built-in dialog boxes—file open, file save, and so on—now have their own separate controls as well, so instead of using a single **CommonDialog** control, there are a number of new built-in dialog boxes, such as print preview and page setup. And printing has changed also, as we'll see.

Menus

Every Windows user is familiar with menus; you wouldn't get far in Windows without them. Menus are those controls that allow the user to make selections and also hide away those selections when they're not needed, saving space in Windows applications, which is always at a premium. (Imagine replacing all the menu items in a real-world Windows application with buttons in the main window.)

In Visual Basic, the **MainMenu** control represents the container for the menu structure of a form; you can assign a control of this type to a form's **Menu** property at run time. Menus are made up of **MenuItem** objects that represent the individual parts of a menu—menu items can be a parent menu or a menu item in a menu. You can see one of the menu applications we'll develop in this chapter, Menus on the CD-ROM, in Figure 9.1. Here, I've opened the File menu in the menu bar, and opened a submenu two levels deep.

There are all kinds of options here—you can add submenus to menus that will pop up when the user clicks an arrow in a menu item, display check marks, create menu separators (horizontal bars used in menus to group menu items), assign shortcut keys (like Ctrl+H) to menu items, even draw the appearance of menu items yourself. These actions are actually supported by **MenuItem** objects, not **MainMenu** objects.

Figure 9.1   The Menus application.

TIP: *Don't forget that there are many menu conventions in Windows that you should adhere to if you're going to release your programs for public consumption. For example, if a menu item opens a dialog box, you should add an ellipsis (...) after its name (such as Print...). Many shortcuts are already standard, such as Ctrl+S for Save, Ctrl+X for Cut, Ctrl+V for Paste/View, Ctrl+C for Copy, and so on. The File menu should be the first menu, and an Exit item should be at the bottom of that menu. Menus in the menu bar that don't open a menu but instead perform some action immediately, sometimes called bang menus, should have an exclamation point (!) after their names (such as Connect!), and so on.*

Menu Items

Menus like File or Edit and the actual items in such menus are supported with the **MenuItem** class. This class supports the actual controls in your menu system, and it's their **Click** event that you add code to in order to make that menu system active.

This class provides properties that enable you to configure the appearance and functionality of a menu item. To display a checkmark next to a menu item, use the **Checked** property. You can use this feature to identify a menu item that is selected in a list of mutually exclusive menu items. You can use the **Shortcut** property to define a keyboard combination (like Ctrl+X) that can be pressed to select the menu item, and set the **ShowShortcut** property to **True** to display that key combination in the menu item's caption. **MenuItem** objects themselves also can have other **MenuItem** objects attached to them to display submenus.

To set the caption of a menu or menu item, you use the **Text** property. Setting the **Text** property to a hyphen (-) converts the menu item into a menu separator, one of those horizontal bars that help group menu items together. (You can even have separators in menu bars, in which case they're vertical.) Prefacing a character in a menu item's caption with an ampersand (&) underlines that character and makes it into an access key, which means the user can select that item by pressing Alt and that character. For example, giving a menu item the caption "E&xit" makes X into the access key for this menu item. You can enable and disable menu items with the **Enabled** property, and show or hide them with the **Visible** property.

Note that for a **MenuItem** to be displayed, you have to add it to a **MainMenu** (or **ContextMenu**) object.

MenuItem objects in a Multiple Document Interface (MDI) application work in a special way. When an MDI child window appears, its menu is merged with the MDI parent window (so no menu system appears in the child). You can specify how menu items should be added to the MDI parent window with the **MergeOrder** and **MergeType** properties. You can also use the **MergeMenu** method to specify how this merging occurs.

TIP: ***MenuItem*** *objects cannot be used in multiple places at the same time, such as in a **MainMenu** object and a **ContextMenu** object. However, you can use the **CloneMenu** method to create a copy of a **MenuItem** object for use in another location.*

The most common menu item event that you handle is **Click**, which means the user has clicked a menu item and your code should respond to it. However, there are other events here as well—the **Popup** event lets you to perform tasks before a menu is displayed, because it happens just before a menu item is displayed. And the **Select** event happens when a menu item is selected (that is, highlighted). This enables you to perform tasks like displaying help for menu items when the user places the mouse cursor over those items.

Context Menus

Another popular type of menus is *context menus*. You use **ContextMenu** controls to give users access to frequently used menu commands, and bring them up by right-clicking another control. You can see a context menu at work in the ContextMenus example on the CD-ROM in Figure 9.2. You usually use context menus to display control-specific options, such as Cut, Copy, and Paste in text boxes.

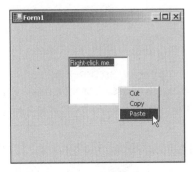

Figure 9.2 A context menu.

You associate context menus with other controls by setting the control's **ContextMenu** property to the **ContextMenu** control. The central property of the **ContextMenu** control is the **MenuItems** property; you can add menu items to a context menu at design time or in code by creating **MenuItem** objects and adding them to the **MenuItems** collection of the context menu.

As with main menus, context menu items can be disabled, hidden, or deleted. You also can show and hide context menus yourself with the **ContextMenu** control's **Show** and **Hide** methods. You can handle the menu item's **Click**, **Select**, and **Popup** events, as you can in main menus. In fact, the only major difference here is that context menus are not divided into separate menus, like File, Edit, Window, and so on.

TIP: A context menu can be associated with a number of other controls, but as you'd expect, each control can have only one context menu.

NOTE: You can reuse **MenuItem** objects from a main menu in a context menu if you use the **CloneMenu** method of the **MenuItem** class.

The Built-in Dialog Boxes

There are a number of built-in dialog boxes in Visual Basic, which is great, because developing your own file open, file save, and other dialog boxes not only takes a lot of work, but gives your program a different look from what Windows users are already used to. We'll look at these dialogs in this chapter; here they are:

- Open File dialogs
- Save File dialogs
- Font dialogs
- Color dialogs
- Print Preview dialogs
- Page Setup dialogs
- Print dialogs

You use the **ShowDialog** method to display the dialog at run time and can check its return value (such as **DialogResult.OK** or **DialogResult.Cancel**) to see which button the user has clicked. Here are the possible return values from this method, from the **DialogResult** enumeration:

- **Abort**—The dialog box return value is **Abort** (usually from a button labeled Abort).

- **Cancel**—The dialog box return value is **Cancel** (usually from a button labeled Cancel).

- **Ignore**—The dialog box return value is **Ignore** (usually from a button labeled Ignore).

- **No**—The dialog box return value is **No** (usually from a button labeled No).

- **None**—Nothing is returned from the dialog box. This means that the modal dialog continues running.

- **OK**—The dialog box return value is **OK** (usually from a button labeled OK).

- **Retry**—The dialog box return value is **Retry** (usually from a button labeled Retry).

- **Yes**—The dialog box return value is **Yes** (usually from a button labeled Yes).

I'll take a closer look at these dialogs now.

Open File Dialogs

As you'd expect from its name, the Open File dialog lets the user select a file to open. In fact, it's the same Open File dialog used by Windows itself. You can see this dialog box in Figure 9.3, as displayed in the OpenFileDialog example on the CD-ROM.

Open File dialogs are supported with the **OpenFileDialog** class. You can let users select multiple files with the **Multiselect** property. You can use the **ShowReadOnly** property to determine if a read-only checkbox appears in the dialog box. The **ReadOnlyChecked** property indicates whether the read-only checkbox is selected. And the **Filter** property sets the current file name filter string, which determines the choices that appear in the "Files of type" box in the

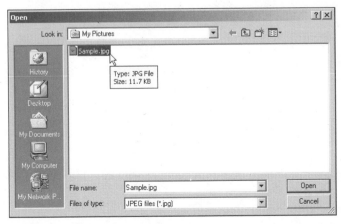

Figure 9.3   An Open File dialog box.

dialog box. The name and path the user selected is stored in the **FileName** property of the **OpenFileDialog** object—and there's a neat shortcut here: you can use the **OpenFile** method to open the selected file directly.

Save File Dialogs

Save File dialogs are supported by the **SaveFileDialog** class. These dialogs let the user specify the name of a file to save data to. These dialogs are the same as the standard Save File dialog box used by Windows; you can see a Save File dialog in Figure 9.4 from the SaveFileDialog project on the CD-ROM.

You can use the **ShowDialog** method to display the dialog box at run time. You can use the **FileName** property to get the file the user selected, open a file in read-write mode using the **OpenFile** method, and so on.

TIP: You also can set the handy **CheckFileExists** and **CheckPathExists** properties to **True** to check if a specified file or path already exists, and if it should be created otherwise.

Font Dialogs

Font dialogs let the user select a font size, face, color, and so on. You can see a font dialog box at work in Figure 9.5 from the FontDialog example on the CD-ROM.

What's handy about these dialogs, besides the fact that they're the same as those used by Windows, is that they return **Font** and **Color** objects directly (using the properties of the same name), ready for installation in controls that can use them, like rich text boxes. This saves you the trouble of creating and configuring these objects from scratch.

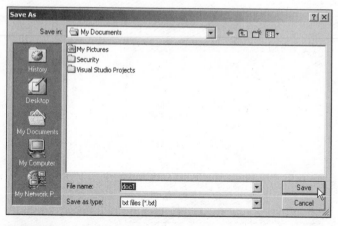

Figure 9.4   A Save As dialog box.

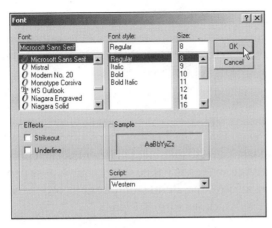

Figure 9.5   A font dialog box.

To display the font dialog box, call the **ShowDialog** method. This dialog shows list boxes for **Font**, **Style**, and **Size**, checkboxes for effects like **Strikeout** and **Underline**, a drop-down list for **Script** (**Script** refers to different character scripts that are available for a given font—for example, Hebrew), and a sample of how the font will appear. You can recover these settings using properties of the same names of the **Font** object returned by the **Font** property.

Color Dialogs

Color dialogs let the user select a color in an easy way. The principal property you use of these dialogs is the **Color** property, which returns a **Color** object, ready for use. You can see a color dialog box at work in Figure 9.6.

In Figure 9.6, I've opened the color dialog fully (by clicking Define Custom Colors) to let the user define their own colors with color values and hue, saturation, and lumi-

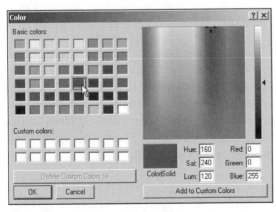

Figure 9.6   A color dialog box.

nosity. If you set the **AllowFullOpen** property to **False**, on the other hand, the Define Custom Colors button is disabled and the user can select colors only from the predefined colors in the palette. Note also that if you set the **SolidColorOnly** property to **True**, the user can select only solid (not dithered) colors.

Printing Documents

The way you print documents in Visual Basic has become fairly involved, revolving around the **PrintDocument** class. You add an object of this class to a project, and then handle events like **PrintPage**, which is called every time a new page is to be printed. When it is added to a form, the **PrintDocument** component appears in the tray at the bottom of the Windows form designer.

You're responsible for handling the printing yourself—you are passed a **Graphics** object, and you use the methods of that object, like **DrawString**, which draws strings of text, to draw the document you want printed. Because this graphics object corresponds to the printer, what you draw with it will appear in the printer.

For some reason, all the examples you see on this topic only print out a single page, so I'll make it a point here to show how you handle multipage documents as well. In this case, our example, called Printing on the CD-ROM, is designed to print out two pages, one with a red rectangle, and one with a blue rectangle. You'll find Print, Print Preview, and Page Setup menu items in that example's File menu.

Besides **PrintDocument** objects, there are a number of dialog boxes you use to support printing. The first of these is the Print dialog itself.

Print Dialogs

Print dialogs let the user print documents, and these dialogs are supported with the **PrintDialog** class. Before displaying a Print dialog, you set the **Document** property of a **PrintDialog** object to a **PrintDocument** object, and the **PrinterSettings** property to a **PrinterSettings** object of the kind set by Page Setup dialogs.

When the dialog is closed, you can print the document by assigning the **PrintDialog** object's **PrinterSettings** property (which returns a **PrinterSettings** object as configured by the user, indicating the number of copies to print, the printer to use, and so on) to the **PrinterSettings** property of the **PrintDocument** object and use the **PrintDocument** object's **Print** method to actually print the document. Here's how that might look in code:

```
Private Sub MenuItem1_Click(ByVal sender As System.Object, _
    ByVal e As System.EventArgs) Handles MenuItem1.Click
```

```
    PrintDialog1.Document = PrintDocument1
    PrintDialog1.PrinterSettings = PrintDocument1.PrinterSettings
    PrintDialog1.AllowSomePages = True
    If PrintDialog1.ShowDialog = DialogResult.OK Then
        PrintDocument1.PrinterSettings = PrintDialog1.PrinterSettings
        PrintDocument1.Print()
    End If
End Sub
```

You can see a Print dialog in Figure 9.7—this one comes from the Printing example on the CD-ROM.

Print Preview Dialogs

You use Print Preview dialogs to let the user see what a document will look like when it's printed. This dialog is supported with the **PrintPreviewDialog** class. This dialog contains buttons for printing, zooming in, displaying one or multiple pages, and closing the dialog box. You can see it at work in Figure 9.8 from the Printing example on the CD-ROM.

The dialog's major property is **Document**, which sets the document to be previewed, and the document must be a **PrintDocument** object. There's not much else to do here—this dialog simply displays the document as it will be printed. Print Preview dialogs are based on the **PrintPreviewControl** object (see the next topic), and you can set some of the properties of that control directly, such as the **Columns** and **Rows** properties (which set the number of pages displayed horizontally and vertically) with properties like **PrintPreviewDialog1.PrintPreview Control.Columns** or **PrintPreviewDialog1.PrintPreview Control.Rows**. You also can use **PrintPreviewControl** objects directly to create your own custom print preview dialog boxes—see the next topic for the details.

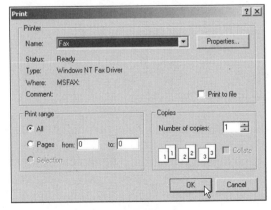

Figure 9.7 The Print dialog.

Figure 9.8   The Print Preview dialog.

Custom Print Previews

You can use a **PrintPreviewControl** to display a **PrintDocument** as it will appear when printed. Note that this control has no buttons or other user interface elements, so you usually use this control only if you wish to write your own print preview user interface. You can see a print preview control at work in Figure 9.9 from the Printing example on the CD-ROM. Here, the control is showing the first page that the Printing example prints out, which just displays a red rectangle.

Page Setup Dialogs

You also can use Page Setup dialogs to specify page details for printing. You can let users set border and margin adjustments, headers and footers, and portrait or landscape orientation, and so on. You can see a Page Setup dialog in Figure 9.10 from the Printing example on the CD-ROM.

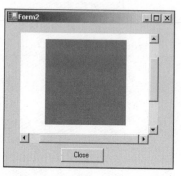

Figure 9.9   A Print Preview control.

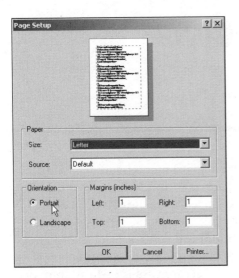

Figure 9.10   A Page Setup dialog.

You can use the **PrinterSettings** property of this dialog box to get a **Printer Settings** object that holds the settings that the user specified, and assign that object to a **PrintDocument** object's **PrinterSettings** property to make sure the settings the user wants are assigned to the document itself. Here's how that might look in code:

```
Private Sub MenuItem2_Click(ByVal sender As System.Object, _
    ByVal e As System.EventArgs) Handles MenuItem2.Click
    PageSetupDialog1.Document = PrintDocument1
    PageSetupDialog1.PrinterSettings = PrintDocument1.PrinterSettings
    If PageSetupDialog1.ShowDialog = DialogResult.OK Then
        PrintDocument1.PrinterSettings = PageSetupDialog1.PrinterSettings
    End If
End Sub
```

That gives us a look at what we'll be covering in this chapter. Now it's time to start looking at individual points in the Immediate Solutions section.

Immediate Solutions

Using the MainMenu Class

There are two main classes involved in standard menu handling—**MainMenu**, which lets you assign objects of this type to a form's **Menu** class to install the corresponding menu system, and **MenuItem**, which is the class that actually supports the items in a menu system (including the menus, like File and Edit). At design time, you only need to drag a **MainMenu** control from the toolbox to a form—the Windows form designer will add any additional menu items you want to that menu automatically. Here's the class hierarchy of the **MainMenu** class:

```
Object
    MarshalByRefObject
        Component
            Menu
                MainMenu
```

You can find the notable public properties of **MainMenu** objects in Table 9.1 and the notable public methods of this class in Table 9.2.

To create a working menu system, you need menu items. See the next topic for the details.

Table 9.1   Noteworthy public properties of MainMenu objects.

Property	Means
IsParent	Holds a value that is **True** if this menu contains any menu items.
MdiListItem	Holds a value that is **True** if the **MenuItem** is used to display a list of MDI child windows.
MenuItems	Holds the collection of **MenuItem** objects for this menu.

Table 9.2   Noteworthy public methods of MainMenu objects.

Method	Means
GetContextMenu	Gets the **ContextMenu** that contains this menu.
GetForm	Gets the **Form** that contains this menu.
GetMainMenu	Gets the **MainMenu** that contains this menu.
MergeMenu	Merges the **MenuItem** objects of a menu with the current menu.

Using the **MenuItem** Class

The actual menus and menu items in a menu system are supported by the **MenuItem** class—these are the objects that you handle **Click** events for in a menu system. Here's the hierarchy of this class:

```
Object
    MarshalByRefObject
        Component
            Menu
                MenuItem
```

You can see the notable public properties of objects of the **MenuItem** class in Table 9.3, the notable methods in Table 9.4, and the notable events in Table 9.5.

Table 9.3 Noteworthy public properties of **MenuItem** objects.

Property	Means
Break	Gets/sets whether the item is displayed on a new line (for menu items added to a **MainMenu** object) or in a new column (for items or submenu items displayed in a **ContextMenu**).
Checked	Gets/sets if a checkmark should appear next to a menu item.
DefaultItem	Gets/sets if the menu item is the default menu item.
Enabled	Gets/sets if the menu item is enabled.
Index	Gets/sets the position of the menu item in its parent menu.
IsParent	Gets if the menu item contains child menu items.
MdiList	Gets/sets if the menu item will be automatically filled with a list of Multiple Document Interface (MDI) child windows that are displayed in the associated form.
MdiListItem	Gets the menu item used to display a list of Multiple Document Interface (MDI) child forms.
MenuItems	Gets the collection of menu item objects for the menu.
MergeOrder	Gets/sets the relative position of the menu item when it is merged with another menu.
MergeType	Gets/sets the behavior of this menu item when its menu is merged with another menu.
Mnemonic	Gets the mnemonic character for this menu item.
OwnerDraw	Gets/sets whether you will draw this item in code or not.
Parent	Returns the menu that contains this menu item.
RadioCheck	Gets/sets whether the menu item, if checked, displays a radio-button (instead of a checkmark).
Shortcut	Gets/sets the shortcut key for the menu item.
ShowShortcut	Gets/sets whether a shortcut key for the menu item is displayed next to the menu item.
Text	Gets/sets the caption of the menu item.
Visible	Gets/sets whether the menu item is visible.

Table 9.4   Noteworthy public methods of MenuItem objects.

Method	Means
CloneMenu	Creates a copy of a menu item.
GetContextMenu	Gets the **ContextMenu** that contains this menu.
GetMainMenu	Gets the **MainMenu** that contains this menu.
MergeMenu	Merges this menu item with another menu item.
PerformClick	Creates a **Click** event for the menu item.
PerformSelect	Creates a **Select** event for this menu item.

Table 9.5   Noteworthy public events of MenuItem objects.

Event	Means
Click	Occurs when the menu item is clicked or selected using a shortcut key or access key for the menu item.
DrawItem	Occurs when the **OwnerDraw** property of a menu item is set to **True** and the menu item should be drawn.
MeasureItem	Occurs when Visual Basic wants to know the size of a menu item before drawing it (usually happens before the **DrawItem** event).
Popup	Occurs before a menu item's list of menu items is displayed.
Select	Occurs when the user moves the cursor over a menu item.

Creating Menus

So how do you actually create menus in Visual Basic? The simplest way to do so is at design time, because all you have to do is to add a **MainMenu** control from the toolbox to a Windows form. When you do so, the **MainMenu** control appears in the component tray under the form designer, as you see in Figure 9.11. (In fact, it would be more proper to call this a **MainMenu** component, because it does not inherit the **Control** class, and it appears in the component tray, but Visual Basic calls this a **MainMenu** control.)

Note the text "Type Here" in Figure 9.11. To create a new menu, you just have to double-click that text to open a text box which you can use to enter the caption for menus and menu items. When you're creating a new menu item, "Type Here" boxes appear in all the other places you can enter text. To create a new menu in the menu bar, add a submenu to the current menu item, and so on, as you see in Figure 9.12,

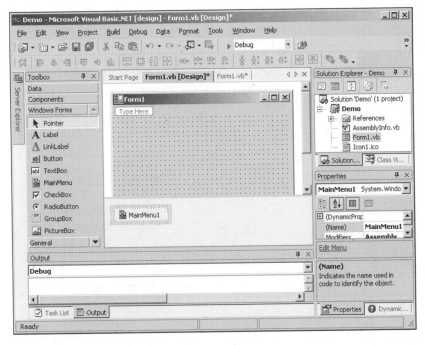

Figure 9.11   Adding a menu system to a form.

where I'm editing the menu system in the Menus example on the CD-ROM. Using this control is intuitive and easy—all you have to do is to enter text in the "Type Here" boxes and double-click the resulting menus and menu items to add code to their **Click** events in the corresponding code designer. To drag menu items around, repositioning them after you've given them a caption, just use the mouse.

How do you make the menu items you've added to a menu system active? For each menu and menu item you add at design time, Visual Basic creates a **MenuItem** object, and you can handle its **Click** event. For example, the last menu item in the File menu is the Exit item in the Menus project. It turns out that this item is **MenuItem4** in this example, so when I double-click it in the form designer, its **Click** event opens in the code designer, and I can use the **End** statement to end the program:

```
Private Sub MenuItem4_Click(ByVal sender As System.Object, _
    ByVal e As System.EventArgs) Handles MenuItem4.Click
    End
End Sub
```

Now when the user clicks the Exit menu item at run time, the program will terminate.

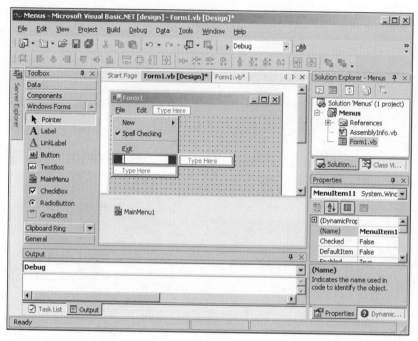

Figure 9.12   Adding menu items to a form.

Creating Submenus

In the previous topic, we got our start with menus, creating simple menu items. You also can create submenus, which involves giving menu items to menu items. When a menu item has a submenu, a right pointing arrow appears in that menu item at run time, as you see in Figure 9.1. Clicking that arrow opens the submenu, displaying additional menu items. And submenus can have submenus, which can have other submenus, and so on.

It's easy to create submenus—you just create the menu item you want to add a submenu to, then select it in a form designer. Doing so opens a "Type Here" box to the right of that menu item; you can enter the captions for the submenu items, as you see in Figure 9.13. Selecting the first item in the submenu opens a "Type Here" box for the next item under it, as well as another "Type Here" box for a new submenu to the right of it. All you have to do is to enter the caption of the submenu items you want, then double-click them to open their **Click** event in the matching code designer.

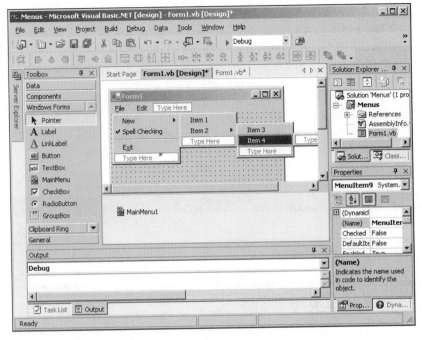

Figure 9.13 Adding submenu items to a form.

For example, you can add code to display a message box when a menu item is selected, like this:

```
Private Sub MenuItem6_Click(ByVal sender As System.Object, _
    ByVal e As System.EventArgs) Handles MenuItem6.Click
    MsgBox("You clicked my favorite item!")
End Sub
```

To see this in action, take a look at Figure 9.1, which shows how the submenus work in the Menus example on the CD-ROM.

Adding Checkmarks to Menu Items

You can also add a checkmark to a menu item, which you usually use to indicate to the user that a specific option has been selected—you can see an example in front of the Spell Checking menu item in Figure 9.1 in the Menus example on the CD-ROM. To add a checkmark to a menu item at design time, just click to the left of its caption. There's a checkbox there, and if you click it, you'll toggle a checkmark on and off; you can see the checkmark in Figure 9.13.

You can use the **Checked** property of a **MenuItem** object to toggle the checkmark; **True** means the checkmark is displayed, **False** means it's hidden. In the Menus example on the CD-ROM, the checkmark in front of the Spell Checking item toggles on and off when you select that item, because I flip the logical sense of the **Checked** property with the **Not** operator that we saw in Chapter 2:

```
Private Sub MenuItem7_Click(ByVal sender As System.Object, _
    ByVal e As System.EventArgs) Handles MenuItem7.Click
    MenuItem7.Checked = Not MenuItem7.Checked
End Sub
```

Related solution:	Found on page:
Using Visual Basic Operators	88

Creating Menu Access Keys

Access keys make it possible to select menu items from the keyboard using the Alt key. For example, if you make the "F" in the File menu's caption an access key and the "x" in the Exit menu item an access key, the user can select the Exit item by typing Alt+F to open the File menu, then Alt+X to select the Exit item.

To give an item an access key, you precede the access key in its caption with an ampersand (&). In this example, that means using the captions "&File" and "E&xit". Access keys are underlined in menu captions, as you see in Figure 9.13, as visual cues to the user.

Note that you still have to open a menu item's menu to be able to use its access key—if you want to assign a key to a menu item that can be used without first opening that item's menu, use a shortcut instead—see the next topic.

Creating Menu Shortcuts

You can create shortcuts for menu items, which are key combinations that, when pressed, will select that item, making its **Click** event happen. You set a shortcut with the **Shortcut** property. To display the shortcut next to the menu item's caption at run time, you set the **ShowShortcut** property to **True** (it's **True** by default).

For example, in the Menus example on the CD-ROM, I've given the Exit item in the File menu a shortcut of Ctrl+X, as you can see next to its caption in Figure 9.1. When the user presses Ctrl+X, this item is activated. To assign a shortcut key combination to a menu item at design time, just select a shortcut key combination from the list that appears when you select the **Shortcut** property of any menu item in the properties window. At run time, you can use members of the **Shortcut** enumeration to do the same thing, as in this code:

```
menuItem1.Shortcut = Shortcut.CtrlX
```

Bear in mind that shortcuts will select their corresponding menu item even if no menu is open at the time. If you want to make sure the user must first open the item's menu, use access keys instead; see the previous topic.

Changing a Menu Item's Caption at Run Time

To change a menu item's caption at run time, you only have to set its **Text** property. Here's an example:

```
Private Sub MenuItem1_Popup(ByVal sender As Object, _
    ByVal e As System.EventArgs) Handles MenuItem6.Popup
    MenuItem1.Text = "I've been clicked!"
End Sub
```

Creating Menu Separators

If you take a look at Figure 9.1, you'll see a horizontal line in the File menu above the Exit item. That line is a menu separator, and you can use them to separate the items in a menu into functional groupings.

To create a menu separator, as in the Menus example on the CD-ROM, you can assign a single hyphen (-) to a menu item's **Text** property (just type a hyphen in the "Type Here" box when you're creating the menu item). That's all it takes—Visual Basic will make the menu item into a menu separator for you automatically.

Using the **Popup** Event

The **MenuItem Popup** event occurs when a menu item is about to be displayed, and you can execute code to configure the item in this event's handler. For example, you might have an item that lets the user connect to the Internet, and you might want to set the caption to "Connect" if they are presently disconnected, and "Disconnect" if they're connected. Here's an example that uses this event to display a message box before the corresponding menu item is displayed:

```
Private Sub MenuItem6_Popup(ByVal sender As Object, _
    ByVal e As System.EventArgs) Handles MenuItem6.Popup
    MsgBox("I'm about to open my submenu!")
End Sub
```

Showing and Hiding Menu Items

To show and hide menu items, you can use their **Visible** property (they don't have **Show** or **Hide** methods). Here's an example from the Menus example on the CD-ROM; when you select the item with the caption "Item 4" from the submenu system, the program will hide the menu item with the caption "Item 1":

```
Private Sub MenuItem8_Click(ByVal sender As System.Object, _
    ByVal e As System.EventArgs) Handles MenuItem8.Click
    MsgBox("Hiding item 1...")
    MenuItem5.Visible = False
End Sub
```

Disabling Menu Items

To disable, or "gray out" a menu item, so that it can't be selected, you set its **Enabled** property to **False**. Here's an example:

```
Private Sub MenuItem8_Click(ByVal sender As System.Object, _
    ByVal e As System.EventArgs) Handles MenuItem8.Click
    MsgBox("Disabling item 1...")
    MenuItem5.Enabled = False
End Sub
```

Drawing Menu Items Yourself

Well, your new menu system looks good, but it's just not right. Wouldn't it be much nicer if you could draw people's faces instead of just text?

You can, if that's what you want. To show how this works, take a look at the DrawMenuItem example on the CD-ROM. In this example, I'm drawing an ellipse in a menu item, as you see in Figure 9.14.

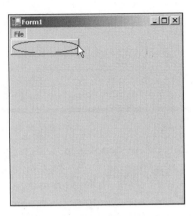

Figure 9.14 Drawing a menu item.

Here's how you do it—you first set the menu item's **OwnerDraw** property to **True**. Next, you add code to the menu item's **MeasureItem** event to let Visual Basic know how big you want to make this item when displayed. To pass this information back to Visual Basic, you are passed an object of the **MeasureItemEventArgs**, and you set this object's **ItemHeight** and **ItemWidth** properties in pixels, like this:

```
Private Sub MenuItem2_MeasureItem(ByVal sender As Object, _
    ByVal e As System.Windows.Forms.MeasureItemEventArgs) _
    Handles MenuItem2.MeasureItem
    e.ItemHeight = 20
    e.ItemWidth = 100
End Sub
```

Next, you actually draw the item with a **Graphics** object passed to you in the menu item's **DrawItem** event. In this case, I'll do that by creating a black pen object to draw with and by drawing an ellipse this way. Note in particular that the boundaries that you're supposed to draw inside are passed to you as a **Bounds** object (you can use the **Height** and **Width** properties of this object to get more information):

```
Private Sub MenuItem2_DrawItem(ByVal sender As Object, _
    ByVal e As System.Windows.Forms.DrawItemEventArgs) _
    Handles MenuItem2.DrawItem
    Dim pen As New Pen(Color.Black)
    e.Graphics.DrawEllipse(pen, e.Bounds)
End Sub
```

And, of course, you can handle other events as before for this menu item, such as the **Click** event:

```
Private Sub MenuItem2_Click(ByVal sender As System.Object, _
    ByVal e As System.EventArgs) _
```

```
        Handles MenuItem2.Click
        MsgBox("You clicked item 1")
    End Sub
```

Creating Menus in Code

So far in this chapter, we've designed and built our menu systems at design time, but of course you can create menu systems at run time as well—just create a **MainMenu** object, add the **MenuItem** objects you want to it, and assign the **MainMenu** object to a form's **Menu** property. Here's an example, CreateMenus on the CD-ROM, that does exactly that. You can see the menu system that this example creates when you click its "Create menu" button in Figure 9.15.

Here's the code this example uses to create the menu system you see in Figure 9.15—note that all you really have to do is to create **MenuItem** objects and use the **MenuItems** collection's **Add** method to add them to menus or other menu items:

```
Dim mainMenu1 As New MainMenu()

Dim WithEvents menuItem1 As New MenuItem()
Dim WithEvents menuItem2 As New MenuItem()
Dim WithEvents menuItem3 As New MenuItem()
Dim WithEvents menuItem4 As New MenuItem()

Private Sub Button1_Click(ByVal sender As System.Object, _
    ByVal e As System.EventArgs) Handles Button1.Click
    menuItem1.Text = "File"
    menuItem2.Text = "New"
    menuItem3.Text = "Text File..."
    menuItem3.Checked = True
    menuItem3.Shortcut = Shortcut.CtrlT
    menuItem4.Text = "Image..."
    menuItem4.Shortcut = Shortcut.CtrlI
    menuItem2.MenuItems.Add(menuItem3)
    menuItem2.MenuItems.Add(menuItem4)
    AddHandler menuItem3.Click, AddressOf MenuItem3_Click
    menuItem1.MenuItems.Add(menuItem2)
    mainMenu1.MenuItems.Add(menuItem1)
    Menu = mainMenu1
End Sub

Private Sub MenuItem3_Click(ByVal sender As System.Object, _
    ByVal e As System.EventArgs) Handles menuItem2.Click
    MsgBox("You clicked me!")
End Sub
```

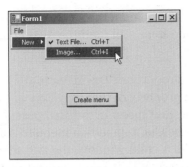

Figure 9.15   Creating menus from code.

Merging MDI Menus

Here's a problem—let's say you have an MDI program that does spell checking, but of course, you don't want any spell checking done unless a document is open. To make matters worse, MDI children are not supposed to display their own menu systems at all. How can you set things up so that a Spell Checking menu item appears in the main menu system only when an MDI child window is open?

You could create the Spell Checking menu item and keep track if any MDI children are open or not, and use the menu item's **Visible** property to make it appear or disappear as appropriate, but there's an easier way. All you need to do is to give the MDI children menus, and specify how to *merge* those menus with the MDI parent when a child MDI window appears in the MDI parent. This way, new menu items will appear in the parent's menu system as appropriate when child windows are open.

There are two properties that specify how MDI child menus merge with the MDI parent's menu system: **MergeType** and **MergeOrder**, which are properties of **MenuItem** objects. **MergeType** specifies how a menu item will be merged with its parent's menu system, and can take these values from the **MenuMerge** enumeration:

- **Add**—The menu item is added to the existing menu items in a merged menu.

- **MergeItems**—All submenu items of this menu item are merged with those of existing menu items (at the same position) in a merged menu.

- **Remove**—The menu item is not to be included in a merged menu.

- **Replace**—The menu item replaces an existing menu item at the same position.

And the **MergeOrder** property sets the order of the merged items, in case you want to specify that order.

You can see how this works in the MDIMenus example on the CD-ROM. In this case, I've given the MDI parent's Edit menu one item: Cut, and the MDI child's Edit menu one item: Copy.

To merge these menus, I set the **MergeType** property of the MDI child's Edit menu to **MergeItems**, and set the **MergeType** property of the Copy item in that menu to **Add**. Then I set the **MergeType** of the Edit menu in the MDI parent to **MergeItems** and the **MergeType** property of the Cut item in that menu to **Add**. Now when I run the program and display an MDI child window, the two menu items, Cut and Copy, are merged in the MDI parent's Edit menu, as you see in Figure 9.16, and the MDI child doesn't display any menu system at all.

TIP: You can also use the **MergeMenu** method to merge menu items in code.

Related solution:	Found on page:
Creating Multiple Document Interface (MDI) Applications	186

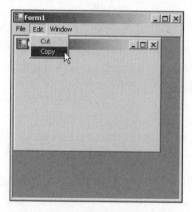

Figure 9.16   Merging MDI menu items.

Creating MDI Window Menus

MDI applications often have a Window menu that displays a list of the currently open MDI child windows, with a check in front of the currently active window. You can support that easily with Visual Basic—all you have to do is to create a Window menu and set the **MdiList** property to **True** for that menu. Setting this property to **True** automatically adds a list of the currently open MDI windows to the end of the current menu. You can see the results in Figure 9.17—selecting a window from this list will give that window the focus.

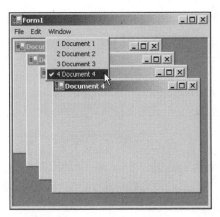

Figure 9.17   Creating an MDI Window menu.

Using the ContextMenu Class

Context menus are those handy menus that pop up over controls, usually when you right-click them. They're called context menus because they appear over specific controls—that is, in the context of that control, and so can be tailored to that control. They're supported by the **ContextMenu** class, which has this class hierarchy:

```
Object
    MarshalByRefObject
        Component
            Menu
                ContextMenu
```

You can find the notable public properties of **ContextMenu** objects in Table 9.6, their notable methods in Table 9.7, and their notable events in Table 9.8.

Table 9.6   Noteworthy public properties of **ContextMenu** objects.

Property	Means
IsParent	**True** if this menu contains any menu items. This property is read-only.
MdiListItem	Holds the **MenuItem** that is used to display a list of MDI child forms.
MenuItems	Holds the collection of **MenuItem** objects associated with the menu.
SourceControl	Holds the control that is displaying the shortcut menu.

Table 9.7   Noteworthy public methods of ContextMenu objects.

Method	Means
GetContextMenu	Gets the context menu that contains this menu.
GetMainMenu	Gets the **MainMenu** object that contains this menu.
MergeMenu	Merges the **MenuItem** objects of one menu with the another menu.
Show	Displays the shortcut menu.

Table 9.8   Noteworthy public events of ContextMenu objects.

Event	Means
Popup	Occurs before the context menu is displayed.

Creating Context Menus

Creating context menus is much like creating standard menus—you only need to add a **ContextMenu** control to a Windows form, as you see in Figure 9.18. The caption for this context menu is simply "Context Menu", but everything else is the same as creating any standard menu (see "Creating Menus" in this chapter)—just give the items in the menu the captions you want, as you also see in Figure 9.18.

Now you can connect code to the context menu items as you can with any click events:

```
Private Sub MenuItem3_Click(ByVal sender As System.Object, _
    ByVal e As System.EventArgs) Handles MenuItem3.Click
    MsgBox("You clicked the Paste item")
End Sub


Private Sub MenuItem2_Click(ByVal sender As System.Object, _
    ByVal e As System.EventArgs) Handles MenuItem2.Click
    MsgBox("You clicked the Copy item")
End Sub


Private Sub MenuItem1_Click(ByVal sender As System.Object, _
    ByVal e As System.EventArgs) Handles MenuItem1.Click
    MsgBox("You clicked the Cut item")
End Sub
```

Finally, assign the context menu control, such as **ContextMenu1**, to the **ContextMenu** property of the control you want to connect it to. In the

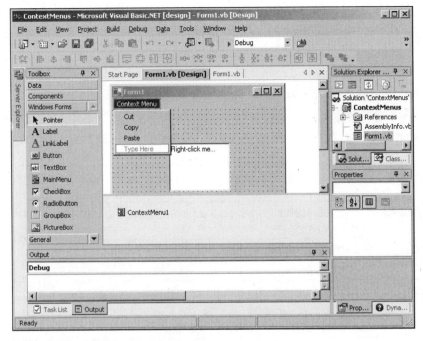

Figure 9.18   Creating a context menu.

ContextMenus example on the CD-ROM, I've connected this context menu to a multiline text box; when the user right-clicks this text box, the context menu appears, as you see in Figure 9.2, and you can select the items in that menu.

*TIP: You also can make context menus appear whenever you want to—just set their **Visible** property to **True**.*

Using the **OpenFileDialog** Class

As discussed in the In Depth section of this chapter, Open File dialogs let you get the name or names of files to open from the user. They're based on the **OpenFileDialog** class, which has this class hierarchy:

```
Object
    MarshalByRefObject
        Component
            CommonDialog
                FileDialog
                    OpenFileDialog
```

You can find the notable public properties of **OpenFileDialog** objects in Table 9.9, the notable public methods in Table 9.10, and the notable public events in Table 9.11.

Table 9.9   Noteworthy public properties of OpenFileDialog objects.

Property	Means
AddExtension	Gets/sets if the dialog box adds an extension to file names if the user doesn't supply the extension.
CheckFileExists	Gets/sets if the dialog box displays a warning if the user specifies a nonexistent file.
CheckPathExists	Gets/sets whether the dialog box displays a warning if the user gives a path that does not exist.
DefaultExt	Gets/sets the default file extension.
FileName	Gets/sets the file name selected in the file dialog box.
FileNames	Gets the file names of all selected files.
Filter	Gets/sets the current file name filter string, which sets the choices that appear in the "Save as file type" or "Files of type" box.
FilterIndex	Gets/sets the index of the filter selected in the file dialog box.
InitialDirectory	Gets/sets the initial directory used in the file dialog box.
Multiselect	Gets/sets whether the dialog box allows multiple file selections.
ReadOnlyChecked	Gets/sets whether the read-only checkbox is checked.
RestoreDirectory	Gets/sets whether the dialog box should restore the original directory before closing.
ShowHelp	Gets/sets whether the Help button should be displayed.
ShowReadOnly	Gets/sets whether the dialog displays a read-only check box.
Title	Gets/sets the file dialog box title.
ValidateNames	Gets/sets a value specifying if the dialog box accepts only valid (that is, Win32) file names.

Table 9.10   Noteworthy public methods of OpenFileDialog objects.

Method	Means
OpenFile	Opens the file selected by the user, with read-only permission. The file is specified by the **FileName** property.
Reset	Resets all options to their default values.
ShowDialog	Shows the dialog box.

Table 9.11 Noteworthy public events of OpenFileDialog objects.

Event	Means
FileOk	Occurs when the user clicks the Open or Save button.
HelpRequest	Occurs when the user clicks the Help button.

Creating Open File Dialogs

Open File dialogs let you get the name and the path of files the user wants to open. You create these dialogs with the **OpenFileDialog** class, and you can see an example in the OpenFileDialog example on the CD-ROM.

This example lets the user open an image in a picture box. To configure the Open File dialog, I add an **OpenFileDialog** control to the project. To specify that I want the user to be able to open JPEG or GIF files, I use the **Filter** property of this control, which sets the possible file types this dialog can open. In this case, I'll set that property to this string at design time: "JPEG files (*.jpg)|*.jpg|GIF files (*.gif)|*.gif|All files (*.*)|*.*". This gives the user three prompts, "JPEG files (*.jpg)", "GIF files (*.gif)", and "All files (*.*)" in the "Files of type" box in the dialog box, and informs the program what file extensions to use by separating information with upright bars (|).

If the user did not click the Cancel button, I can determine which file they want to open from the **FileName** property, and load the corresponding image into the picture box in this example this way:

```
Private Sub Button1_Click(ByVal sender As System.Object, _
    ByVal e As System.EventArgs) Handles Button1.Click
    If OpenFileDialog1.ShowDialog() <> DialogResult.Cancel Then
        PictureBox1.Image = Image.FromFile(OpenFileDialog1.FileName)
    End If
End Sub
```

TIP: *If you've set the dialog box's **Multiselect** property to **True**, the user can select multiple files—and you can recover their file names from the **FileNames** property, which returns an array of strings. Want to see an example? Take a look at "Adding Images to Image Lists in Code" in Chapter 10.*

Another useful property to know about is the **InitialDirectory** property, which lets you set the directory that the Open File dialog box first shows; here's an example:

```
openFileDialog1.InitialDirectory = "c:\datafiles"
```

9. Windows Forms:
Menus, Built-in Dialog
Boxes, and Printing

And here's another good one—if you set the dialog's **ShowHelp** property to **True**, it'll display a Help button. If that button is clicked, a **HelpRequest** event occurs, and you can display a help window when it does.

TIP: Don't forget that you can set the dialog box's title with the **Title** property in case you don't want it just to say "Open".

You can see the File Open dialog created in the OpenFileDialog example from the CD-ROM, which is shown in Figure 9.3.

Related solution:	Found on page:
Adding Images to Image Lists in Code	441

Using the **SaveFileDialog** Class

As discussed in the In Depth section of this chapter, you can use Save File dialogs to get the name of the file that the user wants to save data to. Here is the class hierarchy for this class:

```
Object
    MarshalByRefObject
        Component
            CommonDialog
                FileDialog
                    SaveFileDialog
```

You can find the notable public properties of **SaveFileDialog** objects in Table 9.12, the notable public methods in Table 9.13, and the notable public events in Table 9.14.

Table 9.12   Noteworthy public properties of SaveFileDialog objects.

Property	Means
AddExtension	Gets/sets whether the dialog will add an extension to a file name if the user doesn't supply an extension.
CheckFileExists	Gets/sets whether the dialog box displays a warning if the user specifies a file that does not exist.
CheckPathExists	Gets/sets whether the dialog box displays a warning if the user specifies a path that does not exist.
CreatePrompt	Gets/sets whether the dialog box asks the user if it should create a file if the user specifies a nonexistent file.

(continued)

Table 9.12   Noteworthy public properties of SaveFileDialog objects (continued).

Property	Means
DefaultExt	Gets/sets the default file extension.
FileName	Gets/sets the file name selected in the file dialog box.
FileNames	Gets the file names of all selected files.
Filter	Gets/sets the current file name filter string, which sets the choices that appear in the "Save as file type" or "Files of type" box.
FilterIndex	Gets/sets the index of the filter selected in the file dialog box.
InitialDirectory	Gets/sets the initial directory used in the file dialog box.
OverwritePrompt	Gets/sets whether the dialog displays a warning if the user specifies a name that already exists.
RestoreDirectory	Gets/sets whether the dialog box should restore the original directory before closing.
ShowHelp	Gets/sets whether the Help button should be displayed.
Title	Gets/sets the file dialog box title.
ValidateNames	Gets/sets whether the dialog box accepts only valid (that is, Win32) file names.

Table 9.13   Noteworthy public methods of SaveFileDialog objects.

Method	Means
OpenFile	Opens the file with read/write permission selected by the user.
Reset	Resets all dialog options to their default values.
ShowDialog	Shows the dialog.

Table 9.14   Noteworthy public events of SaveFileDialog objects.

Event	Means
FileOk	Occurs when the user clicks the Open or Save button.
HelpRequest	Occurs when the user clicks the Help button.

Creating Save File Dialogs

You can use the **SaveFileDialog** class to display a Save File dialog and get the name of the file the user wants to save data to. You can see an example in the SaveFileDialog example on the CD-ROM. Here's how that works in code; I'm checking the return value from the **ShowDialog** method, and if it's anything but **DialogResult.Cancel**, I display the filename that the user selected in a message box:

```
Private Sub Button1_Click(ByVal sender As System.Object, _
    ByVal e As System.EventArgs) Handles Button1.Click
    If SaveFileDialog1.ShowDialog <> DialogResult.Cancel Then
        MsgBox("You chose " & SaveFileDialog1.FileName)
    End If
End Sub
```

TIP: *You can use the **CreatePrompt** property to display a prompt asking the user if a file that does not exist should be created, and the **OverwritePrompt** property to ask the user if an existing file should be overwritten.*

You can see the Save File dialog that the SaveFileDialog example from the CD-ROM creates in Figure 9.4.

TIP: *Don't forget that you can set the dialog box's title with the **Title** property in case you don't want it just to say "Save As".*

Using the **FontDialog** Class

As discussed in the In Depth section of this chapter, the **FontDialog** class displays a dialog box that lets the user select a font. It returns a **Font** object in the **Font** property, and a **Color** object in the **Color** property. **Font** dialogs are supported by the **FontDialog** class. Here is the class hierarchy for that class:

```
Object
    MarshalByRefObject
        Component
            CommonDialog
                FontDialog
```

You can find the notable public properties of **FontDialog** objects in Table 9.15, the notable public methods in Table 9.16, and the notable public events in Table 9.17.

Table 9.15   Noteworthy public properties of FontDialog objects.

Property	Means
AllowSimulations	Gets/sets whether the dialog box allows graphics device interface font simulations.
AllowVectorFonts	Gets/sets whether the dialog box allows vector font selections.
AllowVerticalFonts	Gets/sets whether the dialog box displays both vertical and horizontal fonts or only horizontal fonts.
Color	Gets/sets the selected font color.
FixedPitchOnly	Gets/sets whether the dialog box allows only the selection of fixed-pitch fonts.
Font	Gets/sets the selected font.
FontMustExist	Gets/sets whether the dialog box specifies an error condition if the user attempts to select a font or style that does not exist.
MaxSize	Gets/sets the maximum point size a user can select.
MinSize	Gets/sets the minimum point size a user can select.
ShowApply	Gets/sets whether the dialog box contains an Apply button.
ShowColor	Gets/sets whether the dialog box displays the color choice.
ShowEffects	Gets/sets whether the dialog box contains controls that allow the user to specify strikethrough, underline, and text color options.
ShowHelp	Gets/sets whether the dialog box displays a Help button.

Table 9.16   Noteworthy public methods of FontDialog objects.

Method	Means
Reset	Resets all dialog options to default values.
ShowDialog	Shows the dialog.

Table 9.17   Noteworthy public events of FontDialog objects.

Event	Means
Apply	Occurs when the user clicks the Apply button.
HelpRequest	Occurs when the user clicks the Help button.

Creating Font Dialogs

The great thing about **Font** dialogs is that they return **Font** and **Color** objects, saving you the trouble of configuring those objects from scratch. This is handy because you can assign these objects directly to the properties of controls that can use them.

Here's an example, called FontDialog on the CD-ROM. In this case, I'll set the font used in a rich text box simply by assigning the **Font** and **Color** properties of a Font dialog to the **Font** and **ForeColor** properties of the rich text box, unless the user has clicked the Cancel button in that dialog:

```
Private Sub Button1_Click(ByVal sender As System.Object, _
    ByVal e As System.EventArgs) Handles Button1.Click
    If FontDialog1.ShowDialog <> DialogResult.Cancel Then
        RichTextBox1.Font = FontDialog1.Font
        RichTextBox1.ForeColor = FontDialog1.Color
    End If
End Sub
```

You can see the Font dialog that this example creates in Figure 9.5. In the FontDialog example, you click a button labeled "Select font" to display this dialog, and when you dismiss it, the new font is assigned to the rich text box, as you see in Figure 9.19.

Figure 9.19   Setting the font in a rich text box.

Using the **ColorDialog** Class

As discussed in the In Depth section of this chapter, Color dialogs let the user select a color, which is returned in the dialog object's **Color** property. Here is the class hierarchy for Color dialog boxes:

```
Object
    MarshalByRefObject
        Component
            CommonDialog
                ColorDialog
```

You can find the notable public properties of **ColorDialog** objects in Table 9.18, the notable public methods in Table 9.19, and the notable public events in Table 9.20.

Table 9.18   Noteworthy public properties of ColorDialog objects.

Property	Means
AllowFullOpen	Gets/sets whether the user can use the dialog box to define custom colors.
AnyColor	Gets/sets whether the dialog box displays all available colors in the set of basic colors.
Color	Gets/sets the color selected by the user.
CustomColors	Gets/sets the set of custom colors shown in the dialog box.
FullOpen	Gets/sets whether the controls used to create custom colors are visible when the dialog box is opened
ShowHelp	Gets/sets whether a Help button appears in the color dialog box.
SolidColorOnly	Gets/sets whether the dialog box will restrict users to selecting solid colors only.

Table 9.19   Noteworthy public methods of ColorDialog objects.

Method	Means
Reset	Resets all dialog options to their default values.
ShowDialog	Shows the dialog.

Table 9.20   Noteworthy public events of ColorDialog objects.

Event	Means
HelpRequest	Occurs when the user clicks the Help button.

Creating Color Dialogs

You can see an example using Color dialogs on the CD-ROM; it's named ColorDialog. This example lets the user use a Color dialog to set the background color of a label control. In code, all you have to do is to assign the **Color** object returned by the dialog box's **Color** property to the label's **BackColor** property like this—I'm also changing the label's text (originally "Change my color!") to "Here's my new color!" for a little additional excitement:

```
Private Sub Button1_Click(ByVal sender As System.Object, _
    ByVal e As System.EventArgs) Handles Button1.Click
    If ColorDialog1.ShowDialog <> DialogResult.Cancel Then
        Label1.Text = "Here's my new color!"
        Label1.BackColor = ColorDialog1.Color
    End If
End Sub
```

Figure 9.20   Setting a label's background color.

The Color dialog that this example displays appears in Figure 9.6. You can use it to set the new background color of the label, as you see in Figure 9.20. You can't see it in the black-and-white figure, but I've set the background color to an appealing aqua blue there.

Printing with the Printing Example

The support for printing has become fairly elaborate in Visual Basic, including all kinds of new objects and dialogs. To bring it all together, I've created the Printing example on the CD-ROM; you can see this example at work in Figure 9.21. By selecting various options in the File menu, you can see how Page Setup, Print Preview, Custom Print Preview, and Print dialogs look and work. This example includes a multipage print document that displays a red rectangle on the first page (which you can see in the Print Preview dialog in Figure 9.8) and a blue rectangle on the second page. The rest of this chapter is based on the Printing example program.

Figure 9.21   The Printing example.

Using the **PrintDocument** and **PrintSetting** Classes

As discussed in the In Depth section of this chapter, **PrintDocument** objects support the actual events and operations of printing in Visual Basic. You handle the **PrintPage** event of these objects to print pages, for example. Here is the hierarchy of this class:

```
Object
   MarshalByRefObject
      Component
         PrintDocument
```

You can find the notable public properties of **PrintDocument** objects in Table 9.21, the notable public methods in Table 9.22, and the notable public events in Table 9.23. The most important method is **Print**, which actually prints the document. When the print job starts, a **BeginPrint** event occurs, followed by a **PrintPage** event for each page (set the **HasMorePages** property of the object passed to you to **True** if you want to indicate that there are more pages to print), followed by an **EndPrint** event when the whole job is complete.

Table 9.21   Noteworthy public properties of PrintDocument objects.

Property	Means
DefaultPageSettings	Gets/sets the default settings that apply to a single, printed page of the document.
DocumentName	Gets/sets the document name to display while printing the document, as in a print status dialog box or printer queue.
PrinterSettings	Gets/sets the printer that prints the document.

Table 9.22   Noteworthy public methods of PrintDocument objects.

Method	Means
Print	Prints the document.

Table 9.23   Noteworthy public events of PrintDocument objects.

Event	Means
BeginPrint	Happens when the **Print** method is called to start a print job.
EndPrint	Happens when the last page of the document has printed.
PrintPage	Happens for each page to print—you draw the page in this event's handler.
QueryPageSettings	Happens before each **PrintPage** event.

9. Windows Forms: Menus, Built-in Dialog Boxes, and Printing

You also use the **PrintSettings** class to configure how a document will be printed—on what printer, how many copies, from what page to what page, and so on. You can find the public class properties of **PrintSettings** in Table 9.24 (that is, static, shared properties you can use with the class name, without an object, like this: **PrinterSettings.InstalledPrinters**), the notable public properties of **Printer Settings** objects in Table 9.25, and the notable public methods in Table 9.26.

Table 9.24   Noteworthy class (static/shared) properties of the PrintSettings class.

Event	Means
InstalledPrinters	Returns the names of all printers installed on the computer.

Table 9.25   Noteworthy public properties of PrintSettings objects.

Event	Means
CanDuplex	**True** if the printer supports double-sided printing.
Collate	Gets/sets whether the printed document is collated.
Copies	Gets/sets the number of copies of the document to print.
DefaultPageSettings	Gets the default page settings for this printer.
Duplex	Gets/sets the printer setting for double-sided printing.
FromPage	Gets/sets the page number of the first page to print.
IsPlotter	Returns whether the printer is a plotter.
IsValid	Returns whether the **PrinterName** property designates a valid printer.
LandscapeAngle	Holds the angle, in degrees, used for landscape orientation.
MaximumCopies	Holds the maximum number of copies that the printer allows you to print at one time.
MaximumPage	Gets/sets the maximum **FromPage** or **ToPage** that can be selected in a **PrintDialog**.
MinimumPage	Gets/sets the minimum **FromPage** or **ToPage** that can be selected in a **PrintDialog**.
PaperSizes	Holds the paper sizes that are supported by this printer.
PaperSources	Holds the paper source trays that are available on the printer.
PrinterName	Gets/sets the name of the printer to use.
PrinterResolutions	Gets the resolutions supported by this printer.
PrintRange	Gets/sets the page numbers to print, as specified by the user.
PrintToFile	Gets/sets whether the printing output is sent to a file instead of a port.
SupportsColor	Returns whether this printer supports color printing.
ToPage	Gets/sets the number of the last page to print.

Table 9.26 Noteworthy public methods of PrintSettings objects.

Method	Means
CreateMeasurementGraphics	Gets a **Graphics** object that contains printer information.

Using the PrintDialog Class

So how does one actually print a document? You start with a Print dialog, which displays the actual Print button, and is supported by the **PrintDialog** class; here is the hierarchy of that class:

```
Object
    MarshalByRefObject
        Component
            CommonDialog
                PrintDialog
```

You can find the notable public properties of **PrintDialog** objects in Table 9.27, the notable public methods in Table 9.28, and the notable events in Table 9.29.

So what happens when the user actually clicks the OK button in a Print dialog? See the next topic.

Table 9.27 Noteworthy public properties of PrintDialog objects.

Property	Means
AllowPrintToFile	Gets/sets whether the Print to file checkbox is enabled.
AllowSelection	Gets/sets whether the Selection radio button is enabled.
AllowSomePages	Gets/sets whether the From... To... Page radio button is enabled.
Document	Gets/sets the **PrintDocument** used to obtain **PrinterSettings**.
PrinterSettings	Gets/sets the **PrinterSettings** dialog box to modify.
PrintToFile	Gets/sets whether the Print to file checkbox is checked.
ShowHelp	Gets/sets whether the Help button is displayed.
ShowNetwork	Gets/sets whether the Network button is displayed.

Table 9.28 Noteworthy public methods of PrintDialog objects.

Method	Means
Reset	Resets all dialog options.
ShowDialog	Shows the dialog.

Table 9.29   Noteworthy public events of PrintDialog objects.

Event	Means
HelpRequest	Occurs when the user clicks the Help button.

Printing

To print a document, you add a **PrintDocument** and a **PrintDialog** object to a form (see the previous two topics), as I've done in the Printing example on the CD-ROM. Before displaying the Print dialog, you assign the **PrintDocument** object to the **PrintDialog** object's **Document** property. In the Printing example, I'm storing all the printer settings (such as what printer to use and what pages to print) in the print document's **PrinterSettings** property, so I assign the **PrinterSettings** object returned by that property to the **PrinterSettings** property of the **PrintDialog** object before displaying that dialog. I also set the print dialog's **AllowSomePages** property to **True** to allow the user to select a range of pages to print, and use the **ShowDialog** method to show the dialog box. You can see what the Print dialog looks like for this example in Figure 9.7.

If the user clicked the OK button in the Print dialog, I copy the settings the user specified in that dialog to the document, and then print the document with the **Print** method:

```
Private Sub MenuItem5_Click(ByVal sender As System.Object, _
    ByVal e As System.EventArgs) Handles MenuItem5.Click
    PrintDialog1.Document = PrintDocument1
    PrintDialog1.PrinterSettings = PrintDocument1.PrinterSettings
    PrintDialog1.AllowSomePages = True
    If PrintDialog1.ShowDialog = DialogResult.OK Then
        PrintDocument1.PrinterSettings = PrintDialog1.PrinterSettings
        PrintDocument1.Print()
    End If
End Sub
```

When you call the **PrintDocument** object's **Print** method, this object's **BeginPrint** event occurs to start the print job, followed by a **PrintPage** event for each page to print, followed by a **EndPrint** event at the end of the printing job. You're responsible for keeping track of the pages and printing them. In the **PrintPage** event, you're passed an object of the **PrintPageEventArgs** class, which has these members:

- **Cancel**—Gets/sets a value indicating whether the print job should be canceled. Setting this value to **True** cancels the print job.

- **Graphics**—The **Graphics** object used to draw the page.

- **HasMorePages**—Gets/sets a value indicating whether an additional page should be printed.

- **MarginBounds**—The rectangular area that represents the portion of the page inside the margins.

- **PageBounds**—The rectangular area that represents the total area of the page.

- **PageSettings**—The page settings for the current page (see "Creating Page Setup Dialogs" later in this chapter for more information on the **PageSetting** class).

All these properties are very useful—for example, when you're done printing one page, you can set the **HasMorePages** property to **True** to indicate that there are more pages yet to print (which means another **PrintPage** event will occur). To print the two pages of rectangles in the Printing example on the CD-ROM, we'll need to keep track of the current page number, which I do by setting an integer, **PageNumber**, to 0 when the **BeginPrint** event happens. Then, in the **PrintPage** event handler, I increment the page number, use the **FillRectangle** method of the **Graphics** object passed to us to draw the rectangles, and set **HasMorePages** to **True** if there are more pages to print:

```
Dim PageNumber As Integer

Private Sub PrintDocument1_BeginPrint(ByVal sender As Object, _
    ByVal e As System.Drawing.Printing.PrintEventArgs) Handles _
    PrintDocument1.BeginPrint
    PageNumber = 0
End Sub

Private Sub PrintDocument1_PrintPage(ByVal sender As _
    System.Object, ByVal e As _
    System.Drawing.Printing.PrintPageEventArgs) _
    Handles PrintDocument1.PrintPage
    PageNumber += 1
    Select Case PageNumber
        Case 1
            e.Graphics.FillRectangle(Brushes.Red, _
                New Rectangle(200, 200, 500, 500))
            e.HasMorePages = True
        Case 2
            e.Graphics.FillRectangle(Brushes.Blue, _
                New Rectangle(200, 200, 500, 500))
            e.HasMorePages = False
    End Select
End Sub
```

9. Windows Forms:
Menus, Built-in Dialog
Boxes, and Printing

NOTE: *This example is not set up to print selected ranges of pages—it just prints the whole document. If you want to handle print ranges, take a look at the* **PrintDocument PrintRange** *property, which holds the range of pages to print.*

And that's it—our output is sent to the printer. If you want to print text, you can use the use the **Graphics** object's **DrawString** method. We'll discuss the **Graphics** class later in the book; for example, if the font you want to print in is represented by the **Font** object **myFont**, you could determine the number of text lines per page this way:

```
numberLinesPerPage = e.MarginBounds.Height / myFont.GetHeight(e.Graphics)
```

Using the PrintPreviewDialog Class

As discussed in the In Depth section of this chapter, you can use Print Preview dialog to let the user see what a document will look like when it's printed. This dialog is supported by the **PrintPreviewDialog** class, which has this class hierarchy:

```
Object
    MarshalByRefObject
        Component
            Control
                ScrollableControl
                    ContainerControl
                        Form
                            PrintPreviewDialog
```

You can find the notable public properties of **PrintPreviewDialog** objects in Table 9.30. Note that I'm not listing those members this class inherits from the **Control** class here (which you can find in Tables 5.1, 5.2, and 5.3) or from the **Form** class (which you can find in Tables 4.1, 4.2, and 4.3).

Table 9.30   Noteworthy public properties of PrintPreviewDialog objects.

Property	Means
AcceptButton	Gets/sets the button that is automatically clicked when the user presses the Enter key.
ControlBox	Gets/sets whether a control box is displayed in the caption bar of the form.
Document	Gets/sets the document to preview.
FormBorderStyle	Gets/sets the border style of the form.

(continued)

Table 9.30   Noteworthy public properties of PrintPreviewDialog objects *(continued)*.

Property	Means
HelpButton	Gets/sets whether a help button should be displayed in the caption box of the form.
MaximizeBox	Gets/sets whether the maximize button is displayed in the caption bar of the form.
MaximumSize	Gets the maximum size the form can be resized to.
MinimizeBox	Gets/sets whether the minimize button is displayed in the caption bar of the form.
MinimumSize	Gets the minimum size the form can be resized to.
PrintPreviewControl	Gets the **PrintPreviewControl** contained in this form.
ShowInTaskbar	Gets/sets whether the form is displayed in the Windows taskbar.
Size	Gets/sets the size of the form.
StartPosition	Gets/sets the starting position of the form at run time.
TopMost	Gets/sets whether the form should be displayed as your application's the topmost form.

Creating Print Preview Dialogs

To display a print preview, all you have to do is to assign a print document to a print preview dialog's **Document** property (and have implemented at least the **PrintPage** event handler of the print document), and use the **ShowDialog** method to show the print preview. Here's how it looks in the Printing example on the CD-ROM:

```
Private Sub MenuItem3_Click(ByVal sender As System.Object, _
    ByVal e As System.EventArgs) Handles MenuItem3.Click
    PrintPreviewDialog1.Document = PrintDocument1
    PrintPreviewDialog1.ShowDialog()
End Sub
```

You can see the print preview dialog in the Printing example in Figure 9.8.

9. Windows Forms: Menus, Built-in Dialog Boxes, and Printing

Using the **PrintPreviewControl** Class

As discussed in the In Depth section of this chapter, you can use **PrintPreview Control** objects to create your own custom print previews. Here's the class hierarchy for this control:

```
Object
    MarshalByRefObject
        Component
            Control
                PrintPreviewControl
```

You can find the notable public properties of **PrintPreviewControl** objects in Table 9.31. Note that I'm not listing the members this class inherits from the **Control** class, which you can find in Tables 5.1, 5.2, and 5.3.

Table 9.31   Noteworthy public properties of PrintPreviewControl objects.

Property	Means
AutoZoom	If **True** (the default), resizing the control automatically zooms to make all contents visible.
Columns	Gets/sets the number of pages displayed horizontally.
Rows	Gets/sets the number of pages displayed vertically.
StartPage	Gets/sets the page number of the upper left page.
Zoom	Gets/sets a value specifying how large the pages will appear.

Creating Custom Print Previews

The **PrintPreviewControl** control displays print previews, and you can use it to create your own custom print preview windows—all you have to do is to assign a print document to its **Document** property (and have at least implemented the print document's **PrintPage** event handler). I've added a second form, **Form2**, to the Printing example on the CD-ROM to show how to create a custom print preview, and placed a print preview control, **PrintPreviewControl1**, in that form (and also added a Close button that closes the form). Here's what the code to launch the custom preview looks like in the Printing example:

```
Private Sub MenuItem4_Click(ByVal sender As System.Object, _
    ByVal e As System.EventArgs) Handles MenuItem4.Click
    Dim preview As New Form2()
```

```
      preview.PrintPreviewControl1.Document = PrintDocument1
      preview.Show()
End Sub
```

You can see the custom print preview dialog in the Printing example in Figure 9.9.

Using the **PageSetupDialog** Class

As discussed in the In Depth section of this chapter, page setup dialogs let you specify page orientation, paper size, margin size, and more; you can see the page setup dialog from the Printing example on the CD-ROM in Figure 9.10. Page setup dialogs are supported by the **PageSetupDialog** class, which has this class hierarchy:

```
Object
    MarshalByRefObject
        Component
            CommonDialog
                PageSetupDialog
```

You can find the notable properties of **PageSetupDialog** objects in Table 9.32, the notable methods in Table 9.33, and the notable events in Table 9.34.

Table 9.32   Noteworthy public properties of PageSetupDialog objects.

Property	Means
AllowMargins	Gets/sets whether the margins section of the dialog box is enabled.
AllowOrientation	Gets/sets whether the orientation section of the dialog box (landscape or portrait) is enabled.
AllowPaper	Gets/sets whether the paper section of the dialog box (paper size and paper source) is enabled.
AllowPrinter	Gets/sets whether the Printer button is enabled.
Document	Gets/sets the **PrintDocument** to get page settings from.
MinMargins	Gets/sets the minimum margins the user is allowed to select. Measured in hundredths of an inch.
PageSettings	Gets/sets the page settings to modify.
PrinterSettings	Gets/sets the printer settings to modify.
ShowHelp	Gets/sets whether the Help button is visible.
ShowNetwork	Gets/sets whether the Network button is visible.

Table 9.33   Noteworthy public methods of PageSetupDialog objects.

Method	Means
Reset	Resets all dialog options.
ShowDialog	Shows the dialog.

Table 9.34   Noteworthy public events of PageSetupDialog objects.

Event	Means
HelpRequest	Occurs when the user clicks the Help button.

Creating Page Setup Dialogs

Page setup dialogs let the user specify the format for the pages that are to be printed, such as setting page orientation (portrait or landscape), margin size, and so on. You can use a Page Setup dialog to modify both the **PrinterSettings** and **PageSettings** objects in a **PrintDocument** object to record the settings the user wants to use for printing.

We've already seen the **PrinterSettings** class (see Tables 9.24, 9.25, and 9.26)—objects of this class can hold the page range to print, the number of copies to print, the printer to use and so on—but we haven't seen the **PageSettings** class yet. Here are the notable properties of this class:

- **Bounds**—Gets the bounds of the page.

- **Color**—Gets/sets a value indicating whether the page should be printed in color.

- **Landscape**—Gets/sets a value indicating whether the page is printed in landscape or portrait orientation.

- **Margins**—Gets/sets the margins for this page.

- **PaperSize**—Gets/sets the paper size for the page.

- **PaperSource**—Gets/sets the page's paper source.

- **PrinterResolution**—Gets/sets the printer resolution for the page.

- **PrinterSettings**—Gets/sets the printer settings associated with the page.

Here's how I let the user display a Page Setup dialog in the Printing example on the CD-ROM, and record the new settings in that example's **PrintDocument** object:

```
Private Sub MenuItem2_Click(ByVal sender As System.Object, _
    ByVal e As System.EventArgs) Handles MenuItem2.Click
```

```
        PageSetupDialog1.Document = PrintDocument1
        PageSetupDialog1.PrinterSettings = PrintDocument1.PrinterSettings
        PageSetupDialog1.PageSettings = PrintDocument1.DefaultPageSettings
        If PageSetupDialog1.ShowDialog = DialogResult.OK Then
            PrintDocument1.PrinterSettings = PageSetupDialog1.PrinterSettings
            PrintDocument1.DefaultPageSettings = PageSetupDialog1.PageSettings
        End If
    End Sub
```

You can see the page setup dialog in the Printing example in Figure 9.10.

Chapter 10

Windows Forms: Image Lists, Tree and List Views, Toolbars, Status and Progress Bars, and Tab Controls

In Depth

In this chapter, we'll take a look at seven popular Windows forms controls—image lists, tree views, list views, toolbars, status bars, progress bars, and tab controls—to round off our study of Windows forms controls (although we'll see the data grid control later, when discussing data handling). There's a lot to cover here, but of course we're going to go beyond the ordinary, using image lists to draw not only in the controls that have an **ImageList** property, but also in virtually any control; seeing how to add not only buttons to tool bars but also to other controls such as combo boxes; taking a look at "hot tracking" in tab controls (which changes tab appearance when the mouse moves over them); and so on.

Image Lists

You use image lists to store images; they form a kind of image repository. This doesn't sound terribly useful, but in fact, there are plenty of controls that are designed to work with image lists: list views, tree views, toolbars, tab controls, checkboxes, buttons, radio buttons, and labels—all of which have an **ImageList** (or **SmallImageList** and **LargeImageList**) and **ImageIndex** property.

When you associate an image list with a control's **ImageList** property, you can specify which image appears in the control with the **ImageIndex** property. The images in an image list are indexed—starting at zero—and you can switch the image displayed in a control at run time by changing the value of the **ImageIndex** property.

However, image list controls weren't really introduced to work with buttons or checkboxes; they appeared along controls that can handle many images at once, like tree views and list views. These kinds of controls may display dozens of images at once (such as the icons for the individual items in a list view), and that's when using image lists start to make sense, because such controls can simply take those images from the image list, one after the next.

The central property in image list controls is **Images**, which contains the pictures to be used by the control; you can access the images in this collection by index. The **ColorDepth** property determines the number of colors that the images are rendered with. Note that images will all be displayed at the same size, as set by the **ImageSize** property. This property is set to 16×16 pixels by default (the size of a small icon), so you should most likely change that when you load your images into the list.

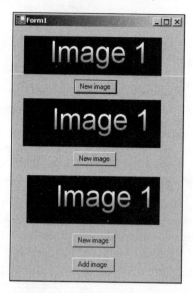

Figure 10.1   An image list at work.

You can see an image list at work in Figure 10.1, which is the ImageLists example on the CD-ROM; I've loaded four images into the image list in this example. The top image is displayed in a label, using the label's **ImageList** property. When you click the "New image" button, the next image appears, simply by changing the label's **ImageIndex** property. The middle image is displayed in a picture box, which doesn't have an **ImageList** property, but we can use the picture box's **Image** property instead if we handle the details of loading new images into that property as needed. The bottom image is actually displayed in a panel, which doesn't have either an **ImageList** or an **Image** property; we're drawing the image in the panel directly, which will take a little bit of cleverness. (Strictly speaking, this isn't necessary, because panels do support a **BackgroundImage** property, but this example shows how to use image list's **Draw** method, which lets you draw in practically any control.)

Tree Views

You use a tree view to display a hierarchy of *nodes*. Each node is not only displayed visually, but also can have child nodes. An example of this is the Windows Explorer, which uses a tree view in its left pane to display the hierarchy of folders on disk. You can expand and collapse parent nodes by clicking them; when expanded, their children are also visible. You can see a tree view control at work in Figure 10.2; this is the TreeViews example on the CD-ROM. Here, the icons you see for nodes are actually stored in an image list that I've added to the project. I've specified which icon to use with what node individually.

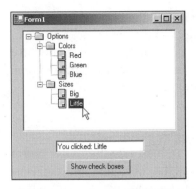

Figure 10.2   A tree view at work.

A tree view also can be displayed with checkboxes next to the nodes, if the tree view's **CheckBoxes** property is set to **True**. You can then check or uncheck nodes by setting the node's **Checked** property to **True** or **False**.

The main properties of tree views are **Nodes** and **SelectedNode**. The **Nodes** property contains the list of nodes in the tree view, and the **SelectedNode** property gets or sets the currently selected node. Nodes themselves are supported by the **TreeNode** class.

The **Nodes** collection for a node holds the node's child **TreeNode** objects. You can add, remove, or clone a **TreeNode**, and when you do, all child tree nodes are added, removed, or cloned at the same time. Each **TreeNode** can contain a collection of other **TreeNode** objects, which means you can use expressions like this: **MyNode.Nodes(3).Nodes(5)** to refer to child nodes (in this case, actually grandchild nodes). You also can use the **FullPath** property to specify nodes in terms of their absolute, not relative, locations. And you can use the **Nodes** collection's **Add** or **Remove** methods to add or remove nodes in code.

You can set the text for each tree node label by setting a **TreeNode** object's **Text** property. And you can display images next to the tree nodes; just assign an **ImageList** to the **ImageList** property of the parent **TreeView** control and assign an image to a node by referencing its index value in the **ImageList** property. Specifically, you set the **ImageIndex** property to the index value of the image you want to display when the **TreeNode** is in an unselected state, and set the **SelectedImageIndex** property to the index value of the image you want to display when the **TreeNode** is selected.

Tree views also support various properties for navigating through them, node by node. In particular, you can use the following properties: **FirstNode**, **LastNode**, **NextNode**, **PrevNode**, **NextVisibleNode**, **PrevVisibleNode**. To select a node from code, just assign the **TreeNode** object to the tree view's **SelectedNode** property.

Tree views are all about showing node hierarchies—the user can expand a node (showing its children) by clicking the plus sign (+) displayed next to it, or collapse a node by clicking the minus sign (-) next to it. You can do the same in code with the **Expand** method to expand a single node, or **ExpandAll** to expand all nodes, and the **Collapse** or **CollapseAll** methods to collapse nodes.

List Views

If tree views are all about displaying node hierarchies, like the folder hierarchy on a disk, then list views are all about displaying lists of items. You can see a list view in the right pane in the Windows Explorer (the part that displays what files are in a folder). You also can see a list view at work in Figure 10.3, which is the ListViews example on the CD-ROM.

List views can display their items in four *view modes*: **View.LargeIcon**, **View.SmallIcon**, **View.List**, and **View.Details**; you set the view by assigning one of those values to the list view's **View** property. You can select all of these views in the ListViews example on the CD-ROM to compare them (use the combo box at lower right). The large icon mode displays large icons (large icons are 32×32 pixels) next to the item text. The small icon mode is the same except that it displays items using small icons (small icons are 16×16 pixels). The list mode displays small icons, always in one column. The report mode (also called the details mode) displays items in multiple columns, displaying column headers as you see in Figure 10.3. All of the view modes can display images from image lists.

The central property of list views is **ListItems**, which contains the items displayed by the control. The **SelectedItems** property contains a collection of the items currently selected in the control. Note that the user can select multiple items if the **MultiSelect** property is set to **True**, and like tree views, list views can display checkboxes next to the items, if the **CheckBoxes** property is set to **True**.

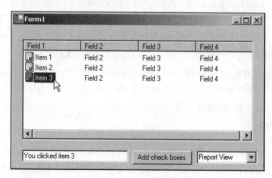

Figure 10.3   A list view at work.

You can use the **SelectedIndexChanged** event to handle item selections, and **ItemCheck** events to handle checkmark events. The **Activation** property sets what action the user must take to activate an item in the list: the options are **Standard**, **OneClick**, and **TwoClick**. **OneClick** requires a single click to activate the item. **TwoClick** requires the user to double-click (a single click changes the color of the item text). **Standard** requires the user to double-click to activate an item (but in this case, the item does not change appearance). You can sort the items in a list view with the **Sorting** property.

Toolbars

Windows users are familiar with toolbars—they're those bars full of buttons that appear under menu bars, as you see in Figure 10.4. There are various kinds of options here for the buttons in a toolbar—you can have standard push buttons, toggle buttons (that can appear up or pressed), drop-down buttons that can display a drop-down menu, and buttons that display images. Buttons also can be converted into separators, which display empty horizontal space to separate other buttons.

Typically, the buttons in a toolbar correspond to the most popular menu items in the application. In such cases, the code for a toolbar button is easy to implement—you just use the corresponding **MenuItem** object's **PerformClick** method, which clicks the menu item just as if the user did.

Although toolbars are usually docked along the top of its parent window, they can actually be docked to any side of a window. Toolbars also can display tool tips when the user points the mouse pointer at a toolbar button. (Note that to display **ToolTips**, the **ShowToolTips** property must be set to **True**.)

When the **Appearance** property is set to **Normal**, the toolbar buttons appear raised (that is, three-dimensional). You can set the **Appearance** property of the toolbar to **Flat** to give the toolbar and its buttons a flat appearance. (Note that when the mouse pointer moves over a flat button, the button's appearance changes to three-dimensional.) The **TextAlign** property specifies the alignment of the text in a button, such as at the top of bottom of the button.

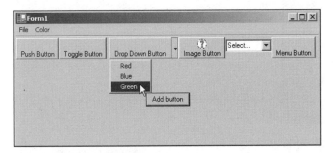

Figure 10.4   A toolbar at work.

The **Toolbar** control allows you to create toolbars by adding **ToolBarButton** objects to the toolbar's **Buttons** collection. At design time, an editor appears to add buttons to a toolbar; each button can have text and/or an image (images come from an image list control). At run time, you can add or remove buttons from the toolbar using the **Add** and **Remove** methods of the **Buttons** property. And here's an interesting fact: The buttons in a toolbar do not get their own **Click** events—instead, you add code to the **ButtonClick** events of the toolbar. (You can tell what button was clicked by checking the **Button** property of the **ToolBarButtonClickEventArgs** argument passed to you.)

To create a collection of **ToolBarButton** controls to display in a toolbar, you add the buttons individually at design time, or at run time using the **Add** method of the **Buttons** property, or using the **AddRange** method to add a number of buttons at once.

Status Bars

Although toolbars usually appear right under menu bars; status bars usually appear at the bottom of a window and give the user some additional information, such as the page number they're editing, or whether or not the program is connected to the Internet, and so on. In Visual Basic, you support status bars with the **StatusBar** control. This control can display panels (if it does not display panels, it's called a *simple* status bar), as you see in Figure 10.5, which is the StatusBars example on the CD-ROM.

To make the status bar into a *simple status bar*, which means that you can display a single message on the status bar, set the **ShowPanels** property to **False** (this is the default) and set the **Text** property of the status bar to the text you want to display. Typically, however, status bars are divided into panels by adding **StatusBarPanel** objects to the status bar and setting the **ShowPanels** property to **True**. You can keep track of panels in a status bar using the **Panels** collection,

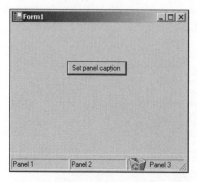

Figure 10.5   A status bar at work.

setting the text in a panel this way, for example: **StatusBar1.Panels(0).Text =** "**Everything's OK**". You can add panels to a status bar at design time by clicking the **Panels** property in the properties window and using the collection editor that appears, or by the **Add** method of the **Panels** collection in code.

Each panel is a **StatusbarPanel** object. You also can set the text in any such object directly, like this: **StatusbarPanel1.Text = "Everything's OK"**. To handle panel clicks, you use the **StatusBar** class's **PanelClick** event; you can determine which panel was clicked with the **StatusBarPanel** property of the **StatusBarPanel ClickEventArgs** event object passed to you in this event's handler.

Progress Bars

Progress bars are those simple controls that show the progress of some operation by displaying rectangles in a horizontal bar, as you see in Figure 10.6, which is the ProgressBars example on the CD-ROM. In this case, the progress bar is being drawn using timer events that start when you click the Start button. When the operation finishes, the progress bar is filled; the idea here is to give the user some visual feedback on how the operation is progressing, and how long it will take.

The main properties of a progress bar are **Value**, **Minimum**, and **Maximum**. You use the **Minimum** and **Maximum** properties to set the maximum and minimum values the progress bar can display. (The minimum is represented by one rectangle.) To change the display, you write code to set the **Value** property. For example, if the **Maximum** property is set to 100, the **Minimum** property is set to 10, and the **Value** property is set to 60, then 6 rectangles will appear.

Tab Controls

As mentioned several times in this book, space is usually at a premium in Windows programs, and the tab control is another one that (like menus, combo boxes, drop-down list boxes, etc.) is designed to help you conserve space. Tab controls work much like the tabs in a set of folders in a filing cabinet; you can click a tab to

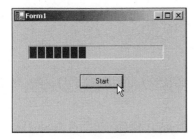

Figure 10.6   A progress bar at work.

Figure 10.7   A tab control at work.

display a whole new client area, and each such client area can display other controls. You can see a tab control at work in Figure 10.7, which is the TabControls example on the CD-ROM. In this case, the first tab displays a page that holds buttons, the next tab's page displays a rich text box, and the third tab's page displays a picture box. Using tabs like this allows you to present page after page of controls, all in the same space. Tabs like these are becoming increasingly popular in dialog boxes that let the user select options. If you've got 2,000 options from which the user may select (as many Microsoft applications seem to have), you can divide them up by category and give each category its own tab page.

The central property of the **TabControl** is **TabPages**, which contains the individual tab pages in the control, each of which is a **TabPage** object. When a tab is clicked, it displays its page and causes a **Click** event for that **TabPage** object. You can add new tab pages with the **TabPages** collection's **Add** method, and remove them with the **Remove** method.

Now it's time to get all the details on these controls in the Immediate Solutions section.

Immediate Solutions

Using the **ImageList** Class

As discussed in the In Depth section of this chapter, image lists, which are components and do not appear at run time, store images for use by various controls, including list views, tree views, toolbars, tab controls, checkboxes, buttons, radio buttons, and labels. Here is the class hierarchy of the **ImageList** component:

```
Object
    MarshalByRefObject
        Component
            ImageList
```

You can find the notable public properties of **ImageList** objects in Table 10.1, and the notable methods in Table 10.2.

Table 10.1   Noteworthy public properties of ImageList objects.

Property	Means
ColorDepth	Gets the color depth for this image list.
Handle	Gets the handle for this image list.
Images	Gets an **ImageCollection** object for this image list.
ImageSize	Gets/sets the image size for images in the list.
TransparentColor	Gets/sets the transparent color for this list.

Table 10.2   Noteworthy public methods of ImageList objects.

Method	Means
Draw	Draws the given image.

Creating Image Lists

In the ImageLists example on the CD-ROM, I've added an **ImageList** component to store images in. When you click the image list's **Images** property in the Properties window, a collection editor opens as you see in Figure 10.8, and you can add

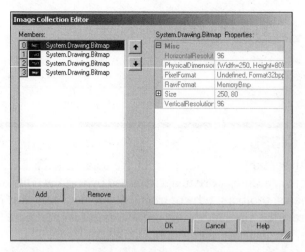

Figure 10.8   Adding images to an image list component.

new images to the image list (all of which should be the same size) by clicking the Add button (which lets you browse for new images) or remove them by clicking the Remove button.

You can set the size of the images in the image list (the default is 16×16 pixels, the size of a small icon) with its **ImageSize** property in the properties window. Of course, you also can add images to image lists in code; see the topic "Adding Images to Image Lists in Code" later in this chapter.

Using Image Lists with **ListView, TreeView, ToolBar, TabControl, Button, CheckBox, RadioButton,** and **Label** Controls

Image list components are designed to work with controls that support two properties: **ImageList** and **ImageIndex.** Those controls are list views, tree views, toolbars, tab controls, checkboxes, buttons, radio buttons, and labels. You associate an image list with the control using the **ImageList** property and set which image from that list is displayed in the control with the **ImageIndex** property (for example, setting **ImageIndex** to 0 makes the control display the first image in the image list).

You can see how this works in the ImageLists example on the CD-ROM, which appears in Figure 10.1—the top image there is displayed in a label whose **ImageList** property is set to the image list component in the example, **ImageList1,** and whose **ImageIndex** property starts off at 0. When the user clicks the "New image" button in that example, I cycle through the available images by changing the **ImageIndex** property, like this:

```
Private Sub Button1_Click(ByVal sender As System.Object, _
    ByVal, e As System.EventArgs) Handles Button1.Click
    If Label1.ImageIndex < ImageList1.Images.Count - 1 Then
        Label1.ImageIndex += 1
    Else
        Label1.ImageIndex = 0
    End If
End Sub
```

You can see the results in Figure 10.9, where I've clicked the "New image" button under the label to display the second image.

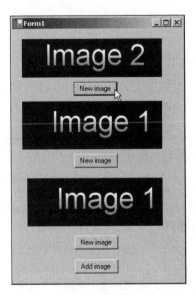

Figure 10.9   Displaying a new image in a label.

Using Image Lists with Picture Boxes and Other Controls with **Image** or **BackgroundImage** Properties

Although image lists were primarily designed to work with controls that have an **ImageList** and **ImageIndex** property (see the previous topic), you also can use image lists with controls that only have **Image** or **BackgroundImage** properties.

For example, picture boxes only have an **Image** property, so to load an image from an image list into a picture box, you have to access images in the list using the **Images** collection. Here's how that works in the ImageLists example on the CD-ROM, where I'm loading image 0 from **ImageList1** into a picture box when the form loads, and cycling through the other images in the image list when the user clicks a "New image" button beneath the picture box:

```
Private Sub Form1_Load(ByVal sender As System.Object, _
    ByVal e As System.EventArgs) Handles MyBase.Load
    PictureBox1.Image = ImageList1.Images(0)
End Sub

Private Sub Button2_Click(ByVal sender As System.Object, _
    ByVal e As System.EventArgs) Handles Button2.Click
    Static ImageIndex As Integer = 0
    If ImageIndex < ImageList1.Images.Count - 1 Then
        ImageIndex += 1
    Else
        ImageIndex = 0
    End If
    PictureBox1.Image = ImageList1.Images(ImageIndex)
End Sub
```

You can see the results of this code in Figure 10.1—the picture box is the one in the middle of the figure.

Using Image Lists with Other Controls

You can use an image list's **Draw** method to draw an image in a control that you wouldn't usually think of to display images, such as a panel control. You can pass the **Draw** method a **Graphics** object to draw in, the X and Y coordinates at which to draw the image, and the index of the image to draw from the internal list of images. To draw in a panel control, you can use the control's **Paint** event, which happens when a control is drawn. Here's how that looks when I draw image 0 from **ImageList1** in **Panel1** in the ImageLists example on the CD-ROM:

```
Private Sub Panel1_Paint(ByVal sender As Object, _
    ByVal e As System.Windows.Forms.PaintEventArgs) Handles Panel1.Paint
    ImageList1.Draw(e.Graphics, 0, 0, 0)
End Sub
```

The panel control appears at the bottom in Figure 10.1. The user also can click the "New image" button under the panel to load a new image into it, and that's a little trickier to implement, because we're not supplied a **Graphics** object. In this case, we can get the Windows *handle* for the panel (a Windows handle is how Windows keeps track of windows internally) with the **Handle** property, and create a **Graphics** object with the **Graphics** class's **FromHandle** method:

```
Dim ImageIndex As Integer = 0

Private Sub Button3_Click(ByVal sender As System.Object, _
    ByVal e As System.EventArgs) Handles Button3.Click
    If ImageIndex < ImageList1.Images.Count - 1 Then
        ImageIndex += 1
    Else
        ImageIndex = 0
    End If
    ImageList1.Draw(Graphics.FromHwnd(Panel1.Handle), 0, 0, ImageIndex)
End Sub
```

Note that this means we should change the **Panel1_Paint** event handler, because as written, it only draws the first image, image 0, so only that image will appear when the panel needs to be redrawn (as when the form is minimized and then restored). We can make it draw the currently selected image by using the **ImageIndex** variable set by the above code instead:

```
Private Sub Panel1_Paint(ByVal sender As Object, _
    ByVal e As System.Windows.Forms.PaintEventArgs) Handles Panel1.Paint
    ImageList1.Draw(e.Graphics, 0, 0, ImageIndex)
End Sub
```

Adding Images to Image Lists in Code

We've already seen that you can add new images to image lists at design time by using a collection editor with the **Images** collection in the image list, but you also can add new images to an image list in code. (Note that the new image should be the same size as the other images in the list, or they'll automatically be resized to the size in the image list's **ImageSize** property.)

To see how that works, take a look at the "Add image" button in Figure 10.1. When the user clicks this button, the program displays a Open File dialog and uses the **Add** method of the image list's **Images** collection to add the newly selected images to the image list. (There's a new image, Image5.jpg, the same size as the others in the image list, in the ImageLists folder on the CD-ROM that you can add to the image list.) Here's how that looks in code—note that I'm allowing the user to make multiple selections in the Open File dialog (in which case you use the dialog's **FileNames** property) as well as single selections (in which case you use the **FileName** property):

```
Private Sub Button4_Click(ByVal sender As System.Object, _
    ByVal e As System.EventArgs) Handles Button4.Click
    If openFileDialog1.ShowDialog() = DialogResult.OK Then
        If Not (openFileDialog1.FileNames Is Nothing) Then
            Dim intLoopIndex As Integer
            For intLoopIndex = 0 To OpenFileDialog1.FileNames.Length - 1
                ImageList1.Images.Add( _
                    Image.FromFile(_
                    OpenFileDialog1.FileNames(intLoopIndex)))
            Next intLoopIndex
        Else
            ImageList1.Images.Add(_
                Image.FromFile(_
                OpenFileDialog1.FileNames(OpenFileDialog1.FileName)))
        End If
    End If
End Sub
```

And that's it—now the user can add new images to the image list at run time.

Related solution:	Found on page:
Creating Open File Dialogs	407

Using the **TreeView** Class

As discussed in the In Depth section of this chapter, tree view controls are designed to display a hierarchy of nodes, much like the left pane in the Windows Explorer. Here is the class hierarchy of the **TreeView** class:

```
Object
    MarshalByRefObject
        Component
            Control
                TreeView
```

You can find the notable public properties of **TreeView** objects in Table 10.3, the notable public methods in Table 10.4, and the notable public events in Table 10.5. Note that I'm omitting those properties, methods, and events **TreeView** objects inherit from the **Control** class—you'll find all that in Chapter 5, Tables 5.1, 5.2, and 5.3.

Table 10.3   Noteworthy public properties of TreeView objects.

Property	Means
BorderStyle	Gets/sets the tree view's border style.
CheckBoxes	Gets/sets whether checkboxes should be displayed next to tree nodes.
FullRowSelect	Gets/sets whether a selection should select the whole width of the tree view.
HideSelection	Gets/sets whether the selected tree node stays highlighted when the tree view loses the focus.
HotTracking	Gets/sets whether a tree node label should change its appearance when the mouse pointer moves over it.
ImageIndex	Gets/sets the image list index of the current image.
ImageList	Gets/sets the image list used with this tree view.
Indent	Gets/sets the distance that each level should be indented.
ItemHeight	Gets/sets the height of tree nodes.
LabelEdit	Gets/sets whether tree node text can be edited.
Nodes	Gets the collection of tree nodes.
PathSeparator	Gets/sets the string the tree node uses as a path delimiter.
Scrollable	Gets/sets whether the tree view should display scroll bars as needed.
SelectedImageIndex	Gets/sets the image index for the image to display when a node is selected.
SelectedNode	Gets/sets the node that is selected.
ShowLines	Gets/sets whether lines are drawn between tree nodes.
ShowPlusMinus	Gets/sets whether plus-sign (+) and minus-sign (-) buttons are shown next to tree nodes with child tree nodes.
ShowRootLines	Gets/sets whether lines should be drawn between the tree nodes and the root node.
Sorted	Gets/sets if the tree nodes should be sorted.
TopNode	Gets the first visible tree node.
VisibleCount	Gets the number of nodes that can be seen currently.

Table 10.4   Noteworthy public methods of TreeView objects.

Method	Means
BeginUpdate	Disables redrawing of the tree view.
CollapseAll	Collapses all nodes.
EndUpdate	Enables redrawing of the tree view.
ExpandAll	Expands all the nodes.
GetNodeAt	Gets the node that is at the given location.
GetNodeCount	Gets the number of nodes.

Table 10.5   Noteworthy public events of TreeView objects.

Event	Means
AfterCheck	Occurs when a node checkbox is checked.
AfterCollapse	Occurs when a tree node is collapsed.
AfterExpand	Occurs when a tree node is expanded.
AfterLabelEdit	Occurs when a tree node label text is edited.
AfterSelect	Occurs when a tree node is selected.
BeforeCheck	Occurs before a node checkbox is checked.
BeforeCollapse	Occurs before a node is collapsed.
BeforeExpand	Occurs before a node is expanded.
BeforeLabelEdit	Occurs before a node label text is edited.
BeforeSelect	Occurs before a node is selected.
ItemDrag	Occurs when an item is dragged into the tree view.

Using the TreeNode Class

Tree views display nodes in a hierarchical structure, and each node in a tree view is a **TreeNode** object. Here is the class hierarchy of the **TreeNode** class:

```
Object
    MarshalByRefObject
        TreeNode
```

You can find the notable public properties of **TreeNode** objects in Table 10.6 and the notable public methods in Table 10.7.

Table 10.6 Noteworthy public properties of TreeNode objects.

Property	Means
Bounds	Gets the actual bounds of the tree node.
Checked	Gets/sets whether the tree node is checked.
FirstNode	Gets the first child tree node.
FullPath	Gets the path from the root node to the current node.
ImageIndex	Gets/sets the image list index of the image displayed for a node.
Index	Gets the location of the node in the node collection.
IsEditing	Gets whether the node can be edited.
IsExpanded	Gets whether the node is expanded.
IsSelected	Gets whether the node is selected.
IsVisible	Gets a value specifying if the node is visible.
LastNode	Gets the last child node.
NextNode	Gets the next sibling node.
NextVisibleNode	Gets the next visible node.
NodeFont	Gets/sets the font for the node.
Nodes	Gets the collection of nodes in the current node.
Parent	Gets the parent node of the current node.
PrevNode	Gets the previous sibling node.
PrevVisibleNode	Gets the previous visible node.
SelectedImageIndex	Gets/sets the image index for the image to display when a node is selected.
Text	Gets/sets the text for a node's label.
TreeView	Gets the node's parent tree view.

Table 10.7 Noteworthy public methods of TreeNode objects.

Method	Means
BeginEdit	Starts editing of the node's label.
Collapse	Collapses a node.
EndEdit	Ends editing of the node's label.
EnsureVisible	Makes sure the node is visible, scrolling the tree view if needed.
Expand	Expands a node.
ExpandAll	Expands all child nodes.
GetNodeCount	Gets the number of child nodes.
Remove	Removes the current node.
Toggle	Toggles the tree node between the expanded and collapsed states.

Creating Tree Views

To create a tree view at design time, just drag a tree view control onto a Windows form, and to add nodes to it, open the **Nodes** property in the properties window, which displays the TreeNode editor you see in Figure 10.10.

The TreeNode Editor in Figure 10.10 is working on the tree view in the TreeViews example on the CD-ROM. To start creating nodes, you use the Add Root button, which adds a top-level node. To add children to that node, you select the node and use the Add Child button. You can add text to any node in the Label box in the TreeNode editor, or double-click the text next to any node directly to edit it.

If you've added an **ImageList** control to the form and stored images in it, you can display those images in the tree view. Just associate an image and a selected image (which is displayed when the node is selected) with each node using the drop-down boxes in the TreeNode Editor. (In the TreeViews example, I'm using icons that come with Visual Basic, and may be found in the Common7\Graphics\ icons directory).

Of course, you may want to add or remove nodes to a tree view in code. See "Creating Tree Views in Code" later in this chapter for more information.

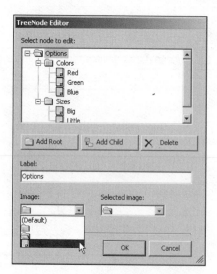

Figure 10.10   The TreeNode Editor.

Handling Tree View Events

Tree views have quite a number of events; see Table 10.5 for the list. The default event is the **AfterSelect** event, which occurs after a node has been selected. This event is an event of the tree view control, not of the **TreeNode** object that was selected, but you can determine which node was selected with the **TreeViewEvent Args** object that is passed to you, because it has a **Node** property that holds the selected node. For example, here's how I display the text of a selected node in a text box:

```
Private Sub TreeView1_AfterSelect(ByVal sender As System.Object, _
    ByVal e As System.Windows.Forms.TreeViewEventArgs) Handles _
    TreeView1.AfterSelect
    TextBox1.Text = "You clicked: " & e.Node.Text
End Sub
```

You can see how this works in Figure 10.11, in the TreeViews example on the CD-ROM, where I've clicked a node, and the program is reporting which one I clicked. To check if the selected node is a particular node in the tree, you can use code, like this: **If e.Node Is TreeView1.Nodes(233) Then....**

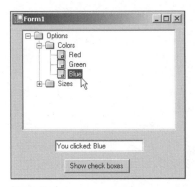

Figure 10.11   Handling tree view events.

Using Checkboxes in Tree Views

Tree views also can display checkboxes, much like those you can use in menu items. You can make checkboxes appear in a tree view by setting the tree view's **CheckBoxes** property to **True**. Here's how that works in the TreeViews example on the CD-ROM, when the user clicks the "Show check boxes" button:

```
Private Sub Button1_Click(ByVal sender As System.Object, _
    ByVal e As System.EventArgs) Handles Button1.Click
```

```
        TreeView1.CheckBoxes = True
End Sub
```

Here's how I display which checkboxes have been checked or unchecked in that example, using the **TreeNode** class's **Checked** property:

```
Private Sub TreeView1_AfterCheck(ByVal sender As Object, _
    ByVal e As System.Windows.Forms.TreeViewEventArgs) _
    Handles TreeView1.AfterCheck
    If e.Node.Checked Then
        TextBox1.Text = "You checked: " & e.Node.Text
    Else
        TextBox1.Text = "You unchecked: " & e.Node.Text
    End If
End Sub
```

You can see the results in Figure 10.12, where I've checked a node, and the program is reporting that fact in the text box.

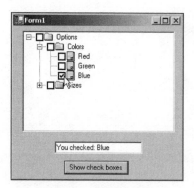

Figure 10.12   Handling tree view checkmark events.

Creating Tree Views in Code

You can create tree views in code as well as at design time. To see an example, take a look at the CreateTreeView program on the CD-ROM—this example creates a tree view of employees, each of whom has several sales account nodes.

The trick here is realizing that the hierarchical nature of tree views means that one node's **Nodes** collection can contain child nodes, which can itself contain child nodes, and so on, so you can refer to nodes using syntax like **MyNode.Nodes(3). Nodes(5)**. To add a new node, you use the **Nodes** collection's **Add** method. Like other controls, you can use the **BeginUpdate** and **EndUpdate** methods to turn off updating of the tree view while you're updating it. Note that this example uses the **Clear** method to clear all nodes in the tree view before refilling it. (Note also that I'm using a few advanced programming techniques here, such as creating our own classes and storing objects in an **ArrayList** collection, which we'll see soon in the book.) Here's the code, showing how to stock a tree view with nodes, and how to give those nodes child nodes, and so on, at run time:

```
Public Class Form1
    Inherits System.Windows.Forms.Form

    'Windows Form Designer generated code

    Private EmployeeArray As New ArrayList()

    Private Sub Button1_Click(ByVal sender As System.Object, _
        ByVal e As System.EventArgs) Handles Button1.Click
        Dim intLoopIndex As Integer
        For intLoopIndex = 0 To 9
            EmployeeArray.Add(New Employee("Employee " & _
                intLoopIndex.ToString()))
        Next intLoopIndex

        Dim EmployeeObject As Employee
        For Each EmployeeObject In EmployeeArray
            For intLoopIndex = 0 To 3
                EmployeeObject.EmployeeAccounts.Add(New _
                    Account("Account " & intLoopIndex.ToString()))
            Next intLoopIndex
        Next EmployeeObject

        TreeView1.BeginUpdate()
        TreeView1.Nodes.Clear()

        Dim RootNode = New TreeNode("Employees")
        TreeView1.Nodes.Add(RootNode)

        For Each EmployeeObject In EmployeeArray
            TreeView1.Nodes(0).Nodes.Add(New _
                TreeNode(EmployeeObject.EmployeeName))

            Dim AccountObject As Account
            For Each AccountObject In EmployeeObject.EmployeeAccounts
```

```
                        TreeView1.Nodes(0).Nodes(_
                            EmployeeArray.IndexOf(EmployeeObject)).Nodes.Add( _
                            New TreeNode(AccountObject.AccountID))
                    Next AccountObject
                Next EmployeeObject

                TreeView1.EndUpdate()
        End Sub
    End Class

    Public Class Employee
        Private Index = 0
        Public EmployeeName As String
        Public EmployeeAccounts As New ArrayList()

        Public Sub New(ByVal Name As String)
            EmployeeName = Name
        End Sub
    End Class

    Public Class Account
        Public AccountID As String
        Public Sub New(ByVal ID As String)
            AccountID = ID
        End Sub
    End Class
```

You can see the results in Figure 10.13; when you click the "Create tree view" button, the code creates the display you see in that figure.

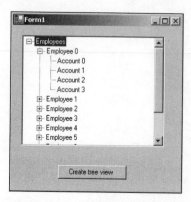

Figure 10.13   Creating a tree view in code.

Using the **ListView** Class

As discussed in the In Depth section of this chapter, list views display lists of items, much like the right pane in the Windows Explorer. List views are supported by the **ListView** class, which has this class hierarchy:

```
Object
    MarshalByRefObject
        Component
            Control
                ListView
```

You can find the notable public properties of **ListView** objects in Table 10.8, the notable public methods in Table 10.9, and the notable public events in Table 10.10. Note that I'm omitting those properties, methods, and events **ListView** objects inherit from the **Control** class—you'll find all that in Tables 5.1, 5.2, and 5.3, Chapter 5.

Table 10.8   Noteworthy public properties of ListView objects.

Property	Means
Activation	Gets/sets the user action to activate this item.
Alignment	Gets/sets the side of a window that items should be aligned to.
AllowColumnReorder	Gets/sets whether the user may drag column headers.
AutoArrange	Gets/sets if items are automatically arranged (using the **Alignment** property).
CheckBoxes	Gets/sets if every item should show a checkbox.
CheckedIndices	Gets the indices of currently checked items.
CheckedItems	Gets the currently checked items.
Columns	Gets a collection of columns.
FocusedItem	Gets the item that has the focus.
FullRowSelect	Gets/sets whether selecting an item will select the entire row.
GridLines	Gets/sets whether grid lines are drawn between items and their subitems.
HeaderStyle	Gets/sets the column header style.
HideSelection	Gets/sets whether selected items should be hidden when the list view loses the focus.
HoverSelection	Gets/sets if items can be selected by mouse hovering.
Items	Gets the list items.
LabelEdit	Gets/sets if the user can edit the item labels.
LabelWrap	Gets/sets whether item labels wrap for icon view.
LargeImageList	Gets/sets the **ImageList** for large icon view.

(continued)

Table 10.8   Noteworthy public properties of ListView objects (continued).

Property	Means
MultiSelect	Gets/sets whether multiple items can be selected.
Scrollable	Gets/sets if scroll bars should be visible.
SelectedIndices	Gets the indices of the selected items.
SelectedItems	Gets the selected items.
SmallImageList	Gets/sets the small icon image list.
Sorting	Gets/sets the sort order for the items.
TopItem	Gets the item at the top of the list.
View	Gets/sets the current view mode.

Table 10.9   Noteworthy public methods of ListView objects.

Method	Means
ArrangeIcons	Arranges the displayed items in Large Icon or Small Icon view.
BeginUpdate	Stops the list view from redrawing.
Clear	Removes all items from the **list view.**
EndUpdate	Allows redrawing of the list view.
EnsureVisible	Makes sure that an item is visible.
GetItemAt	Gets the item corresponding to the given X,Y coordinate.

Table 10.10   Noteworthy public methods of ListView objects.

Event	Means
AfterLabelEdit	Occurs when a label has been edited.
BeforeLabelEdit	Occurs before a label is changed.
ColumnClick	Occurs when a column is clicked.
ItemActivate	Occurs when an item is activated.
ItemCheck	Occurs when an item is checked.
SelectedIndexChanged	Occurs when the selected index changes.

Using the **ListViewItem** Class

The items in a list view are objects of the **ListViewItem** class, and the collection of those items is stored in the list view's **Items** property. Here is the class hierarchy of the **ListViewItem** class:

```
Object
    ListViewItem
```

You can find the notable public properties of **ListViewItem** objects in Table 10.11, and the notable public methods in Table 10.12.

Table 10.11 Noteworthy public properties of ListViewItem objects.

Property	Means
Bounds	Gets the bounding rectangle of an item, including its subitems.
Checked	**True** if the item is checked, **False** otherwise.
Index	Gets the index in the list view of the item.
ListView	Gets the list view that contains this item.
Selected	Gets/sets if the item is selected.
SubItems	Gets a collection of the subitems of this item.
Text	Gets the text for this item.

Table 10.12 Noteworthy public methods of ListViewItem objects.

Method	Means
BeginEdit	Begins the editing of the text in the item's label.
EndEdit	Ends the editing of the text in the item's label.
EnsureVisible	Makes sure that the item is visible.

Creating List Views

You can add list views to a Windows form just like any other control—just drag it from the toolbox to the form at design time. To add items to a list box, open the **Items** property in the Properties window, which displays the ListViewItem Collection Editor that you see in Figure 10.14. This editor is much like the TreeNode editor (see "Creating Tree Views" in this chapter), and works in the same way—to add a new list view item, click Add, to delete one, click Remove. You can set the various properties of list view items in this editor, such as the item's text, its image index in a list view, and so on.

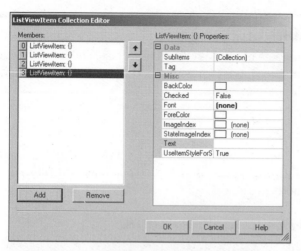

Figure 10.14   The **ListViewItem** Collection Editor.

As discussed in the In Depth section, there are four views you can use in a list view. You select one by assigning a value (**View.LargeIcon**, **View.SmallIcon**, **View.List**, or **View.Details**) to the list view's **View** property:

- *Large icon mode*—displays large icons (large icons are 32×32 pixels) next to the item text.

- *Small icon mode*—is the same as the large icon mode except that it displays items using small icons (small icons are 16×16 pixels).

- *List mode*—displays small icons, and always in one column.

- *Report mode* (also called the *details* mode)—displays items in multiple columns, displaying column headers and fields.

You also can create list views in code—take a look at the next topic to see how.

Creating List Views in Code

You can add items to list views in code, as in the ListViews example on the CD-ROM. In this case, when the form loads, I'll add four items to a list view. As you might expect, you do this with the **Add** method of the list view's **Items** collection, which can take the text of the new item and an image index in an **ImageList** for an icon to display for the item.

In the report mode (also called details mode), a list view can display column headers and fields in each of the columns, as you see in Figure 10.3. You can create column headers with the **Columns** collection of the list view, and add fields to a **ListViewItem** object with its **SubItems** collection. List views display their items with small icons (16×16 pixels), except for large icon mode, which uses large (32×32 pixel) icons. To assign images to list items, you can use the **SmallImageList** property to assign an image list to a list view, which means the first item will use the first image in the image list, the second item the second image, and so on. You also can assign an image list to the **LargeImageList** property for the large icon view; in the ListViews example, I'm using icons that come with Visual Basic in the Common7\Graphics\icons directory. (Each icon file, which ends with .ico, has both a large and small version of the icon stored in it.)

Here's the code where I add list view items to a list view, **ListView1**, in the ListViews example when the main form first loads; note that when you create a column header, you give the text for the column header, as well as the width of the column, and the alignment of its contained text:

```
Private Sub Form1_Load(ByVal eventSender As System.Object, _
    ByVal eventArgs As System.EventArgs) Handles MyBase.Load
    ListView1.Columns.Add("Field 1", ListView1.Width / 4, _
        HorizontalAlignment.Left)
    ListView1.Columns.Add("Field 2", ListView1.Width / 4, _
        HorizontalAlignment.Left)
    ListView1.Columns.Add("Field 3", ListView1.Width / 4, _
        HorizontalAlignment.Left)
    ListView1.Columns.Add("Field 4", ListView1.Width / 4, _
        HorizontalAlignment.Left)

    Dim ListItem1 As ListViewItem
    ListItem1 = ListView1.Items.Add("Item 1", 1)
    ListView1.Items(0).SubItems.Add("Field 2")
    ListView1.Items(0).SubItems.Add("Field 3")
    ListView1.Items(0).SubItems.Add("Field 4")

    Dim ListItem2 As ListViewItem
    ListItem2 = ListView1.Items.Add("Item 2", 1)
    ListView1.Items(1).SubItems.Add("Field 2")
    ListView1.Items(1).SubItems.Add("Field 3")
    ListView1.Items(1).SubItems.Add("Field 4")

    Dim ListItem3 As ListViewItem
    ListItem2 = ListView1.Items.Add("Item 3", 1)
    ListView1.Items(2).SubItems.Add("Field 2")
    ListView1.Items(2).SubItems.Add("Field 3")
```

```
        ListView1.Items(2).SubItems.Add("Field 4")


        ListView1.SmallImageList = ImageList1
        ListView1.LargeImageList = ImageList2
End Sub
```

You can see the results of this code in Figure 10.3. That figure shows the list view operating in details mode, which you can select with the combo box at lower right. See the next topic for the details.

Selecting List View Views

As discussed in the In Depth section of this chapter, and in the topic "Creating List Views" earlier in the Immediate Solutions, there are four different types of views in list views: large icon view, report view (also called details view), small icon view, and list view. You can switch between these views by assigning **View.LargeIcon** (which equals 0), **View.Details** (which equals 1), **View.SmallIcon** (which equals 2), or **View.List** (which equals 3) to a list view's **View** property. To do this in the ListViews example on the CD-ROM, I create a combo box, this way:

```
With ComboBox1
    .Items.Add("Large Icon View")
    .Items.Add("Report View")
    .Items.Add("Small Icon View")
    .Items.Add("List View")
End With
```

Because the index of each combo box item matches the actual value of each item in the **View** enumeration, I can simply assign the index of the combo box's selected item to the list view's **View** property when the user makes a selection:

```
Private Sub ComboBox1_SelectedIndexChanged(ByVal sender As System.Object, _
    ByVal e As System.EventArgs) Handles ComboBox1.SelectedIndexChanged
    ListView1.View = ComboBox1.SelectedIndex
End Sub
```

You can see the results in Figure 10.15, where I've selected large icon view in the ListViews example on the CD-ROM.

Figure 10.15   Selecting a view mode in a list view

Handling List View Item Selections

How can you determine which item was selected by the user in a list view? You can handle the **SelectedIndexChanged** event, and in this event's handler, you can check the list view's **SelectedIndices** to determine which items are currently selected. The **SelectedIndices** property holds the indices of those items that are selected if the list view's **MultiSelect** property is **True**, or of the single selected item, if one is selected, if **MultiSelect** is **False**. The **MultiSelect** property is **False** in the ListViews example on the CD-ROM, so here's how I display the currently selected item in the text box in that example:

```
Private Sub ListView1_SelectedIndexChanged(ByVal sender As System.Object, _
    ByVal e As System.EventArgs) Handles ListView1.SelectedIndexChanged
    If ListView1.SelectedIndices.Count > 0 Then
        TextBox1.Text = "You clicked item " & _
            (ListView1.SelectedIndices(0) + 1)
    End If
End Sub
```

You can see the results in Figure 10.16, where I've clicked item 3 in the ListViews example, and the program is reporting that fact.

TIP: *Besides **SelectedIndices**, you can also use a list view's **SelectedItems** property to get a collection of the selected items themselves.*

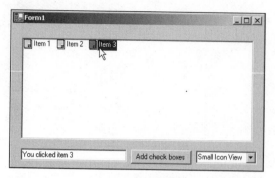

Figure 10.16 Handling list view item selections.

Handling Column Clicks in List Views

In report view (also called details view), list views can display column headers, i.e., the buttons you see in Figure 10.3 above each column. How can you handle column header clicks in a list view? You use the **ColumnClick** event; here's how that looks in the ListViews example on the CD-ROM, where I'm reporting the column header the user clicked:

```
Private Sub ListView1_ColumnClick(ByVal sender As Object, _
    ByVal e As System.Windows.Forms.ColumnClickEventArgs) Handles _
    ListView1.ColumnClick
    TextBox1.Text = "You clicked column " & (e.Column + 1)
End Sub
```

Using Checkboxes in List Views

As with menus, list views can display checkboxes; all you have to do is to set their **CheckBoxes** property to **True**. You can see how this works in the ListViews example on the CD-ROM if you click the "Add check boxes" button, which sets the **CheckBoxes** property of **ListView1** to **True**:

```
Private Sub Button1_Click(ByVal sender As System.Object, _
    ByVal e As System.EventArgs) Handles Button1.Click
    ListView1.CheckBoxes = True
End Sub
```

To handle checkbox events, I add code to the list view's **ItemCheck** event. In that event handler, I can take a look at the new setting of the item by examining the **NewValue** property of the **ItemCheckEventArgs** object passed to us, and get the index of the item in the list view with the **Index** property. Here's how I report what item was checked or unchecked in the ListViews example:

```
Private Sub ListView1_ItemCheck(ByVal sender As Object, _
    ByVal e As System.Windows.Forms.ItemCheckEventArgs) _
    Handles ListView1.ItemCheck
    If e.NewValue = CheckState.Checked Then
        TextBox1.Text = "You checked item " & (e.Index() + 1)
    Else
        TextBox1.Text = "You unchecked item " & (e.Index() + 1)
    End If
End Sub
```

And you can see the results in Figure 10.17, where I've added checkboxes to the list view and checked item 2.

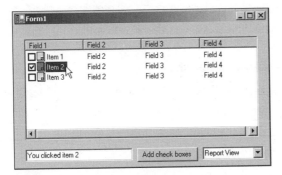

Figure 10.17   Using checkboxes in a list view

Using the **ToolBar** Class

As discussed in the In Depth section of this chapter, this is the **ToolBar** Class; here is the hierarchy of this class:

```
Object
    MarshalByRefObject
        Component
            Control
                ToolBar
```

You can find the notable public properties of **ToolBar** objects in Table 10.13, and the notable public events in Table 10.14. Note that I'm omitting the properties, methods, and events toolbars inherit from the **Control** class, which you can find in Chapter 5, Tables 5.1, 5.2, and 5.3.

Table 10.13   Noteworthy public properties of ToolBar objects.

Property	Means
Appearance	Gets/sets the toolbar's appearance.
AutoSize	Gets/sets whether the toolbar can change its size automatically.
BorderStyle	Gets/sets the toolbar's border style.
Buttons	Gets the collection of buttons in the toolbar.
ButtonSize	Gets/sets the size of buttons in the toolbar.
Divider	Gets/sets whether the toolbar shows a divider.
DropDownArrows	Gets/sets if drop-down buttons display down arrows.
ImageList	Gets/sets the collection of images for the toolbar buttons.
ImageSize	Gets the size of the images in the image list assigned to the toolbar.
ShowToolTips	Gets/sets if the toolbar displays a tool tip for each button.
TextAlign	Gets/sets the alignment of text in the toolbar button controls.
Wrappable	Gets/sets if toolbar buttons wrap to the next line as needed.

Table 10.14   Noteworthy public events of ToolBar objects.

Event	Means
ButtonClick	Occurs when a button in the toolbar is clicked.
ButtonDropDown	Occurs when a drop-down button or its down arrow is clicked.

Using the ToolBarButton Class

The buttons in a toolbar are actually **ToolBarButton** objects. Here is the class hierarchy for the **ToolBarButton** class:

```
Object
   MarshalByRefObject
      Component
         ToolBarButton
```

You can find the notable public properties of **ToolBarButton** objects in Table 10.15.

Table 10.15   Noteworthy public properties of ToolBarButton objects.

Property	Means
DropDownMenu	Gets/sets the menu object for a drop-down button.
Enabled	Gets/sets if the button is enabled.
ImageIndex	Gets/sets the index value of the image for a button.
Parent	Gets the toolbar that the button is a child of.
PartialPush	Gets/sets whether a toggle toolbar button is partially pushed.
Pushed	Gets/sets whether a toggle-style button is pushed.
Rectangle	Gets the bounding rectangle for a toolbar button.
Style	Gets/sets the style of a button.
Text	Gets/sets the text displayed in the button.
ToolTipText	Gets/sets the text for a tool tip for the button.
Visible	Gets/sets if the toolbar button is visible.

Creating Toolbars

After you've added a toolbar to a Windows form, you can dock it on any edge you like—by default, the **Dock** property is set to **Top**, but you can set it to **Top**, **Bottom**, **Fill**, or whatever you prefer. To actually add the buttons to a toolbar at design time, click the **Buttons** property at design time, which opens the **ToolBarButton** Collection Editor you see in Figure 10.18. You can add buttons to the toolbar as with the other editors we've seen (see "Creating Tree Views" and

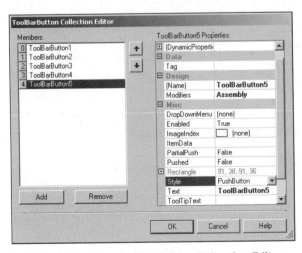

Figure 10.18   The **ToolBarButton** Collection Editor.

"Creating List Views" earlier in this chapter)—just click the Add button to add a new button to the toolbar, and Remove to remove a button.

You also can set the text in a button with the **Text** property in the **ToolBarButton** Collection Editor, the image from an image list to use in a button with the **ImageIndex** property, and the style of the button with the **Style** property, which can take these values:

- **PushButton**—A normal push button.
- **ToggleButton**—A toggle button that toggles between up and down.
- **Separator**—A small space between other buttons, used to space and group buttons.
- **DropDownButton**—A button that can display a drop-down menu.

I've added one of each of these types of buttons to the toolbar in the ToolBars example on the CD-ROM, which you see operating in Figure 10.4. How do you make this toolbar *do* something? See the next topic.

Handling Toolbar Button Clicks

When a button in a toolbar is clicked, the toolbar's **ButtonClick** event happens. (There are no such events for the individual buttons in the toolbar.) You can see which button was clicked by taking a look at the **Button** property of the **ToolBarButtonClickEventArgs** object passed to the **ButtonClick** event handler. Here's how that works in the ToolBars example on the CD-ROM, where I'm reporting the text of the clicked button in a message box:

```
Private Sub ToolBar1_ButtonClick(ByVal sender As System.Object, _
    ByVal e As System.Windows.Forms.ToolBarButtonClickEventArgs) _
    Handles ToolBar1.ButtonClick
    MsgBox("You clicked the " & e.Button.Text)
End Sub
```

Here's how you can check whether a particular button was clicked:

```
If e.Button Is ToolBar1.Buttons(1) Then
        .
        .
        .
End If
```

Creating Toolbar Drop-down Buttons

Drop-down buttons are one of the most useful styles of toolbar buttons; these buttons can display a drop-down menu if you click their down arrow. To add a menu to a drop-down button, you can create a menu, such as a context menu, and assign that menu to the drop-down button's **DropDownMenu** property. To see how this works, take a look at the ToolBars example on the CD-ROM. I've added a context menu, **ContextMenu1**, to that example, with three menu items: Red, Blue, and Green, and implemented the event handlers for these items like this:

```
Private Sub MenuItem1_Click(ByVal sender As System.Object, _
    ByVal e As System.EventArgs) Handles MenuItem1.Click
    MsgBox("You clicked Red")
End Sub

Private Sub MenuItem2_Click(ByVal sender As System.Object, _
    ByVal e As System.EventArgs) Handles MenuItem2.Click
    MsgBox("You clicked Blue")
End Sub

Private Sub MenuItem3_Click(ByVal sender As System.Object, _
    ByVal e As System.EventArgs) Handles MenuItem3.Click
    MsgBox("You clicked Green")
End Sub
```

All that remains is to assign **ContextMenu1** to the **DropDownMenu** property of the drop-down button in the toolbar, which you can do with the ToolBarButton Collection Editor, which you open with the **Buttons** property in the properties window. That's all it takes; you can see the active drop-down button at work in Figure 10.4.

Related solution:	*Found on page:*
Creating Context Menus	404

Connecting Toolbar Buttons to Menu Items

Typically, toolbar buttons correspond to frequently used menu items. To connect a toolbar to a menu item, you can use that menu item's **PerformClick** method to make it seem as though the item itself was clicked:

```
Private Sub ToolBar1_ButtonClick(ByVal sender As System.Object, _
    ByVal e As System.Windows.Forms.ToolBarButtonClickEventArgs) _
```

```
        Handles ToolBar1.ButtonClick
        If e.Button Is ToolBar1.Buttons(1) Then
            MenuItem7.PerformClick()
        End If
    End Sub
```

For example, the button labeled "Menu Button" in the ToolBars example on the CD-ROM (see Figure 10.4) corresponds to the Red item in the Color menu, and clicking that button is the same as clicking the Red menu item.

Creating Toolbar Image Buttons

To display images in a toolbar button, you only need to add an image list component to a form and then set the **ImageIndex** property of the button in the **ToolBarButton** Collection Editor to the image you want to use. You can see an example in the ToolBars example in Figure 10.4, where I'm displaying a small question mark image in a button.

Adding Combo Boxes and Other Controls to Toolbars

One of the common non-button controls you see in toolbars is the combo box control, which lets the user select an item from a list, or type their own entry. In previous versions of Visual Basic, it was difficult to add combo boxes or other such controls to a toolbar, but now it's easy. All you have to do is to leave space in the toolbar for the combo box or other control, and then place a combo box in that space. You can leave space in a toolbar by using separator buttons—that is, toolbar buttons whose style has been set to **Separator**.

That's what I've done in the ToolBars example on the CD-ROM—created some space in the toolbar using multiple separators and placed a combo box, **ComboBox1**, in that space. I've also added a few items to the combo box, Red, Blue, and Green, and added this code to its **SelectedIndexChanged** event handler:

```
Private Sub ComboBox1_SelectedIndexChanged(ByVal sender As System.Object, _
    ByVal e As System.EventArgs) Handles ComboBox1.SelectedIndexChanged
    Dim selectedIndex As Integer
    selectedIndex = ComboBox1.SelectedIndex
```

```
    Dim selectedItem As Object
    selectedItem = ComboBox1.SelectedItem

    MsgBox("Selected item text: " & selectedItem.ToString() & _
        " Selected index: " & selectedIndex.ToString())
End Sub
```

You can see the results of this code in Figure 10.4, where you see the combo box in the toolbar. Besides combo boxes, you can add all kinds of other controls to toolbars as well.

Adding Buttons to a Toolbar at Run Time

As you might expect, you can add buttons to a toolbar at run time. To do that, just click the "Add button" button in the ToolBars example on the CD-ROM; here's how that program adds a new button to the toolbar:

```
Private Sub Button1_Click(ByVal sender As System.Object, _
    ByVal e As System.EventArgs) Handles Button1.Click
    Dim ToolBarButton As New ToolBarButton("New Button")
    ToolBar1.Buttons.Add(ToolBarButton)
End Sub
```

You can see the results in Figure 10.19, where I've added six new buttons to the toolbar.

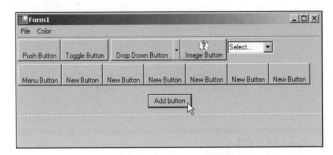

Figure 10.19   Adding buttons to a toolbar at run time.

Using the **StatusBar** Class

As discussed in the In Depth section of this chapter, status bars display status messages, usually at the bottom of forms. This class is supported by the **StatusBar** class, and here is that class's hierarchy:

```
Object
    MarshalByRefObject
        Component
            Control
                StatusBar
```

You can find the notable public properties of **StatusBar** objects in Table 10.16 and the notable public events in Table 10.17. Note that I'm omitting the properties, methods, and events status bars inherit from the **Control** class, which you can find in Chapter 5, Tables 5.1, 5.2, and 5.3.

Table 10.16   Noteworthy public properties of StatusBar objects.

Property	Means
BackgroundImage	Gets/sets the background image in a status bar.
Dock	Gets/sets a status bar's docking behavior.
Font	Gets/sets the font for a status bar.
Panels	Gets the collection of status bar panels in a status bar.
ShowPanels	Gets/sets whether panels should be shown or not.
Text	Gets/sets the status bar text.

Table 10.17   Noteworthy public events of StatusBar objects.

Event	Means
PanelClick	Occurs when a status bar panel is clicked.

Using the **StatusBarPanel** Class

The **StatusBarPanel** class supports status bar panels; here is the hierarchy of this class:

```
Object
    MarshalByRefObject
        Component
            StatusBarPanel
```

You can find the notable public properties of **StatusBarPanel** objects in Table 10.18, and the notable public methods in Table 10.19.

Table 10.18   Noteworthy public properties of StatusBarPanel objects.

Property	Means
Alignment	Gets/sets the panel's alignment.
BorderStyle	Gets/sets the panel's border style.
Icon	Gets/sets the icon for this panel.
MinWidth	Gets/sets the minimum width for the panel.
Parent	Gets the status bar that contains the panel.
Style	Gets/sets the style of the panel.
Text	Gets/sets the text of the panel.
ToolTipText	Gets/sets the panel's ToolTip text.
Width	Gets/sets the width of the panel.

Table 10.19   Noteworthy public methods of StatusBarPanel objects.

Method	Means
BeginInit	Begins the initialization of a panel.
EndInit	Ends the initialization of a panel.

Creating Simple Status Bars

You've added a status bar to your form—now what? By default, status bars only allow you to display a single text string. Such status bars are called *simple status bars*, and you can display text in them using their **Text** property. For example, if I wanted to display mouse actions in the status bar, I could do something like this:

```
Private Sub Form1_MouseEnter(ByVal sender As Object, _
    ByVal e As System.EventArgs) Handles MyBase.MouseEnter
    StatusBar1.Text = "Mouse entered"
End Sub


Private Sub Form1_MouseLeave(ByVal sender As Object, _
    ByVal e As System.EventArgs) Handles MyBase.MouseLeave
    StatusBar1.Text = "Mouse left"
End Sub
```

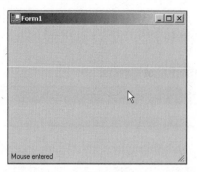

Figure 10.20   Displaying text in a simple status bar.

You can see the results in Figure 10.20, where the simple status bar at the bottom is reporting that the mouse has entered the form. Want to see how to add panels to a status bar? Take a look at the next topic.

Adding Panels to a Status Bar

You can add panels to a status bar at design time by opening the status bar's **Panels** property in the Properties window, which opens the **StatusBarPanel** Collection Editor, which you can see in Figure 10.21. You can use this editor to add new panels to the status bar; just click the Add button to add a new panel and fill in the properties of the panel you want. To remove a panel, use the Remove button.

To add panels to a status bar in code, you use the **StatusBar.Panels.Add** and **StatusBar.Panels.AddRange** methods; to remove panels, you use the **StatusBar.Panels.Remove** and **StatusBar.Panels.RemoveAt** methods.

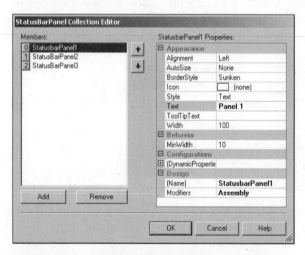

Figure 10.21   The **StatusBarPanel** Collection Editor.

Displaying Text in Status Bar Panels

To display text in a status bar panel, you can simply use the **Text** property of a **StatusbarPanel** object like this, which displays the text "The new text!" when the user clicks a button:

```
Private Sub Button1_Click(ByVal sender As System.Object, _
    ByVal e As System.EventArgs) Handles Button1.Click
    StatusbarPanel1.Text = "The new text!"
End Sub
```

You also can access the **Text** property of a status bar panel using the **Panels** collection of a **StatusBar** object, like this (my preferred method):

```
Private Sub Button1_Click(ByVal sender As System.Object, _
    ByVal e As System.EventArgs) Handles Button1.Click
    StatusBar1.Panels(0).Text = "The new text!"
End Sub
```

You can see the result of this code in Figure 10.22, in the first panel at left in the status bar of the StatusBars example on the CD-ROM.

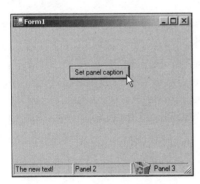

Figure 10.22   Displaying text in a status bar panel.

Displaying Icons in Status Bar Panels

It's easy to add icons to panels in a status bar; at design time, just select the status bar, click the Panels property in the Properties window to open the **StatusBar Panel** Collection Editor. Then select the panel, click the **Icon** property in the **StatusBarPanel** Collection Editor, and browse to the icon file (extension .ico) you want to use.

And you can do the same thing at run time; all you need to do is to assign an **Icon** object to a status bar panel's **Icon** property and you can create an **Icon** object by passing a filename to the **Icon** class's constructor:

```
Private Sub Button1_Click(ByVal sender As System.Object, _
    ByVal e As System.EventArgs) Handles Button1.Click
    StatusbarPanel1.Icon = New Icon("c:\vbnet\ch10\statusbars\waste.ico")
End Sub
```

If you prefer, you can access the status bar panel from the status bar's **Panels** collection:

```
Private Sub Button1_Click(ByVal sender As System.Object, _
    ByVal e As System.EventArgs) Handles Button1.Click
    StatusBar1.Panels(0).Icon = New _
        Icon("c:\vbnet\ch10\statusbars\waste.ico")
End Sub
```

You can see an icon in the third panel of the status bar in Figure 10.22 in the StatusBars example on the CD-ROM.

Handling Status Bar Panel Clicks

To handle status bar panel clicks, you can use the **PanelClick** event. The actual panel that caused the **Click** event is passed to you in the **StatusBarPanel** property of the **StatusBarPanelClickEventArgs** object passed to this event's handler, so you can determine what panel was clicked and take appropriate action:

```
Private Sub StatusBar1_PanelClick(ByVal sender As System.Object, _
    ByVal e As System.Windows.Forms.StatusBarPanelClickEventArgs) _
    Handles StatusBar1.PanelClick
    If e.StatusBarPanel Is StatusBar1.Panels(1) Then
        MsgBox("You clicked " & e.StatusBarPanel.Text)
    End If
End Sub
```

Using the **ProgressBar** Control

As discussed in the In Depth section of this chapter, progress bars display rectangles in a horizontal bar to let the user watch the progress of some operations. Here's the class hierarchy of the **ProgressBar** class:

```
Object
    MarshalByRefObject
        Component
            Control
                ProgressBar
```

You can find the notable public properties of **ProgressBar** objects in Table 10.20, and the notable public methods in Table 10.21. Note that I'm omitting the properties, methods, and events progress bars inherit from the **Control** class, which you can find in Tables 5.1, 5.2, and 5.3 in Chapter 5.

Table 10.20   Noteworthy public properties of ProgressBar objects.

Property	Means
Font	Gets/sets the font of the progress bar's text.
ForeColor	Gets/sets the foreground color of the progress bar.
Maximum	Gets/sets the progress bar's maximum value.
Minimum	Gets/sets the progress bar's minimum value.
Step	Gets/sets the value by which the **PerformStep** method will increase a progress bar's value.
Value	Gets/sets the current value of the progress bar.

Table 10.21   Noteworthy public methods of ProgressBar objects.

Method	Means
Increment	Increments the position of the progress bar by a given amount.
PerformStep	Increments the value of the progress bar by the **Step** property.

Creating Progress Bars

The primary properties of progress bars, much like scroll bars, are **Minimum**, **Maximum**, and **Value**. Here's an example, ProgressBars on the CD-ROM, where I use a timer to steadily increment the **Value** property of **ProgressBar1**, having already set the **Minimum** and **Maximum** properties. The action starts when the user clicks a button labeled Start that enables the timer:

```
Private Sub Button1_Click(ByVal sender As System.Object, _
    ByVal e As System.EventArgs) Handles Button1.Click
    Timer1.Enabled = True
End Sub

Private Sub Timer1_Tick(ByVal sender As System.Object, _
    ByVal e As System.EventArgs) Handles Timer1.Tick
    ProgressBar1.Value += 1
    If ProgressBar1.Value = ProgressBar1.Maximum Then
        Timer1.Enabled = False
    End If
End Sub
```

You can see this example at work in Figure 10.6.

Using the **TabControl** Class

As discussed in the In Depth section of this chapter, tab controls let you divide your display into overlapping tab pages, and each page can contain other controls. Here is the class hierarchy of the **TabControl** class:

```
Object
    MarshalByRefObject
        Component
            Control
                TabControl
```

You can find the notable public properties of **TabControl** objects in Table 10.22, and the notable public events in Table 10.23. Note that I'm omitting the properties, methods, and events tab controls inherit from the **Control** class, which you can find in Chapter 5, Tables 5.1, 5.2, and 5.3.

Table 10.22   Noteworthy public properties of TabControl objects.

Property	Means
Alignment	Gets/sets where the tabs appear (top, left, etc.).
Appearance	Gets/sets the appearance of tabs in a tab control.
DisplayRectangle	Gets the bounding rectangle of the tab pages.
HotTrack	Gets/sets whether the tabs should change appearance when the mouse is over them.
ImageList	Gets/sets the images to show in tabs.
Multiline	Gets/sets whether the tab control can show more than one row of tabs.
RowCount	Gets the number of rows in the tab strip.
SelectedIndex	Gets/sets selected tab page's index.
SelectedTab	Gets/sets the selected tab page.
ShowToolTips	Gets/sets whether a tab's tooltip can be displayed.
TabCount	Gets the number of tabs.
TabPages	Gets the collection of tab pages.

Table 10.23   Noteworthy public events of TabControl objects.

Event	Means
SelectedIndexChanged	Occurs when the **SelectedIndex** property is changed.

Using the **TabPage** Class

As discussed in the In Depth section of this chapter, you use tab pages in tab controls. Tab pages are descended from **Panel** controls, so, as you'd expect, they can contain other controls (and that's the whole point). Here is the class hierarchy of **TabPage**:

```
Object
    MarshalByRefObject
        Component
            Control
                ScrollableControl
                    Panel
                        TabPage
```

You can find the notable public properties of **TabPage** objects in Table 10.24. Note that I'm omitting the properties, methods, and events tab pages inherit from the **Control** class, which you can find in Chapter 5, Tables 5.1, 5.2, and 5.3, and the properties they inherit from **Panel** controls, which you can find in Chapter 6, Table 6.8.

Table 10.24   Noteworthy public properties of **TabPage** objects.

Property	Means
ImageIndex	Gets/sets the index of the image in this tab.
Text	Gets/sets the text to show in the tab.
ToolTipText	Gets/sets the tab's tool tip text.

Creating Tab Controls

After you've added a new tab control to a Windows form at design time, you can add tab pages to it by opening the **TabPages** property in the Properties window, which opens the **TabPage** Collection Editor that you see in Figure 10.23. You can add new tab pages with the Add button, remove them with the Remove button, and set properties in the editor.

After you've added new tab pages to the control, you're free to add other controls to those pages. You can see a tab control at work—specifically, the TabControls example from the CD-ROM—in Figure 10.7, displaying two buttons in a page.

TIP: Tab controls are often used to display pages of options in a dialog box, in which case it's a good idea to dock the tab control so it fills the dialog box.

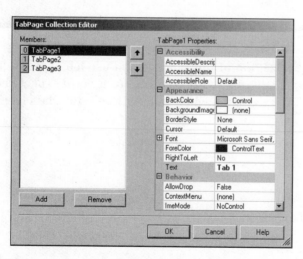

Figure 10.23   The **TabPage** Collection Editor.

Displaying an Icon in a Tab

It's easy to display an image in a tab, but you'll need to add an image list to the form first. After you've done so, just set the **ImageIndex** property of the **TabPage** object to the appropriate image in the list.

Creating Multiple Rows of Tabs

To display multiple rows of tabs in a tab control, just set the control's **Multiline** property to **True**. (If that doesn't make the tabs appear in multiple rows, set the **Width** property of the **TabControl** to be narrower than all the tabs combined.)

Arranging Tabs Sideways or on the Bottom

You can set the **Alignment** property of tab controls to **Left**, **Right**, **Top**, or **Bottom** to specify where the tabs should appear. For example, you can see the TabControls example from the CD-ROM in Figure 10.24, where I've aligned the tabs on the left.

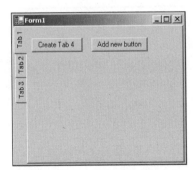

Figure 10.24   Displaying tabs on the left in a tab control.

Displaying Tabs as Buttons

You can make the tabs in a tab control appear as buttons; just set the **Appearance** property of the tab control to either **Buttons** or **FlatButtons**.

Hot-Tracking Tabs

You can hot-track tabs in a tab control, which makes their captions change color as the mouse moves over them. You can see an example in the TabControls example on the CD-ROM (which unfortunately doesn't reproduce here in figures in black and white—when you move the mouse over a tab's caption, the text changes from standard black to blue). To do this, just set the tab control's **HotTrack** property to **True** (the default is **False**).

Adding New Tabs at Run Time

You can add new tabs to a **Tab** control at run time with the **Add** method of the **TabPages** collection. You can see an example of this in the TabControls example on the CD-ROM—when the user clicks the "Create Tab 4" button, a new tab appears, as you see in Figure 10.25.

Here's what it looks like in code:

```
Private Sub Button1_Click(ByVal sender As System.Object, _
    ByVal e As System.EventArgs) Handles Button1.Click
    Dim tabpage As New TabPage()
    tabpage.Text = "Tab 4"
    TabControl1.TabPages.Add(tabpage)
End Sub
```

Now that you've added a new tab page to a tab control, how do you add controls to that page? See the next topic.

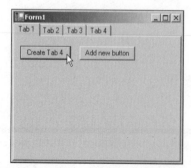

Figure 10.25   Adding a new tab to a tab control at run time.

Adding Controls to Tab Pages at Run Time

How do you add controls to a tab page at run time? You use the **Add** method of the **Controls** collection of the tab page. You can see this at work when you click the "Add new button" button in the TabControls example on the CD-ROM. Here's the code—I'm adding a new button to a tab page, and adding an event handler to the new button so it actually does something when clicked:

```
Dim WithEvents MyButton As New Button()

Private Sub Button2_Click(ByVal sender As System.Object, _
    ByVal e As System.EventArgs) Handles Button2.Click
    AddHandler MyButton.Click, AddressOf MyButton_Click
    MyButton.Size = New Size(88, 23)
    MyButton.Location = New Point(8, 45)
    MyButton.Text = "New button"
    TabControl1.TabPages(0).Controls.Add(MyButton)
End Sub

Private Sub MyButton_Click(ByVal sender As System.Object, _
    ByVal e As System.EventArgs) Handles MyButton.Click
    MsgBox("You clicked the button!")
End Sub
```

You can see the results in Figure 10.26—when you click the "Add new button" button, a new button appears in the tab page.

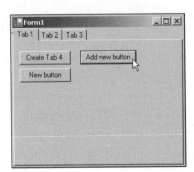

Figure 10.26   Adding a new button to a tab control at run time.

Chapter 11

Object-Oriented Programming

In Depth

Just about everything you do in Visual Basic .NET involves objects in some way—even simple variables are based on the Visual Basic **Object** class. And all your code has to appear in a class of some sort, even if you're using a module or structure, which are also types of classes now. For these reasons, it's important to understand object-oriented programming (OOP) in Visual Basic, and now more than ever before. This and the following chapter are dedicated to OOP.

We haven't looked at OOP in detail until now, because we didn't really need to understand a great deal of the programming aspect of it. Visual Basic comes with thousands of built-in classes, ready to use, so we didn't have to plumb the depths too much. We knew that Windows forms are classes, of course, based on the **System.Windows.Forms.Form** class, and that our code was part of that class:

```
Public Class Form1
    Inherits System.Windows.Forms.Form

    Private Sub Form1_Load(ByVal sender As System.Object, _
    ByVal e As System.EventArgs) Handles MyBase.Load
        .
        .
        .
    End Sub

End Class
```

And we knew, too, that controls such as text boxes are really based on classes, as with the **TextBox** class, as in this example from Chapter 5, CreateTextBox, where we created a new object of that class and used that object's various members to configure it:

```
    Private Sub Button1_Click(ByVal sender As System.Object, _
        ByVal e As System.EventArgs) Handles Button1.Click
        Dim TextBox1 As New TextBox()
        TextBox1.Size = New Size(150, 20)
        TextBox1.Location = New Point(80, 20)
        TextBox1.Text = "Hello from Visual Basic"
        Me.Controls.Add(TextBox1)
    End Sub
```

But that's just a start. To go further, we're going to have to create our own classes and objects.

Classes and Objects

We've already become familiar with the idea behind classes and objects, as discussed in Chapter 2. The idea is that classes are a type, and objects are examples or *instances* of that class. The relationship between classes and objects is much like the relationship between cookie cutters and cookies—you use the cookie cutter to create new cookies. Just think of the numeric data types like **Integer**, which is a type, and a specific integer variable, **myInteger233**, which is an instance of that type. In fact, the **Integer** type is a class in Visual Basic, and variables of that type are in fact objects.

It's easy to create classes and objects in Visual Basic. To create a class, you only need to use the **Class** statement, which, like other compound statements in Visual Basic, needs to end with **End Class**:

```
Public Class DataClass
    .
    .
    .
End Class
```

This creates a new class named **DataClass**. You can create an object of this class, **data**, like this—note that you must use the **New** keyword to create a new instance of a class:

```
Dim data As New DataClass()
```

You also can do this like this:

```
Dim data As DataClass = New DataClass()
```

That's all there is to it, but of course, not much is happening here. It's when you start giving classes their own methods, fields, properties, and events that things become more useful.

Fields, Properties, Methods, and Events

Fields, Properties, Methods, and Events are called the *members* of a class. Inside the class, members are declared as either **Public**, **Private**, **Protected**, **Friend**, or **Protected Friend**:

- **Public**—Gives variables public access, which means there are no restrictions on their accessibility.

- **Private**—Gives variables private access, which means they are accessible only from within their class, including any nested procedures.

- **Protected**—Gives variables protected access, which means they are accessible only from within their own class or from a class derived from that class. Note that you can use **Protected** only at class level (which means you can't use it inside a procedure), because you use it to declare members of a class.

- **Friend**—Gives variables friend access, which means they are accessible from within the program that contains their declaration, as well as anywhere else in the same assembly.

- **Protected Friend**—Gives variables both protected and friend access, which means they can be used by code in the same assembly, as well as by code in derived classes.

The *fields* of a class, also called the class's *data members*, are much like built-in variables (although they also may be constants). For example, I can declare a field named **value** to the **DataClass** class we just saw by declaring a variable with that name:

```
Public Class DataClass
    Public value As Integer
End Class
```

Now I can refer to that field in an object of this class using the familiar *object.field* syntax of Visual Basic:

```
Dim data As New DataClass()
data.value = 5
```

You also can make fields hold constant values with **Const**:

```
Public Class Class1
    Public Const Field1 As Integer = 0
    .
    .
    .
End Class
```

Using fields like this can give you direct access to the data stored inside an object, and that's unusual in OOP because you usually want to check the data being stored in your objects to make sure it's legal first. (For example, you might want to make sure the number of computers stored in your warehouse is not assigned negative numbers, and so on.) An easy way of guarding access to the data in your objects is to use *properties*. We're all familiar with properties of objects, like this in the code we saw earlier in this chapter:

```
TextBox1.Size = New Size(150, 20)
TextBox1.Location = New Point(80, 20)
TextBox1.Text = "Hello from Visual Basic"
```

Properties are retrieved and set like fields, but are handled with the **Property Get** and **Property Set** procedures, which provide more control on how values are set or returned. We've first saw how to create properties in Chapter 3. We'll see more on properties in this chapter, such as creating write-only or read-only properties.

Methods represent the object's built-in procedures. For example, a class named **Animal** may have methods named **Sleeping** and **Eating**. You define methods by adding procedures, either Sub routines or functions, to your class; for example, here's how I might implement the **Sleeping** and **Eating** methods:

```
Public Class Animal
    Public Sub Eating()
        MsgBox("Eating...")
    End Sub

    Public Sub Sleeping()
        MsgBox("Sleeping...")
    End Sub
End Class
```

Now I can create a new object of the **Animal** class and call the **Eating** method in the familiar way:

```
Dim pet As New Animal()
pet.Eating()
```

And, as we all know, *events* allow objects to perform actions whenever a specific occurrence takes place. For example, when you click a button, a **Click** event occurs, and you can handle that event in an event handler, as we already have done so many times. As an example, I'll create a custom event, **ThreeClick**, in this chapter, which will happen when you click a button three times. We'll be able to set up an event handler for that event that looks like this:

```
Private Sub tracker_ThreeClick(ByVal Message As String) _
    Handles tracker.ThreeClick
    TextBox1.Text = Message
End Sub
```

Class vs. Object Members

There's another important distinction to understand when dealing with members in OOP: class members vs. object members. Members that apply to a class and are invoked with the class name are called *shared* or *static* or *class* members; the members that apply to objects created from the class are called *instance* or *object* members. For example, if **TextBox1** is an object, then its **Text** property is an instance or object member, because you use it with the object's name: **TextBox1.Text = "Hello from Visual Basic"**.

On the other hand, you can make members shared or class members, which you use with the class name, if you use the **Shared** keyword. Using this keyword makes a member into a class member, which you can use with just the class name—no object needed. (It also makes all objects share that member, as we'll see in this chapter.) Here's an example; in this case, I'll add a class method named **Add** to a class named **Mathematics**—this method just takes two integers and adds them, returning their sum:

```
Public Class Mathematics
    Shared Function Add(ByVal x As Integer, ByVal y As Integer) _
        As Integer
        Return x + y
    End Function
End Class
```

Now I can use this new class method using the name of the class, **Mathematics**, without needing an object of that class:

```
Private Sub Button1_Click(ByVal sender As System.Object, _
    ByVal e As System.EventArgs) Handles Button1.Click
    TextBox3.Text = Mathematics.Add(TextBox1.Text, TextBox2.Text)
End Sub
```

As we'll see in this chapter, using the keyword **Shared** also means that the shared method or data member is shared across all instances of its class. For example, if a class has a shared data member named **Count**, then every object of that class uses the same exact memory location for **Count**.

Abstraction, Encapsulation, Inheritance, and Polymorphism

Fields, properties, methods, and events are only one part of OOP. Generally speaking, a language like Visual Basic is object oriented if it supports:

- *Abstraction*—The ability to create an abstract representation of a concept in code (as an object named **employee** is an abstraction of a real employee).

- *Encapsulation*—Encapsulation is all about the separation between implementation and interface. In other words, when you encapsulate an object, you make its code and data *internal* and no longer accessible to the outside except through a well-defined interface. This is also called *data hiding*.

- *Polymorphism*—This is all about creating procedures that can operate on objects of different types. For example, if both **person** and **employee** objects have a **last_name** property, a polymorphic procedure can use that property of both objects. Visual Basic handles polymorphism with both late binding and multiple interfaces, both of which we'll cover.

- *Inheritance*—As we've seen, inheritance allows you to derive new classes from other classes. The idea here is that if you were to create, for example, a class for a specific Visual Basic form and then derive a new type of form from that class, the derived class will *inherit* all the base class's functionality, even before you start adding code or customizing the new form.

In fact, inheritance is such an important topic that the next chapter is dedicated to it. Using inheritance, you can derive a new class, the *derived class*, from a *base class*. The derived class inherits all the members of the base class, unless you specifically *override* them. What's that mean? Take a look at the next topic.

Overloading, Overriding, and Shadowing

Overloading, overriding, and shadowing are also important concepts in Visual Basic OOP. All three of these techniques allow you to create multiple members with the same name. Here's how they work, in overview:

- *Overloaded*—members provide different versions of a property or method that have the same name, but that accept a different number of parameters (or parameters of different types).

- *Overridden*—properties and methods are used to replace an inherited property or method. When you override a member from a base class, you replace it. Overridden members must accept the same data type and number of arguments.

• *Shadowed*—members are used to create a local version of a member that has broader scope. You also can shadow a type with any other type. For example, you can declare a property that shadows an inherited method with the same name.

Constructors and Destructors

You create objects with the **New** keyword, as we've seen, like this:

```
Dim data As New DataClass()
```

When you create an object, you might want to customize that object with data—for example, when you create an object of a class named **Employee**, you might want to store the employee's name, phone number, ID number, and so on in that object. To do that, you can use *constructors*, which we first discussed in Chapter 2. You pass data to a constructor by enclosing it in the parentheses following the class name when you're creating an object. The parentheses above are empty because we're not passing anything to a constructor here. (Technically, each class comes with a default constructor built in, which takes no arguments.) However, we might want to store a value, such the integer 5, in an object of a class named **DataClass,** like this:

```
Dim data As New DataClass(5)
```

How do you create a constructor? You add a Sub procedure named **New** to a class—that's all it takes. For example, here's how that might look for the **DataClass** class; in this case, I'm storing the value passed to **New** in a private data member named value, and adding a method named **GetData** to return that stored value as needed:

```
Public Class DataClass
    Private value As Integer

    Public Sub New(ByVal newValue As Integer)
        value = newValue
    End Sub

    Public Function GetData() As Integer
        Return value
    End Function
End Class
```

Now I can store the value 5 inside an object of the **DataClass** class simply by passing 5 to the constructor, and I can retrieve that value with the **GetData** method:

```
Dim data As New DataClass(5)
MsgBox(data.GetData())
```

The life cycle of an object ends when they leave scope or are set to **Nothing** and are released by the .NET framework. Visual Basic controls the release of system resources using procedures called *destructors*. In Visual Basic, objects have constructors far more often than they have destructors in general, because you typically only use destructors to clean up after an object (deallocating resources, for example, or informing other objects that the current object will no longer be available). The **Finalize** destructor is the one you normally use; **Finalize** is called automatically by the system when an object is destroyed (which means that you should not explicitly call **Finalize** yourself). The .NET Framework automatically runs the **Finalize** destructor and destroys objects when the system determines that such objects are no longer needed.

*TIP: The **Sub New** and **Sub Finalize** procedures in Visual Basic .NET replace the **Class_Initialize** and **Class_Terminate** methods used in earlier versions of Visual Basic to initialize and destroy objects.*

However, unlike the **Class_Terminate** procedure of VB6 and earlier, you're not supposed to be able to determine exactly when the .NET Framework will execute the **Finalize** method. You only can be sure that the system will call Sub **Finalize** some time after the last reference to an object is released. The delay between when an object leaves scope and when it is actually destroyed is because the .NET Framework uses a system called *reference-tracing garbage collection* that releases unused resources every now and then. Garbage collection is automatic, and it ensures that unused resources (usually memory) are always released without any extra work on your part.

To get rid of an object, then, you assign it the value **Nothing**. The next time garbage is collected, the object will be removed from memory.

TIP: If you read the Visual Basic documentation, you'll read a great deal about how you can't trigger garbage collection yourself, but the fact is that you can. We'll see how to do so in this chapter in "Triggering Garbage Collection."

An OOP Example

Examples always help, and in fact, we've already seen an example that puts together many of the aspects of OOP in Visual Basic, including custom classes and objects, fields, methods, constructors, and so on in Chapter 7 (see "Storing Objects in a List Box or Combo Box" in that chapter). This example, ComboBoxesData, stores objects in a combo box, and each object holds its name and index in the combo box. When the user selects an item in the combo box, the code recovers the data from the object corresponding to the selected item, and displays that data.

To make this work, I created a class named **DataItem,** which used a **New** constructor to store each item's name and index value as internal, private data:

```
Public Class DataItem
      Private Data As Single
      Private Name As String


      Public Sub New(ByVal NameArgument As String, ByVal Value As Single)
          Name = NameArgument
          Data = Value
      End Sub
      .
      .
      .

End Class
```

I also added two methods to this class—**ToString**, which returns the name of the item (and which actually overrides the **ToString** method built into the **Object** class, which is the ultimate base class of every class), and **GetData**, which returns the index value of the item:

```
Public Class DataItem
      Private Data As Single
      Private Name As String

      Public Sub New(ByVal NameArgument As String, ByVal Value As Single)
          Name = NameArgument
          Data = Value
      End Sub

      Overrides Function ToString() As String
          Return CStr(Name)
      End Function

      Public Function GetData() As Single
          Return Data
      End Function
End Class
```

I created 20 objects of this class and placed them into a combo box with the combo box's **AddRange** method this way when the program's form first loaded:

```
Public Class Form1
    Inherits System.Windows.Forms.Form
```

```
'Windows Form Designer generated code

Private Sub Form1_Load(ByVal sender As System.Object, _
    ByVal e As System.EventArgs) Handles MyBase.Load
    Dim Objects(20) As DataItem
    ComboBox1.BeginUpdate()
    Dim intLoopIndex As Integer
    For intLoopIndex = 0 To 20
        Objects(intLoopIndex) = New DataItem("Item " & intLoopIndex, _
        CSng(intLoopIndex))
    Next
    ComboBox1.Items.AddRange(Objects)
    ComboBox1.EndUpdate()
End Sub
```

Then, when the user changed the selection in the combo box, I recovered the selected item with the combo box's **SelectedItem** property, and used the **GetData** method we have given that item to recover the item's internal data:

```
Public Class Form1
    Inherits System.Windows.Forms.Form

    'Windows Form Designer generated code

    Private Sub Form1_Load(ByVal sender As System.Object, _
        ByVal e As System.EventArgs) Handles MyBase.Load
        Dim Objects(20) As DataItem
        ComboBox1.BeginUpdate()
        Dim intLoopIndex As Integer
        For intLoopIndex = 0 To 20
            Objects(intLoopIndex) = New DataItem("Item " & intLoopIndex, _
            CSng(intLoopIndex))
        Next
        ComboBox1.Items.AddRange(Objects)
        ComboBox1.EndUpdate()
    End Sub

    Private Sub ComboBox1_SelectedIndexChanged(ByVal sender As _
        System.Object, ByVal e As System.EventArgs) Handles _
        ComboBox1.SelectedIndexChanged
        MsgBox("The data for the item you selected is: " & _
            CType(ComboBox1.SelectedItem, DataItem).GetData())
    End Sub
End Class
```

As you see, now we can understand all that's going on in this code. You can see this example, ComboBoxData, at work in Figure 7.15 in Chapter 7.

Structures and Modules

Classes are so popular in OOP that other programming constructs—in particular, structures and modules—are now based on them. Structures were originally a halfway solution between variables and true objects allowing you to create your own data types, much like adding fields to a class. As with classes, however, structures can now support methods. Modules in Visual Basic are designed primarily to hold code, but now they can also support members, just like classes.

Although structures support many of the same features as classes, including the ability to support fields, methods, events, and properties, it's important to realize that the following features of classes are not supported by structures:

- Structures cannot explicitly inherit from any other type.

- Structures cannot inherit from other structures.

- You cannot define a nonshared constructor that doesn't take any arguments for a structure. You can, however, define a nonshared constructor that does take arguments. The reason for this is that every structure has a built-in public constructor without arguments that initializes all the structure's data members to their default values. That means that **Dim employee As EmployeeStruct** is the same as **Dim employee As EmployeeStruct = New EmployeeStruct( )**.

- You cannot override the **Finalize** method in a structure.

- The declarations of data members in a structure cannot include initializers, the **New** keyword, or set initial sizes for arrays.

- If you declare them with **Dim**, the default access of data members in structures is public, not private as in classes and modules.

- Structure members cannot be declared as **Protected**.

- Structures are *value types* rather than *reference types*. This means, for example, that assigning a structure instance to another structure, or passing a structure instance to a **ByVal** argument causes the entire structure to be copied.

TIP: You have to perform equality testing with structures testing member-by-member for equality.

In addition, modules are a reference type similar to classes, but with some important distinctions:

- The members of a module are implicitly shared.

- Modules can never be instantiated.

- Modules do not support inheritance.

- Modules cannot implement interfaces.

- A module can be declared only inside a namespace.

- Modules cannot be nested in other types.

- You can have multiple modules in a project, but note that members with the same name in two or more modules must be qualified with the name of their module when used outside that module.

And now it's time to start digging into the specific details in the Immediate Solutions section of this chapter.

Immediate Solutions

Creating Classes

So how do you actually create a class? You use the **Class** statement:

```
[ <attrlist> ] [ Public | Private | Protected | Friend | Protected Friend ]
[ Shadows ] [ MustInherit | NotInheritable ] Class name
 [ Implements interfacename ]
   [ statements ]
End Class
```

Here are the various parts of this statement:

- *attrlist*—Optional. This is the list of attributes for this class. Separate multiple attributes by commas.

- **Public**—Optional. Classes declared **Public** have public access; there are no restrictions on the use of public classes.

- **Private**—Optional. Classes declared **Private** have private access, which is accessible only within its declaration context.

- **Protected**—Optional. Classes declared **Protected** have protected access, which means they are accessible only from within their own class or from a derived class.

- **Friend**—Optional. Classes declared **Friend** have friend access, which means they are accessible only within the program that contains their declaration.

- **Protected Friend**—Optional. Classes declared **Protected Friend** have both protected and friend accessibility.

- **Shadows**—Optional. Indicates that this class shadows a programming element in a base class.

- **MustInherit**—Optional. Indicates that the class contains methods that must be implemented by a deriving class.

- **NotInheritable**—Optional. Indicates that the class is a class from which no further inheritance is allowed.

- *name*—Required. Name of the class.

- *interfacename*—Optional. The name of the interface implemented by this class.

- **statements**—Optional. The statements that make up the variables, properties, events, and methods of the class.

Each attribute in the *attrlist* part has the following syntax:

```
<attrname [({ attrargs | attrinit })]> Attrlist
```

Here are the parts of the *attrlist* part:

- **attrname**—Required. Name of the attribute.
- **attrargs**—Optional. List of arguments for this attribute. Separate multiple arguments by commas.
- **attrinit**—Optional. List of field or property initializers. Separate multiple initializers by commas.

You place the members of the class inside the class itself. You also can nest class declarations. We've already seen a number of examples; here's how we set up a class named **DataClass**:

```
Public Class DataClass
    Private value As Integer

    Public Sub New(ByVal newValue As Integer)
        value = newValue
    End Sub

    Public Function GetData() As Integer
        Return value
    End Function
End Class
```

Creating Objects

You can create objects of a class using the **Dim** statement; this statement is used at module, class, structure, procedure, or block level:

```
[ <attrlist> ] [{ Public | Protected | Friend | Protected Friend |
Private | Static }] [ Shared ] [ Shadows ] [ ReadOnly ] Dim
[ WithEvents ] name [ (boundlist) ] [ As [ New ] type ] [ = initexpr ]
```

Here are the parts of this statement:

- **attrlist**—A list of attributes that apply to the variables you're declaring in this statement. You separate multiple attributes with commas.

- **Public**—Gives variables public access, which means there are no restrictions on their accessibility. You can use **Public** only at module, namespace, or file level (which means you can't use it inside a procedure). Note that if you specify **Public**, you can omit the **Dim** keyword if you want to.

- **Protected**—Gives variables protected access, which means they are accessible only from within their own class or from a class derived from that class. You can use **Protected** only at class level (which means you can't use it inside a procedure), because you use it to declare members of a class. Note that if you specify **Protected**, you can omit the **Dim** keyword if you want to.

- **Friend**—Gives variables friend access, which means they are accessible from within the program that contains their declaration, as well as anywhere else in the same assembly. You can use **Friend** only at module, namespace, or file level (which means you can't use it inside a procedure). Note that if you specify **Friend**, you can omit the **Dim** keyword if you want to.

- **Protected Friend**—Gives variables both protected and friend access, which means they can be used by code in the same assembly, as well as by code in derived classes.

- **Private**—Gives variables private access, which means they are accessible only from within their declaration context (usually a class), including any nested procedures. You can use **Private** only at module, namespace, or file level (which means you can't use it inside a procedure). Note that if you specify **Private**, you can omit the **Dim** keyword if you want to.

- **Static**—Makes variables static, which means they'll retain their values, even after the procedure in which they're declared ends. You can declare static variables inside a procedure or a block within a procedure, but not at class or module level. Note that if you specify **Static**, you can omit the **Dim** keyword if you want to, but you cannot use either **Shadows** or **Shared**.

- **Shared**—Declares a shared variable, which means it is not associated with a specific instance of a class or structure, but can be shared across many instances. You access a shared variable by referring to it either with its class or structure name, or with the variable name of an instance of the class or structure. You can use **Shared** only at module, namespace, or file level (but not at the procedure level). Note that if you specify **Shared**, you can omit the **Dim** keyword if you want to.

- **Shadows**—Makes this variable a shadow of an identically named programming element in a base class. A shadowed element is unavailable in the derived class that shadows it. You can use **Shadows** only at module, namespace, or file level (but not inside a procedure). This means you can declare shadowing variables in a source file or inside a module, class, or structure, but not inside a procedure. Note that if you specify **Shadows**, you can omit the **Dim** keyword if you want to.

- **ReadOnly**—Means this variable can only be read and not written. This can be useful for creating constant members of reference types, such as an object variable with preset data members. You can use **ReadOnly** only at module, namespace, or file level (but not inside procedures). Note that if you specify **Shadows**, you can omit the **ReadOnly** keyword if you want to.

- **WithEvents**—Specifies that this variable is used to respond to events caused by the instance that was assigned to the variable. Note that you cannot specify both **WithEvents** and **New** in the same variable declaration.

- *name*—The name of the variable. You separate multiple variables by commas. If you specify multiple variables, each variable is declared of the data type given in the first **As** clause encountered after its *name* part.

- *boundlist*—Used to declare arrays; gives the upper bounds of the dimensions of an array variable. Multiple upper bounds are separated by commas. An array can have up to 60 dimensions.

- **New**—Means you want to create a new object immediately. If you use **New** when declaring an object variable, a new instance of the object is created. Note that you cannot use both **WithEvents** and **New** in the same declaration.

- *type*—The data type of the variable. Can be **Boolean**, **Byte**, **Char**, **Date**, **Decimal**, **Double**, **Integer**, **Long**, **Object**, **Short**, **Single**, or **String**; or the name of an enumeration, structure, class, or interface. To specify the type, you use a separate **As** clause for each variable, or you can declare a number of variables of the same type by using common **As** clauses. If you do not specify *type*, the variable takes the data type of *initexpr*. Note that if you don't specify either *type* or *initexpr*, the data type is set to **Object**.

- *initexpr*—An initialization expression which is evaluated and the result is assigned to the variable when it is created. Note that if you declare more than one variable with the same **As** clause, you cannot supply *initexpr* for those variables.

Each attribute in the *attrlist* list must use this syntax:

```
<attrname [({ attrargs | attrinit })]>
```

Here are the parts of the *attrlist* list:

- *attrname*—Name of the attribute.

- *attrargs*—List of arguments for this attribute. Separate multiple arguments with commas.

- *attrinit*—List of field or property initializers for this attribute. Separate multiple arguments with commas.

When you create a new object from a class, you use the **New** keyword. You can do that in either of these ways:

```
Dim employee As New EmployeeClass()
Dim employee As EmployeeClass = New EmployeeClass()
```

If you omit the **New** keyword, you're just declaring a new object, and it's not yet created:

```
Dim employee As EmployeeClass
```

Before using the object, you must explicitly create it with **New**:

```
employee = New EmployeeClass()
```

As discussed in the In Depth section of this chapter, classes often use constructors that let you configure objects with data. You write constructors by giving a method the name **New**, as in the **DataClass** class from the In Depth section of this chapter:

```
Public Class DataClass
    Private value As Integer

    Public Sub New(ByVal newValue As Integer)
        value = newValue
    End Sub

    Public Function GetData() As Integer
        Return value
    End Function
End Class
```

Now I can store the value 5 inside an object of the **DataClass** class simply by passing 5 to the constructor, and I can retrieve that value with the **GetData** method:

```
Dim data As New DataClass(5)
MsgBox(data.GetData())
```

Related solution:	Found on page:
Storing Objects in a List Box or Combo Box	322

Creating Structures

Traditionally, structures were used to let you create your own complex data types. For example, if you wanted to store both an employee's ID value (an integer) and a employee's name (a string) in one variable, you could create a new structure named, say, **Employee**, like this:

```
Public Structure Employee
     Public Name As String
     Public ID As Integer
End Structure
```

This creates a new data type. Now you can declare a variable of this new type, and access the data fields in it, like this:

```
Dim employee As Employee
employee.Name = "Cary Grant"
employee.ID = 101
```

Now, however, structures are much like classes and can support events, methods, and properties as well as fields. To create a structure, you use the **Structure** statement at the module or class level:

```
[ <attrlist> ] [{ Public | Protected | Friend |
Protected Friend | Private }] Structure name
    [ variabledeclarations ]
    [ proceduredeclarations ]
End Structure
```

Here are the parts of this statement:

- *attrlist*—Optional. List of attributes for this structure. Separate multiple attributes by commas.

- **Public**—Optional. Structures declared **Public** have public access; there are no restrictions on the accessibility of public structures.

- **Protected**—Optional. Structures declared **Protected** have protected access, which means they are accessible only from within their own class or from a derived class.

- **Friend**—Optional. Structures declared **Friend** have friend access, which means they are accessible from within the program that contains their declaration and from anywhere else in the same assembly.

- **Protected Friend**—Optional. Structures declared **Protected Friend** have both protected and friend access. They can be used by code in the same assembly, as well as by code in derived classes.

- **Private**—Optional. Structures declared **Private** have private access, which means they are accessible only within their declaration context.

- *name*—Required. Name of the structure.

- *variabledeclarations*—Optional. One or more **Dim**, **Friend**, **Private**, or **Public** statements declaring variables that are the data members of the structure. Note that these declarations follow the same rules as they do outside of a structure.

- *proceduredeclarations*—Optional. One or more declarations of **Function**, **Property**, or **Sub** procedures that are the method members of the structure. Note that these declarations follow the same rules as they do outside of a structure.

Each attribute in the *attrlist* part has the following syntax:

```
<attrname [({ attrargs | attrinit })]> Attrlist
```

Here are the parts of *attrlist*:

- *attrname*—Required. Name of the attribute.

- *attrargs*—Optional. List of positional arguments for this attribute. Separate multiple arguments by commas.

- *attrinit*—Optional. List of field or property initializers for this attribute. Separate multiple initializers by commas.

Note that you must declare every data member of a structure. This means every statement in the *variabledeclarations* part must contain **Dim**, **Friend**, **Private**, or **Public**. If **Option Strict** is **On**, you also must include the **As** clause in every statement. Members declared with **Dim** default to public access, and members declared without the **As** clause default to the **Object** data type.

NOTE: *You cannot initialize the value of any data member of a structure as part of its declaration. You must either initialize a data member by means of a parameterized constructor on the structure, or assign a value to the member after you have created an instance of the structure.*

You can assign one structure variable to another of the same type, and all the members will be copied as well. However, to compare structures, you must compare each member individually currently in Visual Basic, although that may change in the future.

As mentioned, structures support many of the same features as classes. However, as discussed in the In Depth section of this chapter, there are a number of features of classes that are not supported in structures—see the In Depth section for more information.

Also, structures are value types rather than reference types. This means that when you copy a structure, it's copied by value, not reference. And in Visual Basic, it also means that you can't convert from structures to classes, such as the **Object** class. That's often important. For example, in the ComboBoxData example from Chapter 7 that we took a look at in the In Depth section of this chapter (see "An OOP Example"), I created an array of objects named **Objects** and used a combo box's **AddRange** method to add the whole array to the combo box at once:

```
ComboBox1.Items.AddRange(Objects)
```

However, **AddRange** takes an array of type **Object** by default, and an array of structures can't be converted to an array of type **Object**. Instead, I'll add each structure to the combo box one at a time. The rest of the code is the same, except that **DataItem** is now a structure instead of a class, and even supports constructors, methods, and so on, as you can see in the Structures example on the CD-ROM:

```
Public Class Form1
    Inherits System.Windows.Forms.Form

    'Windows Form Designer generated code

    Private Sub Form1_Load(ByVal sender As System.Object, _
        ByVal e As System.EventArgs) Handles MyBase.Load
        Dim Objects(20) As DataItem
        ComboBox1.BeginUpdate()
        Dim intLoopIndex As Integer
        For intLoopIndex = 0 To 20
            Objects(intLoopIndex) = New DataItem("Item " & _
                intLoopIndex, CSng(intLoopIndex))
            ComboBox1.Items.Add(Objects(intLoopIndex))
        Next
        ComboBox1.EndUpdate()
    End Sub

    Private Sub ComboBox1_SelectedIndexChanged(ByVal sender As _
        System.Object, ByVal e As System.EventArgs) Handles _
        ComboBox1.SelectedIndexChanged
        MsgBox("The data for the item you selected is: " & _
            CType(ComboBox1.SelectedItem, DataItem).GetData())
    End Sub
End Class
```

11. Object-Oriented Programming

```
Public Structure DataItem
    Private Data As Single
    Private Name As String
    Public Sub New(ByVal NameArgument As String, ByVal Value As Single)
        Name = NameArgument
        Data = Value
    End Sub

    Overrides Function ToString() As String
        Return CStr(Name)
    End Function

    Public Function GetData() As Single
        Return Data
    End Function
End Structure
```

The Structures example works just as the ComboBoxData example did (which you
can see in Chapter 7, Figure 7.15), except that now the data is stored in structures.

Creating Modules

Traditionally in Visual Basic, you used modules to divide your code up into smaller
units, because modules were designed primarily to hold code. Here's an example
from Chapter 2:

```
Module Module1
    Sub Main()
        System.Console.WriteLine("Hello from Visual Basic")
        System.Console.WriteLine("Press Enter to continue...")
        System.Console.ReadLine()
    End Sub
End Module
```

However, as mentioned earlier, modules can now hold methods, fields, properties,
and events, just as classes can. There are a number of differences between classes
and modules, though—see the In Depth section of this chapter for the details.

You create a module with the **Module** statement:

```
[ <attrilist> ] Module [ Public | Friend ] name
    [ statements ]
End Module
```

Here are the parts of this statement:

- *attrlist*—Optional. List of attributes for this module. Separate multiple attributes by commas.

- **Public**—Optional. Modules declared **Public** have public access, which means there are no restrictions on the accessibility of public modules.

- **Friend**—Optional. Modules declared **Friend** have friend access, which means they are accessible from within the program that contains their declaration and from anywhere else in the same assembly.

- *name*—Required. Name of the module.

- *statements*—Optional. Statements that make up the variables, properties, events, and methods of the module.

- **End Module**—Ends a **Module** block.

Each attribute in the *attrlist* part has the following syntax:

```
<attrname [({ attrargs | attrinit })]> Attrlist
```

Here are the parts of *attrlist*:

- *attrname*—Required. Name of the attribute.

- *attrargs*—Optional. List of arguments for this attribute. Separate multiple arguments by commas.

- *attrinit*—Optional. List of field or property initializers for this attribute. Separate multiple initializers by commas.

Creating Constructors

As discussed in the In Depth section of this chapter, as well as in Chapter 2, constructors are special methods that let you configure the objects you create from a class. We've already dealt with constructors throughout this book, as in this code from Chapter 5, where we're passing data to the constructors for the **Size** and **Point** classes:

```
Private Sub Button1_Click(ByVal sender As System.Object, _
    ByVal e As System.EventArgs) Handles Button1.Click
    Dim TextBox1 As New TextBox()
    TextBox1.Size = New Size(150, 20)
    TextBox1.Location = New Point(80, 20)
    TextBox1.Text = "Hello from Visual Basic"
    Me.Controls.Add(TextBox1)
End Sub
```

So how do you create a constructor? You add a Sub procedure named **New** to a class—that's all it takes. For example, here's how that might look for the class named **DataClass** which we saw in the In Depth section of this chapter; in this case, I'm storing the value passed to **New** in a private data member named **value**:

```
Public Class DataClass
    Private value As Integer

    Public Sub New(ByVal newValue As Integer)
        value = newValue
    End Sub

    Public Function GetData() As Integer
        Return value
    End Function
End Class
```

Now I can store the value 5 inside an object of the **DataClass** class simply by passing 5 to the constructor:

```
Dim data As New DataClass(5)
MsgBox(data.GetData())
```

Note that all classes have a default constructor that doesn't take any arguments; this constructor exists so you can create objects without providing an explicit **New** Sub procedure and doesn't do anything special. (However, if you derive a new class from a base class and add a constructor to the derived class, Visual Basic will complain if you don't call the base class's constructor from the derived class's constructor and there's no explicit base class constructor that takes no arguments.) More on constructors is coming up in the next chapter, when we start deriving classes from base classes.

Using **Is** to Compare Objects

Here's something that's important to know—if you want to know if two objects are really the same object, you should use the **Is** keyword instead of the standard comparison operators. If the two objects you're checking are the same object, **Is** returns

True. Here's an example we saw in Chapter 6, where I'm checking which button of several has been clicked; the clicked button is passed to us in the **sender** argument:

```
Private Sub Button_Click(ByVal sender As System.Object, _
    ByVal e As System.EventArgs)
    If sender Is Button1 Then
        TextBox1.Text = "You clicked button 1"
    End If
    If sender Is Button2 Then
        TextBox1.Text = "You clicked button 2"
    End If
    If sender Is Button3 Then
        TextBox1.Text = "You clicked button 3"
    End If
End Sub
```

Creating Data Members

As discussed in the In Depth section of this chapter, the fields of a class, also called the class's data members, are much like built-in variables. For example, in the In Depth section of this chapter, I declared a field named **value** in a class named **DataClass**:

```
Public Class DataClass
    Public value As Integer
End Class
```

Now I can refer to that field in an object of this class using the familiar *object.field* syntax of Visual Basic:

```
Dim data As New DataClass()
data.value = 5
```

You also can make fields hold constant values with **Const**:

```
Public Class Class1
    Public Const Field1 As Integer = 0

    .

    .

    .

End Class
```

These data members are object data members—you use them with a specific object. However, you also can create class data members; see the next topic for the details.

Related solution:	Found on page:
Declaring Variables	73

Creating Class (Shared) Data Members

You can use the **Shared** keyword to create class data members. You can use a class data member with the name of the class alone, no object needed. For example, say you have a class named **Mathematics**, and declare a shared variable named **Pi**:

```
Public Class Mathematics
    Public Shared Pi As Double = 3.1415926535
End Class
```

Now you can use **Pi** as a class variable with the **Mathematics** class directly, no object needed:

```
integer5 = Mathematics.Pi
```

Pi is more naturally handled as a constant, of course; you can use **Const** instead of **Shared** to create a shared constant that works the same way (except, of course, that you can't assign values to it, because it's a constant):

```
Public Class Mathematics
    Public Const Pi As Double = 3.1415926535
End Class
```

The reason variables you declare with the **Shared** keyword are called shared is because they're shared over all instances of the class. For example, take a look at the Shared example on the CD-ROM—in this case, I'm adding a shared data member named **Data** to the **Mathematics** class, and each instance of this class will now see the same value stored in **Data**. To show this, I'll add a method named **Increment** to the **Mathematics** class, which increments the value in **Data** by 1 and returns the new value:

```
Public Class Mathematics
    Shared Data As Integer = 0
```

```
    Public Function Increment() As Integer
        Data += 1
        Return Data
    End Function
End Class
```

Next, I create two different objects of the **Mathematics** class, **Object1** and **Object2**. Both of these objects will share the same internal **Data** member, which you can see by clicking the buttons in this program—one button uses the **Increment** method of **Object1**, and the other button uses the **Increment** method of **Object2**, but no matter how much you alternate between the buttons, you'll see that the value in **Data** (which appears in a text box) increments steadily because both objects are working on the same value. Here's what the code looks like:

```
Dim Object1, Object2 As New Mathematics()

Private Sub Button2_Click(ByVal sender As System.Object, _
    ByVal e As System.EventArgs) Handles Button2.Click
    TextBox4.Text = "Count = " & Object1.Increment
End Sub

Private Sub Button3_Click(ByVal sender As System.Object, _
    ByVal e As System.EventArgs) Handles Button3.Click
    TextBox4.Text = "Count = " & Object2.Increment
End Sub
```

You can see this program at work in Figure 11.1—the two buttons that use **Object1** and **Object2** are at the bottom, and the text box that reports the new value stored in the **Data** member is beneath them. No matter which button you click, the displayed value increments steadily, demonstrating that indeed, both objects are sharing the same value in **Data**.

Related solution:	*Found on page:*
Declaring Variables	73

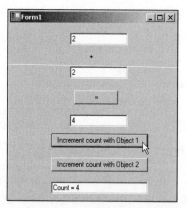

Figure 11.1   Using a shared data member.

Creating Methods

As discussed in the In Depth section of this chapter, methods represent the object's built-in procedures. For example, a class named **Animal** may have methods named **Sleeping** and **Eating**. You define methods by adding procedures, either Sub procedures or functions, to your class; for example, here's how I might implement the **Sleeping** and **Eating** methods:

```
Public Class Animal
    Public Sub Eating()
        MsgBox("Eating...")
    End Sub

    Public Sub Sleeping()
        MsgBox("Sleeping...")
    End Sub
End Class
```

Now I can create a new object of the **Animal** class and call the **Eating** method in the familiar way:

```
Dim pet As New Animal()
pet.Eating()
```

In general, you can add whatever functions or Sub procedures you want to your class, including those that accept parameters and those that return values, as we saw earlier in this chapter:

```
Public Class DataClass
    Private value As Integer

    Public Sub New(ByVal newValue As Integer)
        value = newValue
    End Sub

    Public Function GetData() As Integer
        Return value
    End Function
End Class
```

Note that these methods are object methods—you use them with an object. However, you also can create class methods. See the next topic for the details.

Related solutions:	Found on page:
Creating Sub Procedures	122
Creating Functions	125

Creating Class (Shared) Methods

When you create a class method, you can use it with the class alone, no object needed. For example, in the Shared example on the CD-ROM, I've added a function named **Add** to the **Mathematics** class and made it a class method by using the **Shared** keyword. Now I can use the **Add** method like this: **Mathematics.Add**, that is, with the name of the class alone. Here's how I add two integers in text boxes in the Shared example when the user clicks the button with the equals sign (=) caption you see in Figure 11.1:

```
Private Sub Button1_Click(ByVal sender As System.Object, _
    ByVal e As System.EventArgs) Handles Button1.Click
    TextBox3.Text = Mathematics.Add(TextBox1.Text, TextBox2.Text)
End Sub

Public Class Mathematics
    Shared Function Add(ByVal x As Integer, ByVal y As Integer) _
        As Integer
        Return x + y
    End Function
End Class
```

You can see the results in Figure 11.1, where the numbers in the two text boxes are added and the sum displayed when the user clicks the = button. Note that you can only use shared data in a shared method, or the values that are passed to you, as I've done here, unless you provide a specific object to work with.

Related solutions:	Found on page:
Creating Sub Procedures	122
Creating Functions	125

Creating Properties

As discussed in the In Depth section of this chapter, you often don't want to give code outside an object direct access to the data in the object. Instead, you can use properties, which use methods to set or get an internal value. We saw how to do that in Chapter 3; here's an example from that chapter where I'm adding a property to a module:

```
Module Module2
    Private PropertyValue As String
    Public Property Prop1() As String
        Get
            Return PropertyValue
        End Get
        Set(ByVal Value As String)
            PropertyValue = Value
        End Set
    End Property
End Module
```

See the topic "Creating Properties" in Chapter 3 for all the details, including how to create indexed properties. Note that you can make properties write-only with the **WriteOnly** keyword (and you must omit the **Get** method):

```
Module Module2
    Private PropertyValue As String
    Public WriteOnly Property Prop1() As String
        Set(ByVal Value As String)
            PropertyValue = Value
        End Set
    End Property
End Module
```

You can make properties read-only with the **ReadOnly** keyword (and you must omit the **Set** method):

```
Module Module2
    Private PropertyValue As String
    Public ReadOnly Property Prop1() As String
        Get
            Return PropertyValue
        End Get
    End Property
End Module
```

Related solution:	*Found on page:*
Creating Properties	132

Creating Class (Shared) Properties

You can make properties shared with the **Shared** keyword, which means you can use them with the class name, and don't need a specific object to work with. However, in a shared property, you can only work with shared data, or data passed to you, or you must provide a specific object to work with. Here's an example where I'm creating and working with a shared property:

```
Public Class Mathematics
    Shared Data As Integer = 0
    Shared Property Property1()
        Get
            Return Data
        End Get
        Set(ByVal Value)
            Data = Value
        End Set
    End Property
End Class

Private Sub Button1_Click(ByVal sender As System.Object, _
ByVal e As System.EventArgs) Handles Button1.Click
    Mathematics.Property1 = 5
End Sub

Private Sub Button2_Click(ByVal sender As System.Object, _
ByVal e As System.EventArgs) Handles Button2.Click
    TextBox1.Text = Mathematics.Property1
End Sub
```

Related solution:	Found on page:
Creating Properties	132

Creating Events

You can design and support your own events using OOP in Visual Basic, using the **Event** statement:

```
[ <attrlist> ] [ Public | Private | Protected | Friend |
Protected Friend] [ Shadows ] Event eventname[(arglist)]
[ Implements interfacename.interfaceeventname ]
```

Here are the parts of this statement:

- *attrlist*—Optional. List of attributes that apply to this event. Separate multiple attributes by commas.

- **Public**—Optional. Events declared **Public** have public access, which means there are no restrictions on their use.

- **Private**—Optional. Events declared **Private** have private access, which means they are accessible only within their declaration context.

- **Protected**—Optional. Events declared **Protected** have protected access, which means they are accessible only from within their own class or from a derived class.

- **Friend**—Optional. Events declared **Friend** have friend access, which means they are accessible only within the program that contains the its declaration.

- **Protected Friend**—Optional. Events declared **Protected Friend** have both protected and friend accessibility.

- **Shadows**—Optional. Indicates that this event shadows an identically named programming element in a base class.

- *eventname*—Required. Name of the event.

- *interfacename*—The name of an interface.

- *interfaceeventname*—The name of the event being implemented.

Each attribute in the *attrlist* part has the following syntax:

```
<attrname [({ attrargs | attrinit })]> Attrlist
```

Here are the parts of *attrlist*:

- *attrname*—Required. Name of the attribute.

- **attrargs**—Optional. List of arguments for this attribute. Separate multiple arguments by commas.

- **attrinit**—Optional. List of field or property initializers for this attribute. Separate multiple initializers by commas.

The *arglist* argument has the following syntax:

```
[ <attrlist> ] [ ByVal | ByRef ] varname[ ( ) ] [ As type ] Arglist
```

Here are the parts of *arglist*:

- **attrlist**—Optional. List of attributes for this argument. Separate multiple attributes by commas.

- **ByVal**—Optional. Specifies that the argument is passed by value. (**ByVal** is the default.)

- **ByRef**—Optional. Specifies that the argument is passed by reference.

- **varname**—Required. Name of the variable representing the argument being passed to the procedure.

- **type**—Optional. Data type of the argument passed to the procedure; may be **Byte**, **Boolean**, **Char**, **Short**, **Integer**, **Long**, **Single**, **Double**, **Decimal**, **Date**, **String** (variable length only), **Object**, a user-defined type, or an object type.

Let's see an example; this one is named Events on the CD-ROM. In this case, I'll create a custom event that occurs when you click a button three times, called **ThreeClick**. To keep track of how many times the button has been clicked, I'll use an object called tracker, of a class I'll call **ClickTrack**:

```
Public Class ClickTrack
    .
    .
    .
End Class
```

To implement the **ThreeClick** event, I use the **Event** statement, indicating that the event handler for this event should be passed one argument, a string holding a message (which will just indicate that the event occurred):

```
Public Class ClickTrack
    Public Event ThreeClick(ByVal Message As String)
    .
    .
    .
End Class
```

11. Object-Oriented Programming

How can we make this event actually occur? You just use the **RaiseEvent** method. In this case, you must pass **RaiseEvent** a message you want to associate with this event (if you had given **ThreeClick** two arguments, you'd have to pass **RaiseEvent** two arguments, and so on). I can keep track of the number of button clicks with a Sub procedure named **Click** and raise the **ThreeClick** event when three clicks have occurred, passing that event's handler the string "You clicked three times":

```
Public Class ClickTrack
    Public Event ThreeClick(ByVal Message As String)
    Public Sub Click()
        Static ClickCount As Integer = 0
        ClickCount += 1
        If ClickCount >= 3 Then
            ClickCount = 0
            RaiseEvent ThreeClick("You clicked three times")
        End If
    End Sub
End Class
```

That's how you make a custom event occur—with **RaiseEvent**. I'll need an object of this new **ClickTrack** class, and I'll call that object **tracker**. Note that I declare it using the keyword **WithEvents** to indicate this new object can handle events:

```
Dim WithEvents tracker As New ClickTrack()
```

Now that we've created a new event, you also can write an event handler for it, just make sure you accept the right number of type of arguments and use a **Handles** clause to indicate what event you're handling (which is **tracker.ThreeClick** in this case); when the event occurs, I'll display the message we've associated with the event in a text box:

```
Private Sub tracker_ThreeClick(ByVal Message As String) Handles _
    tracker.ThreeClick
    TextBox1.Text = Message
End Sub
```

All that's left is to keep calling the tracker object's **Click** method until the **ThreeClick** event occurs, and I can do that with a button this way:

```
Private Sub Button1_Click(ByVal sender As System.Object, _
    ByVal e As System.EventArgs) Handles Button1.Click
    tracker.Click()
End Sub
```

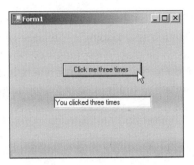

Figure 11.2   Using custom events.

You can see the result in Figure 11.2. Now you're creating and handling custom events.

Creating Class (Shared) Events

Events (see the previous topic to see how to create custom events) also can be declared as **Shared**:

```
Public Shared Event ThreeClick(ByVal Message As String)
```

That's good to know because, for example, shared methods can raise only shared events.

Overloading Methods and Properties

In OOP, methods and properties can be *overloaded*, which means that you can define a method or property multiple times with different argument lists. For example, say you had a method named **Draw** that can draw rectangles and triangles. For rectangles, you might need only four arguments in your argument list—the x and y coordinates of the upper-left and lower-right corners of the rectangle. However, for triangles, you might need six arguments, corresponding to the x and y coordinates of the three vertices of the triangle. To handle this, you can overload **Draw** to handle four or six arguments just by defining the method twice with two different argument lists (note, by the way, that to be different, an argument list need not have a different *number* of arguments—arguments are considered different if they're of different data types too).

TIP: Don't confuse overloading with overriding; overriding is something that happens with inheritance, where a base class member is replaced by different member in the derived class. We'll see overriding in Chapter 12.

Here's an example named Overloading on the CD-ROM. In this case, I'll create a class named **Notifier** with a method named **Display**, which will display a message box. **Display** will have two versions—you pass the text to display in the message box to the first version, and the text and a message box icon to the second. Here, then, is all you do to overload a method—just define it a number of times with different argument lists—note that I'm adding two buttons to call the two versions of **Display**:

```
Dim notifierObject As New Notifier()

Private Sub Button1_Click(ByVal sender As System.Object, _
    ByVal e As System.EventArgs) Handles Button1.Click
    notifierObject.Display("Hello from Visual Basic!")
End Sub

Private Sub Button2_Click(ByVal sender As System.Object, _
    ByVal e As System.EventArgs) Handles Button2.Click
    notifierObject.Display("Hello from Visual Basic!", _
        MsgBoxStyle.Exclamation)
End Sub

Public Class Notifier
    Public Sub Display(ByVal Message As String)
        MsgBox(Message)
    End Sub

    Public Sub Display(ByVal Message As String, ByVal Icon _
        As MsgBoxStyle)
        MsgBox(Message, Icon)
    End Sub
End Class
```

How does Visual Basic know which overloaded version to use? All it has to do is to check the argument list you're passing to the method and find the version of the method that has the same number and types of arguments, in the same order. And that's all it takes—you can see the results in Figure 11.3.

There is also an **Overloads** keyword that you can use to indicate that you're overloading a method or property. You don't need to use **Overloads** when you're overloading members of the same class, but it becomes important when you're working with inheritance.

Related solution:	*Found on page:*
Overloading Base Class Members	548

Figure 11.3   Overloading a method.

Getting Rid of Objects When You're Done with Them

When you're done with an object and want to get rid of it so it no longer takes up memory and other resources, what do you do? (This isn't necessarily such a problem when you have one such object, but imagine if you have an array of 20,000 of them....) The official way to get rid of objects is to assign them the keyword **Nothing**. That might look like this:

```
Dim notifierObject As New Notifier()
notifierObject.Display("Hello from Visual Basic!")
notifierObject = Nothing
```

This tags the object for garbage collection, which was discussed in the In Depth section of this chapter. When the program gets around to collecting the garbage, this object will be destroyed. Note, by the way, that you don't have to do this at all unless you explicitly want to get rid of an object; if an object goes out of scope, it is automatically targeted for garbage collection. The Visual Basic documentation goes on a great deal about how you can't determine when garbage collection happens—but you can. See the next topic.

Triggering Garbage Collection

If you read the Visual Basic documentation, you'll read a lot about how you have no control over when garbage collection happens. But it's a little-known fact that you *do* have control over this if you want it. All you have to do is to go behind the scenes to the garbage collector namespace (which is **GC**) and use the **Collect** method:

```
System.GC.Collect()
```

Creating Class Libraries

Now that we're creating classes, we also can take a look at creating class libraries. When you've got a large number of classes to handle, you can store them in a class library and compile them into a DLL file, which can be used across multiple projects if you wish.

Here's an example, ClassLibraries on the CD-ROM. In this case, I'll create a class library with two classes, imaginatively called **Class1** and **Class2**. These classes are just for demonstration purposes; both of them will have a method named **Display** which displays a message box. You pass the text for the message box to the **Class1 Display** method, and the text and a message box icon to the **Class2 Display** method, that's the only difference between these methods. To create a class library, select the New|Project item, and this time, select the Class Library icon in the New Project dialog, use the name ClassLibraries, and click OK.

This creates and opens the following template in a code designer:

```
Public Class Class1

End Class
```

We want to create two classes here, each with a **Display** method, so add this code:

```
Public Class Class1
    Public Sub Display(ByVal Message As String)
        MsgBox(Message)
    End Sub
End Class

Public Class Class2
    Public Sub Display(ByVal Message As String)
        MsgBox(Message, MsgBoxStyle.Exclamation)
    End Sub
End Class
```

To make this class library available to other projects, you compile it into a DLL (dynamic link library) file using the Build|Build ClassLibraries menu item which creates, in this case, ClassLibraries.dll.

To use this DLL file, I'll create a new project named Displayer now; to do that, use the New|Project menu item and click the "Add to Solution" radio button in the

New Project dialog. Make this a Windows application named Displayer and click OK. Now make this new project the startup project with the Project|Set as Startup Project menu item (that is, you can't run a class library project like ClassLibraries, so you need a startup project to test out our code).

To use the classes in ClassLibraries.dll in the Displayer project, click the Project|Add Reference menu item to open the Add Reference dialog you see in Figure 11.4. Click the Projects tab, then double click the ClassLibraries item to make it appear in the Selected Components box, then click OK.

Now we can use the classes in the ClassLibraries class library; for example, to use **Class1**, you refer to it as **ClassLibraries.Class1**. Here's how I do that in the ClassLibraries example—I create an object of the **ClassLibraries.Class1** class, then use that object's **Display** method like this:

```
Dim cl As New ClassLibraries.Class1()

Private Sub Button1_Click(ByVal sender As System.Object, _
    ByVal e As System.EventArgs) Handles Button1.Click
    cl.Display("Hello from Visual Basic!")
End Sub
```

Now when you click this button, the **Display** method displays a message box as it should, as you see in Figure 11.5.

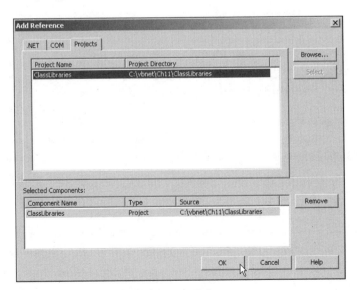

Figure 11.4   The Add Reference dialog.

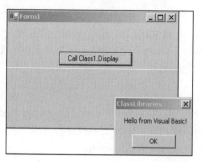

Figure 11.5   Using a class library.

Creating Namespaces

When you're creating a large number of classes, it can be helpful to divide them up into their own namespaces to help organize things. We already know about namespaces; as the name implies, you use them to create separate spaces so that names can't conflict with other names already declared. To create your own namespace, you can use the **Namespace** statement:

```
Namespace {name | name.name}
    componenttypes
End Namespace
```

Here are the parts of this statement:

* *name*—Required. A unique name that identifies the namespace.

* *componenttypes*—Required. Elements that make up the namespace. These include enumerations, structures, interfaces, classes, delegates, and so on.

Note that namespaces are always public, which means that the declaration of a namespace cannot include any access modifiers. (However, the components inside the namespace may have public or friend access; the default access is friend.)

Here's an example that declares two namespaces, one inside another:

```
Namespace Secret         ' Declares a namespace named Secret.
    Namespace TopSecret  ' Declares a namespace named TopSecret in Secret.
        Class Documents  ' Declares the class Secret.TopSecret.Documents
            .
            .
            .
        End Class
    End Namespace
End Namespace
```

Using the **Finalize** Method (Creating Destructors)

We know how to create constructors, but what about *destructors*, which are run when an object is destroyed? You can place code to clean up after the object, such saving state information and closing files, in a destructor. In Visual Basic, you can use the **Finalize** method for this purpose. The **Finalize** method is called automatically when the .NET runtime determines that the object is no longer needed.

Here's a quick example, named Finalize on the CD-ROM. In this case, I'm creating an object of a class named **Class1**, and adding a **Finalize** method that beeps when the object is destroyed. Here's what the code looks like:

```
Public Class Form1
    Inherits System.Windows.Forms.Form

    'Windows Form Designer generated code

    Dim Object1 As New Class1()
End Class

Public Class Class1
    Protected Overrides Sub Finalize()
        Beep()
    End Sub
End Class
```

Note that you have to use the **Overrides** keyword with **Finalize**, because you're actually overriding the **Finalize** method built into the **Object** class. When you run this example, a blank form appears and an object, **Object1**, of **Class1** is created; when you close the form, **Object1** is destroyed and the **Beep** method beeps. The usual code you place in **Finalize** is a little more substantial, of course, and you can use this method to deallocate resources, disconnect from the Internet, inform other objects that the current object is going to be destroyed, and more.

Chapter 12

Object-Oriented Inheritance

In Depth

This chapter is all about inheritance, which is the process you use to derive one class from another. This is more useful than it may sound, because Visual Basic comes with thousands of built-in base classes for you to create derived classes from and then customize. We're already familiar with this process from our work with Windows forms, of course, because we derive our forms from **System.Windows.Forms.Form** and then customize them with buttons and event handlers, like this:

```
Public Class Form1
    Inherits System.Windows.Forms.Form

    'Windows Form Designer generated code

    Private Sub Button1_Click(ByVal sender As System.Object, _
        ByVal e As System.EventArgs) Handles Button1.Click
        .
        .
        .
    End Sub

    Private Sub Button2_Click(ByVal sender As System.Object, _
        ByVal e As System.EventArgs) Handles Button2.Click
        .
        .
        .
    End Sub
End Class
```

The **Inherits** statement you see above is used to declare a new class, called the *derived class*, based on an existing class, known as the *base class*. Derived classes inherit, and can extend, the properties, methods, events, fields, and constants defined in the base class (the exception here are constructors, which are *not* inherited). For example, if you have a class named **Animal** that has a method named **Breathe** and then derive a class named **Dog** from **Animal**, **Dog** will already have the **Breathe** method built in.

By default, any class can serve as a base class unless you explicitly mark it with the **NotInheritable** keyword, as we'll see in this chapter. And in Visual Basic, you can inherit only from one base class, not more. As with Java, Visual Basic allows you to implement multiple *interfaces*, which we'll see in a few pages, and that can accomplish much that multiple inheritance could, but with more work on our part.

Let's take a look at an example, named Inheritance on the CD-ROM, that puts this into a practical light and will give us a good start on inheritance. In fact, here I'll implement the base class **Animal** and the derived class **Dog,** discussed earlier. I start by creating the **Animal** class. This class will have a method named **Breathing**, which displays the text "Breathing..." in a text box in the program's main Windows form. To get access to that form, I can pass that form to the constructor, **New**, which will store it as **MainForm**:

```
Public Class Animal
    Public MainForm As Form1

    Public Sub New(ByVal form1 As Form1)
        MainForm = form1
    End Sub
        .
        .
        .
End Class
```

Now, in **Breathing**, I can use **MainForm** to display the text "Breathing..." in a text box, **TextBox1**, in the main form:

```
Public Class Animal
    Public MainForm As Form1

    Public Sub New(ByVal form1 As Form1)
        MainForm = form1
    End Sub

    Public Sub Breathing()
        MainForm.TextBox1.Text = "Breathing..."
    End Sub
End Class
```

That's simple enough so far. Now I can derive a new class, **Dog**, from **Animal**—note the **Inherits** statement here:

```
Public Class Dog
    Inherits Animal
        .
        .
        .
End Class
```

However, this raises an issue—how do we pass the form to display text into the **Animal** class's constructor so it can store it in **MainForm**? In other words, when you create an object of the **Dog** class, how can you pass necessary data back to the base class's constructor? You can do that with the special **MyBase** keyword, which refers to the base class. This means I can call the base class's constructor as **MyBase.New**. Note that if you do call a base class's constructor, you must do so as the very first line (Visual Basic insists on this) in your derived class's constructor:

```
Public Class Dog
    Inherits Animal

    Public Sub New(ByVal form1 As Form1)
        MyBase.New(form1)
    End Sub
        .
        .
        .
End Class
```

Now the **Dog** class inherits everything the **Animal** class had, such as the **Breathing** method. In addition, it inherits the **MainForm** data member, so we can use that data member when we add a new method to **Dog**, **Barking**:

```
Public Class Dog
    Inherits Animal

    Public Sub New(ByVal form1 As Form1)
        MyBase.New(form1)
    End Sub

    Public Sub Barking()
        MainForm.TextBox1.Text = "Barking..."
    End Sub
End Class
```

In this way, we're augmenting and customizing the base class in the derived class; for example, now **Dog** supports a **Barking** method in addition to the **Breathing** method. To see the **Dog** class at work, I can create a new **Dog** object, passing its constructor the current form so it knows what form to display results in, and calling its **Breathing** method like this (recall that the **Me** keyword, which we first saw in Chapter 4, refers to the current form):

```
Public Class Form1
    Inherits System.Windows.Forms.Form

    'Windows Form Designer generated code
    Dim spot As Dog

    Private Sub Button1_Click(ByVal sender As System.Object, _
        ByVal e As System.EventArgs) Handles Button1.Click
        spot = New Dog(Me)
        spot.Breathing()
    End Sub
End Class
```

This is all in the Inheritance example on the CD-ROM; you can see it at work in Figure 12.1. When you click the "Create a dog..." button, the code creates a new **Dog** object, and the **Dog** class's constructor passes the main form back to the **Animal** base class. When you call the **Breathing** method, which is inherited from the base class, the program displays the text "Breathing..." in the main form, as you see in that figure. Now we're using inheritance.

As we've discussed as far back as Chapter 2, you can control the access that derived classes have to base class members by using *access modifiers*.

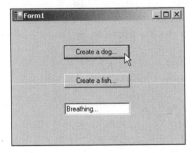

Figure 12.1   The Inheritance example on the CD-ROM.

Access Modifiers

We've been seeing access modifiers throughout the book. You use access modifiers when you declare a class, and when you declare the members of the class. Here they are (note that some of them, like **Protected**, are designed to be used only with inheritance):

- **Public**—Entities declared **Public** have public access. There are no restrictions on the accessibility of public entities. You can use **Public** only at module, namespace, or file level.

- **Protected**—Entities declared **Protected** have protected access. They are accessible only from within their own class or from a derived class. **Protected** access is not a superset of friend access. You can use **Protected** only at class level.

- **Friend**—Entities declared **Friend** have friend access. They are accessible from within the program that contains their declaration and from anywhere else in the same assembly. You can use **Friend** only at module, namespace, or file level.

- **Protected Friend**—Entities declared **Protected Friend** have both protected and friend access. They can be used by code in the same assembly, as well as by code in derived classes. The rules for **Protected** and **Friend** apply to **Protected Friend** as well.

- **Private**—Entities declared **Private** have private access. They are accessible only from within their declaration context, including from any nested procedures. You can use **Private** only at module, namespace, or file level.

Public base class members are available to derived classes and everywhere else, private members are available only in the current class—not in classes derived from that class—protected members are available only in the current class and classes derived from that class, and friend members are available throughout the current assembly. For example, note that I declared the **MainForm** data member in the **Animal** class as **Public**:

```
Public Class Animal
    Public MainForm As Form1

    Public Sub New(ByVal form1 As Form1)
        MainForm = form1
    End Sub
        .
        .
        .
End Class
```

However, this gives **MainForm** more scope than it needs, and it's contrary to the idea of encapsulation and data hiding in OOP, which says that objects should be as self-contained as possible (to avoid unintentional naming conflicts or illegal data access). There's no reason all parts of our code should have access to this variable, but classes derived from this class *will* need access to **MainForm**, so I make **MainForm** *protected*, which restricts its scope to the current class (**Animal**) and any classes derived from it (like **Dog**). This is how **MainForm** is actually declared in the Inheritance example on the CD-ROM:

```
Public Class Animal
    Protected MainForm As Form1

    Public Sub New(ByVal form1 As Form1)
        MainForm = form1
    End Sub
        .
        .
        .
End Class
```

Inheritance Modifiers

By default, all classes can serve as base classes in Visual Basic .NET. However, you can use two class-level modifiers, called inheritance modifiers, to modify that behavior:

- **NotInheritable**—Prevents a class being used as a base class.

- **MustInherit**—Indicates that the class is intended for use as a base class only.

Note that objects of **MustInherit** classes cannot be created directly; they can be created only as base class instances of a derived class.

We'll see both of these modifiers in this chapter.

Overloading, Overriding, and Shadowing

Overloading, overriding, and shadowing are also important concepts in Visual Basic OOP. These techniques allow you to create multiple members with the same name. We've already discussed them in the previous chapter; here's how they work in overview:

- *Overloaded*—Overloaded members provide different versions of a property or method that have the same name, but that accept different number of parameters (or parameters of different types).

- *Overridden*—Overridden properties and methods are used to replace an inherited property or method. When you override a member from a base class, you replace it. Overridden members must accept the same data type and number of arguments.

- *Shadowed*—Shadowed members are used to create a local version of a member that has broader scope. You also can shadow a type with any other type. For example, you can declare a property that shadows an inherited method with the same name.

We saw overloading in the previous chapter, although we'll have a little more to say about it here. In particular, there is an **Overloads** keyword that you can use to indicate that you're overloading a method or property. You don't need to use **Overloads** when you're overloading members of the same class, but it becomes important when you're working with inheritance—see "Overloading Base Class Members" in this chapter.

What's overriding? If an inherited property or method needs to behave differently in the derived class, it can be overridden; that is, you can define a new implementation of the method in the derived class. The following modifiers are used to control how properties and methods are overridden:

- **Overridable**—Allows a property or method in a class to be overridden.

- **Overrides**—Overrides an **Overridable** property or method.

- **NotOverridable**—Prevents a property or method from being overridden. Note that public methods are **NotOverridable** by default.

- **MustOverride**—Requires that a derived class override the property or method. **MustOverride** methods must be declared in **MustInherit** classes.

Let's see an example of overriding at work. In the Inheritance example on the CD-ROM, the base class is **Animal**, and when you call its **Breathing** method, it displays "Breathing...". However, if you were to derive a class named **Fish** from **Animal**, that wouldn't be quite appropriate—you might want this method to display something like "Bubbling..." instead. To do that, you can override the **Animal** class's **Breathing** method in the **Fish** class. All that takes is to mark the **Animal** class's **Breathing** method as **Overridable**, and to use the **Overrides** keyword when defining the **Breathing** method in the **Fish** class:

```
Public Class Animal
    Protected MainForm As Form1
    Public Sub New(ByVal form1 As Form1)
        MainForm = form1
    End Sub
```

```
    Public Overridable Sub Breathing()
        MainForm.TextBox1.Text = "Breathing..."
    End Sub
End Class

Public Class Fish
    Inherits Animal

    Public Sub New(ByVal form1 As Form1)
        MyBase.New(form1)
    End Sub

    Public Overrides Sub Breathing()
        MyBase.MainForm.TextBox1.Text = "Bubbling..."
    End Sub
End Class
```

Now I can declare a **Fish** object named **jaws** and when I use its overriden **Breathing** method, you'll see "Bubbling...", not "Breathing...":

```
    Dim jaws As Fish

    Private Sub Button2_Click(ByVal sender As System.Object, _
        ByVal e As System.EventArgs) Handles Button2.Click
        jaws = New Fish(Me)
        jaws.Breathing()
    End Sub
```

You can see this code at work in the Inheritance example on the CD-ROM in Figure 12.2.

Figure 12.2   Overriding a base class method in the Inheritance example.

Visual Basic Methods Are Virtual

Here's an interesting OOP fact—if you declare an object of the **Animal** class, you can assign any object of a class derived from **Animal**, such as the **Dog** class, to that object:

```
Dim obj As Animal

Private Sub Button2_Click(ByVal sender As System.Object, _
    ByVal e As System.EventArgs) Handles Button2.Click
    obj = New Dog(Me)
    .
    .
    .
End Sub
```

Now you can use all the **Animal** class's members with the **obj** object—but you can't use any members that **Dog** has that **Animal** doesn't (because **obj** is declared as an **Animal** object). For example, the **Dog** class implements its own **Barking** method, so Visual Basic won't let you use **obj.Barking**.

So what happens if you use a derived class that has overridden some base class members? For example, the **Fish** class overrides the **Animal** class's **Breathing** method, so if you use this code, will you see "Breathing..." or "Bubbling..."?

```
Dim obj As Animal

Private Sub Button2_Click(ByVal sender As System.Object, _
    ByVal e As System.EventArgs) Handles Button2.Click
    obj = New Fish(Me)
    obj.Breathing()
End Sub
```

Since **obj** is an **Animal** object, you might expect to see "Breathing...", but in fact, you'll see "Bubbling...". That's because all methods are *virtual* in Visual Basic OOP, which means that objects use the latest overridden method. In this case, that means the **Fish** class's **Breathing** method is used, not the **Animal** base class's **Breathing** method. (This fact forms the basis of *polymorphism*, which we'll also go into in this chapter.)

TIP: *If you are familiar with OOP, it might interest you to know that you also can create pure virtual methods, called* **abstract** *methods, with the Visual Basic* **MustInherit** *keyword. An abstract method can't be used in a base class, but must be implemented in a derived class.*

Creating Interfaces

Although a class can inherit only from one base class, it can *implement* multiple *interfaces*. As in Java, an interface is a *specification* for a set of class members—not an implementation, just a specification. There's an example on the CD-ROM named Interfaces to show how this works. In this example, I'll define an interface named **person** and implement that interface in a class named **employee** to show that implementing interfaces is a little like inheriting from a base class. First, I create the **person** interface with the **Interface** statement, indicating that this interface consists of two methods, **SetName** and **GetName**, which set and get the name of a person:

```
Public Interface person
    Sub SetName(ByVal PersonName As String)
    Function GetName() As String
End Interface
```

Notice that there's no implementation of these methods here, just their declarations. As mentioned above, all an interface does is specify members; when you implement the interface, you must implement all the members yourself. You do that with the **Implements** keyword (which must come after any **Inherits** statements and before any **Dim** statements in a class). Here's how I implement the **person** interface in a class named **employee**; note that I specify which class method implements which interface method using the **Implements** keyword:

```
Public Class employee
    Implements person
    Dim Name As String

    Sub SetName(ByVal PersonName As String) Implements person.SetName
        Name = PersonName
    End Sub

    Function GetName() As String Implements person.GetName
        Return Name
    End Function
End Class
```

Now I can create a new object of the **employee** class named **Edward**:

```
Public Class Form1
    Inherits System.Windows.Forms.Form

    'Windows Form Designer generated code
```

12. Object-Oriented Inheritance

```
    Private Sub Button1_Click(ByVal sender As System.Object, _
        ByVal e As System.EventArgs) Handles Button1.Click
        Dim Edward As New employee()
        Edward.SetName("Edward")
        TextBox1.Text = "You created " & Edward.GetName()
    End Sub
End Class
```

That's how the Interfaces example functions. You can see it at work in Figure 12.3, where the **Edward** object of the **employee** class is created when you click the "Create an employee..." button.

One class also can implement multiple interfaces, which is as close as you're going to come to multiple inheritance in Visual Basic (and it's not all that close). For example, in the Interfaces example, I define an interface named **executive** in addition to the **employee** example; the **executive** interface specifies these methods—**SetTitle**, **GetTitle**, **SetName**, and **GetName**—like this:

```
Public Interface person
    Sub SetName(ByVal PersonName As String)
    Function GetName() As String
End Interface

Public Interface executive
    Sub SetTitle(ByVal PersonName As String)
    Function GetTitle() As String
    Sub SetName(ByVal ExecutiveTitle As String)
    Function GetName() As String
End Interface
```

Now I can create a class that implements the **executive** interface, and I'll call it **vicepresident**. This class will implement both the **person** and **executive** inter-

Figure 12.3   Using an interface.

faces. Here's how it looks—note in particular that one method can implement multiple interface methods at the same time:

```
Public Class vicepresident
    Implements person, executive
    Dim Name As String
    Dim Title As String

    Sub SetTitle(ByVal ExecutiveTitle As String) Implements _
        executive.SetTitle
        Title = ExecutiveTitle
    End Sub

    Function GetTitle() As String Implements executive.GetTitle
        Return Title
    End Function

    Sub SetName(ByVal PersonName As String) Implements person.SetName, _
        executive.SetName
        Name = PersonName
    End Sub

    Function GetName() As String Implements person.GetName, _
        executive.GetName
        Return Name
    End Function
End Class
```

Now when the user clicks the "Create an executive..." button in the Interfaces example, I'll create a new **vicepresident** object named **Sam**, and set Sam's title to "vice president" like this:

```
Public Class Form1
    Inherits System.Windows.Forms.Form

    'Windows Form Designer generated code

    Private Sub Button2_Click(ByVal sender As System.Object, _
        ByVal e As System.EventArgs) Handles Button2.Click
        Dim Sam As New vicepresident()
        Sam.SetName("Sam")
        Sam.SetTitle("vice president")
        TextBox1.Text = "You created " & Sam.GetName() & ", " _
            & Sam.GetTitle ()
    End Sub
End Class
```

Figure 12.4   Using multiple interfaces.

When you click the "Create an executive…" button, the **Sam** object, which implements multiple interfaces, is created, as you see in Figure 12.4.

Polymorphism

Polymorphism is the ability to assume different forms. Polymorphism lets you assign objects of a derived class to variables of the class's base class; we've already seen that like this, where I've assigned an object of the **Dog** class (which is derived from **Animal**) to a variable of the **Animal** class (the **Dog** class's base class):

```
Dim obj As Animal

Private Sub Button2_Click(ByVal sender As System.Object, _
    ByVal e As System.EventArgs) Handles Button2.Click
    obj = New Dog(Me)
    obj.Breathing
    .
    .
    .
End Sub
```

Now I can use the **Animal** class's members with **obj**, even though I've stored a **Dog** class object in **obj**. I cannot, however, use any members that are not part of the **Animal** class with **obj**, such as **Barking**, which is a method added to **Animal** in the **Dog** class (unless the derived class has specifically overridden a base class's method or property, in which case Visual Basic will use the new, overriding version and not the base class version). This is useful, because, for example, you can use one routine to handle objects of a base class and all classes derived from that base class. There are two ways to handle polymorphism in Visual Basic—inheritance-based polymorphism, and interface-based polymorphism. I'll take a look at them here. (You can see both of these techniques in the Polymorphism example on the CD-ROM.)

Inheritance-based Polymorphism

Inheritance-based polymorphism works as we've already seen—you can store objects of a derived class in variables of that class's base class (but you can access only the base class's members using that variable, unless, as mentioned, a derived class has specifically overridden a base class's method or property). Here's how that works in the Polymorphism example on the CD-ROM; there, I declare the **Animal** class with a **Breathe** method that displays "Breathing..." in a message box, and derive a **Fish** class from **Animal** that overrides **Breathe** to display "Bubbling...":

```
Public Class Animal
    Overridable Sub Breathe()
        MsgBox("Breathing...")
    End Sub
End Class

Public Class Fish
    Inherits Animal
    Overrides Sub Breathe()
        MsgBox("Bubbling...")
    End Sub
End Class
```

Here's where the quality of polymorphism comes in handy; I can set up a Sub procedure named **Display** that takes an argument of the **Animal** class and invokes its **Breathe** method:

```
Public Sub Display(ByVal AnimalObject As Animal)
    AnimalObject.Breathe()
End Sub
```

Through polymorphism, I can call **Display** with objects of *either* the **Animal** or **Fish** class:

```
Public Class Form1
    Inherits System.Windows.Forms.Form

    'Windows Form Designer generated code

    Private Sub Button1_Click(ByVal sender As System.Object, _
        ByVal e As System.EventArgs) Handles Button1.Click
        Dim pet1 As New Animal()
        Dim pet2 As New Fish()
        Display(pet1)
        Display(pet2)
    End Sub
```

```
      Public Sub Display(ByVal AnimalObject As Animal)
          AnimalObject.Breathe()
      End Sub
  End Class
```

You can see the results in Figure 12.5 when you click the "Inheritance-based Polymorphism" button.

Interface-based Polymorphism

Interfaces provide another way you can accomplish polymorphism in Visual Basic .NET. To support polymorphism with interfaces, you create an interface and implement it in different ways in various classes. You can then invoke the implemented method of either kind of object in the same way. Here's how that works in the Polymorphism example on the CD-ROM; in this case, I create an interface named **AnimalInterface** with one method, **Breathe**, and implement that method in classes named **Animal2** and **Fish2**:

```
Public Interface AnimalInterface
    Sub Breathe()
End Interface

Public Class Animal2
    Implements AnimalInterface
    Sub Breathe() Implements AnimalInterface.Breathe
        MsgBox("Breathing...")
    End Sub
End Class

Public Class Fish2
    Implements AnimalInterface
    Sub Breathe() Implements AnimalInterface.Breathe
        MsgBox("Bubbling...")
    End Sub
End Class
```

Now I can use one method, **Display2**, to handle both **Animal** and **Fish** objects if I pass it an argument of the **AnimalInterface** type:

```
      Public Sub Display2(ByVal AnimalObject As AnimalInterface)
          AnimalObject.Breathe()
      End Sub
```

Here's how that looks in the Polymorphism example on the CD-ROM. In this case, when the user clicks the "Interface-based Polymorphism" button, the

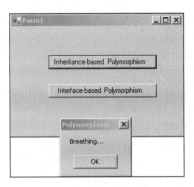

Figure 12.5   Using inheritance-based polymorphism.

code creates an **Animal2** object and a **Fish2** object, and calls **Display2** with both of them:

```
Public Class Form1
    Inherits System.Windows.Forms.Form

    'Windows Form Designer generated code

    Private Sub Button2_Click(ByVal sender As System.Object, _
        ByVal e As System.EventArgs) Handles Button2.Click
        Dim pet1 As New Animal2()
        Dim pet2 As New Fish2()
        Display2(pet1)
        Display2(pet2)
    End Sub

    Public Sub Display2(ByVal AnimalObject As AnimalInterface)
        AnimalObject.Breathe()
    End Sub
End Class
```

The results of this code look just as you see in Figure 12.5, showing that you can indeed produce a form of polymorphism with interfaces, not just straight inheritance.

Early and Late Binding

When you're using a variable of type **Object**, the processing of the expression it's in may be deferred until run time. Deferring processing this way is called *late binding*. This is in contrast to early binding, where Visual Basic knows what the type of an expression is going to be at compile time.

Late binding, on the other hand, allows **Object** variables to be used in a *typeless* way, because how the members are used is based on the runtime type of the value in the variable. In early binding, which is the norm, Visual Basic knows the type of objects it is working with—but if the object is late bound, it doesn't know the type until run time, which is useful, because you can use the code with different objects. In polymorphism, you specify the class of a variable before you use it, so Visual Basic at least knows what kind of class members will be available. (Keep in mind that if you use a variable of a base class and assign a derived class object to it, you can't use members only defined in the derived class.) Here, Visual Basic has no idea what kind of object will be used; it's all done at run time.

TIP: *If you use **Option Strict**, late binding will cause an error.*

You can see this in the LateBinding example on the CD-ROM. In this example, I create **Animal** and **Fish** classes, as we have before:

```
Public Class Animal
    Public Sub Breathe()
        MsgBox("Breathing...")
    End Sub
End Class

Public Class Fish
    Public Sub Breathe()
        MsgBox("Bubbling...")
    End Sub
End Class
```

Now I can pass objects of these classes to a Sub procedure named **Display**, treating the passed argument as an object of class **Object**. In **Display**, I'll call the passed object's **Breathe** method. Because Visual Basic will wait until run time to check if the pass object actually has a **Breathe** method, it can't tell you at design time if you're doing anything wrong, so I'll add a little exception handling just in case the passed object doesn't have a **Breathe** method:

```
    Private Sub Display(ByVal o As Object)
        Try
            o.Breathe()
        Catch
            MsgBox("Sorry, no Breathe method available.")
        End Try
    End Sub
```

Thanks to late binding, I can pass any kind of object to **Display**, and if that object has a **Breathe** method, that method will be invoked:

```
Public Class Form1
    Inherits System.Windows.Forms.Form

    'Windows Form Designer generated code

    Private Sub Button1_Click(ByVal sender As System.Object, _
        ByVal e As System.EventArgs) Handles Button1.Click
        Dim animal As New Animal()
        Dim jaws As New Fish()
        Display(animal)
        Display(jaws)
    End Sub

    Private Sub Display(ByVal o As Object)
        Try
            o.Breathe()
        Catch
            MsgBox("Sorry, no Breathe method available.")
        End Try
    End Sub
End Class
```

And that's how late binding works; I can use **Display** with any kind of object, not just those derived from some specific base class. (This actually works because all classes are derived from **Object** in Visual Basic.)

Now it's time to start looking into some of the more detailed aspects of what we've been discussing, and I'll do that in the Immediate Solutions section of this chapter.

Immediate Solutions

Inheriting from a Base Class

To inherit from a base class in a derived class, you use the Inherits statement, which makes the derived class inherit the attributes, fields, properties, methods, and events from the base class:

```
Inherits classname
```

Here, *classname* is required, and it's the name of a class being inherited by the class in which the **Inherits** statement is used. You use this statement first thing (before any other statement) in a derived class:

```
Public Class Form1
    Inherits System.Windows.Forms.Form
    .
    .
    .
```

As discussed in the In Depth section of this chapter, you can use access modifiers to indicate how the members of a base class will be inherited and what scope they will have. For more information, see the discussion at the beginning of the In Depth section of this chapter.

Related solution:	Found on page:
Creating Classes	492

Using **Public** Inheritance

When you make a member of a class public, there are no restrictions on its scope; it can be used by any part of your program. Public members in a base class become public members of a derived class by default. You make classes and members public with the **Public** keyword (see "Access Modifiers" in the In Depth section of this chapter), as I've done many places in the Inheritance example on the CD-ROM, also discussed in the In Depth section of this chapter:

```
Public Class Form1
    Inherits System.Windows.Forms.Form

    'Windows Form Designer generated code
    Dim spot As Dog

    Private Sub Button1_Click(ByVal sender As System.Object, _
        ByVal e As System.EventArgs) Handles Button1.Click
        spot = New Dog(Me)
        spot.Breathing()
    End Sub
End Class

Public Class Animal
    Protected MainForm As Form1
    Public Sub New(ByVal form1 As Form1)
        MainForm = form1
    End Sub

    Public Sub Breathing()
        MainForm.TextBox1.Text = "Breathing..."
    End Sub
End Class

Public Class Dog
    Inherits Animal

    Public Sub New(ByVal form1 As Form1)
        MyBase.New(form1)
    End Sub

    Public Sub Barking()
        MainForm.TextBox1.Text = "Barking..."
    End Sub
End Class
```

Using **Protected** Inheritance

When you declare a member of a base class protected, it's available throughout that class, and in any derived classes, but nowhere else. You can see an example of this in the Inheritance example on the CD-ROM, as discussed in the In Depth section of this chapter. In that example, I pass the main Windows form of the program to the **Animal** class's constructor (so that class can display text in the main window). That form is stored in the **Animal** class's **MainForm** variable. Because derived classes also will need to use **MainForm**, but no one else will, I made that variable protected (also discussed in the In Depth section of this chapter):

```
Public Class Form1
    Inherits System.Windows.Forms.Form

    'Windows Form Designer generated code
    Dim spot As Dog

    Private Sub Button1_Click(ByVal sender As System.Object, _
        ByVal e As System.EventArgs) Handles Button1.Click
        spot = New Dog(Me)
        spot.Breathing()
    End Sub
End Class

Public Class Animal
    Protected MainForm As Form1
    Public Sub New(ByVal form1 As Form1)
        MainForm = form1
    End Sub

    Public Sub Breathing()
        MainForm.TextBox1.Text = "Breathing..."
    End Sub
End Class

Public Class Dog
    Inherits Animal

    Public Sub New(ByVal form1 As Form1)
        MyBase.New(form1)
    End Sub
```

```
    Public Sub Barking()
        MainForm.TextBox1.Text = "Barking..."
    End Sub
End Class
```

Using **Private** Inheritance

If you make a class member private, it's available only in the present class—not outside that class, and not in any class derived from that class. For example, if I made the **MainForm** member of the **Animal** class private in the Inheritance example on the CD-ROM, as discussed in the previous topic and in the In Depth section of this chapter, then that member would not be available in the derived class named **Dog**. That means this code wouldn't work, because I've made **MainForm** private but tried to use it in the derived **Dog** class (note also that the button event handlers are **private** in the **Form1** class, which means they can't be used in any class derived from **Form1**):

```
Public Class Form1
    Inherits System.Windows.Forms.Form

    'Windows Form Designer generated code

    Dim spot As Dog
    Dim jaws As Fish

    Private Sub Button1_Click(ByVal sender As System.Object, _
        ByVal e As System.EventArgs) Handles Button1.Click
        spot = New Dog(Me)
        spot.Breathing()
    End Sub

    Private Sub Button2_Click(ByVal sender As System.Object, _
        ByVal e As System.EventArgs) Handles Button2.Click
        jaws = New Fish(Me)
        jaws.Breathing()
    End Sub
End Class

Public Class Animal
    Private MainForm As Form1
    Public Sub New(ByVal form1 As Form1)
        MainForm = form1
    End Sub
```

```
        Public Overridable Sub Breathing()
            MainForm.TextBox1.Text = "Breathing..."
        End Sub
End Class

Public Class Dog
    Inherits Animal

    Public Sub New(ByVal form1 As Form1)
        MyBase.New(form1)
    End Sub

    Public Sub Barking()
        MainForm.TextBox1.Text = "Barking..."    'Will not work now!!!
    End Sub
End Class

Public Class Fish
    Inherits Animal

    Public Sub New(ByVal form1 As Form1)
        MyBase.New(form1)
    End Sub

    Public Overrides Sub Breathing()
        MainForm.TextBox1.Text = "Bubbling..."
    End Sub
End Class
```

Note that if you declare a class **Private**, all the members in it are restricted to
that class.

Using Friend Access

The scope of public members is unlimited, but you also can give members friend
scope, which restricts them to the current program (that is, the program that
contains their declaration) and anywhere else in the same assembly (public members, by contrast, are available across assemblies). You can use the **Friend** keyword in these statements:

- **Class** Statement
- **Const** Statement
- **Declare** Statement

- **Dim** Statement

- **Enum** Statement

- **Event** Statement

- **Function** Statement

- **Interface** Statement

- **Module** Statement

- **Property** Statement

- **Structure** Statement

- **Sub** Statement

You can declare friend access just like any other access modifier; here's an example:

```
Public Class Displayer
    Friend Sub Display(ByVal Text As String)
        MsgBox(Text)
    End Sub
End Class


Dim displayer As New displayer()
Private Sub Button1_Click(ByVal sender As System.Object, _
    ByVal e As System.EventArgs) Handles Button1.Click
    displayer.Display("Hello from Visual Basic!")
End Sub
```

Overriding Base Class Members

As discussed in the In Depth section of this chapter, when you inherit from a base class, you can override (replace) base class members in the derived class. We saw how that worked in the In Depth section of this chapter with the Inheritance example from the CD-ROM with the **Fish** class, which overrode the **Animal** base class's **Breathe** method. The **Animal** class's **Breathe** method displayed "Breathing..." but the **Fish** class's version displayed "Bubbling...". I have to make the **Animal** class's version overridable with the **Overridable** keyword and indicate that the **Fish** class's version is overriding it by using the **Overrides** keyword:

```
Public Class Form1
    Inherits System.Windows.Forms.Form

    'Windows Form Designer generated code
```

```
        Dim jaws As Fish
                .
                .
                .

        Private Sub Button2_Click(ByVal sender As System.Object, _
            ByVal e As System.EventArgs) Handles Button2.Click
            jaws = New Fish(Me)
            jaws.Breathing()
        End Sub
    End Class


    Public Class Animal
        Protected MainForm As Form1
        Public Sub New(ByVal form1 As Form1)
            MainForm = form1
        End Sub

        Public Overridable Sub Breathing()
            MainForm.TextBox1.Text = "Breathing..."
        End Sub
    End Class
                .
                .
                .

    Public Class Fish
        Inherits Animal

        Public Sub New(ByVal form1 As Form1)
            MyBase.New(form1)
        End Sub

        Public Overrides Sub Breathing()
            MyBase.MainForm.TextBox1.Text = "Bubbling..."
        End Sub
    End Class
```

You can see the result in Figure 12.2, where the Fish class's Breathe method is displaying "Bubbling...". Don't confuse overriding, which replaces a base class member, with overloading, which we saw in Chapter 11; overloading lets you use different argument lists with methods and properties.

Related solution:	*Found on page:*
Overloading Methods and Properties	513

Inheriting Constructors

By default, constructors are *not* inherited in Visual Basic. The idea here is that initializing a derived class's object will be different from initializing an object of the base class, so you're responsible for creating your own constructor in derived classes, if you want to give them one.

TIP: *Here's an important point—if you give a derived class a constructor, and the base class does not have an explicit constructor that you can call with no arguments, Visual Basic will insist that you call the base class's constructor first thing in the derived class.*

We saw an example of using constructors and inheritance in the Inheritance example on the CD-ROM, as discussed in the In Depth section of this chapter. In that case, I'm deriving the **Dog** class from the **Animal** class. The **Animal** class has a constructor that accepts a form, the main form for the program, and stores it in a protected member named **MainForm**. To pass that form from the **Dog** class's constructor back to the **Animal** class's constructor, I called the **Animal** class's constructor as **MyBase.New** (see the In Depth section of this chapter for more information):

```
Public Class Form1
    Inherits System.Windows.Forms.Form

    'Windows Form Designer generated code

    Dim spot As Dog

    Private Sub Button1_Click(ByVal sender As System.Object, _
        ByVal e As System.EventArgs) Handles Button1.Click
        spot = New Dog(Me)
        spot.Breathing()
    End Sub
End Class

Public Class Animal
    Protected MainForm As Form1

    Public Sub New(ByVal form1 As Form1)
        MainForm = form1
    End Sub

    Public Sub Breathing()
        MainForm.TextBox1.Text = "Breathing..."
```

```
            End Sub
    End Class

    Public Class Dog
        Inherits Animal

        Public Sub New(ByVal form1 As Form1)
            MyBase.New(form1)
        End Sub

        Public Sub Barking()
            MyBase.MainForm.TextBox1.Text = "Barking..."
        End Sub
    End Class
```

Note that if you do call a base class's constructor from a derived class's constructor, that call must be the first line in the derived class's constructor.

Overloading Base Class Members

As mentioned earlier, we took a look at overloading methods and properties in Chapter 11; however, there's more to this subject when inheritance enters the picture. You can use the **Overloads** keyword to indicate that you're overloading a method or property; that keyword isn't necessary when you're overloading a method or property in the same class, but it is when you're overloading a method or property from another class, such as a base class. In that case, you must use the **Overloads** keyword, as in this example, where I'm overloading the **Animal** class's **Breathe** method, which takes no arguments, in the **Fish** class, creating a version that you can pass text to:

```
    Private Sub Button2_Click(ByVal sender As System.Object, _
        ByVal e As System.EventArgs) Handles Button2.Click
        jaws = New Fish(Me)
        jaws.Breathing("Bubbling...")
    End Sub

Public Class Fish
    Inherits Animal

    Public Sub New(ByVal form1 As Form1)
        MyBase.New(form1)
    End Sub
```

```
      Public Overloads Sub Breathing(ByVal Text As String)
          MyBase.MainForm.TextBox1.Text = Text
      End Sub
End Class
```

Related solution:	*Found on page:*
Overloading Methods and Properties	513

Creating Interfaces

As discussed in the In Depth section of this chapter, interfaces can act as specifications for class members; when you implement an interface, you also must implement all the specified members. There's an example on the CD-ROM named Interfaces that shows how this works; in this case, I create an interface named **person** that specifies two members: **SetName** and **GetName**. Then I implement that interface in a class named **employee** with the **Implements** keyword (which must come after **Inherits** statements and before any **Dim** statements):

```
Public Interface person
    Sub SetName(ByVal PersonName As String)
    Function GetName() As String
End Interface

Public Class employee
    Implements person
    Dim Name As String

    Sub SetName(ByVal PersonName As String) Implements person.SetName
        Name = PersonName
    End Sub

    Function GetName() As String Implements person.GetName
        Return Name
    End Function
End Class
```

Now I can create an object of the **employee** class and use it in code, as you see in the Interfaces example:

```
Public Class Form1
    Inherits System.Windows.Forms.Form
```

```
'Windows Form Designer generated code

Private Sub Button1_Click(ByVal sender As System.Object, _
    ByVal e As System.EventArgs) Handles Button1.Click
    Dim Edward As New employee()
    Edward.SetName("Edward")
    TextBox1.Text = "You created " & Edward.GetName()
End Sub
End Class
```

You can see the results of this code in Figure 12.3.

Using Multiple Interfaces

As discussed in the In Depth section of this chapter, Visual Basic does not support multiple inheritance, where you inherit from multiple base classes at the same time. Like Java, however, Visual Basic lets you implement multiple interfaces at the same time, which is a dressed-down version of multiple inheritance. We saw this in the Interfaces example in the In Depth section of this chapter; in this example, we constructed two interfaces, **person** and **executive**:

```
Public Interface person
    Sub SetName(ByVal PersonName As String)
    Function GetName() As String
End Interface

Public Interface executive
    Sub SetTitle(ByVal PersonName As String)
    Function GetTitle() As String
    Sub SetName(ByVal ExecutiveTitle As String)
    Function GetName() As String
End Interface
```

Then I implemented these interfaces in a class named **vicepresident**—note that one method can implement multiple interface methods:

```
Public Class vicepresident
    Implements person, executive
    Dim Name As String
    Dim Title As String
```

```
    Sub SetTitle(ByVal ExecutiveTitle As String) Implements _
        executive.SetTitle
        Title = ExecutiveTitle
    End Sub

    Function GetTitle() As String Implements executive.GetTitle
        Return Title
    End Function

    Sub SetName(ByVal PersonName As String) Implements _
        person.SetName, executive.SetName
        Name = PersonName
    End Sub

    Function GetName() As String Implements person.GetName, _
        executive.GetName
        Return Name
    End Function
End Class
```

I used this new **vicepresident** class in the Interfaces example, like this:

```
Public Class Form1
    Inherits System.Windows.Forms.Form

    'Windows Form Designer generated code

    Private Sub Button2_Click(ByVal sender As System.Object, _
        ByVal e As System.EventArgs) Handles Button2.Click
        Dim Sam As New vicepresident()
        Sam.SetName("Sam")
        Sam.SetTitle("vice president")
        TextBox1.Text = "You created " & Sam.GetName() & ", " & _
            Sam.GetTitle ()
    End Sub
End Class
```

You can see the results of this code in Figure 12.4.

Using the **MustInherit** Keyword (Creating Abstract Classes)

The **MustInherit** keyword is used to declare a class that cannot be instantiated and can be used only as a base class, also called an *abstract base class*. For example, in the Inheritance example on the CD-ROM, I derive two classes, **Fish** and **Dog**, from the **Animal** class. To make **Animal** an abstract class, all I have to do is to use the **MustInherit** keyword:

```
Public MustInherit Class Animal
    Protected MainForm As Form1
    Public Sub New(ByVal form1 As Form1)
        MainForm = form1
    End Sub

    Public Overridable Sub Breathing()
        MainForm.TextBox1.Text = "Breathing..."
    End Sub
End Class

Public Class Dog
    Inherits Animal
        .
        .
        .
End Class

Public Class Fish
    Inherits Animal
        .
        .
        .
End Class
```

Using **MustOverride, Overridable,** and **NotOverridable**

You can specify if class members must be overridden, can be overridden, or may not be overridden, using the **MustOverride**, **Overridable**, and **NotOverridable** keywords, respectively. We've already see in the In Depth section of this chapter in the Inheritance example how to use the **Overridable** keyword to indicate that a method may be overridden:

```
Public Overridable Sub Breathing()
    MainForm.TextBox1.Text = "Breathing..."
End Sub
```

```
Public Overrides Sub Breathing()
    MainForm.TextBox1.Text = "Bubbling..."
End Sub
```

You also can use **MustOverride** to indicate that derived classes must provide their own implementation of a method:

```
Public MustOverride Overridable Sub Breathing()
    MainForm.TextBox1.Text = "Breathing..."
End Sub
```

Using **MustOverride** creates pure **virtual**, also called **abstract**, methods. These methods may not be used directly, but must be overridden; for example, a method that returns the programmer's name must be customized and is best created as an **abstract** method.

You also can indicate that a method may not be overridden (as for a method that returns copyright information) using the **NotOverridable** keyword:

```
Public NotOverridable Sub Breathing()
    MainForm.TextBox1.Text = "Breathing..."
End Sub
```

Creating Shadowing

What's shadowing all about? It turns out that you can have programming elements in the same module, class, or structure with the same name but different scope. When you have two such elements, and the code refers to the name they share, the compiler uses the element with the narrower, closer scope. This is known as *shadowing*.

For example, imagine that a module defines a public variable named **Data**, and a procedure inside the module declares a local variable also named **Data**. When you use the name **Data** in the procedure, you use the local variable, but references to **Data** outside the procedure use the public variable. Here, the procedure-level variable **Data** shadows the module-level variable **Data**.

If a derived class redefines an element from a base class, the redefined element shadows the original element. When you access a shadowed element in a derived class, you can do so by qualifying its name with **Me**. If your derived class shadows the element in the base class, you can access the base class element by qualifying it **MyBase**. How do you redefine elements this way? You use the **Shadows** keyword:

```
Shadows element
```

Here, *element* is the name of the class member being shadowed. Here's an example. In this case, I'm declaring a data member in a base class, **Pi**, that is shadowed by a property of the same name in a derived class—note the use of the **Shadows** keyword:

```
Class Class1
    Public Pi As Double = 3.1415926535
End Class

Class Class2
    Inherits Class1

    Public Shadows ReadOnly Property Pi() As Double
        Get
            Return 3.1415926535
        End Get
    End Property
End Class
```

Using the **MyBase** Keyword

You can use the **MyBase** keyword to access methods in a base class when overriding methods in a derived class. For example, suppose you are designing a derived class that overrides a method inherited from the base class; in this case, the overridden method can call the original method in the base class using **MyBase**. We've already seen this at work in the Inheritance example on the CD-ROM, as discussed in the In Depth section of this chapter, where I'm calling a base class's constructor from a derived class:

```
Public Sub New(ByVal form1 As Form1)
    MyBase.New(form1)
End Sub
```

TIP: Note that **MyBase** is a keyword and not an object, so you can't assign it to a variable. And, of course, you can't use it to access private members of a base class. Nor can you use **MyBase** in modules.

Using the **MyClass** Keyword

The **MyClass** keyword lets you call an **overridable** method in your class while making sure that implementation of the method in your class is called instead of an overridden version of the method. Clear as mud, right? Here's an example—say that you have a class **Animal** with a method named **Breathing** that displays "Breathing..." in a message box:

```
Public Class Animal
    Overridable Sub Breathing()
        MsgBox("Breathing...")
    End Sub
End Class
```

Now suppose you have a method in **Animal** named, say, **Live**, that calls **Breathing**:

```
Public Class Animal
    Sub Live()
        Breathing()
    End Sub

    Overridable Sub Breathing()
        MsgBox("Breathing...")
    End Sub
End Class
```

So far, there's no problem. However, what if you derive a class named **Fish** from **Animal**, and **Fish** overrides **Breathing** with its own version:

```
Public Class Fish
    Inherits Animal

    Overrides Sub Breathing()
        MsgBox("Bubbling...")
    End Sub
End Class
```

Now, when you create a **Fish** object and call the **Live** method, the new overriding version of **Breathing** will be called, not the original version from the **Animal** class. To call the original version in the **Animal** class, you can use **MyClass.Breathing** in the **Animal** class, which I do in a new method named **Live2**:

```
Public Class Animal
    Sub Live()
```

```
        Breathing()
    End Sub

    Sub Live2()
        MyClass.Breathing()
    End Sub

    Overridable Sub Breathing()
        MsgBox("Breathing...")
    End Sub
End Class
```

This is all part of the MyClass example on the CD-ROM; there are two buttons in that example, "Call Breathing" and "Call MyClass.Breathing"; here's how those buttons work:

```
Public Class Form1
    Inherits System.Windows.Forms.Form

    'Windows Form Designer generated code

    Dim jaws As New Fish()
    Private Sub Button1_Click(ByVal sender As System.Object, _
        ByVal e As System.EventArgs) Handles Button1.Click
        jaws.Live()
    End Sub

    Private Sub Button2_Click(ByVal sender As System.Object, _
        ByVal e As System.EventArgs) Handles Button2.Click
        jaws.Live2()
    End Sub
End Class
```

You can see the **MyClass** example at work in Figure 12.6. When you click the "Call Breathing" button, you'll see "Bubbling..." and when you click "Call MyClass.Breathing", you'll see "Breathing...".

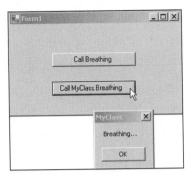

Figure 12.6   Using the **MyClass** keyword.

Inheritance-based Polymorphism

As discussed in the In Depth section of this chapter, polymorphism is a process that lets you store objects of a derived class in variables of a base class. You cannot, however, access any members not in the base class using the derived class variable. (The exception is that if the derived class overrides a base class method or property, the overriding method or property will be used.) The usual way to implement polymorphism is with inheritance. You can see this illustrated in the Polymorphism example on the CD-ROM, as covered in the In Depth section of this chapter. In that example, I create a class named **Animal** and derive a class, **Fish**, from it:

```
Public Class Animal
    Overridable Sub Breathe()
        MsgBox("Breathing...")
    End Sub
End Class

Public Class Fish
    Inherits Animal
    Overrides Sub Breathe()
        MsgBox("Bubbling...")
    End Sub
End Class
```

I also create a method named **Display** that you pass an object of the **Animal** class to:

```
    Public Sub Display(ByVal AnimalObject As Animal)
        AnimalObject.Breathe()
    End Sub
```

Because of polymorphism, we saw that you can pass objects of either **Animal** or **Fish** to the **Display** method:

```
Public Class Form1
    Inherits System.Windows.Forms.Form

    'Windows Form Designer generated code

    Private Sub Button1_Click(ByVal sender As System.Object, _
        ByVal e As System.EventArgs) Handles Button1.Click
        Dim pet1 As New Animal()
        Dim pet2 As New Fish()
        Display(pet1)
        Display(pet2)
    End Sub

    Public Sub Display(ByVal AnimalObject As Animal)
        AnimalObject.Breathe()
    End Sub
End Class
```

You can see this program at work in Figure 12.5; for more details, see the In Depth section of this chapter.

Interface-based Polymorphism

As also discussed in the In Depth section of this chapter, interfaces provide another way you can support polymorphism in Visual Basic .NET. To implement polymorphism with interfaces, you create an interface and implement it in a number of other classes. You can then invoke the implemented method of the various objects you create in the same way. Here's how that works in the Polymorphism example on the CD-ROM; in this case, I create an interface named **AnimalInterface** with one method, **Breathe**, and implement that method in classes named **Animal2** and **Fish2**:

```
Public Class Form1
    Inherits System.Windows.Forms.Form

    'Windows Form Designer generated code

    Private Sub Button2_Click(ByVal sender As System.Object, _
        ByVal e As System.EventArgs) Handles Button2.Click
        Dim pet1 As New Animal2()
```

```
        Dim pet2 As New Fish2()
        Display2(pet1)
        Display2(pet2)
    End Sub

    Public Sub Display2(ByVal AnimalObject As AnimalInterface)
        AnimalObject.Breathe()
    End Sub
End Class

Public Interface AnimalInterface
    Sub Breathe()
End Interface

Public Class Animal2
    Implements AnimalInterface
    Sub Breathe() Implements AnimalInterface.Breathe
        MsgBox("Breathing...")
    End Sub
End Class

Public Class Fish2
    Implements AnimalInterface
    Sub Breathe() Implements AnimalInterface.Breathe
        MsgBox("Bubbling...")
    End Sub
End Class
```

For more details, see the In Depth section of this chapter.

Early and Late Binding

As discussed in the In Depth section of this chapter, when the target of an expression is of type **Object**, the processing of the expression may be deferred until run time. Deferring processing this way is called *late binding*. In early binding, which is the norm, Visual Basic knows the type of an expression at compile time, but in late binding, the type of an expression isn't known until run time. As we saw in the In Depth section of this chapter, using the example called LateBinding on the CD-ROM, you can create a base class and a derived class this way:

```
Public Class Animal
    Public Sub Breathe()
        MsgBox("Breathing...")
```

```
        End Sub
End Class

Public Class Fish
    Public Sub Breathe()
        MsgBox("Bubbling...")
    End Sub
End Class
```

Then you can pass objects of either of these classes to a method if you use an argument of class **Object**:

```
Private Sub Display(ByVal o As Object)
    Try
        o.Breathe()
    Catch
        MsgBox("Sorry, no Breathe method available.")
    End Try
End Sub
```

Here's how this works in the LateBinding example:

```
Public Class Form1
    Inherits System.Windows.Forms.Form

    'Windows Form Designer generated code

    Private Sub Button1_Click(ByVal sender As System.Object, _
        ByVal e As System.EventArgs) Handles Button1.Click
        Dim animal As New Animal()
        Dim jaws As New Fish()
        Display(animal)
        Display(jaws)
    End Sub

    Private Sub Display(ByVal o As Object)
        Try
            o.Breathe()
        Catch
            MsgBox("Sorry, no Breathe method available.")
        End Try
    End Sub
End Class
```

For more on how this example works, take a look at the In Depth section of the chapter.

Chapter 13

Graphics and File Handling

In Depth

In this chapter, we're going to take a look at two popular topics: graphics handling and file handling, both of which have changed since VB6. In VB6 and before, for example, graphics support was spread throughout, and you could use the graphics methods of forms and picture boxes as needed. Now, as with Java, the graphics capability has been lumped together into huge classes, primarily the **Graphics** class. Among other things, this means that the cherished **AutoRedraw** property of forms, which made forms redraw themselves if needed (as when they're uncovered or restored from being minimized) has been stripped out of Visual Basic entirely. This in turn means that redrawing forms is all up to you again (see "Repainting Windows" in this chapter). And, also as with Java, file handling is now based on *streams* in Visual Basic, and is handled with various stream classes. Streams refer to "streams" of data, which may be redirected in various ways. Although Java uses streams, they're probably not going to make life easier for the programmer trying to upgrade to VB .NET from VB6 who already has a lot to contend with, especially as all the old file handling support has been taken out of Visual Basic now.

Graphics Handling

The graphics handling in Visual Basic.NET is based on GDI+ (GDI stands for Graphics Device Interface). A graphics device interface such as GDI+ allows you to display graphics on a screen—or a printer—without having to handle the details of a specific display device. You make calls to methods supported by the GDI+ classes and those methods make the corresponding calls to individual device drivers as needed to handle the screen or printer.

GCI+ support covers these categories:

- 2D vector graphics
- Imaging
- Typography

2D Vector Graphics

Vector graphics are all about drawing "primitive" shapes such as lines, curves, and other similar figures. As you might recall from physics classes, vectors are line segments that have both a length and a direction, and in graphics, you can build more complicated figures, such as rectangles, using these line segments. Everything in 2D graphics is drawn with vectors (which is to say, with line segments) that can be assembled into squares and rectangles and even curves and circles. For example, to draw a rectangle, you need only supply the upper-left corner of the rectangle in X and Y coordinates, and the height and width of the rectangle.

In Visual Basic 2D graphics, the drawing origin (0, 0) is at the upper left of the drawing surface; the positive X axis extends to the right and the positive Y axis downward, much like the way you'd read text on a page (and don't forget that all measurements are in pixels). Using that coordinate system, you can indicate to the vector graphics classes how you want your lines, ellipses, rectangles, and other figures to appear.

GDI+ also supports a **Pen** class that specifies just how you draw figures. In particular, you can customize pens, specifying line color, line width, and line style. When you draw a figure—such as an ellipse—you must create and provide a **Pen** object that GDI+ will use to draw that ellipse.

TIP: *Actually, you don't have to create a **Pen** object from scratch when you want to draw anything—you can use one of the predefined pens in the **Pens** class. See "Using the **Pens** and **Brushes** Classes" later in this chapter.*

Similarly, GDI+ supports a **Brush** class that you can use to fill the figures you've drawn in, as when you want to fill a rectangle or polygon with color. The **Brush** class is actually an abstract class; instead of using it directly, you use one of the classes derived from it:

- **HatchBrush**
- **LinearGradientBrush**
- **PathGradientBrush**
- **SolidBrush**
- **TextureBrush**

TIP: *As with the **Pens** class, there are a number of predefined solid color brushes in the **Brushes** class. See "Using the **Pens** and **Brushes** Classes" later in this chapter.*

However, vector graphics—even the complex Bézier curves that you can now create—are based fundamentally on connecting points with lines, and they're not useful for images. For that, you use the **Bitmap** class.

13. Graphics and File Handling

Imaging

Imagine trying to draw the kind of pictures you see in digital photographs or even icons with vector graphics—you could do it, but assembling such images from lines and curves would be just about impossible. Instead, you store those kinds of images as *bitmaps*, which are simple arrays of points (although they may be compressed when stored on disk) corresponding to pixels on the screen. In other words, bitmaps store the actual pixel settings needed to display the corresponding image.

Handling and working with such bitmaps is actually more complex than simply working with vector graphics, so GDI+ supports the **Bitmap** class, with all kinds of built-in methods to display and handle images.

Typography

Typography is all about displaying text. GDI+ has a lot of support for typography, allowing you to display text using various different fonts, in various sizes, and in various styles (such as italic and bold), as well as in different colors. The typography supported by GDI+ also supports a technique now called *antialiasing*, which makes text appear smoother on the screen, avoiding the jagged edges of text that used to be typical in the early days of personal computing.

The Graphics Class

We'll be working with GDI+ through the Visual Basic **Graphics** class. Working directly with GDI+ is pretty abstract, and the **Graphics** class gives us a drawing surface that we can work with instead. The actual methods we'll be using here, such as **DrawRectangle**, **DrawImage**, and **FillEllipse**, are all methods of the **Graphics** class.

As in Java, the **Graphics** class is a large class, with many methods available to use. In fact, we've already seen this class at work back in Chapter 8, where we scrolled images (see "Scrolling Images" in that chapter's Immediate Solutions section). Now that we're working with the **Graphics** class explicitly, I'll take another look at that example in this chapter. And we'll see how to draw and fill figures in here.

Drawing 2D Figures with Graphics Methods

Drawing 2D figures involves two steps—getting a **Graphics** object for the object you want to draw in (such as a form or picture box), and using the methods of that **Graphics** object to draw the figures you want. You can get a **Graphics** object in two ways—by using one that was passed to you or by creating one from scratch. For example, if you want to draw in a form, you'll get a graphics object in a handler procedure for the form's **Paint** event. This event occurs when the form needs to be drawn (or redrawn) for any reason. However, you might want more control than that, and might not want to wait until the form needs to be drawn or redrawn before displaying your graphics, in which case you can create a **Graphics** object with the form's **CreateGraphics** method. (This is a method of the **Control** class, so it works with all Windows forms and Windows controls.) Here's how that might look in code:

```
Dim g As Graphics

Private Sub Form1_Load(ByVal sender As System.Object, _
    ByVal e As System.EventArgs) Handles MyBase.Load
    g = Me.CreateGraphics()
End Sub
```

TIP: *It's important to realize that you can't draw graphics in a form from its **Load** event, because the form's drawing surface hasn't been created yet. You must use the **Paint** event instead of the **Load** event.*

For example, we're going to create an example named Painter in this chapter that lets you select what graphics figure to draw and then lets you draw that figure with the mouse. You can see the Painter example in Figure 13.1.

Here's how Painter works in overview (we'll see it in more detail in the Immediate Solutions section of this chapter—see "Drawing Figures with Pens")—when you press the mouse button, Painter stores the location of the mouse:

```
Private Sub Form1_MouseDown(ByVal sender As Object, _
    ByVal e As System.Windows.Forms.MouseEventArgs) Handles _
    MyBase.MouseDown
    down = New Point(e.X, e.Y)
End Sub
```

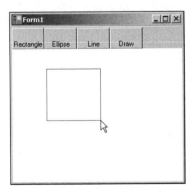

Figure 13.1   The Painter example.

Then you move the mouse to a new location, and when you release the mouse button, Painter will draw the figure you've chosen (lines, rectangles, ellipses, and so on). To do that, it stores the location at which the mouse button went up, then creates a rectangle enclosing the figure with the **Rectangle** class (note the use of **Math.Min** and **Math.Abs** to find the upper-left corner, width, and height of the rectangle):

```
Private Sub Form1_MouseUp(ByVal sender As Object, _
    ByVal e As System.Windows.Forms.MouseEventArgs) _
    Handles MyBase.MouseUp
    up = New Point(e.X, e.Y)
    r = New Rectangle(Math.Min(up.X, down.X), _
        Math.Min(up.Y, down.Y), Math.Abs(up.X - down.X), _
        Math.Abs(up.Y - down.Y))
    .
    .
    .
```

Now all we have to do is to pass that rectangle (or, if we're drawing lines, the beginning and ending points of the line) to the **DrawRectangle**, **DrawEllipse**, or **DrawLine** method. How do we determine what kind of figure to draw? When you click a button in the toolbar you see in Figure 13.1 to select a particular drawing tool (such as the line drawing tool, the rectangle drawing tool, and so on), the Painter program assigns a variable named **Tool** a value from the **Tools** enumeration that we'll create. Then, we need only check the value in **Tool** and draw the corresponding figure—note here that I'm using the predefined **BlueViolet** pen from the **Pens** class to draw with:

```
Private Sub Form1_MouseUp(ByVal sender As Object, _
    ByVal e As System.Windows.Forms.MouseEventArgs) _
        Handles MyBase.MouseUp
    up = New Point(e.X, e.Y)
    r = New Rectangle(Math.Min(up.X, down.X), Math.Min(up.Y, down.Y), _
        Math.Abs(up.X - down.X), Math.Abs(up.Y - down.Y))

    Select Case Tool
        Case Tools.Rectangle
            g.DrawRectangle(Pens.BlueViolet, r)
        Case Tools.Ellipse
            g.DrawEllipse(Pens.BlueViolet, r)
        Case Tools.Line
            g.DrawLine(Pens.BlueViolet, up, down)
    End Select
End Sub
```

You can see the result in Figure 13.1, where I'm drawing a rectangle—now we're drawing in Windows forms.

Filling in 2D Figures with Graphics Methods

In this chapter, you also will see how to fill in figures with brushes. To fill in a figure with a brush, you use methods like **FillEllipse**, **FillRectangle**, and so on. You can see this at work in the FillGraphics example on the CD-ROM, where I'm filling in four circles using various brushes, as you see in Figure 13.2.

There are various brush classes you can use, all derived from the **Brush** class. The **FillGraphics** example uses the **LinearGradientBrush**, **HatchBrush**, **SolidBrush**, and **TextureBrush** classes. To use these classes, you import the **System.Drawing.Drawing2D** namespace. Here's what this example looks like in code—note that the texture brush uses an image to fill a figure. In this case, I'm using the greenstone.bmp image that comes with Windows 2000:

```
Imports System.Drawing.Drawing2D
Public Class Form1
    Inherits System.Windows.Forms.Form

    'Windows Form Designer generated code

    Private Sub Form1_Paint(ByVal sender As Object, _
        ByVal e As System.Windows.Forms.PaintEventArgs) _
        Handles MyBase.Paint
        Dim g As Graphics
        Dim r As Rectangle
        g = Me.CreateGraphics()

        r = New Rectangle(20, 20, 60, 60)
        Dim lb As New LinearGradientBrush( _
            r, Color.Red, Color.Yellow, LinearGradientMode.Horizontal)
        g.FillEllipse(lb, r)

        r = New Rectangle(20, 100, 60, 60)
        Dim hb As New HatchBrush(HatchStyle.DarkDownwardDiagonal, _
            Color.LightBlue)
        g.FillEllipse(hb, r)

        r = New Rectangle(100, 20, 60, 60)
        Dim sb As New SolidBrush(Color.Coral)
        g.FillEllipse(sb, r)

        r = New Rectangle(100, 100, 60, 60)
        Dim tb As New TextureBrush(Bitmap.FromFile("greenstone.bmp"))
        g.FillEllipse(tb, r)
    End Sub
End Class
```

Figure 13.2   Filling in figures using brushes.

You can see the results in Figure 13.2. Using brushes like these, especially texture brushes and linear gradient brushes, can give your program a professional appearance.

File Handling

We'll also take a look at general Visual Basic file handling in this chapter. In Visual Basic .NET, file handling is largely based on the **System.IO** namespace, which encloses a class library that supports string, character, and file manipulation. These classes include properties, methods, and events for creating, copying, moving, and deleting files. The most commonly used classes are **FileStream**, **BinaryReader, BinaryWriter, StreamReader**, and **StreamWriter**, and we'll take a look at all of these classes in this chapter.

---

*TIP: File handling is one of the most error-prone of all possible programming operations. It's best to always enclose your code in **Try/Catch** blocks here to handle problems (although I'll sometimes skip implementing that in this chapter in the interest of brevity).*

The FileStream Class

The **FileStream** class gives you access to files. You start working with a file on disk by opening it or creating it; you can use the members of the **FileAccess**, **FileMode**, and **FileShare** enumerations with the constructors of the **FileStream** class to determine how the file is created, opened, and shared. In addition, the **FileStream** class can open a file in one of two modes, either synchronously or asynchronously, which can have significant performance differences in different circumstances. **FileStream** defaults to opening files synchronously, but also has a constructor to open files asynchronously.

After you've opened or created a file, you can pass its **FileStream** object to the **BinaryReader, BinaryWriter, StreamReader**, and **StreamWriter** classes to actually work with the data in the file.

You also can use the **FileStream Seek** method to move to various locations in a file—this is called moving the read/write position or the read/write pointer. This allows you to break a file up into *records*, each of the same length. For example, if you're keeping track of 2,000 employees, you can create 2,000 records in a file, each with data on the corresponding employee.

Because you know the length of each record, it's easy to move to the beginning of a specific record and read it in—or overwrite it with new data. This record-based process, where you can move around in a file and select the data you want, is called *random access*. The other form of file access, where you just read or write data to a file one item after the other—and so you must read through the first 2001 data items if you want to read the 2002th—is called *sequential access*. The only difference between these types of access from our point of view is that for random access, you use the **Seek** method. You use the **Seek** method by specifying a byte offset to move by; you can specify if you want to move that number of bytes from the beginning of the file, the current position, or the end of the file, as we'll see in this chapter.

As mentioned, after you've connected a **FileStream** object to a file, you can use the **FileStream**, **BinaryReader**, **BinaryWriter**, **StreamReader**, and **Stream Writer** classes with that file, and I'll take a look at those classes next.

Handling Text: The StreamReader and StreamWriter Classes

To work with *text data* in files—that is, storing and reading text to and from files—you can use the **StreamReader** and **StreamWriter** classes. (The **StreamReader** class is actually derived from an abstract class called **TextReader**, which reads characters from a stream, and the **StreamWriter** class is derived from an abstract class called **TextWriter**, which writes characters to a stream.) We'll create an example that uses these classes named **StreamWriterReader**; this example will write text to a file, file.txt, and then read that text back, displaying it in a text box. I start by importing the **System.IO** namespace, and by creating file.txt and connecting a **FileStream** object to it. Next, I can create a **StreamWriter** object and use various methods to move around in and write text to the file.

In this case, I'll use the **Seek** method that we've already seen to move to the beginning of the file (that's not necessary in newly created or opened files because when you open a file, you start at the beginning of the file—here, I'm just showing how **Seek** works), then write a line of text to the file with the **WriteLine** method, and then write some text to the file with the **Write** method (the **WriteLine** method is the same as **Write**, except it adds a carriage-return/linefeed pair at the end of the text it writes).

I'll also use the **Flush** method—because file handling is buffered in Visual Basic, nothing is written to disk until the buffer is *flushed*. This happens automatically when the buffer is full or when you close a file (or when the associated stream object goes out of scope), but you also can use the **Flush** method to explicitly flush data to the disk. (You don't have to use **Flush** at all, because flushing is usually automatic; I'm just using it here to show that this method is available.) Finally, I close the file with the **Close** method; this closes the file on disk, which finishes our work with the file and makes it available to other programs:

```
Imports System
Imports System.IO

Public Class Form1
    Inherits System.Windows.Forms.Form

    'Windows Form Designer generated code

    Private Sub Button1_Click(ByVal sender As System.Object, _
        ByVal e As System.EventArgs) Handles Button1.Click
        Dim fs As New System.IO.FileStream("file.txt", FileMode.Create, _
            FileAccess.Write)

        Dim w As New StreamWriter(fs)
        w.BaseStream.Seek(0, SeekOrigin.End)
        w.WriteLine("Here is the file's text.")
        w.Write("Here is more file text." & ControlChars.CrLf)
        w.WriteLine("And that's about it.")
        w.Flush()
        w.Close()
        .
        .
        .
```

Now that the file, file.txt, has been created and had some text placed in it, I can open it again with another **FileStream** object, then connect a **StreamReader** object to it, and use the **StreamReader** object's methods like **ReadLine** to read data from the file line by line (in text files, "lines" mean text strings of various lengths, marked by a carriage-return/linefeed pair at the end of each). How can you determine if there's still more data to read in the file? You can use the **StreamReader** object's **Peek** method, which tells you how much more data there is remaining in the file. If there's no more data, **Peek** returns a value of -1. If there is more data, I'll keep reading it in and displaying it in a multi-line text box, like this:

```
Imports System
Imports System.IO

Public Class Form1
    Inherits System.Windows.Forms.Form

    'Windows Form Designer generated code

    Private Sub Button1_Click(ByVal sender As System.Object, _
        ByVal e As System.EventArgs) Handles Button1.Click
        Dim fs As New System.IO.FileStream("file.txt", FileMode.Create, _
            FileAccess.Write)

        Dim w As New StreamWriter(fs)
        w.BaseStream.Seek(0, SeekOrigin.End)
        w.WriteLine("Here is the file's text.")
        w.Write("Here is more file text." & ControlChars.CrLf)
        w.WriteLine("And that's about it.")
        w.Flush()
        w.Close()

        fs = New System.IO.FileStream("file.txt", FileMode.Open, _
            FileAccess.Read)

        Dim r As New StreamReader(fs)
        r.BaseStream.Seek(0, SeekOrigin.Begin)
        While r.Peek() > -1
            TextBox1.Text &= r.ReadLine() & ControlChars.CrLf
        End While
        r.Close()
    End Sub
End Class
```

Note in particular the **Seek** statement. You pass this method the number of bytes to move from the current position (this value can be positive or negative), and the origin that you want to move from; and you define the origin with a value from the **SeekOrigin** enumeration: **SeekOrigin.Begin** for the beginning of the file,

Figure 13.3   Writing and reading a text file.

SeekOrigin.Current for the current location in the file, or **SeekOrigin.End** for the end of the file. You can see the results of this code in Figure 13.3, where I've created a new file, file.txt, filled it with text, and read that text back in.

So far, we've handled a text file—but what about binary files such as image files? And what's the difference, anyway? Shouldn't a text file be a binary file as well? It is. The difference is in the way that line endings are handled. In Windows, the end of a line is represented by two characters, a carriage return and a linefeed; if you only have a carriage return in your text, it'll be converted into a carriage return/ linefeed pair when you write your data to disk as a text file. If you write that text to disk as a binary file, you'll get an exact copy of your data on disk—and the carriage return will not be turned into a carriage return/linefeed pair. Because line endings are so important when you're handling data as text, the text-handling **StreamReader** and **StreamWriter** classes are line oriented, using methods such as **WriteLine** and **ReadLine**. But you also can handle data without organizing it into lines; you do that with the **BinaryReader** and **BinaryWriter** classes.

---

*TIP: Both the **StreamReader** and **StreamWriter** classes use Unicode UTF-8 encoding by default. You can set the encoding for **StreamWriter** with the encoding parameter in its constructor.*

Handling Binary Data: The BinaryReader and BinaryWriter Classes

Both **BinaryReader** and **BinaryWriter** read and write data as *binary* (that is, in the raw 0s and 1s that your data is actually stored as in your computer) rather than text. (To handle text, you use **StreamReader** and **StreamWriter** instead.) For example, you use the **BinaryWriter** class's **Write** method to send binary data to a file. To read it back in, you can use the **BinaryReader** class's **Read** method, passing it an array of bytes to store data in, the location in the array to start string data, and the number of bytes you want to read, like this, where I'm reading 1,000 bytes from data.dat:

```
Dim fs As FileStream = New FileStream("data.dat", FileMode.Open)
Dim myBinaryReader As BinaryReader = New BinaryReader(fs)
Dim buffer(1000) As Byte
myBinaryReader.Read(buffer, 0, 1000)
```

However, there are more convenient methods available—for example, if you know you're reading in an **Int32** value, you can use the **BinaryReader** class's **ReadInt32** method, for **Double** values, you can use **ReadDouble**, for **Boolean** values, **ReadBoolean**, and so on. As another example, here's how I write 20 **Int32** values to a file, data.dat, and then read them back in and display them in a text box in the example BinaryWriterReader on the CD-ROM—note that after I write the data to the file, all I have to do is to use **Seek** to move to the beginning of the file and read the data we just wrote:

```
Imports System.IO

Public Class Form1
    Inherits System.Windows.Forms.Form

    'Windows Form Designer generated code

    Private Sub Button1_Click(ByVal sender As System.Object, _
        ByVal e As System.EventArgs) Handles Button1.Click
        Dim fs As FileStream = New FileStream("data.dat", _
            FileMode.OpenOrCreate)
        Dim w As BinaryWriter = New BinaryWriter(fs)
        Dim LoopIndex As Int32

        For LoopIndex = 0 To 19
            w.Write(LoopIndex)
        Next

        w.Seek(0, SeekOrigin.Begin)
        Dim r As BinaryReader = New BinaryReader(fs)

        For LoopIndex = 0 To 19
            TextBox1.Text &= r.ReadInt32() & ControlChars.CrLf
        Next
    End Sub
End Class
```

Why are there multiple reading methods when you can write your data simply with **Write**? The **Write** method is actually overloaded for the various data types, and Visual Basic knows what kind of data type a variable is, so it can write it to the file without problem. But when you open a binary file, it's just a file full of binary bits, 1s and 0s, and Visual Basic has no clue how to divide it into items of a particular data type—which is why the **ReadInt16**, **ReadChar**, **ReadBoolean**, and so on methods exist.

The File and Directory Classes

Two other classes you should know about are **File** and **Directory**. The **File** class lets you handle files without opening them, allowing you to move and copy them, and so on. The **Directory** class lets you work with directories, renaming and creating them. In fact, the methods that let you do this are class methods, so you don't have to create any **File** and **Directory** objects first.

The copier example on the CD-ROM shows how this works. This example first lets you create a directory and then copy a file to it, using **File** and **Directory** methods. First, the user enters the path of a new directory into the text box in this example, and clicks the "Create directory" button, which uses the **Directory** class's **CreateDirectory** method to create the directory:

```
Imports System.IO

Public Class Form1
    Inherits System.Windows.Forms.Form

    'Windows Form Designer generated code

    Private Sub Button1_Click(ByVal sender As System.Object, _
        ByVal e As System.EventArgs) Handles Button1.Click
        Try
            Directory.CreateDirectory(TextBox1.Text)
        Catch
            MsgBox("Could not create directory.")
            Exit Sub
        End Try
        MsgBox("Directory created.")
    End Sub
    .
    .
    .
```

Next, I'll let the user use a Open File dialog to select a file to copy to the new directory, using the **File** class's **Copy** method, like this (note that I'm stripping the pathname off the filename returned by the Open File dialog using the **String** class's **SubString** method):

```
Imports System.IO

Public Class Form1
    Inherits System.Windows.Forms.Form

    'Windows Form Designer generated code

    Private Sub Button1_Click(ByVal sender As System.Object, _
        ByVal e As System.EventArgs) Handles Button1.Click
        Try
            Directory.CreateDirectory(TextBox1.Text)
        Catch
            MsgBox("Could not create directory.")
            Exit Sub
        End Try
        MsgBox("Directory created.")
    End Sub

    Private Sub Button2_Click(ByVal sender As System.Object, _
        ByVal e As System.EventArgs) Handles Button2.Click
        Try
            If OpenFileDialog1.ShowDialog <> DialogResult.Cancel Then
                File.Copy(OpenFileDialog1.FileName, TextBox1.Text & "\" & _
                    OpenFileDialog1.FileName.Substring( _
                    OpenFileDialog1.FileName.LastIndexOf("\")))
            End If
        Catch
            MsgBox("Could not copy file.")
            Exit Sub
        End Try
        MsgBox("File copied.")
    End Sub
End Class
```

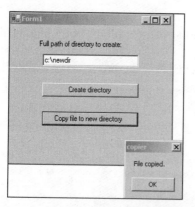

Figure 13.4   Creating a new directory and copying a file to it.

You can see the results in Figure 13.4, where I've created a new directory and have copied a file to it.

And that's it—now it's time to turn to the Immediate Solutions section to get to the various details of these topics.

Immediate Solutions

Using the **Graphics** Class

As its name suggests, and as discussed in the In Depth section of this chapter, you use the **Graphics** class to create graphics. Here's the class hierarchy of the **Graphics** class:

```
Object
    MarshalByRefObject
        Graphics
```

You can find the some notable public class (shared) methods of the **Graphics** class in Table 13.1, the notable public properties of **Graphics** objects in Table 13.2, and their more notable public methods in Table 13.3.

Table 13.1   Noteworthy class (shared) methods of the Graphics class.

Method	Means
FromHwnd	Returns a new **Graphics** object given a Windows handle.
FromImage	Returns a new **Graphics** object given an Image object.

Table 13.2   Noteworthy public properties of Graphics objects.

Property	Means
Clip	Holds the drawing region of this **Graphics** object.
DpiX	Holds the horizontal resolution of this **Graphics** object.
DpiY	Holds the vertical resolution of this **Graphics** object.
IsClipEmpty	**True** if the clip region is empty.
PixelOffsetMode	Indicates how pixels are offset when drawn, affecting both drawing quality and speed.
SmoothingMode	Sets the quality for rendering with this **Graphics** object.

13. Graphics and File Handling

Table 13.3 Noteworthy public methods of **Graphics** objects.

Method	Means
Clear	Clears the drawing surface, filling it with the background color.
Dispose	Deletes and deallocates this **Graphics** object.
DrawArc	Draws an arc.
DrawBezier	Draws a Bézier curve.
DrawBeziers	Draws Bézier curves.
DrawClosedCurve	Draws a closed curve.
DrawCurve	Draws a curve.
DrawEllipse	Draws an ellipse.
DrawIcon	Draws an icon.
DrawIconUnstretched	Draws an icon without scaling the icon.
DrawImage	Draws an image.
DrawImageUnscaled	Draws an image without scaling the image.
DrawLine	Draws a line.
DrawLines	Draws lines.
DrawPath	Draws a graphics path.
DrawPie	Draws a pie section.
DrawPolygon	Draws a polygon.
DrawRectangle	Draws a rectangle.
DrawRectangles	Draws rectangles.
DrawString	Draws a text string.
FillClosedCurve	Fills a closed curve.
FillEllipse	Fills an ellipse.
FillPath	Fills the inside of a path.
FillPie	Fills a pie section.
FillPolygon	Fills a polygon.
FillRectangle	Fills a rectangle.
FillRectangles	Fills rectangles.
FillRegion	Fills the inside of a region.
GetHdc	Gets Windows device context handle for this **Graphics** object.
GetNearestColor	Gets the nearest color to a given color.
MeasureString	Gets the length of a string to display.
Save	Saves this object as a **GraphicsState** object.
SetClip	Sets the clipping region.

Using the **Pen** Class

You use the **Pen** class to draw with in **Graphics** objects. Here is the hierarchy of the **Pen** class:

```
Object
    MarshalByRefObject
        Pen
```

You can find the more notable public properties of **Pen** objects in Table 13.4 and their more notable public methods in Table 13.5.

Table 13.4   Noteworthy public properties of Pen objects.

Property	Means
Alignment	Gets/sets the alignment for drawing objects.
Brush	Gets/sets the **Brush** object of this **Pen**.
Color	Gets/sets the **Pen**'s color.
CompoundArray	Gets/sets an array of dashes and spaces to configure a **Pen**.
CustomEndCap	Gets/sets the cap style used at the end of lines.
CustomStartCap	Gets/sets the cap style used at the beginning of lines.
DashCap	Gets/sets the cap style used at the beginning or end of dashed lines.
DashOffset	Gets/sets the length from the beginning of a line to the beginning of a dash pattern.
DashPattern	Gets/sets an array of dashes and spaces.
DashStyle	Gets/sets the style used for dashed lines.
EndCap	Gets/sets the cap style used at the end of lines.
LineJoin	Gets/sets the style used to join the ends of overlapping lines.
PenType	Gets the style of lines this **Pen** draws.
StartCap	Gets/sets the cap style used at the beginning of lines.
Width	Gets/sets the width of this **Pen** in pixels.

Table 13.5   Noteworthy public methods of Pen objects.

Method	Means
Clone	Creates a copy of this **Pen**.
Dispose	Deallocates and disposes of this **Pen**.
SetLineCap	Sets the style of cap used to end lines.

Specifying Drawing Colors

In Visual Basic, you can specify drawing colors with the **Color** structure. To create a custom color, you can use the **FromArgb** method of this structure. There are a number of overloaded versions of the **FromArgb** method; one allows you to specify the red, green, and blue color values for the new color as bytes (holding values ranging from 0 to 255). For example, white has the (red, green, blue) color values (255, 255, 255), bright green is (0, 255, 0), gray is (128, 128, 128), bright blue is (0, 0, 255), and so on. Here's how I use the **FromArgb** method to create a bright red pen and use it to draw a line:

```
Dim c As Color = Color.FromArgb(255, 0, 0)
Dim RedPen As New Pen(c)
g.DrawLine(RedPen, point1, point2)
```

The **Color** structure also comes with dozens of built-in colors, which are the same as those used in the **Pens** and **Brushes** classes, which you can find in Table 13.6. For example, you can use such colors as **Color.SteelBlue** or **Color.Teal**, and so on.

TIP: You can recover the red, green, and blue values for a color using the **Color** structure's **R**, **G**, and **B** members (these members are read-only).

Drawing Figures with Pens

Here's an example, named Painter on the CD-ROM, that shows how to use the **Graphics** class to draw 2D shapes. As you can see in Figure 13.1, this program lets you select various shapes to draw by clicking buttons in the toolbar. After you've selected a drawing tool, you can use the mouse to draw the figure—just press the mouse button at one corner of the figure, then drag it to the opposite corner and release the button, making the figure appear. I start this example by getting a **Graphics** object for the form using the form's **CreateGraphics** method (as this method is a member of the **Control** class, you can use it with all Windows forms and controls):

```
Dim g As Graphics

Private Sub Form1_Load(ByVal sender As System.Object, _
    ByVal e As System.EventArgs) Handles MyBase.Load
    g = Me.CreateGraphics()
End Sub
```

TIP: *Note that when you get a **Graphics** object for the entire form this way, that object corresponds to the whole form, not just the client area, so the drawing origin is the upper-left corner of the whole form, above the title bar. When a **Graphics** object is passed to you in the **Paint** event handler, that object's origin is at upper left of the client area (that is, the area below the title bar, menu bar, and toolbars, if any).*

Now I can draw using this graphics object as needed. I also define an enumeration named **Tools** that holds these values, corresponding to the buttons in the toolbar:

```
Enum Tools
      Rectangle
      Ellipse
      Line
      Draw
End Enum
```

When the user clicks a toolbar button, I can assign a variable named **Tool** a value from this enumeration to specify what drawing tool (line, rectangle, and so on) we're using currently:

```
Dim Tool As Tools

Private Sub ToolBar1_ButtonClick(ByVal sender As System.Object, _
      ByVal e As System.Windows.Forms.ToolBarButtonClickEventArgs) _
      Handles ToolBar1.ButtonClick
        If (ToolBar1.Buttons(0) Is e.Button) Then
            Tool = Tools.Rectangle
        End If
        If (ToolBar1.Buttons(1) Is e.Button) Then
            Tool = Tools.Ellipse
        End If
        If (ToolBar1.Buttons(2) Is e.Button) Then
            Tool = Tools.Line
        End If
        If (ToolBar1.Buttons(3) Is e.Button) Then
            Tool = Tools.Draw
        End If
    End Sub
```

I record the point at which the mouse button went down in a **Point** variable named **down**, like this:

```
Dim up, down As Point
```

```
Private Sub Form1_MouseDown(ByVal sender As Object, _
    ByVal e As System.Windows.Forms.MouseEventArgs) Handles _
    MyBase.MouseDown
        down = New Point(e.X, e.Y)
End Sub
```

The user now moves the mouse to the opposite corner of the figure's defining rectangle and releases the mouse button. I can now create a rectangle of the **Rectangle** class after finding the figure's upper-left corner, width, and height. Then all I need to do is to check which kind of figure we're drawing (which I can do with the **Tool** variable), and draw the corresponding figure—here, I'm using a predefined blue-violet pen (see "Using the **Pens** and **Brushes** Classes" for the details on predefined pens), but note that you can create pens of any color (see "Specifying Drawing Colors" for the details):

```
Dim up, down As Point
Dim r As Rectangle

Private Sub Form1_MouseUp(ByVal sender As Object, _
    ByVal e As System.Windows.Forms.MouseEventArgs) _
    Handles MyBase.MouseUp
        up = New Point(e.X, e.Y)
        r = New Rectangle(Math.Min(up.X, down.X), _
            Math.Min(up.Y, down.Y), Math.Abs(up.X - down.X), _
            Math.Abs(up.Y - down.Y))

    Select Case Tool
        Case Tools.Rectangle
            g.DrawRectangle(Pens.BlueViolet, r)
        Case Tools.Ellipse
            g.DrawEllipse(Pens.BlueViolet, r)
        Case Tools.Line
            g.DrawLine(Pens.BlueViolet, up, down)
    End Select
End Sub
```

You can see the results in Figure 13.5, where I'm drawing ellipses.

Note that there's also a button labeled "Draw" in Figure 13.1—this button lets you draw freehand with the mouse. To implement that, I'll add code to the **MouseMove** event handler and use the **Graphics** class's **DrawLines** method. You pass this method an array of the points to connect with lines, so all we need to do is to store the points passed to us in **MouseMove**. (A **MouseMove** event is not generated for every pixel the mouse passes over, but rather only so many times a sec-

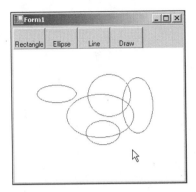

Figure 13.5 Drawing ellipses.

ond, so all we need to do is to connect the dots with short lines using **DrawLines**.)
I'll do that with an array named **Points**—note that since **DrawLines** gets the
number of lines to draw from the length of the array passed to it, I'll need to
redimension this array every time we add a new point to it. Here's how the code
looks to draw freehand with the mouse; note that I don't invoke the **DrawLines**
method unless there are at least two points stored in the **Points** array, which is
the minimum that **DrawLines** requires:

```
Dim Points() As Point
Dim NumberPoints As Integer = 0

Private Sub Form1_MouseMove(ByVal sender As Object, _
    ByVal e As System.Windows.Forms.MouseEventArgs) Handles _
    MyBase.MouseMove
        If Tool = Tools.Draw And e.Button = MouseButtons.Left Then
            Dim p As New Point(e.X, e.Y)

            ReDim Preserve Points(NumberPoints)

            Points(NumberPoints) = p
            NumberPoints += 1

            If NumberPoints >= 2 Then
                g.DrawLines(Pens.BlueViolet, Points)
            End If
        End If
    End Sub
End Class
```

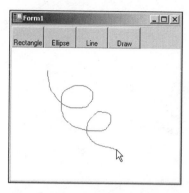

Figure 13.6   Drawing freehand with the mouse.

You can see the results in Figure 13.6, where I'm drawing (well, more or less) with the mouse.

But here's a problem—if you minimize and then restore, or cover and then uncover, Painter, you'll notice that all the graphics disappear. They didn't previously; in VB6, you could use the **AutoRedraw** property to make the window redraw itself, but now you're responsible for that. See the next topic.

Repainting Windows

When you draw graphics in a form and then minimize and then restore the form, or cover and then uncover it, you need to redraw the graphics as well. (As mentioned in the In Depth section, you didn't have to do so in VB6 and earlier, where forms supported the **AutoRedraw** property, but now you do because that property no longer exists.) You can do that in the form's **Paint** event handler, which is called when the form needs to be drawn or *painted*. As an example, I can redraw the most recent graphics figure in the Painter example this way, using the **Paint** event:

```
Private Sub Form1_Paint(ByVal sender As Object, _
    ByVal e As System.Windows.Forms.PaintEventArgs) _
        Handles MyBase.Paint
    Select Case Tool
        Case Tools.Rectangle
            g.DrawRectangle(Pens.BlueViolet, r)
        Case Tools.Ellipse
            g.DrawEllipse(Pens.BlueViolet, r)
```

```
            Case Tools.Line
                    g.DrawLine(Pens.BlueViolet, up, down)
            Case Tools.Draw
                If NumberPoints >= 2 Then
                        g.DrawLines(Pens.BlueViolet, Points)
                End If
        End Select
    End Sub
```

Now when you minimize and then restore Painter, the most recent figure reappears (to redraw all the figures the user has drawn, you can store their dimensions and types and redraw them all one by one, of course).

Using **Brush** Classes

You use brushes to fill in figures that you've drawn with the **Graphics** class. **Brush** is actually an abstract class—in practice, you use the classes derived from it, and here they are:

```
Object
    MarshalByRefObject
        Brush
            HatchBrush
            LinearGradientBrush
            PathGradientBrush
            SolidBrush
            TextureBrush
```

To see a number of these brushes at work, take a look at the next topic.

Filling Figures with Brushes

You use brushes to fill in graphics figures. (See the previous topic and the discussion in the In Depth section of this chapter.) To illustrate, take a look at the FillGraphics example on the CD-ROM, which you can see at work in Figure 13.2. This example draws four ellipses and fills them in with the **FillEllipse** method using various brushes—**LinearGradientBrush**, **HatchBrush**, **SolidBrush**, and **TextureBrush**. To use these classes, you import the **System.Drawing. Drawing2D** namespace. Here's what this example looks like in code; note that the texture brush uses an image to fill a figure. In this case, I'm using the greenstone.bmp image that comes with Windows 2000:

```
Imports System.Drawing.Drawing2D
Public Class Form1
    Inherits System.Windows.Forms.Form

    'Windows Form Designer generated code

    Private Sub Form1_Paint(ByVal sender As Object, _
        ByVal e As System.Windows.Forms.PaintEventArgs) _
        Handles MyBase.Paint
        Dim g As Graphics
        Dim r As Rectangle
        g = Me.CreateGraphics()

        r = New Rectangle(20, 20, 60, 60)
        Dim lb As New LinearGradientBrush( _
            r, Color.Red, Color.Yellow, LinearGradientMode.Horizontal)
        g.FillEllipse(lb, r)

        r = New Rectangle(20, 100, 60, 60)
        Dim hb As New HatchBrush(HatchStyle.DarkDownwardDiagonal, _
            Color.LightBlue)
        g.FillEllipse(hb, r)

        r = New Rectangle(100, 20, 60, 60)
        Dim sb As New SolidBrush(Color.Coral)
        g.FillEllipse(sb, r)

        r = New Rectangle(100, 100, 60, 60)
        Dim tb As New TextureBrush(Bitmap.FromFile("greenstone.bmp"))
        g.FillEllipse(tb, r)
    End Sub
End Class
```

To use a **Pen**, you use the **DrawXXX** method of the **Graphics** class, and to fill the figure in using a brush, you use the **FillXXX** methods. For more on setting the colors of brushes, see "Specifying Drawing Colors," and to see how to use predefined brushes, see "Using the **Pens** and **Brushes** Classes," both in this chapter.

Using the **Pens** and **Brushes** Classes

When you draw using the **Graphics** class's methods, you need to supply a **Pen** object. Rather than creating a pen from scratch, you can use a predefined pen from the **Pens** class. These pens have a width of one pixel, and you can refer to them as **Pens.ForestGreen**, **Pens.LightSeaGreen**, and so on. And instead of creating a brush from scratch, you can use a solid color brush from the **Brushes** class like this: **Brushes.Coral**, **Brushes.Moccasin**, and so on. The possible colors for use with these classes appear in Table 13.6.

Table 13.6   Colors of the Pens and Brushes classes.

AliceBlue	AntiqueWhite	Aqua	Aquamarine
Azure	Beige	Bisque	Black
BlanchedAlmond	Blue	BlueViolet	Brown
BurlyWood	CadetBlue	Chartreuse	Chocolate
Coral	CornflowerBlue	Cornsilk	Crimson
Cyan	DarkBlue	DarkCyan	DarkGoldenrod
DarkGray	DarkGreen	DarkKhaki	DarkMagenta
DarkOliveGreen	DarkOrange	DarkOrchid	DarkRed
DarkSalmon	DarkSeaGreen	DarkSlateBlue	DarkSlateGray
DarkTurquoise	DarkViolet	DeepPink	DeepSkyBlue
DimGray	DodgerBlue	Firebrick	FloralWhite
ForestGreen	Fuchsia	Gainsboro	GhostWhite
Gold	Goldenrod	Gray	Green
GreenYellow	Honeydew	HotPink	IndianRed
Indigo	Ivory	Khaki	Lavender
LavenderBlush	LawnGreen	LemonChiffon	LightBlue
LightCoral	LightCyan	LightGoldenrodYellow	LightGray
LightGreen	LightPink	LightSalmon	LightSeaGreen
LightSkyBlue	LightSlateGray	LightSteelBlue	LightYellow
Lime	LimeGreen	Linen	Magenta
Maroon	MediumAquamarine	MediumBlue	MediumOrchid
MediumPurple	MediumSeaGreen	MediumSlateBlue	MediumSpringGreen
MediumTurquoise	MediumVioletRed	MidnightBlue	MintCream
MistyRose	Moccasin	NavajoWhite	Navy
OldLace	Olive	OliveDrab	Orange
OrangeRed	Orchid	PaleGoldenrod	PaleGreen
PaleTurquoise	PaleVioletRed	PapayaWhip	PeachPuff
Peru	Pink	Plum	PowderBlue
Purple	Red	RosyBrown	RoyalBlue
SaddleBrown	Salmon	SandyBrown	SeaGreen
SeaShell	Sienna	Silver	SkyBlue

13. Graphics and File Handling

(continued)

Table 13.6 Colors of the Pens and Brushes classes (continued).

SlateBlue	SlateGray	Snow	SpringGreen
SteelBlue	Tan	Teal	Thistle
Tomato	Transparent	Turquoise	Violet
Wheat	White	WhiteSmoke	Yellow
YellowGreen			

Handling Images

To handle images using the **Graphics** class, you can use methods like **DrawImage**, which draws images where you want them. We've already seen an example showing how that works; that example is named ScrollImage in Chapter 8 (see "Scrolling Images" in the Immediate Solutions section of that chapter). Now that we know more about the **Graphics** class, I'll take another look at that example's code here. There are many overloaded forms of **DrawImage;** with the one I'm using here, you pass the **Image** object to work with, the destination rectangle to draw in, the source rectangle to copy pixels from, and the graphics units (which are pixels). To scroll the image, you use the scrollbar positions and simply redraw the image, like this:

```
Imports System.Drawing
Public Class Form1
    Inherits System.Windows.Forms.Form

    'Windows Form Designer generated code

    Private Sub ShowScrollBars()
        VScrollBar1.Visible = True
        HScrollBar1.Visible = True

        If PictureBox1.Height > PictureBox1.Image.Height Then
            VScrollBar1.Visible = False
        End If

        If PictureBox1.Width > PictureBox1.Image.Width Then
            HScrollBar1.Visible = False
        End If
    End Sub

    Public Sub ScrollBars_Scroll(ByVal sender As Object, _
        ByVal se As ScrollEventArgs)
        Dim graphics As Graphics = PictureBox1.CreateGraphics()
        graphics.DrawImage(PictureBox1.Image, New Rectangle(0, 0, _
            PictureBox1.Width - HScrollBar1.Height, _
```

13. Graphics and File Handling

```
              PictureBox1.Height - VScrollBar1.Width), _
              New Rectangle(HScrollBar1.Value, VScrollBar1.Value, _
              PictureBox1.Width - HScrollBar1.Height, _
              PictureBox1.Height - VScrollBar1.Width), GraphicsUnit.Pixel)
    End Sub

    Private Sub Form1_Load(ByVal sender As System.Object, _
        ByVal e As System.EventArgs) Handles MyBase.Load
        AddHandler HScrollBar1.Scroll, AddressOf ScrollBars_Scroll
        AddHandler VScrollBar1.Scroll, AddressOf ScrollBars_Scroll
    End Sub

    Private Sub Button1_Click(ByVal sender As System.Object, _
        ByVal e As System.EventArgs) Handles Button1.Click
        If OpenFileDialog1.ShowDialog() <> DialogResult.Cancel Then
            PictureBox1.Image = Image.FromFile(OpenFileDialog1.FileName)
            HScrollBar1.Maximum = PictureBox1.Image.Width - _
                PictureBox1.Width
            VScrollBar1.Maximum = PictureBox1.Image.Height - _
                PictureBox1.Height
            ShowScrollBars()
        End If
    End Sub
End Class
```

Note that all I'm doing is to use the picture box's **CreateGraphics** method to create a **Graphics** object (recall that because **CreateGraphics** is a **Control** class method, it's supported in Windows forms and controls), and then using that **Graphics** object to scroll the image. That's all it takes. You can see this example at work in Figure 13.7.

Related solution:	Found on page:
Scrolling Images	349

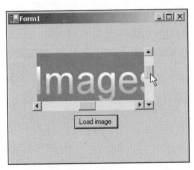

Figure 13.7   Scrolling an image using the **DrawImage** method.

Using the **FileStream** Class

As discussed in the In Depth section of this chapter, you can use the **FileStream** class to open or create files, and then use other classes, like **BinaryWriter** and **BinaryReader**, to work with the data in the file. Here's the hierarchy of the **FileStream** class:

```
Object
    MarshalByRefObject
        Stream
            FileStream
```

You can find the more notable public properties of **FileStream** objects in Table 13.7 and the more notable public methods in Table 13.8.

Table 13.7   Noteworthy public properties of FileStream objects.

Property	Means
CanRead	Determines if the stream supports reading.
CanSeek	Determines if the stream supports seeking.
CanWrite	Determines if the stream supports writing.
Handle	Gets the operating system file handle for the stream's file.
IsAsync	Determines if the stream was opened asynchronously or synchronously.
Length	Gets the length of the stream in bytes.
Name	Gets the name of the file stream passed to the constructor.
Position	Gets/sets the position in this stream.

Table 13.8   Noteworthy public methods of FileStream objects.

Method	Means
BeginRead	Starts an asynchronous read operation.
BeginWrite	Starts an asynchronous write operation.
Close	Closes a file, making it available in Windows to any other program.
EndRead	Waits for an asynchronous read operation to finish.
EndWrite	Ends an asynchronous write operation, waiting until the operation has finished.
Flush	Flushes all buffers for this stream, writing any buffered data out to its target (such as a disk file).
Lock	Withholds any access to the file to other processes.
Read	Reads a block of bytes.

(continued)

13. Graphics and File Handling

Table 13.8   Noteworthy public methods of FileStream objects *(continued)*.

Method	Means
ReadByte	Reads a byte from the file.
Seek	Sets the current read/write position.
SetLength	Sets the length of the stream.
Unlock	Gives access to other processes to a file that had been locked.
Write	Writes a block of bytes to this stream.
WriteByte	Writes a byte to the current read/write position.

Using the **FileMode** Enumeration

When you open a file with the **FileStream** class, you specify the file mode you want to use—for example, if you want to create a new file, you use the file mode **FileMode.Create**. The various possible file modes are part of the **FileMode** enumeration; you can find the members of this enumeration in Table 13.9.

Table 13.9   Members of the FileMode enumeration.

Member	Means
Append	Opens a file and moves to the end of the file (or creates a new file if the specified file doesn't exist). Note that you can only use **FileMode.Append** with **FileAccess.Write**.
Create	Creates a new file; if the file already exists, it is overwritten.
CreateNew	Creates a new file; if the file already exists, an **IOException** is thrown.
Open	Opens an existing file.
OpenOrCreate	Open a file if it exists; or create a new file.
Truncate	Open an existing file, and truncate it to zero length so you can write over its data.

Using the **FileAccess** Enumeration

When you open files with the **FileStream** class, you can specify the file mode (see the previous topic) and *access*. The access indicates the way you're going to use the file—to read from, to write to, or both. To indicate the type of file access you want, you use members of the **FileAccess** enumeration. You can find the members of the **FileAccess** enumeration in Table 13.10.

Table 13.10   Members of the FileAccess enumeration.

Member	Means
Read	Gives read access to the file, which means you can read data from the file.
ReadWrite	Gives both read and write access to the file, which means you can both read and write to and from a file.
Write	Gives write access to the file, which means you can write to the file.

Using the FileShare Enumeration

When you open a file, you can specify the file-sharing mode you want to use in some of the **FileStream** constructors (you don't have to specify a file-sharing mode with other **FileStream** constructors). For example, if you want to allow other programs to read a file at the same time you're working with it, you use the file-sharing mode **FileShare.Read**. The various possible file-sharing modes are part of the **FileShare** enumeration, and you can find the members of this enumeration in Table 13.11.

Table 13.11   Members of the FileShare enumeration.

Member	Means
None	The file cannot be shared. Other processes cannot access it.
Read	The file also may be opened by other processes for reading.
ReadWrite	The file also may be opened by other processes for reading and writing.
Write	The file also may be opened by other processes for writing.

Opening or Creating a File with the FileStream Class

When you want to open or create a file, you use the **FileStream** class, which has many constructors, allowing you to specify the file mode (for example, **FileMode.Create**), file access (such as **FileAccess.Write**), and/or the file-sharing mode (such as **FileShare.None**), like this (these are only a few of the **FileStream** constructors):

```
Dim fs As New System.IO.FileStream(String, FileMode)
Dim fs As New System.IO.FileStream(String, FileMode, FileAccess)
Dim fs As New System.IO.FileStream(String, FileMode, FileAccess, FileShare)
```

The StreamWriterReader example on the CD-ROM shows how this works—in that example, I'm creating a file named file.txt and opening it for writing with a **FileStream** object; note that I'm setting the file mode to **Create** to create this new file, and explicitly setting the file access to **Write** so we can write to the file:

```
Imports System
Imports System.IO

Public Class Form1
    Inherits System.Windows.Forms.Form

    'Windows Form Designer generated code

    Private Sub Button1_Click(ByVal sender As System.Object, _
        ByVal e As System.EventArgs) Handles Button1.Click
        Dim fs As New System.IO.FileStream("file.txt", FileMode.Create, _
            FileAccess.Write)
        .
        .
        .
```

To actually do something with this new **FileStream** object, I'll use the **StreamWriter** class, coming up next.

Using the **StreamWriter** Class

After you've opened a file for writing using the **FileStream** class (see "Using the **FileStream** Class" in this chapter), you can create a **StreamWriter** object to write text to the file. Here is the hierarchy of the **StreamWriter** class:

```
Object
   MarshalByRefObject
      TextWriter
         StreamWriter
```

You can find the more notable public properties of the **StreamWriter** class in Table 13.12, and the more notable methods in Table 13.13.

Table 13.12   Noteworthy public properties of StreamWriter objects.

Property	Means
AutoFlush	Gets/sets if the **StreamWriter** will flush its buffer after **Write** or **WriteLine** operation.
BaseStream	Gets the base stream for this stream, giving you access to the base stream's properties and methods.
Encoding	Gets the character encoding for this stream.

Table 13.13   Noteworthy public methods of StreamWriter objects.

Method	Means
Close	Closes the current stream.
Flush	Flushes all buffers for the stream writer, writing any buffered data to the base stream.
Write	Writes data to the stream.

Writing Text with the **StreamWriter** Class

As discussed in the In Depth section of this chapter, you can use the **StreamWriter** class to write text to a file. In the topic "Opening or Creating a File with the **FileStream** Class" in this chapter, I used a **FileStream** object to create a file for writing in the StreamWriterReader example on the CD-ROM. In this topic, I can continue that example by using that **FileStream** object to create a **StreamWriter** object and use **StreamWriter** methods to write sample text to the file. Here's how this looks (note that I've discussed these methods in the In Depth section of this chapter; for example, **Write** just writes text, while **WriteLine** follows the text it writes with a carriage-return/linefeed pair):

```
Imports System
Imports System.IO

Public Class Form1
    Inherits System.Windows.Forms.Form

    'Windows Form Designer generated code

    Private Sub Button1_Click(ByVal sender As System.Object, _
        ByVal e As System.EventArgs) Handles Button1.Click
        Dim fs As New System.IO.FileStream("file.txt", FileMode.Create, _
            FileAccess.Write)
```

```
        Dim w As New StreamWriter(fs)
        w.BaseStream.Seek(0, SeekOrigin.End)
        w.WriteLine("Here is the file's text.")
        w.Write("Here is more file text." & ControlChars.CrLf)
        w.WriteLine("And that's about it.")
        w.Flush()
        w.Close()
          .
          .
          .

    End Sub
End Class
```

*TIP: I'm using the **Flush** method here—as mentioned in the In Depth section of this chapter—because file handling is buffered in Visual Basic, nothing is written to disk until the buffer is flushed. This happens automatically when the buffer is full or when you close a file (or when the associated stream object goes out of scope) so you don't have to use **Flush**, but you can use the **Flush** method to explicitly flush data to the disk. I'm using it here just to show that it exists.*

At the end of this code, I close the file, which makes it available to other programs. We also can open the file again and read the text data back in, using the **StreamReader** class. I'll do that in the next two topics.

Using the **StreamReader** Class

You can use the **StreamReader** class to read text data from files; here's the hierarchy of this class:

```
Object
    MarshalByRefObject
        TextReader
            StreamReader
```

You can find the more notable public properties of the **StreamReader** class in Table 13.14 and the more notable methods of this class in Table 13.15.

Table 13.14   Noteworthy public properties of StreamReader objects.

Property	Means
BaseStream	Holds the underlying stream, giving you access to that stream's properties and methods.
CurrentEncoding	Gets the character encoding for the stream reader.

Table 13.15   Noteworthy public methods of StreamReader objects.

Method	Means
Close	Closes the stream reader.
DiscardBufferedData	Discards the data in the buffer.
Peek	Looks ahead and returns the next available character (but does not actually read it as **Read** would, so does not advance the read/write position). Returns -1 if there is no more data waiting to be read.
Read	Reads the next character or characters.
ReadLine	Reads a line of text from the stream, returning that data as a string.
ReadToEnd	Reads from the current position to the end of the stream.

Reading Text with the **StreamReader** Class

In the topic "Writing Text with the **StreamWriter** Class" in this chapter, I used the **StreamWriter** class to write text to a file in the StreamWriterReader example on the CD-ROM. You also can use the **StreamReader** class to read that text back in, and I do that in the **StreamWriterReader** example like this, as discussed in the In Depth section of this chapter:

```
Imports System
Imports System.IO

Public Class Form1
    Inherits System.Windows.Forms.Form

    'Windows Form Designer generated code

    Private Sub Button1_Click(ByVal sender As System.Object, _
        ByVal e As System.EventArgs) Handles Button1.Click
        Dim fs As New System.IO.FileStream("file.txt", FileMode.Create, _
            FileAccess.Write)

        Dim w As New StreamWriter(fs)
        w.BaseStream.Seek(0, SeekOrigin.End)
        w.WriteLine("Here is the file's text.")
        w.Write("Here is more file text." & ControlChars.CrLf)
        w.WriteLine("And that's about it.")
        w.Flush()
        w.Close()
```

```
        fs = New System.IO.FileStream("file.txt", FileMode.Open, _
            FileAccess.Read)

        Dim r As New StreamReader(fs)
        r.BaseStream.Seek(0, SeekOrigin.Begin)
        While r.Peek() > -1
            TextBox1.Text &= r.ReadLine() & ControlChars.CrLf
        End While
        r.Close()
    End Sub
End Class
```

This code reads the text we've written to the file file.txt and displays it in a text box, as you see in Figure 13.3. As discussed in the In Depth section of this chapter, you use **StreamWriter** and **StreamReader** with text—if you want to handle binary data, use **BinaryWriter** and **BinaryReader** (see the next few topics).

Using the **BinaryWriter** Class

As discussed in the In Depth section of this chapter, after you have a **FileStream** object, you can use the **BinaryWriter** class to write binary data to a file. Here is the hierarchy of the **BinaryWriter** class:

```
Object
    BinaryWriter
```

You can find the more notable public properties of the **BinaryWriter** class in Table 13.16 and the more notable methods of this class in Table 13.17.

Table 13.16 Noteworthy public properties of BinaryWriter objects.

Property	Means
BaseStream	Gets the underlying stream, giving you access to that stream's properties and methods.

Table 13.17 Noteworthy public methods of BinaryWriter objects.

Method	Means
Close	Closes the binary writer as well as the underlying stream.
Flush	Flushes the buffer of the binary writer and writes out any buffered data.
Seek	Sets the read/write position in the stream.
Write	Writes data to the stream.

Writing Binary Data with the **BinaryWriter** Class

As discussed in the In Depth section of this chapter, once you have a **FileStream** object, you can use the **BinaryWriter** class to write binary data to a file. The BinaryWriterReader example on the CD-ROM shows how to do this, and this topic is also discussed in the In Depth section of this chapter. That example uses the **BinaryWriter** class's **Write** method to write 20 **Int32** values to a file, data.dat:

```
Imports System.IO

Public Class Form1
    Inherits System.Windows.Forms.Form

    'Windows Form Designer generated code

    Private Sub Button1_Click(ByVal sender As System.Object, _
        ByVal e As System.EventArgs) Handles Button1.Click
        Dim fs As FileStream = New FileStream("data.dat", _
            FileMode.OpenOrCreate)
        Dim w As BinaryWriter = New BinaryWriter(fs)
        Dim LoopIndex As Int32

        For LoopIndex = 0 To 19
            w.Write(LoopIndex)
        Next
        .
        .
        .

    End Sub
End Class
```

After writing those values to the file, you also can read them back with the **BinaryReader** class. See the next two topics for the details.

Using the **BinaryReader** Class

As discussed in the In Depth section of this chapter, you can use the **BinaryClass** class to read binary data from files once you have a **FileStream** object; here's this class's hierarchy:

```
Object
    BinaryReader
```

You can find the more notable public properties of the **BinaryReader** class in Table 13.18 and the more notable methods in Table 13.19.

Table 13.18   Noteworthy public properties of BinaryReader objects.

Property	Means
BaseStream	Holds the underlying stream of the binary reader, giving you access to that stream's properties and methods.

Table 13.19   Noteworthy public methods of BinaryReader objects.

Method	Means
Close	Closes the binary reader as well as the underlying stream.
PeekChar	Peeks ahead and returns the next available character (but does not advance the read/write position).
Read	Reads characters from the underlying stream and advances the current position of the stream.
ReadBoolean	Reads a **Boolean** from the stream.
ReadByte	Reads the next byte from the stream.
ReadBytes	Reads a number of bytes from the stream into a byte array.
ReadChar	Reads the next character from the stream.
ReadChars	Reads a number of characters from the stream.
ReadDecimal	Reads a decimal value from the stream.
ReadDouble	Reads an 8-byte floating-point value from the stream.
ReadInt16	Reads a 2-byte signed integer from the stream.
ReadInt32	Reads a 4-byte signed integer from the stream.
ReadInt64	Reads an 8-byte signed integer from the stream.
ReadSByte	Reads a signed byte from the stream.
ReadSingle	Reads a 4-byte floating-point value from the stream.
ReadString	Reads a string from the current stream.
ReadUInt16	Reads a 2-byte unsigned integer from the stream.
ReadUInt32	Reads a 4-byte unsigned integer from the stream.
ReadUInt64	Reads an 8-byte unsigned integer from the stream.

13. Graphics and File Handling

Reading Binary Data with the **BinaryReader** Class

As discussed in the In Depth section of this chapter, if you have a **FileStream** object, you can use the **BinaryReader** class to read binary data from files. In the BinaryWriterReader example on the CD-ROM, I first write 20 **Int32** values to a file and then read them back with a **BinaryReader** object like this, using the **ReadInt32** method, and display them in a text box:

```
Imports System.IO

Public Class Form1
    Inherits System.Windows.Forms.Form

    'Windows Form Designer generated code

    Private Sub Button1_Click(ByVal sender As System.Object, _
        ByVal e As System.EventArgs) Handles Button1.Click
        Dim fs As FileStream = New FileStream("data.dat", _
            FileMode.OpenOrCreate)
        Dim w As BinaryWriter = New BinaryWriter(fs)
        Dim LoopIndex As Int32

        For LoopIndex = 0 To 19
            w.Write(LoopIndex)
        Next

        w.Seek(0, SeekOrigin.Begin)
        Dim r As BinaryReader = New BinaryReader(fs)

        For LoopIndex = 0 To 19
            TextBox1.Text &= r.ReadInt32() & ControlChars.CrLf
        Next
    End Sub
End Class
```

You can see the results of this code in Figure 13.8, where the integers appear in the text box after having been written to the data.dat file and then read back in.

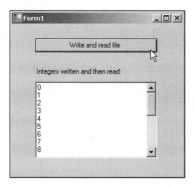

Figure 13.8   Writing and reading binary data to and from a file.

Using the **File** Class

The **File** class lets you work with files, copying, deleting, and creating them. Here is the hierarchy for this class:

```
Object
    File
```

You can find the public class (shared) methods of this class in Table 13.20.

Table 13.20   Noteworthy public class (shared) methods of the **File** class.

Method	Means
AppendText	Appends text to a file, or creates the file if it does not exist.
Copy	Copies a file to a new file.
Create	Creates a file.
CreateText	Creates a **StreamWriter** object that writes a new text file.
Delete	Deletes a file.
Exists	Determines if a file exists.
GetAttributes	Gets the file attributes of a file.
GetCreationTime	Gets a file's date and time.
GetLastAccessTime	Gets the date and time a file was last accessed.
GetLastWriteTime	Gets the date and time a file was last written.
Move	Moves a file to a new location.
Open	Opens a **FileStream** object for the file.

(continued)

13. Graphics and File Handling

Table 13.20   Noteworthy public class (shared) methods of the File class _(continued)_.

Method	Means
OpenRead	Creates a read-only file.
OpenText	Creates a **StreamReader** object that reads from a text file.
OpenWrite	Creates a read/write stream for a file.
SetAttributes	Sets file attributes for a file.
SetCreationTime	Sets a file's date and time.
SetLastAccessTime	Sets a file's last access date and time.
SetLastWriteTime	Sets a file's last written date and time.

Using the **Directory** class

Visual Basic .NET allows you to work with folders and drives via the **Directory** class. This class gives you the ability to create, edit, and delete folders, as well as maintain the drives on your system. Here is the hierarchy of this class:

```
Object
    Directory
```

You can find the public class (shared) methods of this class in Table 13.21.

Table 13.21   Noteworthy public class (shared) methods of the Directory class.

Method	Means
CreateDirectory	Creates directories.
Delete	Deletes a directory (and any directory contents!).
Exists	**True** if a directory exists.
GetCreationTime	Gets a directory's creation date and time.
GetCurrentDirectory	Gets the current (default) directory.
GetDirectories	Gets the directories in the current directory.
GetDirectoryRoot	Gets the root part of a path.
GetFiles	Gets the files in a directory.
GetFileSystemEntries	Gets the file system entries for a path.
GetLastAccessTime	Gets the date and time a directory was last accessed.
GetLastWriteTime	Gets the date and time a directory was last written.
GetLogicalDrives	Gets the names of the computer's logical drives.

(continued)

Table 13.21 Noteworthy public class (shared) methods of the Directory class *(continued).*

Method	Means
GetParent	Gets the parent directory.
Move	Moves a directory (including its contents).
SetCreationTime	Sets a directory's creation time.
SetCurrentDirectory	Sets the current directory.
SetLastAccessTime	Sets a directory's last accessed date and time.
SetLastWriteTime	Sets a directory's last written-to date and time.

Putting the **File** and **Directory** Classes to Work

You'll find an example showing how to use the **File** and **Directory** classes on the CD-ROM. This example is called copier, and it lets you create a directory and then copy a file to that new directory. As discussed in the In Depth section of this chapter, to use the **File** and **Directory** classes, I first import the **System.IO** namespace, then use the **Directory** class's **CreateDirectory** method to create a new directory, using the path the user has entered into a text box. Then I use an Open File dialog box to determine what file the user wants to copy, and use the **File** class's **Copy** method to actually copy the file:

```
Imports System.IO

Public Class Form1
    Inherits System.Windows.Forms.Form

    'Windows Form Designer generated code

    Private Sub Button1_Click(ByVal sender As System.Object, _
        ByVal e As System.EventArgs) Handles Button1.Click
        Try
            Directory.CreateDirectory(TextBox1.Text)
        Catch
            MsgBox("Could not create directory.")
            Exit Sub
        End Try
        MsgBox("Directory created.")
    End Sub

    Private Sub Button2_Click(ByVal sender As System.Object, _
        ByVal e As System.EventArgs) Handles Button2.Click
```

13. Graphics and File Handling

```
    Try
        If OpenFileDialog1.ShowDialog <> DialogResult.Cancel Then
            File.Copy(OpenFileDialog1.FileName, TextBox1.Text & "\" & _
                OpenFileDialog1.FileName.Substring( _
                OpenFileDialog1.FileName.LastIndexOf("\")))
        End If
    Catch
        MsgBox("Could not copy file.")
        Exit Sub
    End Try
    MsgBox("File copied.")
End Sub
End Class
```

And that's all it takes—I didn't need to open the file, or even create objects of the **File** and **Directory** classes. You can see the results of this code after the files has been copied to the new directory in Figure 13.4.

Chapter 14

Web Forms

In Depth

In this chapter, we begin our work with Web applications. One of the most important features of Visual Basic .NET is the ability to create distributed applications centered around the Web, so prepare to be amazed. In this chapter, I'll take a look at creating Web applications with Web forms. This represents quite a change from Windows forms, and there's an amazing amount of programming power coming up.

Working with Web Forms

Web forms are based on ASP.NET (ASP stands for Active Server Pages). Visual Basic will handle the details of working with ASP.NET for us, so in the end, it feels much like you're working with a standard Windows Visual Basic project. But the difference is that you're creating a Web page or pages that can be accessed by any browser on the Internet. These Web pages are given the extension .aspx, so, for example, if your program is called CalculateRates, you might end up simply directing users to a Web page called CalculateRates.aspx, which they can open in their browsers.

To create Web applications, you'll need a computer with the Microsoft Internet Information Services (IIS) version 5.0 or later installed (either locally or on a remote server).

IIS must be running on a Windows machine with the .NET framework installed so your Visual Basic code can run. Note that for development purposes, you can use IIS locally if you install it on the same machine that you develop programs on. (IIS comes pre-installed in some Windows operating systems like Windows 2000 Server, and it comes on the CDs for it, but still has to be installed in others, such as Windows 2000 Professional.)

The Web forms you create need not run in Internet Explorer, but if they don't, a number of features will usually be disabled, because they need Internet Explorer to work (see the topic "Detecting Browser Type and Capabilities" in the Immediate Solutions section of this chapter). In Web forms, the user interface programming is divided into two distinct pieces: the visual component, which is the Web page itself (this can include scripting code, such as JavaScript—or

JScript, the Internet Explorer equivalent—to run in the browser), and the Visual Basic code behind that page (which runs on the server). The visual component has the extension .aspx, and the code that runs on the server has the extension .aspx.vb.

Working with Web Form Controls

Developing a Web form-based application is much like developing a Windows form-based application. Visual Basic will manage the files on the server automatically, and you don't have to explicitly upload or download anything, and that's very cool because we can make use of all that Visual Basic already offers us, such as drag-and-drop programming, IntelliSense code prompts, what-you-see-is-what-you-get (WYSIWYG) visual interface designing, project management, and so on. You can fill your Web forms with Web controls, just as you can place Windows controls in a Windows form. But because they run in browsers, Web forms and Web controls are more limited than the Windows variety.

Web Server Controls

In fact, there are two varieties of Web form controls—server controls and client controls. *Web server controls* run not in the browser, but back in the server. That means that when an event occurs, the Web page has to be sent back to the Web server to handle the event. For that reason, Microsoft has restricted Web server control events greatly, mostly handling only **Click**-type events. And by default, many events—like **SelectedIndexChanged** events in list boxes—are not sent back to the server at all, but wait until the whole page is sent ("posted" is the Web term) back to the server (which happens when you click a control that is always handled on the server, such as buttons). However, you *can* force Web server control events like **SelectedIndex Changed** to be sent back to the server at the time they occur if you set the control's **AutoPostBack** property to **True** (see "Forcing Event Handling" in the Immediate Solutions section of this chapter).

Because Web server controls like these are handled back at the server, you can connect Visual Basic code to them. Web server controls often support more functionality than standard HTML controls—but note that they still must run in a browser, so they're actually made up from HTML controls, sometimes in combination with others. You can find the Web server controls—many of which you'll recognize from Windows forms—in Table 14.1. When you want to add these controls to a Web form, you select the Web Forms tab in the toolbox.

Table 14.1   Web server controls.

Control	Does this
Label	A label control.
TextBox	A text box control.
DropDownList	A control that allows users to select items from a list or enter text directly.
ListBox	A list box control.
Image	A control that simply displays an image.
AdRotator	A control that displays ad banners.
CheckBox	A checkbox control.
CheckBoxList	A control that supports a group of checkboxes.
RadioButton	A radio button control.
RadioButtonList	A control that supports a group of radio buttons.
Calendar	A control that displays a calendar for choosing dates.
Button	A button control.
LinkButton	A button that looks like a hyperlink but lets you handle **Click** events like any other button.
ImageButton	A button that displays an image.
HyperLink	A control that displays a hyperlink.
Table	A control that creates an HTML table.
TableCell	A cell in an HTML table.
TableRow	A row in an HTML table.
Panel	A panel control.
Repeater	A data control that displays information from a data set using HTML elements.
DataList	A control that displays data with more formatting options than a Repeater control.
DataGrid	A control that displays data in a table of columns.

HTML Server Controls

Visual Basic creates some Web server controls especially for Web forms, but it also supports the standard HTML controls such as HTML text fields and HTML buttons. You can turn all standard HTML controls into *HTML server controls*, whose events are handled back at the server. To do that, you right-click a control and select the "Run As Server Control" item. When you do, you can handle such HTML server controls in Visual Basic code in your program by connecting event-handling code to them just as you would in Windows forms. You can find the HTML server controls in Table 14.2. When you want to add these controls to a Web form, you use the HTML tab in the toolbox.

Table 14.2   HTML server controls.

Control	Does this
HtmlForm	Creates an HTML form.
HtmlInputText	Creates an HTML text field. (You also can use this control to create password fields.)
HtmlTextArea	Creates an HTML text area (two-dimensional text field).
HtmlAnchor	Creates an **<a>** element for navigation.
HtmlButton	Creates an HTML button using the **<button>** element.
HtmlInputButton	Creates an HTML button using the **<input>** element.
HtmlInputImage	Creates an HTML button that displays images.
HtmlSelect	Creates an HTML select control.
HtmlImage	Creates an HTML **<img>** element.
HtmlInputHidden	Creates an HTML hidden control.
HtmlInputCheckbox	Creates an HTML checkbox.
HtmlInputRadioButton	Creates an HTML radio button.
HtmlTable	Creates an HTML table.
HtmlTableRow	Creates a row in an HTML table.
HtmlTableCell	Creates a cell in an HTML table.
HtmlInputFile	Creates an HTML file upload control.
HtmlGenericControl	Creates a basic control for an HTML element.

HTML Client Controls

HTML controls don't run on the server by default; they only do so if you right-click a control and select the Run As Server Control menu item. By default, they are handled in the browser, out of the reach of Visual Basic code. There is an advantage to operating this way; if you handle events in the Web client (the browser) instead of the Web server, the whole page doesn't have to make the round trip to the server, which saves a lot of time. Visual Basic refers to controls handled this way as *HTML client controls*. Because they run in the browser (as such controls might in any Web page), you have to program them with a language the browser understands, such as JavaScript. You do that with the Visual Basic HTML editor, which allows you to edit the HTML of the Web page directly; we'll see an example of this in this chapter. You add these controls to a Web form just as you add HTML server controls—with the HTML tab in the toolbox—but you don't select the Run As Server Control menu item here.

Validation Controls

Besides Web server controls, HTML server controls, and HTML client controls, you also can work with *validation controls* in Web forms. A validation control lets you test a user's input—for example, you can make sure that the user has entered text into a text field. You also can perform more complex tests, such as comparing what's been entered against a pattern of characters or numbers to make sure things are in the right format. To make these more specific tests, validation controls support *regular expressions*, which are special expressions used to check text against a pattern to see how well they match that pattern. You can find the validation controls in Table 14.3.

TIP: *We'll cover regular expressions in this book, but for the full story, take a look at the Coriolis* Perl Black Book, *which examines regular expressions in great detail.*

User Controls

User controls are controls that you create as Web forms pages. You can embed user controls in Web forms, giving you an easy way to create menus, toolbars, and other elements that users are familiar with from Windows forms.

Saving a Web Application's State

Here's another place where Web form programming differs from Windows form programming—in saving the current *state* of the data in controls. The problem here is that your data is in a Web page, and the code that works on them is back on the server. Visual Basic makes automatic provision to store the data in Web server controls using HTML hidden fields (that is, HTML **<input>** elements with the **type** attribute set to "hidden"), so you don't have to worry about the data in each Web server control (such as the text in a text box). However, what about the

Table 14.3   Validation controls.

Control	Does this
RequiredFieldValidator	Makes sure the user enters data in this field.
CompareValidator	Uses comparison operators to compare user-entered data to a constant value.
RangeValidator	Makes sure that user-entered data is in a range between given lower and upper boundaries.
RegularExpressionValidator	Makes sure that user-entered data matches a regular-expression pattern.
CustomValidator	Makes sure user-entered data passes validation criteria that you set yourself.

variables in your program code? They're reset to their default value each time the page is sent on a round trip to the server, so making sure that the data in your variables is stored is up to you. To see how to do this, see "Saving Program Data across Server Round Trips" in the Immediate Solutions section of this chapter.

There are two possible places to store the data in a page: in the page itself—that is, in the client—and in the server. To see how this works, take a look at "Saving Program Data across Server Round Trips" in this chapter; I'll also take a look at them in overview here.

TIP: *For another example showing how to persist (that is, save) data across server round trips using HTML hidden controls, see "Adding Items to List Boxes at Run Time" in Chapter 17.*

Saving State in the Client

If you save data in the client, then that data isn't stored on the server. This means the page has to store all the data in each control itself so it can be sent back to the server when the page is posted back to the server. This is the easier way of doing things, because the server doesn't have to "remember" the state of all the applications that it is working with.

The default way of saving the state of the data in Visual Basic controls in Web applications is to use HTML hidden fields. A hidden field stores text data (it's supported with the HTML **<input type = "hidden">** element), and in this case, all the data in the controls is stored in encoded text. For example, a Web application page may have a hidden HTML field (which doesn't appear in the browser) that looks like this in HTML:

```
<input type="hidden" name="__VIEWSTATE"
value="dDwxMzI1NzI5NjA3OztsPEltYWdlQnV0dG9uMTs+Pg=="/>
```

Note that this element uses an XML-style self-closing tag, which ends with />. You'll see this syntax in several places in the HTML that Visual Basic generates. This is the same as if you had explicitly added a closing tag, like this:

```
<input type="hidden" name="__VIEWSTATE"
value="dDwxMzI1NzI5NjA3OztsPEltYWdlQnV0dG9uMTs+Pg=="></input>
```

You can create and use your own hidden fields to store data in, or if you use the **ViewState** property, you can use the hidden field that Visual Basic uses for the Web form—see "Saving Program Data across Server Round Trips" later in this chapter for the details.

Besides hidden fields, you also can use browser cookies to store the state of a page in Web applications. There's another option too, if you prefer: Web applications can use query strings, which are made up of information appended to the end of a page's URL after a question mark (?), something like this:

```
http://www.starpowder.com/checkout.aspx?item=1019&price=399
```

Saving State in the Server

In fact, you also can store an application's state on the server, which provides you with much more security than the client-side options. ASP .NET lets you store an application's state using an *application state object* (which is an object the **HttpApplicationState** class) for each active Web application. In this case, the application object is a global storage mechanism accessible from all pages in the Web application and is thus useful for storing information that needs to be maintained between server round trips and between pages.

Besides application state objects, ASP .NET also can store session states using a *session state object*, which is an object of the **HttpSessionState** class for each active Web application session. Once you add your session-specific information to the session state object, the Web server manages this object from then on.

Web Forms and HTML

Web forms are written in HTML, so to work with them (and customize them), you should have a working knowledge of HTML. They also include Active Server Pages (ASP) elements, but Visual Basic manages them for us, so it's less necessary to know ASP in detail. However, if you want to implement client-side scripting of HTML elements in your Web forms, you also should know a scripting language that the target browser can use, such as JavaScript. A good book for both HTML and JavaScript is the Coriolis *HTML Black Book*, which not only includes all HTML elements and how to use them, but also has a number of chapters on JavaScript, as well as how to use JavaScript with HTML controls. For reference, I'm including a quick listing of all the HTML tags in HTML 4.01 in Table 14.4.

Table 14.4   HTML 4.01 tags.

Tag	Use for:
<!-->	Comments and server-side includes
<!doctype>	Starting an HTML page
<a>	Creating a hyperlink or anchor
<abbr>	Displaying abbreviations

(continued)

Table 14.4   HTML 4.01 tags *(continued)*.

Tag	Use for:
<acronym>	Displaying acronyms
<address>	Displaying an address
<applet>	Embedding applets in Web pages
<area>	Creating clickable regions in image maps
<b>	Creating bold text
<base>	Setting the base for hyperlinks
<basefont>	Setting the base font
<bdo>	Overriding the bidirectional character algorithm
<bgsound>	Adding background sounds
<big>	Creating big text
<blink>	Making text blink
<blockquote>	Indenting quotations
<body>	Creating a Web page's body
** **	Inserting line breaks
<button>	Creating a customizable button
<caption>	Creating a table caption
<center>	Centering text
<cite>	Creating a citation
<code>	Displaying program code
<col>	Defining a column
<colgroup>	Grouping and formatting columns
<dd>	Creating definition list definitions
<del>	Displaying text as deleted
<dfn>	Defining new terms
<dir>	Creating a list (obsolete)
<div>	Formatting block text
<dl>	Creating definition lists
<dt>	Creating definition list terms
<em>	Emphasizing text
<embed>	Embedding multimedia and plug-ins in a Web page
<fieldset>	Grouping form elements
<font>	Specifying a font

(continued)

14. Web Forms

Table 14.4   HTML 4.01 tags *(continued)*.

Tag	Use for:
\<form>	Creating HTML forms
\<frame>	Creating frames
\<frameset>	Creating frames
\<h1> through \<h6>	Creating Web page headings
\<head>	Creating a Web page's head
\<hr>	Creating horizontal rules
\<html>	Starting an HTML page
\<i>	Creating italic text
\<iframe>	Creating inline or floating frames
\<ilayer>	Creating inline layers
\<img>	Adding an image to a Web page
\<input type=button>	Creating buttons
\<input type=checkbox>	Creating checkboxes
\<input type=file>	Creating file input for a form
\<input type=hidden>	Creating hidden data
\<input type=image>	Creating image submit buttons
\<input type=password>	Creating password controls
\<input type=radio>	Creating radio buttons
\<input type=reset>	Creating reset buttons
\<input type=submit>	Creating submit buttons
\<input type=text>	Creating text fields
\<ins>	Displaying inserted text
\<isindex>	Using an index
\<kbd>	Displaying text the user is to type
\<keygen>	Processing secure transactions
\<label>	Labeling form elements
\<layer>	Arranging text in layers
\<legend>	Creating a legend for form elements
\<li>	Creating list items
\<link>	Setting link information
\<map>	Creating client-side image maps
\<marquee>	Displaying text in a scrolling marquee

(continued)

14. Web Forms

Table 14.4   HTML 4.01 tags *(continued)*.

Tag	Use for:
<menu>	Creating a list (obsolete)
<meta>	Giving more information about your Web page
<multicol>	Creating columns
<nobr>	Avoiding line breaks
<noembed>	Handling browsers that don't handle embedding
<nolayer>	Handling browsers that don't handle layers
<noscript>	Handling browsers that don't handle JavaScript
<object>	Placing an object into a Web page
<ol>	Creating ordered lists
<optgroup>	Creating a select control item group
<option>	Creating a select control item
<p>	Creating paragraphs
<param>	Specifying a parameter
<pre>	Displaying preformatted text
<q>	Displaying short quotations
<rt>	Creating ruby text
<ruby>	Creating rubies
<s> And <strike>	Striking text out
<samp>	Displaying sample program output
<script>	Creating a script
<select>	Creating a select control
<server>	Running server-side JavaScript scripts
<small>	Creating small text
<spacer>	Controlling horizontal and vertical spacing
<span>	Formatting inline text
<strong>	Strongly emphasizing text
<style>	Using embedded style sheets
<sub>	Creating subscripts
<sup>	Creating superscripts
<table>	Creating a table
<tbody>	Create a table body when grouping rows
<td>	Creating table data

(continued)

14. Web Forms

Table 14.4   HTML 4.01 tags *(continued)*.

Tag	Use for:
<textarea>	Creating text areas
<tfoot>	Create a table foot when grouping rows
<th>	Creating table headings
<thead>	Creating a table head when grouping rows
<title>	Giving a Web page a title
<tr>	Creating a table row
<tt>	Creating "teletype" text
<u>	Underlining text
<ul>	Creating unordered lists
<var>	Displaying program variables and arguments
<wbr>	Allowing word breaks
<xml>	Accessing XML data with an XML data island

You should be familiar enough with HTML to know, for example, that HTML elements start with an opening tag, **<h1>** here, and often end with a closing tag, **</h1>**, such as this example, where I'm creating an **h1** heading with the text "Here is a heading!":

```
<h1>Here is a heading!</h1>
```

You also should be familiar enough with HTML to know, for example, that this **<input>** element creates a 40-character long text field with the name "text1", which can take 60 characters maximum, and that this **input** element has four attributes—**type**, **name**, **size**, and **maxlength**:

```
<input type= "text" name = "text1" size = "40" maxlength = "60">
```

TIP: *For the sake of reference, I've written and included on the CD-ROM an HTML file (open it in your browser) named htmlref.html, which is a complete HTML element reference. It includes all the HTML 4.01 elements (and additional ones that are browser-specific), all their attributes, what they mean, where you can use them, and in which browsers. Hopefully, that'll be all the reference you need, but if not, check out a good book on the subject, such as the* HTML Black Book *referred to earlier.*

Creating a Web Application

Before you create a Web application, you must have the Internet Information Server (IIS) running on the target server (which also must have the .NET Framework installed) that will host your application. The reason IIS must be running on the target server is that Visual Basic will create the files you need and host them directly on the server when you create the Web application (usually in the IIS directory named wwwroot).

To create a new Web application, select the File|New menu item in Visual Basic, just as you would to create a new Windows application. This time, however, select the ASP .NET Web Application icon, as shown in Figure 14.1. You can enter the name for the new application as you see in that figure. I'm going to call this first application WebApplication1.

Instead of specifying a local or network disk location in the Location box, you enter the location you want to use on a Web server. I'm using a local server (that is, a server on my computer) named STEVE in Figure 14.1, so the location is "http://STEVE". If I had wanted to store the application in a directory such as Ch14 (for Chapter 14), I could have entered the location "http://STEVE/Ch14". That would make the URL for the main Web form in the application, which is **WebForm1**, "http://STEVE/Ch14/applicationname/WebForm1.aspx". That's the URL that gets launched when I (or someone else) want to run the application. For applications on the Internet, that URL might look something like this: "http://www.starpowder.com/Ch14/applicationname/WebForm1.aspx". If you're unsure what server you want to use, click the Browse button next to the Location box in Figure 14.1. To create the Web application, click the OK button.

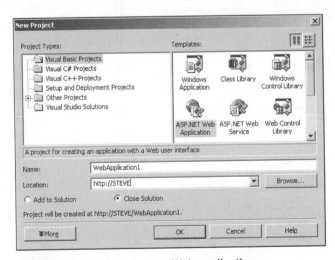

Figure 14.1   Creating a new Web application.

Similarly, to open a Web application that you've already created, use the File|Open Project From Web menu item (not the File|Open menu item). Visual Basic will ask for the URL of the server to use, then open the Open Project dialog you see in Figure 14.2. You can browse to the VBPROJ file you want and click Open to open it.

Once you've created the WebApplication1 application, you'll see the main Web form, WebForm1.aspx, open in the Visual Basic IDE, as shown in Figure 14.3. This new project is in fact like a Windows application project in many ways; for example, you can set project options—like debugging versus release versions— the same way you would with Windows projects.

You'll also see some new files in the Solution Explorer; here's an overview of what they do:

- *AssemblyInfo.vb* contains all the information for your assembly, such as versioning and dependencies.

- *Global.asax* handles application level ASP requests.

- *Styles.css* can be used to define default HTML style settings.

- *Web.config* contains application settings for the ASP .NET application.

- *Projectname.vsdisco* is an XML file that contains links about an ASP .NET Web application.

- *WebForm.aspx* is the Web form itself.

- References to these .NET Framework namespaces: **System**, **System.Data**, **System.Drawing**, **System.Web**, **System.Web.Services**, and **System.Xml**.

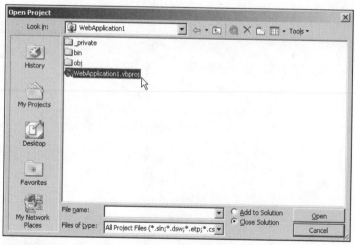

Figure 14.2   Opening a Web application.

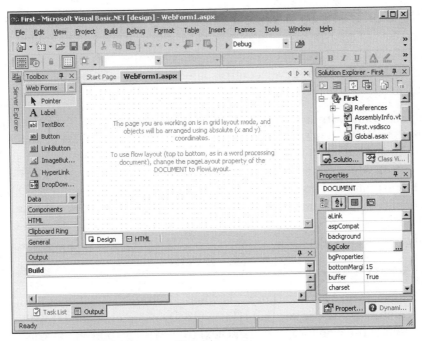

Figure 14.3   Designing a new Web form.

There is also a VBPROJ file on the server in the application's folder for the Visual Basic project itself, and you can open the application in Visual Basic using that VBPROJ file. When you start adding Visual Basic code to the application, a file with the extension .aspx.vb is created as well.

Note that the text in Figure 14.3 in the Web form indicates that it is in *grid layout mode*, which means you can place controls where you want them in the Web form, just as you would in a Windows form. The other layout option, which you set with the **pageLayout** property, is *flow layout*, which is the layout that browsers usually use. With flow layout, the controls you add to a Web form "flow," much like the words in a word processor's page, changing position when the page changes size. To anchor your controls, use grid layout. You can set the Web form's properties in the Properties window, like **bgColor**, to set the form's background color, just as you can for Windows controls.

NOTE: *There's a difference between the properties you'll see in the Properties window for Web forms versus Windows forms—Web forms support properties that you'll normally find in HTML pages, like **bgColor** (for the background color), **vLink** (for the color of hyperlinks the user has already visited), **text** (for the foreground color used for text), and so on. And note that these properties start with lowercase letters, unlike Windows forms properties, which start with capital letters.*

Adding Controls to a Web Form

You can now add controls to the Web form, just as you can with Windows forms. In this case, we'll use Web server controls, so click the Web Forms tab in the toolbox, making the Web server controls appear in the toolbox, as you see in Figure 14.4.

Just as you would with a Windows form, add two text boxes, **TextBox1** and **TextBox2**, to **WebForm1**, and a button with the caption "Click Me", as you see in Figure 14.4. (The small boxed arrow at upper left in each control indicates a server control, which is run at the server.) Also, add a list box control, **ListBox1**, to **WebForm1**, and add six items to it as you would to a Windows form list box; click the ellipsis ("...") button in the Items entry in the Properties window, and enter "Item 0" to "Item 5" in the ListItem Collection Editor dialog. This gives you the result you see in Figure 14.4.

Using HTML Views

The Web form itself, WebForm1.aspx, is where the actual HTML that browsers will open is stored. You can see that HTML directly if you click the HTML button at the bottom of the Web form designer (next to the Design button), as you see in Figure 14.5.

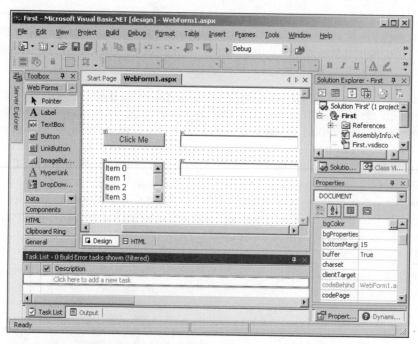

Figure 14.4   Adding Web server controls to a new Web form.

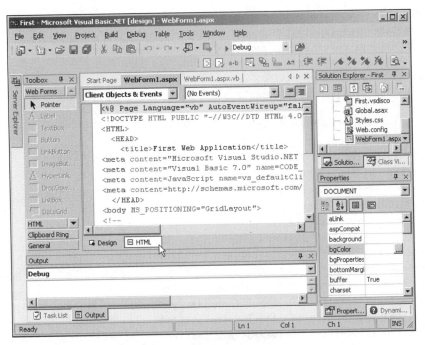

Figure 14.5   The HTML code for WebForm1.aspx.

This is close to the HTML that a Web browser will open, and you can edit this HTML directly (which we'll do later in this chapter). Note the ASP elements in this document, which begin here with **<%@** and **<asp:**. These ASP elements will be executed by IIS, which will create standard HTML from them. This HTML is then sent to the browser—that's how ASP works: ASP elements are executed in the server, which creates the HTML corresponding to the various ASP commands. That creates the final HTML that the browser actually sees, without any ASP elements in it.

Looking at WebForm1.aspx

Here's what WebForm1.aspx looks like—as you can see, this is just standard HTML, with ASP elements embedded in it for IIS (note in particular the **Codebehind** attribute, which connects this code to the appropriate Visual Basic code):

```
<%@ Page Language="vb" AutoEventWireup="false"
Codebehind="WebForm1.aspx.vb" Inherits="First.WebForm1"%>
<!DOCTYPE HTML PUBLIC "-//W3C//DTD HTML 4.0 Transitional//EN">
<HTML>
  <HEAD>
    <title>First Web Application</title>
    <meta name="GENERATOR" content="Microsoft Visual Studio .NET 7.0">
```

```
        <meta name="CODE_LANGUAGE" content="Visual Basic 7.0">
        <meta name=vs_defaultClientScript content="JavaScript">
        <meta name=vs_targetSchema content="http://schemas.microsoft.com/ _
            intellisense/ie5">
    </HEAD>
    <body MS_POSITIONING="GridLayout">

        <form id="Form1" method="post" runat="server">
<asp:Button id=Button1 style="Z-INDEX: 101; LEFT: 108px;
POSITION: absolute; TOP: 77px" runat="server"
Text="Button" Width="106px"Height="23px"></asp:Button>
<asp:TextBox id=TextBox2 style="Z-INDEX: 104; LEFT: 240px; POSITION:
absolute; TOP: 124px" runat="server" Width="205px"
Height="24px"></asp:TextBox>
<asp:ListBox id=ListBox1 style="Z-INDEX: 103; LEFT: 107px; POSITION:
absolute; TOP: 125px" runat="server" Width="107px" Height="71px"
AutoPostBack="True">
<asp:ListItem Value="Item 0">Item 0</asp:ListItem>
<asp:ListItem Value="Item 1">Item 1</asp:ListItem>
<asp:ListItem Value="Item 2">Item 2</asp:ListItem>
<asp:ListItem Value="Item 3">Item 3</asp:ListItem>
<asp:ListItem Value="Item 4">Item 4</asp:ListItem>
<asp:ListItem Value="Item 5">Item 5</asp:ListItem>
</asp:ListBox>
<asp:TextBox id=TextBox1 style="Z-INDEX: 102; LEFT: 240px;
POSITION: absolute; TOP: 78px" runat="server" Width="204px"
Height="22px"></asp:TextBox>

    </form>

  </body>
</HTML>
```

This doesn't look much like the Visual Basic code we've been working with throughout the book. That will appear in another file, WebForm1.aspx.vb.

Handling Events in Code

Double-click the button in **WebForm1** now. Doing so opens the code designer you see in Figure 14.6; the code here is definitely Visual Basic, and it runs on the server.

TIP: As with Windows forms, you also can select events to add code to in a code designer by selecting the object (such as a control or Web form) to work with in the left drop-down list box, and the event you want to handle in the right drop-down list box.

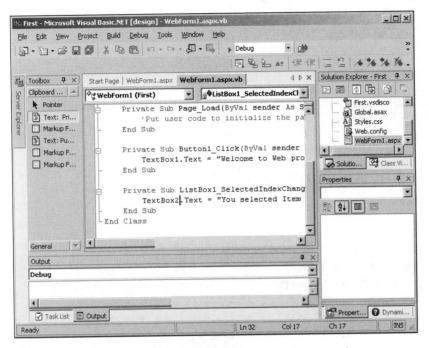

Figure 14.6   Code designer for WebForm1.

The Visual Basic code is stored in a file named WebForm1.aspx.vb. (This is also called the "code-behind" file.) Now that you've double-clicked the button in the Web form, the corresponding **Click** event handler opens in the code designer:

```
Private Sub Button1_Click(ByVal sender As System.Object, _
    ByVal e As System.EventArgs) Handles Button1.Click
    .
    .
    .

End Sub
```

You can enter code for this button just as you can in Windows forms. For example, to display the message "Welcome to Web programming" in the text box when the button is clicked, you can use this code:

```
Private Sub Button1_Click(ByVal sender As System.Object, _
    ByVal e As System.EventArgs) Handles Button1.Click
    TextBox1.Text = "Welcome to Web programming."
End Sub
```

In the same way, I'll add code to display the current selection, when that selection changes, in the list box's **SelectedIndexChanged** event handler:

```
        Private Sub ListBox1_SelectedIndexChanged(ByVal sender As _
            System.Object, ByVal e As System.EventArgs) Handles _
            ListBox1.SelectedIndexChanged
                TextBox2.Text = "You selected Item " & sender.SelectedIndex
        End Sub
```

TIP: *In fact, it's possible to embed Visual Basic code directly in ASPX files—no ASPXVB "code-behind" file needed. Take a look at "Embedding Visual Basic Code in Web Pages" in the Immediate Solutions section of this chapter for the details.*

Looking at WebForm1.aspx.vb

Here's what the whole file, WebForm1.aspx.vb, looks like when you've added this code:

```
Public Class WebForm1
    Inherits System.Web.UI.Page
    Protected WithEvents TextBox1 As System.Web.UI.WebControls.TextBox
    Protected WithEvents ListBox1 As System.Web.UI.WebControls.ListBox
    Protected WithEvents TextBox2 As System.Web.UI.WebControls.TextBox
    Protected WithEvents Button1 As System.Web.UI.WebControls.Button

#Region " Web Form Designer Generated Code "

    'This call is required by the Web Form Designer.
    <System.Diagnostics.DebuggerStepThrough()> Private Sub _
        InitializeComponent()

    End Sub

    Private Sub Page_Init(ByVal sender As System.Object, _
        ByVal e As System.EventArgs) Handles MyBase.Init
        'CODEGEN: This method call is required by the Web Form Designer
        'Do not modify it using the code editor.
        InitializeComponent()
    End Sub

#End Region

    Private Sub Page_Load(ByVal sender As System.Object, _
        ByVal e As System.EventArgs) Handles MyBase.Load
        'Put user code to initialize the page here
    End Sub

    Private Sub Button1_Click(ByVal sender As System.Object, _
        ByVal e As System.EventArgs) Handles Button1.Click
```

```
        TextBox1.Text = "Welcome to Web programming."
    End Sub

    Private Sub ListBox1_SelectedIndexChanged(ByVal sender As _
        System.Object, ByVal e As System.EventArgs) Handles _
        ListBox1.SelectedIndexChanged
        TextBox2.Text = "You selected Item " & sender.SelectedIndex
    End Sub
End Class
```

These two files, WebForm1.aspx and WebForm1.aspx.vb, form the core of the WebApplication1 application from a programming point of view. There are some other important files as well; I'll take a look at them, too.

Looking at AssemblyInfo.vb, Web.config, and Styles.css

As in Windows applications, the AssemblyInfo.vb file includes information about the assembly itself, and you can set version and other information here:

```
Imports System.Reflection
Imports System.Runtime.InteropServices

' General Information about an assembly is controlled through the following
' set of attributes. Change these attribute values to modify the
' information associated with an assembly.

' Review the values of the assembly attributes

<Assembly: AssemblyTitle("")>
<Assembly: AssemblyDescription("")>
<Assembly: AssemblyCompany("")>
<Assembly: AssemblyProduct("")>
<Assembly: AssemblyCopyright("")>
<Assembly: AssemblyTrademark("")>
<Assembly: CLSCompliant(True)>

'The following GUID is for the ID of the typelib if this project is _
    exposed to COM
<Assembly: Guid("3499736A-B472-459D-A21D-539E8DF8CA6B")>

' Version information for an assembly consists of the following four _
    values:
'
'       Major Version
'       Minor Version
'       Build Number
```

```
'       Revision
'
' You can specify all the values or you can default the _
     Build and Revision Numbers by using the '*' as shown below:
```

```
<Assembly: AssemblyVersion("1.0.*")>
```

The Web.config file contains information on how the server will handle your project. You can set options for tracing, security, and permission here, including how to make sure that no one can download your code from the server. This file is written in XML, and here's what it looks like:

```
<?xml version="1.0" encoding="utf-8" ?>
<configuration>

  <system.web>

    <!--  DYNAMIC DEBUG COMPILATION
    Set compilation debug="true" to insert debugging symbols
    (.pdb information) into the compiled page. Because this creates
    a larger file that executes more slowly, you should set this
    value to true only when debugging and to false at all other times.
    For more information, refer to the documentation
    about debugging ASP .NET files.
    -->
    <compilation defaultLanguage="vb" debug="true" />

    <!--  CUSTOM ERROR MESSAGES
        Set customErrors mode="On" or "RemoteOnly" to enable custom error
        messages, "Off" to disable.
        Add <error> tags for each of the errors you want to handle.
    -->
    <customErrors mode="RemoteOnly" />

    <!--  AUTHENTICATION
        This section sets the authentication policies of the application.
        Possible modes are "Windows",
        "Forms", "Passport" and "None"
    -->
    <authentication mode="Windows" />
```

```
<!--   AUTHORIZATION
This section sets the authorization policies of the application.
You can allow or deny access to application resources by user or
role. Wildcards: "*" means everyone, "?" means anonymous
(unauthenticated) users.
-->
<authorization>
    <allow users="*" /> <!-- Allow all users -->

        <!--  <allow     users="[comma separated list of users]"
                          roles="[comma separated list of roles]"/>
              <deny      users="[comma separated list of users]"
                          roles="[comma separated list of roles]"/>

        -->
</authorization>


<!--   APPLICATION-LEVEL TRACE LOGGING
Application-level tracing enables trace log output for every page
within an application. Set trace enabled="true" to enable application
trace logging.  If pageOutput="true", the trace information will be
displayed at the bottom of each page.  Otherwise, you can view the
application trace log by browsing the "trace.axd" page from your
Web application root.
-->
<trace enabled="false" requestLimit="10" pageOutput="false"
    traceMode="SortByTime" localOnly="true" />


<!--   SESSION STATE SETTINGS
By default ASP .NET uses cookies to identify which requests belong to
a particular session. If cookies are not available, a session can be
tracked by adding a session identifier to the URL. To disable cookies,
set sessionState cookieless="true".
-->
<sessionState
        mode="InProc"
        stateConnectionString="tcpip=127.0.0.1:42424"
        sqlConnectionString=
        "data source=127.0.0.1;user id=sa;password="
        cookieless="false"
        timeout="20"
    />
```

```
<!--   PREVENT SOURCE CODE DOWNLOAD
       This section sets the types of files that will not be downloaded.
       As well as entering a httphandler for a file type, you also must
       associate that file type with the xspisapi.dll in the App
       Mappings property of the Web site, or the file can be downloaded
       It is recommended that you use this section to prevent your
       sources being downloaded.
  -->
  <httpHandlers>
        <add verb="*" path="*.vb"
            type="System.Web.HttpNotFoundHandler,System.Web" />
        <add verb="*" path="*.cs"
            type="System.Web.HttpNotFoundHandler,System.Web" />
        <add verb="*" path="*.vbproj"
            type="System.Web.HttpNotFoundHandler,System.Web" />
        <add verb="*" path="*.csproj"
            type="System.Web.HttpNotFoundHandler,System.Web" />
        <add verb="*" path="*.webinfo"
            type="System.Web.HttpNotFoundHandler,System.Web" />
  </httpHandlers>


  <!--   GLOBALIZATION
         This section sets the globalization settings of the application.
  -->
  <globalization requestEncoding="utf-8" responseEncoding="utf-8" />
 </system.web>
</configuration>
```

Finally, the Styles.css file holds the Cascading Style Sheet (CSS) styles for the page. This is an important file when you want to start customizing your Web application's appearance in the browser, because it sets the styles used. CSS is the usual way to set styles for Web pages, but using CSS takes a little getting used to. For the details, check out a book on the subject—the *HTML Black Book* (The Coriolis Group) covers CSS styles in depth. Here's what Styles.css looks like; note that you can set the style (including font, font weight, and so on) for many HTML elements:

```
/* Default CSS Stylesheet for a new Web Application project */

BODY
{
    BACKGROUND-COLOR: white;
    FONT-FAMILY: Verdana, Helvetica, sans-serif;
    FONT-SIZE: .8em;
    FONT-WEIGHT: normal;
    LETTER-SPACING: normal;
    TEXT-TRANSFORM: none;
    WORD-SPACING: normal
```

```
}

H1, H2, H3, H4, H5, TH, THEAD, TFOOT
{
    COLOR: #003366;
}
H1    {
    font-family: Verdana, Arial, Helvetica, sans-serif;
    font-size:    2em;
    font-weight:    700;
    font-style:    normal;
    text-decoration:    none;
    word-spacing:    normal;
    letter-spacing:    normal;
    text-transform:    none;
    }

H2    {
    font-family: Verdana, Arial, Helvetica, sans-serif;
    font-size:    1.75em;
    font-weight:    700;
    font-style:    normal;
    text-decoration:    none;
    word-spacing:    normal;
    letter-spacing:    normal;
    text-transform:    none;
    }

H3    {
    font-family: Verdana, Arial, Helvetica, sans-serif;
    font-size:    1.58em;
    font-weight:    500;
    font-style:    normal;
    text-decoration:    none;
    word-spacing:    normal;
    letter-spacing:    normal;
    text-transform:    none;
    }

H4    {
    font-family: Verdana, Arial, Helvetica, sans-serif;
    font-size:    1.33em;
    font-weight:    500;
    text-decoration:    none;
    word-spacing:    normal;
    letter-spacing:    normal;
    text-transform:    none;
    }
```

```
H5, DT     {
    font-family: Verdana, Arial, Helvetica, sans-serif;
    font-size:    1em;
    font-weight:   700;
    font-style:    normal;
    text-decoration:   none;
    word-spacing:   normal;
    letter-spacing:    normal;
    text-transform:    none;
    }


H6     {
    font-family: Verdana, Arial, Helvetica, sans-serif;
    font-size:    .8em;
    font-weight:   700;
    font-style:    normal;
    text-decoration:   none;
    word-spacing:   normal;
    letter-spacing:    normal;
    text-transform:    none;
    }


TFOOT, THEAD    {
    font-size:    1em;
    word-spacing:   normal;
    letter-spacing:    normal;
    text-transform:    none;
    font-family: Arial, Helvetica, sans-serif;
    }


TH    {
    vertical-align:    baseline;
    font-size:    1em;
    font-weight:    bold;
    word-spacing:   normal;
    letter-spacing:    normal;
    text-transform:    none;
    font-family: Arial, Helvetica, sans-serif;
    }


A:link    {
    text-decoration:    none;
    color:    #3333cc;
    }
```

14. Web Forms

```
A:visited    {
   text-decoration:    none;
   color:    #333399;
   }


A:active    {
   text-decoration:    none;
   color:    #333399;
   }


A:hover    {
   text-decoration:    underline;
   color:    #3333cc;
   }


SMALL    {
   font-size:    .7em;
   }


BIG    {
   font-size:    1.17em;
   }


BLOCKQUOTE, PRE    {
   font-family:    Courier New, monospace;
   }


UL LI    {
   list-style-type:    square ;
   }


UL LI LI    {
   list-style-type:    disc;
   }


UL LI LI LI    {
   list-style-type:    circle;
   }


OL LI    {
   list-style-type:    decimal;
   }


OL OL LI    {
   list-style-type:    lower-alpha;
   }
```

```
OL OL OL LI    {
    list-style-type:    lower-roman;
    }

IMG    {
    margin-top: 5px;
    margin-left: 10px;
    margin-right: 10px;
    }
```

As you proceed in Web application programming, you'll probably want to customize this file to set the way various HTML elements are displayed.

Running a Web Application

Now we've written our first Web application, called First. You run it as you would a Windows application—for example, you can use the Debug|Start menu item in the Visual Basic IDE. Doing so starts the application—but this time, it'll appear not in a standard window, but in your default browser, as you see in Figure 14.7.

Of course, you don't need Visual Basic to run a Web application; you also can start the application simply by using a browser and navigating to its startup ASPX form on the server (that's http://STEVE/Ch14/First/WebForm1.aspx here; if you were running this page on a Web server named, say, starpowder.com, that could be http://www.starpowder.com/Ch14/First/WebForm1.aspx). The server will do the rest.

You can see the new Web application at work in Figure 14.7, looking a lot like a Visual Basic Windows application. Now you can click the button and the message "Welcome to Web programming" appears in the text box, as it should—although note it takes a round trip to the server to make that happen. You can see the results in Figure 14.7.

Now, try clicking an item in the list box. When you do, *nothing happens*. Why? I included a list box in this example to show that not all Web server control events are automatically sent back to the server when they occur (to save time by avoiding trips to the server). **Click** events usually are sent back to the server for processing, but not an event such as a list box's **SelectedIndexChanged** event.

Events like **SelectedIndexChanged** are handled the next time the page is sent back to the server. If you were to change the selection in the list box and then click the Click Me button, that would send the form's data back to the server, and when it reappeared, the message "Welcome to Web programming" would appear in the top text box—but the code for the **SelectedIndexChanged** event also would have run, so the bottom text box would indicate which item you selected.

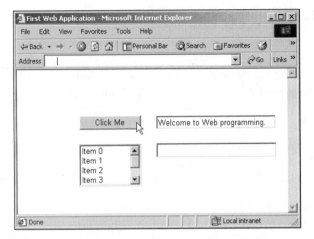

Figure 14.7   Running a Web application.

Sometimes, you don't want to wait until the form is sent back to the server by other events before handling events like the **SelectedIndexChanged** event. It turns out that you can *force* events like **SelectedIndexChanged** to be handled on the server at the time they occur if you set the control's **AutoPostBack** property to **True**. To see how that works, set the list box's **AutoPostBack** property to **True** and run the application again. When you do and when you change the selection in the list box by clicking a new selection, a message like "You selected Item 1" appears in the bottom text box, without your having to wait until some other event sends the form back to the server. You can see this in Figure 14.8.

And that's it—pretty cool, huh? To close the application, you close the Web browser, or select the Debug|Stop Debugging menu item.

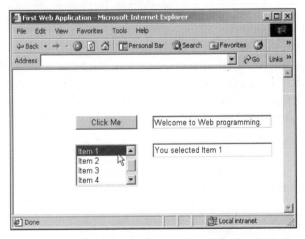

Figure 14.8   Enabling a Web application after **AutoPostBack**.

Using the HTML Editor to Customize Web Pages

One of the most important things to consider when designing your Web applications is your Web pages' *appearance*. You can customize their appearance in several ways. For instance, you can change the styles used in a Web application to display HTML elements in the Styles.css file. You can set the properties of a Web form in the Properties window, setting text color, background color, and so on. You also can edit the HTML in a Web form's ASPX file directly, and the Visual Basic IDE can operate as a great HTML editor for this purpose.

To edit HTML directly, click the HTML button at the bottom of the code designer for WebForm1.aspx in the First project we just created. When you click the Design button, you see what your HTML page will look like when it appears in a browser; when you click the HTML button, you see the actual HTML for the page (complete with ASP elements, of course). When you're looking at the HTML for the page, you can edit it just as you can edit Visual Basic code—and all the HTML syntax is already built into this editor.

For example, say that I wanted to display text in a centered **<h1>** header—the biggest HTML header there is—in a Web form. I can center the **<h1>** element with a **<div>** element, and when I type a **<div>** tag into the HTML, the HTML editor automatically adds a closing **</div>** tag. And when I add an **align** attribute, IntelliSense lists the possible values this attribute can take, as you see in Figure 14.9.

TIP: Why don't I use the more familiar **<center>** element to center this header? As of HTML 4.0, **<center>** is obsolete, and the Visual Basic HTML editor will mark it as a syntax error—the modern replacement is to use a **<div>** element with the **align** attribute set to "center".

Next, I add the **<h1>** element inside the **<div>** element, just by typing it in. To set the style for this element, you can add a **style** attribute to the element by typing that in, which makes IntelliSense display a button with the text "Build Style", which, when you click it, brings up the Style Builder (as you can see in Figure 14.10), which you can use to build CSS styles for individual elements. This is very useful indeed, because you don't have to remember what styles apply to which elements.

TIP: If you ever want to paste HTML into the HTML editor, use the Edit|Paste as HTML menu item, not simply Edit|Paste. The Edit|Paste item will convert elements like **<div>** to "<div>", but the Edit|Paste as HTML item will paste the HTML intact.

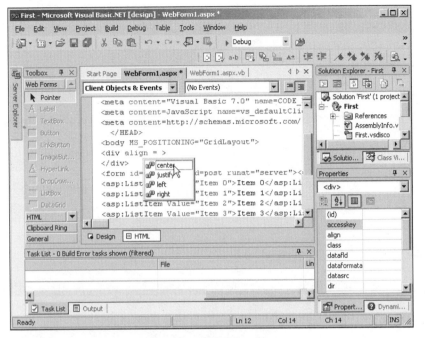

Figure 14.9 Using IntelliSense in the HTML editor.

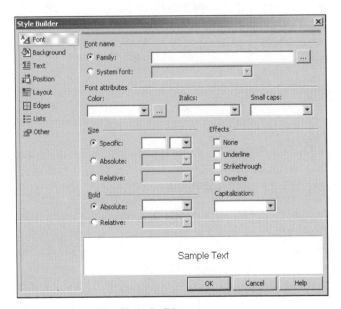

Figure 14.10 The Style Builder.

Using the HTML editor, then, I can add HTML to WebForm1.aspx to display the text "Web Forms" in an **<h1>** header like this:

```
<%@ Page Language="vb" AutoEventWireup="false"
Codebehind="WebForm1.aspx.vb" Inherits="First.WebForm1"%>
<!DOCTYPE HTML PUBLIC "-//W3C//DTD HTML 4.0 Transitional//EN">
<HTML>
  <HEAD>
    <title>First Web Application</title>
<meta content="Microsoft Visual Studio .NET 7.0" name=GENERATOR>
<meta content="Visual Basic 7.0" name=CODE_LANGUAGE>
<meta content=JavaScript name=vs_defaultClientScript>
<meta content=http://schemas.microsoft.com/intellisense/ie5
name=vs_targetSchema>
  </HEAD>
<body MS_POSITIONING="GridLayout">
<div align=center>
<h1 style ="FONT-SIZE: 36pt; FONT-FAMILY: 'Times New Roman'">Web Forms</h1>
</div>
<form id=Form1 method=post runat="server"><asp:button id=Button1
style="Z-INDEX: 101; LEFT: 108px; POSITION: absolute; TOP: 77px"
runat="server" Text="Button" Width="106px" Height="23px"></asp:button>
<asp:textbox id=TextBox2 style="Z-INDEX: 104; LEFT: 240px;
POSITION: absolute; TOP: 124px" runat="server" Width="205px"
Height="24px"></asp:textbox><asp:listbox id=ListBox1 style="Z-INDEX:
103; LEFT: 107px; POSITION: absolute; TOP: 125px" runat="server"
Width="107px" Height="71px" AutoPostBack="True">
        .
        .
        .
```

You can see how this header will appear in the Web page immediately; just click the Design button to switch to design view, as you see in Figure 14.11. In this way, we've been able to directly edit the HTML of **WebForm1**.

Of course, you don't have to edit any HTML directly if you don't want to; you can design much of a Web page's appearance by setting properties for the Web form in the Properties window, and you can display headers like the one in this example using label controls. However, it's important to know that you can work with a Web form's HTML directly and customize what's going on—if you want to and know how to.

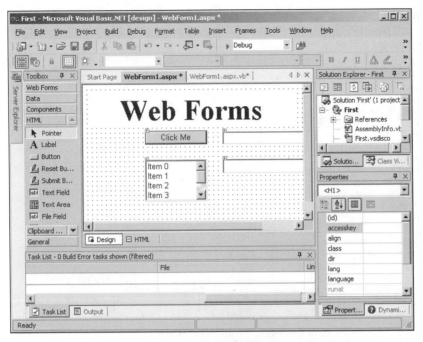

Figure 14.11   Looking at new HTML in a Web page.

Creating a Multiform Web Project

As in Windows applications, you can add multiple forms to a Web application. To see how this works, I'll create a new example here, called Multiform on the CD-ROM. This example will put to work a few Web server controls we'll see in the following chapters, but whose use is very like what we've seen with Windows controls. In the main form, **WebForm1**, I add a Web server label control with the text "Web Form 1", as you see in Figure 14.12. (Set the **Font** property of this label to XX-Large.) Next, add two hyperlink controls with the HyperLink tool in the toolbox. Set the text of HyperLink1 to "Web form 2" and the text of HyperLink2 to "See HTML Page 1", as you see in that figure.

Now we can add a new Web form to the project—just select the Project|Add Web Form menu item and click Open in the Add New Item dialog box that appears. This adds **WebForm2** to the project (just as we might have added **Form2** to a Windows project). Besides Web forms, you also can add simple HTML pages to our project. To see how that works, select the Project|Add HTML Page menu item and click Open, creating **HTMLPage1** and adding it to our project.

All that's left is to navigate to the new Web form and HTML page when the user clicks the corresponding hyperlink. To connect **HyperLink1** to **WebForm2**, select

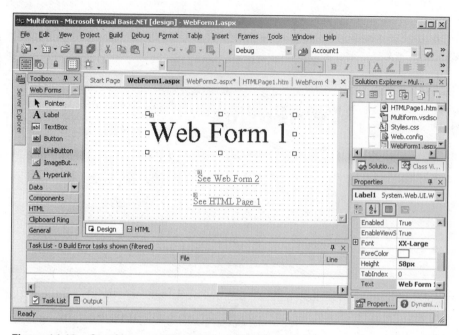

Figure 14.12 Starting a multiform Web application.

HyperLink1 and select the ellipsis ("...") button in the **NavigateURL** property in the Properties window to open the Select URL dialog box you see in Figure 14.13. This dialog lists the other files in our project—select WebForm2.aspx and click OK to connect the hyperlink to **WebForm2**.

Also, set the **NavigateURL** property for the second hyperlink, **HyperLink1**, to HTMLPage1.htm, connecting that hyperlink to the simple HTML page.

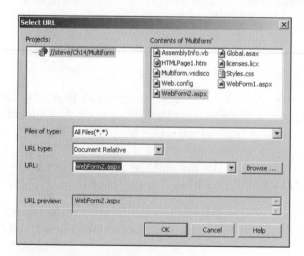

Figure 14.13 The Select URL dialog box.

Next, you have to set the hyperlinks' *target*. In HTML, a link's target specifies where the data the hyperlink points to will appear, and that's especially valuable when you're working with HTML frames. If you don't set the hyperlinks' **Target** properties, **WebForm2** and **HTMLPage1** will appear in new browser windows when you click them. To make them appear in the same browser window as **WebForm1** (so they replace **WebForm1** when they appear), set the **Target** property of each hyperlink to "_self" in the drop-down list that appears in the Properties window for this property ("_self" is the HTML term for the current window).

When you run this example, you see the two hyperlinks, now active, as shown in Figure 14.14.

When you click a hyperlink, such as the one to **WebForm2**, that new form appears in the browser as you see in Figure 14.15. (I've added a label like the one in **WebForm1** to this form so we can tell what form we're looking at.)

In this way, we're able to support multiple forms in a Web application. (Note that we'll take a closer look at hyperlink and label controls in upcoming chapters.)

Handling Client Events

The kind of events we've been dealing with until now are handled on the server, not in the browser. However, it can be a tedious process to wait for events to be handled on the server, so you also can add scripting to your Web pages that can support client-side events. Usually, we'll stick with server-side code in our Web applications, but it's good to know that you also can let the browser handle some events on the client side.

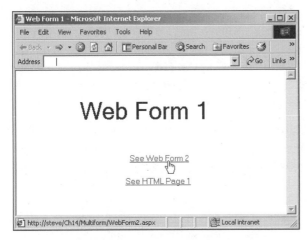

Figure 14.14   Hyperlinks for navigating to a new form.

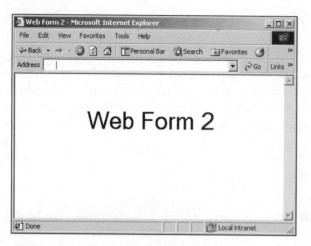

Figure 14.15   Navigating to a new form.

Because you'll be handling events in the browser and not with Visual Basic on the server, you must use a scripting language that the browser can understand. And note that we'll also be using HTML client controls here (that is, just standard HTML controls), not Web server controls or HTML server controls. As mentioned, we'll almost always stick with server controls in this book (this is a book about Visual Basic, not JavaScript), but it's also good to know how to do a little client-side scripting.

To see an example, I'll create a new project here, named ClientEvents on the CD-ROM. In this case, I'll just add an HTML button and an HTML text field (Visual Basic text controls are called text boxes, but the HTML equivalents are called text fields) to a Web form, then use client-side JavaScript to display text in the text field when the button is clicked.

Start by clicking the HTML tab in the toolbox, and adding an HTML button and an HTML text field to **WebForm1** of our project. These controls are not given names by default, so enter "Button1" and "Text1" in the **(id)** property in the Properties window for the button and text field respectively. After you've given these controls an ID, you can refer to them in JavaScript.

Note that these are indeed HTML controls, not Web server controls; I could make sure their events are handled on the server by right-clicking them and selecting the Run As Server Control item, but in this case, we want them to remain as client controls. To add JavaScript code for the button's **Click** event, which is called **onclick** in HTML, you can use the drop-down list boxes in the main Web form's code designer, just as you add event handlers for Windows controls or Web Server controls. Here, however, you select the main Web form and click the HTML button so the code will be added to the Web form's HTML, not the Web form's Visual Basic code. When you can see the Web form's HTML, select the button, **Button1**, in the left drop-down list above the code designer, and the **onclick** event in the right drop-down list, as shown in Figure 14.16.

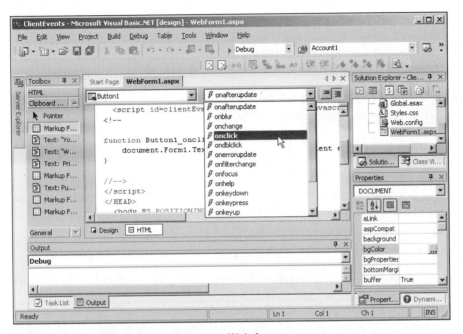

Figure 14.16   Adding a client event to a Web form.

This adds a JavaScript event handler to the HTML for our Web form like this:

```
<%@ Page Language="vb" AutoEventWireup="false"
Codebehind="WebForm1.aspx.vb" Inherits="ClientEvents.WebForm1"%>
<!DOCTYPE HTML PUBLIC "-//W3C//DTD HTML 4.0 Transitional//EN">
<HTML>
  <HEAD>
    <title>Handling Client Events</title>
    <meta name="GENERATOR" content="Microsoft Visual Studio .NET 7.0">
    <meta name="CODE_LANGUAGE" content="Visual Basic 7.0">
    <meta name=vs_defaultClientScript content="JavaScript">
    <meta name=vs_targetSchema content="http://schemas.microsoft.com/ _
        intellisense/ie5">
  <script id=clientEventHandlersJS language=javascript>
<!--

function Button1_onclick() {

}

//-->
</script>
</HEAD>
  <body MS_POSITIONING="GridLayout">
```

```
    <form id="Form1" method="post" runat="server">
<INPUT id=Button1 style="Z-INDEX: 101; LEFT: 125px; POSITION: absolute;
    TOP: 85px" type=button value="Click me" language=javascript
    onclick="return Button1_onclick()">
<INPUT
id=Text1 style="Z-INDEX: 102; LEFT: 208px; WIDTH: 155px;
POSITION: absolute; TOP: 86px; HEIGHT: 22px" type=text>
    </form>
  </body>
</HTML>
```

Now when the button is clicked, the code in the JavaScript **Button1_onclick** event handler is run. I can place a line of JavaScript to display the text "Handling client events!" into **text1**, in this way:

```
function Button1_onclick() {
    document.Form1.Text1.value = "Handling client events!"
}
```

And that's all it takes—except here, we're writing code in JavaScript, not Visual Basic, because we want this code to execute in the client (that is, the browser). You can see this code at work in Figure 14.17. When you click the button, the text "Handling client events!" appears in **text1**, as you see in that figure—and all without a round trip to the server. Our code will usually use a round trip to the server, and use Visual Basic instead of JavaScript, but it's worth knowing that you also can handle client events in this way.

And that's it—now it's time to start getting into the additional details of all this in the Immediate Solutions section.

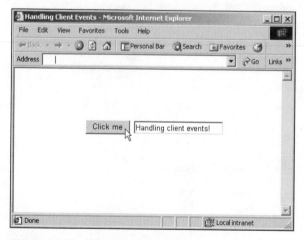

Figure 14.17   Handling client events.

Immediate Solutions

Using the **System.Web.UI.Page** Class

Any Web page requested from a server hosting the .NET framework, whether it contains .NET code or only HTML text, is actually based on the **System.Web.UI. Page** class; this is the class that our Web forms inherit from:

```
Public Class WebForm1
    Inherits System.Web.UI.Page
        .
        .
        .
```

Here is the class hierarchy for the **Page** class (note that the **Control** class here is the ASP .NET **Control** class, not the Windows application's **Control** class):

```
Object
   Control
      TemplateControl
         Page
```

You can find the notable public properties of **Page** objects in Table 14.5, the notable methods in Table 14.6, and the notable events in Table 14.7. Note that I'm not including all the properties, methods, and events that the **Page** class inherits from the **System.Web.UI.Control** class—you can find them in Chapter 15, Tables 15.1, 15.2, and 15.3. (The **Page** class doesn't inherit members from the **TemplateControl** class that you normally deal with directly.)

Table 14.5   Noteworthy public properties of Page objects.

Property	Means
Application	Gets an **Application** object.
ClientTarget	Gets/sets if you want to override automatic browser capabilities detection and handle page rendering for specific browsers.
ErrorPage	Gets/sets an error page's URL in case there are unhandled page exceptions.
IsPostBack	Indicates if a page was created after a client postback, or if it is being loaded for the first time.

(continued)

Table 14.5   Noteworthy public properties of Page objects *(continued)*.

Property	Means
IsValid	Indicates if a page validation was successful.
Request	Gets the current HTTP **Request** object.
Response	Gets the current HTTP **Response** object.
Server	Gets the current **Server** object.
Session	Gets the current **Session** object.
Site	Gets Web site data.
User	Gets data about the user.
Validators	Gets a collection of the validation controls in the page.

Table 14.6   Noteworthy public methods of Page objects.

Method	Means
HasControls	Indicates if the form has any child controls.
LoadControl	Gets a **UserControl** object.
MapPath	Connects a virtual path to an actual path.
ResolveUrl	Converts a relative URL to an absolute URL.
Validate	Validates data using validation control in the page.

Table 14.7   Noteworthy public events of Page objects.

Event	Means
Disposed	Occurs when a Web form is disposed.
Error	Occurs when an unhandled exception has occurred.
Init	Occurs when the Web form is initialized.
Load	Occurs when the Web form is loaded.
Unload	Occurs when the server control is unloaded.

Initializing a Web Form at Run Time

In Windows forms, you can place code in the **Form_Load** event to initialize the form when it first loads; in Web forms, you use the **Page_Load** event instead:

```
Private Sub Page_Load(ByVal sender As System.Object, _
    ByVal e As System.EventArgs) Handles MyBase.Load
```

```
        'Put user code to initialize the page here
    End Sub
```

For an example, see "Writing HTML to a Web Form at Run Time" later in this chapter.

Setting Control Layout

You can set the page layout for controls two ways in Web forms, using the **pageLayout** property:

- **GridLayout**—This layout is the kind of layout you see in Windows forms. Using grid layout, you can place your controls where you want them, and they'll appear there in your Web page. You can call this kind of positioning *absolute positioning*.

- **FlowLayout**—This layout is the standard layout for controls in HTML pages; the browser can move controls as it wants, letting them "flow." Here, controls follow the same layout as words in a page in a word processor—as the page is resized, the words flow to match. You can call this kind of positioning *relative positioning*.

Forcing Event Handling

As discussed in the In Depth section of this chapter, some events, like **Click**, cause a Web form to be sent back to the server for event processing, and some, like **SelectedIndexChanged** in a list box, don't. Sending a Web form back to the server for processing is called posting it back to the server. Events that aren't automatically posted back to the server are stored and processed when the form is posted back to the server (so, for example, a **SelectedIndexChanged** event would be handled when a **Click** event occurs elsewhere in the page).

To force a control's events to be automatically posted back to the server, and so handled at once, you set the control's **AutoPostBack** property to **True**. That's all it takes. (This adds the attribute **runat = "server"** to the control's HTML.)

Setting Colors in Web Forms and HTML Pages

A number of properties in Web forms can be set to colors (such as **link**, **text**, **bgColor**, and so on). Colors can be specified in HTML pages in two ways: by using a color name (such as "Red" or "Blue" or "Magenta," which are predefined color names supported by the browser), or by using numbers to denote an RGB color value. In HTML, an RGB color value consists of three two-digit hexadecimal (base 16) numbers (range: 0 to 255, which is to say #00 to #FF in hexadecimal, where # indicates a hexadecimal number) specifying the intensity of the corresponding color, in this order: "#*RRGGBB*", where *RR* is the red color value, *GG* is the green color value, and *BB* is the blue color value (see the *HTML Black Book* for more details and examples). For example, "#FFFFFF" is pure white, "#000000" pure black, "#FF0000" is pure red, "#00FF00" is pure green, "#0000FF" is pure blue, "#FF7F50" is coral, magenta is "#FF00FF", maroon is "#800000", and so on. Note also that when you select a property that can be set to a color in the Properties window, a color picker dialog opens automatically, allowing you to set colors at design time easily.

Setting Title Bar Text

By default, you'll see the URL of a Web form in the browser's title bar when the Web form is being displayed. If that's not what you want (and it probably won't be), you should give the Web form a title, using the **title** property. For example, I've set this property to "First Web Application" in Figure 14.7.

Related solution:	*Found on page:*
Setting Title Bar Text	170

Setting Hyperlink Colors

You can set the colors used for hyperlinks in a Web form with these Web form properties, taken from HTML:

- **vlink**—The color used for links the user has already visited.

- **alink**—The color used for active links—those in the process of being clicked, for example.

- **link**—The color used for links before they've been activated or visited.

NOTE: *See "Setting Colors in Web Forms and HTML Pages" in this chapter for more information on setting colors.*

Setting Page Margins

You can set the size of the page margins surrounding the content in a Web form and other HTML pages with these properties (measured in pixels):

- **rightMargin**—Sets the right margin.
- **leftMargin**—Sets the left margin.
- **topMargin**—Sets the top margin.
- **bottomMargin**—Sets the bottom margin.

Setting Text Color

You can set the "foreground" color (that is, the default color of text) used in Web forms and HTML pages with the **text** property, mirroring the attribute of the same name in HTML pages.

NOTE: *See "Setting Colors in Web Forms and HTML Pages" in this chapter for more information on setting colors.*

Creating an Error Page

You can add an error page to jump to when there's an unhandled page exception with the **Page** class's **errorPage** property. Just assign this property the URL of the error page you want to use.

Setting Background Images

As in other Web pages, you can set the background image used in Web forms and HTML pages, using the **background** property. You can set this property to the URL of an image at run time; at design time, you can browse to an image file to assign to this property.

Setting Background Color

In HTML, you set the background color using the **bgColor** attribute, and in Web forms and HTML pages, you can use the property of the same name.

NOTE: See "Setting Colors in Web Forms and HTML Pages" in this chapter for more information on setting colors.

Setting Background Properties

The Internet Explorer supports a property for an HTML page's background that other browsers don't: fixed backgrounds. When you make a page's background fixed, it won't scroll when the rest of the page does. This provides a nice effect, rather as though the rest of the page is on a sheet of glass, moving over the background. To make the background fixed in a Web form or HTML page in VB .NET, set its **bgProperties** property to **Fixed**.

Setting Content Type

You can set the HTTP content type of a document using the **contentType** property in VB .NET. For Web forms, the default is "text/html", but you can use any legal MIME type here, such as "text/xml". This is not something you have to worry about if you're just creating standard Web applications and services.

Setting Search Engine Keywords

Web search engines look for words to list your Web page under using keywords stored in a **<meta>** element. You can add those keywords using the **keywords** property of the page in VB .NET. For example, if I want to use the keyword "VB" for a Web form, I can do that by setting the **keywords** property of the form to **VB**, which adds this **<meta>** element to the form:

```
<meta name=keywords content="VB">
```

If a search engine adds your page to its store, it will match if a user searches for "VB".

Adding a New Web Form

You can add a new Web form to a Web application with the Project|Add Web Form menu item. Here's the code for the Web form added to your project:

```
<%@ Page Language="vb" AutoEventWireup="false"
    Codebehind="WebForm2.aspx.vb" Inherits="ProjectName.WebForm2"%>
<!DOCTYPE HTML PUBLIC "-//W3C//DTD HTML 4.0 Transitional//EN">
<html>
  <head>
    <title></title>
    <meta name="GENERATOR" content="Microsoft Visual Studio .NET 7.0">
    <meta name="CODE_LANGUAGE" content="Visual Basic 7.0">
    <meta name=vs_defaultClientScript content="JavaScript">
    <meta name=vs_targetSchema
        content="http://schemas.microsoft.com/intellisense/ie5">
  </head>
  <body MS_POSITIONING="GridLayout">

    <form id="Form2" method="post" runat="server">

    </form>

  </body>
</html>
```

For more information, see "Creating a Multiform Web Project" in the In Depth section of this chapter.

Adding a New HTML Page

You can add a new HTML page to a Web application with the Project|Add HTML Page menu item. Here's the code for the HTML page added to your project:

```
<!DOCTYPE HTML PUBLIC "-//W3C//DTD HTML 4.0 Transitional//EN">
<html>
<head>
<meta name=vs_defaultClientScript content="JavaScript">
<meta name=vs_targetSchema content="http://schemas.microsoft.com/
intellisense/ie5">
<meta name="GENERATOR" content="Microsoft Visual Studio .NET 7.0">
```

```
<meta name=ProgId content=VisualStudio.HTML>
<meta name=Originator content="Microsoft Visual Studio .NET 7.0">
</head>
<body MS_POSITIONING="GridLayout">

</body>
</html>
```

For more information, see "Creating a Multiform Web Project" in the In Depth section of this chapter.

Navigating to Another Form

An easy way to let users navigate among the documents in a Web application is to use hyperlinks, as we did in the "Creating a MultiForm Web Project" topic in this chapter. We'll take a closer look at hyperlinks later in this book; to create one, you use the **HyperLink** tool in the toolbox, and set the hyperlink's **navigationURL** property to the URL you want to navigate to. By default, clicking a hyperlink will open a new browser window; to replace the current page with the new page without opening a new window, set the hyperlink's **target** property to "_self".

For more information, see "Creating a Multiform Web Project" in the In Depth section of this chapter.

Redirecting to Another Form

You may want to redirect users from one Web forms page to another, if, for example, you are upgrading a page and don't want to display it. To redirect users to another page, you add a line of code to a Web application, for example in the **Page_Load** event handler:

```
Response.Redirect("http://www.starpowder.com/steve.html")
```

Writing HTML to a Web Form at Run Time

You can write HTML to a Web form at run time with the **Write** method of the ASP .NET **Response** object. For example, to write the **<h1>** header "Welcome to my page!" in a Web form at run time (not design time), place this line in the **Page_Load** event handler:

```
Response.Write("<h1>Welcome to my page!</h1>")
```

You can see this at work in the WriteHTML example on the CD-ROM, as you see in Figure 14.18.

Figure 14.18   Writing HTML at run time.

Detecting Browser Type and Capabilities

Web applications can appear in various types of browsers, but the capabilities of your application may be restricted in browsers VB .NET calls "downlevel." A downlevel browser is one that only supports HTML 3.2. Uplevel browsers, on the other hand, support:

- ECMAScript (the formal name for JavaScript) version 1.2
- HTML version 4.0
- The Microsoft Document Object Model (MSDOM)
- Cascading style sheets (CSS)

To determine the type and capabilities of the target browser, you can use the properties of the **Request.Browser** object in the **Page_Load** event. You can find these properties in Table 14.8; these properties hold either text or a **Boolean** value (for example, **Request.Browser.Frames** returns a value of **True** if the browser supports frames, while **Request.Browser.Browser** will hold the text "IE" if the browser is the Internet Explorer).

Table 14.8   Request.Browser properties.

To find this:	Use this:
Browser type (example: IE6)	**Request.Browser.Type**
Browser name (example: IE)	**Request.Browser.Browser**
Version (example: 6.0b)	**Request.Browser.Version**
Major version (example: 6)	**Request.Browser.MajorVersion**
Minor version (example: 0)	**Request.Browser.MinorVersion**
Platform (example: WinNT)	**Request.Browser.Platform**
Is a beta version?	**Request.Browser.Beta**
Is an AOL browser?	**Request.Browser.AOL**
Is Win16?	**Request.Browser.Win16**
Is Win32?	**Request.Browser.Win32**
Supports frames?	**Request.Browser.Frames**
Supports tables?	**Request.Browser.Tables**
Supports cookies?	**Request.Browser.Cookies**
Supports VB Script?	**Request.Browser.VBScript**
Supports JavaScript?	**Request.Browser.JavaScript**
Supports Java Applets?	**Request.Browser.JavaApplets**
Supports ActiveX Controls?	**Request.Browser.ActiveXControls**

Embedding Visual Basic Code in Web Pages

In fact, it's possible to embed Visual Basic code directly in ASPX files—no ASPXVB "code-behind" file needed. However, in this case, you're responsible for writing all the code yourself—the Visual Basic IDE won't help with IntelliSense and other features.

There's an example, EmbeddedVB, on the CD-ROM showing how this works. You can see this example at work in Figure 14.19—just click the Click Me button and the message "Hello from Visual Basic!" appears in the text box after a round trip to the server.

To make this work, I've written WebForm1.aspx for this example by hand. In this case, I've created a button and a text box using the **<asp:Button>** and **<asp:TextBox>** elements, and made them into server controls by setting their **runat** attributes to "server". I've also placed the Visual Basic code for the button's event handler, **Button1_Click**, in the ASPX file itself, in an HTML **<script>** ele-

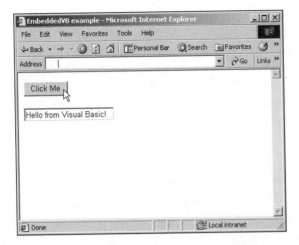

Figure 14.19 Using Visual Basic code embedded in a Web page.

ment with the language attribute set to "VB" and the **runat** attribute set to "server" so this Visual Basic code is run back at the server. I've also connected the button's **Click** event to this event handler by setting the **onclick** attribute of the **<asp:Button>** element to "Button1_Click", like this:

```
<%@ Page Language="vb" AutoEventWireup="false"
Inherits="EmbeddedVB.WebForm1"%>
<!DOCTYPE HTML PUBLIC "-//W3C//DTD HTML 4.0 Transitional//EN">
<HTML>
  <HEAD><meta name=vs_targetSchema content="http://schemas.microsoft.com/ _
      intellisense/ie5">
<TITLE>EmbeddedVB example</TITLE>
   <script language="VB" runat="server">
   Private Sub Button1_Click(ByVal sender As System.Object, _
      ByVal e As System.EventArgs)
        TextBox1.Text = "Hello from Visual Basic!"
   End Sub
   </script>
</HEAD>
<body>
   <form runat="server" ID="Form1">

<asp:Button id="Button1" Text="Click Me" OnClick="Button1_Click"
   runat="server"/>
<P>
<asp:TextBox id=TextBox1 runat="server"></asp:TextBox></P>
   </form>
</body>
</HTML>
```

And that's all it takes—now the Visual Basic code in the button's event handler will be run back at the server, even though this code is actually stored in the Web page itself, not in a ASPXVB code-behind file on the server. Whether or not you write your code this way is a matter of choice—if you consider yourself an ASP .NET programmer, this is often the primary way you'll write code. Visual Basic programmers, however, often prefer to stick with the Visual Basic code and code designers that they already know how to use.

Saving Program Data across Server Round Trips

As discussed in the In Depth section of this chapter, all the data in a Web form isn't necessarily preserved between round trips to the server. By default, Visual Basic stores the data in Web server controls and HTML server controls in an HTML hidden field in the Web page (that is, HTML **<input>** elements with the **type** attribute set to "hidden"), so that data is preserved between round trips to the server. However, what about the variables in your code? That data isn't stored automatically, so after the page goes to the server and comes back, the values in your variables will be reset to their default values (usually 0).

However, you can make sure the data in your variables is stored over server round trips, and you can do so in several different ways. For example, say you have a variable named **value1** that you increment every time the user clicks a button, displaying the new value. If you didn't save the value in **value1** between server round trips, it would be set to 0 after every such trip, and if you incremented it and displayed the resulting value, the user would always see a value of 1, no matter how many times they clicked the button. How do you fix this problem?

I'll take a look at a couple of ways of saving the value in **value1** during server round trips in the RoundTrip example from the CD-ROM, which you see in Figure 14.20. When you click any of the three buttons in that example, the code increments one of three counters, whose value is preserved between trips to the server; you'll see "New value: 1", then "New value: 2", then "New value: 3", and so on as you keep clicking a button.

The first technique I'll take a look at, illustrated by the first button in this example, is a server-side technique, where you store data on the server, using the ASP .NET **Session** object. Each time someone works with your Web application, a new session is created and given a long randomly generated ID value. You can

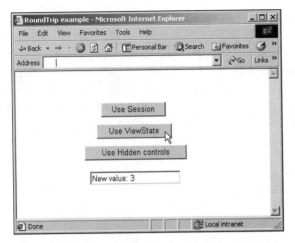

Figure 14.20   Saving program data across server round trips.

store and retrieve values using the **Session** object in Visual Basic code; here's how that looks when the user clicks the first button (caption: "Use Session"):

```
Private Sub Button1_Click(ByVal sender As System.Object, _
    ByVal e As System.EventArgs) Handles Button1.Click
    Dim value1 As Integer = Session("value1")
    value1 += 1
    TextBox1.Text = "New value: " & value1
    Session("value1") = value1
End Sub
```

Besides saving values on the server, you also can save them in the Web page itself. By default, Visual Basic stores data in an HTML hidden control in a Web page. The data in that control corresponds to a **StateBag** object, and you can reach that object yourself using a control's **ViewState** property. Because Web forms are based on the **Control** class, you can use the Web form's **ViewState** property to store and retrieve your data across server round trips. Here's how that works when the user clicks the second button in the RoundTrips example (caption: "Use ViewState"):

```
Private Sub Button2_Click(ByVal sender As System.Object, _
    ByVal e As System.EventArgs) Handles Button2.Click
    Dim value1 As Integer = Me.ViewState("value1")
    value1 += 1
    TextBox1.Text = "New value: " & value1
    Me.ViewState("value1") = value1
End Sub
```

You also can create your own HTML hidden field in a Web form and use that to store data in. You can add a hidden field to a Web form by clicking the HTML tab in the toolbox and double-clicking the Hidden tool. You need to make this field into a server control so its data will be preserved across server round trips, so right-click it and select the Run As Server Control item. Finally, give it an ID value, using the **(id)** property in the Properties window, of **Hidden1**. Now you can access the data in this hidden control as **Hidden1.Value**, so here's how I use this control with the third button in the example (caption: "Use Hidden controls"):

```
Private Sub Button3_Click(ByVal sender As System.Object, _
    ByVal e As System.EventArgs) Handles Button3.Click
    Hidden1.Value += 1
    TextBox1.Text = "New value: " & Hidden1.Value
End Sub
```

Related solution:	Found on page:
Navigating in Datasets	1000

Chapter 15

Web Forms: Buttons, Text Boxes, Labels, Literals, and Place Holders

In Depth

This chapter begins our study of the Visual Basic .NET Web server controls. Web server controls are the ones that have been most closely designed to resemble standard Visual Basic Windows forms controls, and in this and the following chapters, we're going to examine these controls in detail. Web server controls are expressly designed to be handled back on the server, using Visual Basic code.

NOTE: *If you're in doubt about which are the Web server controls, see "Web Server Controls" in the In Depth section of Chapter 14.*

It's fortunate that the standard Windows forms controls in Visual Basic so closely resemble the controls you see in browsers already, because that's what makes the whole transition to Web forms possible. Certainly not all Windows form controls can be displayed using the controls native to Web browsers, but many—such as text boxes, list boxes, labels, and others—can. And that's what makes the whole thing work—the fact that Web browsers already support controls that match what Visual Basic offers us in Windows forms in many ways.

We've already seen how to work with Web server controls in a basic way in the previous chapter. All you have to do is to add these controls to a Web form, set their properties in the Properties window, and add server code to them with the appropriate code designer. (Note that you can't add Windows controls to a Web form, because those controls won't work.) To add code to a control's handler, just double-click the control to open its code designer, as with Windows forms.

You also can add Web server controls to a Web form by editing its HTML directly—just switch to HTML view with the HTML button. For example, this code creates a Web server button:

```
<asp:Button id=Button1 style="Z-INDEX: 101; LEFT: 95px; POSITION:
absolute; TOP: 75px" runat="server" Text="Click me" Width="125px"
Height="24px"></asp:Button>
```

Note the syntax here—this element uses the prefix "asp" as a sort of XML-style namespace to indicate that the Web server should handle this element, producing the required HTML. In this case, the server will actually create an HTML Submit button, because when the button is clicked, the entire Web page should be sent back to the server to handle the **Click** event. Note also the required attribute **runat**, which is set to "server", indicating that this control's code is to be run back at the server. In addition, note the **style** attribute, which sets the position mode to "absolute", which means you can set the location of the control yourself (this is how server controls work in grid layout), using the **top** and **left** style members to set the location of the upper-left corner of the control, measured in pixels. The **text** attribute here sets the caption of the button, and the **width** and **height** attributes set the dimensions of the button.

It's important to understand the difference between the ID and name of a control. In your server-side Visual Basic code, you refer to the control with the **Name** property, but in the browser, you refer to the control with its **ID** attribute's value (which is why the button's **ID** attribute is set in the above code). In other words, in Visual Basic code on the server, you refer to a control by name; if you're going to add script (such as JavaScript) to it to be run in the browser, you use the control's ID. Usually for server controls, the name and ID are set to the same value.

Web server controls like this button are based on the **Control** class, but this isn't the **Control** class we've seen for Windows controls; this is the **System.Web.UI. Control** class. Because this class is the base class for the controls we'll be working with in the next few chapters, it's important to know the members of the **Control** class, because they're available in the Web controls derived from this class (which includes the Web form **Page** class we saw in the previous chapter), and we'll rely on them. For that reason, I'll take a look at the **Control** class now.

The Control Class

The **System.Web.UI.Control** class is the base class for Web server controls, and for the Web form **Page** class as well. This class is derived directly from the **Object** class:

```
Object
    Control
```

You can find the notable public properties of **Control** objects in Table 15.1, the notable methods in Table 15.2, and the notable events in Table 15.3. These tables are worth a look, because they list many of the properties, methods, and events we'll be using with server controls. It's worth noting the **EnableViewState** property, which specifies if the control saves its state between round trips to the server (the default setting for this property is **True**). Note also the **Init** and **Load** events, which you can use to initialize your controls.

Table 15.1   Noteworthy public properties of Control objects.

Property	Means
ClientID	Gets the ASP.NET control identifier for the control.
Controls	Gets a collection of child controls in the control.
EnableViewState	Gets/sets whether the control maintains its state between round trips to the server.
ID	Gets/sets the ID for the control.
Page	Gets the **Page** object that contains the control.
Parent	Gets the control's parent control.
Site	Gets the control's Web site.
UniqueID	Gets the unique ID for the control.
Visible	Gets/sets whether the control is visible or not.

Table 15.2   Noteworthy public methods of Control objects.

Method	Means
DataBind	Binds the control to a data source.
Dispose	Disposes of the control.
FindControl	Searches a container for a control.
HasControls	**True** if the control contains child controls.
RenderControl	Draws the control, using HTML.
ResolveUrl	Resolves relative URLs to absolute URLs, based on the location of the control's containing page.

Table 15.3   Noteworthy public events of Control objects.

Event	Means
DataBinding	Occurs when data source is bound to a control.
Disposed	Occurs when a control is disposed of.
Init	Occurs when a control is initialized (this is the first event you can use for controls).
Load	Occurs when a control is loaded into a **Page** object.
PreRender	Occurs when a control is about to be drawn in a **Page** object.
Unload	Occurs when a control is unloaded.

In fact, there's another class to discuss here, because Web server controls aren't based directly on the **Control** class—they are based on the **WebControl** class, which is based on the **Control** class.

The WebControl Class

Here's the class hierarchy of the **WebControl** class, which is based on the **Control** class:

```
Object
   Control
      WebControl
```

You can find the notable public properties of **WebControl** objects in Table 15.4 and the notable methods in Table 15.5. (Note there's no table of events here—**WebControl** inherits all its events from the **Control** class.)

Table 15.4   Noteworthy public properties of WebControl objects.

Property	Means
AccessKey	Gets/Sets the access key for the control.
Attributes	Gets a collection of attributes used to render the control. (These attributes are the ones that do not correspond to control properties.)
BackColor	Gets/sets the control's background color.
BorderColor	Gets/sets the control's border color.
BorderStyle	Gets/sets the control's border style.
BorderWidth	Gets/sets the control's border width.
ControlStyle	Gets the control's style.
CssClass	Gets/sets control's CSS class.
Enabled	Gets/sets whether the control is enabled.
Font	Gets/sets font information for the control.
ForeColor	Gets/sets the control's foreground color.
Height	Gets/sets the control's height.
Style	Gets the HTML style of the control as a collection of text attributes.
TabIndex	Gets/sets the control's tab index.
ToolTip	Gets/sets the control's tool tip text.
Width	Gets/sets the control's width.

Table 15.5   Noteworthy public methods of WebControl objects.

Method	Means
CopyBaseAttributes	Copies base attributes (that is, the **AccessKey**, **Enabled**, **ToolTip**, **Tab Index**, and **Attributes** properties) from a source control to the current control.
RenderBeginTag	Renders the HTML starting tag of the control.
RenderEndTag	Renders the HTML ending tag of the control.

15. Web Forms: Buttons, Text Boxes, Labels, Literals

And now that we've gotten the **Control** and **WebControl** classes in hand, we can turn to the actual Web server controls, starting with buttons.

Creating Buttons

You use the **Button** control to create a button in a Web page. Here is the class hierarchy of this control; note that it's based on the **WebControl** class, which in turn is based on the **Control** class:

```
Object
    Control
        WebControl
            Button
```

Web server button controls post their data back to the server when they're clicked, so by default, they're made into Submit buttons in HTML by the Web server. (Submit buttons are the ones you click expressly to send data to the server.) Here's what a typical button looks like in HTML:

```
<input type="submit" name="Button1" value="Click me" id="Button1"
style="height:24px;width:125px;Z-INDEX: 101; LEFT: 95px; POSITION:
absolute; TOP: 75px" />
```

That's the HTML representation of the button, but in code, you can stick to Visual Basic; in fact, the **Click** event handler for buttons looks exactly as it would in a Windows forms project, with the same two arguments passed to this Sub procedure:

```
Private Sub Button1_Click(ByVal sender As System.Object, _
    ByVal e As System.EventArgs) Handles Button1.Click
    TextBox1.Text = "You clicked the button."
End Sub
```

You also can add a command name to a button to create a *command button.* (VB .NET makes a distinction between simple buttons, which are Submit buttons, and command buttons.) You can add a command name to a button with the **CommandName** property, and a command argument with the **Command Argument** properties. Both of these properties can hold text; you can recover that text in your Visual Basic code. This is useful, for example, if you want to use only one button event handler for all the buttons in your Web page (which you can do if you embed your Visual Basic in the Web page—see "Embedding Visual Basic Code in Web Pages" in Chapter 14 for more details). To determine which button was clicked, you can just check the **CommandName** property of the button that caused the event.

The big event for buttons, of course, is the **Click** event; we'll put that event to work in this chapter. The other main event is the **Command** event, which you add code to if you're working with command buttons that have a command name. For our purposes, working with Web server buttons will be much like working with Windows buttons, which gives you an indication of how well Microsoft has been able to port the functionality of button controls to Web forms.

Creating Text Boxes

As with Windows forms, the **TextBox** Web server control is an input control that lets you enter text. Here is the class hierarchy of this class:

```
Object
    Control
        WebControl
            TextBox
```

This control is usually converted into a standard HTML text field, using an HTML **<input>** element with the **type** attribute set to "text" to create a text field—here's an example:

```
<input name="TextBox1" type="text" id="TextBox1" style="Z-INDEX: 104; LEFT:
239px; POSITION: absolute; TOP: 127px" />
```

You can set the style of the text box using the **TextMode** property. By default, the **TextMode** property is set to **SingleLine** to create a single-line HTML text field, but it also can be set to **MultiLine** for a multiline text box, or **Password** to create a password control. As with other Web server controls, these also are supported with HTML controls; a multiline text box, for example, is actually an HTML text area control. Here's an example created by VB .NET:

```
<textarea name="TextBox2" id="TextBox2" style="height:74px;width:157px;
Z-INDEX: 103; LEFT: 233px; POSITION: absolute; TOP: 117px"></textarea>
```

You set the display width of a text box with its **Columns** property. And if it's a multiline text box, the display height is set with the **Rows** property. As we'll see in this chapter, using Web server text boxes is much like using Windows forms text boxes. Of course, the properties, methods, and events are often different to fit the Web browser environment, but the basic functionality is similar. For example, to recover the text in a text box, you can use its **Text** property in Visual Basic code; it has a **TextChanged** event to handle the case where the user changes the text in the text box.

Creating Labels

You use the Web server **Label** control to display text that the user isn't supposed to change. Here's the class hierarchy for this class:

```
Object
    Control
        WebControl
            Label
```

You can change the displayed text with the **Text** property in code, as you can in Windows forms (just bear in mind that it takes a round trip to the server to change that text). In HTML, Web server labels become **<span>** elements that enclose text. Here's an example, created by VB .NET; this label is displaying the text "Hello!", surrounded by a dashed border:

```
<span id="Label1" style="border-style:Dashed;font-size:XX-
Large;height:118px;width:203px;Z-INDEX: 101; LEFT: 250px; POSITION:
absolute; TOP: 79px">Hello!</span>
```

Creating Literals

Visual Basic also gives you a way of adding HTML in a Web page while using a standard Visual Basic IDE code designer (that is, without having to switch to the .aspx page and click the HTML button to edit the HTML directly)—you can use a **Literal** Web server control. You just assign text to a literal control's **Text** property, and that text is inserted directly into the Web form. Here's the class hierarchy of this class:

```
Object
    Control
        Literal
```

This control doesn't have any visual appearance in a Web page—you just set the **Text** property, and that text is inserted into the Web form. For example, here's how I insert the HTML for an **<h1>** header into a Web form, using a literal:

```
Literal1.Text = "<div align='center'><h1>Hello</h1></div>"
```

The only part of this literal control that appears in the final Web form is the HTML:

```
<div align='center'><h1>Hello</h1></div>
```

> **TIP:** *Note the quoted text **" <h1>Hello</h1> "** that I'm assigning to the **Text** property here. When you quote HTML that itself contains quotes, as in this case, you should make sure that you make the inner quotes into single quotes (') so VB .NET doesn't get confused about where your quoted text ends. Note that the Unix way of doing this, which is to "escape" double as \" instead of just ", won't work here.*

Creating Place Holders

The last control we'll take a look at in this chapter is the **PlaceHolder** control. This control is intended to be used as a place holder when you add controls to a Web form at run time, as we'll do in this chapter. Here is the class hierarchy for the **PlaceHolder** class:

```
Object
    Control
        PlaceHolder
```

As with the literal control, the **PlaceHolder** control does not produce any visible output. This control is used only as a container for other controls on the Web page, and especially when you add new controls.

Now it's time to get to the specific case-by-case details on these first Web server controls in the Immediate Solutions section of this chapter. I'll start with an example named Controls that shows how to use many of the properties of Web server controls in general to enable or disable, add tool tips to, or move those controls in a Web form at run time.

Immediate Solutions

Enabling and Disabling Controls

To see how to work with a number of important aspects of Web server controls, take a look at the Controls example on the CD-ROM. You can see this example at work in Figure 15.1. You can use the various buttons to work on the text box that appears in the bottom of the page, such as moving the text box to a new position.

Here is Webform1.aspx from this example, the actual Web page sent by the server (after it handles the ASP elements in this page) to the server:

```
<%@ Page Language="vb" AutoEventWireup="false"
Codebehind="WebForm1.aspx.vb" Inherits="Controls.WebForm1"%>
<!DOCTYPE HTML PUBLIC "-//W3C//DTD HTML 4.0 Transitional//EN">
<HTML>
  <HEAD>
    <title></title>
<meta content="Microsoft Visual Studio.NET 7.0" name=GENERATOR>
<meta content="Visual Basic 7.0" name=CODE_LANGUAGE>
<meta content=JavaScript name=vs_defaultClientScript>
<meta content=http://schemas.microsoft.com/intellisense/ie5
name=vs_targetSchema>
  </HEAD>
<body MS_POSITIONING="GridLayout">
<form id=Form1 method=post runat="server">
<asp:button id=Button1 style="Z-INDEX: 101; LEFT: 170px;
POSITION: absolute; TOP: 47px" runat="server"
Text="Enable/disable text box" Width="164px" Height="24px"
ToolTip="This is a button"></asp:button>
<asp:Button id=Button4 style="Z-INDEX: 105; LEFT: 190px;
POSITION: absolute; TOP: 165px" runat="server"
Text="Move text box"></asp:Button>
<asp:button id=Button3 style="Z-INDEX: 104; LEFT: 152px;
POSITION: absolute; TOP: 128px" runat="server"
Text="Change text box's style">
</asp:button>
<asp:button id=Button2 style="Z-INDEX: 103; LEFT: 162px;
POSITION: absolute; TOP: 88px" tabIndex=1 runat="server"
Text="Make text box visible/invisible" Width="184px" Height="24px">
</asp:button><asp:textbox id=TextBox1 style="Z-INDEX: 102; LEFT:
```

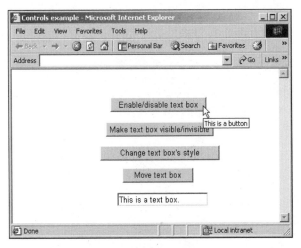

Figure 15.1   The Controls example.

```
181px; POSITION: absolute; TOP: 206px" tabIndex=2 runat="server"
accessKey=T>
This is a text box.</asp:textbox></form>

  </body>
</HTML>
```

And here is WebForm1.aspx.vb, the Visual Basic code for this Web application:

```
Public Class WebForm1
    Inherits System.Web.UI.Page
    Protected WithEvents Button1 As System.Web.UI.WebControls.Button
    Protected WithEvents Button2 As System.Web.UI.WebControls.Button
    Protected WithEvents Button3 As System.Web.UI.WebControls.Button
    Protected WithEvents Button4 As System.Web.UI.WebControls.Button
    Protected WithEvents TextBox1 As System.Web.UI.WebControls.TextBox

#Region " Web Form Designer Generated Code "

    'This call is required by the Web Form Designer.
    <System.Diagnostics.DebuggerStepThrough()> Private Sub
InitializeComponent()

    End Sub

    Private Sub Page_Init(ByVal sender As System.Object, _
        ByVal e As System.EventArgs) Handles MyBase.Init
        'CODEGEN: This method call is required by the Web Form Designer
        'Do not modify it using the code editor.
```

15. Web Forms:
Buttons, Text Boxes,
Labels, Literals

```
                InitializeComponent()
        End Sub

#End Region

    Private Sub Page_Load(ByVal sender As System.Object, _
        ByVal e As System.EventArgs) Handles MyBase.Load
        'Put user code to initialize the page here
    End Sub

    Private Sub Button1_Click(ByVal sender As System.Object, _
        ByVal e As System.EventArgs) Handles Button1.Click
        TextBox1.Enabled = Not TextBox1.Enabled
    End Sub

    Private Sub Button2_Click(ByVal sender As System.Object, _
        ByVal e As System.EventArgs) Handles Button2.Click
        TextBox1.Visible = Not TextBox1.Visible
    End Sub

    Private Sub Button3_Click(ByVal sender As System.Object, _
        ByVal e As System.EventArgs) Handles Button3.Click
        TextBox1.Style("BACKGROUND-COLOR") = "aqua"
    End Sub

    Private Sub Button4_Click(ByVal sender As System.Object, _
        ByVal e As System.EventArgs) Handles Button4.Click
        TextBox1.Style("Left") = "300px"
    End Sub
End Class
```

The first thing I'll do with this example is show how controls can be enabled and
disabled, just as they can in Windows forms. You use the **Enabled** property to
enable or disable controls; when you click the "Enable/disable text box" button,
I'll toggle the Boolean value of this property, like this:

```
    Private Sub Button1_Click(ByVal sender As System.Object, _
        ByVal e As System.EventArgs) Handles Button1.Click
        TextBox1.Enabled = Not TextBox1.Enabled
    End Sub
```

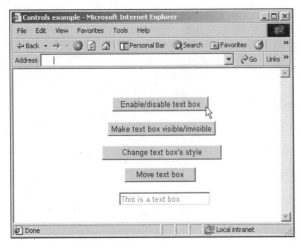

Figure 15.2   Disabling a text box.

You can see the result in Figure 15.2, where the text box has been disabled; that is, grayed out and made inaccessible so it can no longer accept the keyboard focus, which means the user can't change the text in the control.

Making Controls Visible and Invisible

Using the Controls example on the CD-ROM (introduced in the previous topic), you can make a text box visible and invisible, using its **Visible** property, which all Web server controls support. When you click the "Make text box visible/invisible" button in this example, the code toggles the **Visible** property of the text box, like this:

```
Private Sub Button2_Click(ByVal sender As System.Object, _
    ByVal e As System.EventArgs) Handles Button2.Click
    TextBox1.Visible = Not TextBox1.Visible
End Sub
```

You can see the results in Figure 15.3, where the text box has been made invisible.

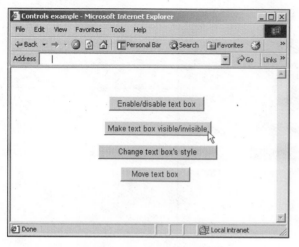

Figure 15.3   Making a text box invisible.

Giving Controls Tool Tips

Using the Controls example on the CD-ROM developed in the first topic of the Immediate Solutions section of this chapter, you can see that you add a tool tip to a control with the **ToolTip** property. In that example, I've added a tool tip to the top button with the text "This is a button". You can see that tool tip in operation in Figure 15.1.

Setting a Control's Style

One important method you can use for customizing your applications is changing the style of a Web form or the controls it contains. This demands knowledge of cascading style sheets, CSS, which you can pick up in a book such as the *HTML Black Book* (Coriolis Group, 2000). To handle styles, you can use the **Style** property of Web forms and Web server controls.

For example, in the Controls example on the CD-ROM, I change the background color of the displayed text box by accessing the background color part of its style as **TextBox1.Style("BACKGROUND-COLOR")**. In the Controls example, I set the text box's background color to aqua this way (this works because "aqua" is a predefined color in the Internet Explorer):

```
Private Sub Button3_Click(ByVal sender As System.Object, _
    ByVal e As System.EventArgs) Handles Button3.Click
    TextBox1.Style("BACKGROUND-COLOR") = "aqua"
End Sub
```

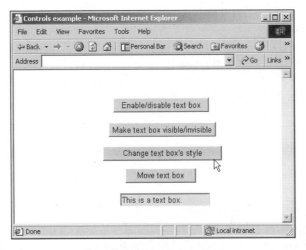

Figure 15.4   Changing a text box's style

You can see the result in Figure 15.4 (although the aqua background isn't very evident in the black-and-white figure).

In this way, you can change all style attributes of controls. (For an example, refer to the topic "Moving Controls" in this chapter to see how to set the position of controls using styles.)

TIP: *You can set the **CssClass** property of a control to a CSS style class defined in the Styles.css file that is a part of Web applications.*

Giving a Control an Access Key

As with Windows forms controls, you can give Web form controls access keys. When you press Alt and the access key (such as Alt+T), the corresponding control gets the focus. You can see this at work in the Controls example on the CD-ROM (which appears in Figure 15.1), where I've given the text box the access key T, so when you press Alt+T, the text box gets the focus.

Moving Controls

There are several ways to move controls in Windows forms, but things are more restricted with Web server controls, which don't have **Top** and **Left** properties to position controls. Instead, Web server controls are positioned using CSS styles.

In particular, you can use the **Style("LEFT")** and **Style("TOP")** properties to move a control.

You can see how this works in the Controls example on the CD-ROM; when you click the "Move text box" button, the code moves the text box this way, where I'm setting the left edge's position of the text box to 300 pixels:

```
Private Sub Button4_Click(ByVal sender As System.Object, _
    ByVal e As System.EventArgs) Handles Button4.Click
    TextBox1.Style("Left") = "300px"
End Sub
```

You can see the result in Figure 15.5, where the text box has been moved to the right. Note that you must be using grid layout for this to work, which means that the **Position** style attribute has been set to "absolute". In this way, you can move the controls around in your Web forms, but keep in mind that it takes a round trip to the server to do it this way. (You can set the style of HTML controls in browser script like JavaScript, but not Web server controls.) For another example of moving controls, see "Adding Controls at Run Time" in this chapter.

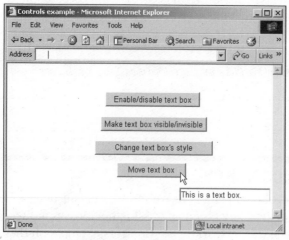

Figure 15.5   Moving a text box.

Setting Control Fonts

You can set the fonts used in Web server controls that display text with their **Font** property. This property returns an object that has these properties (although note that not all properties will be supported by all browsers):

• **Bold**—Gets/sets whether the font is bold.

- **Italic**—Gets/sets whether the font is italic.

- **Name**—Gets/sets the main font name.

- **Names**—Gets/sets an array of font names.

- **Overline**—Gets/sets whether the font is overlined.

- **Size**—Gets/sets the font size.

- **Strikeout**—Gets/sets whether the font is struck out.

- **Underline**—Gets/sets whether the font is underlined.

The **Size** property here matches the kind of sizes you can use in Web browsers, and can take these values:

- **Large**—New size is two sizes larger than the default font size.

- **Larger**—New size is one size larger than in the parent element.

- **Medium**—New size is one size larger than the default font size.

- **Small**—The default font size.

- **Smaller**—New size is one size smaller than the parent element.

- **XLarge**—New size is three sizes larger than the base font size.

- **XSmall**—New size is one size smaller than the base font size.

- **XXLarge**—New size is four sizes larger than the base font size.

- **XXSmall**—New size is two sizes smaller than the base font size.

For example, here's how you might underline text in a label:

```
Label1.Font.Underline = True
```

Setting Control Border Style

A number of Web server controls, such as labels and text boxes, let you set their border style (although note that not all border styles will be supported by all browsers). You set the **BorderStyle** property to one of these values:

- **Dashed**—A dashed line border.

- **Dotted**—A dotted line border.

- **Double**—A double solid line border.

- **Groove**—A grooved border.

- **Inset**—An inset border.

- **None**—No border.

- **NotSet**—No set border style.
- **Outset**—An outset border.
- **Ridge**—A ridged border.
- **Solid**—A solid line border.

Using the **Button** Class

We've already seen the Web server **System.Web.UI.WebControls.Button** class at work in this and the previous chapter; here is the hierarchy of this class:

```
Object
    Control
        WebControl
            Button
```

You can find the notable public properties of **Button** objects in Table 15.6, and the notable events in Table 15.7. (Note there's no table of methods here—**Button** inherits all its methods from the **WebControl** class.) Note that as with other Web server controls, I am not listing the notable properties, methods, and events this class inherits from the **Control** and **WebControl** classes—you can find them in Tables 15.1 to 15.5.

Related solution:	Found on page:
All About Buttons	256

Table 15.6   Noteworthy public properties of Button objects.

Property	Means
CausesValidation	Gets/sets the button that causes validation.
CommandArgument	Gets/sets the command argument, which is passed to the **Command** event handler.
CommandName	Gets/sets the command name, which is passed to the **Command** event handler.
Text	Gets/sets the caption in the button.

Table 15.7   Noteworthy public events of Button objects.

Event	Means
Click	Occurs when a button is clicked.
Command	Occurs when a command button is clicked.

Creating Buttons

Using buttons in Web forms is similar to using buttons in Windows forms, as you can see in the Buttons example on the CD-ROM. You can see this example at work in Figure 15.6; when you click the button labeled "Click me", the text "Hello from Visual Basic" appears in a text box.

For reference, here is WebForm1.aspx from the Buttons example:

```
<%@ Page Language="vb" AutoEventWireup="false" Codebehind=
"WebForm1.aspx.vb" Inherits="Buttons.WebForm1"%>
<!DOCTYPE HTML PUBLIC "-//W3C//DTD HTML 4.0 Transitional//EN">
<HTML>
  <HEAD>
    <title></title>
    <meta name="GENERATOR" content="Microsoft Visual Studio.NET 7.0">
    <meta name="CODE_LANGUAGE" content="Visual Basic 7.0">
    <meta name=vs_defaultClientScript content="JavaScript">
    <meta name=vs_targetSchema content="http://schemas.microsoft.com/
intellisense/ie5">
  </HEAD>
  <body MS_POSITIONING="GridLayout">

    <form id="Form1" method="post" runat="server">
<asp:Button id=Button1 style="Z-INDEX: 101; LEFT: 95px;
POSITION: absolute; TOP: 75px" runat="server" Text="Click me"
Width="125px" Height="24px"></asp:Button>
<asp:TextBox id=TextBox2 style="Z-INDEX: 104; LEFT: 239px;
POSITION: absolute; TOP: 127px" runat="server"></asp:TextBox>
<asp:Button id=Button2 style="Z-INDEX: 103; LEFT: 95px;
POSITION: absolute; TOP: 125px" runat="server" Text="Click me too"
Width="125px" Height="24px" CommandArgument="You clicked Button2"
CommandName="Button2"></asp:Button>
<asp:TextBox id=TextBox1 style="Z-INDEX: 102; LEFT: 239px; POSITION:
absolute; TOP: 76px" runat="server"></asp:TextBox>

    </form>

  </body>
</HTML>
```

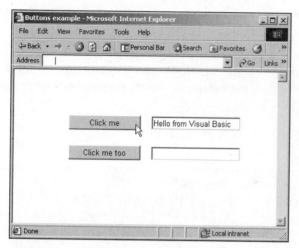

Figure 15.6   The Buttons example.

And here is WebForm1.aspx.vb, which holds the Visual Basic code in the Buttons example:

```
Public Class WebForm1
    Inherits System.Web.UI.Page
    Protected WithEvents Button1 As System.Web.UI.WebControls.Button
    Protected WithEvents Button2 As System.Web.UI.WebControls.Button
    Protected WithEvents TextBox2 As System.Web.UI.WebControls.TextBox
    Protected WithEvents TextBox1 As System.Web.UI.WebControls.TextBox

#Region " Web Form Designer Generated Code "

    'This call is required by the Web Form Designer.
    <System.Diagnostics.DebuggerStepThrough()> Private Sub
InitializeComponent()

    End Sub

    Private Sub Page_Init(ByVal sender As System.Object, ByVal e As _
        System.EventArgs) Handles MyBase.Init
        'CODEGEN: This method call is required by the Web Form Designer
        'Do not modify it using the code editor.
        InitializeComponent()
    End Sub

#End Region
```

```
    Private Sub Page_Load(ByVal sender As System.Object, ByVal e As _
        System.EventArgs) Handles MyBase.Load
        'Put user code to initialize the page here
    End Sub

    Private Sub Button1_Click(ByVal sender As System.Object, ByVal e As _
        System.EventArgs) Handles Button1.Click
        TextBox1.Text = "Hello from Visual Basic"
    End Sub

    Private Sub Button2_Command(ByVal sender As Object, ByVal e As _
        System.Web.UI.WebControls.CommandEventArgs) Handles Button2.Command
        TextBox2.Text = e.CommandArgument
    End Sub
End Class
```

By default, buttons are supported as HTML Submit buttons; here is the actual HTML sent from the server to the Web browser:

```
<input type="submit" name="Button1" value="Click me" id="Button1"
style="height:24px;width:125px;Z-INDEX: 101; LEFT: 95px; POSITION:
absolute; TOP: 75px" />
```

In the Visual Basic code, you can handle the button's **Click** event just as you would in a Windows form; just double-click a button to bring up this code in a code designer:

```
    Private Sub Button1_Click(ByVal sender As System.Object, ByVal e As _
        System.EventArgs) Handles Button1.Click
            .
            .
            .
    End Sub
```

This is reassuringly like what Windows programmers are used to, even though this button will appear in a Web browser. To display the text in the text box you see in Figure 15.6, you only need to add this code to the event handler and run the application:

```
    Private Sub Button1_Click(ByVal sender As System.Object, ByVal e As _
        System.EventArgs) Handles Button1.Click
            TextBox1.Text = "Hello from Visual Basic"
    End Sub
```

15. Web Forms:
Buttons, Text Boxes,
Labels, Literals

Creating Command Buttons

Besides creating buttons that work as Submit buttons, you also can create command buttons, as discussed in the In Depth section of this chapter. You make a button into a command button by assigning text to its **CommandName** property, and you also can assign text to its **CommandArgument** property (following the lead of buttons in Java).

In the Buttons example, which you can see in Figure 15.6, I've set the bottom button's **CommandName** property to "Button2" and its **CommandArgument** property to "You clicked Button2". To recover those values, you add code to the **Command** event of this property, not the **Click** event. Here's what that event handler looks like:

```
Private Sub Button2_Command(ByVal sender As Object, ByVal e As _
    System.Web.UI.WebControls.CommandEventArgs) Handles Button2.Command
        .
        .
        .
End Sub
```

The **CommandEventArgs** object passed to us has both a **CommandName** and **CommandArgument** property, so I can display the command argument for this button in the text box in this example this way:

```
Private Sub Button2_Command(ByVal sender As Object, ByVal e As _
    System.Web.UI.WebControls.CommandEventArgs) Handles Button2.Command
    TextBox2.Text = e.CommandArgument
End Sub
```

You can see the result in Figure 15.7, where I've clicked the bottom button.

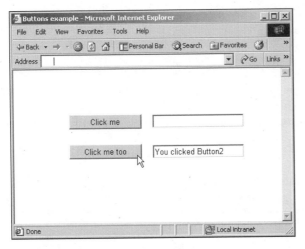

Figure 15.7   Using a command button.

Using the **TextBox** Class

We've already used the **System.Web.UI.WebControls.TextBox** class quite a bit; this class displays a text box in a Web form. Here is the hierarchy of this class:

```
Object
    Control
        WebControl
            TextBox
```

You can find the notable public properties of **TextBox** objects in Table 15.8 and the notable events in Table 15.9. (Note there's no table of methods here—**TextBox** inherits all its methods from the **WebControl** class.) Note that as with other Web server controls, I am not listing the notable properties, methods, and events this class inherits from the **Control** and **WebControl** classes—you can find them in Tables 15.1 to 15.5.

Table 15.8   Noteworthy public properties of **TextBox** objects.

Property	Means
AutoPostBack	Gets/sets whether events will be automatically posted back to the server.
Columns	Gets/sets the text box's width in characters.
MaxLength	Gets/sets the maximum number of characters that may be displayed in the text box.

(continued)

15. Web Forms:
Buttons, Text Boxes,
Labels, Literals

Table 15.8   Noteworthy public properties of TextBox objects *(continued)*.

Property	Means
ReadOnly	Gets/sets whether the text box is read-only.
Rows	Gets/sets a multiline text box's display height.
Text	Gets/sets the text in a text box.
TextMode	Gets/sets whether a text box should be single line, multiline, or a password control.
Wrap	Gets/sets whether text wraps in the text box.

Table 15.9   Noteworthy public events of TextBox objects.

Event	Means
TextChanged	Occurs when the text in the text box is changed.

Creating Text Boxes

We've been working with text boxes in this and the previous chapter already; because text boxes in Web forms work much like they do in Windows forms, they're easy to handle. For example, the TextBoxes example on the CD-ROM shows several ways to work with text boxes, as you see in Figure 15.8. This example shows how to work with single-line text boxes, multiline text boxes, and password controls. When you click the button in this example, the message "You clicked the button." appears in a single-line text box and a multiline text box. In addition, the masked text in a password control is copied and displayed in a text box under that control.

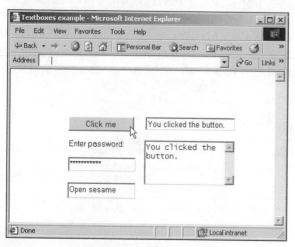

Figure 15.8   The Textboxes example.

Here is WebForm1.aspx from the Textboxes example:

```
<%@ Page Language="vb" AutoEventWireup="false" Codebehind=
"WebForm1.aspx.vb" Inherits="TextBoxes.WebForm1"%>
<!DOCTYPE HTML PUBLIC "-//W3C//DTD HTML 4.0 Transitional//EN">
<HTML>
  <HEAD>
    <title></title>
    <meta name="GENERATOR" content="Microsoft Visual Studio.NET 7.0">
    <meta name="CODE_LANGUAGE" content="Visual Basic 7.0">
    <meta name=vs_defaultClientScript content="JavaScript">
    <meta name=vs_targetSchema content="http://schemas.microsoft.com/ _
        intellisense/ie5">
  </HEAD>
  <body MS_POSITIONING="GridLayout">

    <form id="Form1" method="post" runat="server">
<asp:Button id=Button1 style="Z-INDEX: 101; LEFT: 101px;
POSITION: absolute; TOP: 78px" runat="server" Text="Click me"
Width="114px" Height="24px"></asp:Button>
<asp:Label id=Label1 style="Z-INDEX: 106; LEFT: 102px;
POSITION: absolute; TOP: 115px" runat="server">
Enter password:</asp:Label>
<asp:TextBox id=TextBox4 style="Z-INDEX: 105; LEFT:
100px; POSITION: absolute; TOP: 188px" runat="server"
Width="119px" Height="27px"></asp:TextBox>
<asp:TextBox id=TextBox3 style="Z-INDEX: 104; LEFT: 101px;
POSITION: absolute; TOP: 146px" runat="server" Width="118px"
Height="24px" TextMode="Password"></asp:TextBox>
<asp:TextBox id=TextBox2 style="Z-INDEX: 103; LEFT: 233px;
POSITION: absolute; TOP: 117px" runat="server" Width="157px"
Height="74px" TextMode="MultiLine"></asp:TextBox>
<asp:TextBox id=TextBox1 style="Z-INDEX: 102; LEFT: 235px;
POSITION: absolute; TOP: 78px" runat="server" AutoPostBack="True">
</asp:TextBox>

    </form>
  </body>
</HTML>
```

And here is WebForm1.aspx.vb from this example:

```
Public Class WebForm1
    Inherits System.Web.UI.Page
    Protected WithEvents Button1 As System.Web.UI.WebControls.Button
    Protected WithEvents TextBox2 As System.Web.UI.WebControls.TextBox
    Protected WithEvents TextBox3 As System.Web.UI.WebControls.TextBox
```

```
        Protected WithEvents TextBox4 As System.Web.UI.WebControls.TextBox
        Protected WithEvents Label1 As System.Web.UI.WebControls.Label
        Protected WithEvents TextBox1 As System.Web.UI.WebControls.TextBox

    #Region " Web Form Designer Generated Code "

        'This call is required by the Web Form Designer.
        <System.Diagnostics.DebuggerStepThrough()> _
            Private Sub InitializeComponent()

        End Sub

        Private Sub Page_Init(ByVal sender As System.Object, _
            ByVal e As System.EventArgs) Handles MyBase.Init
            'CODEGEN: This method call is required by the Web Form Designer
            'Do not modify it using the code editor.
            InitializeComponent()
        End Sub

    #End Region

        Private Sub Page_Load(ByVal sender As System.Object, _
            ByVal e As System.EventArgs) Handles MyBase.Load
            'Put user code to initialize the page here
        End Sub

        Private Sub Button1_Click(ByVal sender As System.Object, _
            ByVal e As System.EventArgs) Handles Button1.Click
            TextBox1.Text = "You clicked the button."
            TextBox2.Text = "You clicked the button."
            TextBox4.Text = TextBox3.Text
        End Sub

        Private Sub TextBox1_TextChanged(ByVal sender As _
            System.Object, ByVal e As System.EventArgs) Handles _
            TextBox1.TextChanged
            TextBox1.Text = "You changed the text."
        End Sub
    End Class
```

As discussed in the In Depth section of this chapter, a single-line text box actually becomes an HTML **<input>** control with the **type** attribute set to "text", which is called a *text field* in HTML:

```
<input name="TextBox1" type="text" id="TextBox1" style="Z-INDEX: 104; LEFT:
239px; POSITION: absolute; TOP: 127px" />
```

Most work one does with a text box is done with the **Text** property and the **TextChanged** event. Here's how I use the **Text** property to place text into the single-line text box in the Textboxes example when the user clicks the button:

```
Private Sub Button1_Click(ByVal sender As System.Object, _
    ByVal e As System.EventArgs) Handles Button1.Click
        TextBox1.Text = "You clicked the button."
        .
        .
        .
    End Sub
```

If you want to use a text box event like **TextChanged**, which occurs when the text in the text box is changed, note that text box events are not automatically posted back to the server when they occur. If you want that to happen, set the text box's **AutoPostBack** property to **True** first (see "Forcing Event Handling" in Chapter 14 for more information). I've added code to the top text box's **TextChanged** event in the Textboxes example so if you change that text, the message "You changed the text." appears in that text box (note that to trigger a **TextChanged** event, you must first change the text and then click another control so the text box loses the focus):

```
Private Sub TextBox1_TextChanged(ByVal sender As _
    System.Object, ByVal e As System.EventArgs) Handles _
    TextBox1.TextChanged
        TextBox1.Text = "You changed the text."
    End Sub
```

Related solution:	Found on page:
Forcing Event Handling	645

Creating Multiline Text Boxes

If you set the **TextMode** property of a Web server text box to **MultiLine**, you can create a multiline text box. You can size the multiline text box at design time by stretching it into place, or with the **Rows** and **Columns** properties.

Multiline text boxes are really HTML text areas; you can see one in the Textboxes example you see in Figure 15.8. Here's the HTML text area created in the Textboxes example:

```
<textarea name="TextBox2" id="TextBox2"
style="height:74px;width:157px;Z-INDEX: 103; LEFT: 233px;
POSITION: absolute; TOP: 117px"></textarea>
```

Even though you handle the text in HTML text areas differently from HTML text fields (which is how single-line text boxes are supported in Web forms), VB .NET hides that detail; you can just use the **Text** property of a multiline text box to work with its text, just as you can with a single-line text box. Here's how that works in the Textboxes example on the CD-ROM, where **TextBox2** is a multiline text box:

```
Private Sub Button1_Click(ByVal sender As System.Object, _
    ByVal e As System.EventArgs) Handles Button1.Click
    TextBox1.Text = "You clicked the button."
    TextBox2.Text = "You clicked the button."
        .
        .
        .
End Sub
```

Creating Password Controls

You can convert a text box into a password control, where the text the user types is masked with asterisks (*). You can see this in the Textboxes example on the CD-ROM in Figure 15.8. You create a password control by setting a text box's **TextMode** property to **Password**, as I've done for the text box under the button in the Textboxes example. In HTML, this becomes an **<input>** element with the **type** attribute set to "password":

```
<input name="TextBox3" type="password" id="TextBox3"
style="height:24px;width:118px;Z-INDEX: 104; LEFT: 101px;
POSITION: absolute; TOP: 146px" />
```

In code, you can read the text in the password control using the control's **Text** property, as I do in the Textboxes example, where I transfer the text from the password control to the text box under it, like this:

```
Private Sub Button1_Click(ByVal sender As System.Object, _
    ByVal e As System.EventArgs) Handles Button1.Click
    TextBox1.Text = "You clicked the button."
    TextBox2.Text = "You clicked the button."
    TextBox4.Text = TextBox3.Text
End Sub
```

You can see the result in Figure 15.8.

TIP: *Although the security of password controls isn't to be relied on too heavily, it's worth noting that the browser is smart enough to thwart someone who just tries to copy the masked password and paste it into another application to read it; you can't actually copy password text, because nothing is placed into the clipboard when you try.*

Creating Read-only Text Boxes

You can also make text boxes read-only, where the user can't change the text in the control, by setting their **ReadOnly** property to **True**. That's all it takes.

Setting Text Box Columns and Rows

With the **Columns** property, you can set the number of characters a text box will display in multiline text boxes. You also can use the **Rows** property to set the number of rows.

Using the **Label** Class

The **Label** class is much like the labels you use in Windows forms. Here's the hierarchy of this class:

```
Object
    Control
        WebControl
            Label
```

The only notable non-inherited property of this class is the **Text** property, which gets and sets the text in the label (this control has no non-inherited methods or events). Note that as with other Web server controls, I am not listing the notable properties, methods, and events this class inherits from the **Control** and **WebControl** classes—you can find them in Tables 15.1 to 15.5.

Creating Labels

You can use the **Label** class just as you use labels in Windows forms—to display text. You can change that text with the **Text** property in code if you want, but the user can't edit the text in a label control directly.

There's an example called Labels on the CD-ROM that puts a label to work; you can see this example in Figure 15.9. When you click the "Click me" button in this example, the code places the text "Hello!" in a label and adds a dashed border to the label, as shown in that figure.

Here is WebForm1.aspx from the Labels example:

```
<%@ Page Language="vb" AutoEventWireup="false"
Codebehind="WebForm1.aspx.vb" Inherits="Labels.WebForm1"%>
<!DOCTYPE HTML PUBLIC "-//W3C//DTD HTML 4.0 Transitional//EN">
<HTML>
  <HEAD>
    <title></title>
    <meta name="GENERATOR" content="Microsoft Visual Studio.NET 7.0">
    <meta name="CODE_LANGUAGE" content="Visual Basic 7.0">
    <meta name=vs_defaultClientScript content="JavaScript">
    <meta name=vs_targetSchema content="http://schemas.microsoft.com/ _
        intellisense/ie5">
  </HEAD>
  <body MS_POSITIONING="GridLayout">

    <form id="Form1" method="post" runat="server">
<asp:Label id=Label1 style="Z-INDEX: 101; LEFT: 250px;
POSITION: absolute; TOP: 79px" runat="server" Width="203px"
Height="118px" Font-Size="XX-Large"></asp:Label>
<asp:Button id=Button1 style="Z-INDEX: 102; LEFT: 127px;
POSITION: absolute; TOP: 107px" runat="server" Text="Click me">
</asp:Button>

    </form>
  </body>
</HTML>
```

And here is WebForm1.aspx.vb from the same example:

```
Public Class WebForm1
    Inherits System.Web.UI.Page
    Protected WithEvents Label1 As System.Web.UI.WebControls.Label
    Protected WithEvents Button1 As System.Web.UI.WebControls.Button
```

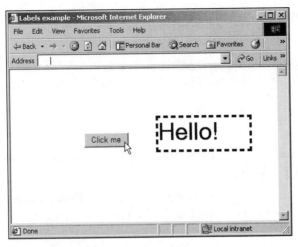

Figure 15.9   **The Labels example.**

```
#Region " Web Form Designer Generated Code "

    'This call is required by the Web Form Designer.
    <System.Diagnostics.DebuggerStepThrough()> _
        Private Sub InitializeComponent()

    End Sub

    Private Sub Page_Init(ByVal sender As System.Object, _
        ByVal e As System.EventArgs) Handles MyBase.Init
        'CODEGEN: This method call is required by the Web Form Designer
        'Do not modify it using the code editor.
        InitializeComponent()
    End Sub

#End Region

    Private Sub Page_Load(ByVal sender As System.Object, _
        ByVal e As System.EventArgs) Handles MyBase.Load
        'Put user code to initialize the page here
    End Sub

    Private Sub Button1_Click(ByVal sender As System.Object, _
        ByVal e As System.EventArgs) Handles Button1.Click
        Label1.Text = "Hello!"
        Label1.BorderStyle = BorderStyle.Dashed
    End Sub
End Class
```

In HTML, labels are supported by **<span>** elements; here's the one generated in the Labels example:

```
<span id="Label1" style="border-style:Dashed;font-size:XX-
Large;height:118px;width:203px;Z-INDEX: 101; LEFT: 250px; POSITION:
absolute; TOP: 79px">Hello!</span>
```

Setting Label Text and Style

As in Windows forms, you can set the text in a label with the **Text** property of **Label** objects. Here's how that looks in the Labels example when you click the button in that example:

```
Private Sub Button1_Click(ByVal sender As System.Object, _
    ByVal e As System.EventArgs) Handles Button1.Click
    Label1.Text = "Hello!"
        .
        .
        .
End Sub
```

You can see the results of this code in Figure 15.9.

NOTE: The text in this label is pretty big—I've set it to XX-Large, in fact; see "Setting Control Fonts" in this chapter for the details.

You also can set the border style of labels with the **BorderStyle** property, and the border width with the **BorderWidth** property. For example, I'm setting the **BorderStyle** property of the label in the Labels example on the CD-ROM to a dashed border:

```
Private Sub Button1_Click(ByVal sender As System.Object, _
    ByVal e As System.EventArgs) Handles Button1.Click
    Label1.Text = "Hello!"
    Label1.BorderStyle = BorderStyle.Dashed
End Sub
```

NOTE: To see what types of borders are available, see "Setting Control Border Style" in this chapter.

Using the **Literal** Class

You use the Literal class to insert literal text, often HTML, into a Web form. Here is the hierarchy of this class:

```
Object
    Control
        Literal
```

This class's only notable property is the **Text** property, with which you assign the text you want to insert into a Web form's HTML—it has no methods or events that are not inherited from the **WebControl** class. Note that as with other Web server controls, I am not listing the notable properties, methods, and events this class inherits from the **Control** and **WebControl** classes—you can find them in Tables 15.1 to 15.5.

Creating Literals

You can see the **Literal** class at work in the Literals example on the CD-ROM. When you click the button in this example, the code inserts the HTML needed to display the word "Hello" in a centered HTML **<h1>** header—** <h1>Hello</h1> **—into the Web form, as you can see in Figure 15.10.

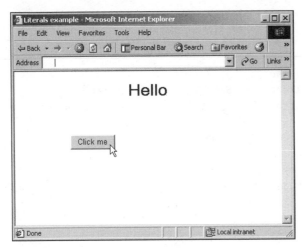

Figure 15.10   The Literals example.

Here's Webform1.aspx from the Literals example:

```
<%@ Page Language="vb" AutoEventWireup="false" Codebehind=
"WebForm1.aspx.vb" Inherits="Literals.WebForm1"%>
<!DOCTYPE HTML PUBLIC "-//W3C//DTD HTML 4.0 Transitional//EN">
<HTML>
  <HEAD>
    <title></title>
    <meta name="GENERATOR" content="Microsoft Visual Studio.NET 7.0">
    <meta name="CODE_LANGUAGE" content="Visual Basic 7.0">
    <meta name=vs_defaultClientScript content="JavaScript">
    <meta name=vs_targetSchema
    content="http://schemas.microsoft.com/intellisense/ie5">
  </HEAD>
  <body MS_POSITIONING="GridLayout">

    <form id="Form1" method="post" runat="server">
<asp:Button id=Button1 style="Z-INDEX: 101; LEFT: 96px;
POSITION: absolute; TOP: 106px" runat="server" Text="Click me">
</asp:Button>
<asp:Literal id=Literal1 runat="server"></asp:Literal>

    </form>

  </body>
</HTML>
```

And here's WebForm1.aspx.vb from the same project:

```
Public Class WebForm1
    Inherits System.Web.UI.Page
    Protected WithEvents Literal1 As System.Web.UI.WebControls.Literal
    Protected WithEvents Button1 As System.Web.UI.WebControls.Button

#Region " Web Form Designer Generated Code "

    'This call is required by the Web Form Designer.
    <System.Diagnostics.DebuggerStepThrough()> _
        Private Sub InitializeComponent()

    End Sub

    Private Sub Page_Init(ByVal sender As System.Object, _
        ByVal e As System.EventArgs) Handles MyBase.Init
```

```
            'CODEGEN: This method call is required by the Web Form Designer
            'Do not modify it using the code editor.
            InitializeComponent()
        End Sub

#End Region

    Private Sub Page_Load(ByVal sender As System.Object, _
        ByVal e As System.EventArgs) Handles MyBase.Load
        'Put user code to initialize the page here
    End Sub

    Private Sub Button1_Click(ByVal sender As System.Object, _
        ByVal e As System.EventArgs) Handles Button1.Click
        Literal1.Text = "<div align='center'><h1>Hello</h1></div>"
    End Sub
End Class
```

Here's how the code inserts the **<h1>** header when you click the button in this example:

```
    Private Sub Button1_Click(ByVal sender As System.Object, _
        ByVal e As System.EventArgs) Handles Button1.Click
        Literal1.Text = "<div align='center'><h1>Hello</h1></div>"
    End Sub
```

Using the **PlaceHolder** Class

The **PlaceHolder** class is designed to store server controls you add to a Web page at run time. Here's the hierarchy of this class:

```
Object
    Control
        PlaceHolder
```

This class doesn't have any non-inherited members; to add controls to a place holder, you use its **Controls** collection's **Add** member. See the next topic for an example. Note that as with other Web server controls, I am not listing the notable properties, methods, and events this class inherits from the **Control** and **WebControl** classes—you can find them in Tables 15.1 to 15.5.

Adding Controls at Run Time

A control can contain other controls. You might want to read this twice: Controls based on the **Control** class contain a **Controls** collection that holds the controls contained in the control, if any. For example, the Web form **Page** class is derived from the **Control** class, so you can add controls to a Web form with the form's **Controls.Add** method. In fact, placeholder controls are designed to be used this way—they don't insert any HTML into a Web page themselves, but you can add controls to them with their **Controls.Add** method.

You can see how this works in the AddControls example on the CD-ROM, which you can see in Figure 15.11. When you click the button in this example, two text boxes are added to the Web form. One text box is added to a place holder, and one to a panel control, which is also used for this purpose.

Here is the WebForm1.aspx file for the AddControls project:

```
<%@ Page Language="vb" AutoEventWireup="false" Codebehind=
"WebForm1.aspx.vb" Inherits="AddControls.WebForm1"%>
<!DOCTYPE HTML PUBLIC "-//W3C//DTD HTML 4.0 Transitional//EN">
<HTML>
  <HEAD>
    <title></title>
    <meta name="GENERATOR" content="Microsoft Visual Studio.NET 7.0">
    <meta name="CODE_LANGUAGE" content="Visual Basic 7.0">
    <meta name=vs_defaultClientScript content="JavaScript">
    <meta name=vs_targetSchema
        content="http://schemas.microsoft.com/intellisense/ie5">
  </HEAD>
  <body MS_POSITIONING="GridLayout">

    <form id="Form1" method="post" runat="server">
<asp:Button id=Button1 style="Z-INDEX: 101; LEFT: 99px;
POSITION: absolute; TOP: 105px" runat="server" Text="Click me">
</asp:Button>
<asp:Panel id=Panel1 style="Z-INDEX: 102; LEFT: 275px;
POSITION: absolute; TOP: 105px" runat="server" Width="128px"
Height="26px"></asp:Panel>
<asp:PlaceHolder id=PlaceHolder1 runat="server">
</asp:PlaceHolder>

    </form>
  </body>
</HTML>
```

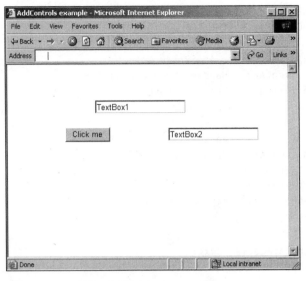

Figure 15.11   The AddControls example.

And here's the WebForm1.aspx.vb file:

```
Public Class WebForm1
    Inherits System.Web.UI.Page
    Protected WithEvents Button1 As System.Web.UI.WebControls.Button
    Protected WithEvents PlaceHolder1 As _
        System.Web.UI.WebControls.PlaceHolder
    Protected WithEvents Panel1 As System.Web.UI.WebControls.Panel

#Region " Web Form Designer Generated Code "

    'This call is required by the Web Form Designer.
    <System.Diagnostics.DebuggerStepThrough()> _
        Private Sub InitializeComponent()

    End Sub

    Private Sub Page_Init(ByVal sender As System.Object, _
        ByVal e As System.EventArgs) Handles MyBase.Init
        'CODEGEN: This method call is required by the Web Form Designer
        'Do not modify it using the code editor.
        InitializeComponent()
    End Sub

#End Region
```

```
Dim TextBox1, TextBox2 As New _
    System.Web.UI.WebControls.TextBox()

Private Sub Page_Load(ByVal sender As System.Object, _
    ByVal e As System.EventArgs) Handles MyBase.Load
    'Put user code to initialize the page here
End Sub

Private Sub Button1_Click(ByVal sender As System.Object, _
    ByVal e As System.EventArgs) Handles Button1.Click
    TextBox1.Text = "TextBox1"
    TextBox2.Text = "TextBox2"
    TextBox1.Style("POSITION") = "ABSOLUTE"
    TextBox1.Style("TOP") = "60px"
    TextBox1.Style("LEFT") = "150px"
    PlaceHolder1.Controls.Add(TextBox1)
    Panel1.Controls.Add(TextBox2)
End Sub
End Class
```

In this example, I've added a placeholder control, **PlaceHolder1**, and a panel control, **Panel1**. Web form panels act just like Windows form panels, and they're frequently used as a container control for other controls. (We'll see Web form panels in Chapter 16.) Here's how this example works—the code creates two text boxes, like this:

```
Dim TextBox1, TextBox2, TextBox3 As New _
    System.Web.UI.WebControls.TextBox()

Private Sub Button1_Click(ByVal sender As System.Object, _
    ByVal e As System.EventArgs) Handles Button1.Click
    TextBox1.Text = "TextBox1"
    TextBox2.Text = "TextBox2"
        .
        .
        .
End Sub
```

Then I add a new control to the place holder and to the panel using the **Controls.Add** method. By default, place holders don't have a position in the Web page, so note that I also position the text box inserted into the place using its

Style property to place the text box in the position I want (see "Moving Controls" in this chapter for more information):

```
Dim TextBox1, TextBox2 As New _
    System.Web.UI.WebControls.TextBox()

Private Sub Button1_Click(ByVal sender As System.Object, _
    ByVal e As System.EventArgs) Handles Button1.Click
    TextBox1.Text = "TextBox1"
    TextBox2.Text = "TextBox2"
    TextBox1.Style("POSITION") = "ABSOLUTE"
    TextBox1.Style("TOP") = "60px"
    TextBox1.Style("LEFT") = "150px"
    PlaceHolder1.Controls.Add(TextBox1)
    Panel1.Controls.Add(TextBox2)
End Sub
```

And that's all it takes. If you want to add an event handler to a new control, use the **AddHandler** method, as we've done in Windows forms.

Related solution:	Found on page:
Adding and Removing Controls at Run Time	196

Chapter 16

Web Forms: Checkboxes, Radio Buttons, Tables, and Panels

In Depth

In this chapter, I'll take a look at a number of popular Web server controls: checkboxes, checkbox lists, radio buttons, radio button lists, tables, and panels. These are all basic controls that you find yourself using quite a lot, and we'll add them to our programming arsenal in this chapter.

Checkboxes

We all know what checkboxes are—those square controls that toggle a checkmark when clicked and that can display caption text. For example, you can see checkboxes in the CheckBoxes example on the CD-ROM, as shown in Figure 16.1. This example is intended to help the user design a sandwich, and as you can see in that figure, they've chosen whole wheat bread, sausage, and so on. Checkboxes like these are good for specifying non-exclusive options; that is, a single sandwich can have not only whole wheat bread, but also sesame seeds so, unlike radio buttons, the checkboxes in Figure 16.1 will stay checked when you check and uncheck other checkboxes.

Web server checkboxes look and act very much like the ones you'll see in Windows forms, but of course there are many differences. Web server checkboxes cannot be made three-state, they do not have a **Select** method, they do not have **Show** or **Hide** methods, you need to set their **AutoPostBack** property to **True** if you want to handle their events when they happen, and there are many other differences as well.

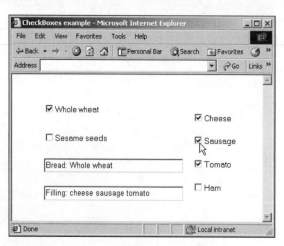

Figure 16.1   The CheckBoxes example.

In fact, only the two checkboxes at left in Figure 16.1 are standalone checkboxes—the other checkboxes you see are part of a *checkbox list*.

Checkbox Lists

You can use a checkbox list control to display a number of checkboxes at once. (This is often useful when you want to bind data from a data source to checkboxes.) This control has an **Items** collection (inherited from the **ListControl** class) with members corresponding to checkboxes in the list. Each item in the **Items** collection is an object of the **ListItem** class (see "Using the **ListItem** Class" in this chapter), and you can use the **ListItem** class's **Value**, **Text**, and **Selected** properties to work with the individual checkboxes in the list, like this: **CheckBoxList1. Items(5).Selected**. To find out which checkboxes are checked, you can loop through the list and test the **Selected** property of each item.

TIP: *You also can use the **SelectedItem** or **SelectedIndex** properties in checkbox lists, but note that these lists can support multiple selections. If multiple items are selected, the **SelectedItem** and **SelectedIndex** properties hold the selected item with the lowest index value, and the index value of the selected item with the lowest index value, which tells you nothing about the other selected items. You usually use the **SelectedItem** or **SelectedIndex** properties with radio button lists, coming up in this chapter, which only support a single selected item.*

You can specify the way the list is actually displayed by using the **RepeatLayout** and **RepeatDirection** properties. For example, if **RepeatLayout** is set to **RepeatLayout.Table** (which is the default), the list is drawn in an HTML table. If it is set to **RepeatLayout.Flow**, on the other hand, the list is drawn without a table. And by default, **RepeatDirection** is set to **RepeatDirection.Vertical**. Setting this property to **RepeatDirection.Horizontal** draws the list horizontally.

Radio Buttons

Just like checkboxes, we all know what radio buttons are—they're those round controls that toggle a dot in the middle. You can see radio buttons at work in Figure 16.2, where I'm selecting various options for a new vehicle to buy. In this case, I'm selecting a car and making its color red.

Unlike checkboxes, radio buttons form exclusive groups, where only one radio button can be selected (that is, display a dot in its center) at a time. In Windows forms, radio buttons are grouped automatically by container, but in Web forms, you have to set radio buttons' **GroupName** property to the same value to associate them into a group. Radio buttons in Web forms are much like radio buttons in Windows forms, but they have the same differences that checkboxes have—you need to set the **AutoPostBack** property to handle their events when they occur, for example.

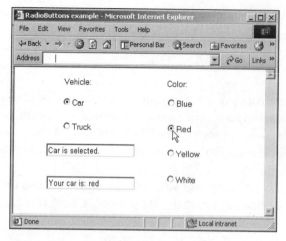

Figure 16.2 The RadioButtons example.

Besides standalone radio buttons, Web forms also support *radio buttons lists*; in fact, the radio buttons at right in Figure 16.2 are in a radio button list control.

Radio Button Lists

Radio button list controls give you an easy way to display a single-selection radio button group. One useful aspect of this control is that lists of radio buttons can be generated at run time with data binding. As with checkbox controls, this control has an **Items** collection (inherited from the **ListControl** class) that holds the individual radio buttons in the list. Each item in the **Items** collection is an object of the **ListItem** class (see "Using the **ListItem** Class" in this chapter). You can use the **ListItem** class's **Value**, **Text**, and **Selected** properties to work with the individual radio buttons in the list, like this: **RadioButtonList1.Items(5). Selected**. To determine which item is selected, you can test the **SelectedItem** property of the list. You don't need to loop over each item (although, like each item in checkbox lists, each item also has a **Selected** property). You also can find the selected item's index with the **SelectedIndex** property.

And, as with checkbox lists, you can specify the way the list is actually displayed by using the **RepeatLayout** and **RepeatDirection** properties (see the In Depth section "Checkbox Lists" for the details).

Tables

Another Web server control is the **Table** control, which just displays an HTML table. This control is a good one if you want to visually organize what's going on in a Web page using rows and columns, usually to present data in tabular form. Previously, Web designers often used tables to get a measure of control over where elements were placed in Web pages, but now that you can position elements in an absolute manner, that's no longer needed.

You can create a table at design time or at run time. Doing so at run time is often useful because you can build a table by binding it to a data source. You can see a table at work in the Tables example in Figure 16.3, where I am listing the name, length of day, radius, and perihelion (farthest distance from the sun) of several planets.

To create a table using a **Table** control, it helps to know how HTML tables are created, because your table will be drawn as an HTML table. You create a table in HTML with the **<table>** element, and an object of the **Table** class in VB .NET. You add rows to the table in HTML with **<tr>** (table row) elements, and with objects of the **TableRow** class in Visual Basic. And you add the cells in an HTML table with the **<td>** (table data) element, and with **TableCell** objects in Visual Basic. Here's what the generated HTML for the table in Figure 16.3 looks like:

```
<table id="Table1" bordercolor="Black" border="0"
style="border-color:Black;border-width:2px;
border-style:Solid;height:163px;width:313px;
Z-INDEX: 101; LEFT: 96px; POSITION: absolute; TOP: 63px">
    <tr align="Center">
        <td style=
                "border-width:1px;border-style:Solid;font-weight:bold;">
            Name
        </td><td style=
                "border-width:1px;border-style:Solid;font-weight:bold;">
            Day
        </td><td style=
                "border-width:1px;border-style:Solid;font-weight:bold;">
            Radius (miles)
        </td><td style=
                "border-width:1px;border-style:Solid;font-weight:bold;">
            Perihelion (million miles)
        </td>
    </tr><tr align="Center">
        <td style="border-width:1px;border-style:Solid;">
            Mercury
        </td><td style="border-width:1px;border-style:Solid;">
            58.65
        </td><td style="border-width:1px;border-style:Solid;">
            1516
        </td><td style="border-width:1px;border-style:Solid;">
            43.4
        </td>
    </tr><tr align="Center">
```

```
    <td style="border-width:1px;border-style:Solid;">
        Venus
    </td><td style="border-width:1px;border-style:Solid;">
        116.75
    </td><td style="border-width:1px;border-style:Solid;">
        3716
    </td><td style="border-width:1px;border-style:Solid;">
        66.8
    </td>
</tr><tr align="Center">
    <td style="border-width:1px;border-style:Solid;">
        Earth
    </td><td style="border-width:1px;border-style:Solid;">
        1
    </td><td style="border-width:1px;border-style:Solid;">
        2107
    </td><td style="border-width:1px;border-style:Solid;">
        128.4
    </td>
</tr>
</table>
```

To help create the **TableRow** and **TableCell** objects you need in a table, the Visual Basic IDE uses collection editors, as we'll see in this chapter. In code, you can add contents to a table cell by adding literal controls or other controls to its **Controls** collection. Then you add the **TableCell** objects you've created to a table row's **Cells** collection. After that, you add the **TableRow** objects to the table's **Rows** collection, and you're all set.

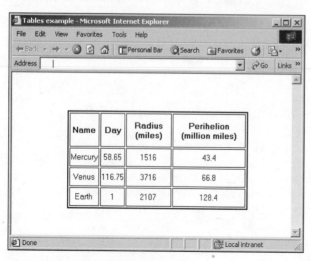

Figure 16.3   The Tables example.

TIP: *It is important to know that any additions to modification of table rows or cells in code will not persist after you post the page back to the server. This is because table rows and cells are controls of their own, and not properties of controls.*

Panels

Panel controls are most often used as—and are intended as—containers for other controls. They're often useful when you want to show or hide a group of controls at once, or when you want to add controls to a Web page in code. In fact, we've already seen how to use panels to add controls to a Web page; see "Adding Controls at Run Time" in Chapter 15. To see how panels are used to group controls, notice the Panels example, which is shown in Figure 16.4. This example presents a very basic color-picker type application, which lets you use radio buttons to select a color. That's a panel I'm using at the bottom of the application you see in Figure 16.4 to display the selected color (using the panel's **BackColor** property).

If you click the Custom radio button in the Panels example, a panel that was previously hidden appears, as you see in Figure 16.5; you can use all the controls that now appear to set a custom color. I'll go over this example in more depth later in the chapter—see "Creating Panels" for the details.

And those are the controls that this chapter covers. It's time to turn to the Immediate Solutions section of the chapter to start working things out detail by detail.

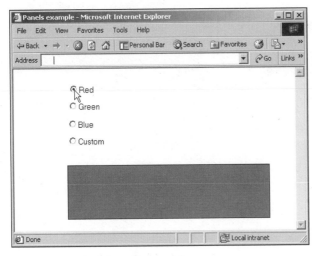

Figure 16.4   The Panels example.

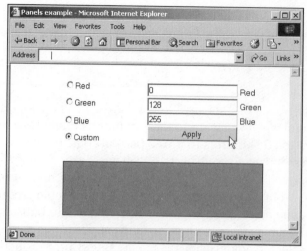

Figure 16.5   The Panels example showing the previously hidden panel.

Immediate Solutions

Using the **CheckBox** Class

Checkboxes display checkmarks that allow the user to toggle a **True** or **False** condition. Here is the class hierarchy of the **CheckBox** class:

```
Object
   Control
      WebControl
         CheckBox
```

You can find the notable public properties of **CheckBox** objects in Table 16.1, the notable public methods in Table 16.2, and the notable public events in Table 16.3. Note that as with other Web server controls, I am not listing the notable properties, methods, and events this class inherits from the **Control** and **WebControl** classes—you can find them in Chapter 15, Tables 15.1 to 15.5.

Table 16.1 Noteworthy public properties of **CheckBox** objects.

Property	Means
AutoPostBack	Gets/sets whether the checkbox automatically posts the page back to the server.
Checked	Gets/sets whether the checkbox displays a check.
Text	Gets/sets the text caption for the checkbox.
TextAlign	Gets/sets the alignment of the text caption.

Table 16.2 Noteworthy public methods of **CheckBox** objects.

Method	Means
DataBind	Binds the checkbox to a data source.
Dispose	Disposes of the checkbox control.

Table 16.3 Noteworthy public events of **CheckBox** objects.

Event	Means
CheckedChanged	Occurs when the **Checked** property changes.
Load	Occurs when the checkbox is loaded.
Unload	Occurs when the checkbox is unloaded.

16. Web Forms: Checkboxes Radio Buttons, Tables

Creating Checkboxes

Checkboxes display checkmarks—which the user can toggle with a click—and caption text. To see how this works in Web applications, take a look at the CheckBoxes example on the CD-ROM; you can see it at work in Figure 16.1. This example is intended to help the user design a sandwich, and as you can see in that figure, they've chosen whole wheat bread, sausage, and so on.

For reference, here's what WebForm1.aspx in the CheckBoxes example looks like:

```
<%@ Page Language="vb" AutoEventWireup="false"
Codebehind="WebForm1.aspx.vb" Inherits="CheckBoxes.WebForm1"%>
<!DOCTYPE HTML PUBLIC "-//W3C//DTD HTML 4.0 Transitional//EN">
<HTML>
  <HEAD>
    <title>CheckBoxes example</title>
    <meta name="GENERATOR" content="Microsoft Visual Studio.NET 7.0">
    <meta name="CODE_LANGUAGE" content="Visual Basic 7.0">
    <meta name=vs_defaultClientScript content="JavaScript">
    <meta name=vs_targetSchema content="http://schemas.microsoft.com/ _
        intellisense/ie5">
  </HEAD>
  <body MS_POSITIONING="GridLayout">

    <form id="Form1" method="post" runat="server">
<asp:CheckBox id=CheckBox1 style="Z-INDEX: 101; LEFT: 54px;
POSITION: absolute; TOP: 47px" runat="server" Text="Whole wheat"
AutoPostBack="True"></asp:CheckBox>
<asp:CheckBoxList id=CheckBoxList1 style="Z-INDEX: 105; LEFT:
310px; POSITION: absolute; TOP: 51px" runat="server" Width="126px"
Height="157px" AutoPostBack="True">
<asp:ListItem Value="cheese">Cheese</asp:ListItem>
<asp:ListItem Value="sausage">Sausage</asp:ListItem>
<asp:ListItem Value="tomato">Tomato</asp:ListItem>
<asp:ListItem Value="ham">Ham</asp:ListItem>
</asp:CheckBoxList>
<asp:TextBox id=TextBox2 style="Z-INDEX: 104; LEFT: 55px;
POSITION: absolute; TOP: 186px" runat="server" Width="243px"
Height="25px"></asp:TextBox>
<asp:TextBox id=TextBox1 style="Z-INDEX: 103; LEFT: 55px;
POSITION: absolute; TOP: 140px" runat="server" Width="243px"
Height="24px"></asp:TextBox>
<asp:CheckBox id=CheckBox2 style="Z-INDEX: 102; LEFT: 54px;
POSITION: absolute; TOP: 95px" runat="server" Text="Sesame seeds"
AutoPostBack="True"></asp:CheckBox>
```

```
        </form>
      </body>
</HTML>
```

And here's what WebForm1.aspx.vb looks like:

```
Public Class WebForm1
    Inherits System.Web.UI.Page
    Protected WithEvents CheckBox1 As System.Web.UI.WebControls.CheckBox
    Protected WithEvents CheckBox2 As System.Web.UI.WebControls.CheckBox
    Protected WithEvents TextBox1 As System.Web.UI.WebControls.TextBox
    Protected WithEvents CheckBoxList1 As _
        System.Web.UI.WebControls.CheckBoxList
    Protected WithEvents TextBox2 As System.Web.UI.WebControls.TextBox


#Region " Web Form Designer Generated Code "

    'This call is required by the Web Form Designer.
    <System.Diagnostics.DebuggerStepThrough()> _
        Private Sub InitializeComponent()

    End Sub

    Private Sub Page_Init(ByVal sender As System.Object, _
        ByVal e As System.EventArgs) Handles MyBase.Init
        'CODEGEN: This method call is required by the Web Form Designer
        'Do not modify it using the code editor.
        InitializeComponent()
    End Sub

#End Region

    Private Sub Page_Load(ByVal sender As System.Object, _
        ByVal e As System.EventArgs) Handles MyBase.Load
        'Put user code to initialize the page here
    End Sub

    Private Sub CheckBox1_CheckedChanged(ByVal sender As System.Object, _
        ByVal e As System.EventArgs) Handles CheckBox1.CheckedChanged
        If CType(sender, CheckBox).Checked Then
            TextBox1.Text = "Bread: Whole wheat"
        Else
            TextBox1.Text = "Bread: White"
        End If
```

```
            If CheckBox2.Checked Then
                TextBox1.Text += " with sesame seeds"
            End If
        End Sub

        Private Sub CheckBox2_CheckedChanged(ByVal sender As System.Object, _
            ByVal e As System.EventArgs) Handles CheckBox2.CheckedChanged
            If CheckBox1.Checked Then
                TextBox1.Text = "Bread: Whole wheat"
            Else
                TextBox1.Text = "Bread: White"
            End If

            If CType(sender, CheckBox).Checked Then
                TextBox1.Text += " with sesame seeds"
            End If
        End Sub

        Private Sub CheckBoxList1_SelectedIndexChanged(ByVal sender _
            As System.Object, ByVal e As System.EventArgs) Handles _
            CheckBoxList1.SelectedIndexChanged
            Dim LoopIndex As Integer
            TextBox2.Text = "Filling: "

            For LoopIndex = 0 To 3
                If CheckBoxList1.Items(LoopIndex).Selected Then
                    TextBox2.Text &= _
                        CheckBoxList1.Items(LoopIndex).Value & " "
                End If
            Next
        End Sub
    End Class
```

In this example, the two checkboxes appear at left, where you can select the bread type. (The other checkboxes are part of a checkbox list control.) When the user clicks the "Whole wheat" checkbox, for example, we can display the type of bread selected, whole wheat if the box is checked, or the default—white bread— if the box is not checked. To display the type of bread, I'll handle the checkbox's **CheckChanged** event; to determine if a checkbox is selected or not, you just use its **Checked** property. Note that I also take a look at the other checkbox, **CheckBox2**, to see if the user wants sesame seeds, and add them as well, if needed:

```
    Private Sub CheckBox1_CheckedChanged(ByVal sender As System.Object, _
        ByVal e As System.EventArgs) Handles CheckBox1.CheckedChanged
```

```
        If CType(sender, CheckBox).Checked Then
            TextBox1.Text = "Bread: Whole wheat"
        Else
            TextBox1.Text = "Bread: White"
        End If

        If CheckBox2.Checked Then
            TextBox1.Text += " with sesame seeds"
        End If
    End Sub
```

The other checkboxes, at right in this example, are part of a checkbox list control—coming up right after the **ListControl** class which the **CheckBoxList** class is based on.

NOTE: *Don't forget—if you want to handle this control's events immediately, you must set its **AutoPostBack** property to **True**.*

Using the ListControl Class

The **ListControl** class is an abstract base class which supports the properties, methods, and events common for all list-type controls, including the ones we'll see in this chapter—checkbox lists and radio button lists. Here's the hierarchy of this class:

```
Object
    Control
        WebControl
            ListControl
```

You can find the notable public properties of **ListControl** objects in Table 16.4 and their notable public events in Table 16.5. (This class has no non-inherited methods.) Note that as with other Web server controls, I am not listing the notable properties, methods, and events this class inherits from the **Control** and **WebControl** classes—you can find them in Chapter 15, Tables 15.1 to 15.5.

Note that the **ListControl** control's **Items** property returns a collection of **ListItem** objects that you can use to access an item in a list control. See the next topic for the details.

TIP: *To add items to a control based on the **ListControl** class, you use the **Items** collection's **Add** method.*

Table 16.4   Noteworthy public properties of **ListControl** objects.

Property	Means
AutoPostBack	Gets/sets whether the page is posted back to the server when the user changes the list selection.
Items	Gets the collection of items that are in this list control.
SelectedIndex	Gets/sets the index of the selected item in the list. If more than one item is selected, this value is the lowest selected index.
SelectedItem	Gets the selected item in the list control. If more than one item is selected, this property holds the item with the lowest index.

Table 16.5   Noteworthy public events of **ListControl** objects.

Event	Means
SelectedIndexChanged	Occurs when the list selection changes.

Related solution:	Found on page:
5Adding Items to List Boxes at Run Time	753

Using the ListItem Class

A **ListItem** object represents an individual data item within a list control, such as a CheckBoxList control or a RadioButtonList control. Here is the inheritance hierarchy of this control:

```
Object
    ListItem
```

You can find the notable public properties of **ListItem** objects in Table 16.6. (This class has no non-inherited methods or events.)

Table 16.6   Noteworthy public properties of **ListItem** objects.

Property	Means
Selected	**True** if the item is selected.
Text	Gets/sets the text list item's displayed text.
Value	Gets/sets the list item's value.

Using the **CheckBoxList** Class

Checkbox list controls create multiselection checkbox groups. You can create these at run time by binding these controls to a data source. Here is the hierarchy of the **CheckBoxList** class:

```
Object
   Control
      WebControl
         ListControl
            CheckBoxList
```

To find out which items are checked in this control, you can loop through the list and test the **Selected** property of each item. Each item in the checkbox list's **Items** collection (inherited from the **ListControl** class) is an object of the **ListItem** class (see "Using the **ListItem** Class" in this chapter). You can use the **ListItem** class's **Value**, **Text**, and **Selected** properties to work with the checkboxes in the list, like this: **CheckBoxList1.Items(5).Selected**. And, as discussed in the In Depth section of this chapter, you can specify the way the list is displayed using the **RepeatLayout** and **RepeatDirection** properties. If **RepeatLayout** is set to **RepeatLayout.Table** (which is the default), the list is drawn in an HTML table. If it is set to **RepeatLayout.Flow**, on the other hand, the list is drawn without a table. And by default, **RepeatDirection** is set to **RepeatDirection.Vertical**. Setting this property to **RepeatDirection.Horizontal** draws the list horizontally.

You can find the notable public properties of **CheckBoxList** objects in Table 16.7, the notable methods in Table 16.8, and the notable public events in Table 16.9. Note that as with other Web server controls, I am not listing the notable properties, methods, and events this class inherits from the **Control** and **WebControl** classes—you can find them in Chapter 15, Tables 15.1 to 15.5. And this class is also based on the **ListControl** class—you can find the properties and events (it has no non-inherited methods) of that class in Tables 16.4 and 16.5.

Table 16.7   Noteworthy public properties of CheckBoxList objects.

Property	Means
CellPadding	Gets/sets the distance between the checkbox and the table cell that contains it, in pixels.
CellSpacing	Gets/sets the distance between the table cells the checkboxes are displayed in, in pixels.
RepeatColumns	Gets/sets the number of columns in the checkbox list.
RepeatDirection	Gets/sets whether checkboxes are arranged vertically or horizontally.
RepeatLayout	Gets/sets the checkbox layout.
TextAlign	Gets/sets the alignment of the caption text for the checkboxes.

Table 16.8   Noteworthy public methods of CheckBoxList objects.

Method	Means
DataBind	Binds the checkbox list to a data source.
Dispose	Disposes of the checkbox list.

Table 16.9   Noteworthy public events of CheckBoxList objects.

Event	Means
DataBinding	Occurs when the checkbox list is bound to a data source.
Load	Occurs when the checkbox list is loaded.
Unload	Occurs when the checkbox list is unloaded.

Creating Checkbox Lists

You can see a checkbox list at work in the CheckBoxes example on the CD-ROM, and in Figure 16.1. The checkbox list is on the right, showing the items Cheese, Sausage, Tomato, and Ham. To add items like that to a checkbox list, click the ellipsis ("...") button in the **Items** property in the Properties window.

Clicking the ellipsis button opens the ListItem Collection Editor, as you see in Figure 16.6. This collection editor works much like other collection editors—to add a new item to the checkbox list control, click the Add button, and fill in its **Text** (the checkbox's caption), **Value** (holds optional text associated with the

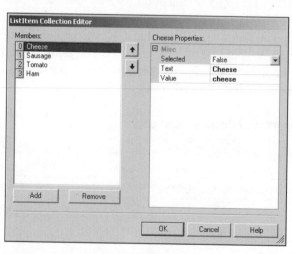

Figure 16.6   The ListItem Collection Editor.

checkbox), and **Selected** (set this to **True** to make the corresponding checkbox appear selected initially) properties. You also can add checkboxes to a checkbox list at run time, using the **Add** method of the control's **Items** collection.

To determine which items in a checkbox list are checked, you can loop over the items in the control and examine their **Selected** properties. Here's how that works in the CheckBoxes example on the CD-ROM, which you see at work in Figure 16.1. (You can view the full code for this example in "Creating Checkboxes" in this chapter.) When the user clicks an item in the checkbox list, the **SelectedIndex** event occurs, and in that event's handler, I loop over the items in the control and display the values of those selected in a text box, this way:

```
Private Sub CheckBoxList1_SelectedIndexChanged(ByVal sender _
    As System.Object, ByVal e As System.EventArgs) Handles _
    CheckBoxList1.SelectedIndexChanged
    Dim LoopIndex As Integer
    TextBox2.Text = "Filling: "

    For LoopIndex = 0 To 3
        If CheckBoxList1.Items(LoopIndex).Selected Then
            TextBox2.Text &= _
                CheckBoxList1.Items(LoopIndex).Value & " "
        End If
    Next
End Sub
```

*TIP: As mentioned in the In Depth section of this chapter, you also can use the **SelectedItem** or **SelectedIndex** properties in checkbox lists, but note that these lists can support multiple selections. If multiple items are selected, the **SelectedItem** and **SelectedIndex** properties hold the selected item with the lowest index value, and the index value of the selected item with the lowest index value, which tells you nothing about the other selected items.*

*NOTE: Don't forget—if you want to handle this control's events immediately, you must set its **AutoPostBack** property to **True**.*

Using the **RadioButton** Class

The **RadioButton** class supports radio buttons. Here is the hierarchy of this class:

```
Object
   Control
      WebControl
         CheckBox
            RadioButton
```

You can find the notable public properties of **RadioButton** objects in Table 16.10, the notable methods in Table 16.11, and the notable public events in Table 16.12. Note that as with other Web server controls, I am not listing the notable properties, methods, and events this class inherits from the **Control** and **WebControl** classes—you can find them in Chapter 15, Tables 15.1 to 15.5. This class also inherits from the **CheckBox** class—you'll find the **CheckBox** class's notable properties, methods, and events in Tables 16.1, 16.2, and 16.3.

Table 16.10   Noteworthy public properties of RadioButton objects.

Property	Means
GroupName	Gets/sets the radio button's group; the radio button will act in concert with other members of the group.
Text	Gets/sets the text caption for with the radio button.

Table 16.11   Noteworthy public methods of RadioButton objects.

Method	Means
Dispose	Disposes of the radio button.

Table 16.12   Noteworthy public events of RadioButton objects.

Event	Means
CheckedChanged	Occurs when the **Checked** property changes.

Creating Radio Buttons

You create and work with radio buttons in Web forms much as you do in Windows forms. However, you can't just group Web server radio buttons together by container here; you must set their **GroupName** property to the same value to group them together. When radio buttons are grouped together logically in this way, you don't have to place them next to each other; they can be anywhere in the Web page.

To see how to work with Web server radio buttons, take a look at the RadioButtons example on the CD-ROM, which you can see at work in Figure 16.2. This example shows you where I'm selecting various options for a new vehicle to buy; in the figure, I'm selecting a car and choosing the color red.

For reference, here is WebForm1.aspx for this example:

```
<%@ Page Language="vb" AutoEventWireup="false"
Codebehind="WebForm1.aspx.vb" Inherits="RadioButtons.WebForm1"%>
<!DOCTYPE HTML PUBLIC "-//W3C//DTD HTML 4.0 Transitional//EN">
<HTML>
  <HEAD>
    <title>RadioButtons example</title>
<meta content="Microsoft Visual Studio.NET 7.0" name=GENERATOR>
<meta content="Visual Basic 7.0" name=CODE_LANGUAGE>
<meta content=JavaScript name=vs_defaultClientScript>
<meta content=http://schemas.microsoft.com/intellisense/ie5
name=vs_targetSchema>
  </HEAD>
<body MS_POSITIONING="GridLayout">
<form id=Form1 method=post runat="server"><asp:radiobuttonlist
id=RadioButtonList1 style="Z-INDEX: 101; LEFT: 259px; POSITION:
absolute; TOP: 36px" runat="server" Width="116px" Height="172px"
AutoPostBack="True">
<asp:ListItem Value="blue" Selected="True">Blue</asp:ListItem>
<asp:ListItem Value="red">Red</asp:ListItem>
<asp:ListItem Value="yellow">Yellow</asp:ListItem>
<asp:ListItem Value="white">White</asp:ListItem>
</asp:RadioButtonList>
<asp:Label id=Label2 style="Z-INDEX: 107; LEFT: 265px; POSITION:
absolute; TOP: 18px" runat="server">Color:</asp:Label>
<asp:Label id=Label1 style="Z-INDEX: 106; LEFT: 86px; POSITION:
absolute; TOP: 16px" runat="server">Vehicle:</asp:Label><asp:textbox
id=TextBox2 style="Z-INDEX: 105; LEFT: 57px; POSITION: absolute;
TOP: 182px" runat="server"></asp:TextBox><asp:radiobutton
id=RadioButton2 style="Z-INDEX: 104; LEFT: 80px; POSITION:
absolute; TOP: 88px" runat="server" Text="Truck" AutoPostBack="True"
GroupName="Type"></asp:RadioButton>
<asp:radiobutton id=RadioButton1 style="Z-INDEX: 103; LEFT: 80px;
POSITION: absolute; TOP: 48px" runat="server" Text="Car"
AutoPostBack="True" GroupName="Type" Checked="True">
</asp:RadioButton><asp:textbox id=TextBox1 style="Z-INDEX: 102;
LEFT: 56px; POSITION: absolute; TOP: 128px"
runat="server"></asp:TextBox></FORM>

  </body>
</HTML>
```

And here is WebForm1.aspx.vb in this example:

```
Public Class WebForm1
    Inherits System.Web.UI.Page
    Protected WithEvents TextBox1 As _
        System.Web.UI.WebControls.TextBox
    Protected WithEvents RadioButton1 As _
        System.Web.UI.WebControls.RadioButton
    Protected WithEvents RadioButton2 As _
        System.Web.UI.WebControls.RadioButton
    Protected WithEvents TextBox2 As _
        System.Web.UI.WebControls.TextBox
    Protected WithEvents Label1 As System.Web.UI.WebControls.Label
    Protected WithEvents Label2 As System.Web.UI.WebControls.Label
    Protected WithEvents RadioButtonList1 As _
        System.Web.UI.WebControls.RadioButtonList

#Region " Web Form Designer Generated Code "

    'This call is required by the Web Form Designer.
    <System.Diagnostics.DebuggerStepThrough()> _
        Private Sub InitializeComponent()

    End Sub

    Private Sub Page_Init(ByVal sender As System.Object, _
        ByVal e As System.EventArgs) Handles MyBase.Init
        'CODEGEN: This method call is required by the Web Form Designer
        'Do not modify it using the code editor.
        InitializeComponent()
    End Sub

#End Region

    Private Sub Page_Load(ByVal sender As System.Object, _
        ByVal e As System.EventArgs) Handles MyBase.Load
        If RadioButton1.Checked Then
            TextBox1.Text = "Car is selected."
            TextBox2.Text = "Your car is: blue"
        End If
    End Sub

    Private Sub RadioButtonList1_SelectedIndexChanged(ByVal sender _
        As System.Object, ByVal e As System.EventArgs) Handles _
        RadioButtonList1.SelectedIndexChanged
```

```
        If RadioButton1.Checked Then
            TextBox2.Text = "Your car is: "
        Else
            TextBox2.Text = "Your truck is: "
        End If

        TextBox2.Text &= RadioButtonList1.SelectedItem.Value
    End Sub

    Private Sub RadioButton1_CheckedChanged(ByVal sender As _
        System.Object, ByVal e As System.EventArgs) Handles _
        RadioButton1.CheckedChanged
        If CType(sender, RadioButton).Checked Then
            TextBox1.Text = "Car is selected."
        End If

        If RadioButton1.Checked Then
            TextBox2.Text = "Your car is: "
        Else
            TextBox2.Text = "Your truck is: "
        End If

        TextBox2.Text &= RadioButtonList1.SelectedItem.Value
    End Sub

    Private Sub RadioButton2_CheckedChanged(ByVal sender As _
        System.Object, ByVal e As System.EventArgs) Handles _
        RadioButton2.CheckedChanged
        If CType(sender, RadioButton).Checked Then
            TextBox1.Text = "Truck is selected."
        End If

        If RadioButton1.Checked Then
            TextBox2.Text = "Your car is: "
        Else
            TextBox2.Text = "Your truck is: "
        End If

        TextBox2.Text &= RadioButtonList1.SelectedItem.Value
    End Sub
End Class
```

In the RadioButtons example, the user can click the radio buttons labeled "Car" or "Truck", and when they do, the code updates the text displayed in the text box immediately under the radio buttons (e.g., "Truck is selected."). The code does this in the **CheckChanged** event handler. If the control's **Checked** property is **True**, the radio button is selected, and the code will display the message "Car is selected" when the user selects radio button 1, and "Truck is selected" when the user clicks radio button 2:

```
Private Sub RadioButton1_CheckedChanged(ByVal sender As _
        System.Object, ByVal e As System.EventArgs) Handles _
        RadioButton1.CheckedChanged
        If CType(sender, RadioButton).Checked Then
            TextBox1.Text = "Car is selected."
        End If
End Sub


Private Sub RadioButton2_CheckedChanged(ByVal sender As _
        System.Object, ByVal e As System.EventArgs) Handles _
        RadioButton2.CheckedChanged
        If CType(sender, RadioButton).Checked Then
            TextBox1.Text = "Truck is selected."
        End If
End Sub
```

The reason this code works is that I have grouped these two radio buttons in the same group by setting their **GroupName** properties to the same value—I've used the name "Type" (for type of vehicle) here. When you click one radio button and so select it, the others in the same group are deselected. (The browser does this; it doesn't take a round trip to the server.)

You also can set a radio button's **Checked** property to make it appear selected when it's first displayed, as I do in the RadioButtons example. In the **Page_Load** event, I also initialize the text boxes to display the text corresponding to the initially selected radio buttons:

```
Private Sub Page_Load(ByVal sender As System.Object, _
    ByVal e As System.EventArgs) Handles MyBase.Load
    If RadioButton1.Checked Then
        TextBox1.Text = "Car is selected."
        TextBox2.Text = "Your car is: blue"
    End If
End Sub
```

NOTE: Don't forget—if you want to handle this control's events immediately, you must set its **AutoPostBack** property to **True**.

As discussed in the In Depth section of this chapter, the radio buttons at right in this example—the Blue, Red, Yellow, and White radio buttons—are actually items in a radio button list control, not individual radio buttons. See the next two topics for the details.

Using the **RadioButtonList** Class

The **RadioButtonList** control lets you display a list of radio buttons. Here is the inheritance hierarchy of this class:

```
Object
    Control
        WebControl
            ListControl
                RadioButtonList
```

To determine which item is selected in a radio button control, you can test the **SelectedItem** property of the list. You also can determine the index of the selected item with the **SelectedIndex** property. Each item in the radio button list's **Items** collection (inherited from the **ListControl** class) is an object of the **ListItem** class (see "Using the **ListItem** Class" in this chapter), and you can use the **ListItem** class's **Value**, **Text**, and **Selected** properties to work with the radio buttons in the list like this: **RadioButtonList1.Items(5).Selected**.

You can customize how the list is displayed using the **RepeatLayout** and **RepeatDirection** properties. If **RepeatLayout** is set to **RepeatLayout.Table** (which is the default), the list is drawn in an HTML table. If it is set to **RepeatLayout.Flow**, on the other hand, the list is drawn without a table. And by default, **RepeatDirection** is set to **RepeatDirection.Vertical**. Setting this property to **RepeatDirection.Horizontal** draws the list horizontally.

You can find the notable public properties of **RadioButtonList** objects in Table 16.13, the notable methods in Table 16.14, and the notable public events in Table 16.15. Note that as with other Web server controls, I am not listing the notable properties, methods, and events this class inherits from the **Control** and **WebControl** classes; you can find them in Tables 15.1 to 15.5 in Chapter 15. This class also inherits from the **ListControl** class you can find the notable public properties of **ListControl** objects in Table 16.4, and their notable public events in Table 16.5. (This class has no non-inherited methods.)

Table 16.13   Noteworthy public properties of RadioButtonList objects.

Property	Means
CellPadding	Gets/sets the distance between the radio button and the table cell that contains it, in pixels.
CellSpacing	Gets/sets the distance between the table cells the radio buttons are displayed in, in pixels.
RepeatColumns	Gets/sets the number of displayed columns in the radio button list.
RepeatDirection	Gets/sets the display direction of radio buttons.
RepeatLayout	Gets/sets the radio button layout.
TextAlign	Gets/sets the radio button's caption text alignment.

Table 16.14   Noteworthy public methods of RadioButtonList objects.

Method	Means
DataBind	Binds a radio button list to a data source.

Table 16.15   Noteworthy public events of RadioButtonList objects.

Event	Means
SelectedIndexChanged	Occurs when the selection in the radio button list changes.

Creating Radio Button Lists

At design time, you can add items to a radio button list by clicking the **Items** property in the Properties window, opening the ListItem Collection Editor you see in Figure 16.7, where I'm using it on the radio button list in the RadioButtons example on the CD-ROM which appears in Figure 16.2. (You can see the code for this example in "Creating Radio Buttons" in this chapter.) This collection editor works much like other collection editors—to add a new item to the radio button list control, click the Add button, and fill in its **Text** (the checkbox's caption), **Value** (holds optional text associated with the checkbox), and **Selected** (set this to **True** to make the corresponding checkbox appear selected initially) properties. You also can add radio buttons to a radio button list at run time, using the **Add** method of the control's **Items** collection.

How can you handle selection events in a radio button list? You can use the **SelectedIndexChanged** event, and use the radio button list's **SelectedIndex** and **SelectedItem** properties to get the selected index and item respectively.

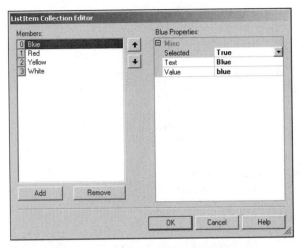

Figure 16.7 The ListItem Collection Editor.

You can see this at work in the RadioButtons example. In this case, to display the selected color of the car or truck the user has selected, I just use the **SelectedItem** property to get the selected item in the radio button list (only one item can be selected at a time, of course), and use that item's **Value** property to get the selected color:

```
Private Sub RadioButtonList1_SelectedIndexChanged(ByVal sender _
    As System.Object, ByVal e As System.EventArgs) Handles _
    RadioButtonList1.SelectedIndexChanged
    If RadioButton1.Checked Then
        TextBox2.Text = "Your car is: "
    Else
        TextBox2.Text = "Your truck is: "
    End If

    TextBox2.Text &= RadioButtonList1.SelectedItem.Value
End Sub

Private Sub RadioButton1_CheckedChanged(ByVal sender As _
    System.Object, ByVal e As System.EventArgs) Handles _
    RadioButton1.CheckedChanged
    If CType(sender, RadioButton).Checked Then
        TextBox1.Text = "Car is selected."
    End If

    If RadioButton1.Checked Then
        TextBox2.Text = "Your car is: "
```

```
        Else
            TextBox2.Text = "Your truck is: "
        End If

        TextBox2.Text &= RadioButtonList1.SelectedItem.Value
    End Sub

    Private Sub RadioButton2_CheckedChanged(ByVal sender As _
        System.Object, ByVal e As System.EventArgs) Handles _
        RadioButton2.CheckedChanged
        If CType(sender, RadioButton).Checked Then
            TextBox1.Text = "Truck is selected."
        End If

        If RadioButton1.Checked Then
            TextBox2.Text = "Your car is: "
        Else
            TextBox2.Text = "Your truck is: "
        End If

        TextBox2.Text &= RadioButtonList1.SelectedItem.Value
    End Sub
```

And that's all it takes—you can see the results of this code in Figure 16.2.

NOTE: *Don't forget—if you want to handle this control's events immediately, you must set its **AutoPostBack** property to **True**.*

Using the Table Class

You can use the **Table** class to create an HTML table. Here is the hierarchy of this class:

```
Object
    Control
        WebControl
            Table
```

Table objects correspond to **<table>** elements in Web pages; to create an entire table, you'll also need **TableRow** and **TableCell** objects, as discussed in the In Depth section of this chapter.

Table 16.16   Noteworthy public properties of Table objects.

Property	Means
BackImageUrl	Indicates the URL of the background image to display behind the table. The image will be tiled if it is smaller than the table.
CellPadding	Gets/sets the distance (in pixels) between the border and the contents of the table cell.
CellSpacing	Gets/sets the distance (in pixels) between table cells.
GridLines	Gets/sets the gridlines property of the **Table** class.
HorizontalAlign	Gets/sets the horizontal alignment of the table within the page.
Rows	Gets the collection of rows within the table.

You can find the notable public properties of **Table** objects in Table 16.16. (This class has no non-inherited methods or properties.) Note that as with other Web server controls, I am not listing the notable properties, methods, and events this class inherits from the **Control** and **WebControl** classes—you can find them in Chapter 15, in Tables 15.1 to 15.5.

Using the TableRow Class

You use the **TableRow** class to create the table rows you use in Table objects. Here's the inheritance hierarchy for the **TableRow** class:

```
Object
    Control
        WebControl
            TableRow
```

You can use the **TableRow** class to control how the contents of a table row are displayed. The alignment of the contents in the row is specified by setting the **HorizontalAlign** and **VerticalAlign** properties. You can manage the cells in the row in code by using the **Cells** collection. The **Cells** collection is a collection of **TableCell** objects that represent the cells in the row.

You can find the notable public properties of **TableRow** objects in Table 16.17. (This class has no non-inherited methods or events.) Note that as with other Web server controls, I am not listing the notable properties, methods, and events this class inherits from the **Control** and **WebControl** classes; you can find them in Tables 15.1 to 15.5 in Chapter 15.

Table 16.17   Noteworthy public properties of TableRow objects.

Property	Means
Cells	Gets a collection of the table cells for this table row, each of which is a **TableCell** object.
HorizontalAlign	Gets/sets the horizontal alignment of the row contents.
VerticalAlign	Gets/sets the vertical alignment of the row contents.

Using the TableCell Class

The **TableCell** class represents a cell in a **Table** control. Here is the inheritance hierarchy of this class:

```
Object
    Control
        WebControl
            TableCell
```

You can use the **Text** property to get or set the contents of the cell. You can specify the contents in the cell with the **HorizontalAlign** and **VerticalAlign** properties, and use the **Wrap** property to specify whether the contents of the cell wrap in the cell. And you also can specify how many rows or columns in the **Table** control are occupied by one single cell with the **RowSpan** and **ColumnSpan** properties, which set, respectively, how many rows and columns should be spanned by that cell.

You can find the notable public properties of **TableCell** objects in Table 16.18. (This class has no non-inherited methods or events.) Note that as with other Web server controls, I am not listing the notable properties, methods, and events this class inherits from the **Control** and **WebControl** classes you can find them in Chapter 15, Tables 15.1 to 15.5.

Table 16.18   Noteworthy public properties of TableCell objects.

Property	Means
ColumnSpan	Gets/sets the number of columns the cell spans.
HorizontalAlign	Gets/sets the cell content's horizontal alignment.
RowSpan	Gets/sets the number of rows the cell spans.
Text	Gets/sets the text in the cell.
VerticalAlign	Gets/sets the cell content's vertical alignment.
Wrap	Gets/sets whether the cell content wraps.

Creating a Table

To see how to use the **Table**, **TableRow**, and **TableCell** classes, I'll take a look at the Tables example on the CD-ROM, which was discussed in the In Depth section of this chapter. You can see the table created in that example, which displays data on several planets, in Figure 16.3.

You can design tables in the Visual Basic IDE. Just add a **Table** control to a Web page, and click its **Rows** property in the Properties window to open a TableRow Collection Editor, as you see in Figure 16.8. You can add new table rows to the table by clicking the Add button, as in other collection editors; you set the properties of each row in on the right side of the editor.

To add table cells to a table row, click the **Cells** property's ellipsis ("...") button in the TableRow Collection Editor, opening the TableCell Collection Editor you see in Figure 16.9. You can add cells to a row by clicking the Add button, just as you'd add items to any collection, and you can set the properties of the various cells, such as font properties, in the editor as well. I've made the font in the top row of the table bold to make it stand out as a table header, and you can do that either by setting the **Font** property on a cell-by-cell or row-by-row basis.

---

*TIP: There is a **TableHeaderCell** class, which corresponds to the **<th>** element that you use for table headers (this element displays its text in bold), but the TableRow Collection and TableCell Collection Editors don't support this class, so in this example, I've used the **Bold** property to bold the text in the top row of the table.*

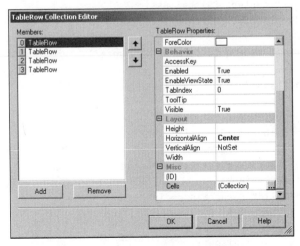

Figure 16.8   The TableRow Collection Editor.

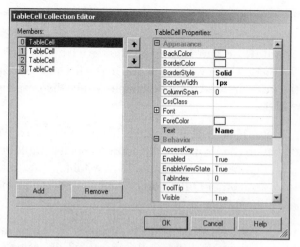

Figure 16.9   The TableCell Collection Editor.

Here's the HTML created by this example and displayed in the browser:

```
<%@ Page Language="vb" AutoEventWireup="false"
Codebehind="WebForm1.aspx.vb" Inherits="Tables.WebForm1"%>
<!DOCTYPE HTML PUBLIC "-//W3C//DTD HTML 4.0 Transitional//EN">
<HTML>
  <HEAD>
    <title>Tables example</title>
    <meta name="GENERATOR" content="Microsoft Visual Studio.NET 7.0">
    <meta name="CODE_LANGUAGE" content="Visual Basic 7.0">
    <meta name=vs_defaultClientScript content="JavaScript">
    <meta name=vs_targetSchema
        content="http://schemas.microsoft.com/intellisense/ie5">
  </HEAD>
  <body MS_POSITIONING="GridLayout">

    <form id="Form1" method="post" runat="server">
<asp:Table id=Table1 style="Z-INDEX: 101; LEFT: 96px;
POSITION: absolute; TOP: 63px" runat="server" BorderStyle="Solid"
 Height="163px" Width="313px" BorderColor="Black" BorderWidth="2px">
<asp:TableRow HorizontalAlign="Center">
<asp:TableCell BorderStyle="Solid" BorderWidth="1px"
Font-Bold="True" Text="Name"></asp:TableCell>
<asp:TableCell BorderStyle="Solid" BorderWidth="1px"
Font-Bold="True" Text="Day"></asp:TableCell>
<asp:TableCell BorderStyle="Solid" BorderWidth="1px"
Font-Bold="True" Text="Radius (miles)"></asp:TableCell>
<asp:TableCell BorderStyle="Solid" BorderWidth="1px"
```

```
Font-Bold="True" Text="Perihelion (million miles)"></asp:TableCell>
</asp:TableRow>
<asp:TableRow HorizontalAlign="Center">
<asp:TableCell BorderStyle="Solid" BorderWidth="1px" Text="Mercury">
</asp:TableCell>
<asp:TableCell BorderStyle="Solid" BorderWidth="1px" Text="58.65">
</asp:TableCell>
<asp:TableCell BorderStyle="Solid" BorderWidth="1px" Text="1516">
</asp:TableCell>
<asp:TableCell BorderStyle="Solid" BorderWidth="1px" Text="43.4">
</asp:TableCell>
</asp:TableRow>
<asp:TableRow HorizontalAlign="Center">
<asp:TableCell BorderStyle="Solid" BorderWidth="1px" Text="Venus">
</asp:TableCell>
<asp:TableCell BorderStyle="Solid" BorderWidth="1px" Text="116.75">
</asp:TableCell>
<asp:TableCell BorderStyle="Solid" BorderWidth="1px" Text="3716">
</asp:TableCell>
<asp:TableCell BorderStyle="Solid" BorderWidth="1px" Text="66.8">
</asp:TableCell>
</asp:TableRow>
<asp:TableRow HorizontalAlign="Center">
<asp:TableCell BorderStyle="Solid" BorderWidth="1px" Text="Earth">
</asp:TableCell>
<asp:TableCell BorderStyle="Solid" BorderWidth="1px" Text="1">
</asp:TableCell>
<asp:TableCell BorderStyle="Solid" BorderWidth="1px" Text="2107">
</asp:TableCell>
<asp:TableCell BorderStyle="Solid" BorderWidth="1px" Text="128.4">
</asp:TableCell>
</asp:TableRow>
</asp:Table>

    </form>
  </body>
</HTML>
```

You can see the table created by this example in Figure 16.3.

You also can add rows to a **Table** object in code, of course, with the **Rows** collection's **Add** method:

```
Dim Table1 As New Table()
Dim TableRow1 As New TableRow()
Table1.Rows.Add(TableRow1)
```

And you can add new cells to a row, then add that row to a table in a like manner. To add cells to a row, just use the row's **Cells** collection's **Add** method:

```
Dim Table1 As New Table()
Dim TableRow1 As New TableRow()
Dim TableCell1 As New TableCell()
TableRow1.Cells.Add(TableCell1)
Table1.Rows.Add(TableRow1)
```

Using the **Panel** Class

The **Panel** control is usually used as a container for other controls. It is especially useful when you want to create controls in code, or show and hide a group of controls at once. Here is the inheritance hierarchy of the **Panel** class:

```
Object
    Control
        WebControl
            Panel
```

You can find the notable public properties of **Panel** objects in Table 16.19. (This class has no non-inherited methods or events.) Note that as with other Web server controls, I am not listing the notable properties, methods, and events this class inherits from the **Control** and **WebControl** classes—you can find them in Chapter 15, Tables 15.1 to 15.5.

Table 16.19   Noteworthy public properties of Panel objects.

Property	Means
BackImageUrl	Gets/sets the background image's URL for the panel.
HorizontalAlign	Gets/sets the horizontal alignment of the panel's contents.
Wrap	Gets/sets whether the panel's content wraps.

Creating Panels

There are various ways to use panels (see "Adding Controls at Run Time" in Chapter 15 to see how to use panels as containers that the code adds controls to). The Panels example on the CD-ROM also puts a couple of panels to work, as discussed in the In Depth section of this chapter, by letting the user select a color and displaying that color in a panel. You can see this example at work in Figures 16.4 and 16.5.

You can add a panel to a Web application as you would any other Web server control; just use the Web Forms tab in the toolbox, and add the panel to a Web form. When you create a panel, the text "Panel" appears in it; to remove this text, you don't use the **Text** property (there isn't one)—you just select the text in the panel and delete it. You can add controls to a panel just by dragging them on top of the panel (or by using the **Controls** collection's **Add** method—see "Adding Controls at Run Time" in Chapter 15). As you can see in Figure 16.10, I've added three text boxes, a set of labels ("Red", "Green", and "Blue"), as well as a button, to a panel, **Panel2** (**Panel1** appears at the bottom of the application, and, as discussed in the In Depth section of this chapter, this where the new color the user has selected appears, using the panel's **BackColor** property).

The user can select colors in this example by clicking one of the Red, Green, or Blue radio buttons, but they also can click the Custom radio button to display the

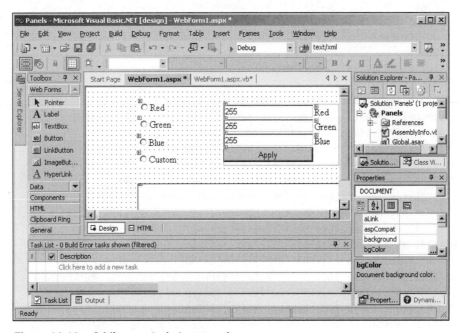

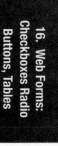

Figure 16.10   Adding controls to a panel.

controls in the panel (see Figure 16.5). That's done very simply—all I have to do is to set the panel's **Visible** property to **True** to display it, and **False** to hide it:

```
Private Sub RadioButton4_CheckedChanged(ByVal sender As _
    System.Object, ByVal e As System.EventArgs) Handles _
    RadioButton4.CheckedChanged
    If CType(sender, RadioButton).Checked Then
        Panel2.Visible = True
    Else
        Panel2.Visible = False
    End If
End Sub
```

That's all it takes. Here's the Panels example's code in WebForm1.aspx:

```
<%@ Page Language="vb" AutoEventWireup="false"
Codebehind="WebForm1.aspx.vb" Inherits="Panels.WebForm1"%>
<!DOCTYPE HTML PUBLIC "-//W3C//DTD HTML 4.0 Transitional//EN">
<HTML>
  <HEAD>
    <title>Panels example</title>
    <meta name="GENERATOR" content="Microsoft Visual Studio.NET 7.0">
    <meta name="CODE_LANGUAGE" content="Visual Basic 7.0">
    <meta name=vs_defaultClientScript content="JavaScript">
    <meta name=vs_targetSchema
        content="http://schemas.microsoft.com/intellisense/ie5">
  </HEAD>
  <body MS_POSITIONING="GridLayout">

    <form id="Form1" method="post" runat="server">
<asp:Panel id=Panel1 style="Z-INDEX: 101; LEFT: 92px; POSITION:
absolute; TOP: 161px" runat="server" Width="346px" Height="90px"
BorderStyle="Solid" BorderWidth="1px"></asp:Panel>
<asp:RadioButton id=RadioButton4 style="Z-INDEX: 106; LEFT: 91px;
POSITION: absolute; TOP: 110px" runat="server" GroupName="ColorGroup"
Text="Custom" AutoPostBack="True"></asp:RadioButton>
<asp:RadioButton id=RadioButton3 style="Z-INDEX: 105; LEFT: 91px;
POSITION: absolute; TOP: 82px" runat="server" GroupName="ColorGroup"
Text="Blue" AutoPostBack="True"></asp:RadioButton>
<asp:RadioButton id=RadioButton2 style="Z-INDEX: 104; LEFT: 92px;
POSITION: absolute; TOP: 52px" runat="server" GroupName="ColorGroup"
Text="Green" AutoPostBack="True"></asp:RadioButton>
<asp:RadioButton id=RadioButton1 style="Z-INDEX: 103; LEFT: 93px;
POSITION: absolute; TOP: 24px" runat="server" GroupName="ColorGroup"
Text="Red" AutoPostBack="True"></asp:RadioButton>
```

```
<asp:Panel id=Panel2 style="Z-INDEX: 102; LEFT: 239px; POSITION:
absolute; TOP: 29px" runat="server" Width="198px" Height="102px"
Visible="False">
<asp:TextBox id=TextBox1 runat="server">255</asp:TextBox>
<asp:Label id=Label1 runat="server">Red</asp:Label>
<asp:TextBox id=TextBox2 runat="server">255</asp:TextBox>
<asp:Label id=Label2 runat="server">Green</asp:Label>
<asp:TextBox id=TextBox3 runat="server">255</asp:TextBox>
<asp:Label id=Label3 runat="server">Blue</asp:Label>
<asp:Button id=Button1 runat="server" Width="154px" Height="24px"
Text="Apply"></asp:Button></asp:Panel>

    </form>
  </body>
</HTML>
```

And here's what WebForm1.aspx.vb looks like in this example:

```
Public Class WebForm1
    Inherits System.Web.UI.Page
    Protected WithEvents Panel1 As System.Web.UI.WebControls.Panel
    Protected WithEvents RadioButton1 As _
        System.Web.UI.WebControls.RadioButton
    Protected WithEvents RadioButton2 As _
        System.Web.UI.WebControls.RadioButton
    Protected WithEvents RadioButton3 As _
        System.Web.UI.WebControls.RadioButton
    Protected WithEvents RadioButton4 As _
        System.Web.UI.WebControls.RadioButton
    Protected WithEvents TextBox1 As System.Web.UI.WebControls.TextBox
    Protected WithEvents Label1 As System.Web.UI.WebControls.Label
    Protected WithEvents TextBox2 As System.Web.UI.WebControls.TextBox
    Protected WithEvents Label2 As System.Web.UI.WebControls.Label
    Protected WithEvents TextBox3 As System.Web.UI.WebControls.TextBox
    Protected WithEvents Label3 As System.Web.UI.WebControls.Label
    Protected WithEvents Button1 As System.Web.UI.WebControls.Button
    Protected WithEvents Panel2 As System.Web.UI.WebControls.Panel

#Region " Web Form Designer Generated Code "

    'This call is required by the Web Form Designer.
    <System.Diagnostics.DebuggerStepThrough()> _
        Private Sub InitializeComponent()

    End Sub
```

```
        Private Sub Page_Init(ByVal sender As System.Object, ByVal e As _
            System.EventArgs) Handles MyBase.Init
            'CODEGEN: This method call is required by the Web Form Designer
            'Do not modify it using the code editor.
            InitializeComponent()
        End Sub

    #End Region

        Private Sub RadioButton1_CheckedChanged(ByVal sender As _
            System.Object, ByVal e As System.EventArgs) Handles _
            RadioButton1.CheckedChanged
            If CType(sender, RadioButton).Checked Then
                Panel1.BackColor = Color.Red
            End If
        End Sub

        Private Sub RadioButton2_CheckedChanged(ByVal sender As _
            System.Object, ByVal e As System.EventArgs) Handles _
            RadioButton2.CheckedChanged
            If CType(sender, RadioButton).Checked Then
                Panel1.BackColor = Color.Green
            End If
        End Sub

        Private Sub RadioButton3_CheckedChanged(ByVal sender As _
            System.Object, ByVal e As System.EventArgs) Handles _
            RadioButton3.CheckedChanged
            If CType(sender, RadioButton).Checked Then
                Panel1.BackColor = Color.Blue
            End If
        End Sub

        Private Sub RadioButton4_CheckedChanged(ByVal sender As _
            System.Object, ByVal e As System.EventArgs) Handles _
            RadioButton4.CheckedChanged
            If CType(sender, RadioButton).Checked Then
                Panel2.Visible = True
            Else
                Panel2.Visible = False
            End If
        End Sub

        Private Sub Button1_Click(ByVal sender As System.Object, _
            ByVal e As System.EventArgs) Handles Button1.Click
```

```
        Panel1.BackColor = Color.FromArgb(TextBox1.Text, _
            TextBox2.Text, TextBox3.Text)
    End Sub

    Private Sub Page_Load(ByVal sender As System.Object, ByVal e _
        As System.EventArgs) Handles MyBase.Load

    End Sub
End Class
```

Related solution:	Found on page:
Adding Controls at Run Time	692

Chapter 17

Images, Image Buttons, List Boxes, Drop-down Lists, Hyperlinks, and Link Buttons

In Depth

In this chapter, we're going to take a look at quite a number of Web server controls: image controls, image buttons, list boxes, drop-down lists, hyperlinks, and link buttons. Some of these controls are similar to each other; in fact, they're sometimes supported by variations of the same HTML element. For example, hyperlinks and link buttons are both supported with the **<a>** element, and list boxes and drop-down lists are both supported by the **<select>** element. I'll look at these controls in more depth now.

Image Controls

As you can guess from its name, you use Image controls to display images in Web applications. You set the URL of the image with the **ImageUrl** property. The alignment of the image in relation to other elements on the Web page is specified by setting **ImageAlign** property (see a book on HTML like the Coriolis *HTML Black Book* for more on setting image alignment). You can specify the text to display in place of an image if the image is not available by setting the **AlternateText** property. You can see an Image control at work in Figure 17.1, from the Images example on the CD-ROM.

There's not really all that much going on in Image controls—they're simply translated to **<img>** elements. Here's the HTML that displays the image in Figure 17.1:

```
<img id="Image1" src="Image.jpg" border="0" style="height:150px;width:
300px;Z-INDEX: 101; LEFT: 107px; POSITION: absolute; TOP: 73px" />
```

TIP: *Image controls only display images—if you want to work with* ***Click*** *events and images, use an* ***ImageButton*** *control instead, coming up next.*

Image Buttons

You use image buttons to display an image that responds to mouse clicks. This control is supported with **<input>** HTML elements where the **type** attribute is set to "image" (in other words, an image map). As with other Web server controls, image buttons support both **Click** and **Command** events.

Figure 17.1   Using an Image control.

When you handle **Click** events, you are passed the actual location of the mouse in the image, which is great when you want to create an image map where the user can click various parts of an image and your code undertakes appropriate action. The position of the mouse is recorded in pixels, and the origin (0, 0) is at the upper-left corner of the image.

You can use **Command** event handlers to make the **ImageButton** control work like command buttons. That is, you can associate a command name with the control by using the **CommandName** property. And the **CommandArgument** property also can be used to pass additional information about the command.

You can see an image button at work in Figure 17.2, where the ImageButtons example on the CD-ROM is displaying the location of the mouse when you click the image.

Here's the HTML created to support the image button you see in Figure 17.2:

```
<input type="image" name="ImageButton1" id="ImageButton1"
src="ButtonImage.jpg" border="0" style="Z-INDEX: 101; LEFT: 101px;
POSITION: absolute; TOP: 59px" />
```

List Boxes

As in Windows forms, you use list boxes to create a control that allows single or multiple selection of items. You can see both a single-selection list box (at left) in Figure 17.3 and a multiple-selection list box (at right) in the ListBoxes example on the CD-ROM.

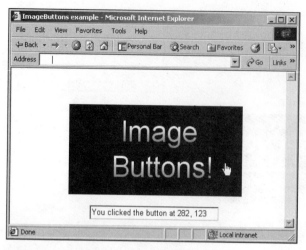

Figure 17.2   Using an image button.

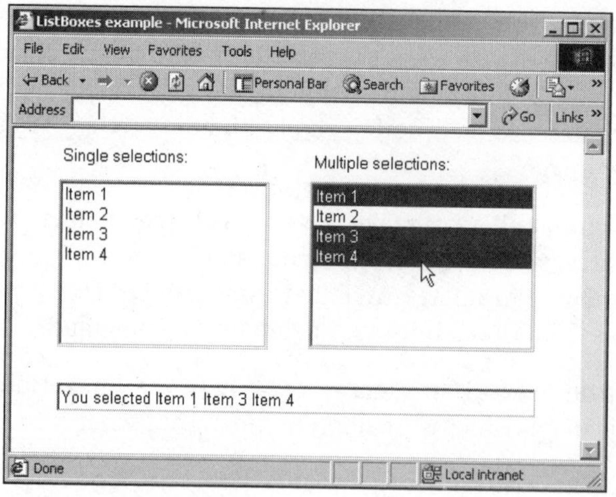

Figure 17.3   A list box.

TIP: *How do you make multiple selections in a list box? The same way as you would in other Windows controls—you can use the Shift key with the mouse to select a range of items, or the Ctrl key to select multiple items, clicking one after the other.*

You use the **Rows** property to specify the height of the control. To enable multiple item selection, you set the **SelectionMode** property to **ListSelectionMode. Multiple**. You can find the selected item in a single-selection list box with the **SelectedItem** and **SelectedIndex** properties. The **SelectedItem** property returns the selected item as a ListItem object, which supports **Text**, **Value**, and **Selected** properties—see "Using the **ListItem** Class" in Chapter 16. In multiple-selection list boxes, you loop over the Items collection of **ListItem** objects, checking each item's **Selected** property to see if that item is selected.

List boxes are supported with the HTML **<select>** control. Here's the HTML that creates the single-selection list box you see at left in Figure 17.3:

```
<select name="ListBox1" id="ListBox1" size="4"
onchange="__doPostBack('ListBox1','')" language="javascript"
style="height:142px;width:176px;Z-INDEX: 101; LEFT: 38px;
POSITION: absolute; TOP: 41px">
    <option value="Item 1">Item 1</option>
    <option value="Item 2">Item 2</option>
    <option value="Item 3">Item 3</option>
    <option value="Item 4">Item 4</option>
</select>
```

The HTML for the multiple-selection list box at right in Figure 17.3 is almost the same, except for the addition of the **multiple** attribute (this attribute is a standalone attribute which means you don't have to assign it a value, but following the lead of the XHTML specification, Visual Basic assigns it the value "multiple" to make the HTML more compatible with XML, which does not support standalone attributes):

```
<select name="ListBox2" id="ListBox2" size="4" multiple="multiple"
onchange="__doPostBack('ListBox2','')" language="javascript"
style="height:134px;width:188px;Z-INDEX: 103; LEFT: 248px;
POSITION: absolute; TOP: 40px">
    <option selected="selected" value="Item 1">Item 1</option>
    <option value="Item 2">Item 2</option>
    <option selected="selected" value="Item 3">Item 3</option>
    <option selected="selected" value="Item 4">Item 4</option>
</select>
```

Drop-down Lists

You use drop-down lists to create a single-selection drop-down list control. (You can't select multiple items in this control because when you make a selection from the list, the list closes automatically.) You can see a drop-down list at work in Figure 17.4; this is the DropDownLists example on the CD-ROM—where I'm making a selection.

After you've selected an item in a drop-down list, you can use the control's **SelectedItem** and **SelectedIndex** properties to work with the selection. The DropDownLists example displays the selection you've made, as you see in Figure 17.5.

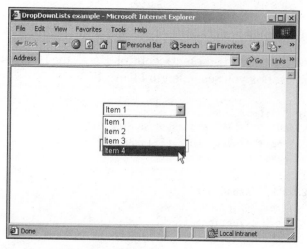

Figure 17.4   A drop-down list.

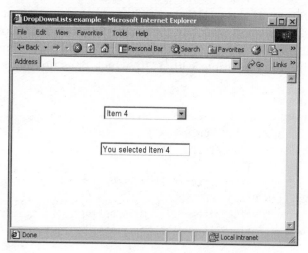

Figure 17.5   Making a selection in a drop-down list.

As with Web server list boxes, drop-down lists are supported with **<select>** controls; here, the **<select>** controls are drawn to display only one item in the list at a time. Here's the HTML that creates the drop-down list you see in Figure 17.5:

```
<select name="DropDownList1" id="DropDownList1"
onchange="__doPostBack('DropDownList1','')" language="javascript"
style="height:22px;width:144px;Z-INDEX: 101; LEFT: 160px;
POSITION: absolute; TOP: 58px">
    <option value="Item 1">Item 1</option>
    <option value="Item 2">Item 2</option>
```

```
      <option value="Item 3">Item 3</option>
      <option value="Item 4">Item 4</option>
</select>
```

Hyperlinks

You use the **HyperLink** control to create a link to another Web page, which can be a page in your Web application, or a page anywhere on the World Wide Web. You can specify the location of the linked page in an absolute way, where you use the linked page's complete URL, or in a relative way, with respect to the current page. You can see both types of links in Figure 17.6, in the HyperLinks example on the CD-ROM; in this example, I've created hyperlinks both to the Visual Basic technical page at Microsoft (using an absolute URL: **http://msdn.microsoft.com/ vbasic/technical/articles.asp**) and to another Web form in the same project (using a relative URL: **WebForm2.aspx**).

TIP: *If terms like absolute and relative URLs are confusing to you, you might want to take a look at an HTML book like the Coriolis HTML Black Book.*

The text in the hyperlink control is specified with the **Text** property. You also can display an image as specified by the **ImageUrl** property.

TIP: *If both the **Text** and **ImageUrl** properties are set, the **ImageUrl** property is used. If the image is not available, the text in the **Text** property is displayed. Also, in browsers that support tool tips, the **Text** property also becomes the tool tip.*

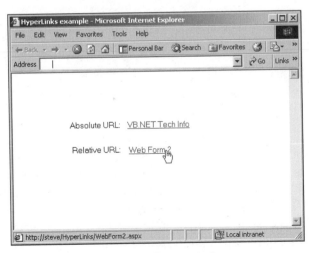

Figure 17.6   Using a hyperlink control.

You set the URL that the link navigates to with the **NavigateUrl** property. And there's more to the story than that; you also need to consider how you want to set the **Target** property. The link target specifies where the new content will be displayed; by default, when you click a hyperlink control, the linked-to content appears in a new browser window. You can set the **Target** property to the name of a window or frame (you set those names in HTML), or one of these values (which are HTML constants):

- **_blank**—Displays the linked content in a new window without frames.
- **_parent**—Displays the linked content in the immediate frameset parent.
- **_self**—Displays the linked content in the frame with focus.
- **_top**—Displays the linked content in the full window without frames.

TIP: *You also can customize the appearance of hyperlinks in a page by setting that page's **link**, **alink**, and **vlink** properties in the properties window. See "Setting Hyperlink Colors" in Chapter 14.*

The HTML to support hyperlinks is, of course, the **<a>** element; here's the HTML for the two hyperlinks you see in Figure 17.6:

```
<a id="HyperLink1" href="http://msdn.microsoft.com/vbasic/technical/_
    articles.asp"
target="_self" style="Z-INDEX: 101; LEFT: 196px; POSITION:
absolute; TOP: 80px">VB.NET Tech Info</a>
            .
            .
            .
<a id="HyperLink2" href="/HyperLinks/WebForm2.aspx"
target="_blank" style="Z-INDEX: 103; LEFT: 198px; POSITION:
absolute; TOP: 122px">Web Form 2</a>
<span id="Label1" style="Z-INDEX: 102; LEFT: 98px; POSITION:
absolute; TOP: 80px">Absolute URL:</span>
```

Link Buttons

Hyperlinks are fine, but as a programmer, you have relatively little control over what happens when the user clicks them, because the browser takes over. However, Visual Basic also provides link buttons, which look just like hyperlinks, but act like buttons, with both **Click** and **Command** events. When the corresponding hyperlink is clicked, you can take some action in code, not just have the browser navigate to a new page. For example, the LinkButtons example on the CD-ROM makes a label with a border visible when you click the link button, as you see in Figure 17.7.

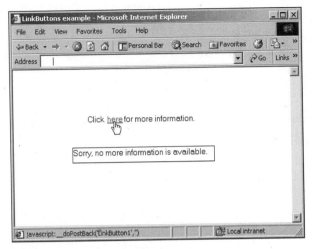

Figure 17.7   Using a link button.

Link buttons are supported with HTML **<a>** elements, just as hyperlink controls are, but the code for link buttons is processed back at the server. Here's what the HTML for the link button you see in Figure 17.7 looks like:

```
<a id="LinkButton1" href="javascript:__doPostBack('LinkButton1','')"
style="Z-INDEX: 101; LEFT: 162px; POSITION: absolute; TOP: 75px">
here</a>
```

And that's what the Web server controls we'll work with in this chapter look like. It's time to see more details now in the Immediate Solutions section of this chapter.

Immediate Solutions

Using the Image Class

As discussed in the In Depth section, you use Image controls to display an image in a Web page. Here's the inheritance hierarchy for this class:

```
Object
    Control
        WebControl
            Image
```

You can find the notable public properties of **Image** objects in Table 17.1 (this class has no non-inherited methods or events). Note that as with other Web server controls, I am not listing the notable properties, methods, and events this class inherits from the **Control** and **WebControl** classes—you can find them in Tables 15.1 to 15.5, Chapter 15.

Table 17.1   Noteworthy public properties of Image objects.

Property	Means
AlternateText	Gets/sets the text to display in an Image control when the image is not available. Note also that in browsers that display tool tips, this text will become the tool tip text.
Font	Gets/sets the alternate text's font.
ImageAlign	Gets/sets the image alignment of the Image control (as set with regard to other HTML elements in the Web page).
ImageUrl	Gets/sets the URL of the image you want to display.

Creating Image Controls

Image controls are very simple—they just display an image in a Web page. You can see this at work in the Images example on the CD-ROM, as discussed in the In Depth section of this chapter, and as shown in Figure 17.1. To associate an image with an Image control, you just assign the image's URL to the

Image control's **ImageUrl** property. (You can browse to the image you want to use by clicking this property in the Properties window at design time. If the image file is local to the project, you just set the **ImageUrl** property to the name of the image file.) You also can set the image's width and height with the **Width** and **Height** properties.

Here's WebForm1.aspx from the Images example:

```
<%@ Page Language="vb" AutoEventWireup="false"
Codebehind="WebForm1.aspx.vb" Inherits="Images.WebForm1"%>
<!DOCTYPE HTML PUBLIC "-//W3C//DTD HTML 4.0 Transitional//EN">
<HTML>
  <HEAD>
    <title>Images example</title>
    <meta name="GENERATOR" content="Microsoft Visual Studio.NET 7.0">
    <meta name="CODE_LANGUAGE" content="Visual Basic 7.0">
    <meta name=vs_defaultClientScript content="JavaScript">
    <meta name=vs_targetSchema
        content="http://schemas.microsoft.com/intellisense/ie5">
  </HEAD>
  <body MS_POSITIONING="GridLayout">

    <form id="Form1" method="post" runat="server">
<asp:Image id=Image1 style="Z-INDEX: 101; LEFT: 107px; POSITION:
absolute; TOP: 73px" runat="server" Width="300px" Height="150px"
ImageUrl="file:///C:\inetpub\wwwroot\images\Image.jpg"></asp:Image>

    </form>
  </body>
</HTML>
```

Here's the HTML generated for the HTML **<img>** element that actually displays the image in the Images example (the image file I'm using is called Image.jpg):

```
<img id="Image1" src="Image.jpg" border="0" style=
"height:150px;width:300px;Z-INDEX: 101; LEFT: 107px;
POSITION: absolute; TOP: 73px" />
```

TIP: *Image controls only display images. If you want to work with **Click** events and images, use an image button control instead, coming up next.*

Using the **ImageButton** Class

As discussed in the In Depth section of this chapter, you can use image button controls to display images that also can handle click events. This is particularly useful if you want to create image maps—those clickable images that initiate various actions depending on where you click them. Image buttons are supported with the **ImageButton** class; here is the inheritance hierarchy of this class:

```
Object
    Control
        WebControl
            Image
                ImageButton
```

You can find the notable public properties of **ImageButton** objects in Table 17.2, and the notable public events in Table 17.3. (This class has no non-inherited methods.) Note that as with other Web server controls, I am not listing the notable properties, methods, and events this class inherits from the **Control** and **WebControl** classes—you can find them in Chapter 15, Tables 15.1 to 15.5. This class also inherits the **Image** class; you can find the public properties of the **Image** class in Table 17.1.

Table 17.2   Noteworthy public properties of ImageButton objects.

Property	Means
CausesValidation	Gets/sets whether this image button causes validation in other controls.
CommandArgument	Gets/sets an optional argument holding data about the command specified with **CommandName**.
CommandName	Gets/sets the command name for this image button.

Table 17.3   Noteworthy public events of ImageButton objects.

Event	Means
Click	Occurs when the image button was clicked.
Command	Occurs when the image button was clicked—use a **Command** event handler for this one.

Creating Image Buttons

You can see the image button in the ImageButtons example from the CD-ROM at work in Figure 17.2. As discussed in the In Depth section of this chapter, when you click this image button, the code displays the location at which you clicked, as you can see in the figure.

As with Image controls, you set the URL of the image to be used to the **ImageUrl** property. (To set the **ImageUrl** property at design time, click this property in the Properties window and browse to the image you want to use.) You also can set the image's width and height with the **Width** and **Height** properties. And you can add code to the image button's **Click** and **Command** events as you would for any button.

Here's WebForm1.aspx for the ImageButtons example on the CD-ROM:

```
<%@ Page Language="vb" AutoEventWireup="false"
Codebehind="WebForm1.aspx.vb" Inherits="ImageButtons.WebForm1"%>
<!DOCTYPE HTML PUBLIC "-//W3C//DTD HTML 4.0 Transitional//EN">
<HTML>
  <HEAD>
    <title>ImageButtons example</title>
    <meta name="GENERATOR" content="Microsoft Visual Studio.NET 7.0">
    <meta name="CODE_LANGUAGE" content="Visual Basic 7.0">
    <meta name=vs_defaultClientScript content="JavaScript">
    <meta name=vs_targetSchema
        content="http://schemas.microsoft.com/intellisense/ie5">
  </HEAD>
  <body MS_POSITIONING="GridLayout">

    <form id="Form1" method="post" runat="server">
<asp:ImageButton id=ImageButton1 style="Z-INDEX: 101; LEFT: 101px;
POSITION: absolute; TOP: 59px" runat="server"
ImageUrl="file:///C:\inetpub\wwwroot\ImageButtons\ButtonImage.jpg">
</asp:ImageButton>
<asp:TextBox id=TextBox1 style="Z-INDEX: 102; LEFT: 139px; POSITION:
absolute; TOP: 227px" runat="server" Width="223px" Height="24px">
</asp:TextBox>

    </form>

  </body>
</HTML>
```

And here's WebForm1.aspx.vb for the ImageButtons example:

```
Public Class WebForm1
    Inherits System.Web.UI.Page
    Protected WithEvents TextBox1 As System.Web.UI.WebControls.TextBox
    Protected WithEvents ImageButton1 As _
        System.Web.UI.WebControls.ImageButton

#Region " Web Form Designer Generated Code "
```

```
                   'This call is required by the Web Form Designer.
                   <System.Diagnostics.DebuggerStepThrough()> _
                       Private Sub InitializeComponent()

                   End Sub

                   Private Sub Page_Init(ByVal sender As System.Object, ByVal e As_
                       System.EventArgs) Handles MyBase.Init
                       'CODEGEN: This method call is required by the Web Form Designer
                       'Do not modify it using the code editor.
                       InitializeComponent()
                   End Sub

               #End Region

                   Private Sub Page_Load(ByVal sender As System.Object, ByVal e As _
                       System.EventArgs) Handles MyBase.Load
                       'Put user code to initialize the page here
                   End Sub

                   Private Sub ImageButton1_Click(ByVal sender As System.Object, _
                       ByVal e As System.Web.UI.ImageClickEventArgs) Handles _
                       ImageButton1.Click
                       TextBox1.Text = "You clicked the button at " & e.X & ", " & e.Y
                   End Sub
               End Class
```

The **Click** event handler for image buttons is passed an object of the
ImageClickEventArgs class; you can use the **X** and **Y** members of that class to
get the location at which the mouse was clicked. Here's how I display that information in a text box in the ImageButtons example:

```
                   Private Sub ImageButton1_Click(ByVal sender As System.Object, _
                       ByVal e As System.Web.UI.ImageClickEventArgs) Handles _
                       ImageButton1.Click
                       TextBox1.Text = "You clicked the button at " & e.X & ", " & e.Y
                   End Sub
```

You can see the result in Figure 17.2. Image buttons are supported in HTML with
<input> elements with the **type** attribute set to "image"; here's what the HTML
looks like for the image button in Figure 17.2:

```
<input type="image" name="ImageButton1" id="ImageButton1"
src="ButtonImage.jpg" border="0" style="Z-INDEX: 101; LEFT: 101px;
POSITION: absolute; TOP: 59px" />
```

Using the **ListBox** Class

As in Windows forms, you use Web server list boxes to display a list of items the user can select from. Here's the inheritance hierarchy for the **ListBox** class:

```
Object
    Control
        WebControl
            ListControl
                ListBox
```

As discussed in the In Depth section of this chapter, you can create both single-selection and multiple-selection list boxes.

You can find the notable public properties of **ListBox** objects in Table 17.4. (This class has no non-inherited methods or events.) Note that as with other Web server controls, I am not listing the notable properties, methods, and events this class inherits from the **Control** and **WebControl** classes—you can find them in Chapter 15, Tables 15.1 to 15.5. This class inherits the **ListControl** class, and you can find the notable public properties of **ListControl** objects in Chapter 16, Table 16.4, and their notable public events in Table 16.5. (The **ListControl** class has no non-inherited methods.) Note that the **ListControl** class's **Items** property returns a collection of **ListItem** objects which you can use to access an item in a list box. You can find the notable public properties of **ListItem** objects in Table 16.6. (The **ListItem** class has no non-inherited methods or events.)

*TIP: Don't forget—if you want to handle this control's events immediately, you must set its **AutoPostBack** property to **True**.*

Table 17.4   Noteworthy public properties of ListBox objects.

Property	Means
Rows	Gets/sets the number of rows in the list box.
SelectionMode	Gets/sets the list box's selection mode: single or multiple.
ToolTip	Gets/sets the tool tip text for this list box.

Creating Single-Selection List Boxes

By default, Web server list boxes are single-selection list boxes, allowing the user to make one selection at a time, which is to say that the **SelectionMode** property of list boxes is set to **Single** by default. To create a multiple-selection list box, set this property to **Multiple**. In single-selection list boxes, you can determine which item (an object of the **ListItem** class; see Table 16.6 in Chapter 16) is selected with the list box's **SelectedItem** property, and the index of the item in the list with the **SelectedIndex** property.

You can see this at work in the ListBoxes example on the CD-ROM, as discussed in the In Depth section of this chapter. This example displays two list boxes: a single-selection list box on the left, and a multiple-selection list box on the right. When you make selections in these list boxes, the item(s) you've selected appears in a text box.

To handle selections in a single-selection list box, you can work with the **SelectedIndexChanged** event. In the ListBoxes example, we just want to display the selected item, which I can do like this with the list box's **SelectedItem** property:

```
Private Sub ListBox1_SelectedIndexChanged(ByVal sender As _
    System.Object, ByVal e As System.EventArgs) Handles _
    ListBox1.SelectedIndexChanged
    TextBox1.Text = "You selected " & ListBox1.SelectedItem.Text
End Sub
```

You can see the results in Figure 17.8, where I've selected an item in the single-selection list box, and the code displays my choice in the text box.

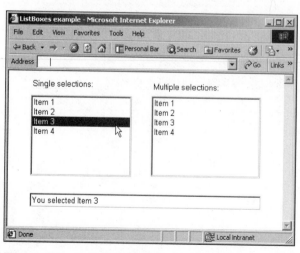

Figure 17.8   Selecting one item in a list box.

Here is WebForm1.aspx for the ListBoxes example:

```
<%@ Page Language="vb" AutoEventWireup="false"
Codebehind="WebForm1.aspx.vb" Inherits="ListBoxes.WebForm1"%>
<!DOCTYPE HTML PUBLIC "-//W3C//DTD HTML 4.0 Transitional//EN">
<HTML>
  <HEAD>
    <title>ListBoxes example</title>
    <meta name="GENERATOR" content="Microsoft Visual Studio.NET 7.0">
    <meta name="CODE_LANGUAGE" content="Visual Basic 7.0">
    <meta name=vs_defaultClientScript content="JavaScript">
    <meta name=vs_targetSchema content=
        "http://schemas.microsoft.com/intellisense/ie5">
  </HEAD>
  <body MS_POSITIONING="GridLayout">

    <form id="Form1" method="post" runat="server">
<asp:ListBox id=ListBox1 style="Z-INDEX: 101; LEFT: 38px;
POSITION: absolute; TOP: 41px" runat="server" Width="176px"
Height="142px" AutoPostBack="True" >
<asp:ListItem Value="Item 1">Item 1</asp:ListItem>
<asp:ListItem Value="Item 2">Item 2</asp:ListItem>
<asp:ListItem Value="Item 3">Item 3</asp:ListItem>
<asp:ListItem Value="Item 4">Item 4</asp:ListItem>
</asp:ListBox>
<asp:Label id=Label2 style="Z-INDEX: 105; LEFT: 251px; POSITION:
absolute; TOP: 16px" runat="server">Multiple selections:</asp:Label>
<asp:Label id=Label1 style="Z-INDEX: 104; LEFT: 41px; POSITION:
absolute; TOP: 13px" runat="server">Single selections:</asp:Label>
<asp:ListBox id=ListBox2 style="Z-INDEX: 103; LEFT: 248px; POSITION:
absolute; TOP: 40px" runat="server" Width="188px" Height="134px"
AutoPostBack="True" SelectionMode="Multiple">
<asp:ListItem Value="Item 1">Item 1</asp:ListItem>
<asp:ListItem Value="Item 2">Item 2</asp:ListItem>
<asp:ListItem Value="Item 3">Item 3</asp:ListItem>
<asp:ListItem Value="Item 4">Item 4</asp:ListItem>
</asp:ListBox>
<asp:TextBox id=TextBox1 style="Z-INDEX: 102; LEFT: 38px; POSITION:
absolute; TOP: 204px" runat="server" Width="400px" Height="23px">
</asp:TextBox>
    </form>
  </body>
</HTML>
```

And here is WebForm1.aspx.vb for the ListBoxes example:

```
Public Class WebForm1
    Inherits System.Web.UI.Page
    Protected WithEvents ListBox1 As System.Web.UI.WebControls.ListBox
    Protected WithEvents ListBox2 As System.Web.UI.WebControls.ListBox
    Protected WithEvents Label1 As System.Web.UI.WebControls.Label
    Protected WithEvents Label2 As System.Web.UI.WebControls.Label
    Protected WithEvents TextBox1 As System.Web.UI.WebControls.TextBox

#Region " Web Form Designer Generated Code "

    'This call is required by the Web Form Designer.
    <System.Diagnostics.DebuggerStepThrough()> _
        Private Sub InitializeComponent()

    End Sub

    Private Sub Page_Init(ByVal sender As System.Object, _
        ByVal e As System.EventArgs) Handles MyBase.Init
        'CODEGEN: This method call is required by the Web Form Designer
        'Do not modify it using the code editor.
        InitializeComponent()
    End Sub

#End Region

    Private Sub Page_Load(ByVal sender As System.Object, _
        ByVal e As System.EventArgs) Handles MyBase.Load
        'Put user code to initialize the page here
    End Sub

    Private Sub ListBox1_SelectedIndexChanged(ByVal sender As _
        System.Object, ByVal e As System.EventArgs) Handles _
        ListBox1.SelectedIndexChanged
        TextBox1.Text = "You selected " & ListBox1.SelectedItem.Text
    End Sub

    Private Sub ListBox2_SelectedIndexChanged(ByVal sender As _
        System.Object, ByVal e As System.EventArgs) Handles _
        ListBox2.SelectedIndexChanged
        Dim LoopIndex As Integer
        TextBox1.Text = "You selected "
        For LoopIndex = 0 To ListBox2.Items.Count - 1
            If ListBox2.Items(LoopIndex).Selected Then
                TextBox1.Text &= ListBox2.Items(LoopIndex).Text & " "
```

```
            End If
        Next
    End Sub
End Class
```

Creating Multiple-Selection List Boxes

By default, Web server list boxes let you select only one item at a time, but if you set the **SelectionMode** property to **Multiple**, the list box will support multiple selections. You can see the multiple-selection list box in the ListBoxes example on the CD-ROM at work in Figure 17.3.

When the user makes a new selection in a multiple-selection list box, a **SelectedIndexChanged** event occurs. To determine which items are selected, you can loop over the list box's **Items** collection, checking each item's **Selected** property. Here's how I display the selected items in the multiple-selection list box in the ListBoxes example:

```
Private Sub ListBox2_SelectedIndexChanged(ByVal sender As _
    System.Object, ByVal e As System.EventArgs) Handles _
    ListBox2.SelectedIndexChanged
    Dim LoopIndex As Integer
    TextBox1.Text = "You selected "
    For LoopIndex = 0 To ListBox2.Items.Count - 1
        If ListBox2.Items(LoopIndex).Selected Then
            TextBox1.Text &= ListBox2.Items(LoopIndex).Text & " "
        End If
    Next
End Sub
```

And that's all you need.

Adding Items to List Boxes at Run Time

As with any Web server control based on the **ListControl** class, you can use the **Items** collection's **Add** method to add items to list boxes at run time. The **Items** collection is a collection of **ListItem** objects (see "Using the **ListItem** Class" in Chapter 16), so you can pass either a **ListItem** object to the **Add** method, or the text you want to give to the new item. To see how this works, take a look at the AddItems example on the CD-ROM. You can see this example at work in Figure 17.9—when you click the "Add a new item" button, a new item is added to the list box.

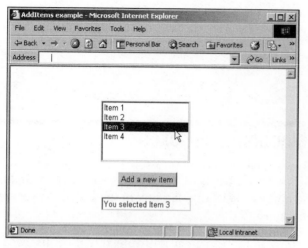

Figure 17.9   The AddItems example.

In this example, there's more going on than just using the **Items** collection's **Add** method, however—we'll have to keep track of the number of items added to the list box between round trips to the server to be able to increment the caption of newly added items (for example, from "Item 1" to "Item 2"). To do that, I'll use an HTML hidden control (see "Saving Program Data across Server Round Trips" in Chapter 14 for more details).

In the AddItems example, I've given the new hidden control the ID **Hidden1** in the Properties window. To make sure the hidden control's data is sent back to the server, and is accessible to your Visual Basic code, you must make it a server control, so right-click it and select the "Run As Server Control". Finally, assign its value property the value 0 in the Properties window. The data in this control, **Hidden1.Value**, will be stored in the Web page and sent back to the server, so I can store the number of items I've added to the list box and set the caption of new items like this:

```
Private Sub Button1_Click(ByVal sender As System.Object, _
    ByVal e As System.EventArgs) Handles Button1.Click
        Hidden1.Value += 1
        ListBox1.Items.Add("Item " & Hidden1.Value)
    End Sub
```

That's all there is to it. I also can add code to the list box's **SelectedIndexChanged** event handler like this:

```
Private Sub ListBox1_SelectedIndexChanged(ByVal sender As _
    System.Object, ByVal e As System.EventArgs) Handles _
    ListBox1.SelectedIndexChanged
        TextBox1.Text = "You selected " & ListBox1.SelectedItem.Text
    End Sub
```

You can see the results in Figure 17.9. For reference, here is WebForm1.aspx from the AddItems example:

```
<%@ Page Language="vb" AutoEventWireup="false"
Codebehind="WebForm1.aspx.vb" Inherits="AddItems.WebForm1"%>
<!DOCTYPE HTML PUBLIC "-//W3C//DTD HTML 4.0 Transitional//EN">
<HTML>
  <HEAD>
    <title>AddItems example</title>
<meta content="Microsoft Visual Studio.NET 7.0" name=GENERATOR>
<meta content="Visual Basic 7.0" name=CODE_LANGUAGE>
<meta content=JavaScript name=vs_defaultClientScript>
<meta content=
    http://schemas.microsoft.com/intellisense/ie5 name=vs_targetSchema>
  </HEAD>
<body MS_POSITIONING="GridLayout">
<form id=Form1 method=post runat="server">
<asp:listbox id=ListBox1 style="Z-INDEX: 101; LEFT: 158px; POSITION:
absolute; TOP: 56px" runat="server" Width="154px" Height="112px"
AutoPostBack="True"></asp:listbox>
<INPUT id=Hidden1 style="Z-INDEX: 104; LEFT: 159px; POSITION:
absolute; TOP: 250px" type=hidden value=0 runat="server">
<asp:button id=Button1 style="Z-INDEX: 103; LEFT: 188px; POSITION:
absolute; TOP: 174px" runat="server" Width="103px" Height="24px"
Text="Add a new item">
</asp:button>
<asp:textbox id=TextBox1 style="Z-INDEX: 102; LEFT: 160px;
POSITION: absolute; TOP: 217px" runat="server"></asp:textbox>
</form>

  </body>
</HTML>
```

And here is WebForm1.aspx.vb from this example:

```
Public Class WebForm1
    Inherits System.Web.UI.Page
    Protected WithEvents ListBox1 As System.Web.UI.WebControls.ListBox
    Protected WithEvents TextBox1 As System.Web.UI.WebControls.TextBox
    Protected WithEvents Hidden1 As _
        System.Web.UI.HtmlControls.HtmlInputHidden
    Protected WithEvents Button1 As System.Web.UI.WebControls.Button

#Region " Web Form Designer Generated Code "
```

```
'This call is required by the Web Form Designer.
<System.Diagnostics.DebuggerStepThrough()> _
    Private Sub InitializeComponent()

End Sub

Private Sub Page_Init(ByVal sender As System.Object, _
    ByVal e As System.EventArgs) Handles MyBase.Init
    'CODEGEN: This method call is required by the Web Form Designer
    'Do not modify it using the code editor.
    InitializeComponent()
End Sub

#End Region

Private Sub Page_Load(ByVal sender As System.Object, _
    ByVal e As System.EventArgs) Handles MyBase.Load
End Sub

Private Sub Button1_Click(ByVal sender As System.Object, _
    ByVal e As System.EventArgs) Handles Button1.Click
    Hidden1.Value += 1
    ListBox1.Items.Add("Item " & Hidden1.Value)
End Sub

Private Sub ListBox1_SelectedIndexChanged(ByVal sender As _
    System.Object, ByVal e As System.EventArgs) Handles _
    ListBox1.SelectedIndexChanged
    TextBox1.Text = "You selected " & ListBox1.SelectedItem.Text
End Sub
End Class
```

Using the **DropDownList** Class

As discussed in the In Depth section of this chapter, these controls are the same as list boxes, except that they can support only single selections, and they display their lists in a drop-down manner. This control is supported with the **DropDownList** class, and here is the inheritance hierarchy of this class:

```
Object
   Control
      WebControl
         ListControl
            DropDownList
```

You can find the notable public properties of **DropDownList** objects in Table 17.5. (This control has no non-inherited methods or events.) Note that as with other Web server controls, I am not listing the notable properties, methods, and events this class inherits from the **Control** and **WebControl** classes—you can find them in Chapter 15, Tables 15.1 to 15.5. This class inherits the **ListControl** class, and you can find the notable public properties of **ListControl** objects in Table 16.4, and their notable public events in Table 16.5. (The **ListControl** class has no non-inherited methods.) Note that the **ListControl** class's **Items** property returns a collection of **ListItem** objects that you can use to access an item in a list box. You can find the notable public properties of **ListItem** objects in Table 16.6. (The **ListItem** class has no non-inherited methods or events.)

TIP: *Don't forget—if you want to handle this control's events immediately, you must set its **AutoPostBack** property to **True**.*

Table 17.5   Noteworthy public properties of DropDownList objects.

Property	Means
SelectedIndex	Gets/sets selected item's index.
ToolTip	Gets/sets the tool tip text for the drop-down list.

Creating Drop-down Lists

To see how to work with drop-down list boxes, take a look at the DropDownLists example on the CD-ROM. You can see this example at work in Figure 17.4, where I'm selecting an item in a drop-down list, and in Figure 17.5, where the application is displaying the selection I've made.

Determining the selection the user has made in a drop-down list is easy; because you can only select one item at a time in a drop-down list, you use the **SelectedItem** and **SelectedIndex** properties of this control. Here's how that works in the DropDownLists example, where I'm reporting the selection the user made by displaying a message in a text box:

```
Private Sub DropDownList1_SelectedIndexChanged(ByVal sender As _
    System.Object, ByVal e As System.EventArgs) Handles _
    DropDownList1.SelectedIndexChanged
        TextBox1.Text = "You selected " & _
            DropDownList1.SelectedItem.Text
    End Sub
```

And that's all there is to it. Here's WebForm1.aspx for the DropDownLists example:

```
<%@ Page Language="vb" AutoEventWireup="false"
Codebehind="WebForm1.aspx.vb" Inherits="DropDownLists.WebForm1"%>
<!DOCTYPE HTML PUBLIC "-//W3C//DTD HTML 4.0 Transitional//EN">
<HTML>
  <HEAD>
    <title>DropDownLists example</title>
    <meta name="GENERATOR" content="Microsoft Visual Studio.NET 7.0">
    <meta name="CODE_LANGUAGE" content="Visual Basic 7.0">
    <meta name=vs_defaultClientScript content="JavaScript">
    <meta name=vs_targetSchema content=
        "http://schemas.microsoft.com/intellisense/ie5">
  </HEAD>
  <body MS_POSITIONING="GridLayout">

    <form id="Form1" method="post" runat="server">
<asp:DropDownList id=DropDownList1 style="Z-INDEX: 101; LEFT: 160px;
    POSITION: absolute; TOP: 58px" runat="server" Width="144px"
    Height="22px" AutoPostBack="True">
<asp:ListItem Value="Item 1">Item 1</asp:ListItem>
<asp:ListItem Value="Item 2">Item 2</asp:ListItem>
<asp:ListItem Value="Item 3">Item 3</asp:ListItem>
<asp:ListItem Value="Item 4">Item 4</asp:ListItem>
</asp:DropDownList>
<asp:TextBox id=TextBox1 style="Z-INDEX: 102; LEFT: 155px; POSITION:
    absolute; TOP: 118px" runat="server"></asp:TextBox>

    </form>

  </body>
</HTML>
```

And here's WebForm1.aspx.vb for this example:

```
Public Class WebForm1
    Inherits System.Web.UI.Page
```

```
    Protected WithEvents DropDownList1 As _
        System.Web.UI.WebControls.DropDownList
    Protected WithEvents TextBox1 As System.Web.UI.WebControls.TextBox

#Region " Web Form Designer Generated Code "

    'This call is required by the Web Form Designer.
    <System.Diagnostics.DebuggerStepThrough()> _
        Private Sub InitializeComponent()

    End Sub

    Private Sub Page_Init(ByVal sender As System.Object, ByVal e As _
        System.EventArgs) Handles MyBase.Init
        'CODEGEN: This method call is required by the Web Form Designer
        'Do not modify it using the code editor.
        InitializeComponent()
    End Sub

#End Region

    Private Sub Page_Load(ByVal sender As System.Object, ByVal e _
        As System.EventArgs) Handles MyBase.Load
        'Put user code to initialize the page here
    End Sub

    Private Sub DropDownList1_SelectedIndexChanged(ByVal sender As _
        System.Object, ByVal e As System.EventArgs) Handles _
        DropDownList1.SelectedIndexChanged
        TextBox1.Text = "You selected " & _
            DropDownList1.SelectedItem.Text
    End Sub
End Class
```

Using the **HyperLink** Class

You use the **HyperLink** class to create hyperlinks in Web applications. Here is the inheritance hierarchy of this class:

```
Object
    Control
        WebControl
            HyperLink
```

Table 17.6   Noteworthy public properties of HyperLink objects.

Property	Means
ImageUrl	Gets/sets the URL of an image you want to use in the hyperlink.
NavigateUrl	Gets/sets the URL to navigate to when the hyperlink is clicked.
Target	Gets/sets the target window or frame to display the new content in when the hyperlink is clicked.
Text	Gets/sets the text for the hyperlink.

You can find the notable public properties of **HyperLink** objects in Table 17.6. (This class has no non-inherited methods or events.) Note that as with other Web server controls, I am not listing the notable properties, methods, and events this class inherits from the **Control** and **WebControl** classes—you can find them in Chapter 15, Tables 15.1 to 15.5.

Creating Hyperlinks

You can create hyperlinks in Web forms with hyperlink controls. You can see hyperlinks at work in Figure 17.6 in the HyperLinks example on the CD-ROM—to see how to set the various properties of hyperlinks, see the In Depth section of this chapter.

In the HyperLinks example on the CD-ROM, the two most important properties of the hyperlinks in the application, **HyperLink1** and **HyperLink2**, are the **Text** and **NavigateUrl** properties. You set the **Text** property to the text you want the hyperlink to display at run time, and the **NavigateUrl** property to the URL you want the browser to navigate to when the hyperlink is clicked.

To assign a value to the **NavigateUrl** property at design time, click that property in the Properties window, opening the Select URL dialog you see in Figure 17.10. As you see in that dialog, you can select the URL type, which can be **Absolute** or **Relative**. You use **Absolute** if you want to specify an entire URL, and **Relative** if you want to specify an URL with respect to the current page (which you usually do if the URL is for another page in the same project). In this example, I'm creating hyperlinks both to the Visual Basic technical page at Microsoft (using an absolute URL: **http://msdn.microsoft.com/vbasic/technical/articles.asp**) and to another Web form in the same project (using a relative URL: **WebForm2.aspx**).

---

*TIP: Note that there are other properties you might want to set when working with hyperlinks, such as the **Target** property of the hyperlink, as well as the **link**, **alink**, and **vlink** properties of the Web form. See "Setting Hyperlink Colors" in Chapter 14.*

Figure 17.10   The Select URL dialog box.

Figure 17.11   The Visual Basic technical page.

Now when the user clicks the "VB.NET Tech Info" link, for example, the browser will navigate to the Visual Basic technical page, as you see in Figure 17.11. (Note that in this case, I've set the hyperlink's **Target** property to **_self**, which means that the linked-to page replaces the current page when the user clicks the hyperlink.)

For reference, here is WebForm1.aspx for the HyperLinks example on the CD-ROM (this example needs no Visual Basic code):

```
<%@ Page Language="vb" AutoEventWireup="false"
Codebehind="WebForm1.aspx.vb" Inherits="HyperLinks.WebForm1"%>
<!DOCTYPE HTML PUBLIC "-//W3C//DTD HTML 4.0 Transitional//EN">
```

```
<HTML>
  <HEAD>
    <title>HyperLinks example</title>
    <meta name="GENERATOR" content="Microsoft Visual Studio.NET 7.0">
    <meta name="CODE_LANGUAGE" content="Visual Basic 7.0">
    <meta name=vs_defaultClientScript content="JavaScript">
    <meta name=vs_targetSchema content=
        "http://schemas.microsoft.com/intellisense/ie5">
  </HEAD>
  <body MS_POSITIONING="GridLayout">

    <form id="Form1" method="post" runat="server">
<asp:HyperLink id=HyperLink1 style="Z-INDEX: 101; LEFT: 196px;
POSITION: absolute; TOP: 80px" runat="server" Target="_self"
NavigateUrl="http://msdn.microsoft.com/vbasic/technical/articles.asp">
VB.NET Tech Info</asp:HyperLink>
<asp:Label id=Label2 style="Z-INDEX: 104; LEFT: 101px; POSITION:
absolute; TOP: 121px" runat="server">Relative URL:</asp:Label>
<asp:HyperLink id=HyperLink2 style="Z-INDEX: 103; LEFT: 198px;
POSITION: absolute; TOP: 122px" runat="server" Target="_blank"
NavigateUrl="WebForm2.aspx">Web Form 2</asp:HyperLink>
<asp:Label id=Label1 style="Z-INDEX: 102; LEFT: 98px; POSITION:
absolute; TOP: 80px" runat="server">Absolute URL:</asp:Label>

    </form>

  </body>
</HTML>
```

Using the **LinkButton** Class

As discussed in the In Depth section of this chapter, link buttons look like standard hyperlinks, but actually work like buttons, letting you handle them in Visual Basic code. Link buttons are supported with the **LinkButton** class; here's the inheritance hierarchy for this class:

```
Object
    Control
        WebControl
            LinkButton
```

You can find the notable public properties of **LinkButton** objects in Table 17.7, and their notable public events in Table 17.8. (This class has no non-inherited methods.) Note that as with other Web server controls, I am not listing the no-

Table 17.7 Noteworthy public properties of **LinkButton** objects.

Property	Means
CausesValidation	Gets/sets whether the link button performs validation in other controls.
CommandArgument	Gets/sets an optional argument holding data about the command specified with **CommandName**.
CommandName	Gets/sets the command name for this image button.
Text	Gets/sets the text displayed in the link button.

Table 17.8 Noteworthy public events of **LinkButton** objects.

Event	Means
Click	Occurs when the image button was clicked.
Command	Occurs when the image button was clicked—use a **Command** event handler for this one.

table properties, methods, and events this class inherits from the **Control** and **WebControl** classes—you can find them in Chapter 15, Tables 15.1 to 15.5.

Creating Link Buttons

Link buttons let you handle hyperlinks with Visual Basic code. As with hyperlink controls, you set the text in a link button with the **Text** property, and as with hyperlink controls, link buttons are supported with HTML **<a>** elements. However, you can add code to the **Click** and **Command** event handlers for link buttons, which you can't do for hyperlink controls.

You can see a link button at work in the LinkButtons example on the CD-ROM in Figure 17.7. In this case, when the user clicks the hyperlink, I make a label with the text "Sorry, no more information is available" and a solid border visible, as you can see in that figure. To make that label visible, all I need to do is to add this code to the link button's **Click** event:

```
Private Sub LinkButton1_Click(ByVal sender As System.Object, _
    ByVal e As System.EventArgs) Handles LinkButton1.Click
    Label1.Visible = True
End Sub
```

And that's all it takes. Here's WebForm1.aspx for the LinkButtons example:

```
<%@ Page Language="vb" AutoEventWireup="false"
Codebehind="WebForm1.aspx.vb" Inherits="LinkButtons.WebForm1"%>
```

```
<!DOCTYPE HTML PUBLIC "-//W3C//DTD HTML 4.0 Transitional//EN">
<HTML>
  <HEAD>
    <title>LinkButtons example</title>
    <meta name="GENERATOR" content="Microsoft Visual Studio.NET 7.0">
    <meta name="CODE_LANGUAGE" content="Visual Basic 7.0">
    <meta name=vs_defaultClientScript content="JavaScript">
    <meta name=vs_targetSchema content=
    "http://schemas.microsoft.com/intellisense/ie5">
  </HEAD>
  <body MS_POSITIONING="GridLayout">

    <form id="Form1" method="post" runat="server">
<asp:LinkButton id=LinkButton1 style="Z-INDEX: 101; LEFT: 162px;
POSITION: absolute; TOP: 75px" runat="server">here</asp:LinkButton>
<asp:Label id=Label3 style="Z-INDEX: 104; LEFT: 191px; POSITION:
absolute; TOP: 75px" runat="server">for more information.</asp:Label>
<asp:Label id=Label2 style="Z-INDEX: 103; LEFT: 128px; POSITION:
absolute; TOP: 75px" runat="server">Click</asp:Label>
<asp:Label id=Label1 style="Z-INDEX: 102; LEFT: 101px; POSITION:
absolute; TOP: 130px" runat="server" Width="243px" Height="26px"
BorderStyle="Solid" BorderWidth="1px" Visible="False">Sorry, no more
information is available.</asp:Label>

    </form>

  </body>
</HTML>
```

And here's WebForm1.aspx.vb for the LinkButtons example:

```
Public Class WebForm1
    Inherits System.Web.UI.Page
    Protected WithEvents Label1 As System.Web.UI.WebControls.Label
    Protected WithEvents Label2 As System.Web.UI.WebControls.Label
    Protected WithEvents Label3 As System.Web.UI.WebControls.Label
    Protected WithEvents LinkButton1 As _
        System.Web.UI.WebControls.LinkButton

#Region " Web Form Designer Generated Code "

    'This call is required by the Web Form Designer.
    <System.Diagnostics.DebuggerStepThrough()> _
        Private Sub InitializeComponent()
```

```
    End Sub

    Private Sub Page_Init(ByVal sender As System.Object, ByVal _
        e As System.EventArgs) Handles MyBase.Init
        'CODEGEN: This method call is required by the Web Form Designer
        'Do not modify it using the code editor.
        InitializeComponent()
    End Sub

#End Region

    Private Sub Page_Load(ByVal sender As System.Object, ByVal _
        e As System.EventArgs) Handles MyBase.Load
        'Put user code to initialize the page here
    End Sub

    Private Sub LinkButton1_Click(ByVal sender As System.Object, _
        ByVal e As System.EventArgs) Handles LinkButton1.Click
        Label1.Visible = True
    End Sub
End Class
```

Chapter 18

Validation Controls, Calendars, and Ad Rotators

In Depth

In this chapter, we're going to take a look at validation controls, calendar controls, and ad rotators. You use validation controls to check data the user has entered into a Web page, calendar controls to let the user select dates, and ad rotators to display banner ads. (I can hear Internet purists exclaiming: not banner ads! But, yes indeed; that's exactly what ad rotators let you do—display advertising in your applications.)

Validation Controls

Round trips to the server can take a lot of time, as everyone knows. (Right now, I'm on the fourth attempt to try to load the morning edition of my favorite newspaper into Internet Explorer and realizing that it just doesn't want to appear.) Validation controls were invented to help avoid losing some of that valuable time. They do their work in the client if the client browser can support JavaScript and some simple dynamic HTML (DHTML), checking the data that the user has entered before sending it to the server. (DHTML is used to make the error message visible without a server roundtrip—note that if the browser can't support the scripting and DHTML requirements, the validation is actually done on the server.) This is a common thing for Web pages to do, and you're probably familiar with warnings like "You must enter a valid phone number" and so on.

For an example, take a look at the ValidationControls example on the CD-ROM, which you can see in Figure 18.1. This example is all about applying to college, and asks for your class rank, class size, and so on. In this case, I've entered a class rank, number 44, but made the class size 43, and the Web page is smart enough to know that's not possible, and says so before the users can click the "Admit me to college!" button and waste both their time and ours with invalid data.

Client-side validation like this is done with validation controls, and there is one different type of validation control for each text box you see in Figure 18.1. You tie a validation control to a data-entry control like text boxes (or two data-entry controls in case you want to use a compare validation control to compare two entered values). The user enters data into the data-entry control and when that control loses the focus (as when the user clicks another control to give it the keyboard focus), or a button in the page is clicked, the validation control checks the entered data as you've set it up to do. If there is a problem—if the user omit-

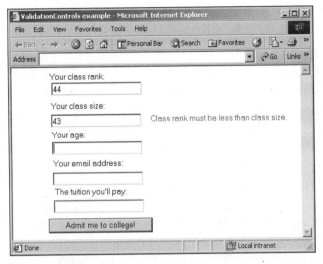

Figure 18.1   The ValidationControls example.

ted to enter some data in a required text box, for example—the validation control displays an error message, as you see in Figure 18.1. Validation controls are based on label controls; they are invisible by default until they determine that there's been an error, in which case they'll display their error message.

As soon as the user fixes the error and the data-entry control loses the focus or the user clicks a button, the validation control checks the new data, and, if the data is OK, makes its error message invisible again—no round trip to the server needed.

You can find the validation controls, and what they do, in Table 18.1. I'll go through them one by one in a page or two. We'll see them all in the Immediate Solutions section of this chapter.

Table 18.1   Validation controls.

Control	Does this
RequiredFieldValidator	Makes sure the user enters data in the associated data-entry control.
CompareValidator	Uses comparison operators to compare user-entered data to a constant value or the value in another data-entry control.
RangeValidator	Makes sure that user-entered data is in a range between given lower and upper boundaries.
RegularExpressionValidator	Makes sure that user-entered data matches a regular-expression pattern.
CustomValidator	Makes sure user-entered data passes validation criteria that you set yourself.

TIP: *You can assign more than one validation control to the same data-entry control in case you want to check multiple conditions at the same time.*

Want to work with the validation controls in a Web page yourself in client-side script? You can loop through the page's **Validators** collection to work with each validation control in the page, checking their **IsValid** property to see if their validation test was successful. And you can use the whole page's **IsValid** property to see if all validation tests were successful. You also can force any validation control to check its data by using the control's **Validate** method.

I'll take a look at the individual validation controls in detail now. To use these controls, you typically set the **ErrorMessage** property to the error message you want to display, and the **ControlToValidate** property to the control you want to check. You can see the various validators in the ValidationControls example at design time, as you see in Figure 18.2, showing their error messages.

Required Field Validators

The simplest validation control is the **RequiredFieldValidator** control, which simply makes sure that the users have entered data into a data-entry control. For example, you may want to make sure that the users enter the number of shoes they want to buy. If they omit to enter a value, this validation control will display its error message.

This control has a property named **InitialValue**, set to an empty string ("") by default. If the data has not changed from that value when validation occurs, the control displays its error message. The required field validator in the **ValidationControls** example makes sure that the user has entered a class rank in the top text box you see in Figure 18.1.

TIP: *Here's a little known fact that can save you some frustration: If a data-entry control is empty, no validation is performed by any of the validation controls except for required field validators, and by default, that means that validation succeeds. To avoid this problem, you should use a required field validator to make sure the user enters data into the data-entry control before checking that data.*

Comparison Validators

You use comparison validators to compare the value entered by the user into a data-entry control with the value entered into another data-entry control or with a constant value. As usual for validation controls, you indicate the data-entry control to validate by setting the **ControlToValidate** property. If you want to compare a specific data-entry control with another data-entry control, set the **ControlToCompare** property to specify the control to compare with.

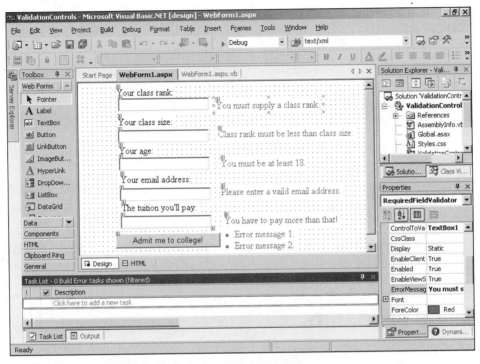

Figure 18.2   The ValidationControls example at design time.

Instead of comparing the value of a data-entry control with another data-entry control, you can compare the value of a data-entry control to a constant value. In this case, you specify the constant value to compare with by setting the **ValueToCompare** property.

TIP: Don't set both the **ControlToCompare** and **ValueToCompare** properties at the same time, because they conflict. If you do, the **ControlToCompare** property takes precedence.

Use the **Operator** property to specify the type of comparison to perform. Here are the possibilities:

- **Equal**—Checks if the compared values are equal.
- **NotEqual**—Checks if the compared values are not equal.
- **GreaterThan**—Checks for a greater than relationship.
- **GreaterThanEqual**—Checks for a greater than or equal to relationship.
- **LessThan**— Checks for a less than relationship.
- **LessThanEqual**—Checks for a less than or equal to relationship.
- **DataTypeCheck**—Compares data types between the value entered into the data-entry control being validated and the data type specified by the **Type** property.

You use the **Type** property to specify the data type of both comparison values. (This type is **String** by default, so don't forget to set this property yourself if you're comparing numbers—otherwise you'll find, for example, that a value of 150 is less than 16 in string terms.) Both values are automatically converted to this data type before the comparison operation is performed. Here are the different data types that you can use:

- **String**—A string data type.
- **Integer**—An integer data type.
- **Double**—A double data type.
- **Date**—A date data type.
- **Currency**—A currency data type.

There's a comparison validator next to the second text box in Figure 18.2. This is the validator that compares class rank with class size and makes sure that the users' rank is less than or equal to their class size.

Range Validators

A range validator tests if the value of a data-entry control is inside a specified range of values. You use three main properties here—the **ControlToValidate** property contains the data-entry control to validate, and the **MinimumValue** and **MaximumValue** properties hold the minimum and maximum values of the valid range. If you set one of the **MinimumValue** and **MaximumValue** properties, you also must set the other. Also, don't forget to set the **Type** property to the data type of the values to compare; the possible values are the same as for comparison validators.

There's a range validator next to the third text box in Figure 18.2—this validator is checking to make sure that the applicant's age is between 18 and 150. As you can see, range validators can be useful for all kinds of ranges, from temperatures to number of items in stock, allowing you, for example, to make sure that the temperature in a freezer is less than freezing, or the number of items in a purchase order is greater than zero.

Regular Expression Validators

You use a **RegularExpressionValidator** control to check if the value in a data-entry control matches a pattern defined by a *regular expression*. You use regular expressions to see if text matches a certain pattern, which is a great way to check if the user has entered text in the way you want. Unfortunately, regular expressions are not easy to work with. There's an entire chapter in the Coriolis *Perl Black Book* dedicated to showing how regular expressions work.

In general, regular expressions are made up of text with embedded codes that start with a backslash (\) as well as other control codes. For example, the code for a word boundary (where a word ends or starts) is **\b**, and a "character class" is a set of characters surrounded with [and] that lets you specify what characters you want to accept, so this regular expression will match a word made up of uppercase and/or lowercase letters only (the + stands for "one or more of", so we're matching one or more uppercase and/or lowercase letters here):

```
\b[A-Za-z]+\b
```

That's hardly scratching the surface of regular expressions, though; for example, here's the regular expression Visual Basic uses to determine if text matches a valid email address—**\w** stands for a word character (such as letter scores and so on), and * means "zero or more of":

```
\w+([-+.]\w+)*@\w+([-.]\w+)*\.\w+([-.]\w+)*
```

As you can see, regular expressions can get pretty co nately, Visual Basic includes some pre-built regular e. match well-known sequences of characters, such as socia addresses, telephone numbers, postal codes, and so on. T sion validator next to the email address text box—the f ValidationControls example on the CD-ROM that you see ...e 18.2 using precisely the above expression to check for valid email addresses.

Custom Validators

As we've seen, there are different types of validators and they do different things, but sometimes they just can't check your data in as specific a way as you might like. For example—what if you wanted to find out whether a number was odd or even? You can't use a range or comparison validator for that. However, you can use a *custom validator*.

With a custom validator, you set the **ClientValidationFunction** property to the name of a script function, such as a JavaScript or VBScript function (VBScript is a Microsoft scripting language that supports a tiny subset of Visual Basic), both of which are supported in the Internet Explorer. This function will be passed two arguments, **source**, giving the source control to validate, and **arguments**, which holds the data to validate as **arguments.Value**. If you validate the data, you set **arguments.IsValid** to **True**, but to **False** otherwise.

There's a custom validator in the ValidationControls example on the CD-ROM that you see in Figure 18.2, next to the fifth text box. This validator will check the amount of tuition people enter into that text box to make sure that they're going to pay enough. Using custom validators is perhaps the most powerful way to use validators that there is—beyond the simple range checking and field checking validators, custom validators let you write your own customization code.

Validation Summaries

There is another validation control that you also should know about—the **ValidationSummary** control, which summarizes the error messages from all validators on a Web page in one location. The summary can be displayed as a list, as a bulleted list, or as a single paragraph, based on the **DisplayMode** property. You also can specify if the summary should be displayed in the Web page and in a message box by setting the **ShowSummary** and **ShowMessageBox** properties, respectively. There's a validation summary in the ValidationControls example; we'll see how to use it in this chapter.

Calendars

You use the **Calendar** control to display a single month of a calendar on a Web page. This control allows you to select dates and move to the next or previous month. You can choose whether the **Calendar** control allows users to select a single day, week, or month by setting the **SelectionMode** property.

By default, the control displays the days of the month, day headings for the days of the week, a title with the month name, and arrow characters for navigating to the next and previous month. You can customize the appearance of the **Calendar** control by setting the properties that control the style for different parts of the control. Here are the properties that you can use to customize a calendar control:

- **DayHeaderStyle**—Sets the style for the days of the week.
- **DayStyle**—Sets the style for the dates in a month.
- **NextPrevStyle**—Sets the style for the navigation controls.
- **OtherMonthStyle**—Sets the style for dates not in the displayed month.
- **SelectedDayStyle**—Sets the style for the selected dates.
- **SelectorStyle**—Sets the style for the week and month selection column.
- **TitleStyle**—Sets the style for titles.
- **TodayDayStyle**—Sets the style for today's date.
- **WeekendDayStyle**—Sets the style for weekend dates.

It's also worth knowing that you can show or hide different parts of a calendar. Here are the properties to use for this:

- **ShowDayHeader**—Shows or hides the days of the week.

- **ShowGridLines**—Shows or hides grid lines (displayed between the days of the month).

- **ShowNextPrevMonth**—Shows or hides the navigation controls to the next or previous month.

- **ShowTitle**—Shows or hides the title.

When the user makes a selection, you can use the **SelectionChanged** event and the **SelectedDate** property to find the new selected date. That's how the Calendars example on the CD-ROM, which you can see in Figure 18.3, works. As it shows, I'm selecting a date.

Ad Rotators

Visual Basic Web applications even support banner ads, which, as mentioned earlier, is something Internet purists may not be happy to hear. These ads, which all Internet users are familiar with, are image files in GIF, JPEG, or other formats, that the user can click to cause the browser to navigate to the advertiser's Web site.

Using an ad rotator, you can automatically cycle through a series of ad banners. The ad rotator automates the cycling process, changing the displayed ad when the page is refreshed. Note also that ads can be "weighted" to control how often they appear compared with others. And, if you prefer, you also can write custom logic that cycles through the ads.

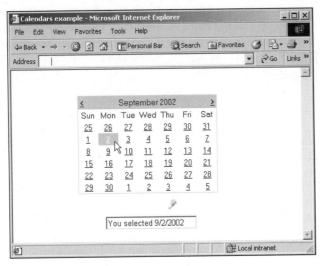

Figure 18.3   The Calendars example.

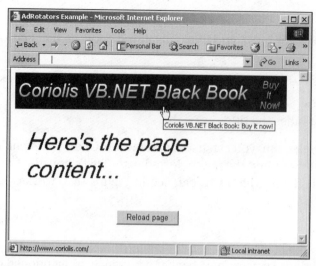

Figure 18.4   The AdRotators example.

You can see an ad rotator at work in Figure 18.4 and in the AdRotators example on the CD-ROM (shamelessly displaying an ad for this book). When you click the button in this example, the page reloads and displays various ads.

There are two ways to specify the ad banners for an ad rotator—you can use an XML file or write your own code to select an ad banner in the **AdCreated** event. Here's what the XML file, ads.xml, for the AdRotators example on the CD-ROM looks like. You can see that for each ad, I'm specifying the URL of the ad banner, the URL to navigate to if the user clicks the ad, the alternate text to display if the ad banner isn't available (this text is also used as a tooltip, as you see in Figure 18.4), the number of impressions (the number of times the ad should be shown), and a keyword to use in selecting ads (you can use the **KeyWordFilter** property to filter ads for target audiences):

```
<Advertisements>
    <Ad>
        <ImageUrl>banner1.jpg</ImageUrl>
        <NavigateUrl>http://www.coriolis.com</NavigateUrl>
        <AlternateText>Coriolis VB.NET Black Book: Buy it now!
        </AlternateText>
        <Impressions>80</Impressions>
        <Keyword>VB.NET</Keyword>
    </Ad>

    <Ad>
        <ImageUrl>banner2.jpg</ImageUrl>
        <NavigateUrl>http://www.coriolis.com</NavigateUrl>
```

```
        <AlternateText>Coriolis Perl Black Book: Buy it now!
        </AlternateText>
        <Impressions>80</Impressions>
        <Keyword>Perl</Keyword>
    </Ad>

    <Ad>
        <ImageUrl>banner3.jpg</ImageUrl>
        <NavigateUrl>http://www.coriolis.com</NavigateUrl>
        <AlternateText>Coriolis HTML Black Book: Buy it now!
        </AlternateText>
        <Impressions>80</Impressions>
        <Keyword>HTML</Keyword>
    </Ad>
</Advertisements>
```

And now it's time to turn to the Immediate Solutions section of this chapter, to see how to handle specific details.

Immediate Solutions

Using Validators

As discussed in the In Depth section of this chapter, validation controls, also called validators, let you check the data a user has entered in a Web application. We've discussed the validation controls available in the In Depth section of this chapter; you can see them all at work in the ValidationControls example on the CD-ROM, which appears in Figure 18.1. This example is a mock-up of a Web application that lets users apply to college, letting them enter data for their class rank, class size, and so on—and checking that data before sending it to the server.

Here is WebForm1.aspx for the ValidationControls example, for reference:

```
<%@ Page Language="vb" AutoEventWireup="false"
Codebehind="WebForm1.aspx.vb" Inherits="ValidationControls.WebForm1"%>
<!DOCTYPE HTML PUBLIC "-//W3C//DTD HTML 4.0 Transitional//EN">
<HTML>
  <HEAD>
    <title>ValidationControls example</title>
<meta content="Microsoft Visual Studio.NET 7.0" name=GENERATOR>
<meta content="Visual Basic 7.0" name=CODE_LANGUAGE>
<meta content=JavaScript name=vs_defaultClientScript>
<meta content=http://schemas.microsoft.com/intellisense/ie5
    name=vs_targetSchema>
<script language=vbscript>

    Sub Validate(source, arguments)

        If (arguments.Value > 20000) Then
            arguments.IsValid = True
        Else
            arguments.IsValid = False
        End If

    End Sub

</script>
</HEAD>
<body MS_POSITIONING="GridLayout">
```

```
      <form id="Form1" method="post" runat="server">
<asp:RequiredFieldValidator id=RequiredFieldValidator1
style="Z-INDEX: 101; LEFT: 235px; POSITION: absolute; TOP: 30px"
runat="server" ErrorMessage="You must supply a class rank."
ControlToValidate="TextBox1"></asp:RequiredFieldValidator>
<asp:Label id=Label5 style="Z-INDEX: 117; LEFT: 73px; POSITION:
absolute; TOP: 199px" runat="server">The tuition you'll pay:</asp:Label>
<asp:TextBox id=TextBox5 style="Z-INDEX: 116; LEFT: 71px; POSITION:
absolute; TOP: 221px" runat="server"></asp:TextBox>
<asp:Label id=Label4 style="Z-INDEX: 115; LEFT: 71px; POSITION:
absolute; TOP: 152px" runat="server">Your email address:</asp:Label>
<asp:Label id=Label3 style="Z-INDEX: 114; LEFT: 69px; POSITION:
absolute; TOP: 104px" runat="server">Your age:</asp:Label>
<asp:Label id=Label2 style="Z-INDEX: 113; LEFT: 68px; POSITION:
absolute; TOP: 56px" runat="server">Your class size:</asp:Label>
<asp:Label id=Label1 style="Z-INDEX: 112; LEFT: 66px; POSITION:
absolute; TOP: 7px" runat="server">Your class rank:</asp:Label>
<asp:TextBox id=TextBox4 style="Z-INDEX: 111; LEFT: 70px; POSITION:
absolute; TOP: 175px" runat="server"></asp:TextBox>
<asp:TextBox id=TextBox3 style="Z-INDEX: 110; LEFT: 69px; POSITION:
absolute; TOP: 124px" runat="server"></asp:TextBox>
<asp:TextBox id=TextBox2 style="Z-INDEX: 109; LEFT: 68px; POSITION:
absolute; TOP: 78px" runat="server"></asp:TextBox>
<asp:Button id=Button1 style="Z-INDEX: 108; LEFT: 62px; POSITION:
absolute; TOP: 252px" runat="server" Text="Admit me to college!">
</asp:Button>
<asp:TextBox id=TextBox1 style="Z-INDEX: 107; LEFT: 69px; POSITION:
absolute; TOP: 25px" runat="server"></asp:TextBox>
<asp:ValidationSummary id=ValidationSummary1 style="Z-INDEX: 106; LEFT:
224px; POSITION: absolute; TOP: 245px" runat="server" Width="149px"
Height="49px"></asp:ValidationSummary>
<asp:CustomValidator id=CustomValidator1 style="Z-INDEX: 105; LEFT:
247px; POSITION: absolute; TOP: 222px" runat="server" ErrorMessage=
"You have to pay more than that!" ControlToValidate="TextBox5"
ClientValidationFunction="Validate"></asp:CustomValidator>
<asp:RegularExpressionValidator id=RegularExpressionValidator1
style="Z-INDEX: 104; LEFT: 242px; POSITION: absolute; TOP: 174px"
runat="server" ErrorMessage="Please enter a valid email address."
ControlToValidate="TextBox4" ValidationExpression=
"\w+([-+.]\w+)*@\w+([-.]\w+)*\.\w+([-.]\w+)*">
</asp:RegularExpressionValidator>
<asp:RangeValidator id=RangeValidator1 style="Z-INDEX: 103; LEFT: 242px;
POSITION: absolute; TOP: 127px" runat="server" ErrorMessage="You must be at
least 18." ControlToValidate="TextBox3" MinimumValue="18" MaximumValue=
"150" Type="Integer"></asp:RangeValidator>
```

```
<asp:CompareValidator id=CompareValidator1 style="Z-INDEX: 102; LEFT:
238px; POSITION: absolute; TOP: 78px" runat="server" ErrorMessage=
"Class rank must be less than class size." ControlToValidate="TextBox2"
ControlToCompare="TextBox1"
Operator="GreaterThanEqual" Width="235px" Height="26px"
Type="Integer"></asp:CompareValidator>

    </form>

  </body>
</HTML>
```

And here is WebForm1.aspx.vb for the ValidationControls example:

```
Public Class WebForm1
    Inherits System.Web.UI.Page
    Protected WithEvents RequiredFieldValidator1 As _
        System.Web.UI.WebControls.RequiredFieldValidator
    Protected WithEvents CompareValidator1 As _
        System.Web.UI.WebControls.CompareValidator
    Protected WithEvents RangeValidator1 As _
        System.Web.UI.WebControls.RangeValidator
    Protected WithEvents RegularExpressionValidator1 As _
        System.Web.UI.WebControls.RegularExpressionValidator
    Protected WithEvents CustomValidator1 As _
        System.Web.UI.WebControls.CustomValidator
    Protected WithEvents ValidationSummary1 As _
        System.Web.UI.WebControls.ValidationSummary
    Protected WithEvents TextBox1 As System.Web.UI.WebControls.TextBox
    Protected WithEvents TextBox2 As System.Web.UI.WebControls.TextBox
    Protected WithEvents TextBox3 As System.Web.UI.WebControls.TextBox
    Protected WithEvents TextBox4 As System.Web.UI.WebControls.TextBox
    Protected WithEvents Label1 As System.Web.UI.WebControls.Label
    Protected WithEvents Label2 As System.Web.UI.WebControls.Label
    Protected WithEvents Label3 As System.Web.UI.WebControls.Label
    Protected WithEvents Label4 As System.Web.UI.WebControls.Label
    Protected WithEvents TextBox5 As System.Web.UI.WebControls.TextBox
    Protected WithEvents Label5 As System.Web.UI.WebControls.Label
    Protected WithEvents Button1 As System.Web.UI.WebControls.Button

#Region " Web Form Designer Generated Code "

    'This call is required by the Web Form Designer.
    <System.Diagnostics.DebuggerStepThrough()> _
        Private Sub InitializeComponent()

    End Sub
```

```
    Private Sub Page_Init(ByVal sender As System.Object, _
        ByVal e As System.EventArgs) Handles MyBase.Init
        'CODEGEN: This method call is required by the Web Form Designer
        'Do not modify it using the code editor.
        InitializeComponent()
    End Sub

#End Region

    Private Sub Page_Load(ByVal sender As System.Object, _
        ByVal e As System.EventArgs) Handles MyBase.Load
        'Put user code to initialize the page here
    End Sub

End Class
```

To see how to use the various validators in this program, take a look at the following topics.

Using the **BaseValidator** Class

The **BaseValidator** class provides the basic implementation needed for all validation controls. Here is the inheritance hierarchy of this class:

```
Object
    Control
        WebControl
            Label
                BaseValidator
```

You can find the notable public properties of **BaseValidator** objects in Table 18.2 and their notable public methods in Table 18.3. (This class has no non-inherited events.) Note that as with other Web server controls, I am not listing the notable properties, methods, and events this class inherits from the **Control** and **WebControl** classes—you can find them in Chapter 15, Tables 15.1 to 15.5. This class also inherits the **Label** class; the **Label** class has only one non-inherited public member—the **Text** property.

Related solution:	Found on page:
Using the **Label** Class	685

18. Validation Controls, Calendars, and Ad Rotators

Table 18.2   Noteworthy public properties of BaseValidator objects.

Property	Means
ControlToValidate	Gets/sets the data-entry control to validate.
Display	Gets/sets how error messages are displayed.
EnableClientScript	Gets/sets whether validation is enabled.
Enabled	Gets/sets whether the validator is enabled.
ErrorMessage	Gets/sets the error message text.
ForeColor	Gets/sets the color of the error message.
IsValid	Gets/sets whether the connected data-entry control is validated.

Table 18.3   Noteworthy public methods of BaseValidator objects.

Method	Means
Validate	Checks the connected data-entry control, as well as updating the **IsValid** property.

Using the RequiredFieldValidator Class

As discussed in the In Depth section of this chapter, required field validators can determine if the user has entered data into a data-entry control or not. This validator is supported by the **RequiredFieldValidator** class; here is the inheritance hierarchy for that class:

```
Object
    Control
        WebControl
            Label
                BaseValidator
                    RequiredFieldValidator
```

You can find the notable public properties of **RequiredFieldValidator** objects in Table 18.4. (This class has no non-inherited methods or events.) Note that as with other Web server controls, I am not listing the notable properties, methods, and events this class inherits from the **Control** and **WebControl** classes—you can find them in Chapter 15, Tables 15.1 to 15.5. This class inherits the **BaseValidator** class, which you can see in Tables 18.2 and 18.3, and this class also inherits the **Label** class; the **Label** class has only one non-inherited public member—the **Text** property, which holds the text the label displays.

Table 18.4   Noteworthy public properties of RequiredFieldValidator objects.

Property	Means
InitialValue	Gets/sets the initial value in the connected data-entry control.

Creating Required Field Validators

You can see a required field validator in the ValidationControls example on the CD-ROM and in Figure 18.2 at design time. Here, I've given this control the error message "You must supply a class rank" using its **ErrorMessage** property. I also have set the **ControlToValidate** property of this control to **TextBox1**, the top text box in the example.

If the user doesn't enter any data into that text box and then clicks the button at the bottom of the example, which sends the page back to the server, the required field validator displays its error message and stops the page from being sent to the server, as you see in Figure 18.5. The user can enter text in the text box and try again, all without a round trip to the server.

TIP: *Note that validators, except for the required field validator, will validate controls that are left empty, so it's a good idea to use required field validators in addition to any other validators you use to make sure that the validation you're performing is meaningful.*

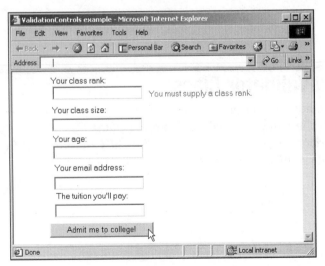

Figure 18.5   Using a required field validator.

Using the **BaseCompareValidator** Class

The **BaseCompareValidator** class is an abstract base class for a number of validation controls that perform comparisons, such as the comparison validator. Here is the inheritance hierarchy for the **BaseCompareValidator** class:

```
Object
    Control
        WebControl
            Label
                BaseValidator
                    BaseCompareValidator
```

You can find the notable public properties of **BaseCompareValidator** objects in Table 18.5. (This class has no non-inherited methods or events.) Note that as with other Web server controls, I am not listing the notable properties, methods, and events this class inherits from the **Control** and **WebControl** classes—you can find them in Chapter 15, Tables 15.1 to 15.5. This class inherits the **BaseValidator** class, which you can find in Tables 18.2 and 18.3, as well as the **Label** class; the **Label** class has only one non-inherited public member—the **Text** property, which holds the text the label displays.

Table 18.5   Noteworthy public properties of BaseCompareValidator objects.

Property	Means
Type	Gets/sets the type of data being compared.

Using the **CompareValidator** Class

You use a comparison validator to compare the value entered by the user into an data-entry control with the value entered into another data-entry control or a constant value. Comparison validators are supported by the **CompareValidator** class, and here is the inheritance hierarchy for this class:

```
Object
    Control
        WebControl
            Label
                BaseValidator
                    BaseCompareValidator
                        CompareValidator
```

Table 18.6   Noteworthy public properties of CompareValidator objects.

Property	Means
ControlToCompare	Gets/sets the data-entry control you want to compare to the data-entry control you want to validate.
Operator	Gets/sets the comparison operation you want to use.
ValueToCompare	Gets/sets the constant value you want to compare with the value in the data-entry control you want to validate.

You can find the notable public properties of **CompareValidator** objects in Table 18.6. (This class has no non-inherited methods or events.) Note that as with other Web server controls, I am not listing the notable properties, methods, and events this class inherits from the **Control** and **WebControl** classes—you can find them in Chapter 15, Tables 15.1 to 15.5. This class inherits the **BaseValidator** class, which you can find in Tables 18.2 and 18.3, the **BaseCompareValidator** class, which you can see in Table 18.5, as well as the **Label** class; the **Label** class has only one non-inherited public member—the **Text** property, which holds the text the label displays.

Creating Comparison Validators

As discussed in the In Depth section of this chapter, comparison validators let you compare a value in a data-entry control to another value, either in another data-entry control or a constant value.

You can see this comparison validator at work in Figure 18.2 and in the ValidationControls example on the CD-ROM, where the code is checking the value the users have entered for class rank and making sure that it's less than the value they've entered for their class size.

Here, I've set the comparison validator's **ControlToValidate** property to **TextBox2**, and its **ControlToCompare** property to **TextBox1**. I've also set the **Type** property to **Integer** and the **Operator** property to **GreaterThanEqual** (see the In Depth section of this chapter for other options on these properties). You also can compare to a constant value—just use the **ValueToCompare** property. And, as with other validation controls, you set the **ControlToValidate** property to set the control whose data you want to validate, and place the error message in the **ErrorMessage** property.

In Figure 18.2, you can see the comparison validator displaying its error message—when the user corrects the situation in one or the other text boxes and the text box loses the focus, the comparison validator will test the data again.

18. Validation Controls, Calendars, and Ad Rotators

Using the **RangeValidator** Class

You use range validators to check if the value of a data-entry control is in a specified range of values. Range validators are supported by the **RangeValidator** class, and here is the inheritance hierarchy for that class:

```
Object
    Control
        WebControl
            Label
                BaseValidator
                    BaseCompareValidator
                        RangeValidator
```

You can find the notable public properties of **RangeValidator** objects in Table 18.7. (This class has no non-inherited methods or events.) Note that as with other Web server controls, I am not listing the notable properties, methods, and events this class inherits from the **Control** and **WebControl** classes—you can find them in Chapter 15, Tables 15.1 to 15.5. This class inherits the **BaseValidator** class, which you can find in Tables 18.2 and 18.3, the **BaseCompareValidator** class, which you can see in Table 18.5, as well as the **Label** class; the **Label** class has only one non-inherited public member—the **Text** property, which holds the text the label displays.

Table 18.7   Noteworthy public properties of RangeValidator objects.

Property	Means
MaximumValue	Gets/sets the allowed range's maximum value.
MinimumValue	Gets/sets the allowed range's minimum value.

Creating Range Validators

As discussed in the In Depth section of this chapter, range validators test if the value of a data-entry control is inside a specified range of values. You use three main properties here—the **ControlToValidate** property contains the data-entry control to validate, and the **MinimumValue** and **MaximumValue** properties specify the minimum and maximum values of the valid range. If you set one of the **MinimumValue** and **MaximumValue** properties, you also must set the other. Also, don't forget to set the **Type** property to the data type of the values to compare; the possible values are the same as for comparison validators. And, as with other validation controls, you set the **ControlToValidate** property to set the control whose data you want to validate, and place the error message in the **ErrorMessage** property.

You can see a range validator at work in the ValidationControls example on the CD-ROM and in Figure 18.6. Here, I've set the validator's **MinimumValue** property to 18 and its **MaximumValue** property to 150. The user has entered an age under 18, so the validator is displaying its error message, as shown in Figure 18.6.

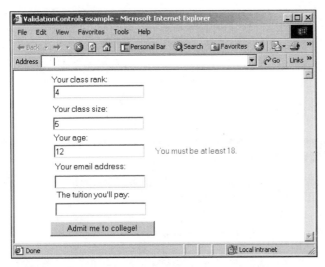

Figure 18.6   Using a range validator.

Using the **RegularExpressionValidator** Class

As discussed in the In Depth section of this chapter, you can use regular expression validators to check if the value of a data-entry control matches the pattern specified by a regular expression. This control is supported by the **RegularExpressionValidator** class, and here is the inheritance hierarchy of this class:

```
Object
    Control
        WebControl
            Label
                BaseValidator
                    RegularExpressionValidator
```

You can find the notable public properties of **RegularExpressionValidator** objects in Table 18.8. (This class has no non-inherited methods or events.) Note that as with other Web server controls, I am not listing the notable properties, methods, and events this class inherits from the **Control** and **WebControl** classes—you can find them in Chapter 15, Tables 15.1 to 15.5. This class inherits the **BaseValidator** class, which you can find in Tables 18.2 and 18.3, as well as the **Label** class; the **Label** class has only one non-inherited public member—the **Text** property, which holds the text the label displays.

Table 18.8 Noteworthy public properties of RegularExpressionValidator objects.

Property	Means
ValidationExpression	Gets/sets the regular expression you want to match data against for validation.

Creating Regular Expression Validators

You can see a regular expression validator at work in the ValidationControls example on the CD-ROM and in Figure 18.7. Here, the code is checking to make sure the users have entered a valid email address—and because they have not, the regular expression validator is displaying an error message as you see in that figure.

As with other validation controls, you set the **ControlToValidate** property to set the control whose data you want to validate, and place the error message in the **ErrorMessage** property. To set the regular expression to use, you use the

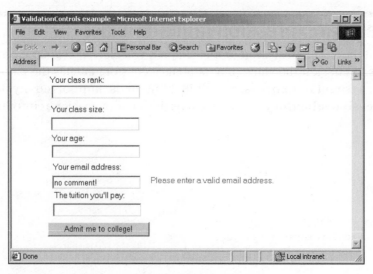

Figure 18.7   Using a regular expression validator.

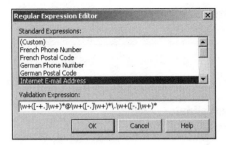

Figure 18.8   Using a regular expression validator.

ValidationExpression property, and Visual Basic lets you choose from some preset regular expressions in the Regular Expression Editor you see in Figure 18.8, which opens when you click the **ValidationExpression** property in the properties window.

In the ValidationControls example, I use this regular expression to match email addresses:

```
\w+([-+.]\w+)*@\w+([-.]\w+)*\.\w+([-.]\w+)*
```

And that's all it takes. In general, creating regular expressions yourself is not the easiest task, but you can get used to working with them. For a complete treatment of regular expressions, showing how to create them in detail, see the Coriolis *Perl Black Book*.

Using the **CustomValidator** Class

You use custom validators to perform your own validation for the data in a data-entry control. This control is supported by the **CustomValidator** class, and here is the inheritance hierarchy of this class:

```
Object
    Control
        WebControl
            Label
                BaseValidator
                    CustomValidator
```

You can find the notable public properties of **CustomValidator** objects in Table 18.9 and their notable events in Table 18.10. Note that as with other Web server controls, I am not listing the notable properties, methods, and events this class

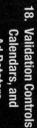

Table 18.9   Noteworthy public properties of CustomValidator objects.

Property	Means
ClientValidationFunction	Gets/sets the name of the script function you've placed in the Web page for validation.

Table 18.10   Noteworthy public events of CustomValidator objects.

Event	Means
ServerValidate	Occurs when validation takes place on the server.

inherits from the **Control** and **WebControl** classes—you can find them in Chapter 15, Tables 15.1 to 15.5. This class inherits the **BaseValidator** class, which you can find in Tables 18.2 and 18.3, as well as the **Label** class; the **Label** class has only one non-inherited public member—the **Text** property, which holds the text the label displays.

Creating Custom Validators

As discussed in the In Depth section of this chapter, to use a custom validator, you set the **ClientValidationFunction** property to the name of a script function, such as a JavaScript or VBScript function (VBScript is a Microsoft scripting language that supports a tiny subset of Visual Basic), both of which are supported in the Internet Explorer. This function will be passed two arguments, **source**, giving the source control to validate, and **arguments**, which holds the data to validate as **arguments.Value**. If you validate the data, you set **arguments.IsValid** to **True**, and to **False** otherwise. And as with other validation controls, you set the **ControlToValidate** property to set the control whose data you want to validate, and place the error message in the **ErrorMessage** property.

There's a custom validator in the ValidationControls example on the CD-ROM, next to the fifth text box from the top. This example lets the users apply for college, and the custom validator checks the amount of tuition they're willing to pay. In this case, I've added this script, written in VBScript, to the ValidationControls example's WebForm1.aspx file:

```
<script language=vbscript>

    Sub Validate(source, arguments)
        If (arguments.Value > 20000) Then
            arguments.IsValid = True
        Else
            arguments.IsValid = False
```

```
      End If
    End Sub

</script>
```

TIP: *To see more on how to write scripts in Web pages, see references such as the Coriolis* HTML Black Book.

In this script, I've created a procedure named **Validate**, where I'm just checking to make sure that the value the user has entered is greater than 20,000. To connect that to the custom validator in the ValidationControls example, you set the validator's **ClientValidationFunction** property to **Validate**. Because the value the user has entered is less than 20,000 in Figure 18.9, the custom validator is displaying its error message.

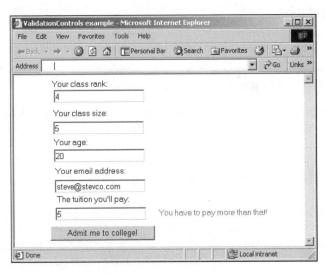

Figure 18.9   Using a custom validator.

Using the **ValidationSummary** Class

As discussed in the In Depth section of this chapter, you can use validation summary controls to display a summary of all validation errors on a Web page, in a message box, or both. This control is supported by the **ValidationSummary** class; here is the inheritance hierarchy of this class:

```
Object
   Control
      WebControl
         ValidationSummary
```

Table 18.11   Noteworthy public properties of ValidationSummary objects.

Property	Means
DisplayMode	Gets/sets the summary's display mode.
EnableClientScript	Gets/sets whether validation should be attempted in the browser.
HeaderText	Gets/sets the text displayed at the top of the summary.
ShowMessageBox	Gets/sets whether a message box displays the validation summary.
ShowSummary	Gets/sets whether the summary is displayed in the Web page.

You can find the notable public properties of **ValidationSummary** objects in Table 18.11. (This class has no non-inherited methods or events.) Note that as with other Web server controls, I am not listing the notable properties, methods, and events this class inherits from the **Control** and **WebControl** classes—you can find them in Chapter 15, Tables 15.1 to 15.5.

Creating a Validation Summary

As discussed in the In Depth section of this chapter, validation summaries display a summary of the errors that have occurred in a Web page. This summary can be displayed as a list, as a bulleted list, or as a single paragraph, depending on the **DisplayMode** property. You also can specify if the summary should be displayed in the Web page and in a message box with the **ShowSummary** and **ShowMessage Box** properties, respectively.

There's a validation summary control in the ValidationControls example on the CD-ROM. When errors occur in other validation controls in the Web page, the validation summary control displays all the errors that have occurred, as you see in Figure 18.10. As you can see, a summary like this is great to bring all the errors in the page into one place.

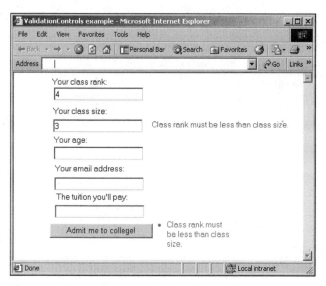

Figure 18.10   Using a validation summary.

Using the **Calendar** Class

You use the **Calendar** class to display a single-month calendar that allows the user to select dates and move to the next or previous month. Here is the inheritance diagram for this class:

```
Object
    Control
        WebControl
            Calendar
```

You can find the notable public properties of **Calendar** objects in Table 18.12, and their notable public events in Table 18.13. (This class has no non-inherited methods.) Note that as with other Web server controls, I am not listing the notable properties, methods, and events this class inherits from the **Control** and **WebControl** classes—you can find them in Chapter 15, Tables 15.1 to 15.5.

Table 18.12   Noteworthy public properties of Calendar objects.

Property	Means
CellPadding	Gets/sets the space used for cell padding in the calendar.
CellSpacing	Gets/sets the space between cells in the calendar.
DayHeaderStyle	Gets the style for the day of the week.

(continued)

Table 18.12   Noteworthy public properties of Calendar objects (continued).

Property	Means
DayNameFormat	Gets/sets the day of the week's name format.
DayStyle	Gets the style for days.
FirstDayOfWeek	Gets/sets the day of the week displayed in the first column.
NextMonthText	Gets/sets the text labeling the next month navigation control.
NextPrevFormat	Gets/sets the format of both the next and previous month navigation controls.
NextPrevStyle	Gets/sets the style for the next and previous month navigation controls.
OtherMonthDayStyle	Gets the style for the days not in the displayed month.
PrevMonthText	Gets/sets the text for the previous month navigation control.
SelectedDate	Gets/sets the selected date.
SelectedDates	Gets a collection of DateTime objects for the selected dates.
SelectedDayStyle	Gets the style for selected dates.
SelectionMode	Gets/sets the date selection mode, determining if you can select a day, a week, or a month.
SelectMonthText	Gets/sets the text for the month selection element.
SelectorStyle	Gets the style for the week and month selector.
SelectWeekText	Gets/sets the text for week selection elements.
ShowDayHeader	Gets/sets whether the day of the week header is shown.
ShowGridLines	Gets/sets whether grid lines should appear between days.
ShowNextPrevMonth	Gets/sets whether to display next and previous month navigation controls.
ShowTitle	Gets/sets if the title should be displayed.
TitleFormat	Gets/sets the format for the title.
TitleStyle	Gets the style of the title.
TodayDayStyle	Gets the style for today's date.
TodaysDate	Gets/sets today's date.
VisibleDate	Gets/sets a date, making sure it's visible.
WeekendDayStyle	Gets the style for weekend dates.

Table 18.13   Noteworthy public events of Calendar objects.

Event	Means
DayRender	Occurs when each day is displayed.
SelectionChanged	Occurs when the user selects a date.
VisibleMonthChanged	Occurs when the user moves to a different month from the one currently displayed.

Creating Calendars

You can see a calendar control in the Calendars example on the CD-ROM, which is also shown in Figure 18.3. By clicking the arrow buttons at top left and right in the calendar control, you can select a month, and by double-clicking the control, you can select a day, causing a **SelectionChanged** event. To determine the selected date, you can use the **SelectedDate** property, as I do in the Calendars example:

```
Private Sub Calendar1_SelectionChanged(ByVal sender As _
    System.Object, ByVal e As System.EventArgs) Handles _
    Calendar1.SelectionChanged
    TextBox1.Text = "You selected " & Calendar1.SelectedDate
End Sub
```

To find more details on the properties and events of calendar Web server controls, see the In Depth section of this chapter. Here's the code for WebForm1.aspx for the Calendars example:

```
<%@ Page Language="vb" AutoEventWireup="false"
Codebehind="WebForm1.aspx.vb" Inherits="Calendars.WebForm1"%>
<!DOCTYPE HTML PUBLIC "-//W3C//DTD HTML 4.0 Transitional//EN">
<HTML>
  <HEAD>
    <title>Calendars example</title>
    <meta name="GENERATOR" content="Microsoft Visual Studio.NET 7.0">
    <meta name="CODE_LANGUAGE" content="Visual Basic 7.0">
    <meta name=vs_defaultClientScript content="JavaScript">
    <meta name=vs_targetSchema
        content="http://schemas.microsoft.com/intellisense/ie5">
  </HEAD>
  <body MS_POSITIONING="GridLayout">

    <form id="Form1" method="post" runat="server">
<asp:Calendar id=Calendar1 style="Z-INDEX: 101; LEFT: 114px;
POSITION: absolute; TOP: 43px" runat="server"></asp:Calendar>
<asp:TextBox id=TextBox1 style="Z-INDEX: 102; LEFT: 160px;
POSITION: absolute; TOP: 245px" runat="server"></asp:TextBox>
    </form>
  </body>
</HTML>
```

And here's the code for the WebForm1.aspx.vb file in this example:

```
Public Class WebForm1
    Inherits System.Web.UI.Page
    Protected WithEvents TextBox1 As System.Web.UI.WebControls.TextBox
    Protected WithEvents Calendar1 As _
        System.Web.UI.WebControls.Calendar

#Region " Web Form Designer Generated Code "

    'This call is required by the Web Form Designer.
    <System.Diagnostics.DebuggerStepThrough()> _
        Private Sub InitializeComponent()

    End Sub

    Private Sub Page_Init(ByVal sender As System.Object, _
        ByVal e As System.EventArgs) Handles MyBase.Init
        'CODEGEN: This method call is required by the Web Form Designer
        'Do not modify it using the code editor.
        InitializeComponent()
    End Sub

#End Region

    Private Sub Page_Load(ByVal sender As System.Object, _
        ByVal e As System.EventArgs) Handles MyBase.Load
        'Put user code to initialize the page here
    End Sub

    Private Sub Calendar1_SelectionChanged(ByVal sender As _
        System.Object, ByVal e As System.EventArgs) Handles _
        Calendar1.SelectionChanged
        TextBox1.Text = "You selected " & Calendar1.SelectedDate
    End Sub
End Class
```

Using the **AdRotator** Class

You use the ad rotator control to display an advertisement banner in a Web page. This control is supported with the **AdRotator** class, and here is the inheritance hierarchy of that class:

```
Object
   Control
      WebControl
         AdRotator
```

You can find the notable public properties of **AdRotator** objects in Table 18.14 and their events in Table 18.15. (This class has no non-inherited methods.) Note that as with other Web server controls, I am not listing the notable properties, methods, and events this class inherits from the **Control** and **WebControl** classes—you can find them in Chapter 15, Tables 15.1 to 15.5.

Table 18.14   Noteworthy public properties of **AdRotator** objects.

Property	Means
AdvertisementFile	Gets/sets the XML file with information on the ads and ad banners.
KeywordFilter	Gets/sets a keyword to filter for types of ads.
Target	Gets/sets the name of the browser window or frame that displays linked-to Web pages when a banner is clicked.

Table 18.15   Noteworthy public events of **AdRotator** objects.

Event	Means
AdCreated	Occurs before the Web page is displayed, allowing you to customize ad displays.

Creating Ad Rotators

Ad rotators let you display banner ads in your applications; you can see an ad rotator in Figure 18.4 displaying a non-subtle ad to buy this book. When you click the button in this example, the page reloads and displays various ads. Using an ad rotator is fairly easy—you just add this control to your Web page (it docks to the top of the page by default), and set up the banners you want to show. You can set those ads up in the **AdCreated** event, or, more commonly, with an XML file.

Although this file is written in XML, you don't need any special knowledge to adapt it for yourself—adapting it or adding other ads is straightforward enough. Here's what the XML file, ads.xml, for the AdRotators example on the CD-ROM looks like. You can see that for each ad, I'm specifying the URL of the ad banner, the URL to navigate to if the user clicks the ad, the alternate text to display if the ad banner isn't available (this text is also used as a tool tip, as you see in Figure 18.4), the number of impressions (the number of times the ad should be shown), and a keyword to use in selecting ads (you can use the **KeyWordFilter** property to filter ads for target audiences):

```
<Advertisements>
    <Ad>
        <ImageUrl>banner1.jpg</ImageUrl>
        <NavigateUrl>http://www.coriolis.com</NavigateUrl>
        <AlternateText>Coriolis VB.NET Black Book: Buy it now!
        </AlternateText>
        <Impressions>80</Impressions>
        <Keyword>VB.NET</Keyword>
    </Ad>

    <Ad>
        <ImageUrl>banner2.jpg</ImageUrl>
        <NavigateUrl>http://www.coriolis.com</NavigateUrl>
        <AlternateText>Coriolis Perl Black Book: Buy it now!
        </AlternateText>
        <Impressions>80</Impressions>
        <Keyword>Perl</Keyword>
    </Ad>

    <Ad>
        <ImageUrl>banner3.jpg</ImageUrl>
        <NavigateUrl>http://www.coriolis.com</NavigateUrl>
        <AlternateText>Coriolis HTML Black Book: Buy it now!
        </AlternateText>
        <Impressions>80</Impressions>
        <Keyword>HTML</Keyword>
    </Ad>
</Advertisements>
```

I place ads.xml in the folder for this example in the server's folder for the AdRotator example, then point to that XML file with the **AdvertisementFile** property of the ad rotator (which I simply set to "ads.xml", because that file is in the AdRotator example's main directory). I also load the banner ads that I'll use for this example, banner1.jpg, banner2.jpg, and banner3.jpg, to the same directory. The result appears in Figure 18.4, where you can see the ad rotator doing its work.

Here is WebForms1.aspx for this project:

```
<%@ Page Language="vb" AutoEventWireup="false" _
    Codebehind="WebForm1.aspx.vb" Inherits="AdRotators.WebForm1"%>
<!DOCTYPE HTML PUBLIC "-//W3C//DTD HTML 4.0 Transitional//EN">
<HTML>
  <HEAD>
    <title>AdRotators Example</title>
    <meta name="GENERATOR" content="Microsoft Visual Studio.NET 7.0">
    <meta name="CODE_LANGUAGE" content="Visual Basic 7.0">
    <meta name=vs_defaultClientScript content="JavaScript">
    <meta name=vs_targetSchema
        content="http://schemas.microsoft.com/intellisense/ie5">
  </HEAD>
  <body MS_POSITIONING="GridLayout">

    <form id="Form1" method="post" runat="server">
<asp:AdRotator id=AdRotator1 style="Z-INDEX: 101; LEFT: 8px;
POSITION: absolute; TOP: 8px" runat="server" Width="468px"
Height="60px" AdvertisementFile="ads.xml"></asp:AdRotator>
<asp:Button id=Button1 style="Z-INDEX: 103; LEFT: 186px; POSITION:
absolute; TOP: 235px" runat="server" Text="Reload page"></asp:Button>
<asp:Label id=Label1 style="Z-INDEX: 102; LEFT: 27px; POSITION:
absolute; TOP: 99px" runat="server" Width="446px" Height="57px"
Font-Italic="True" Font-Size="XX-Large">Here's the page content...
</asp:Label>

    </form>

  </body>
</HTML>
```

And here is WebForm1.aspx.vb:

```
Public Class WebForm1
    Inherits System.Web.UI.Page
    Protected WithEvents Label1 As System.Web.UI.WebControls.Label
    Protected WithEvents Button1 As System.Web.UI.WebControls.Button
    Protected WithEvents AdRotator1 As _
        System.Web.UI.WebControls.AdRotator

#Region " Web Form Designer Generated Code "

    'This call is required by the Web Form Designer.
    <System.Diagnostics.DebuggerStepThrough()> _
        Private Sub InitializeComponent()
```

```vbnet
        End Sub

        Private Sub Page_Init(ByVal sender As System.Object, _
            ByVal e As System.EventArgs) Handles MyBase.Init
            'CODEGEN: This method call is required by the Web Form Designer
            'Do not modify it using the code editor.
            InitializeComponent()
        End Sub

#End Region

        Private Sub Page_Load(ByVal sender As System.Object, _
            ByVal e As System.EventArgs) Handles MyBase.Load
            'Put user code to initialize the page here
        End Sub
    End Class
```

Chapter 19

Web Forms: HTML Controls

In Depth

In addition to the Web server controls we've been working with in the previous chapters, Visual Basic supports straight HTML controls, which are derived directly from HTML browser controls. These controls are less like standard Visual Basic controls, of course, and you have to know some HTML to work with them. (For example, HTML text field controls don't have a **Text** property as text boxes do in Visual Basic; they use a **value** attribute instead.) In this chapter, we'll be working with these HTML controls directly. They're less like the Web server controls that we're used to, and more like the HTML controls that you work with in script in Web pages. But you can work with these controls in Visual Basic as well.

Client and Server HTML Controls

There are two ways to work with these controls—in the client browser (HTML client controls) and in the server (HTML server controls). In the client, you must use a scripting language, such as JavaScript. You can make these controls run at the server and so handle them with Visual Basic code, but they only support very limited events that can be handled on the server—typically, just an event named **ServerClick** or **ServerChange** (to differentiate them from the **Click** or **Change** events that are handled in the browser).

You can find the HTML controls available in the Visual Basic toolbox when you click the HTML tab (as opposed to the Web Forms tab we've been using up to now). It's important to start off by noting that, although these controls are client HTML controls run in the browser by default, you can turn *any* HTML control into an HTML server control—whose events are handled back at the server—by right-clicking them in a Web page and selecting the Run As Server Control menu item.

I'll take a look at working with these controls in the client, using JavaScript, to show how it's done, but our topic is Visual Basic, of course, so for the most part, we'll work with these controls in Visual Basic on the server. (When you specify that these controls should be handled back on the server as HTML server controls, they become available not only in the Web page's .aspx file, but also in the .aspx.vb file you can work with in a code designer.) If you want an in-depth treatment of working with HTML controls and JavaScript, take a look at the Coriolis *HTML Black Book*, which has three full chapters on the topic and teaches JavaScript along the way, not assuming any prior JavaScript knowledge.

When you add an HTML control to a Web form, by default, it's an HTML client control and only available for scripting in the Web page itself. To make it available to script code in the browser, you must give it an ID value, which you do with the **(id)** property in the Properties window; you can then refer to the control by ID in your script code.

When you turn the control into an HTML server control, on the other hand, Visual Basic gives it a default name, as it does with other controls you can access in Visual Basic code—although those names might be different than what you might expect. For example, the first text field gets the name **Text1** (not **TextBox1**), the first radio button the name **Radio1** (not **RadioButton1**), and so on. You can use this name to refer to the control in your Visual Basic code on the server; the control will have a **Name** property that holds this name. In other words, you use a control's ID in client code, and its **Name** in server-side code; for HTML server controls, these values are the same by default.

Some, but certainly not all, attributes of the HTML controls we'll work with become properties that you also can work with in Visual Basic code back on the server. You can, however, access all the HTML attributes of these controls using their **Attributes** property, which holds a collection of their HTML attributes, as we'll look at in this chapter. Keep in mind that not all attributes will be handled by all browsers. To see which attributes are handled in which browser, see the htmlref.html document on the CD-ROM. We'll see that these controls support fewer properties than the Web server controls we've been working with already, and which were specifically designed for Visual Basic .NET; the controls in this chapter are derived from the **HtmlControl** class, not the **WebControl** class.

Here's another thing to realize—these controls have no **AutoPostBack** property, which means that events have to wait to be processed until the user clicks a standard button or a Submit button, just as in other, standard Web pages you see on the Internet. So don't forget to add a Submit button to the pages you construct with these controls. You can create a Submit button with the Submit button tool in the toolbox—no additional code needed—so when the button is clicked, it'll send the page back to the server for processing. In addition, all values are stored as strings in HTML documents, so there's no data type safety here, and, because everything is available in the browser, there's a lot less security. On the other hand, using HTML controls is good when you want to handle a control both on the server and in the client, because you can write code for the same control in both locations.

You can see a number of the HTML server controls we'll discuss in this chapter in the HTMLControls example on the CD-ROM, which you see in Figure 19.1.

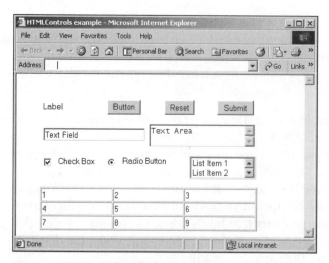

Figure 19.1   The HTMLControls example.

HTML Server Control Classes

When you make an HTML control into a server control, Visual Basic uses the HTML Server Control classes to support that control in code. These classes include such classes as **HtmlTextArea** for HTML **<textarea>** controls, **HtmlInputButton** for HTML buttons created with **<input type="button">** elements, **HtmlInputText** for HTML text fields created with **<input type="text">** elements, and so on. Working with HTML server controls in Visual Basic really means working with objects of these support classes, which you can handle directly in Visual Basic code.

When you work with an HTML server control in the Visual Basic IDE, you'll see that its available properties are in lower case, indicating that these properties correspond directly to HTML attributes, and will appear in the .aspx page as you set them. Not all attributes have corresponding properties in the HTML server control classes, but many do, and they're supported by properties of these classes with the usual Visual Basic capitalization. For example, you can set the caption of an HTML server button at design time using the **value** property, which corresponds to the corresponding HTML **<input>** element's **value** attribute. But at run time, back on the server, this attribute is supported by the **HtmlInputButton** class's **Value** property. Because we're working with an object of the **HtmlInputButton** class on the server, the capitalization of property names in server code adheres to the Visual Basic standard, so don't get confused if you see references to both a **value** property (used in an element at design time or in client-side code) and a **Value** property (used in the element's corresponding object in server-side code).

It's important to realize that there is not a complete one-to-one correspondence with the HTML Server Control classes and the actual HTML controls you see in the HTML toolbox. For example, the **HtmlInputButton** class is used not just for buttons, but also for reset buttons (which sets the value in HTML controls back to their default values), as well as submit buttons. These buttons are all created using an HTML **<input>** element, and they differ only in the setting of the type HTML attribute in that element (a standard button uses **<input type="button">**, a reset button uses **<input type="reset">,** and a submit button uses **<input type="submit">**).

You can find the HTML server control classes in Table 19.1.

TIP: *Note that there's an* **HtmlForm** *class in Table 19.1. HTML programmers know that HTML controls must be in an HTML form to be sent back to the server. However, when creating a Web form in the Visual Basic IDE, you don't have to create the HTML form explicitly—Visual Basic does that as soon as you add input controls to the form.*

I'll look at these various classes in more detail and how to work with them in code in this chapter. You can find the notable properties, methods, and events of these classes in the Immediate Solutions section of this chapter. As mentioned, the HTML classes you see in Table 19.1 are not based on the **WebControl** class we've seen in previous chapters, but on the **HtmlControl** class. I'll start with that.

Table 19.1   HTML server control classes.

Control	Does this
HtmlForm	Creates an HTML form.
HtmlInputText	Creates an HTML text field. (You also can use this control to create password fields).
HtmlTextArea	Creates an HTML text area (two-dimensional text field).
HtmlAnchor	Creates an **<a>** element for navigation.
HtmlButton	Creates an HTML button using the **<button>** element.
HtmlInputButton	Creates an HTML button using the **<input>** element.
HtmlInputImage	Creates an HTML button that displays images.
HtmlSelect	Creates an HTML select control.
HtmlImage	Creates an HTML **<img>** element.
HtmlInputHidden	Creates an HTML hidden control.
HtmlInputCheckbox	Creates an HTML checkbox.
HtmlInputRadioButton	Creates an HTML radio button.
HtmlTable	Creates an HTML table.
HtmlTableRow	Creates an HTML row in a table.
HtmlTableCell	Creates an HTML cell in a table.
HtmlInputFile	Creates an HTML file upload control.
HtmlGenericControl	Creates a basic control for an HTML element.

The HtmlControl Class

The **HtmlControl** class is the basis for all HTML server controls in Visual Basic. You don't use it directly—instead, you use classes derived from it, or, more usually, classes derived from them. Here are the classes derived from the **HtmlControl** class:

```
Object
    Control
        HtmlControl
            HtmlContainerControl
            HtmlImage
            HtmlInputControl
```

The real purpose of the **HtmlControl** class is to provide a set of properties shared by all HTML server controls:

- **Attributes**—Holds all attribute name and value pairs for the server control's HTML element.

- **Disabled**—Gets/sets whether the **disabled** attribute is included when an HTML control is displayed in the browser.

- **Style**—Gets all cascading style sheet (CSS) properties for the specified HTML server control.

- **TagName**—Gets the element name that contains the **runat=server** attribute.

The classes derived from **HtmlControl**—in particular the **HtmlContainerControl** and **HtmlInputControl** classes—form the basis of the HTML server control classes.

The HtmlContainerControl Class

The **HtmlContainerControl** class defines the methods, properties, and events available to all HTML server controls that can act as a container (in HTML terms, these elements all require a closing tag). This class is the base class for the **HtmlTableCell**, **HtmlTable**, **HtmlTableRow**, **HtmlButton**, **HtmlForm**, **HtmlAnchor**, **HtmlGenericControl**, **HtmlSelect**, and **HtmlTextArea** classes, all of which share these properties:

- **InnerHtml**—Gets/sets the content between the opening and closing tags of the HTML control.

- **InnerText**—Gets/sets all text between the opening and closing tags of the specified HTML control. (Note that unlike the **InnerHtml** property, **InnerText** supports automatic HTML encoding and decoding.)

The HtmlInputControl Class

The **HtmlInputControl** class serves as the abstract base class that defines the methods, properties, and events common to all HTML input controls, such as the

<input type="text">, **<input type="submit">**, and other elements that the user can enter data into. The classes derived from the **HtmlInputControl** class are the **HtmlInputText**, **HtmlInputButton**, **HtmlInputCheckBox**, **HtmlInputImage**, **HtmlInputHidden**, **HtmlInputFile**, and **HtmlInputRadioButton** classes, all of which share the following properties:

- **Name**—Gets/sets a unique name for the input control.
- **Value**—Gets/sets the contents of an input control.
- **Type**—Gets the type of an input control.

The HtmlForm Class

You use the **HtmlForm** class if you want to create an HTML form. You don't need to create a form yourself to work with the HTML controls, because as soon as you add an input control to a form, Visual Basic creates a form for you. However, you can create additional forms using this class if you want to; all server controls that post back to the server must be placed between the opening and closing tags of an HTML form.

The HtmlInputText Class

You use the **HtmlInputText** class to support HTML text fields. You also can use this class to create password fields. Text fields are single-line text boxes that allow the user to enter text or a password. Use the **MaxLength** property to specify the maximum number of characters that can be entered in the text box. The **Size** property allows you to specify the width of the text box. You can see a text field in the HTMLControls example on the CD-ROM and in Figure 19.1.

To use a multiline text box, use the **HtmlTextArea** class instead, coming up next.

The HtmlTextArea Class

You use the **HtmlTextArea** control to create an HTML text area (a two-dimensional text field). This is the control you use to accept multiline input in a Web page. You can see a text area in the HTMLControls example on the CD-ROM, as shown in Figure 19.1.

The HtmlAnchor Class

You use the **HtmlAnchor** class to creates an anchor, **<a>**, element for navigation. There are two ways to use the **HtmlAnchor** class—the first is for navigation: using the **HRef** property to define the location of the page to link to. The second is for postback events: using the **ServerClick** event to programmatically handle the case when the user clicks a link.

The HtmlButton Class

The **HtmlButton** class creates an HTML button using the HTML **<button>** element, which displays buttons that also can display images. Note that the **<button>** element is defined in the HTML 4.0 specification and is supported only in relatively recent browsers. To create image buttons for use in other browsers, you can use the **HtmlInputImage** class.

The HtmlInputButton Class

The **HtmlInputButton** class creates an HTML button using an HTML **<input>** element. This control is similar to **<button>** elements, except it's available in all browsers. You can set the caption of an input button with its **value** property and can handle clicks with code on the server using the **ServerClick** event.

The HtmlInputImage Class

The **HtmlInputImage** class creates an HTML button that displays images. You can handle clicks on the image by providing an event handler for the **ServerClick** event.

The coordinates that indicate where the user clicked an input image control can be found by using the **ImageClickEventArgs.X** and **ImageClickEventArgs.Y** properties of the **ImageClickEventArgs** object that is passed as a parameter to the control's event handler.

The HtmlSelect Class

The **HtmlSelect** class creates an HTML select control, which can display as either a list box (use the ListBox tool in the toolbox) or a drop-down list box (use the DropDown tool in the toolbox).

You can see a list box in the HTMLControls example in Figure 19.1. The items in a select control are stored in **<option>** elements inside the **<select>** element; when you add a list box or drop-down list box to a Web form using HTML server controls, Visual Basic adds a default, empty **<option>** element to the **<select>** element:

```
<SELECT style="Z-INDEX: 111; LEFT: 301px; WIDTH: 114px; POSITION: absolute;
TOP: 136px; HEIGHT: 38px" size=2>
<OPTION></OPTION>
</SELECT>
```

To add the items you want to display, you can edit the HTML directly:

```
<SELECT style="Z-INDEX: 111; LEFT: 301px; WIDTH: 114px; POSITION: absolute;
TOP: 136px; HEIGHT: 38px" size=2>
<OPTION>List Item 1</OPTION>
```

```
<OPTION>List Item 2</OPTION>
<OPTION>List Item 3</OPTION>
</SELECT>
```

The HtmlImage Class

This class creates an HTML **<img>** element, used to display images. Using the properties of this class, you change the image displayed and the image size, as well as the alignment of the image with respect to other HTML elements.

The HtmlInputHidden Class

This class creates an HTML hidden control. You can use an HTML hidden control to hold text that the user doesn't see; this text is sent when the Web page is posted back to the server. (As you know, the Web Forms page framework uses HTML hidden controls to automatically load and persist the view state of server controls on a page by default.)

The HtmlInputCheckbox Class

This class creates an HTML checkbox. As with other checkboxes, you use checkboxes in HTML to let the user toggle a setting on or off.

You can see an HTML checkbox in the HTMLControls example on the CD-ROM, as shown in Figure 19.1. This checkbox appears checked when it first appears, because I've set its checked property to **True**. When you make this control into a server control, you can handle the **ServerChange** event, which lets you examine the **Checked** property to see if the checkbox is selected or not.

The HtmlInputRadioButton Class

This class creates an HTML radio button. You can group radio button controls together by specifying a common value for the **Name** property of each radio button control that you want to include in the group. When you group radio buttons together, only one radio button in the group can be selected at a time.

You can see an HTML radio button in the HTMLControls example on the CD-ROM, as shown in Figure 19.1. When you make this control into a server control, you can handle the **ServerChange** event, which lets you examine the **Checked** property to see if the radio button is selected or not.

The HtmlTable Class

You use this class to create an HTML table. You can dynamically change the appearance of the **<table>** element by setting the **BgColor**, **Border**, **BorderColor**, **Height**, and **Width** properties in code. You also can control how the content of a cell is displayed by setting the **Align**, **CellPadding**, and **CellSpacing** properties. You can see an **HtmlTable** control in Figure 19.1 and in the HTMLControls example on the CD-ROM.

The rows of the **HtmlTable** control are stored in the **Rows** collection. This allows you to access the individual rows of the table in code.

---

*TIP: Although HTML 4.0 supports a complex table model, this model is not supported in Visual Basic yet. That is, you cannot have a **HtmlTable** control that nests **<caption>**, **<col>**, **<colgroup>**, **<tbody>**, **<thead>**, or **<tfoot>** elements.*

The HtmlTableRow Class

This class creates an HTML row in a table. It's designed to give you access on the server to individual HTML **<tr>** elements within an **HtmlTable** control.

Usually, there is no need to use this class unless you want control over a table in code. When you add an HTML table control to a Web page, you can edit the values in the rows and cells directly, placing text in the cells, as you like.

The HtmlTableCell Class

This class creates an HTML cell in a table. You use the **HtmlTableCell** class to access individual HTML **<td>** and **<th>** elements in server code. (The **<td>** element represents a data cell in a table and the **<th>** element represents a table heading cell.)

As with the **HtmlTableRow** class, usually, there is no need to use this class yourself, unless you want control over a table in code. When you add an HTML table control to a Web page, you can edit the values in the rows and cells directly, placing text in the cells, as you like.

The HtmlInputFile Class

This class creates an HTML file upload control, which you can use to handle uploading binary or text files from a browser client to the server. This control includes a text box and a browse button to let the user browse for files to upload.

---

*TIP: If you're going to use this class, you should realize that it will work only if the **Enctype** property of an **HtmlForm** is set to "multipart/form-data".*

The HtmlGenericControl Class

This class creates a basic control for an HTML element. You can use it to create an HTML server control not directly represented by a .NET Framework class, such as **<span>**, **<div>**, **<body>**, and **<font>**. This is the class Visual Basic uses to display labels, using **<div>** elements.

Now we've seen the classes Visual Basic uses with HTML controls. To make all this clearer, I'll take a look at two examples next, showing how to use these controls both as HTML client controls and as HTML server controls.

Working with HTML Client Controls

To see an example using HTML client controls with JavaScript, take a look at the JavaScript example on the CD-ROM, which you can see at work in Figure 19.2. When you click the button, the text "Welcome to client coding!" appears in the text field.

In this example, I click the HTML tab in the toolbox and add both a text field and an HTML input button to a Web form. I have to give both of these controls an ID value explicitly, which I do by setting their **(id)** property in the properties window to **Text1** and **Button1**. Now I can refer to these controls in client-side code.

The button is created with an **<input>** element, which looks like this:

```
<INPUT id=Button1 style="Z-INDEX: 101; LEFT: 125px; POSITION:
absolute; TOP: 85px" type=button value="Click me">
```

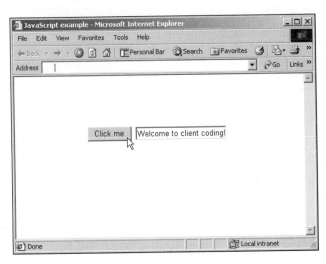

Figure 19.2   The JavaScript example.

To connect this to a JavaScript function I'll name **Button1_onclick**, I use the **language** and **onclick** HTML attributes of this button:

```
<INPUT id=Button1 style="Z-INDEX: 101; LEFT: 125px; POSITION:
absolute; TOP: 85px" type=button value="Click me"
language="javascript" onclick="return Button1_onclick()">
```

And I also add a **<script>** element to the Web page's header that defines the **Button1_onclick** function, which in turn displays the message:

```
<script language="javascript">
<!--


function Button1_onclick() {
    document.Form1.Text1.value = "Welcome to client coding!"
}


//-->
</script>
```

And that completes the example; when you run this code, you see the result in Figure 19.2, where the message appears in the text field when the user clicks the button, all using HTML client controls in the browser, no server roundtrip needed.

Here is the code for WebForm1.aspx for this example:

```
<%@ Page Language="vb" AutoEventWireup="false"
Codebehind="WebForm1.aspx.vb" Inherits="JavaScript.WebForm1"%>
<!DOCTYPE HTML PUBLIC "-//W3C//DTD HTML 4.0 Transitional//EN">
<HTML>
  <HEAD>
    <title>JavaScript example</title>
    <meta name="GENERATOR" content="Microsoft Visual Studio.NET 7.0">
    <meta name="CODE_LANGUAGE" content="Visual Basic 7.0">
    <meta name=vs_defaultClientScript content="JavaScript">
    <meta name=vs_targetSchema
        content="http://schemas.microsoft.com/intellisense/ie5">
  <script language=javascript>
<!--

function Button1_onclick() {
    document.Form1.Text1.value = "Welcome to client coding!"
}
```

```
//-->
</script>
</HEAD>
  <body MS_POSITIONING="GridLayout">

    <form id="Form1" method="post" runat="server">
<INPUT id=Button1 style="Z-INDEX: 101; LEFT: 125px; POSITION:
absolute; TOP: 85px" type=button value="Click me"
language=javascript onclick="return Button1_onclick()">
    
<INPUT
id=Text1
style="Z-INDEX: 102; LEFT: 208px; WIDTH: 155px; POSITION:
absolute; TOP: 86px; HEIGHT: 22px"
type=text>

    </form>

  </body>
</HTML>
```

That's the way you can work with HTML client controls—in the browser, with code that the browser understands, such as JavaScript.

Working with HTML Server Controls

To work with HTML controls using Visual Basic code, you must make them into HTML server controls and handle them on the server. When you make them into server controls, those controls become available in a project's .aspx.vb code for your use, although only limited events are available (and the user must click a standard button or submit button before the page gets sent back to the server for event handling).

You can see how this works in the HTMLControls example that appears in Figure 19.1—all the controls you see in that figure have been made into server controls, and Visual Basic gives them names automatically, like **Button1** and **Text1**. When you click the button (caption: Button) in this example, the text "You clicked the button" appears in the text field. To make this happen, you can use the **ServerClick** event, which is the default event for HTML server buttons; just double-click the button in the Web form designer to open the event handler for the **ServerClick** event:

```
Private Sub Button1_ServerClick(ByVal sender As System.Object, _
    ByVal e As System.EventArgs) Handles Button1.ServerClick

End Sub
```

And I add this code to assign the text "You clicked the button" to the text field's **Value** property (note that we're dealing with HTML controls here—with Web server controls, you'd use the **Text** property of this control, but because this control corresponds to an HTML text field, you must use the **Value** property):

```
Private Sub Button1_ServerClick(ByVal sender As System.Object, _
    ByVal e As System.EventArgs) Handles Button1.ServerClick
        Text1.Value = "You clicked the button."
End Sub
```

In the same way, you can handle the **ServerChange** event of the checkbox, **Checkbox1**, like this, making it display the message "You clicked the check box":

```
Private Sub Checkbox1_ServerChange(ByVal sender As System.Object, _
    ByVal e As System.EventArgs) Handles Checkbox1.ServerChange
        Text1.Value = "You clicked the check box."
End Sub
```

It's important to bear in mind that what we're working with here are really HTML server controls, not Visual Basic's Web server controls (which look a lot like any other Visual Basic controls). All these HTML controls have plenty of attributes that are not reflected in Visual Basic properties; however, you can reach those attributes with the **Attributes** property. This property returns a collection of the attributes in the control, which you can work with as you like. For example, in the HTMLControls example, I use the **onblur** attribute of the text field to display an alert box (such as a message box, but displayed by the browser) when the text field loses the focus (as when you've been typing in the text field and then click somewhere else). I do that by connecting JavaScript to the **onblur** attribute, like this:

```
Private Sub Page_Load(ByVal sender As System.Object, _
    ByVal e As System.EventArgs) Handles MyBase.Load
        Text1.Attributes("onblur") = _
            "javascript:alert('Text field lost the focus');"
End Sub
```

And in this way, you can gain access to all the attributes of HTML server controls, and even add client-side code to them. Here's what WebForm1.aspx looks like for this example:

```
<%@ Page Language="vb" AutoEventWireup="false"
Codebehind="WebForm1.aspx.vb" Inherits="HTMLControls.WebForm1"%>
<!DOCTYPE HTML PUBLIC "-//W3C//DTD HTML 4.0 Transitional//EN">
<HTML>
  <HEAD>
```

```
    <title>HTMLControls example</title>
<meta content="Microsoft Visual Studio.NET 7.0" name=GENERATOR>
<meta content="Visual Basic 7.0" name=CODE_LANGUAGE>
<meta content=JavaScript name=vs_defaultClientScript>
<meta content=http://schemas.microsoft.com/intellisense/ie5
    name=vs_targetSchema>
  </HEAD>
<body MS_POSITIONING="GridLayout">
<form id=Form1 method=post
runat="server">
<DIV
style="DISPLAY: inline; Z-INDEX: 102; LEFT: 46px; WIDTH: 70px;
POSITION: absolute; TOP: 46px; HEIGHT: 15px"
ms_positioning="FlowLayout" id=DIV1 runat="server">Label</DIV>
<DIV
style="DISPLAY: inline; Z-INDEX: 113; LEFT: 72px; WIDTH: 70px;
BORDER-TOP-STYLE: none; BORDER-RIGHT-STYLE: none; BORDER-LEFT-STYLE:
none; POSITION: absolute; TOP: 137px; HEIGHT: 15px;
BORDER-BOTTOM-STYLE: none" ms_positioning="FlowLayout">
Check Box</DIV><SELECT style="Z-INDEX: 111; LEFT: 301px; WIDTH:
114px; POSITION: absolute; TOP: 136px; HEIGHT: 38px"
size=2> <OPTION>List Item 1</OPTION><OPTION>List Item 2</OPTION>
<OPTION>List Item 3</OPTION></SELECT>
<TABLE
style="Z-INDEX: 110; LEFT: 41px; WIDTH: 376px; POSITION: absolute;
TOP: 188px; HEIGHT: 72px"
cellSpacing=1 cellPadding=1 width=376 border=1>
  <TR>
    <TD id=TD1 runat="server">1</TD>
    <TD>2</TD>
    <TD>3</TD></TR>
  <TR>
    <TD>4</TD>
    <TD>5</TD>
    <TD>6</TD></TR>
  <TR>
    <TD>7</TD>
    <TD>8</TD>
    <TD>9</TD></TR></TABLE>
<INPUT
style="Z-INDEX: 109; LEFT: 154px; WIDTH: 20px; POSITION: absolute;
TOP: 137px; HEIGHT: 20px" type=radio id=Radio1 title="" CHECKED
value=Radio1 name="" runat="server">
<INPUT style="Z-INDEX: 108; LEFT: 44px; POSITION: absolute; TOP:
137px" type=checkbox id=Checkbox1 title="Check Box" name=Checkbox1
```

```
runat="server" CHECKED>
<TEXTAREA style="Z-INDEX: 107; LEFT: 231px; WIDTH: 183px;
POSITION: absolute; TOP: 83px; HEIGHT: 38px" rows=2 cols=20
id=TEXTAREA1 name=TEXTAREA1 runat="server">
Text Area</TEXTAREA>
<INPUT
style="Z-INDEX: 106; LEFT: 47px; WIDTH: 155px; POSITION: absolute;
TOP: 90px; HEIGHT: 22px" type=text value="Text Field" id=Text1
name=Text1 runat="server">
<INPUT style="Z-INDEX: 105; LEFT: 348px; WIDTH: 63px; POSITION:
absolute; TOP: 43px; HEIGHT: 24px" type=submit value=Submit
id=Submit1 name=Submit1 runat="server">
<INPUT style="Z-INDEX: 104; LEFT: 257px; WIDTH: 52px; POSITION:
absolute; TOP: 43px; HEIGHT: 24px" type=reset value=Reset id=Reset1
name=Reset1 runat="server">       
<INPUT style="Z-INDEX: 103; LEFT: 158px; POSITION: absolute; TOP: 43px"
type=button value=Button id=Button1 name=Button1 runat="server"> 

<DIV
style="DISPLAY: inline; Z-INDEX: 114; LEFT: 183px; WIDTH: 94px;
POSITION: absolute; TOP: 136px; HEIGHT: 22px"
ms_positioning="FlowLayout">Radio Button</DIV> </form>
  </body>
</HTML>
```

And here's what WebForm1.aspx.vb looks like for this example:

```
Public Class WebForm1
    Inherits System.Web.UI.Page
    Protected WithEvents DIV1 As _
        System.Web.UI.HtmlControls.HtmlGenericControl
    Protected WithEvents Button1 As _
        System.Web.UI.HtmlControls.HtmlInputButton
    Protected WithEvents Reset1 As _
        System.Web.UI.HtmlControls.HtmlInputButton
    Protected WithEvents Submit1 As _
        System.Web.UI.HtmlControls.HtmlInputButton
    Protected WithEvents Text1 As System.Web.UI.HtmlControls.HtmlInputText
    Protected WithEvents TD1 As System.Web.UI.HtmlControls.HtmlTableCell
    Protected WithEvents Checkbox1 As _
        System.Web.UI.HtmlControls.HtmlInputCheckBox
    Protected WithEvents Radio1 As _
        System.Web.UI.HtmlControls.HtmlInputRadioButton
    Protected WithEvents TEXTAREA1 As _
        System.Web.UI.HtmlControls.HtmlTextArea
```

```
#Region " Web Form Designer Generated Code "

    'This call is required by the Web Form Designer.
    <System.Diagnostics.DebuggerStepThrough()> _
        Private Sub InitializeComponent()

    End Sub

    Private Sub Page_Init(ByVal sender As System.Object, _
        ByVal e As System.EventArgs) Handles MyBase.Init
        'CODEGEN: This method call is required by the Web Form Designer
        'Do not modify it using the code editor.
        InitializeComponent()
    End Sub

#End Region

    Private Sub Page_Load(ByVal sender As System.Object, _
        ByVal e As System.EventArgs) Handles MyBase.Load
        'Put user code to initialize the page here
        Text1.Attributes("onblur") = _
            "javascript:alert('Text field lost the focus');"
    End Sub

    Private Sub Button1_ServerClick(ByVal sender As System.Object, _
        ByVal e As System.EventArgs) Handles Button1.ServerClick
        Text1.Value = "You clicked the button."
    End Sub

    Private Sub Checkbox1_ServerChange(ByVal sender As System.Object, _
        ByVal e As System.EventArgs) Handles Checkbox1.ServerChange
        Text1.Value = "You clicked the check box."
    End Sub
End Class
```

And now it's time to turn to the specific details of the HTML server controls classes in the Immediate Solutions section.

Immediate Solutions

Using the **HtmlControl** Class

As discussed in the In Depth section of this chapter, the **HtmlControl** class defines the methods, properties, and events common to all HTML server controls in the Web Forms page framework. Here is the inheritance hierarchy for this class:

```
Object
    Control
        HtmlControl
```

You can find the noteworthy public properties of the **HtmlControl** class in Table 19.2.

Table 19.2   Noteworthy public properties of HTMLControl objects.

Property	Means
Attributes	Holds all attribute name and value pairs for the server control's HTML element.
Disabled	Gets/sets whether the disabled attribute is included when an HTML control is displayed in the browser.
Style	Gets all cascading style sheet (CSS) properties for the specified HTML server control.
TagName	Gets the element name that contains the **runat=server** attribute.

Using the **HtmlContainerControl** Class

As discussed in the In Depth section of this chapter, the **HtmlContainerControl** class defines the methods, properties, and events available to all HTML server controls that are containers. Here is the inheritance hierarchy of this class:

```
Object
    Control
        HtmlControl
            HtmlContainerControl
```

This class allows you to work with the contents between the opening and closing tags of HTML server controls that inherit from this class. You can find the notable public properties of **HtmlContainerControl** objects in Table 19.3. (This class has no non-inherited methods or events.) Note that as with other HTML server controls, I am not listing the notable properties, methods, and events this class inherits from the **Control** class—you can find them in Chapter 15, Tables 15.1 to 15.3. This class also inherits the **HtmlControl** class; you can find that class in Table 19.2.

Table 19.3   Noteworthy public properties of HtmlContainerControl objects.

Property	Means
InnerHtml	Gets/sets the content between the opening and closing tags of the HTML control.
InnerText	Gets/sets all text between the opening and closing tags of the specified HTML control. (Note that, unlike the **InnerHtml** property, **InnerText** supports automatic HTML encoding and decoding.)

Using the **HtmlInputControl** Class

This class forms the basis of input HTML server controls. Here is the inheritance hierarchy for this class:

```
Object
    Control
        HtmlControl
            HtmlInputControl
```

You can find the notable public properties of **HtmlInputControl** objects in Table 19.4. (This class has no non-inherited methods or events.) Note that as with other HTML server controls, I am not listing the notable properties, methods, and events this class inherits from the **Control** class—you can find them in Chapter 15, Tables 15.1 to 15.3. This class also inherits the **HtmlControl** class; you can find that class in Table 19.2.

Table 19.4   Noteworthy public properties of HtmlInputControl objects.

Property	Means
Name	Gets/sets a name for the input control.
Type	Gets the type of an input control.
Value	Gets/sets the contents of an input control.

Using the **HtmlForm** Class

You can use the **HtmlForm** class to get access to the HTML **<form>** element on the server. Here is the inheritance hierarchy of this class:

```
Object
    Control
        HtmlControl
            HtmlContainerControl
                HtmlForm
```

You can find the notable public properties of **HtmlForm** objects in Table 19.5. (This class has no non-inherited methods or events.) Note that as with other HTML server controls, I am not listing the notable properties, methods, and events this class inherits from the **Control** class—you can find them in Tables 15.1 to 15.3 in Chapter 15. This class also inherits the **HtmlControl** class—you can find that class in Table 19.2—and the **HtmlContainerControl** class, which you can see in Table 19.3.

Table 19.5   Noteworthy public properties of HtmlForm objects.

Property	Means
Enctype	Gets/sets the encoding type used when the browser posts the form to the server.
Method	Gets/sets how a browser posts form data to the server for processing.
Name	Gets the name for the form.
Target	Gets/sets the frame or window to display results in.

Using the **HtmlInputText** Class

This class creates an HTML text field, and you also can use this control to create password fields, using the **<input type= "text">** and **<input type= "password">** HTML elements. Here is the inheritance hierarchy of this class:

```
Object
    Control
        HtmlControl
            HtmlInputControl
                HtmlInputText
```

You can find the notable public properties of **HtmlInputText** objects in Table 19.6 and their notable events in Table 19.7. (This class has no non-inherited methods.) Note that as with other HTML server controls, I am not listing the notable properties, methods, and events this class inherits from the **Control** class; you can find them in Chapter 15, Tables 15.1 to 15.3. This class also inherits the **HtmlControl** class—you can find that class in Table 19.2—and the **HtmlInput Control** class, which you can find in Table 19.4.

Table 19.6   Noteworthy public properties of HtmlInputText objects.

Property	Means
MaxLength	Gets/sets the maximum number of characters the user can enter into the text field.
Size	Gets/sets the size (that is, the width) of the text field.
Value	Overridden. Gets/sets the contents of the text field.

Table 19.7   Noteworthy public events of HtmlInputText objects.

Event	Means
ServerChange	Occurs when the **Value** property changes on the server.

Using the **HtmlTextArea** Class

The **HtmlTextArea** class gives you access to the HTML **<textarea>** element on the server. Here is the inheritance hierarchy for this class:

```
Object
   Control
      HtmlControl
         HtmlContainerControl
            HtmlTextArea
```

You can find the notable public properties of **HtmlTextArea** objects in Table 19.8 and their notable events in Table 19.9. (This class has no non-inherited methods.) Note that as with other HTML server controls, I am not listing the notable properties, methods, and events this class inherits from the **Control** class; you can find them in Tables 15.1 to 15.3 in Chapter 15. This class also inherits the **HtmlControl** class—you can find that class in Table 19.2—and the **HtmlInput Control** class, which you can find in Table 19.4.

Table 19.8   Noteworthy public properties of HtmlTextArea objects.

Property	Means
Cols	Gets/sets the text area's width.
Rows	Gets/sets the text area's height of the text area.
Value	Gets/sets the text area's text content.

Table 19.9   Noteworthy public events of HtmlTextArea objects.

Event	Means
ServerChange	Occurs when the **Value** property changes on the server.

Using the **HtmlAnchor** Class

This class gives you access to the HTML **<a>** tag in server code. Here is the inheritance hierarchy of this class:

```
Object
    Control
        HtmlControl
            HtmlContainerControl
                HtmlAnchor
```

You can find the notable public properties of **HtmlAnchor** objects in Table 19.10 and their notable events in Table 19.11. (This class has no non-inherited methods.) Note that as with other HTML server controls, I am not listing the notable properties, methods, and events this class inherits from the **Control** class; you can find them in Tables 15.1 to 15.3. This class also inherits the **HtmlControl** class—you can find that class in Table 19.2—and the **HtmlContainerControl** class, which you can find in Table 19.3.

Table 19.10   Noteworthy public properties of HtmlAnchor objects.

Property	Means
HRef	Gets/sets the target of the link (set to an URL).
Name	Gets/sets the anchor's bookmark name.
Target	Gets/sets the link's target window or frame to display new information in.

Table 19.11   Noteworthy public events of HtmlAnchor objects.

Event	Means
ServerClick	Occurs when the user clicks an anchor control in the browser. This event is handled in the server.

Using the **HtmlButton** Class

This class gives you access to the HTML **<button>** tag in server code. Here is the inheritance hierarchy of this class:

```
Object
    Control
        HtmlControl
            HtmlContainerControl
                HtmlButton
```

You can find the notable public properties of **HtmlButton** objects in Table 19.12 and their notable events in Table 19.13. (This class has no non-inherited methods.) Note that as with other HTML server controls, I am not listing the notable properties, methods, and events this class inherits from the **Control** class; you can find them in Tables 15.1 to 15.3 in Chapter 15. This class also inherits the **HtmlControl** class—you can find that class in Table 19.2—and the **HtmlContainerControl** class, which you can find in Table 19.3.

Related solution:	Found on page:
Using the **Button** Class	674

Table 19.12 Noteworthy public properties of HtmlButton objects.

Property	Means
CausesValidation	Gets/sets whether validation is performed by this button.

Table 19.13 Noteworthy public events of HtmlButton objects.

Event	Means
ServerClick	Occurs when the user clicks a button. Handle this event on the server.

Using the **HtmlInputButton** Class

This class gives you access to HTML **<input type= "button">**, **<input type= "submit">**, and **<input type= "reset">** in server code. Here is the inheritance hierarchy for this class:

```
Object
    Control
        HtmlControl
```

```
HtmlInputControl
    HtmlInputButton
```

You can find the notable public properties of **HtmlInputButton** objects in Table 19.14 and their notable events in Table 19.15. (This class has no non-inherited methods.) Note that as with other HTML server controls, I am not listing the notable properties, methods, and events this class inherits from the **Control** class; you can find them in Chapter 15, Tables 15.1 to 15.3. This class also inherits the **HtmlControl** class—you can find that class in Table 19.2—and the **HtmlInput Control** class, which you can find in Table 19.4.

Table 19.14   Noteworthy public properties of HtmlInputButton objects.

Property	Means
CausesValidation	Gets/sets whether this button performs validation.

Table 19.15   Noteworthy public events of HtmlInputButton objects.

Event	Means
ServerClick	Occurs when an input button is clicked. Handle this event on the server.

Using the **HtmlInputImage** Class

This class gives you access to HTML **<input type= "image">** elements in server code. Here is the inheritance hierarchy of this class:

```
Object
    Control
        HtmlControl
            HtmlInputControl
                HtmlInputImage
```

You can find the notable public properties of **HtmlInputImage** objects in Table 19.16 and their notable events in Table 19.17. (This class has no non-inherited methods.) Note that as with other HTML server controls, I am not listing the notable properties, methods, and events this class inherits from the **Control** class; you can find them in Chapter 15, Tables 15.1 to 15.3. This class also inherits the **HtmlControl** class—you can find that class in Table 19.2—and the **HtmlInput Control**, which you can find in Table 19.4.

Table 19.16   Noteworthy public properties of HtmlInputImage objects.

Property	Means
Align	Gets/sets the input image's alignment with respect to the other HTML elements.
Alt	Gets/sets the input image's alternative text displayed if the image cannot be displayed.
Border	Gets/sets the input image's border width.
CausesValidation	Gets/sets whether this input image performs validation.
Src	Gets/sets the URL of the image.

Table 19.17   Noteworthy public events of HtmlInputImage objects.

Event	Means
ServerClick	Occurs when the user clicks an input image control. Handle this event on the server.

Using the **HtmlSelect** Class

This class gives you access to HTML **<select>** elements in server code. Here is the inheritance hierarchy of this class:

```
Object
    Control
        HtmlControl
            HtmlContainerControl
                HtmlSelect
```

You can find the notable public properties of **HtmlSelect** objects in Table 19.18 and their events in Table 19.19. (This class has no non-inherited methods.) Note that as with other HTML server controls, I am not listing the notable properties, methods, and events this class inherits from the **Control** class; you can find them in Tables 15.1 to 15.3 in Chapter 15. This class also inherits the **HtmlControl** class—you can find that class in Table 19.2—and the **HtmlContainerControl** class, which you see in Table 19.3.

Table 19.18   Noteworthy public properties of HtmlSelect objects.

Property	Means
Items	Gets the list of option elements in the select control.
Multiple	Gets/sets whether multiple option elements can be selected at once.

(continued)

Table 19.18   Noteworthy public properties of HtmlSelect objects (continued).

Property	Means
SelectedIndex	Gets/sets the index of the selected option element.
Size	Gets/sets the number of option elements visible at one time. Note that if you set this to a value of more than one, browsers will usually show a scrolling list.
Value	Gets/sets the item selected in the select control.

Table 19.19   Noteworthy public events of HtmlSelect objects.

Event	Means
ServerChange	Occurs when a select control is changed. Handle this event on the server.

Using the HtmlImage Class

Gives you access to HTML **<img>** elements in server code. Here is the inheritance hierarchy of this class:

```
Object
    Control
        HtmlControl
            HtmlImage
```

You can find the notable public properties of **HtmlImage** objects in Table 19.20. (This class has no non-inherited methods or events.) Note that as with other HTML server controls, I am not listing the notable properties, methods, and events this class inherits from the **Control** class; you can find them in Chapter 15, Tables 15.1 to 15.3. This class also inherits the **HtmlControl** class; you can find that class in Table 19.2.

Table 19.20   Noteworthy public properties of HtmlImage objects.

Property	Means
Align	Gets/sets the image's alignment with respect to other HTML elements.
Alt	Gets/sets the alternative text to display if an image cannot be displayed.
Border	Gets/sets the width of the image's border.
Height	Gets/sets the image's height.
Src	Gets/sets the URL of the image.
Width	Gets/sets the image's width.

Using the **HtmlInputHidden** Class

This class gives you access to HTML **<input type= "hidden">** elements in server code. Here is the inheritance hierarchy of this class:

```
Object
    Control
        HtmlControl
            HtmlInputControl
                HtmlInputHidden
```

You can find the notable public events of **HtmlInputHidden** objects in Table 19.21. (This class has no non-inherited properties or methods.) Note that as with other HTML server controls, I am not listing the notable properties, methods, and events this class inherits from the **Control** class; you can find them in Tables 15.1 to 15.3 in Chapter 15. This class also inherits the **HtmlControl** class—you can find that class in Table 19.2—and the **HtmlInputControl** class, which you can find in Table 19.4.

Table 19.21   Noteworthy public events of HtmlInputHidden objects.

Event	Means
ServerChange	Occurs when the **Value** property changes—handle this event on the server.

Using the **HtmlInputCheckbox** Class

This class gives you access to HTML **<input type= "checkbox">** elements in server code. Here is the inheritance hierarchy for this class:

```
Object
    Control
        HtmlControl
            HtmlInputControl
                HtmlInputCheckBox
```

You can find the notable public properties of **HtmlInputCheckbox** objects in Table 19.22 and their notable events in Table 19.23. (This class has no non-inherited methods.) Note that as with other HTML server controls, I am not listing the notable properties, methods, and events this class inherits from the **Control** class; you can find them in Chapter 15, Tables 15.1 to 15.3. This class also inherits the **HtmlControl** class—you can find that class in Table 19.2—and the **HtmlInputControl** class, which you can find in Table 19.4.

Table 19.22   Noteworthy public properties of HtmlInputCheckbox objects.

Property	Means
Checked	Gets/sets whether the checkbox is checked.

Table 19.23   Noteworthy public events of HtmlInputCheckbox objects.

Event	Means
ServerChange	Occurs when the checkbox changes state from a previous post.

Using the HtmlInputRadioButton Class

This class gives you access to HTML **<input type= "radio">** elements in server code. Here is the inheritance hierarchy for this class:

```
Object
    Control
        HtmlControl
            HtmlInputControl
                HtmlInputRadioButton
```

You can find the notable public properties of **HtmlInputRadioButton** objects in Table 19.24 and their notable events in Table 19.25. (This class has no non-inherited methods.) Note that as with other HTML server controls, I am not listing the notable properties, methods, and events this class inherits from the **Control** class; you can find them in Tables 15.1 to 15.3, Chapter 15. This class also inherits the **HtmlControl** class—you can find that class in Table 19.2—and the **HtmlInput Control** class, which you can find in Table 19.4.

Table 19.24   Noteworthy public properties of HtmlInputRadioButton objects.

Property	Means
Checked	Gets/sets whether the radio button is selected.

Table 19.25   Noteworthy public events of HtmlInputRadioButton objects.

Event	Means
ServerChange	Occurs when the checkbox changes state from a previous post.

Using the **HtmlTable** Class

This class gives you access to HTML **<table>** elements in server code. Here is the inheritance hierarchy for this class:

```
Object
    Control
        HtmlControl
            HtmlContainerControl
                HtmlTable
```

You can find the notable public properties of **HtmlTable** objects in Table 19.26. (This class has no non-inherited methods or events.) Note that as with other HTML server controls, I am not listing the notable properties, methods, and events this class inherits from the **Control** class; you can find them in Chapter 15, Tables 15.1 to 15.3. This class also inherits the **HtmlControl** class—you can find that class in Table 19.2—and the **HtmlContainerControl** class, which you can find in Table 19.3.

Table 19.26   Noteworthy public properties of HtmlTable objects.

Property	Means
Align	Gets/sets the alignment of table contents in a table.
BgColor	Gets/sets the background color of a table.
Border	Gets/sets the width of the border of a table (in pixels).
BorderColor	Gets/sets the border color of a table.
CellPadding	Gets/sets the cell padding for a table (in pixels).
CellSpacing	Gets/sets the cell spacing for a table (in pixels).
Height	Gets/sets the height of a table.
Rows	Gets a collection of all the rows in a table.
Width	Gets/sets the width of a table.

Using the **HtmlTableRow** Class

This class gives you access to individual HTML **<tr>** elements enclosed within an **HtmlTable** control in server code. Here is the inheritance hierarchy for this class:

```
Object
    Control
        HtmlControl
            HtmlContainerControl
                HtmlTableRow
```

Table 19.27   Noteworthy public properties of HtmlTableRow objects.

Property	Means
Align	Gets/sets the horizontal alignment of cells in a table row.
BgColor	Gets/sets the background color of a table row.
BorderColor	Gets/sets the border color of a table row.
Cells	Gets/sets the table cells in a table row.
Height	Gets/sets the height of a table row.
VAlign	Gets/sets the vertical alignment of cells in a table row.

You can find the notable public properties of **HtmlTableRow** objects in Table 19.27. (This class has no non-inherited methods or events.) Note that as with other HTML server controls, I am not listing the notable properties, methods, and events this class inherits from the **Control** class; you can find them in Chapter 15, Tables 15.1 to 15.3. This class also inherits the **HtmlControl** class—you can find that class in Table 19.2—and the **HtmlContainerControl** class, which you can find in Table 19.3.

Using the HtmlTableCell Class

This class gives you access to individual HTML **<td>** and **<th>** elements enclosed within an **HtmlTableRow** control in server code. Here is the inheritance hierarchy for this class:

```
Object
    Control
        HtmlControl
            HtmlContainerControl
                HtmlTableCell
```

You can find the notable public properties of **HtmlTableCell** objects in Table 19.28. (This class has no non-inherited methods or events.) Note that as with other HTML server controls, I am not listing the notable properties, methods, and events this class inherits from the **Control** class; you can find them in Chapter 15, Tables 15.1 to 15.3. This class also inherits the **HtmlControl** class—you can find that class in Table 19.2—and the **HtmlContainerControl** class, which you can find in Table 19.3.

Table 19.28   Noteworthy public properties of HtmlTableCell objects.

Property	Means
Align	Gets/sets the horizontal alignment of a table's content.
BgColor	Gets/sets the background color of a table cell.
BorderColor	Gets/sets the border color of a table cell.
ColSpan	Gets/sets the number of columns spanned by the table cell.
Height	Gets/sets the height of a table cell (in pixels).
NoWrap	Gets/sets whether text in a table cell wraps.
RowSpan	Gets/sets the number of rows spanned by a table cell.
VAlign	Gets/sets the vertical alignment of a table's content.
Width	Gets/sets the width of a table cell (in pixels).

Using the **HtmlInputFile** Class

This class gives you access to HTML **<input type= "file">** elements in server code. As discussed in the In Depth section of this chapter, this control lets the user upload files (you can use the **PostedFile** property to get access to the uploaded file). Here is the inheritance hierarchy for this class:

```
Object
   Control
      HtmlControl
         HtmlInputControl
            HtmlInputFile
```

You can find the notable public properties of **HtmlInputFile** objects in Table 19.29. (This class has no non-inherited methods or events.) Note that as with other HTML server controls, I am not listing the notable properties, methods, and events this class inherits from the **Control** class; you can find them in Tables 15.1 to 15.3 in Chapter 15. This class also inherits the **HtmlControl** class—you can find that class in Table 19.2—and the **HtmlInputControl** class, which you can find in Table 19.4.

Table 19.29   Noteworthy public properties of HtmlInputFile objects.

Property	Means
Accept	Gets/sets a list of MIME encodings the control can accept.
MaxLength	Gets/sets the maximum length of the file to upload.
PostedFile	Gives you access to the uploaded file.
Size	Gets/sets the width of the file path text box.

Using the **HtmlGenericControl** Class

This class creates a basic control for an HTML element. It defines the methods, properties, and events for all HTML server control tags not represented by a specific .NET Framework class. Here is the inheritance hierarchy for this class:

```
Object
    Control
        HtmlControl
            HtmlContainerControl
                HtmlGenericControl
```

You can find the notable public properties of **HtmlGenericControl** objects in Table 19.30. (This class has no non-inherited methods or events.) Note that as with other HTML server controls, I am not listing the notable properties, methods, and events this class inherits from the **Control** class; you can find them in Chapter 15, Tables 15.1 to 15.3. This class also inherits the **HtmlControl** class—you can find that class in Table 19.2—and the **HtmlContainerControl** class, which you can find in Table 19.3.

Table 19.30   Noteworthy public properties of HtmlGenericControl objects.

Property	Means
TagName	Gets/sets the tag name of an element.

Chapter 20

Data Access with ADO.NET

In Depth

This is our first chapter on databases, one of the biggest topics in Visual Basic programming. In this and the next chapter, I'll take a look at handling databases with visual tools, and in the chapter following, I'll take a look at handling databases in code, using Visual Basic objects.

What Are Databases?

We can begin this discussion on databases by asking just what they are. It's probable that you've already worked with databases and so know well what they are and what they do, but for the sake of readers who have less expertise, a brief introduction to the topic will be useful.

Databases have become more complex over the years, as have many other programming concepts, but the fundamental concept is still a simple one. Say, for example, that you are in charge of teaching a class and are supposed to allot a grade for each student. You might make up a table much like the one in Figure 20.1 to record the grades.

In fact, you've already created a database—or more specifically, a database *table*. (We'll even put this particular table from Figure 20.1 to work when we see how to connect MS Jet databases of the kind created by Microsoft Access to Visual Basic applications; see "Connecting to an MS Jet Database" later in this chapter). The

Grade	Name
A	Mark
B	Ann
A-	Barbara
B+	Sam
A-	Franklin
A+	Tamsen

Figure 20.1   A table of data.

transition from a table on paper to one in a computer is natural—with a computer, you can sort, index, update, and organize large tables of data in an easy way (and without a great waste of paper).

Each individual data entry in a table, such as a student's name, goes into a *field* in the table. Here are the data types you can use for fields in Visual Basic: **Boolean**, **Byte**, **Char**, **DateTime**, **Decimal**, **Double**, **Int16**, **Int32**, **Int64**, **SByte**, **Single**, and **String**. An entry in a table is made up of a set of fields, such as the Name and Grade fields for a particular student; this is called a *record*. Each record gets its own row in a table, and each column in that row represents a different field.

A collection of records—that is, rows of records, where each column is a field— becomes a table. What, then, is a *database*? In its most common form, a database is just a collection of one or more tables. A simple collection of tables such as this is a certain type of database—a *flat* or *flat-file* database. There is a second type of database as well—*relational* database, so called because they are set up to relate the data in multiple tables together. To make a table relational, you choose certain fields to be *primary keys* and *foreign keys*.

The primary key in a table is usually the most important one—the one you might use to sort by, for instance. The foreign key usually represents the primary key in another table, which gives you access to that table in an organized way. For example, we might add a field called student ID to our student grade table. That same field, student ID, may be the primary key in the school registrar's database table, which lists all students. In our table, then, the student ID field is a foreign key, allowing us to specify individual records in the registrar's table. For more on relational databases, see "Using Relational Databases" later in this chapter.

Now that you've set up a database, how do you work with the data in that database? One popular way is to use Structured Query Language (SQL), which we'll see more about later in the Immediate Solutions (see "Using Basic SQL" in this chapter). You use SQL to set up a *query*, which, when applied to a database, typically returns a *dataset* of records that matched your SQL query—for example, you may have asked for all students that got a grade of B or better. You can do a great many things with databases using SQL—you can insert new records, create new tables, get datasets that match specific criteria (such as all your customers in Hawaii, or philosophers who lived more than 1,000 years ago, and so on).

TIP: *To get the actual documents that define SQL, as standardized by the International Organization for Standardization (ISO), see **www.iso.org/iso/en/prods-services/catalogue/intstandards/CatalogueListPage. CatalogueList?ICS1=35&ICS2=60**, which lists the ISO's catalogue for SQL documents—they're not free, though. (Note that this URL may have changed by the time you read this—in that case, go to the ISO site, click the link for Information Technology, followed by the link for "Languages Used in Information Technology.")*

So that's how the process works—you use SQL to work with the data in a database, filtering out the records you don't want, and working on the records you do. If you don't know SQL, don't panic; Visual Basic has a built-in tool (the Query Builder) that lets you create SQL statements visually. We'll see that tool at work later; see "Using Relational Databases" in this chapter (also see "Using Basic SQL" in this chapter).

Connections, Data Adapters, and Datasets

Visual Basic .NET uses ADO.NET (ADO stands for ActiveX Data Objects) as its primary data access and manipulation protocol. We'll be getting familiar with ADO.NET in this and the next few chapters. There are plenty of objects available in ADO.NET, but at root, they're not difficult to use in practice.

Here's what happens—you first get a *connection* to a data source, which means using a *data provider* to access a database. The default data provider that Visual Basic .NET works with is Microsoft's SQL Server, version 7.0 or later, and I'll use that data provider in this book. However, Visual Basic also can work with any data provider that can support Open Database Connectivity (ODBC), such as Oracle. To work with SQL server, you use ADO.NET **SQLConnection** objects, and to work with any other data provider, you use ADO.NET **OleDbConnection** objects. We'll see how to create connection objects such as these visually in just a moment.

TIP: *Studies have shown that data access with Visual Basic .NET is up to 70 percent faster with SQL Server connections than with standard OLE-DB connections.*

After you have a connection to a data source, you create a *data adapter* to work with that data. You need a data adapter because datasets do not maintain any active connection to the database—they are *disconnected* from the database. The data adapter is what actually applies your SQL statements to a database and causes your datasets to fill with data. Data adapters are new in Visual Basic, but don't let them throw you. They're just there to apply your commands to the database—because datasets are disconnected from that database—and they're fundamental to the whole process. To work with the SQL Server data provider, you use **SQLDataAdapter** objects, and to work with ODBC data providers, you use **OleDbAdapter** objects.

Once you have a data adapter, you can generate a *dataset* using that adapter. Datasets are what you actually work with in your code when you want to use data from databases. (Although, note that in addition to datasets, there are also *data readers*, which are fast, read-only mini-datasets that you can only move through records with in ascending order; see "Using a Data Reader" in Chapter 22.) For example, if I wanted to get access to the data in the table in Figure 20.1, I would first create a connection to the database the table was stored in, then create an adapter with the SQL to retrieve that table (for example, if the table was named **students**, that SQL might be "SELECT * FROM students"), and then fill a **DataSet** object using that adapter. Note that each data adapter can handle only one SQL query at a time, but **DataSet** objects can store multiple tables, and to place multiple tables in a dataset, you can use multiple data adapters—see "Adding Multiple Tables to a Dataset" in this chapter.

TIP: *The names of tables and fields in datasets are case-insensitive, so the **students** table is the same as the **Students** table or the **STUDENTS** table.*

So those are the three objects that it's essential to know about: data connections to connect to the database, data adapters to execute SQL with, and datasets to store the data—as returned from data adapters—that your code will actually work on. That's a simplified view, because there are many other objects, but it fits the majority of scenarios. In Figure 20.2, you can see an overview these and a few other data objects we'll come across.

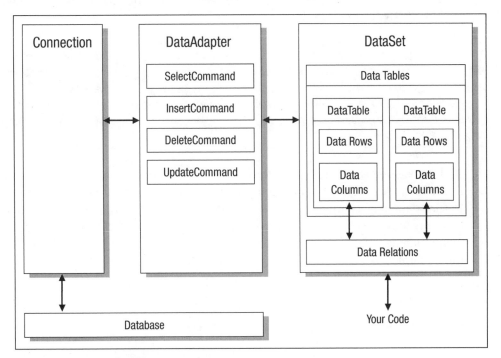

Figure 20.2   ADO.NET data objects.

TIP: *In this chapter, we're going to work with the ADO.NET objects visually, using the tools that VB .NET offers for that purpose. We'll work with ADO.NET connection, adapter, and dataset objects, and others, in code in Chapter 22.*

Of course, the easiest way to understand all this is by looking at an example. Visual Basic has a number of visual tools to make working with databases easier, and that gives us a natural place to start, because Visual Basic will create all the objects we need automatically. The easiest way to do all this is with the Server Explorer, and I'll use that tool first to display the data in a database table. This example is called EasyAccess on the CD-ROM; to follow along, create a new Windows forms application with that name now.

Accessing Data with the Server Explorer

To work with a database, you need a connection to that database. In Visual Basic, the Server Explorer lets you work with connections to various data sources. To display the Server Explorer if it's not already visible, use the View|Server Explorer menu item, or press Ctrl+Alt+S. You can see the Server Explorer in Figure 20.3, where I've docked it to the left edge of the Visual Basic IDE (by clicking the thumbtack icon). This tool lets you create and examine data connections, including connections to Web servers; you can see connections to various databases in the Server Explorer already.

TIP: *When Visual Basic .NET is installed, it searches your local computer for database servers and adds them to the Server Explorer automatically. To add additional servers to the Server Explorer, you select the Tools|Connect to Server menu item or right-click the Servers node that appears at the bottom of the Server Explorer, and select the Add Server menu item. This opens the Add Server dialog, which lets you enter new database servers by computer name or IP address on the Internet. When you subsequently create data connections, you can specify what server to use, as you see in the drop-down list box in Figure 20.4.*

In the EasyAccess example, I'm going to display the data from the **authors** table in the Microsoft SQL Server's pubs sample database, so we'll need a connection to that database. (I'll use the pubs database frequently in this and the next few chapters to make it easy to get the example code on the CD-ROM to work on your own machine, because all you'll need is a connection to that one database to run the examples; see the readme file on the CD-ROM for more information.)

TIP: *A red X over a database's icon in the Server Explorer means a connection is closed; you can open the connection by clicking the plus sign (+) next to the connection in the Server Explorer.*

To create that connection, right-click the Data Connections icon in the Server Explorer and select the Add Connection item, or use the Tools|Connect to Database menu item. Doing so opens the Data Link Properties dialog you see in Figure 20.4.

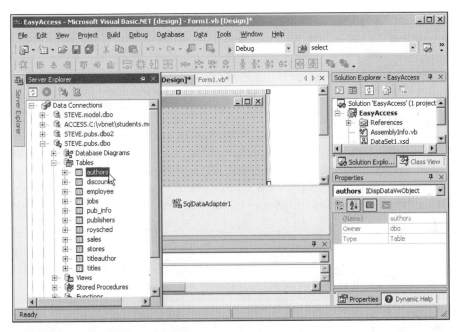

Figure 20.3   The Server Explorer.

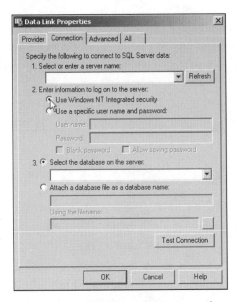

Figure 20.4   Creating a data connection.

In the Data Link Properties dialog, you can enter the name of the server you want to work with, as well as your login name and password, if applicable. (Here, I'm going to use Windows NT integrated security, because SQL Server is on the same machine as VB .NET in my case, but you can choose a server name and enter a user name and password in the Data Link Properties dialog, if you prefer.) You can choose a database already on the server with the "Select the database on the server" option, or another database file with the "Attach a database file as a database name" option. In this case, we'll use the pubs example database that comes with SQL Server, so select the first option here and choose the pubs database, as you see in Figure 20.5.

What if you're not using SQL Server, but, say, Oracle to connect to a database? In that case, you click the Provider tab in the Data Link Properties dialog, as you see in Figure 20.6, and select the type of provider you're working with—Oracle, MS Jet, and so on (the default is SQL Server). Then you go back to the Connection tab and choose the specific database file you want to work with. For an example, see "Connecting to an MS Jet Database" in this chapter.

When you've specified the database file to work with, click the Connection tab and the Test Connection button you see in Figure 20.5. If the connection is working, you'll see a message box with the message "Test connection succeeded" (and if not, a message box will appear, explaining what went wrong).

When the connection is set, click the OK button to close the Data Link Properties dialog. Doing so adds a new connection to the pubs database to the Server Explorer, as you see in Figure 20.3. You can open that connection (assuming, in this case, that SQL Server is running) and take a look what tables are in the database, as you also see in Figure 20.3. Our data connection is ready to work with. Note that this connection is now part of your Visual Basic working environment; it's not specific to the application you're working on at the moment. You can access this connection in the Server Explorer at any time, even when working on other applications.

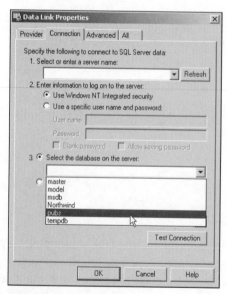

Figure 20.5   Connecting to the pubs database.

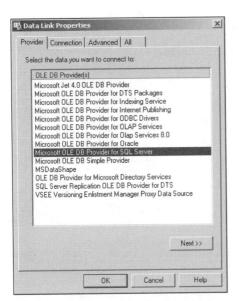

Figure 20.6   The Provider tab in the Data Link Properties dialog.

TIP: *To delete a data connection, just right-click it in the Server Explorer and select the Delete menu item.*

In this example, we want to display the data in the **authors** table of the pubs database, and this is where the Server Explorer makes life easy for us. To create both the data connection and adapter objects we'll need to work with this table, just drag the **authors** table onto the main form. This automatically creates the **SqlConnection1** and **SqlDataAdapter1** objects you see in the component tray in Figure 20.7. (If we had been working with another data provider, Visual Basic would have created **OleDbConnection1** and **OleDbDataAdapter1** objects.)

That was easy enough—Visual Basic created the data connection and data adapter objects we need. (Note that in this case we wanted the whole **authors** table, which means we could simply drag that table onto a form. If we wanted to work with only specific fields, we'd have to generate an SQL query in a data adapter object ourselves, and we'll do that by dragging a data adapter onto a form in the next example.) Now it's time to generate the dataset that holds the data from the data adapter. To do that, just select the Data|Generate Dataset menu item, or right-click **SqlDataAdapter1** and select the Generate Dataset menu item. This displays the Generate Dataset dialog you see in Figure 20.8.

TIP: *If the Data menu is not showing, click the main form in the application to bring it up—this menu only appears when a target that can contain data objects is visible in a designer.*

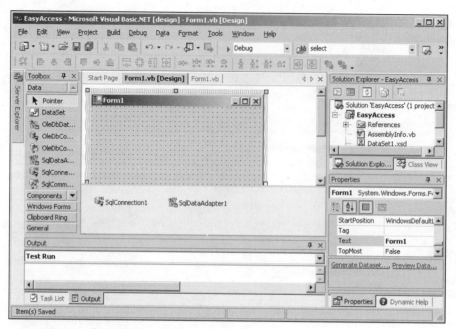

Figure 20.7   Creating data connection and data adapter objects.

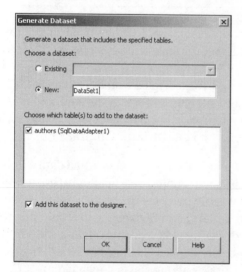

Figure 20.8   The Generate Dataset dialog.

In this case, click the New option to create a new dataset. I'll stick with the default name given to this new dataset object, **DataSet1,** as you see in the figure; make sure the **authors** table checkbox is checked, as well as the "Add this dataset to the designer" checkbox, then click OK. Doing so adds a new dataset, **DataSet11**, to the form designer's component tray, as you see in Figure 20.9. This is the dataset we'll work with.

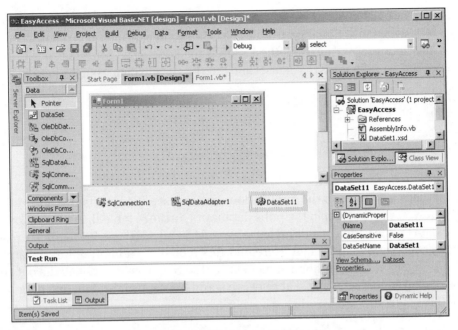

Figure 20.9 A new dataset object in the component tray.

TIP: *You can get an immediate look at the data in the dataset by clicking the dataset object, **DataSet11**, selecting the DatalPreview Data menu item, and then clicking the Fill DataSet button. This will display all the data in the **authors** table in a dialog box. This data preview feature is great, and one you will find yourself using a lot. See "Previewing Data from Data Adapters" in this chapter for more details.*

To display the data in the dataset, I'll use a data grid control, which we'll see more of in the next chapter (see "Using the **DataGrid** Class" in Chapter 21). This control is designed to display entire database tables, so find the DataGrid tool in the Window Forms tab in the toolbox, and drag a new data grid to the main form, sizing it to fit the form. (You can use its **Dock** property to make that sizing easy if you prefer.)

Set the data grid's **DataSource** property to **Data11** (not **DataSet11.authors**, which also will be displayed as an option in the Properties window), and its **DataMember** property to **authors**, which will be displayed automatically as an option when you click that property. This connects the data in the dataset to the data grid.

We're almost done. The final step (which wasn't necessary in Visual Basic 6.0 or earlier) is that you must specifically use the data adapter to fill the dataset with data. The reason you must do this is because the dataset is disconnected from the data provider; it just holds a local copy of the data you're working with. To fill the dataset with data from the data adapter (and remember that our data adapter is already set up to get its data from the **authors** table of the pubs database), you use the data adapter's **Fill** method. Here's the code to add to the **Form1_Load** method; this code clears the dataset and then fills it with data from the data adapter:

```
Private Sub Form1_Load(ByVal sender As System.Object, _
    ByVal e As System.EventArgs) Handles MyBase.Load
    DataSet11.Clear()
    SqlDataAdapter1.Fill(DataSet11)
End Sub
```

And that's it—now run the application. You can see the results in Figure 20.10, where you see the data in the pubs database's **authors** table displayed, showing the data for the various fields in that table, such as au_id (this is the name Microsoft has given to this field when it created this table—it's a contraction of "author ID"), au_lname (for "author last name"), and so on. (Note that not all the data can be displayed in the data grid at once, so scroll bars appear at right and at bottom of this control.)

In summary, here are the steps we've taken:

1. Create a data connection or use an existing data connection.
2. Drag a table from the Server Explorer onto a form; this adds a data connection and a data adapter to the form.
3. Generate a dataset.
4. Bind the dataset to controls.
5. Fill the dataset from a data adapter in code.

That gives us just about the easiest, most painless introduction to working with data access in Visual Basic .NET. Notice, however, that this was a special example, because here, we wanted to look at the entire **authors** table all at once. But what if we had wanted to look at only a few fields of the **authors** table? In that case, we'd have to configure the data adapter ourselves, and I'll show how that works with another example now. This new example is named DataAccess on the CD-ROM, and if you want to follow along, create a Windows Forms application of that name now.

TIP: *In fact, it's worth noting that you can configure the data adapter in the EasyAccess example to select only a few fields in the **authors** table, or otherwise work on that table. Just right-click the adapter object and select the Configure Data Adapter menu item, which opens the same Data Adapter Configuration Wizard we're about to use to create the SQL to extract the data we want to work with from the database. See the next topic for more details.*

---

20. Data Access with ADO.NET

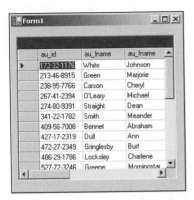

Figure 20.10   Displaying a data table.

Accessing Data with Data Adaptors and Datasets

In the previous example, we dragged an entire data table from the Server Explorer to a form, but often you'll want to look at only a few fields in a table, or otherwise customize what you want to do with a table before working with its data. To do that, you can create a data adapter yourself. It's easy to do.

To see how this works, just click the Data tab in the toolbox now. In this case, I'll drag an **OleDbDataAdapter** object from the toolbox to the main form. (I'm going to use an **OleDbDataAdapter** here only because we already used an **SqlDataAdapter** in the previous example—the rest of the operations here are the same no matter what type of data adapter you use.) Doing so opens the Data Adapter Configuration Wizard that you see in Figure 20.11. This wizard will let you customize your data adapter as you want, which usually means creating the SQL statement this adapter will use. (You can always right-click a data adapter and select the Configure Data Adapter menu item to change an adapter's configuration, including its SQL.)

Click the Next button in the Data Adapter Configuration Wizard to choose the data connection you want to use, as you see in Figure 20.12. You can use an existing data connection of the type we've already created, or click the New Connection button to create a new data connection. (Clicking this button will open the Data Link Properties dialog that we've already used to create a new connection; you can see this dialog in Figure 20.5.) In this case, I'll use the connection we've already made to the pubs database, as you see in Figure 20.12.

Click Next to choose a query type for the adapter, as you see in Figure 20.13. Here, I'll specify that we're going to create an SQL statement, as you see in the figure, but notice that you can either create new or use existing stored SQL pro-

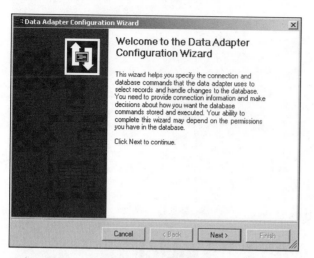

Figure 20.11   The Data Adapter Configuration Wizard.

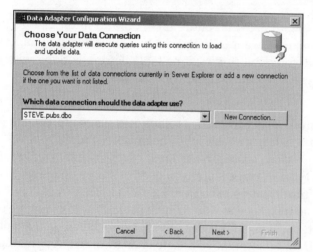

Figure 20.12   Choosing a data adapter's data connection.

cedures. (Using stored procedures is a common SQL technique, and they're great, because they not only hold the SQL you want to use, but they also are stored in the database and can be used over and over by many different applications.)

Click Next to display the dialog you see in Figure 20.14, where we'll generate the SQL statement we'll use in this data adapter.

To make writing the SQL easy, click the Query Builder button now. This displays the Add Table dialog that you see in Figure 20.15. An SQL statement can work with several tables at the same time (as when you join them together), so here you select the tables you want to work with and click the Add button. When you've selected all the tables you want to work with in this way, click the Close button.

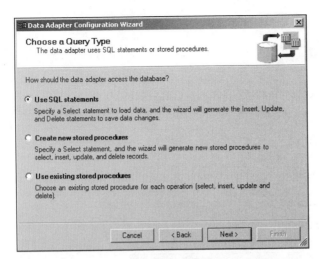

Figure 20.13   Choosing a data adapter's query type.

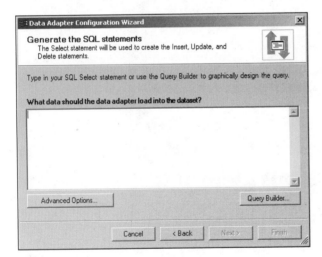

Figure 20.14   Generating a data adapter's SQL.

TIP: *For more on working with multiple tables at once, see "Adding Multiple Tables to a Dataset" in this chapter.*

In this example, we're going to display a few fields from the **authors** table, so just select that table and click Add in the Add Table dialog, then click Close. This opens the Query Builder itself, as you see in Figure 20.16.

At top in Figure 20.16, you can see a window displaying fields in the **authors** table. If you were working with more than one table, you'd see them all open in windows in the query builder, and you'd also see lines indicating any relations connecting primary and foreign keys between the tables (see "Using Relational

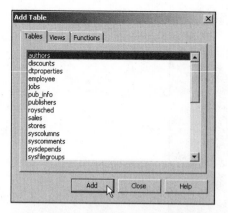

Figure 20.15   The Add Table dialog.

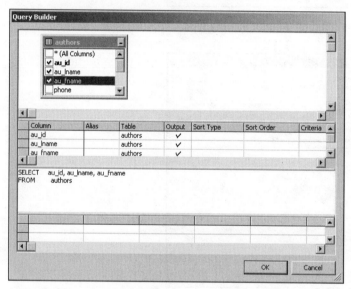

Figure 20.16   The Query Builder.

Databases" in this chapter for an example). You add a field to the generated SQL statement by clicking the checkboxes in a table's window. In Figure 20.16, I've checked the au_id, au_lname, and au_fname fields. (Again, note that these are the names Microsoft gave to these fields when the authors table was created—these names are not created by Visual Basic.) You also can select all fields in a table by checking the checkbox labeled with an asterisk (*), which specifies all fields in SQL. Note that you must select at least one field when creating the SQL for a data adapter, or the Query Builder won't be able to create working SQL.

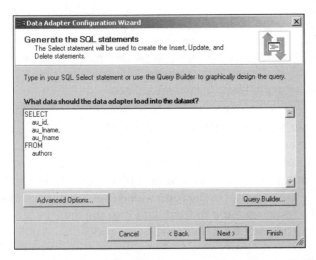

Figure 20.17   A SQL statement in the Data Adapter Configuration Wizard.

Now click the OK button, creating the SQL statement you see in the Data Adapter Configuration Wizard in Figure 20.17. This is the SQL this adapter will use to retrieve data from the database, as well as update the database when you want to, delete records if you want to, and so on.

When you click Next in the Data Adapter Configuration Wizard, the wizard configures the data adapter and reports on the results, as you see in Figure 20.18. We're done—just click the Finish button to dismiss the Data Adapter Configuration Wizard.

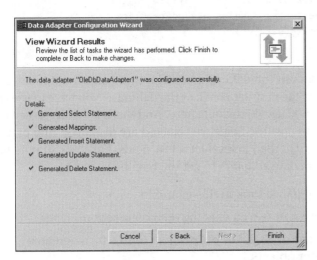

Figure 20.18   Data Adapter Configuration Wizard results.

TIP: *For some SQL statements, like inner joins, the Data Adapter Configuration Wizard won't be able to create some SQL successfully, such as the SQL used to insert rows (which you can't do with an inner join). If this happens, click the Advanced Options button you see in Figure 20.14, and deselect the checkbox for the type of statements that are giving you trouble. In this case, that means deselecting the "Generate Insert, Update, and Delete statements" checkbox. Then click OK and Next to have the Data Adapter Configuration Wizard create the appropriate SQL.*

That creates the data adapter we'll need, **OleDataAdapter1**. Now create a new dataset using this data adapter, as we've done before (i.e., use the Data|Generate Dataset menu item), and connect the new dataset to a data grid using the **DataSource** and **DataMember** properties, also as before. Previously, I filled the data grid with data from the data adapter in the form's load event, but you'll often see "Load" buttons that the user can click to load data into the dataset (and so also the data grid), so I'll use a Load button here, with this code:

```
Private Sub btnLoad_Click(ByVal sender As System.Object, _
    ByVal e As System.EventArgs) Handles btnLoad.Click
    DataSet11.Clear()
    OleDbDataAdapter1.Fill(DataSet11)
End Sub
```

The user can edit the data in a data grid directly, and update the database with it if you want to allow such operations. To make that happen, I'll add a button with the caption "Update" and use the data adapter's **Update** method—like this—to update the database with the edited data in the data grid:

```
Private Sub btnUpdate_Click(ByVal sender As System.Object, _
    ByVal e As System.EventArgs) Handles btnUpdate.Click
    OleDbDataAdapter1.Update(DataSet11)
End Sub
```

When the user edits the data in the data grid control, that control automatically updates the dataset. To send the new data back to the database, you have to use the data adapter's **Update** method, as we're doing here. And that's it—you can see the results in Figure 20.19, where just the fields we selected are displayed. You can, of course, do a lot more with SQL than just select a few fields, but this example has shown us how to use SQL in data adapters to get the results we want.

Here's a summary of the steps we took in this example:

1. Create a data connection or use an existing data connection.

2. Drag an **OleDBAdaptor** or **SQLAdaptor** object onto a form; creates connection and adaptor objects.

3. Use the Data Adapter Configuration Wizard to configure the data adapter and create the SQL you want.

Figure 20.19 Displaying selected fields of the **authors** table.

4. Generate a dataset.

5. Bind the dataset to controls.

6. Fill the dataset in code.

Now we've seen for ourselves the main objects you use in Visual Basic .NET data access, and we've put them to work, giving us some direct familiarity with the whole process. Armed with that firsthand knowledge, we're ready to take a look at the larger picture now, seeing what objects make up the Visual Basic data access world.

Working with ADO.NET

ADO.NET is the main data access system and protocol that Visual Basic .NET uses. As we've already mentioned, it uses a disconnected data architecture, which means that the data you work with is just a copy of the data in the data in the actual database. There are a number of reasons that Microsoft chose this disconnected data architecture; in traditional client/server applications, you get a connection to a database and keep it open while the application is running. However, maintaining those connections takes up a lot of server resources, and, of course, when you want to migrate to the Internet, you have to maintain disconnected datasets instead of maintaining direct and continuous connections.

TIP: *If you need a continuous connection to a database—as when other applications are making changes to the same database that you need to be appraised of (you might be selling theater tickets, for example)—you should know that you actually can use traditional ADO (instead of ADO.NET) objects in Visual Basic .NET. To work with these objects, you use the Project/Add Reference menu item, click the COM tab in the Add Reference dialog, and select one of the ADO libraries. You're then free to use ADO objects in your code.*

To store the data you work with in your application, you use datasets, which represent a sort of data cache of records. (It would be impractical to access the database each time you need a new record.) The data in the dataset is usually a much-reduced version of what is in the database. However, you can work with it in much the same way you do the real data. While you are doing so, you remain disconnected from the database, which lets it perform other tasks. You will probably need to update data in the database, and using data adapters, you can perform update operations on the dataset, and these can be written through to the underlying database.

Datasets are really just passive containers for data. To actually get data from a database and write it back, you use data adapters. A data adapter contains the instructions for populating a single table in the dataset and updating the corresponding table in the database. The instructions are methods that encapsulate either SQL commands or references to stored procedures.

Note that because a dataset exists only locally, it does not necessarily reflect the current state of the database. Although a dataset acts as a cache for data drawn from a database, the dataset has no actual direct relationship with the database. The dataset is a container; it is filled by SQL commands or stored procedures executed from a data adapter. If you want to see the latest changes made by other users, you can refresh the dataset by calling the **Fill** method.

How does the data actually get from the data source to the dataset? ADO.NET uses XML as the format for transferring data. Similarly, if data needs to be saved, which Microsoft calls "persisting," it is stored as XML, the data description language developed by the World Wide Web Consortium (W3C; see **www.w3.org**). This is handy in some cases; for example, if you have an XML file, you can use it as you would any data source and create a dataset from it. You don't have to know how to use XML yourself, of course. Visual Basic .NET will handle the details for you.

TIP: *For more on XML and how to write it, see the Coriolis* HTML Black Book.

One of those details is that ADO.NET needs some way of defining the structure of a dataset using XML. The actual structure—that is, what tables, columns, data types, constraints, and so on are in the dataset—is set up with an *XML schema*. Like XML, XML schemas have been developed by the W3C (although Microsoft uses a proprietary version of XML schemas). They're used to describe the format of an XML file so an application can verify that the XML data is valid. However, that's not usually something you have to worry about directly, because the Visual Studio .NET tools will generate and update schemas as needed, based on what you do in visual designers. To see what such schema look like, take a look at "Examining Dataset Schema" in this chapter.

TIP: *For all the details on XML and XML schema, see* **www.w3.org/TR/REC-xml** *and* **www.w3.org/TR/xmlschema-0/**, *respectively. These are the official W3C documents on these topics.*

As we've seen while working with data connections, data adapters, and datasets, ADO.NET handles data with a series of objects. It's going to crucial to know these objects and what they do in the coming chapters, so I'll go over them now in overview to give us a good foundation in ADO.NET.

Overview of ADO.NET Objects

Here's a list of the most common ADO.NET objects:

- *Data connection objects*—To start working with a database, you must have a data connection. A data adapter needs a connection to a data source to read and write data, and it uses **OleDbConnection** or **SqlConnection** objects to communicate with a data source.

- *Data adapters*—Data adapters are a very important part of ADO.NET. You use them to communicate between a data source and a dataset. You typically configure a data adapter with SQL to execute against the data source. The two types of data adapters are **OleDbDataAdapter** and **SqlDataAdapter** objects.

- *Command objects*—Data adapters can read, add, update, and delete records in a data source. To allow you to specify how each of these operations work, a data adapter contains command objects for each of them. Data adapters support four properties that give you access to these command objects: **SelectCommand**, **InsertCommand**, **UpdateCommand**, and **DeleteCommand**.

- *Datasets*—Datasets store data in a disconnected cache. The structure of a dataset is similar to that of a relational database; it gives you access to an object model of tables, rows, and columns, and it contains constraints and relationships defined for the dataset. Datasets are supported with **DataSet** objects.

- *DataTable objects*—**DataTable** objects hold a data table from a data source. Data tables contain two important properties: **Columns**, which is a collection of the **DataColumn** objects that represent the columns of data in a table, and **Rows**, which is a collection of **DataRow** objects, representing the rows of data in a table.

- *Data readers*—**DataReader** objects hold a read-only, forward-only (i.e., you can only move from one record to the succeeding record, not backwards) set of data from a database. Using a data reader can increase speed because only one row of data is in memory at a time. See "Using a Data Reader" in Chapter 22

- *Data views*—Data views represent a customized view of a single table that can be filtered, searched, or sorted. In other words, a data view, supported by the **DataView** class, is a data "snapshot" that takes up few resources. See "Using Data Views" in this chapter.

- *Constraint objects*—Datasets support constraints to check data integrity. A constraint, supported by the **Constraint** class, is a rule that can be used when rows are inserted, updated, or deleted to check the affected table after the operation. There are two types of constraints: *unique constraints* check that the new values in a column are unique throughout the table, and *foreign-key constraints* specify how related records should be updated when a record in another table is updated.

- ***DataRelation*** *objects*—**DataRelation** objects specify a relationship between parent and child tables, based on a key that both tables share. See "Using Master/Detail Relationships and Data Relation Objects" in Chapter 21.

- ***DataRow*** *objects*—**DataRow** objects correspond to a particular row in a data table. You use the **Item** property to get or set a value in a particular field in the row. See "Creating Data Rows in Code" in Chapter 22.

- ***DataColumn*** *objects*—**DataColumn** objects correspond to the columns in a table. Each object has a **DataType** property that specifies the kind of data each column contains, such as integers or string values. See "Creating Data Columns in Code" in Chapter 22.

We'll put these objects to work in this and the next several chapters. In fact, it's time to turn to the Immediate Solutions section now to start working with specific details of ADO.NET.

Immediate Solutions

Using Basic SQL

As we've seen in the In Depth section of this chapter, you can use Structured Query Language (SQL) in data adapters to configure what those data adapters do. Although SQL is beyond the scope of this book, and Visual Basic itself is able to write SQL for you in many cases, it won't hurt to see an overview of basic SQL here.

In this case, I'll suppose that we're working with a database that contains a table named **Customers** that holds customer IDs, addresses, and so on, and a table named **Orders**, that holds customer orders. This database is based on the Northwind example database that comes with SQL Server 7.0, but you don't need to have that example database to follow along in this topic. In this topic, I'll just work through some basic SQL to get us started; the foundation of SQL is the **SELECT** statement, and I'm going to start with that.

Using the **SELECT** Statement

You use the **SELECT** statement to get fields from a table; here's an example where I'm getting all the records in the **Customers** table, using the wildcard character *:

```
SELECT * FROM Customers
```

This returns a dataset that holds all the records in the **Customers** table. You also can use the **SELECT** statement to select specific fields from a table, like this, where I'm selecting the CustomerID, Address, and City fields of all the records in the **Customers** table:

```
SELECT CustomerID, Address, City FROM Customers
```

This returns a dataset that holds all the records in the **Customers** table, and each record will have a CustomerID, Address, and City field.

Using **Where** Clauses

In SQL, you can use the **WHERE** clause to specify criteria that you want records to meet. For example, to select all the records in the **Customers** table where the City field holds "Boston", you can execute this statement:

```
SELECT * FROM Customers WHERE City = "Boston"
```

You don't have to use an equals sign here; you can test fields using these operators:

- **<** (less than)
- **<=** (less than or equal to)
- **>** (greater than)
- **>=** (greater than or equal to)
- **BETWEEN**
- **IN**
- **LIKE**

The logical comparisons, such as **<** and **>** are familiar, of course, but what about **BETWEEN**, **IN,** and **LIKE**? They're coming up next.

Using the **BETWEEN** Clause

You can use the **BETWEEN** clause to indicate a range of values you will accept. For example, here's how to select all the records from the **Customers** table where the CustomerID record starts with the letter H (the CustomerID field is alphabetic, not numeric, in this table):

```
SELECT * FROM Customers WHERE CustomerID BETWEEN
"H*" AND "I*"
```

Note the use of wildcard characters: "H*" and "I*". Using these wildcards lets you specify that you want all the CustomerID values that start with the letter H.

Using the **IN** Clause

In SQL, you can use the **IN** clause to specify a set of values that fields can match, which is very helpful if you know exactly what you're looking for. For example, here's how I get records that have values in the City field that match Boston or York:

```
SELECT * FROM Customers WHERE City IN ("Boston",
"York")
```

Using the **LIKE** Clause

In SQL, the **LIKE** clause lets you use partial string matching, which you can specify with wildcards. Here's an example, where I'm selecting all the records from the **Customers** table where the City field matches the wildcard string "Los*":

```
SELECT * FROM Customers WHERE City LIKE "Los*"
```

This creates a dataset with records whose City fields match names ""Los*", such as Los Angeles or Los Altos.

Using the **DISTINCT** Clause

Sometimes, a database may hold duplicate values in the fields of the records of a table; for example, several customers come from the same cities, so they'd have the same value in the City field. You might want to take a look at all the cities represented, without duplicates, and you can use the **DISTINCT** clause for that, like this:

```
SELECT DISTINCT City FROM Customers
```

Using Logical Operations

You also can use logical operations on the clauses in your SQL statements. Here's an example in which I'm specifying two criteria: the City field cannot be either Boston or York, and there must be some value in the Fax field (note that I'm using the **NULL** keyword to test if there's anything in a field):

```
SELECT * FROM Customers WHERE City NOT IN ("Boston",
"York") AND Fax IS NOT NULL
```

You can use these logical operators to connect clauses: **AND**, **OR**, and **NOT**. Using **AND** means that both clauses must be **True**, using **OR** means either one can be **True**, and using **NOT** flips the value of a clause from **True** to **False** or from **False** to **True**.

Using the **ORDER BY** Clause

You can order the records in the dataset using an SQL statement. For example, here's how I order the records in the **Customers** table by CustomerID:

```
SELECT * FROM Customers ORDER BY CustomerID
```

You can also sort in descending order with the **Desc** keyword:

```
SELECT * FROM Customers ORDER BY CustomerID Desc
```

Using the **AS** Clause

Here's a handy one. The names of the fields in a dataset are the same as the names they had in the original table. You might want to change those names; for example, labeling a field "Name" might be more descriptive to the user than "au_lname". You can *alias* a field's name with the **AS** clause like this, where I'm changing ContactName to just Name for the purposes of the returned dataset:

```
SELECT ContactName AS Name FROM Customers
```

Now in the dataset, the ContactName field will be called Name.

Using Built-in Functions

It's also worth noting that SQL comes with a number of built-in functions such as **COUNT**, **SUM**, **MIN**, **MAX**, and **AVG** that let you work with the records in a dataset. Here is what these functions can do for you:

- **COUNT**—gets a count of records.
- **SUM**—adds values over records.
- **MIN**—finds the minimum value of a set of records.
- **MAX**—finds the maximum value of a set of records.
- **AVG**—finds the average value of a set of records.

Here's how you can use these functions in an SQL statement:

```
SELECT COUNT(EmployeeID) AS NumberEmployees,
AVG(DateOfBirth) AS AverageDateOfBirth, SUM(DateOfBirth)
AS TotalYears, MIN(DateOfBirth) AS MinDateOfBirth,
MAX(DateOfBirth) AS MaxDateOfBirth FROM Employees
```

Using the **GROUP BY** Clause

Here's another useful one—you can group records with the **GROUP BY** clause like this, where I'm grouping them by city:

```
SELECT * FROM Customers GROUP BY City
```

Using the **HAVING** Clause

You can use the SQL **HAVING** clause with **GROUP BY**; this clause is like the **WHERE** clause, but is used only with **GROUP BY**. This clause lets you specify additional criteria that records must meet, like this, where I'm specifying only records with cities that begin with "Los":

```
SELECT * FROM Customers GROUP BY City HAVING City LIKE "Los*"
```

Using the **DELETE** Statement

Although we've been using SQL in data adapters, note that not all SQL statements are designed to return datasets. For example, you can use the **DELETE** statement to delete records like this, where I'm deleting every record from the **Customers** table that has City values that are not Boston or York:

```
DELETE * FROM Customers WHERE City NOT IN ("Boston", "York")
```

Using the **UPDATE** Statement

You can use the **UPDATE** statement to update a database. Although Visual Basic will do the updating for us, it's worth noting that you can use SQL to do updates as well. Here's an example where I'm changing the City to Boston in all records where it's York now:

```
UPDATE Customers SET City = "Boston" WHERE City = "York"
```

Joining Tables

There's much more you can do with SQL. For example, you can work with relational databases—say you wanted to create a new dataset with customer contact names from the **Customers** table and the IDs of the items they've ordered from the **Orders** table. The key that relates these two tables is CustomerID, so you can set up the SQL query like this, making sure that the CustomerID field matches in each record you're joining:

```
SELECT Customers.ContactName, Orders.OrderID FROM
Customers, Orders WHERE Customers.CustomerID =
Orders.CustomerID
```

You also can do *inner joins*, where records must be in both tables, or *outer joins*, where records can be in either table.

This topic has just given us an introduction to SQL; of course, there's plenty more power available. But now we have all the SQL we'll need here—and more—under our belts.

TIP: *As mentioned in the In Depth section of this chapter, to get the actual documents that define SQL, as standardized by the International Organization for Standardization (ISO), go to **www.iso.org/iso/en/prods-services/catalogue/ intstandards/CatalogueListPage.CatalogueList?ICS1=35&ICS2=60**, which (as of this writing) lists the ISO's catalogue for SQL documents. Note that they're not free, however.*

Using the Server Explorer

You need a data connection to work with the data in a data source, and, as discussed in the In Depth section of this chapter, the Server Explorer is a great tool for working with data connections. To display the Server Explorer if it's not already visible, use the View|Server Explorer menu item, or press Ctrl+Alt+S.

You can explore a database with the Server Explorer, as you see in Figure 20.3; this tool works a lot like the Windows Explorer. You can see the tables, stored SQL procedures, data views, and other entities in a database using the Server Explorer. You can manage the data in a database with the Server Explorer as well. For example, if you right-click a table, you can add a new table to the database by selecting the New Table menu item.

Creating a New Data Connection

You need a data connection to a data source before you can work with data from that database. As we saw in the EasyAccess example in the In Depth section of this chapter, you can create a new data connection in the Server Explorer by right-clicking the Data Connections icon in the Server Explorer and selecting the Add Connection item (or use the Tools|Connect to Database menu item). This opens the Data Link Properties dialog you see in Figure 20.4; you can use this dialog to create a new data connection.

To delete a data connection, right-click it in the Server Explorer and click Delete.

Dragging Tables from the Server Explorer to a Form

As we saw in the EasyAccess example in the In Depth section of this chapter, you can drag whole data entities—such as tables—from the Server Explorer onto a form. In that example, we dragged a whole table, the **authors** table, to a Windows form, and Visual Basic created a data connection and data adapter object for us automatically. We then generated a new dataset with the Data|Generate Dataset menu item, added code to fill the data set from the data adapter, and connected that dataset to a data grid, as you see in Figure 20.10.

Behind the scenes, Visual Basic added a tremendous amount of code to Form1.vb when we performed these actions. Take a look at the next topic for the details.

Creating a Dataset

To create a dataset using a data adapter, you can use the Data|Generate Dataset menu item or right-click a data adapter and choose the Generate Dataset menu item. We did this in the EasyAccess example in the In Depth section of this chapter, as you can see in the Generate Dataset dialog in Figure 20.8. As shown in that figure, all you have to do is to select the table you want to add to the dataset, give it a name if you don't want to accept the default name that Visual Basic has given it, and click OK. Doing so creates a new **DataSet** object and adds it to the form under design.

TIP: You also can add dataset objects to a form from the toolbox—just click the Data tab and use the DataSet tool.

Although the EasyAccess example made creating a data connection, data adapter, and dataset look easy, there's really a great deal of code that's been added to our program. To see what this example looks like in code, here's Form1.vb from the EasyAccess example; it's worth taking a look at the various parts of this application:

```
Public Class Form1
    Inherits System.Windows.Forms.Form

#Region " Windows Form Designer generated code "

    Public Sub New()
        MyBase.New()

        'This call is required by the Windows Form Designer.
        InitializeComponent()

        'Add any initialization after the InitializeComponent() call

    End Sub

    'Form overrides dispose to clean up the component list.
    Protected Overloads Overrides Sub Dispose(ByVal disposing As Boolean)
        If disposing Then
            If Not (components Is Nothing) Then
                components.Dispose()
            End If
        End If
        MyBase.Dispose(disposing)
    End Sub
    Friend WithEvents SqlSelectCommand1 As System.Data.SqlClient.SqlCommand
```

```
Friend WithEvents SqlInsertCommand1 As System.Data.SqlClient.SqlCommand
Friend WithEvents SqlUpdateCommand1 As System.Data.SqlClient.SqlCommand
Friend WithEvents SqlDeleteCommand1 As System.Data.SqlClient.SqlCommand
Friend WithEvents SqlConnection1 As System.Data.SqlClient.SqlConnection
Friend WithEvents SqlDataAdapter1 As _
    System.Data.SqlClient.SqlDataAdapter
Friend WithEvents DataSet11 As EasyAccess.DataSet1
Friend WithEvents DataGrid1 As System.Windows.Forms.DataGrid

'Required by the Windows Form Designer
Private components As System.ComponentModel.Container

'NOTE: The following procedure is required by the Windows Form Designer
'It can be modified using the Windows Form Designer.
'Do not modify it using the code editor.
<System.Diagnostics.DebuggerStepThrough()> Private Sub _
    InitializeComponent()
    Me.SqlDataAdapter1 = New System.Data.SqlClient.SqlDataAdapter()
    Me.SqlDeleteCommand1 = New System.Data.SqlClient.SqlCommand()
    Me.SqlConnection1 = New System.Data.SqlClient.SqlConnection()
    Me.SqlInsertCommand1 = New System.Data.SqlClient.SqlCommand()
    Me.SqlSelectCommand1 = New System.Data.SqlClient.SqlCommand()
    Me.SqlUpdateCommand1 = New System.Data.SqlClient.SqlCommand()
    Me.DataSet11 = New EasyAccess.DataSet1()
    Me.DataGrid1 = New System.Windows.Forms.DataGrid()
    CType(Me.DataSet11, _
        System.ComponentModel.ISupportInitialize).BeginInit()
    CType(Me.DataGrid1, _
        System.ComponentModel.ISupportInitialize).BeginInit()
    Me.SuspendLayout()
    '
    'SqlDataAdapter1
    '
    Me.SqlDataAdapter1.DeleteCommand = Me.SqlDeleteCommand1
    Me.SqlDataAdapter1.InsertCommand = Me.SqlInsertCommand1
    Me.SqlDataAdapter1.SelectCommand = Me.SqlSelectCommand1
    Me.SqlDataAdapter1.TableMappings.AddRange(New _
        System.Data.Common.DataTableMapping() {New _
        System.Data.Common.DataTableMapping("Table", "authors", New _
        System.Data.Common.DataColumnMapping() {New _
        System.Data.Common.DataColumnMapping("au_id", "au_id"), New _
        System.Data.Common.DataColumnMapping("au_lname", "au_lname"), _
        New System.Data.Common.DataColumnMapping("au_fname", _
        "au_fname"), New System.Data.Common.DataColumnMapping(
        "phone", "phone"), New _
```

```
        System.Data.Common.DataColumnMapping("address", _
        "address"), New System.Data.Common.DataColumnMapping("city", _
        "city"), New System.Data.Common.DataColumnMapping("state", _
        "state"), New System.Data.Common.DataColumnMapping("zip", _
        "zip"), New System.Data.Common.DataColumnMapping("contract", _
        "contract")})})
Me.SqlDataAdapter1.UpdateCommand = Me.SqlUpdateCommand1
'
'SqlDeleteCommand1
'
Me.SqlDeleteCommand1.CommandText = "DELETE FROM authors WHERE " & _
"(au_id = @au_id) AND (address = @address OR @address1 I" & _
"S NULL AND address IS NULL) AND (au_fname = @au_fname) AND " & _
"(au_lname = @au_lname) AND (city = @city OR @city1 IS NULL " & _
"AND city IS NULL) AND (contract = @contract) AND " & _
"(phone = @phone) AND (state = @state OR @state1 IS NULL AND " & _
"state IS NULL) AND (zip = @zip OR @zip1 IS NULL AND zip IS NULL)"
Me.SqlDeleteCommand1.Connection = Me.SqlConnection1
Me.SqlDeleteCommand1.Parameters.Add(New
    System.Data.SqlClient.SqlParameter("@au_id", _
    System.Data.SqlDbType.Char, 11, _
    System.Data.ParameterDirection.Input, False, CType(0, Byte), _
    CType(0, Byte), "au_id", System.Data.DataRowVersion.Original, _
    Nothing))
Me.SqlDeleteCommand1.Parameters.Add(New _
    System.Data.SqlClient.SqlParameter("@address", _
    System.Data.SqlDbType.VarChar, 40, _
    System.Data.ParameterDirection.Input, True, CType(0, Byte), _
    CType(0, Byte), "address", _
    System.Data.DataRowVersion.Original, Nothing))
Me.SqlDeleteCommand1.Parameters.Add(New _
    System.Data.SqlClient.SqlParameter("@address1", _
    System.Data.SqlDbType.VarChar, 40, _
    System.Data.ParameterDirection.Input, True, CType(0, Byte), _
    CType(0, Byte), "address", _
    System.Data.DataRowVersion.Original, Nothing))
Me.SqlDeleteCommand1.Parameters.Add(New _
    System.Data.SqlClient.SqlParameter("@au_fname", _
    System.Data.SqlDbType.VarChar, 20, _
    System.Data.ParameterDirection.Input, False, _
    CType(0, Byte), CType(0, Byte), "au_fname", _
    System.Data.DataRowVersion.Original, Nothing))
Me.SqlDeleteCommand1.Parameters.Add(New _
    System.Data.SqlClient.SqlParameter("@au_lname", _
    System.Data.SqlDbType.VarChar, 40, _
```

```
                         System.Data.ParameterDirection.Input, False, CType(0, Byte), _
                         CType(0, Byte), "au_lname", _
                         System.Data.DataRowVersion.Original, Nothing))
            Me.SqlDeleteCommand1.Parameters.Add(New _
                         System.Data.SqlClient.SqlParameter("@city", _
                         System.Data.SqlDbType.VarChar, 20, _
                         System.Data.ParameterDirection.Input, True, CType(0, Byte), _
                         CType(0, Byte), "city", System.Data.DataRowVersion.Original, _
                         Nothing))
            Me.SqlDeleteCommand1.Parameters.Add(New _
                         System.Data.SqlClient.SqlParameter("@city1", _
                         System.Data.SqlDbType.VarChar, 20, _
                         System.Data.ParameterDirection.Input, True, CType(0, Byte), _
                         CType(0, Byte), "city", System.Data.DataRowVersion.Original, _
                         Nothing))
            Me.SqlDeleteCommand1.Parameters.Add(New _
                         System.Data.SqlClient.SqlParameter("@contract", _
                         System.Data.SqlDbType.Bit, 1, _
                         System.Data.ParameterDirection.Input, False, CType(0, Byte), _
                         CType(0, Byte), "contract", _
                         System.Data.DataRowVersion.Original, Nothing))
            Me.SqlDeleteCommand1.Parameters.Add(New _
                         System.Data.SqlClient.SqlParameter("@phone", _
                         System.Data.SqlDbType.Char, 12, _
                         System.Data.ParameterDirection.Input, False, CType(0, Byte), _
                         CType(0, Byte), "phone", System.Data.DataRowVersion.Original, _
                         Nothing))
            Me.SqlDeleteCommand1.Parameters.Add(New _
                         System.Data.SqlClient.SqlParameter("@state", _
                         System.Data.SqlDbType.Char, 2, _
                         System.Data.ParameterDirection.Input, True, CType(0, Byte), _
                         CType(0, Byte), "state", _
                         System.Data.DataRowVersion.Original, Nothing))

            Me.SqlDeleteCommand1.Parameters.Add(New _
                         System.Data.SqlClient.SqlParameter("@state1", _
                         System.Data.SqlDbType.Char, 2, _
                         System.Data.ParameterDirection.Input, True, CType(0, Byte), _
                         CType(0, Byte), "state", _
                         System.Data.DataRowVersion.Original, Nothing))
            Me.SqlDeleteCommand1.Parameters.Add(New _
                         System.Data.SqlClient.SqlParameter("@zip", _
                         System.Data.SqlDbType.Char, 5, _
                         System.Data.ParameterDirection.Input, True, CType(0, Byte), _
                         CType(0, Byte), "zip", System.Data.DataRowVersion.Original, _
```

```
     Nothing))
Me.SqlDeleteCommand1.Parameters.Add(New _
    System.Data.SqlClient.SqlParameter("@zip1", _
    System.Data.SqlDbType.Char, 5, _
    System.Data.ParameterDirection.Input, True, CType(0, Byte), _
    CType(0, Byte), "zip", System.Data.DataRowVersion.Original, _
    Nothing))
'
'SqlConnection1
'
Me.SqlConnection1.ConnectionString = _
    "data source=(local);initial " & _
    "catalog=pubs;integrated security=SSPI;persist securit" & _
    "y info=False;workstation id=STEVE;packet size=4096"
'
'SqlInsertCommand1
'
Me.SqlInsertCommand1.CommandText = "INSERT INTO authors(au_id, " &_
    au_lname, au_fname, phone, address, city, state, zip, " & _
    "contract) VALUES (@au_id, @au_lname, @au_fname, @phone, " & _
    "@address, @city, @state," & _
    " @zip, @contract); SELECT au_id, au_lname, au_fname, " & _
    "phone, address, city, state" & _
    ", zip, contract FROM authors WHERE (au_id = @Select_au_id)" & _
Me.SqlInsertCommand1.Connection = Me.SqlConnection1
Me.SqlInsertCommand1.Parameters.Add(New _
    System.Data.SqlClient.SqlParameter("@au_id", _
    System.Data.SqlDbType.Char, 11, _
    System.Data.ParameterDirection.Input, False, CType(0, Byte), _
    CType(0, Byte), "au_id", System.Data.DataRowVersion.Current, _
    Nothing))
Me.SqlInsertCommand1.Parameters.Add(New _
    System.Data.SqlClient.SqlParameter("@au_lname", _
    System.Data.SqlDbType.VarChar, 40, _
    System.Data.ParameterDirection.Input, False, CType(0, Byte), _
    CType(0, Byte), "au_lname", _
    System.Data.DataRowVersion.Current, Nothing))
Me.SqlInsertCommand1.Parameters.Add(New _
    System.Data.SqlClient.SqlParameter("@au_fname", _
    System.Data.SqlDbType.VarChar, 20, _
    System.Data.ParameterDirection.Input, False, CType(0, Byte), _
    CType(0, Byte), "au_fname", _
    System.Data.DataRowVersion.Current, Nothing))
Me.SqlInsertCommand1.Parameters.Add(New _
    System.Data.SqlClient.SqlParameter("@phone", _
```

```
              System.Data.SqlDbType.Char, 12, _
           System.Data.ParameterDirection.Input, False, CType(0, Byte), _
           CType(0, Byte), "phone", System.Data.DataRowVersion.Current, _
           Nothing))
      Me.SqlInsertCommand1.Parameters.Add(New _
           System.Data.SqlClient.SqlParameter("@address", _
           System.Data.SqlDbType.VarChar, 40, _
           System.Data.ParameterDirection.Input, True, CType(0, Byte), _
           CType(0, Byte), "address", _
           System.Data.DataRowVersion.Current, Nothing))
      Me.SqlInsertCommand1.Parameters.Add(New _
           System.Data.SqlClient.SqlParameter("@city", _
           System.Data.SqlDbType.VarChar, 20, _
           System.Data.ParameterDirection.Input, True, CType(0, Byte), _
           CType(0, Byte), "city", System.Data.DataRowVersion.Current, _
           Nothing))
      Me.SqlInsertCommand1.Parameters.Add(New _
           System.Data.SqlClient.SqlParameter("@state", _
           System.Data.SqlDbType.Char, 2, _
           System.Data.ParameterDirection.Input, True, CType(0, Byte), _
           CType(0, Byte), "state", _
           System.Data.DataRowVersion.Current, Nothing))
      Me.SqlInsertCommand1.Parameters.Add(New _
           System.Data.SqlClient.SqlParameter("@zip", _
           System.Data.SqlDbType.Char, 5, _
           System.Data.ParameterDirection.Input, True, CType(0, Byte), _
           CType(0, Byte), "zip", System.Data.DataRowVersion.Current, _
           Nothing))
      Me.SqlInsertCommand1.Parameters.Add(New _
           System.Data.SqlClient.SqlParameter("@contract", _
           System.Data.SqlDbType.Bit, 1, _
           System.Data.ParameterDirection.Input, False, _
           CType(0, Byte), CType(0, Byte), "contract", _
           System.Data.DataRowVersion.Current, Nothing))
      Me.SqlInsertCommand1.Parameters.Add(New _
           System.Data.SqlClient.SqlParameter("@Select_au_id", _
           System.Data.SqlDbType.Char, 11, _
           System.Data.ParameterDirection.Input, False, CType(0, Byte), _
           CType(0, Byte), "au_id", System.Data.DataRowVersion.Current, _
           Nothing))
      '
      'SqlSelectCommand1
      '
      Me.SqlSelectCommand1.CommandText = "SELECT au_id, au_lname, _
           au_fname, phone, address, city, state, zip, contract FROM" & _
```

```
" authors"
Me.SqlSelectCommand1.Connection = Me.SqlConnection1
'
'SqlUpdateCommand1
'
Me.SqlUpdateCommand1.CommandText = _
"UPDATE authors SET au_id = " & _
"@au_id, au_lname = @au_lname, au_fname = @au_fname, ph" & _
"one = @phone, address = @address, city = @city, state = " & _
"@state, zip = @zip, cont" & _
"ract = @contract WHERE (au_id = @Original_au_id) AND " & _
"(address = @Original_addres" & _
"s OR @Original_address1 IS NULL AND address IS NULL) AND " & _
"(au_fname = @Original_a" & _
"u_fname) AND (au_lname = @Original_au_lname) AND (city = " & _
"@Original_city OR @Orig" & _
"inal_city1 IS NULL AND city IS NULL) AND (contract = " &_
"@Original_contract) AND (ph" & _
"one = @Original_phone) AND (state = @Original_state OR " & _
"@Original_state1 IS NULL " & _
"AND state IS NULL) AND (zip = @Original_zip " & _
"OR @Original_zip1 " & _
" NULL); SELECT au_id, au_lname, au_fname, phone, address, " & _
"city, state, zip, cont" & _
"ract FROM authors WHERE (au_id = @Select_au_id)"
Me.SqlUpdateCommand1.Connection = Me.SqlConnection1
Me.SqlUpdateCommand1.Parameters.Add(New _
    System.Data.SqlClient.SqlParameter("@au_id", _
    System.Data.SqlDbType.Char, 11, _
    System.Data.ParameterDirection.Input, False, CType(0, Byte), _
    CType(0, Byte), "au_id", System.Data.DataRowVersion.Current, _
    Nothing))
Me.SqlUpdateCommand1.Parameters.Add(New _
    System.Data.SqlClient.SqlParameter("@au_lname", _
    System.Data.SqlDbType.VarChar, 40, _
    System.Data.ParameterDirection.Input, False, CType(0, Byte), _
    CType(0, Byte), "au_lname", _
    System.Data.DataRowVersion.Current, Nothing))
Me.SqlUpdateCommand1.Parameters.Add(New _
    System.Data.SqlClient.SqlParameter("@au_fname", _
    System.Data.SqlDbType.VarChar, 20, _
    System.Data.ParameterDirection.Input, False, CType(0, Byte), _
    CType(0, Byte), "au_fname", _
    System.Data.DataRowVersion.Current, Nothing))
Me.SqlUpdateCommand1.Parameters.Add(New _
```

```
            System.Data.SqlClient.SqlParameter("@phone", _
            System.Data.SqlDbType.Char, 12, _
            System.Data.ParameterDirection.Input, False, CType(0, Byte), _
            CType(0, Byte), "phone", System.Data.DataRowVersion.Current, _
            Nothing))
Me.SqlUpdateCommand1.Parameters.Add(New _
            System.Data.SqlClient.SqlParameter("@address", _
            System.Data.SqlDbType.VarChar, 40, _
            System.Data.ParameterDirection.Input, True, CType(0, Byte), _
            CType(0, Byte), "address", _
            System.Data.DataRowVersion.Current, Nothing))
Me.SqlUpdateCommand1.Parameters.Add(New _
            System.Data.SqlClient.SqlParameter("@city", _
            System.Data.SqlDbType.VarChar, 20, _
            System.Data.ParameterDirection.Input, True, CType(0, Byte), _
            CType(0, Byte), "city", System.Data.DataRowVersion.Current, _
            Nothing))
Me.SqlUpdateCommand1.Parameters.Add(New _
            System.Data.SqlClient.SqlParameter("@state", _
            System.Data.SqlDbType.Char, 2, _
            System.Data.ParameterDirection.Input, True, CType(0, Byte), _
            CType(0, Byte), "state", System.Data.DataRowVersion.Current, _
            Nothing))
Me.SqlUpdateCommand1.Parameters.Add(New _
            System.Data.SqlClient.SqlParameter("@zip", _
            System.Data.SqlDbType.Char, 5, _
            System.Data.ParameterDirection.Input, True, CType(0, Byte), _
            CType(0, Byte), "zip", System.Data.DataRowVersion.Current, _
            Nothing))
Me.SqlUpdateCommand1.Parameters.Add(New _
            System.Data.SqlClient.SqlParameter("@contract", _
            System.Data.SqlDbType.Bit, 1, _
            System.Data.ParameterDirection.Input, False, CType(0, Byte), _
            CType(0, Byte), "contract", _
            System.Data.DataRowVersion.Current, Nothing))
Me.SqlUpdateCommand1.Parameters.Add(New _
            System.Data.SqlClient.SqlParameter("@Original_au_id", _
            System.Data.SqlDbType.Char, 11, _
            System.Data.ParameterDirection.Input, False, CType(0, Byte), _
            CType(0, Byte), "au_id", System.Data.DataRowVersion.Original, _
            Nothing))
Me.SqlUpdateCommand1.Parameters.Add(New _
            System.Data.SqlClient.SqlParameter("@Original_address", _
            System.Data.SqlDbType.VarChar, 40, _
            System.Data.ParameterDirection.Input, True, CType(0, Byte), _
            CType(0, Byte), "address", _
```

```
         System.Data.DataRowVersion.Original, Nothing))
Me.SqlUpdateCommand1.Parameters.Add(New _
     System.Data.SqlClient.SqlParameter("@Original_address1", _
     System.Data.SqlDbType.VarChar, 40, _
     System.Data.ParameterDirection.Input, True, CType(0, Byte), _
     CType(0, Byte), "address", _
     System.Data.DataRowVersion.Original, Nothing))
Me.SqlUpdateCommand1.Parameters.Add(New _
     System.Data.SqlClient.SqlParameter("@Original_au_fname", _
     System.Data.SqlDbType.VarChar, 20, _
     System.Data.ParameterDirection.Input, False, CType(0, Byte), _
     CType(0, Byte), "au_fname", _
     System.Data.DataRowVersion.Original, Nothing))
Me.SqlUpdateCommand1.Parameters.Add(New _
     System.Data.SqlClient.SqlParameter("@Original_au_lname", _
     System.Data.SqlDbType.VarChar, 40, _
     System.Data.ParameterDirection.Input, False, CType(0, Byte), _
     CType(0, Byte), "au_lname", _
     System.Data.DataRowVersion.Original, Nothing))
Me.SqlUpdateCommand1.Parameters.Add(New _
     System.Data.SqlClient.SqlParameter("@Original_city", _
     System.Data.SqlDbType.VarChar, 20, _
     System.Data.ParameterDirection.Input, True, CType(0, Byte), _
     CType(0, Byte), "city", _
     System.Data.DataRowVersion.Original, Nothing))
Me.SqlUpdateCommand1.Parameters.Add(New _
     System.Data.SqlClient.SqlParameter("@Original_city1", _
     System.Data.SqlDbType.VarChar, 20, _
     System.Data.ParameterDirection.Input, True, CType(0, Byte), _
     CType(0, Byte), "city", _
     System.Data.DataRowVersion.Original, Nothing))
Me.SqlUpdateCommand1.Parameters.Add(New _
     System.Data.SqlClient.SqlParameter("@Original_contract", _
     System.Data.SqlDbType.Bit, 1, _
     System.Data.ParameterDirection.Input, False, _
     CType(0, Byte), CType(0, Byte), "contract", _
     System.Data.DataRowVersion.Original, Nothing))
Me.SqlUpdateCommand1.Parameters.Add(New _
     System.Data.SqlClient.SqlParameter("@Original_phone", _
     System.Data.SqlDbType.Char, 12, _
     System.Data.ParameterDirection.Input, False, CType(0, Byte), _
     CType(0, Byte), "phone", _
     System.Data.DataRowVersion.Original, Nothing))
Me.SqlUpdateCommand1.Parameters.Add(New _
     System.Data.SqlClient.SqlParameter("@Original_state", _
     System.Data.SqlDbType.Char, 2, _
```

```
                System.Data.ParameterDirection.Input, True, CType(0, Byte), _
                CType(0, Byte), "state", _
                System.Data.DataRowVersion.Original, Nothing))
    Me.SqlUpdateCommand1.Parameters.Add(New _
                System.Data.SqlClient.SqlParameter("@Original_state1", _
                System.Data.SqlDbType.Char, 2, _
                System.Data.ParameterDirection.Input, True, CType(0, Byte), _
                CType(0, Byte), "state", _
                System.Data.DataRowVersion.Original, Nothing))
    Me.SqlUpdateCommand1.Parameters.Add(New _
                System.Data.SqlClient.SqlParameter("@Original_zip", _
                System.Data.SqlDbType.Char, 5, _
                System.Data.ParameterDirection.Input, True, CType(0, Byte), _
                CType(0, Byte), "zip", _
                System.Data.DataRowVersion.Original, Nothing))
    Me.SqlUpdateCommand1.Parameters.Add(New _
                System.Data.SqlClient.SqlParameter("@Original_zip1", _
                System.Data.SqlDbType.Char, 5, _
                System.Data.ParameterDirection.Input, True, _
                CType(0, Byte), CType(0, Byte), "zip", _
                System.Data.DataRowVersion.Original, Nothing))
    Me.SqlUpdateCommand1.Parameters.Add(New _
                System.Data.SqlClient.SqlParameter("@Select_au_id", _
                System.Data.SqlDbType.Char, 11, _
                System.Data.ParameterDirection.Input, False, CType(0, Byte), _
                CType(0, Byte), "au_id", _
                System.Data.DataRowVersion.Current, Nothing))
    '
    'DataSet11
    '
    Me.DataSet11.DataSetName = "DataSet1"
    Me.DataSet11.Locale = New System.Globalization.CultureInfo("en-US")
    Me.DataSet11.Namespace = "http://www.tempuri.org/DataSet1.xsd"
    '
    'DataGrid1
    '
    Me.DataGrid1.DataMember = "authors"
    Me.DataGrid1.DataSource = Me.DataSet11
    Me.DataGrid1.Location = New System.Drawing.Point(8, 16)
    Me.DataGrid1.Name = "DataGrid1"
    Me.DataGrid1.Size = New System.Drawing.Size(272, 240)
    Me.DataGrid1.TabIndex = 0
    '
    'Form1
    '
    Me.AutoScaleBaseSize = New System.Drawing.Size(5, 13)
    Me.ClientSize = New System.Drawing.Size(292, 273)
```

```
        Me.Controls.AddRange(New System.Windows.Forms.Control() _
            {Me.DataGrid1})
        Me.Name = "Form1"
        Me.Text = "Form1"
        CType(Me.DataSet11, _
            System.ComponentModel.ISupportInitialize).EndInit()
        CType(Me.DataGrid1, _
            System.ComponentModel.ISupportInitialize).EndInit()
        Me.ResumeLayout(False)

    End Sub

#End Region

    Private Sub Form1_Load(ByVal sender As System.Object, _
        ByVal e As System.EventArgs) Handles MyBase.Load
        DataSet11.Clear()
        SqlDataAdapter1.Fill(DataSet11)
    End Sub
End Class
```

Related solution:	Found on page:
Creating a Dataset in Code	956

Populating a Dataset

Datasets are disconnected from data sources, and to populate them with data, you must use a data adapter. As shown in the EasyAccess example discussed in the In Depth section of this chapter, you can use a data adapter's **Fill** method to fill a dataset:

```
DataSet11.Clear()
SqlDataAdapter1.Fill(DataSet11)
```

Displaying Data in a Data Grid

Also as shown in the EasyAccess example, you can connect a data grid control to a dataset, using the data grid's **DataSource** and **DataMember** properties. Data grids are especially useful, because they can display an entire table at once. (You also can click a column header to sort the data on the corresponding field.)

You can see a data grid at work in Figure 20.10, in the EasyAccess example. We'll cover data grids in depth in Chapter 21—see "Using the **DataGrid** Class" in that chapter.

Selecting a Data Provider (SQL Server, MS Jet, and so on)

By default, Visual Basic assumes that you're working with SQL Server when you create a data connection. However, you can change that when you create a connection by informing Visual Basic of your actual data provider.

You can tell Visual Basic which data provider you're using when you create a data connection (see "Creating a New Data Connection" in this chapter), which you do using the Data Link Properties dialog. Simply click the dialog's Provider tab, as you see in Figure 20.6, and select the data provider you want to work with.

For an example that uses MS Jet 4.0 as a data provider, see "Connecting to an MS Jet Database" in this chapter.

Data Access Using Data Adapter Controls

As we saw in the DataAccess example in the In Depth section of this chapter, you can drag either a **SqlDataAdapter** or **OleDbDataAdapter** control to a form from the Data tab of the toolbox. When you do, the Data Adapter Configuration Wizard opens, as you see in Figure 20.11. You use this wizard to configure the new data adapter—see the coverage of the DataAccess example for all the details.

Related solution:	*Found on page:*
Creating a Data Adapter in Code	958

Previewing Data from Data Adapters

After you've set up a data adapter, you can get a quick look at the data it provides with the Data Adapter Preview dialog. Just click the Data|Preview Data menu item, or right-click an adapter and select the Preview Data menu item, to open this dialog, as you see in Figure 20.20, and click the Fill Dataset button to display the data from the adapter.

Getting a data preview such as this is very helpful to make sure you know what data the adapter will provide to your program, without having to actually run your program. See also "Examining Dataset Properties" in this chapter, coming up next.

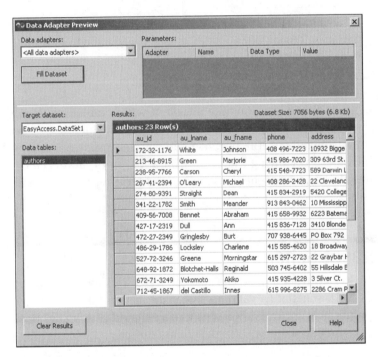

Figure 20.20   Previewing data in the EasyAccess example.

Examining Dataset Properties

You can take a look at the Dataset properties for the dataset(s) in an application by using the Data|Dataset Properties menu item, or by right-clicking a dataset and selecting the Dataset Properties item, opening the Dataset Properties dialog you see in Figure 20.21.

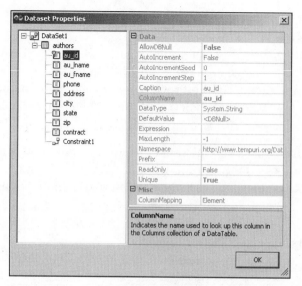

Figure 20.21   Dataset Properties in the EasyAccess example.

The Dataset Properties dialog lets you take a look at which tables are in which datasets, as well as which fields and constraints are in which tables, as you see in Figure 20.21. This is especially useful, because you can determine not only what fields are in a table (see "Previewing Data From Data Adapters" in this chapter), but also get the detailed format of the data in each field in every table this way.

Examining Dataset Schema

As discussed in the In Depth section of this chapter, ADO.NET uses XML to transfer data, and uses XML schema to validate that data. If you know what you're doing in XML, you might want to edit or check the schema that Visual Basic is using for your data; you can work with such schema directly.

To do that, you need a dataset. To take a look at the XML schema Visual Basic is using for a particular dataset, use the Data|View Dataset Schema menu item, or right-click a dataset and select the View Schema menu item. This opens the dataset's schema, which is a file with the extension .xsd, in a Visual Basic designer, as you see in Figure 20.22. As you see in that figure, you can work with the XML of the schema directly in that designer.

You can toggle between XML and Dataset view by clicking the buttons at the bottom of the designer—in XML view, you see the actual XML of the schema, and in Dataset view, you see the resulting types, field by field, for the dataset, as shown in Figure 20.23.

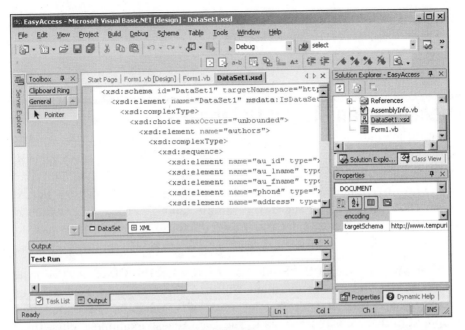

Figure 20.22 A dataset's schema in XML view.

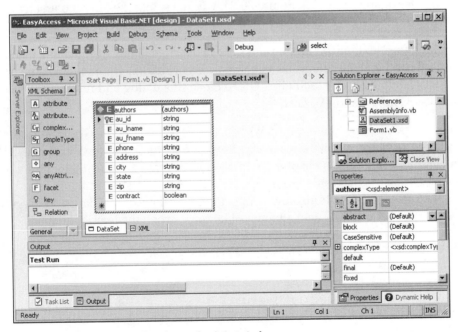

Figure 20.23 A dataset's schema in dataset view.

Related solution:	Found on page:
Writing Datasets to XML and Reading Datasets from XML	966

Connecting to an MS Jet Database

Visual Basic's data access was originally built to work with the Microsoft Jet data access engine, which is the engine in Microsoft Access. Plenty of people still use Jet databases, often because they use MS Access to create them, so I'll take a look at how to connect a Jet database to your Visual Basic code here. In particular, I'll enter the data you see in the sample table in Figure 20.1, which holds students' names and grades, into an MS Jet database named students.mdb, using MS Access.

Next, as you can see in the Students example on the CD-ROM, I've dragged **anOleDbDataAdapter** to the main Windows form, as we've also done in the DataAccess example in the In Depth section of this chapter. This opens the Data Adapter Configuration Wizard, as in the DataAccess example. I click the New Connection button in the second window of this wizard to open the Data Link Properties dialog you see in Figure 20.24, where I select the MS Jet data engine in the Provider tab.

Clicking the Next button in the Data Link Properties dialog displays the Connection tab in the same dialog, as you see in Figure 20.25. Here, I navigate to the students.mdb database, and click OK to close this dialog and return to the Data Adapter Configuration Wizard.

In the Data Adapter Configuration Wizard, I select the Name and Grade fields of the **Students** table, in much the same way as we did in the DataAccess example in the In Depth section of this chapter. Then, also as in that example, I generate a new dataset using the **Students** table with the Data|Generate Dataset menu item, naming that dataset **dsStudents**, and connect the new dataset to a data grid. Finally, I fill the data set from the data adapter—like this—when the main form loads:

```
Private Sub Form1_Load(ByVal sender As System.Object, _
    ByVal e As System.EventArgs) Handles MyBase.Load
    dsStudents1.Clear()
    OleDbDataAdapter1.Fill(dsStudents1)
End Sub
```

And that's all it takes—you can see the result in Figure 20.26, where this example is displaying the data in the **Students** table.

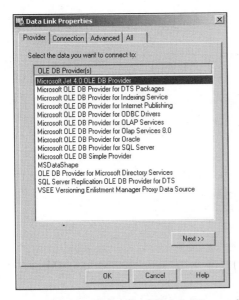

Figure 20.24   Using the MS Jet data provider.

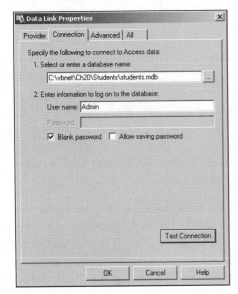

Figure 20.25   Accessing an MS Jet database.

Figure 20.26   The Students example at work.

Using Relational Databases

As discussed in the In Depth section of this chapter, relational databases are powerful databases that connect tables with specific keys, and by using relational concepts, you can perform many SQL operations. You can see how this works in the Relational example on the CD-ROM.

In that example, I've dragged a data adapter onto the main form, which opens the Data Adapter Configuration Wizard. To configure the adapter's SQL statement, I click the Query Builder button, as we did earlier in the DataAccess example in the In Depth section of this chapter, and use the Add Table dialog to add two tables to the Query Builder from the SQL Server pubs database: **authors** and **titleauthor**. These two tables share a key, au_id (Author ID), which relates the records of one table to the records of the other table. The Query Builder displays this relation graphically, as you see in Figure 20.27.

I select a number of fields from both tables to add to the data adapter, as you see in Figure 20.27, and click OK to close the Query Builder. Because we're dealing with two tables at once with an SQL **JOIN** operation, Visual Basic can't generate SQL for updating that data, so click the Advanced Options button in the Data Adapter Configuration Wizard and deselect the "Generate Insert, Update, and Delete Statements" checkbox. (If you didn't do so and tried to move on to the next step of the wizard, Visual Basic would inform you of the error, and you could move back, click the Advanced Options button, and remove the offending statements.) This generates the following SQL:

```
SELECT
    authors.au_id,
    authors.au_lname,
```

```
    titleauthor.au_id AS Expr1,
    titleauthor.title_id,
    titleauthor.au_ord,
    titleauthor.royaltyper,
    authors.au_fname
FROM
    authors INNER
JOIN
    titleauthor ON
        authors.au_id = titleauthor.au_id
```

You can see the result in a datagrid in Figure 20.28. Note how this works—some authors in the **authors** table have multiple entries in the **titleauthor** table, so, for example, you can see that Green has two different title_id entries, as does Locksley, and so on. In this way, the **authors** and **titleauthors** tables have been *joined*, using their common key, au_id.

This example uses one SQL query to join two related table, but there's another way of working with related tables—you can create a data relation object to make the relationship explicit, while still working with the two tables independently (without joining them)—see "Using Master/Detail Relationships and Data Relation Objects" in the next chapter.

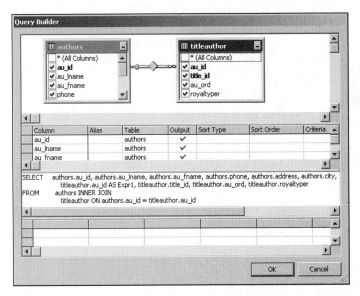

Figure 20.27   The Query Builder, showing a relation between two tables.

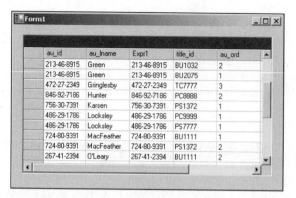

Figure 20.28   Using related tables.

Adding Multiple Tables to a Dataset

A single dataset can contain multiple tables. You can see how this works in the
MultiTable example on the CD-ROM. In this case, I've added two **SqlDataAdapter**
controls to the main form, and connected one to the **authors** table in the SQL
Server pubs database, and the second to the **publishers** table in the same data-
base. Now when I create a dataset (using the Data|Generate Dataset item menu
item), I add both those tables to the dataset, as you see in the Generate Dataset
dialog in Figure 20.29.

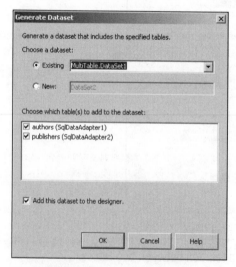

Figure 20.29   Using multiple tables.

That's all it takes; that's the way to add both tables to the same dataset. Now I can bind two data grids to the same dataset, displaying a different table in each data grid. (After setting the data grids' **DataSource** property to the new dataset, I've set the **DataMember** property of the first data grid to authors and the **DataMember** property of the second data grid to publishers.) You can see the result in Figure 20.30.

Related solution:	*Found on page:*
Creating a Data Table in Code	960

Figure 20.30   Working with multiple tables from the same dataset.

Using Data Views

We've worked with datasets primarily in this chapter, but, as discussed in the In Depth section, you also can use data views to get a snapshot of the data in a table and work with it. Data views are much like read-only mini-datasets; you typically load only a subset of a dataset into a data view.

There's an example named DataViews on the CD-ROM. In that example, I've connected an SQL data adapter to the **authors** table in the SQL Server pubs database, and created a dataset, **DataSet11**, from that table. Next, I add a data view, **DataView1**, to this example, by clicking the Data tab in the toolbox and dragging a data view to the example's main form. To specify where the data view should get its data from, I set the data view's **Table** property to **DataSet11.authors**. (When you click the **Table** property in the Properties window, Visual Basic will list the available tables to work with.)

Next, I add a data grid to the main form, and set the data grid's **DataSource** property to **DataView1** (without setting the data grid's **DataMember** property). This connects the data grid to the data view, and if we did nothing more, the data grid would pass the entire **authors** table on to the data grid. However, you usually use data views to work with just a subset of the data in a table, and you can specify what subset you want using the **RowFilter** property. For example, to get only authors with the last name White, I'll set the data view's **RowFilter** property to **au_lname = "White"**. And, as usual, I add code to populate the data set from a data adapter:

```
Private Sub Form1_Load(ByVal sender As System.Object, _
    ByVal e As System.EventArgs) Handles MyBase.Load
    DataSet11.Clear()
    SqlDataAdapter1.Fill(DataSet11)
End Sub
```

You can see the results in Figure 20.31, where the only author whose last name is White is displayed. In this way, we've loaded a filtered snapshot of our data into a data view and bound it to a data grid.

You also can use a data view's **DataViewRowState** property to add rows to a data view depending on their *state*. For example, you can place rows that have been deleted or are new in a data view using this property. Here are the possible state values you can use, and the types of rows they match, from the **DataViewRowState** enumeration:

- **Added**—Added rows.

- **CurrentRows**—Current rows including unchanged, new, and modified rows.

- **Deleted**—Deleted rows.

- **ModifiedCurrent**—The current rows, a modified version of the original data.

Figure 20.31   The DataViews example at work.

- **ModifiedOriginal**—The original rows which have since been modified; the modified rows are available in **ModifiedCurrent**.

- **None**—No rows.

- **OriginalRows**—Original rows, including unchanged and deleted rows.

- **Unchanged**—Unchanged rows.

For example, here's how I make sure that only rows that have been added to a table appear in a data view:

```
Private Sub Form1_Load(ByVal sender As System.Object, _
    ByVal e As System.EventArgs) Handles MyBase.Load
    DataSet11.Clear()
    SqlDataAdapter1.Fill(DataSet11)
    DataView1.RowStateFilter = DataViewRowState.Added
End Sub
```

Chapter 21

Binding Controls to Databases

If you need an immediate solution to:	*See page:*
Using the **DataBindings** Property for Data Binding	905
Using the **ControlBindingsCollection** Class	905
Using the **Binding** Class	907
Creating Simple Data Binding	908
Creating Complex Data Binding	908
Binding Text Boxes	909
Binding Buttons	910
Binding Checkboxes	910
Binding Radio Buttons	911
Binding Combo Boxes	911
Binding List Boxes	912
Binding Checked List Boxes	912
Using the **DisplayMember** and **ValueMember** Properties	913
Using the **DataGrid** Class	913
Binding Data Grids	916
Using the **BindingContext** Class	917
Navigating in Datasets	917
Creating Data Forms Automatically	918
Using Parameterized SQL Queries	919
Using Master/Detail Relationships and Data Relation Objects	919
Using the **ErrorProvider** Class	923
Performing Data Validation in Controls	924

In Depth

In this chapter, we're going to take a look at binding controls to data sources. This usually means binding controls to data from databases; for example, you might bind a text box to the last names of authors (that is, the au_lname field) from the **authors** table of the pubs database, which would make the text box display those names automatically as you moved through the database. Or you might bind the whole **authors** table to a data grid, as we did in the previous chapter. However, data binding has gone far beyond the traditional. In Windows forms, you can now bind controls not to just data in databases, but to just about any programming construct that holds data. For example, you can bind control properties to an array of values, the data you read from a file, or to the properties of another control.

You also can now bind any property of any control to a data source. For example, not only can you bind the **Text** property of a text box to a data source, but also the size and image in a picture box, the background color of a label, even whether or not a list box has a border. In Visual Basic .NET, data binding has become an automatic way of setting any property that you can access at run time of any control in a form.

There are plenty of ways to use data binding in Visual Basic applications; here are some common scenarios:

- *Navigation*—When you bind a data source to controls, you can display the data in that source and allow the user to move through that data, record by record. This is a great way to give the user easy access to your data.

- *Data Entry*—Using data binding, you can create data-entry forms, letting the user enter data that is then sent to a database. The user can enter data using, for example, text boxes, radio buttons, list boxes, drop-down list boxes, and checkboxes, making it easy to work with what otherwise might be a complex database system.

- *Master/Detail Applications*—When you have a data relation that ties tables together, binding that data to controls can let you make use of that relation. For example, you may display the names of publishers from the **publishers** table in the pubs database in a combo box, and, when the user selects one of the publishers, the titles they've published, from the table named **titles**, come up in a data grid. (The connection between the two tables is supported with the pub_id field; see "Using Master/Detail Relationships and Data Relation Objects" in this chapter for an example of this at work.) This is called a master/detail, or parent/child, relation between the tables.

- *Data Lookups*—Your code may deal with product ID and SKU codes, but you may want to display the actual names of the products you're dealing with. For example, it's going to be a lot easier to understand "Lawn Tennis Kit" than ID 438583920, and using data binding, you can display a user-friendly name like "Lawn Tennis Kit" while at the same time working with the associated code-friendly values like 438583920 behind the scenes in your program. This is supported with the **ValueMember** and **DisplayMember** properties that controls such as list boxes support; when the user chooses their lawn tennis kit, your code can actually read 438583920 from the list box.

We're going to see how all of these techniques work in this chapter, with examples. Before we start actually doing some data binding, we first have to understand that there are two ways of binding data in Visual Basic—simple and complex. And there are advantages and disadvantages to both these techniques.

Simple Binding

Simple binding lets you to display *one* data element, such as a field's value from a data table, in a control. In Visual Basic .NET, you can simple-bind *any* property of a control to a data value.

For example, to bind a text box's **Text** property to the au_lname field in the **authors** table from the pubs database in a dataset, **DataSet11**, you select the text box and expand its **(DataBindings)** property in the Properties window. You'll see the most commonly bound properties already listed, such as the **Tag** and **Text** properties for a text box, as shown in Figure 21.1. You can select a field in a dataset to bind to just by clicking a property and selecting a table from the drop-down list that appears.

As mentioned, you can bind to any property of a control. To do that, click the ellipsis button that appears when you click the **(Advanced)** entry in the **(DataBindings)** property, opening the Advanced Data Binding dialog you see in Figure 21.2.

Using the Advanced Data Binding dialog, you can bind any property of a control to a data source.

Note that because simple-bound controls show only one data element at a time (such as the current author's last name), it's usual to include navigation controls in a Windows form with simple-bound controls; we'll do that in this chapter in the DataBinding example on the CD-ROM. The navigation controls will let the user move from record to record just by clicking buttons, and all the data in the bound controls will be updated automatically to match.

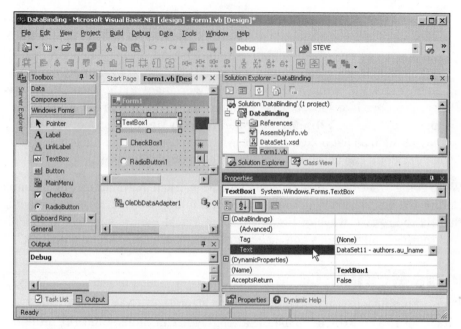

Figure 21.1   Binding a text box to a data table.

Figure 21.2   The Advanced Data Binding dialog.

You also can perform simple binding in code, using a control's **DataBindings** property (see "Using the **DataBindings** Property for Data Binding" in this chapter), which holds a collection of **Binding** objects (see "Using the **Binding** Class" in this chapter) corresponding to the bindings for the control. For example, in code, we could bind the text box to the same au_lname field that we just bound it to at design time. Using the collection's **Add** method, you pass this method the property to bind, the data source to use, and the specific field you want to bind:

```
TextBox1.DataBindings.Add("Text", DataSet11, "authors.au_lname")
```

The **Add** method is overloaded so that you can pass it a **Binding** object directly, as in this example, where I'm binding a date-time picker's **Value** property to a field in a data table:

```
DateTimePicker1.DataBindings.Add _
    (New Binding("Value", DataSet11, "customers.DeliveryDate"))
```

You can even bind one control to another in code this way. Here, I'm binding the **Text** property of one text box to another, which means that if you change the text in the source text box, the text in the bound text box will change immediately to match:

```
TextBox2.DataBindings.Add("Text", TextBox1, "Text")
```

Complex Binding

Simple data binding binds to one data item at a time, such as a name displayed in a text box, but complex data binding allows a control to bind to more than one data element, such as more than one record in a database, at the same time. We've seen complex binding at work in the previous chapter, where we bound an entire data table to a data grid. Instead of displaying just one data item at a time, the data grid displayed the entire table at once, including all the fields and field data (see "Using the **DataGrid** Class" in this chapter). Most controls support only simple data binding but some, such as data grids and list boxes, support complex data binding.

Complex data binding revolves around these properties:

- **DataSource**—The data source, typically a dataset such as **DataSet11**.

- **DataMember**—The data member you want to work with in the data source, typically a table in a dataset such as the **authors** table in the pubs database. Data grids use this property to determine which table they should display.

- **DisplayMember**—The field you want a control to display, such as the author's last name, au_lname. List boxes use the **DisplayMember** and **ValueMember** properties instead of a **DataMember** property.

- **ValueMember**—The field you want the control to return in properties like **SelectedValue**, such as au_id. List boxes use the **DisplayMember** and **ValueMember** properties instead of a **DataMember** property.

We've seen the **DataSource** and **DataMember** properties when we worked with data grids in the previous chapter, but what about **DisplayMember** and **ValueMember**? These handy properties are designed to let you display data in a user-friendly way. For example, you might have a checked list box, as we do in the DataBinding example coming up next, and want to get the ID of the author the user selects. However, it's a little rough asking the user to select the author they want from a list of values like 172-32-1176, which is how author IDs are stored in the **authors** table in the pubs database. Instead, you can set the checked list box's **DisplayMember** property to the au_lname field to display the author's last name in the control, and the **ValueMember** property to the au_id field so that when the user makes a selection, you can use the **SelectedValue** property of the control to get the selected author's ID (see "Binding List Boxes" and "Using the **DisplayMember** and **ValueMember** Properties" in this chapter).

Setting the above four properties at run time is also easy—you just assign them a new value. For example, here's how I bind a dataset, **DataSet11**, to a data grid in code, showing the **authors** table:

```
DataGrid1.DataSource = DataSet11
DataGrid1.DataMember = "authors"
```

You also can use the built-in data grid method named **SetDataBinding** for this (data grids are the only controls that have this method):

```
DataGrid1.SetDataBinding(dsDataSet, "authors")
```

And here's how I bind the **dsDataSet** dataset to a list box using the **DisplayMember** property, using the au_lname field in the **authors** table; note the syntax used to specify a field in a table: authors.au_lname:

```
ListBox1.DataSource = dsDataSet
ListBox1.DisplayMember = "authors.au_lname"
```

And that's all the overview we need—now it's time to get to some real code as we work with the DataBinding example.

Binding Data to Controls

The DataBinding example on the CD-ROM shows how to perform data binding, both simple and complex. As you can see in Figure 21.3, this example uses a number of different data-bound controls; in this case, we're binding to the **authors** table of the SQL Server example pubs database.

Figure 21.3   The DataBinding example.

All I'm doing here is using simple and complex data binding as we've already seen. In this case, I've created a dataset, **DataSet11**, and filled it with data from the **authors** table in the pubs database, and bound it to various controls. For example, I've bound the **Text** property of the text box at upper left to the authors.au_lname field, the **Checked** property of the checkbox to the authors.contract field (which is a field of type **Boolean**, holding **True/False** values), the **Text** property of the radio button to the authors.au_lname field, the entire **authors** table to the data grid at upper right, the **DisplayMember** of the list box to the authors.au_lname field, and so on.

This works fine, and you'll see the data you've bound to the various controls when you run the program, but there's a problem—the simple-bound controls such as text boxes only display one data item (for example, the current author's last name) at a time. How can the user move to the next record?

Navigating in Datasets

You usually add navigation controls, such as the buttons at the bottom of the DataBinding example in Figure 21.3, to let the user move from record to record. When the user clicks the > button, for example, the bound data from the next field is displayed in the text box, so the name displayed in the text box changes from the first author's last name, White, to the last name of the next author, Green. The >> button moves to the last record, as you'd expect; the << button moves to the first record, and so on. And note that the code also displays the user's current location in a label control at the bottom.

To set the current record bound to the various controls in a form, you use the form's **BindingContext** property (see "Using the **BindingContext** Class" in this chapter), which is inherited from the **Control** class. The binding context sets the location in various data sources that are bound in the form. To see how to use the binding context, I'll start by seeing how the code displays the current location in the **authors** table.

TIP: *Note that, unlike in ADO's record sets, ADO.NET's datasets do not use the concept of a current record. To work with the record currently displayed in simple data-bound controls, you use a form's **BindingContext** property instead.*

Displaying the Current Location

When the DataBinding example first loads, it fills its dataset from its data adapter, as we've done in the previous chapter. It also displays the current position in the dataset's binding context for the **authors** table by using the form's **Binding Context** property's **Position** and **Count** members, like this:

```
Private Sub Form1_Load(ByVal sender As System.Object, ByVal _
    e As System.EventArgs) Handles MyBase.Load
    DataSet11.Clear()
    OleDbDataAdapter1.Fill(DataSet11)
    Label1.Text = (Me.BindingContext(DataSet11, "authors").Position + _
        1).ToString & " of  " & Me.BindingContext(DataSet11, _
        "authors").Count.ToString
End Sub
```

This code gives you the "3 of 23" text you see in the bottom of Figure 21.3 as the user moves through the dataset.

Moving to the Next Record

So how does the user actually move through the dataset? They use the arrow buttons in the DataBinding example for navigation; when the user clicks the > arrow, I just increment the **Position** property of the binding context for the **authors** table, and then display the new location in the label between the navigation buttons:

```
Private Sub Button3_Click(ByVal sender As System.Object, _
    ByVal e As System.EventArgs) Handles Button3.Click
    Me.BindingContext(DataSet11, "authors").Position = _
        (Me.BindingContext(DataSet11, "authors").Position + 1)
    Label1.Text = (((Me.BindingContext(DataSet11, "authors").Position _
        + 1).ToString & " of  ") & Me.BindingContext(DataSet11, _
        "authors").Count.ToString)
End Sub
```

Note that if you try to move beyond the end of the record set, the **Position** property isn't incremented.

Moving to the Previous Record

In the same way, when the user clicks the < button to move to the previous record, the code simply decrements the **Position** value:

```
Private Sub Button2_Click(ByVal sender As System.Object, _
    ByVal e As System.EventArgs) Handles Button2.Click
    Me.BindingContext(DataSet11, "authors").Position = _
        (Me.BindingContext(DataSet11, "authors").Position - 1)
    Label1.Text = (((Me.BindingContext(DataSet11, "authors").Position _
        + 1).ToString & " of  ") & Me.BindingContext(DataSet11, _
        "authors").Count.ToString)
End Sub
```

Moving to the First Record

Moving to the first record in the binding context for the **authors** table is easy; you just set the **Position** property to **0**:

```
Private Sub Button4_Click(ByVal sender As System.Object, _
    ByVal e As System.EventArgs) Handles Button4.Click
    Me.BindingContext(DataSet11, "authors").Position = 0
    Label1.Text = (((Me.BindingContext(DataSet11, "authors").Position _
        + 1).ToString & " of  ") & Me.BindingContext(DataSet11, _
        "authors").Count.ToString)
End Sub
```

Moving to the Last Record

Moving to the last record is also easy, because we know that the **Count** property returns the total number of records in the table:

```
Private Sub Button5_Click(ByVal sender As System.Object, _
    ByVal e As System.EventArgs) Handles Button5.Click
    Me.BindingContext(DataSet11, "authors").Position = _
        Me.BindingContext(DataSet11, "authors").Count - 1
    Label1.Text = (((Me.BindingContext(DataSet11, "authors").Position _
        + 1).ToString & " of  ") & Me.BindingContext(DataSet11, _
        "authors").Count.ToString)
End Sub
```

And that gives us a good introduction to using navigation controls to move around in a dataset simply bound to controls. You also might note that even the controls that are complex-bound display the current binding context record; as you see in Figure 21.3, the current record is highlighted in the checked list box and in the list box. Also, the data grid at the upper right of the figure displays a small arrow indicating the current record.

The DataBinding example illustrates one more point that is good to know as well—the difference between the **DisplayMember** and **ValueMember** properties, and I'll take a look at that now.

Using the DisplayMember and ValueMember Properties

If you take a look at the checked list box at lower left in the DataBinding example in Figure 21.3, you'll note that this control is displaying the authors' last names. However, when the user makes a selection in the checked list box, the program displays the author's ID value in the text box just below the checked list box, as you can see in Figure 21.3.

As we know, list boxes use **DisplayMember** and **ValueMember** properties to bind to a specific data field. In the DataBinding example, I've bound the checked list box's **DisplayMember** property to the authors.au_lname field, and the **ValueMember** property to the authors.au_id field. That means the program will show the author's last name in the checked list box, but when the user clicks an author in that control, I'll use the control's **SelectedValue** property to get the actual author's ID value and display it:

```
Private Sub CheckedListBox1_SelectedIndexChanged(ByVal sender _
    As System.Object, ByVal e As System.EventArgs) Handles _
    CheckedListBox1.SelectedIndexChanged
    TextBox2.Text = "Selected ID: " & CheckedListBox1.SelectedValue
End Sub
```

In this way, as discussed earlier in this chapter, the checked list box can display user-friendly names, while actually returning code-friendly ID values.

That completes the DataBinding example on the CD-ROM. But there's more to cover—for example, what if the user wanted to edit the data in bound controls and send the new data back to the data store? In that case, you'd want a data entry form—and Visual Basic has a great tool to let you create data entry forms automatically—the Data Form Wizard.

Creating Data Forms with the Data Form Wizard

There's an easy way to create a data-entry form in Visual Basic—just use the Data Form Wizard. I'll do that in the DataForm example on the CD-ROM, which creates a data-entry form for the **authors** table in the pubs database.

A data form is a new form added to your project, so to create such a form, DataForm1.vb, use the Project|Add New Item menu item, then select the Data Form Wizard icon in the Templates pane and click OK. This opens the Data Form Wizard you see in Figure 21.4.

Click the Next button in the Data Form Wizard to move to the pane you see in Figure 21.5, where the Wizard is asking for the name of a dataset to create (or you can use an existing dataset); I'll name the new dataset **dsDataSet1** here.

In the next pane, the Wizard asks what data connection to use (or allows you to create a new connection), and I'll use a connection to the pubs database, as you see in Figure 21.6.

In the next pane, you can choose which table(s) to add to the data form, and I'll add the **authors** table, as you see in Figure 21.7.

If you are working with multiple tables, you can create a master/detail relationship between the tables (see "Using Master/Detail Relationships and Data Relation Objects" in this chapter) in the next pane, as you see in Figure 21.8. I'll just click next to move on to the next pane here.

Figure 21.4   The Data Form Wizard.

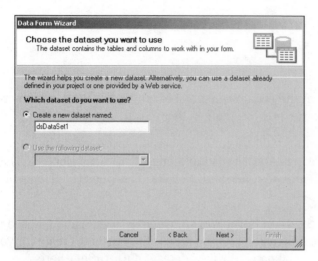

Figure 21.5   Creating a dataset.

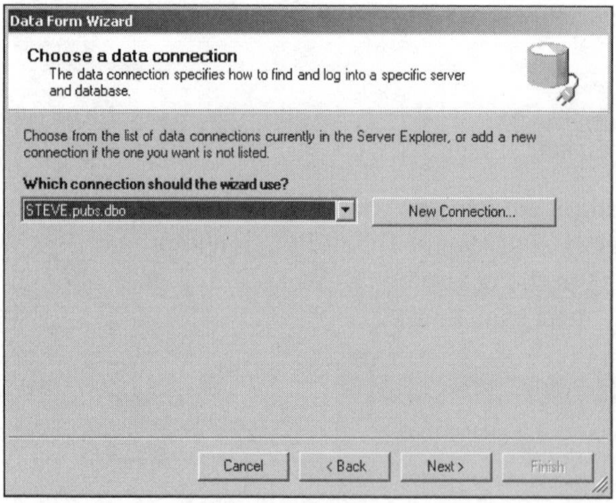

Figure 21.6   Specifying a data connection.

In the next pane, you can select the display style—whether the data form will use a data grid or separate, simply bound controls. I'll specify separate controls here; as you can see in Figure 21.9, that means the data form also can contain Add, Delete, and other controls.

Finally, click the Finish button to create the data form, DataForm1.vb, and add it to the project. What does this data form look like? You can see it in Figure 21.10,

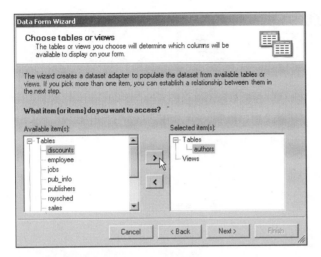

Figure 21.7 Selecting a data table.

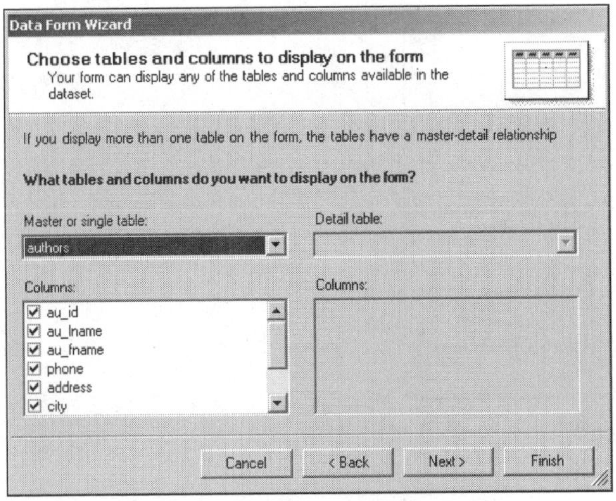

Figure 21.8 Selecting a data table to display.

where I've clicked the Load button to load the **authors** table. In this case, I've added code to the main form to make the data form visible:

```
Private Sub Form1_Load(ByVal sender As System.Object, _
    ByVal e As System.EventArgs) Handles MyBase.Load
    Dim d As New DataForm1()
    d.Show()
End Sub
```

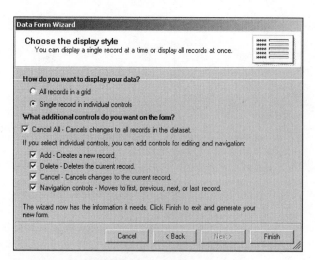

Figure 21.9 Selecting the display style.

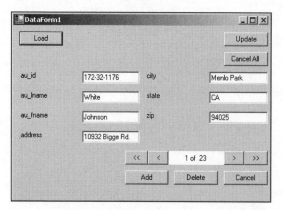

Figure 21.10 A data form at work.

In the data form, you can see all the data in the current record displayed (you can move the controls around in a data form if the default layout doesn't suit you, of course), as well as navigation buttons, and Add, Delete, Cancel, and Update buttons.

The Add, Delete, Cancel, and Update buttons let you edit the data in the dataset in the form, and send it back to the database. When the user changes the data in the bound controls, the changed data is sent back to the dataset immediately, starting an *edit operation* in the dataset—note that any changes to the dataset are only sent back to the database when the user clicks the Update button. The Add button adds a new empty record to the end of the dataset, the Delete button deletes a record, and the Cancel button cancels any edit operation in the dataset that hasn't been sent back to the database yet. I'll take a look at the data form code for these various operations here.

Adding Records to a Dataset

Adding records to a dataset is easy, as you can see in the code the data form uses for this purpose—all you have to do is to use the **BindingContext** object's **AddNew** method:

```
Private Sub btnAdd_Click(ByVal sender As System.Object, _
    ByVal e As System.EventArgs) Handles btnAdd.Click
    Try
        'Clear out the current edits
        Me.BindingContext(objdsDataSet1, "authors").EndCurrentEdit()
        Me.BindingContext(objdsDataSet1, "authors").AddNew()
    Catch eEndEdit As System.Exception
        System.Windows.Forms.MessageBox.Show(eEndEdit.Message)
    End Try
    Me.objdsDataSet1_PositionChanged()
End Sub
```

Note also the call to the **objdsDataSet1_PositionChanged** Sub procedure—all this procedure does is to update the "1 of 23" text at the bottom of the data form:

```
Private Sub objdsDataSet1_PositionChanged()
    Me.lblNavLocation.Text = _
        (((Me.BindingContext(objdsDataSet1, _
        "authors").Position + 1).ToString + " of  ") _
        + Me.BindingContext(objdsDataSet1, _
        "authors").Count.ToString)
    End Sub
```

Deleting Records from a Dataset

To delete a record from the dataset, all you have to do is to use the **RemoveAt** method of the binding context:

```
Private Sub btnDelete_Click(ByVal sender As System.Object, _
    ByVal e As System.EventArgs) Handles btnDelete.Click
    If (Me.BindingContext(objdsDataSet1, "authors").Count > 0) Then
        Me.BindingContext(objdsDataSet1, _
            "authors").RemoveAt(Me.BindingContext(objdsDataSet1, _
            "authors").Position)
        Me.objdsDataSet1_PositionChanged()
    End If
End Sub
```

Canceling a Dataset Edit

When you begin to change the data in the controls bound to a dataset, that in turn starts an edit operation in the dataset. The next time the Update button is clicked, the edited records will be sent to the database itself. If you want to cancel the current edit operation, you can click the Cancel button, which uses the **CancelCurrentEdit** method:

```
Private Sub btnCancel_Click(ByVal sender As System.Object, _
    ByVal e As System.EventArgs) Handles btnCancel.Click
    Me.BindingContext(objdsDataSet1, "authors").CancelCurrentEdit()
    Me.objdsDataSet1_PositionChanged()
End Sub
```

Updating the Underlying Data Store

Working with the dataset is fairly easy, but when it comes to sending the changes back to the database itself, things get more complex, as you can see by taking a look at the code for the Update button in the data form. This code starts by calling a Sub procedure named **UpdateDataSet**:

```
Private Sub btnUpdate_Click(ByVal sender As System.Object, _
    ByVal e As System.EventArgs) Handles btnUpdate.Click
    Try
        Me.UpdateDataSet()
    Catch eUpdate As System.Exception
        System.Windows.Forms.MessageBox.Show(eUpdate.Message)
    End Try
    Me.objdsDataSet1_PositionChanged()
End Sub
```

In the **UpdateDataSet** Sub procedure, we want to send the changes that have been made back to the database, so the code starts by creating a new dataset that holds only the changed records, using the current dataset's **GetChanges** method. Then it sends that new dataset to a Sub procedure called **UpdateDataSource** to update the data source. After the call to **UpdateDataSource**, the code calls the **AcceptChanges** method of the main dataset so the current edit operation ends and the changed records are no longer considered "changed" records, but simply normal records:

```
Public Sub UpdateDataSet()
    'Create a new dataset to hold the changes that have been made
    'to the main dataset.
    Dim objDataSetChanges As DataForm.dsDataSet1 = _
        New DataForm.dsDataSet1()
```

```
        'Stop any current edits.
        Me.BindingContext(objdsDataSet1, "authors").EndCurrentEdit()
        'Get the changes that have been made to the main dataset.
        objDataSetChanges = CType(objdsDataSet1.GetChanges, _
            DataForm.dsDataSet1)
        'Check to see if any changes have been made.
        If (Not (objDataSetChanges) Is Nothing) Then
            Try
                'There are changes that need to be made, so attempt
                'to update the datasource by
                'calling the update method and passing the dataset and
                  any parameters.
                    Me.UpdateDataSource(objDataSetChanges)
                    objdsDataSet1.Merge(objDataSetChanges)
                    objdsDataSet1.AcceptChanges()
            Catch eUpdate As System.Exception
                'Add your error handling code here.
                Throw eUpdate
            End Try
            'Add your code to check the returned dataset
            'for any errors that may have been
            'pushed into the row object's error.
        End If
End Sub
```

TIP: *Note also the use of the **Merge** method in the code above; when you send the dataset of changes to the data provider, the data provider may make changes in that dataset (such as updating fields that hold calculated values, or adding primary keys) and return a new dataset, which this code then merges into the main dataset in the program, using the dataset's **Merge** method, before calling the **AcceptChanges** method.*

To actually pass the changes back to the database, the code uses the **Update** data adapter method. Here's how that works in the **UpdateDataSource** Sub procedure:

```
Public Sub UpdateDataSource(ByVal ChangedRows As DataForm.dsDataSet1)
    Try
        'The data source only needs to be updated if there are
        'changes pending.
        If (Not (ChangedRows) Is Nothing) Then
            'Open the connection.
            Me.OleDbConnection1.Open()
            'Attempt to update the data source.
            OleDbDataAdapter1.Update(ChangedRows)
        End If
    Catch updateException As System.Exception
```

```
            'Add your error handling code here.
            Throw updateException
        Finally
            'Close the connection whether or not the exception was thrown.
            Me.OleDbConnection1.Close()
        End Try
End Sub
```

And that's it—now the user can edit data and update the database with it, creating a true data-entry form.

Using SQL Parameters

Here's another example that uses data-bound controls, the ParameterizedQueries example on the CD-ROM, which also will give us more insight into working with SQL in Visual Basic data adapters. In this case, I'll use two data adapters and two datasets to let the user select the authors they want to view by state. You can see how it works in Figure 21.11. When the program loads, the states of the authors in the **authors** table of the pubs database are loaded into a dataset bound to the drop-down list you see in Figure 21.11. The user can then select a state from the list, and click the "Load data" button to load all the authors from that state into a second dataset, whose data is displayed in the text boxes in the figure.

Loading the state data from the **authors** table is easy in the first data adapter, **OleDbDataAdapter1**—I just give that data adapter this SQL in the Data Adapter Configuration Wizard (see "Accessing Data with Data Adaptors and DataSets" in the previous chapter):

```
SELECT DISTINCT state FROM authors
```

Note that I've added the keyword **DISTINCT** here so that only unique states are placed in the corresponding dataset—no state will be listed more than once.

After the user selects a state, how do we tell the second data adapter, **OleDbDataAdapter2** (which fills the dataset, **DataSet12**, for the rest of the controls) how to use that selection to choose its data? We can do that with a *SQL parameter*, which is much like a variable in other programming languages. Here's how that works; I'm using a parameter, indicated by the question mark (?), for the state field in a **WHERE** clause in the SQL for the second data adapter:

```
SELECT au_id, au_lname, state FROM authors WHERE (state = ?)
```

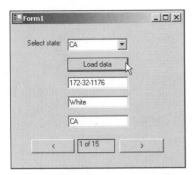

Figure 21.11   The ParameterizedQueries example.

In this case, I'm indicating that I want to set the value of the state field at run time, using a SQL parameter. You can either enter this SQL for **OleDbDataAdapter2** directly into the Data Adapter Configuration Wizard, or use the Query Builder in the Wizard, setting the Criteria column to a **?** (which Visual Basic immediately changes to the more proper SQL "**=?**") for the state field, as you see in Figure 21.12.

How do we place a value into the SQL parameter corresponding to the state field at run time? That's easy enough—you just refer to that parameter as

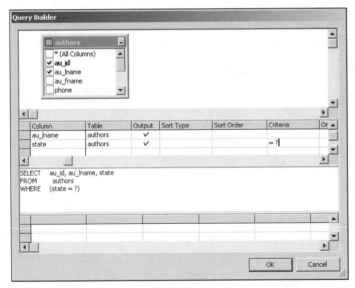

Figure 21.12   Adding a SQL parameter to a data adapter.

OleDbDataAdapter2.SelectCommand.Parameters("state"), and I'll set it to the state the user has selected in the combo box, then use the data adapter to fill the form's main dataset, like this:

```
Private Sub Button1_Click(ByVal sender As System.Object, _
    ByVal e As System.EventArgs) Handles Button1.Click
    OleDbDataAdapter2.SelectCommand.Parameters("state").Value = _
        ComboBox1.Text
    DataSet12.Clear()
    OleDbDataAdapter2.Fill(DataSet12)
    ShowPosition()
End Sub
```

And that's all it takes—now we're using SQL parameters with bound controls to let the user select the author's state. In fact, what we've created here is like a master/detail example, letting the user filter the records they want to see, but in this case, we're only using one data table. We'll see a true master/detail example soon—see "Using Master/Detail Relationships and Data Relation Objects" in the Immediate Solutions. Now that we're creating data-entry forms, I'll also take a look at validating data in controls with built-in events like **Validating** and **Validated** in this chapter—see "Performing Data Validation in Controls" in the Immediate Solutions.

And now it's time to start working with the Immediate Solutions.

Immediate Solutions

Using the **DataBindings** Property for Data Binding

You use the **DataBindings** property to access the data bindings for a control, including a Windows form. This property returns an object of the **ControlBindings Collection** class:

```
Public ReadOnly Property DataBindings As ControlBindingsCollection
```

By adding **Binding** objects to the returned collection, you can data-bind any property of a control to the property of an object. We saw this example in the In Depth section of this chapter:

```
DateTimePicker1.DataBindings.Add _
    (New Binding("Value", DataSet11, "customers.DeliveryDate"))
```

You also can use another overloaded form of the **Add** method to create a simple data binding, like this:

```
TextBox1.DataBindings.Add("Text", DataSet11, "authors.au_lname")
```

Using the **ControlBindingsCollection** Class

The **ControlBindingsCollection** class holds a collection of **Binding** objects for a control. Here is the inheritance hierarchy for this class:

```
Object
    MarshalByRefObject
        BaseCollection
            BindingsCollection
                ControlBindingsCollection
```

You perform simple data binding by adding **Binding** objects to a **ControlBindingsCollection**. The **ControlBindingsCollection** contains standard collection methods such as **Add**, **Clear**, and **Remove**. As mentioned in the previous topic, we saw this example in the In Depth section of this chapter:

```
DateTimePicker1.DataBindings.Add _
    (New Binding("Value", DataSet11, "customers.DeliveryDate"))
```

And you also can use another overloaded form of the **Add** method to create a simple data binding, like this:

```
TextBox1.DataBindings.Add("Text", DataSet11, "authors.au_lname")
```

You can find the more notable public properties of **ControlBindingsCollection** objects in Table 21.1, their more notable methods in Table 21.2, and their more notable events in Table 21.3.

Table 21.1   Noteworthy public properties of ControlBindingsCollection objects.

Property	Means
Control	Gets the collection's associated control.
Count	Gets the number of items in the collection.
Item	Gets a binding.

Table 21.2   Noteworthy public methods of ControlBindingsCollection objects.

Method	Means
Add	Adds a binding.
Clear	Clears the collection.
Remove	Deletes a binding.
RemoveAt	Deletes a binding for the specified item.

Table 21.3   Noteworthy public events of ControlBindingsCollection objects.

Event	Means
CollectionChanged	Occurs when collection changes.

Using the **Binding** Class

The **Binding** class represents the simple binding between the property value of an object and the property value of a control. Here is the inheritance hierarchy for this class:

```
Object
    Binding
```

As discussed in the In Depth section of this chapter, you use the **Binding** class to support a simple binding between the property of a control and either the property of an object or the property of the current object in a list of objects. We saw this example in the In Depth section of this chapter:

```
DateTimePicker1.DataBindings.Add _
    (New Binding("Value", DataSet11, "customers.DeliveryDate"))
```

The **Binding** class also lets you format values for display with the **Format** event and to read formatted values with the **Parse** event.

You can find the more notable public properties of **Binding** objects in Table 21.4, and their more notable events in Table 21.5. (This class has no non-inherited methods.)

Table 21.4 Noteworthy public properties of Binding objects.

Property	Means
BindingMemberInfo	Gets an object that contains binding information.
Control	Gets the associated control.
DataSource	Gets the binding's data source.
IsBinding	Gets whether the binding is active.
PropertyName	Gets/sets the control's data-bound property.

Table 21.5 Noteworthy public events of Binding objects.

Event	Means
Format	Occurs when a property is bound to a data value.
Parse	Occurs when a data-bound control's value changes.

Creating Simple Data Binding

As discussed in the In Depth section of this chapter, simple binding lets you display one data element, such as a field's value from a data table, in a control. In Visual Basic .NET, you can simple-bind *any* property of a control to a data value.

At design time, for example, to bind a text box's **Text** property to the au_lname field in the **authors** table from the pubs database in a dataset, you select the text box and expand its **(DataBindings)** property in the Properties window. You'll see the most commonly bound properties already listed, such as the **Tag** and **Text** properties for a text box, as shown in Figure 21.1. You can select a field in a dataset to bind to just by clicking a property and selecting a table from the drop-down list that appears.

You also can bind to any property of a control, and to do that, click the ellipsis button that appears when you click the **(Advanced)** entry in the **(DataBindings)** property, opening the Advanced Data Binding dialog you see in Figure 21.2.

You also can perform simple binding in code, using a control's **DataBindings** property (see the "Using the **DataBindings** Property for Data Binding" solution), which holds a collection of **Binding** objects (see the "Using the **Binding** Class" solution in this chapter) corresponding to the bindings for the control. For example, as we saw in the In Depth section of this chapter, to bind the text box to the same au_lname field that we just bound it to at design time, we could do this in code, using the collection's **Add** method; you pass this method the property to bind, the data source to use, and the specific field you want to bind:

```
TextBox1.DataBindings.Add("Text", DataSet11, "authors.au_lname")
```

For more information on simple binding, see the In Depth section of this chapter.

Creating Complex Data Binding

As discussed in the In Depth section of this chapter, complex data binding allows a control to bind to more than one data element, such as an entire table in a database, at the same time. And as we saw in the In Depth section of this chapter, complex data binding revolves around the **DataSource**, **DataMember**, **DisplayMember**, and **ValueMember** properties.

Although you often set these properties at design time, you also can set them at run time, as in this example, where I'm binding a dataset to a data grid in code and displaying the **authors** table:

```
DataGrid1.DataSource = DataSet11
DataGrid1.DataMember = "authors"
```

You also can use the built-in data grid method named **SetDataBinding** for this (data grids are the only controls that have this method):

```
DataGrid1.SetDataBinding(dsDataSet, "authors")
```

And here's how to bind the **dsDataSet** dataset to a list box using the **DisplayMember** property, using the au_lname field in the **authors** table, authors. au_lname:

```
ListBox1.DataSource = dsDataSet
ListBox1.DisplayMember = "authors.au_lname"
```

For more information on complex binding, see the In Depth section of this chapter.

Binding Text Boxes

Text boxes are simple data-binding controls. Here are the commonly bound properties displayed when you expand the **(DataBindings)** property:

- **Tag**
- **Text**

You can, of course, bind any property; just click the **(Advanced)** entry in the **(DataBindings)** property. You can see an example of data binding with this control in the DataBinding example on the CD-ROM in Figure 21.3, where I've bound the **Text** property to the authors.au_lname field in the pubs database.

Related solution:	*Found on page:*
Text Boxes	219

Binding Buttons

Buttons are simple data-binding controls. Here are the commonly bound properties displayed when you expand the **(DataBindings)** property:

- **Tag**
- **Text**

You can, of course, bind any property; just click the Advanced item in the **(DataBindings)** property. You can see an example of data binding with this control in the DataBinding example on the CD-ROM in Figure 21.3, where I've bound the **Text** property to the authors.au_lname field in the pubs database.

Related solution:	*Found on page:*
All About Buttons	256

Binding Checkboxes

Checkboxes are simple data-binding controls. Here are the commonly bound properties displayed when you expand the **(DataBindings)** property:

- **CheckAlign**
- **Checked**
- **CheckState**
- **Tag**
- **Text**

You can, of course, bind any property; just click the Advanced item in the **(DataBindings)** property. You can see an example of data binding with this control in the DataBinding example on the CD-ROM in Figure 21.3, where I've bound the **Checked** property to the authors.contract field in the pubs database.

Related solution:	*Found on page:*
Using the **CheckBox** Class	273

Binding Radio Buttons

Radio buttons are simple data-binding controls. Here are the commonly bound properties displayed when you expand the **(DataBindings)** property:

- **CheckAlign**

- **Tag**

- **Text**

You can, of course, bind any property; just click the Advanced item in the **(DataBindings)** property. You can see an example of data binding with this control in the DataBinding example on the CD-ROM in Figure 21.3, where I've bound the **Text** property to the authors.au_lname field in the pubs database.

Related solution:	*Found on page:*
Using the **RadioButton** Class	276

Binding Combo Boxes

Combo boxes are complex data-binding controls. Here are the properties you use to bind this control to a data source (for more on these properties, see the In Depth section of this chapter):

- **DataSource**

- **DisplayMember**

- **ValueMember**

You can see an example of data binding with this control in the DataBinding example on the CD-ROM in Figure 21.3, where I've bound a combo box to the authors.au_lname field in the pubs database. For an example using the **DisplayMember** and **ValueMember** properties, see "Using the **DisplayMember** and **ValueMember** Properties" later in this chapter.

Related solution:	*Found on page:*
Using the **ComboBox** Class	314

Binding List Boxes

List boxes are complex data-binding controls. Here are the properties you use to bind this control to a data source (for more on these properties, see the In Depth section of this chapter):

- **DataSource**
- **DisplayMember**
- **ValueMember**

You can see an example of data binding with this control in the DataBinding example on the CD-ROM in Figure 21.3, where I've bound a list box to the authors.au_lname field in the pubs database. For an example using the **DisplayMember** and **ValueMember** properties, see "Using the **DisplayMember** and **ValueMember** Properties" later in this chapter.

Related solution:	*Found on page:*
Using the **ListBox** Class	295

Binding Checked List Boxes

Checked list boxes are complex data-binding controls. Here are the properties you use to bind this control to a data source (for more on these properties, see the In Depth section of this chapter):

- **DataSource**
- **DisplayMember**
- **ValueMember**

You can see an example of data binding with this control in the DataBinding example on the CD-ROM in Figure 21.3, where I've bound a list box to the authors.au_lname field in the pubs database. For an example using the **DisplayMember** and **ValueMember** properties, see the "Using the **Display Member** and **ValueMember** Properties" solution, coming up next.

Related solution:	*Found on page:*
Using the **CheckedListBox** Class	307

Using the **DisplayMember** and **ValueMember** Properties

As discussed in the In Depth section of this chapter, the **DisplayMember** and **ValueMember** properties let you display data in a user-friendly way. In the DataBinding example, there's a checked list box that lets the user select an author from the **authors** table of the pubs database by last name—but we want to get the ID of the author the user has selected. To do this, I set the checked list box's **DisplayMember** property to the au_lname field to display the author's last name in the control, and the **ValueMember** property to the au_id field so that when the user makes a selection, you can use the **SelectedValue** property of the control to get the selected author's ID:

```
Private Sub CheckedListBox1_SelectedIndexChanged(ByVal sender _
    As System.Object, ByVal e As System.EventArgs) Handles _
    CheckedListBox1.SelectedIndexChanged
    TextBox2.Text = "Selected ID: " & CheckedListBox1.SelectedValue
End Sub
```

In this way, as discussed earlier in this chapter, the checked list box can display user-friendly names, while actually returning code-friendly ID values.

Using the **DataGrid** Class

We've already put the data grid control to work in the previous chapter, and in the DataBinding example in this chapter. This control displays a data table all at once in a scrollable grid format and is supported by the **DataGrid** class. Here is the inheritance hierarchy of this class:

```
Object
    MarshalByRefObject
        Component
            Control
                DataGrid
```

You also can display hierarchical datasets in data grids. In a hierarchical dataset, fields themselves can display Web-like links to child tables. You can click a link to navigate to the child table. When a child table is displayed, a back button appears in the caption that can be clicked to navigate back to the parent table.

You can find the more notable public properties of **DataGrid** objects in Table 21.6, their more notable methods in Table 21.7, and the more notable events in Table 21.8. Note that as with other Windows controls, I am not listing the notable properties, methods, and events **ListBox** inherits from the **Control** class, such as the **Click** event—you can see all that in Chapter 5, Tables 5.1, 5.2, and 5.3.

Table 21.6   Noteworthy public properties of DataGrid objects.

Property	Means
AllowNavigation	Gets/sets if navigation is possible.
AllowSorting	Gets/sets if the grid can be sorted when the user clicks a column header.
AlternatingBackColor	Gets/sets the background color of alternating rows.
BackColor	Gets/sets the background color of the grid.
BackgroundColor	Gets/sets the color of the non-data part of the data grid.
BorderStyle	Gets/sets the grid's style of border.
CaptionBackColor	Gets/sets the caption's background color.
CaptionFont	Gets/sets the caption's font.
CaptionForeColor	Gets/sets the caption's foreground color.
CaptionText	Gets/sets the caption's text.
CaptionVisible	Gets/sets if the caption is visible.
ColumnHeadersVisible	Gets/sets if the parent rows of a table are visible.
CurrentCell	Gets/sets which cell has the focus.
CurrentRowIndex	Gets/sets the index of the selected row.
DataMember	Gets/sets the table or list of data the data grid should display.
DataSource	Gets/sets the data grid's data source, such as a dataset.
FirstVisibleColumn	Gets the index of the first column visible in the grid.
FlatMode	Gets/sets if the grid is shown flat.
ForeColor	Gets/sets the foreground color.
GridLineColor	Gets/sets the color of grid lines.
GridLineStyle	Gets/sets the grid line style.
HeaderBackColor	Gets/sets the background color of headers.
HeaderFont	Gets/sets the font used for headers.
HeaderForeColor	Gets/sets the foreground color of headers.
Item	Gets/sets the value in a particular cell.
LinkColor	Gets/sets the color of links to child tables.

(continued)

Table 21.6   Noteworthy public properties of DataGrid objects *(continued).*

Property	Means
LinkHoverColor	Gets/sets the color of links when the mouse moves over it.
ParentRowsBackColor	Gets/sets the background color of parent rows.
ParentRowsForeColor	Gets/sets the foreground color of parent rows.
ParentRowsLabelStyle	Gets/sets the style for parent row labels.
ParentRowsVisible	Gets/sets if parent rows are visible.
PreferredColumnWidth	Gets/sets the width of the grid columns (measured in pixels).
PreferredRowHeight	Gets/sets the preferred row height.
ReadOnly	Gets/sets if the grid is read-only.
RowHeadersVisible	Gets/sets if row headers are visible.
RowHeaderWidth	Gets/sets the width of row headers.
SelectionBackColor	Gets/sets selected cell's background color.
SelectionForeColor	Gets/sets selected cell's foreground color.
TableStyles	Gets the table styles in the data grid.
VisibleColumnCount	Gets the number of visible columns.
VisibleRowCount	Gets the number of visible rows.

Table 21.7   Noteworthy public methods of DataGrid objects.

Method	Means
BeginEdit	Allows editing.
Collapse	Collapses child table relations.
EndEdit	Ends editing operations.
Expand	Displays child relations.
GetCellBounds	Gets the **Rectangle** object that specifies a cell.
GetCurrentCellBounds	Gets a **Rectangle** object that specifies the selected cell.
HitTest	Coordinates mouse position with points in the data grid.
IsExpanded	Gets whether a row is expanded or collapsed.
IsSelected	Gets whether a row is selected.
NavigateBack	Navigates to the previous table that was shown in the grid.
NavigateTo	Navigates to a specific table.
Select	Makes a selection.
SetDataBinding	Sets both the **DataSource** and **DataMember** properties. Used at run time.
UnSelect	Unselects a row.

Table 21.8   Noteworthy public events of DataGrid objects.

Event	Means
AllowNavigationChanged	Occurs when the **AllowNavigation** property changes.
CurrentCellChanged	Occurs when the **CurrentCell** property changes.
DataSourceChanged	Occurs when the **DataSource** property value changes.
FlatModeChanged	Occurs when the **FlatMode** changes.
Navigate	Occurs when the user navigates to a new table.
ParentRowsVisibleChanged	Occurs when the **ParentRowsVisible** property value changes.
ReadOnlyChanged	Occurs when the **ReadOnly** property value changes.
Scroll	Occurs when the data grid is scrolled.

Binding Data Grids

As we've already seen, you can use data grids to display entire data tables, as in the DataBinding example on the CD-ROM, as discussed in the In Depth section of this chapter. To bind a data grid to a table, you can set the data grid's **DataSource** property (usually to a dataset, such as **dsDataSet**) and **DataMember** property (usually to text naming a table like "authors"). At run time, you can set both of these properties at once with the built-in data grid method **SetDataBinding** (data grids are the only controls that have this method):

```
DataGrid1.SetDataBinding(dsDataSet, "authors")
```

You can use these data sources with the data grid's **DataSource** property:

- **DataTable** objects
- **DataView** objects
- **DataSet** objects
- **DataViewManager** objects
- single dimension arrays

To determine which cell was selected by the user, use the **CurrentCell** property. You can change the value of any cell using the **Item** property, which can take either the row or column indexes of the cell. And you can use the **CurrentCell Changed** event to determine when the user selects another cell.

You can see an example of data binding with this control in the DataBinding example on the CD-ROM in Figure 21.3, where I've bound the data grid to the **authors** table in the pubs database.

Using the **BindingContext** Class

You use the **BindingContext** class to access the data bindings in a control, including a form. Here is the inheritance hierarchy of this class:

```
Object
    BindingContext
```

Each object that inherits from the **Control** class can have a single **Binding Context** object. Using this object gives you access to the data bindings in a form, which allows you to set the current record displayed in simple-bound controls, using the **Position** property.

You can find the more notable public properties of **BindingContext** objects in Table 21.9, and their more notable methods in Table 21.10. (This class has no non-inherited events.)

Table 21.9   Noteworthy public properties of BindingContext objects.

Property	Means
Item	Gets a particular binding.

Table 21.10   Noteworthy public methods of BindingContext objects.

Method	Means
Contains	Gets whether the **BindingContext** contains the specified item.

Navigating in Datasets

As discussed in the In Depth section of this chapter, you can use a **BindingContext** (see the previous topic) object's **Position** property to move through a dataset, setting the current record that simple-bound controls are bound to and display. In the DataBinding example on the CD-ROM, I used this property to display the current location in a dataset and to navigate through the dataset.

Displaying the Current Location

In the DataBinding example, I displayed the current location in a label, like this:

```
Label1.Text = ((Me.BindingContext(DataSet11, "authors").Position + _
    1).ToString + " of  ") & Me.BindingContext(DataSet11, _
    "authors").Count.ToString
```

Moving to the Next Record

To move to the next record in the DataBinding example, I increment the **Position** property (this property won't increment if we're at the end of the dataset):

```
Me.BindingContext(DataSet11, "authors").Position = _
    Me.BindingContext(DataSet11, "authors").Position + 1
```

Moving to the Previous Record

To move to the previous record in the DataBinding example, I decrement the **Position** property (this property won't decrement if we're at the beginning of the dataset):

```
Me.BindingContext(DataSet11, "authors").Position = _
        Me.BindingContext(DataSet11, "authors").Position - 1
```

Moving to the First Record

To move to the first record in the DataBinding example, I set the **Position** property to **0**:

```
Me.BindingContext(DataSet11, "authors").Position = 0
```

Moving to the Last Record

To move to the last record in the DataBinding example, I only have to set the **Position** property to the total count of the records in the dataset minus one:

```
Me.BindingContext(DataSet11, "authors").Position = _
    Me.BindingContext(DataSet11, "authors").Count - 1
```

Creating Data Forms Automatically

The Data Form Wizard is a great tool that lets you create data-entry forms easily. We took a look at the Data Form Wizard in the In Depth section of this chapter (see "Creating Data Forms with the Data Form Wizard"). You start this wizard with the Project|Add New Item menu item—just select the Data Form Wizard icon in the Templates pane and click Open. You can see the Data Form Wizard starting in Figure 21.4. In the In Depth section of this chapter, I used this wizard to create a data-entry form for the **authors** table in the pubs example database. You can see the resulting data form in Figure 21.10.

Using Parameterized SQL Queries

The ParameterizedQueries example on the CD-ROM uses an SQL parameter in a data adapter, which is much like a variable in other programming languages. Here's the SQL—in this case, I'm using a parameter, indicated by the question mark (?), for the state field in a **WHERE** clause in the SQL for the second data adapter:

```
SELECT au_id, au_lname, state FROM authors WHERE (state = ?)
```

In this case, I'm indicating that I want to set the value of the state field at run time. You can either enter this kind of SQL directly into the Data Adapter Configuration Wizard, or use the Query Builder in the wizard, setting the Criteria column to a **?** (which Visual Basic immediately changes to the more proper SQL "**=?**") for the state field.

The question is: how do we place a value into the SQL parameter corresponding to the state field at run time? That turns out to be easy enough—you just refer to that parameter as **OleDbDataAdapter1.SelectCommand.Parameters ("state")**. In the ParameterizedQueries example, I'll set this parameter to the state the user has selected in a combo box:

```
Private Sub Button1_Click(ByVal sender As System.Object, _
    ByVal e As System.EventArgs) Handles Button1.Click
    OleDbDataAdapter2.SelectCommand.Parameters("state").Value = _
        ComboBox1.Text
    DataSet12.Clear()
    OleDbDataAdapter2.Fill(DataSet12)
    ShowPosition()
End Sub
```

And that's all it takes to use SQL parameters in Visual Basic.

Using Master/Detail Relationships and Data Relation Objects

In the topic "Using Relational Databases" in the previous chapter, I showed how to use a single SQL statement to join the data from two related tables (the **authors** and **titleauthor** tables from the pubs database, which are related using the au_id field). This joined the data from the two tables, and you can see the results in Chapter 20, Figure 20.28.

However, you don't have to merge the data from two tables into one dataset to work with related tables; you can keep the two tables separate, and use a data relation object to relate them. For example, you might want to set up a master/detail relationship, also called a parent/child relationship, between two tables, as you see in the ParentChildData example that appears in Figure 21.13. This example uses the publishers and titles tables in the pubs database, and relates them through the pub_id key. (The **publishers** table lists publishers, and the **titles** table lists published books.) The code displays the publishers.pub_name field in the combo box you see in Figure 21.13 (this is the "master" part), and when the user selects a publisher, the program displays all that publisher's books in the datagrid below (this is the "detail" part).

Although the combo box is bound to the publishers.pub_name field, the data grid is actually bound to a data relation object—**publisherstitle**—that we'll create. Let's see how this works.

To follow along in this example, create a new Windows forms project and drag a SQL data adapter, **SqlDataAdapter1**, to the main form in this project. In the Data Adapter Configuration Wizard, connect this data adapter to all fields in the pubs database's **publishers** table (SQL: "**SELECT * FROM publishers**"). Then create a second SQL data adapter, **SqlDataAdapter2**, to the **titles** table (SQL: "**SELECT * FROM titles**"). Then create a dataset using the Data|Generate Dataset menu item using both tables, as you see in Figure 21.14. This creates the **DataSet1** class, and an object of that class, **DataSet11**.

The new dataset is just a data container, like any dataset, and that means it doesn't know anything about the relationship between the tables. In fact, both tables share a common field, pub_id, the publisher ID, which is a key into both tables. We'll add a data relation object to make this relationship explicit. (Because each publisher in the master table has only one ID, but multiple titles in the **titles** table can have the same publisher ID, this is called a *one-to-many relation*.)

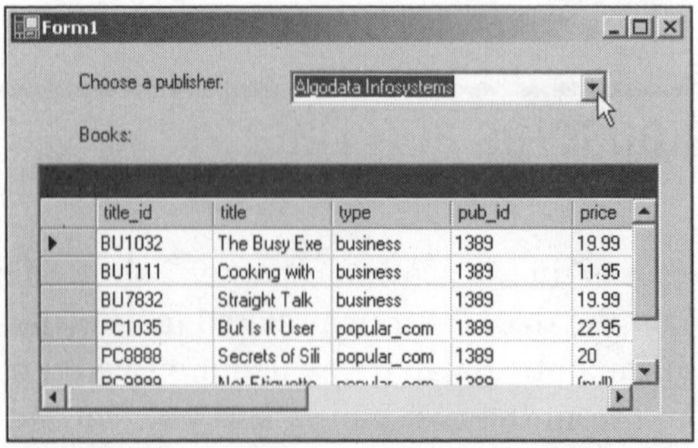

Figure 21.13   The ParentChildData example.

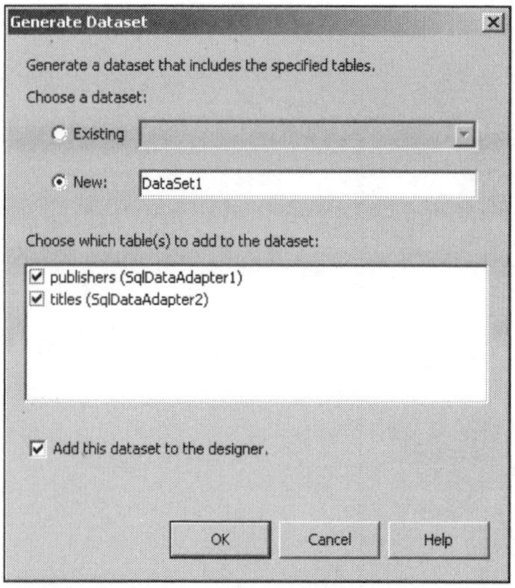

Figure 21.14   Creating **DataSet1**.

We'll create a data relation object named **publisherstitles** relating the two tables we're using. To create this object, find the file DataSet1.xsd, the XML schema for **DataSet1**, in the Solution Explorer and double-click it to open it in the Visual Basic IDE. You'll see the two tables—**publishers** and **titles**—in an XML designer.

When you open the XML schema for **DataSet1**, the toolbox displays and opens an XML Schema tab. Drag a relation object from the toolbox onto the child table, the **titles** table. Doing so opens the Edit Relation dialog you see in Figure 21.15. This dialog creates the data relation object we'll need, and Visual Basic has already given it the default name **publisherstitles** that we'll use. Note that the parent element is already given as the **publishers** table and the child element is given as the **titles** table in Figure 21.15.

Clicking the OK button closes the Edit Relation dialog, and you can now see a data relation object relating the two tables we're using, as you see in Figure 21.16. Now we've added a relation between the two tables in the dataset we've created.

We'll also need code to load the two tables into the dataset from the two data adapters, so add this code to the **Form1_Load** event:

```
Private Sub Form1_Load(ByVal sender As System.Object, _
    ByVal e As System.EventArgs) Handles MyBase.Load
    SqlDataAdapter1.Fill(DataSet11)
    SqlDataAdapter2.Fill(DataSet11)
End Sub
```

Now create a combo box and set its **DataSource** property to **DataSet11**, and its **DisplayMember** property to publishers.pub_name to display the names of pub-

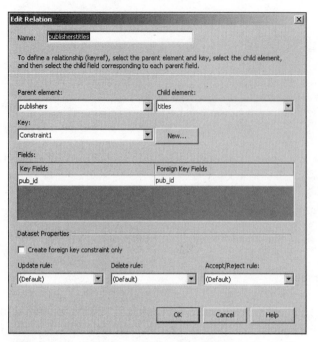

Figure 21.15   Creating a data relation object.

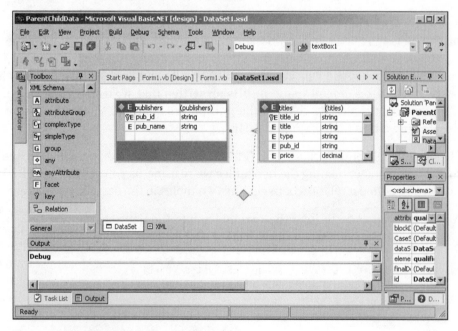

Figure 21.16   A data relation object at work.

lishers, as you see in Figure 21.13. Next, create a data grid and set its **DataSource** property to **DataSet11**, and its **DataMember** property—not to publishers.titles as you might expect—but to the data relation object that we created, publishers.publisherstitles. That's all it takes. Now we've connected the two controls using the data relation object we created, and you see the results in Figure 21.13. When the user selects a publisher in the combo box, the program responds by activating the one-to-many relationship and displaying all the publisher's titles in the data grid.

Related solutions:	Found on page:
Using Relational Databases	878
Creating a Data Relation Object in Code	971

Using the **ErrorProvider** Class

The **ErrorProvider** class gives you a user interface when you want to indicate that there's an error associated with a control in a form; an icon will appear next to the control and an error message in the icon's tool tip. Here is the inheritance hierarchy for this class:

```
Object
    MarshalByRefObject
        Component
            ErrorProvider
```

You can find the more notable public properties of **ErrorProvider** objects in Table 21.11, and their more notable methods in Table 21.12. (This class has no non-inherited events.)

Table 21.11 Noteworthy public properties of ErrorProvider objects.

Property	Means
BlinkRate	Gets/sets the error icon blink rate.
BlinkStyle	Gets/sets if the error icon flashes.
ContainerControl	Gets/sets the parent control for this error provider.
DataMember	Gets/sets the data table to watch.
DataSource	Gets/sets dataset to watch.
Icon	Gets/sets the icon to be displayed next to a control when you've assigned a non-empty string to the error provider.

Table 21.12 Noteworthy public methods of **ErrorProvider** objects.

Method	Means
BindToDataAndErrors	Sets both the **DataSource** and **DataMember** properties at run time.
GetError	Returns the error description string.
GetIconAlignment	Gets the position of the error icon with respect to the control.
GetIconPadding	Gets the space to leave next to the icon.
SetError	Sets the error text.
SetIconAlignment	Sets the position of the error icon with respect to the control.
SetIconPadding	Sets the space to leave next to the icon.
UpdateBinding	Lets you update the data bindings and the text in the error provider.

Performing Data Validation in Controls

Now that we're creating data-entry forms, it's useful to know that you can *validate* the data the user enters into controls. If a control contains data that you think invalid, you can use an error provider (see the previous topic) to indicate what the error is. Here are the control events and properties you use in data validation:

- **Validating Event**—Occurs when the control is validating, which happens when the control loses the focus (if the control's **CausesValidation** property is **True**). Place code to check the control's data here, and throw an exception if there's a problem. You can set an error provider's message here.

- **Validated Event**—Occurs when the control is done validating. This event occurs if no exception was thrown in the **Validating** event. You can clear an error provider's message here.

- **CausesValidation Property**—**True** if entering the control causes validation to be performed on other controls requiring validation when this control gets the focus; otherwise, **False**. The default is **True**.

You can see how this works in the Validation example on the CD-ROM. In that example, I use two text boxes and code that insists that the user enter data into each text box. If the user hasn't entered data into a text box and clicks the other text box (making the current text box lose the focus), the error provider in this example displays an icon with a tool tip indicating what the error was, as you see in Figure 21.17.

To follow along in this example, add two text boxes to a project's main form, and make sure their **CausesValidation** property is set to **True** (this is the default), which means that when either text box receives the focus, it'll cause all the other

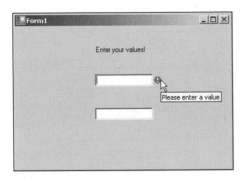

Figure 21.17   Using validation and an error provider.

controls' **Validating** events to occur. Also, add an error provider object, **ErrorProvider1**, from the toolbox.

In the **Validating** event for **TextBox1**, I check to see if the user has entered data into that text box, and if not, use the **SetError** method of the error provider to display an error provider icon next to the text box, with a message, "Please enter a value", which will be displayed in the icon's tool tip, as you see in Figure 21.17. I also throw an exception so Visual Basic knows the data in the control did not validate properly:

```
Private Sub TextBox1_Validating(ByVal sender As Object, _
    ByVal e As System.ComponentModel.CancelEventArgs) Handles _
    TextBox1.Validating
    If TextBox1.Text.Length = 0 Then
        ErrorProvider1.SetError(TextBox1, "Please enter a value")
        Throw New Exception("You must enter a value.")
    End If
End Sub
```

If the text box data did not validate, the icon and tool tip appear, as you see in Figure 21.17. On the other hand, if the data does validate properly, no exception is thrown by the code in the **Validating** event, and the **Validated** event for the control occurs. I'll clear the error provider's error in this event's handler in case the user has corrected a data-entry error and the error icon is showing (this will hide the error icon if it's showing):

```
Private Sub TextBox1_Validated(ByVal sender As Object, _
    ByVal e As System.EventArgs) Handles TextBox1.Validated
    ErrorProvider1.SetError(TextBox1, "")
End Sub
```

And I'll also add error handling for the second text box, **TextBox2**, in the same way:

```
Private Sub TextBox2_Validating(ByVal sender As Object, _
    ByVal e As System.ComponentModel.CancelEventArgs) Handles _
    TextBox2.Validating
    If TextBox2.Text.Length = 0 Then
        ErrorProvider1.SetError(TextBox2, "Please enter a value")
        Throw New Exception("You must enter a value.")
    End If
End Sub

Private Sub TextBox2_Validated(ByVal sender As Object, _
    ByVal e As System.EventArgs) Handles TextBox2.Validated
    ErrorProvider1.SetError(TextBox2, "")
End Sub
```

And that's it—now we're validating the data the user enters into controls, as you see in Figure 21.17.

Chapter 22

Handling Databases in Code

(continued)

In Depth

In this chapter, we're going to focus on working with databases in code. Generally speaking, Visual Basic offers two ways to work with databases—visually and in code. In the preceding two chapters, we've largely seen the visual way at work. Now we're going to focus on doing it all in code.

We're going to work with ADO.NET objects directly in Visual Basic code, creating connections, data adapters, data tables, datasets, and more directly. We'll see how to construct tables from scratch and how to place those tables in datasets. We'll see how to connect to a database by creating our own connection objects, how to place SQL statements in data adapters, and how to execute that SQL in the database. We'll see how to work with data readers, and how to set up data relations between datasets. Here are the objects we'll work with in this chapter:

- Connection objects
- Command objects
- Data adapter objects
- Dataset objects
- Data Reader objects
- Data Table objects
- Data Row objects
- Data Column objects
- Data Relation objects
- The **OleDbConnection** Class

In the In Depth section of this chapter, I'll take a look at each of these objects and how to work with them in code. And we'll put them all to work in the Immediate Solutions section of the chapter. I'll start with data connections; to work with a database in a data provider, you first need a connection to that database. You can use objects of the **OleDbConnection** class and **SqlConnection** class to create that connection.

The OleDbConnection Class

An **OleDbConnection** object supports a connection to an OLE DB data provider. In practice, you usually use OLE DB connections with all data providers except

Microsoft's SQL Server. Note that, depending on the OLE DB data provider, not all properties of an **OleDbConnection** object may be supported.

A central property of connection objects is the **ConnectionString** property, which holds a string full of attribute/value pairs that contain data needed to log on to a data provider and choose a specific database. These attribute/value pairs are specific to the data provider you're using, and make up a list of items separated by semicolons. You can either assign a connection string to the connection's **ConnectionString** property, or you can pass the connection string to the connection object's constructor, like this:

```
Dim ConnectionString As String = "Provider=SQLOLEDB.1;Integrated " & _
    Security=SSPI;Persist Security Info=False;Initial " & _
    "Catalog=pubs;Packet Size=4096;Workstation ID=STEVE;" & _
    "Use Encryption for Data=False"

Dim Connection1 As OleDbConnection = New OleDbConnection(ConnectionString)
```

If you have no idea what a connection string should look like for a specific data provider and database, use the visual tools built into Visual Basic to construct a few sample strings to that data provider, which you can either use directly in code or modify as you need. To do that, create a connection to the source you want to use (see "Creating a New Data Connection" in Chapter 20), then drag a data adapter to a project's main form (see "Data Access Using Data Adapter Controls" in Chapter 20), which creates both data connection and data adapter objects. Then take a look at the connection object's **ConnectionString** property in the Properties window.

TIP: *The most common attribute/value pairs used in OLE DB connection strings are also supported with properties of connection objects, such as **DataSource**, **Database**, **UserId**, and **Password**, which means that when you work with a connection object, you can either set the **ConnectionString** property as a string, or you can set various connection properties one-by-one and let Visual Basic create the connection string for you (unless your OLE DB provider requires data not supported by the connection object's properties).*

After you've created a connection object, you can open it with the **Open** method, and assign it to the **Connection** property of a command object. (To specify the SQL you want to use, you can pass that SQL to the command object's constructor.) Then you can use the command object with a data adapter. For example, you might assign the command object to the **SelectCommand** property of a data adapter, and you can use the data adapter's **Fill** method to execute that command and fill a dataset. When done with the connection, use its **Close** method to close it. (The connection won't be closed otherwise, even if the connection object goes out of scope.)

TIP: *If your application uses a number of connections, you should use connection pooling to improve performance. (Connection pooling lets you keep a cache of connections without having to create new ones all the time.) When you use the OLE DB .NET data provider, connection pooling is enabled automatically.*

The SqlConnection Class

A **SqlConnection** object supports a connection to a SQL Server data source. For the most part, the differences between **SqlConnection** and **OleDbConnection** objects take place behind the scenes, and the programming interface of these two types of objects is very similar.

The main difference here is one of performance—SQL connections to the Microsoft SQL Server have been shown to be up to 70 percent faster than OLE DB connections, so if you're using SQL Server, consider using SQL connections for all your connections.

The OleDbCommand Class

Command objects represent SQL commands or SQL stored procedures that you execute in a database. For example, to retrieve data from a database, you can create a connection object, open the connection with its **Open** method, and then assign the open connection object to the **Connection** property of a command object. You can then assign the command object to a command property of a data adapter, such as the **SelectCommand** property (which lets you retrieve rows of data from the database when you call the data adapter's **Fill** method). Besides the **SelectCommand** property, data adapters also support **UpdateCommand**, **InsertCommand**, and **DeleteCommand** properties, each of which takes connection objects that perform these various functions.

As you can guess, you use **OleDbCommand** objects with OLE DB connections, and **SqlCommand** objects with SQL Server connections. How do you place the SQL you want to use in a command object? You can either assign that text to the command object's **CommandText** property, or you can pass it to the command object's constructor, like this, where I'm selecting all the records in the pubs database's **authors** table:

```
Dim Command1 As OleDbCommand = _
    New OleDbCommand("SELECT * FROM authors")
```

Now I can set the type of the command, which, for SQL statements, is **CommandType.Text** (this is the default), and assign an open connection to the command's **Connection** property:

```
Dim Command1 As OleDbCommand = _
    New OleDbCommand("SELECT * FROM authors")

Command1.CommandType = CommandType.Text

Connection1.Open()
Command1.Connection = Connection1
```

Now this command object is ready to go. In this case, I can assign it to a data adapter's **SelectCommand** property and execute its SQL with the data adapter's **Fill** method.

You also can use the command object's built-in methods to execute commands in a database, no data adapter needed:

- **ExecuteReader**—Executes SQL commands that return rows. Note that this method does *not* return a dataset, it creates a data reader, which is much more simplistic. See "Using a Data Reader" in the Immediate Solutions.

- **ExecuteNonQuery**—Executes commands that do not return data rows (such as **SQL INSERT**, **DELETE**, **UPDATE**, and **SET** statements).

- **ExecuteScalar**—Calculates and returns a single value, such as a sum, from a database.

The SqlCommand Class

SQLCommand objects are very nearly the same as **OleDbCommand** objects, except they're designed to be used with SQL connections, not OLE DB connections. You can use them in the same way as outlined in the previous topic, and **SQLCommand** objects support all the methods listed in that topic, as well as one more: **ExecuteXmlReader**, which creates an **XMLReader** object that makes handling the database with XML easy.

The OleDbDataAdapter Class

OleDbDataAdapter objects act as a bridge between datasets and data sources. As you know, datasets are really just repositories of data; they're not directly connected to a database. **OleDbDataAdapter** objects connect datasets and data sources by supporting the **Fill** method to load data from the data source into the dataset, and the **Update** method to send changes you've made in the dataset back to the data source.

NOTE: See "Populating a Dataset" in Chapter 20 to see how to use the **Fill** method and "Updating the Underlying Data Store" in the In Depth section of Chapter 21 to see how to use the **Update** method.

After you've created a data connection and used it to create a command object, you can assign the command object to one of the command properties of the data adapter—**SelectCommand**, **InsertCommand**, **DeleteCommand**, and **UpdateCommand.** (All these command objects are created automatically when you use the Data Adapter Configuration Wizard—see "Data Access Using Data Adapter Controls" in Chapter 20.) These commands are used as needed by the data adapter.

You also have to specify a *table mapping* when creating a data adapter object. The names of the tables you use in a dataset can be different from those in the database, depending on how you've named them, and a table mapping relates the table names in the database to the names in the dataset. For example, here's how I connect the tables in the database to names I've given them in the dataset:

```
Dim Table1Mappings As New DataTableMappingCollection()
Table1Mappings.Add("authors", "writers")
Table1Mappings.Add("publishers", "company")
```

If you do not specify a **TableName** or a **TableMapping** name when calling the **Fill** or **Update** method of a data adapter, the data adapter searches for a **TableMapping** object named "**Table**". If it can't find that object, the data adapter uses the name "**Table**" for the data source table, and that means you can create a default table mapping by creating a **TableMapping** object using the table name "**Table**". For example, here's how I create a new **OleDbDataAdapter** object, set up the select command object it should use to populate datasets, create a default table mapping, and fill a dataset named **ds** with the **authors** table, using this adapter:

```
Dim OleDbDataAdapter1 As OleDbDataAdapter = New OleDbDataAdapter()

OleDbDataAdapter1.SelectCommand = Command1
OleDbDataAdapter1.TableMappings.Add("Table", "authors")
OleDbDataAdapter1.Fill(ds)
```

The SqlDataAdapter Class

The **SqlDataAdapter** class is the SQL Server counterpart of the **OleDbData Adapter** class. Like the **OleDbDataAdapter** class, the **SqlDataAdapter** class includes the **SelectCommand**, **InsertCommand**, **DeleteCommand**, **Update Command**, and **TableMappings** properties you use for loading and updating data.

The DataSet Class

We've already worked a good deal with the **DataSet** class, which is how datasets are supported in Visual Basic. A dataset is a cache of data retrieved from a database, and, as we know, it's the major component of ADO.NET. A **DataSet** object is made up of a collection of **DataTable** objects that you can relate to each other using **DataRelation** objects. You also can guarantee data integrity with the **UniqueConstraint** and **ForeignKeyConstraint** objects.

As we've discussed in Chapter 20, a dataset reads and writes data and schema as XML documents, which can be transported using the HTTP protocol, which makes it great for the Internet. You can save the schema as an XML schema with the **WriteXmlSchema** method, and the schema and data can be saved using the **WriteXml** method. If you need to read an XML document that includes both schema and data, use the **ReadXml** method that infers and creates a schema from the document. See "Writing Datasets to XML and Reading Datasets from XML" in this chapter.

When the user edits data in data-bound controls (or when you change data values in code), changes are made to the dataset's data immediately. You can use the **GetChanges** method to get a new dataset holding only the rows that have changed, and you typically send this new dataset to the database in the data provider with the data adapter's **Update** method. The data provider may make changes itself in the dataset of changes you send it (such as updating fields that hold calculated values, or adding primary keys) and return a new dataset, which you can then *merge* into the dataset you're working with, using the dataset's **Merge** method. Then you use the **AcceptChanges** method on the original dataset to accept the changes (or use **RejectChanges** to cancel the changes). See "Updating the Underlying Data Store" in the In Depth section of Chapter 21 for more details on this process.

Datasets can be typed or untyped; usually, datasets are typed in Visual Basic. A typed dataset is a dataset that is derived from the **DataSet** class and uses information in an XML schema file (an XSD file). An untyped dataset, on the other hand, has no built-in schema. An untyped dataset can contain tables, columns, and rows, but those are exposed only as collections.

You also can easily navigate through a dataset that's been bound to controls—see "Navigating in Datasets" in Chapter 21.

The OleDbDataReader Class

The **OleDbDataReader** class gives you a way of reading a *forward-only* stream of data rows from a database. Because this stream of data is "forward-only," you can read rows only one after the other, not choose any row you want, or go backward. Data readers are really low-level objects that give you direct access to the data in a database in a way that's not as structured as a dataset, but with faster access. You use this class, the **OleDbDataReader** class, with OLE DB providers.

To create an **OleDbDataReader** object, you call the **ExecuteReader** method of an **OleDbCommand** object—you don't use a class constructor. You use the **Read** method of a data reader to read a new row from a database; you can use methods like **GetString**, **GetInt32**, and **GetBoolean** to read the values of the individual fields in the row, one after the other. You also can read a database's XML schema to determine field names and types. See "Using a Data Reader" in the Immediate Solutions for the details and working code.

The SqlDataReader Class

As you can guess, the **SqlDataReader** class is the SQL Server version of the **OleDbDataReader** class. There are very few difference between the **SqlDataReader** class and the **OleDbDataReader** class; for most practical purposes, you use them the same way—you use the **Read** method to read a new row from a database, and as with the **OleDbDataReader** class, you can use methods like **GetString**, **GetInt32**, and **GetBoolean** to read the values of the individual fields in the row in succession.

The DataTable Class

DataTable objects store data tables, and as such, they're central to datasets and data views (for more on data views, see "Using Data Views" in Chapter 20). In code, you create data tables and then add the fields in each row to them. For example, here's how I create a new table named **Table1** in the DataTableCode example on the CD-ROM that we'll see in the "Creating a Data Table in Code" topic in this chapter. Note that after creating the table, I create a new **DataColumn** object, configure it, and add it to the table's **Columns** collection:

```
Dim Table1 As DataTable
Table1 = New DataTable("Employees")
```

```
Dim FirstName As DataColumn = New DataColumn("First Name")
FirstName.DataType = System.Type.GetType("System.String")
Table1.Columns.Add(FirstName)
     .
     .
     .
```

NOTE: *The DataTableCode example in the "Creating a Data Table in Code" topic creates a data table and uses it to create a dataset, which is then bound to a data grid, so in fact this example creates a dataset from scratch and fills it with data—no connection to a database needed.*

To add rows to a **DataTable**, you use the **NewRow** method to return a new **DataRow** object, because the **NewRow** method returns a row with the schema of the **DataTable**. Then you add data to the fields in the row, referring to them by name or index, and add the row back to the table's **Rows** collection. Here's how that looks in the DataTableCode example:

```
Row1 = Table1.NewRow()

Row1("First Name") = "Ralph"
Row1("Last Name") = "Kramden"
Row1("ID") = 1
Row1("Phone") = "(555) 111-2222"

Table1.Rows.Add(Row1)
```

NOTE: *If you're interested, the maximum number of rows that a data table can have is 16,777,216.*

How do you bind a table in code to a control like a data grid to display it? You can add it to a dataset, and bind that dataset to the data grid, like this:

```
Dim ds As New DataSet()
ds = New DataSet()
ds.Tables.Add(Table1)
DataGrid1.SetDataBinding(ds, "Employees")
```

To find out when changes are made to a table, you can use one of the following events: **RowChanged**, **RowChanging**, **RowDeleting**, and **RowDeleted**.

The DataRow Class

DataRow objects represent rows in a **DataTable** object. You use **DataRow** objects to get access to, insert, delete, and update the records in a table.

To create a new **DataRow** object, you usually use the **NewRow** method of a **DataTable** object, and after configuring the row with data, you can use the **Add** method to add the new **DataRow** to the table. In addition, you also can call the **AcceptChanges** method of the **DataTable** object to make that table treat the new row as it would its original data.

You can delete a **DataRow** from the **Rows** collection in a data table by calling the **Remove** method, or by calling the **Delete** method of the **DataRow** object itself. Note that the **Remove** removes the row from the collection, and the **Delete** method simply marks the **DataRow** for deletion. (The actual deletion occurs when you use the **AcceptChanges** method.)

So how do you actually get the data values stored in a particular field in a row? You can use the **Item** property, referring to the field by name or index. Here's how that looks in the ReadData example on the CD-ROM that we'll see in this chapter (see "Accessing Individual Data Items" in the Immediate Solutions):

```
For RowLoopIndex = 0 To (DataSet11.Tables("authors").Rows.Count - 1)
    For ColLoopIndex = 0 To (DataSet11.Tables("authors").Columns.Count - 1)
        TextBox1.Text &= _
    DataSet11.Tables("authors").Rows(RowLoopIndex).Item(ColLoopIndex) & _
    ControlChars.Tab & ControlChars.Tab
    Next ColLoopIndex
    TextBox1.Text &= ControlChars.CrLf
Next RowLoopIndex
```

The DataColumn Class

DataColumn objects represent the columns, that is, the fields, in a data table. In ADO.NET terms, the columns in a table specify its XML schema. When you create a table and add columns to it, you specify the name of the column and the type of data it stores; see the DataTableCode example in the "Creating a Data Table in Code" topic in this chapter for the details.

TIP: *You can make sure that values in a data column are unique by creating a **UniqueConstraint** object and adding it to the **Constraints** collection of the containing **DataTable** object.*

TIP: *You can use the **Expression** property of data columns to perform operations such as filtering rows, calculating values, or creating sums.*

The DataRelation Class

DataRelation objects relate two data table objects to each other through the use of **DataColumn** objects. Datasets are just simple data repositories, and when you load them, they don't know anything about the relations between tables in a relational database (see "What Are Databases?" in Chapter 20). To make those relations explicit, you have to use **DataRelation** objects.

For example, in Chapter 21, the ParentChildData example used the publishers and titles tables in the pubs database, and related them through the pub_id key in a master/child relationship. The code displayed the publishers.pub_name field in the combo box you see in Figure 21.12 (the "master" part), and when the user selected a publisher, the program displayed all that publisher's books in the datagrid below (the "detail" part). We were able to create a data relation object in that example visually in Visual Basic as we edited the XML schema for the dataset in the example. In this chapter, we'll see how to get the same result by creating a **DataRelation** object in code. See "Creating a Data Relation Object in Code" in the Immediate Solutions for all the details.

TIP: *You can access all the **DataRelation** objects in a dataset with the dataset's **Relations** property, as well as the **ChildRelations** and **ParentRelations** properties of a **DataTable** object.*

And that's it—now it's time to get to the details in this chapter, in the Immediate Solutions section, and work with data objects in code.

Immediate Solutions

Using the **OleDbConnection** Class

The **OleDbDataConnection** class represents a connection to an OLE DB data source. Here is the inheritance hierarchy of this class:

```
Object
    MarshalByRefObject
        Component
            OleDbConnection
```

You can find the more notable public properties of **OleDbConnection** objects in Table 22.1, their more notable methods in Table 22.2, and their more notable events in Table 22.3.

Table 22.1   Noteworthy public properties of OleDbConnection objects.

Property	Means
ConnectionString	Gets/sets the connection string to open a database.
ConnectionTimeout	Gets the amount of time to wait trying to make a connection.
Database	Gets the name of the database to open.
DataSource	Gets the data source (usually the location and file name to open).
Provider	Gets the OLE DB provider's name.
ServerVersion	Gets the version of the server.
State	Gets the connection's current state.

Table 22.2   Noteworthy public methods of OleDbConnection objects.

Method	Means
BeginTransaction	Starts a database transaction.
ChangeDatabase	Changes the current database.
Close	Closes the connection to the data provider.
CreateCommand	Creates an **OleDbCommand** object for this connection.
GetOleDbSchemaTable	Returns the current schema table.
Open	Opens a database connection.

Table 22.3   Noteworthy public events of OleDbConnection objects.

Event	Means
InfoMessage	Occurs if the provider sends a message (including warnings).
StateChange	Occurs when a connection's state changes.

Using the SqlConnection Class

The SqlConnection class represents a connection to a SQL Server database. Here is the inheritance hierarchy of this class:

```
Object
    MarshalByRefObject
        Component
            SqlConnection
```

You can find the more notable public properties of **SqlConnection** objects in Table 22.4, their more notable methods in Table 22.5, and their more notable events in Table 22.6.

Table 22.4   Noteworthy public properties of SqlConnection objects.

Property	Means
ConnectionString	Gets/sets the connection string to open a database.
ConnectionTimeout	Gets the amount of time to wait trying to make a connection.
Database	Gets the name of the database to open.
DataSource	Gets the name of the SQL Server to use.
PacketSize	Gets the size of communication packets to use (in bytes).
ServerVersion	Gets the version of the server.
State	Gets the connection's current state.
WorkstationId	Gets the database client ID.

Table 22.5   Noteworthy public methods of SqlConnection objects.

Method	Means
BeginTransaction	Starts a database transaction.
ChangeDatabase	Changes the current database.
Close	Closes the connection to the data provider.
CreateCommand	Creates an OleDbCommand object for this connection.
Open	Opens a database connection.

Table 22.6   Noteworthy public events of SqlConnection objects.

Event	Means
InfoMessage	Occurs if the provider sends a message (including warnings).
StateChange	Occurs when a connection's state changes.

Using the **OleDbCommand** Class

The **OleDbCommand** class represents a SQL statement or stored procedure that is executed in a database by an OLE DB data provider. Here is the inheritance hierarchy of this class:

```
Object
    MarshalByRefObject
        Component
            OleDbCommand
```

You can find the more notable public properties of **OleDbCommand** objects in Table 22.7 and their more notable methods in Table 22.8. (This class has no non-inherited events.)

Table 22.7   Noteworthy public properties of OleDbCommand objects.

Property	Means
CommandText	Gets/sets the SQL statement (or stored procedure) for this command to execute.
CommandTimeout	Gets the amount of time to wait trying to execute a command.
CommandType	Gets/sets the type of the **CommandText** property (typically set to text for SQL).
Connection	Gets/sets the **OleDbConnection** to use.
DesignTimeVisible	Gets/sets if the command object should be visible in a form designer.
Parameters	Gets the command parameters.
Transaction	Gets/sets the transaction that contains the command.
UpdatedRowSource	Gets/sets how results are used in a data row when you use the **Update** method.

Table 22.8   Noteworthy public methods of OleDbCommand objects.

Method	Means
Cancel	Cancels a command's execution.
CreateParameter	Creates a new parameter.
ExecuteNonQuery	Executes a non-row returning SQL statement, returning the number of affected rows.
ExecuteReader	Creates a data reader using the command.
ExecuteScalar	Executes the command and returns the value in the first column in the first row of the result.
Prepare	Creates a compiled version of the command.
ResetCommandTimeout	Resets the timeout value to the default value.

Using the **SqlCommand** Class

The **SqlCommand** class represents an SQL statement or stored procedure for use in a database using SQL Server. Here is the inheritance hierarchy of this class:

```
Object
    MarshalByRefObject
        Component
            SqlCommand
```

You can find the more notable public properties of **SqlCommand** objects in Table 22.9 and their more notable methods in Table 22.10. (This class has no non-inherited events.)

Table 22.9   Noteworthy public properties of SqlCommand objects.

Property	Means
CommandText	Gets/sets the SQL statement (or stored procedure) for this command to execute.
CommandTimeout	Gets the amount of time to wait trying to execute a command.
CommandType	Gets/sets the type of the **CommandText** property (typically set to text for SQL).
Connection	Gets/sets the **SqlConnection** to use.
DesignTimeVisible	Gets/sets if the command object should be visible in a form designer.
Parameters	Gets the command parameters.
Transaction	Gets/sets the transaction that contains the command.
UpdatedRowSource	Gets/sets how results are used in a data row when you use the **Update** method.

Table 22.10   Noteworthy public methods of SqlCommand objects.

Method	Means
Cancel	Cancels a command's execution.
CreateParameter	Creates a new parameter.
ExecuteNonQuery	Executes a non-row returning SQL statement, returning the number of affected rows.
ExecuteReader	Creates a data reader using the command.
ExecuteScalar	Executes the command and returns the value in the first column in the first row of the result.
ExecuteXmlReader	Builds an **XmlReader** object.
Prepare	Creates a compiled version of the command.
ResetCommandTimeout	Resets the timeout value to the default value.

Using the **DataAdapter** Class

The **DataAdapter** class is the base class for data adapters, which represent a bridge between a dataset and a database in a data provider. Here is the inheritance hierarchy of this class:

```
Object
    MarshalByRefObject
        Component
            DataAdapter
```

You can find the more notable public properties of **DataAdapter** objects in Table 22.11 and their more notable methods in Table 22.12. (This class has no non-inherited events.)

Table 22.11   Noteworthy public properties of DataAdapter objects.

Property	Means
AcceptChangesDuringFill	Gets/sets if a data row's **AcceptChanges** method is called after it is added to a table.
MissingMappingAction	Sets the action taken if there's no table mapping for new data.
MissingSchemaAction	Sets the action taken if new data does not match an existing data schema.
TableMappings	Gets the master mapping between source tables and a data table.

Table 22.12   Noteworthy public methods of DataAdapter objects.

Method	Means
Fill	Adds or updates rows in a data set to match those in the data source. Creates a table named **"Table"** by default.
FillSchema	Adds a table named **"Table"** to the specified **DataSet**, making the table's schema match that in the data source.
GetFillParameters	Gets the parameters to use when executing a **SELECT** statement in SQL.
Update	Updates the data store by calling the **INSERT**, **UPDATE**, or **DELETE** statements for each inserted, updated, or deleted row in the given dataset.

Using the **DbDataAdapter** Class

The **DbDataAdapter** class is the base class for the **OleDbDataAdapter** and **SqlDataAdapter** classes. Here is the inheritance hierarchy of this class:

```
Object
    MarshalByRefObject
        Component
            DataAdapter
                DbDataAdapter
```

You can find the more notable public methods of **DbDataAdapter** objects in Table 22.13 and their more notable events in Table 22.14. (This class has no non-inherited properties.)

Table 22.13   Noteworthy public methods of DbDataAdapter objects.

Method	Means
Fill	Adds or updates rows in a data set to match those in the data source. Creates a table named **"Table"** by default.
FillSchema	Adds a table named **"Table"** to the specified dataset, making the table's schema match that in the data source.
GetFillParameters	Gets the parameters to use when executing a **SELECT** statement in SQL.
Update	Updates the data store by calling the **INSERT**, **UPDATE**, or **DELETE** statements for each inserted, updated, or deleted row in the given dataset.

Table 22.14   Noteworthy public events of DbDataAdapter objects.

Event	Means
FillError	Occurs when an error happens while executing a fill operation.

Using the **OleDbDataAdapter** Class

The **OleDbDataAdapter** class represents a bridge between a dataset and an OLE DB database. Here is the inheritance hierarchy of this class:

```
Object
    MarshalByRefObject
        Component
            DataAdapter
                DbDataAdapter
                    OleDbDataAdapter
```

You can find the more notable public properties of **OleDbDataAdapter** objects in Table 22.15, their more notable methods in Table 22.16, and their more notable events in Table 22.17.

Table 22.15   Noteworthy public properties of OleDbDataAdapter objects.

Property	Means
DeleteCommand	Gets/sets the SQL for deleting records.
InsertCommand	Gets/sets the SQL for inserting new records.
SelectCommand	Gets/sets the SQL for selecting records.
UpdateCommand	Gets/sets the SQL for updating records.

Table 22.16   Noteworthy public methods of OleDbDataAdapter objects.

Method	Means
Fill	Adds or refreshes rows to a dataset to make them match the rows in a data store.

Table 22.17   Noteworthy public events of OleDbDataAdapter objects.

Event	Means
RowUpdated	Occurs when a row is updated.
RowUpdating	Occurs when a row is being updated.

Using the **SqlDataAdapter** Class

The **SqlDataAdapter** class represents a bridge between a dataset and an SQL Server database. Here is the inheritance hierarchy of this class:

```
Object
    MarshalByRefObject
        Component
            DataAdapter
                DbDataAdapter
                    SqlDataAdapter
```

You can find the more notable public properties of **SqlDataAdapter** objects in Table 22.18, their more notable methods in Table 22.19, and their more notable events in Table 22.20.

Table 22.18   Noteworthy public properties of SqlDataAdapter objects.

Property	Means
DeleteCommand	Gets/sets the SQL for deleting records.
InsertCommand	Gets/sets the SQL for inserting new records.
SelectCommand	Gets/sets the SQL for selecting records.
UpdateCommand	Gets/sets the SQL for updating records.

Table 22.19   Noteworthy public methods of SqlDataAdapter objects.

Method	Means
Fill	Adds or refreshes rows to a dataset to make them match the rows in a data store.

Table 22.20   Noteworthy public events of SqlDataAdapter objects.

Event	Means
RowUpdated	Occurs when a row is updated.
RowUpdating	Occurs when a row is being updated.

Using the **DataSet** Class

The **DataSet** class supports datasets, which act as data caches you can access in code. Here is the inheritance hierarchy of this class:

```
Object
    MarshalByValueComponent
        DataSet
```

You can find the more notable public properties of **DataSet** objects in Table 22.21, their more notable methods in Table 22.22, and their more notable events in Table 22.23.

Table 22.21   Noteworthy public properties of DataSet objects.

Property	Means
CaseSensitive	Gets/sets whether string comparisons are case-sensitive.
DataSetName	Gets/sets the name of the dataset.
EnforceConstraints	Gets/sets if constraint rules are enforced.
HasErrors	Indicates if there are errors in any row of any table.
Locale	Gets/sets the locale data to compare strings.
Namespace	Gets/sets the namespace of the dataset.
Relations	Get relation objects that link tables.
Tables	Gets tables in the dataset.

Table 22.22   Noteworthy public methods of DataSet objects.

Method	Means
AcceptChanges	Accepts (commits) the changes made to the dataset.
BeginInit	Begins the initialization of a dataset.
Clear	Clears the dataset by removing all rows in all tables.
Copy	Copies the dataset.
EndInit	Ends the initialization of a dataset.
GetChanges	Gets a dataset containing all changes made to the current dataset.
GetXml	Returns the data in the dataset in XML.
GetXmlSchema	Returns the schema for the dataset.
HasChanges	Indicates if the dataset has changes that have not yet been accepted.
Merge	Merges this dataset with another dataset.
ReadXml	Reads data into a dataset from XML.

(continued)

Table 22.22   Noteworthy public methods of **DataSet** objects *(continued)*.

Method	Means
ReadXmlSchema	Reads an XML schema into a dataset.
RejectChanges	Rolls back the changes made to the dataset since it was created or since the **AcceptChanges** method was called.
Reset	Resets the dataset back to the original state.
WriteXml	Writes the dataset's schema and data to XML.
WriteXmlSchema	Writes the dataset's schema to XML.

Table 22.23   Noteworthy public events of **DataSet** objects.

Event	Means
MergeFailed	Occurs when a **Merge** operation fails.

Using the **OleDbDataReader** Class

The **OleDbDataReader** class creates a data reader for use with an OLE DB data provider. Here is the inheritance hierarchy of this class:

```
Object
    MarshalByRefObject
        OleDbDataReader
```

You can find the more notable public properties of **OleDbDataReader** objects in Table 22.24 and their more notable methods in Table 22.25. (This class has no non-inherited events.)

Table 22.24   Noteworthy public properties of **OleDbDataReader** objects.

Property	Means
Depth	Gets the current row's nesting depth.
FieldCount	Gets the number of columns in the current row.
IsClosed	Indicates if a data reader is closed.
Item	Gets the value in a field.
RecordsAffected	Gets the number of rows changed, inserted, or deleted by an SQL statement.

Table 22.25   Noteworthy public methods of OleDbDataReader objects.

Method	Means
Close	Closes the data reader.
GetBoolean	Gets a field's value as a Boolean.
GetByte	Gets a field's value as a byte.
GetBytes	Reads a stream of bytes.
GetChar	Gets a field's value as a character.
GetChars	Reads a stream of characters.
GetDataTypeName	Gets the name of the source data type.
GetDateTime	Gets a field's value as a **DateTime** object.
GetDecimal	Gets a field's value as a **Decimal** object.
GetDouble	Gets a field's value as a double-precision floating point number.
GetFieldType	Gets the **Type** that is the data type of the object.
GetFloat	Gets a field's value as a single-precision floating point number.
GetGuid	Gets a field's value as a globally unique identifier (GUID).
GetInt16	Gets a field's value as a 16-bit signed integer.
GetInt32	Gets a field's value as a 32-bit signed integer.
GetInt64	Gets a field's value as a 64-bit signed integer.
GetName	Gets the name of the specified column.
GetOrdinal	Gets the column ordinal, given the name of the column.
GetSchemaTable	Returns a schema.
GetString	Gets a field's value as a string.
GetValue	Gets the value of the column in its original format.
GetValues	Gets all the attribute columns in the current row.
IsDBNull	Indicates if a column contains nonexistent (or missing) values.
Read	Advances a data reader to the next record and reads that record.

Using the **SqlDataReader** Class

The **SqlDataReader** class creates a data reader for use with the SQL Server. Here is the inheritance hierarchy of this class:

```
Object
    MarshalByRefObject
        SqlDataReader
```

22. Handling Databases in Code

You can find the more notable public properties of **SqlDataReader** objects in Table 22.26 and their more notable methods in Table 22.27. (This class has no non-inherited events.)

Table 22.26 Noteworthy public properties of SqlDataReader objects.

Property	Means
Depth	Gets the current row's nesting depth.
FieldCount	Gets the number of columns in the current row.
IsClosed	Indicates if a data reader is closed.
Item	Gets the value in a field.
RecordsAffected	Gets the number of rows changed, inserted, or deleted by an SQL statement.

Table 22.27 Noteworthy public methods of SqlDataReader objects.

Method	Means
Close	Closes the data reader.
GetBoolean	Gets a field's value as a Boolean.
GetByte	Gets a field's value as a byte.
GetBytes	Reads a stream of bytes.
GetChar	Gets a field's value as a single character.
GetChars	Reads a stream of characters.
GetData	Not currently supported.
GetDataTypeName	Gets the name of the source data type.
GetDateTime	Gets a field's value as a **DateTime** object.
GetDecimal	Gets a field's value as a **Decimal** object.
GetDouble	Gets a field's value as a double-precision floating point number.
GetFieldType	Gets the **Type** that is the data type of the object.
GetFloat	Gets a field's value as a single-precision floating point number.
GetGuid	Gets a field's value as a globally unique identifier (GUID).
GetInt16	Gets a field's value as a 16-bit signed integer.
GetInt32	Gets a field's value as a 32-bit signed integer.
GetInt64	Gets a field's value as a 64-bit signed integer.
GetName	Gets the name of the specified column.
GetOrdinal	Gets the column ordinal, given the name of the column.
GetSchemaTable	Returns a schema.
GetSqlBinary	Gets a field's value as a **SqlBinary**.

(continued)

Table 22.27   Noteworthy public methods of SqlDataReader objects *(continued)*.

Method	Means
GetSqlByte	Gets a field's value as a **SqlByte**.
GetSqlDateTime	Gets a field's value as a **SqlDateTime**.
GetSqlDecimal	Gets a field's value as a **SqlDecimal**.
GetSqlDouble	Gets a field's value as a **SqlDouble**.
GetSqlGuid	Gets a field's value as a **SqlGuid**.
GetSqlInt16	Gets a field's value as a **SqlInt16**.
GetSqlInt32	Gets a field's value as a **SqlInt32**.
GetSqlInt64	Gets a field's value as a **SqlInt64**.
GetSqlMoney	Gets a field's value as a **SqlMoney**.
GetSqlSingle	Gets a field's value as a **SqlSingle**.
GetSqlString	Gets a field's value as a **SqlString**.
GetSqlValue	Gets an object of **SqlDbType** variant.
GetSqlValues	Gets all the attribute columns in the current row.
GetString	Gets a field's value as a string.
GetValue	Gets a field's value in its native format.
GetValues	Gets all attribute columns in the collection for the current row.
IsDBNull	Indicates if a column contains nonexistent (or missing) values.
Read	Advances a data reader to the next record and reads that record.

Using the **DataTable** Class

The **DataTable** class represents a table of data. Here is the inheritance hierarchy of this class:

```
Object
    MarshalByValueComponent
        DataTable
```

You can find the more notable public properties of **DataTable** objects in Table 22.28, their more notable methods in Table 22.29, and their more notable events in Table 22.30.

22. Handling Databases in Code

Table 22.28   Noteworthy public properties of DataTable objects.

Property	Means
CaseSensitive	Indicates if string comparisons are case-sensitive.
ChildRelations	Gets the child relations for this table.
Columns	Gets columns in this table.
Constraints	Gets constraints for this table.
DataSet	Gets the dataset that this table belongs to.
DefaultView	Gets a customized view of the table.
HasErrors	Indicates if there are errors in any of the rows in the table.
Locale	Gets/sets the locale data used to compare strings.
MinimumCapacity	Gets/sets the table's starting size.
Namespace	Gets/sets the XML namespace for data in the table.
ParentRelations	Gets the parent relations for this table.
PrimaryKey	Gets/sets the columns that act as primary keys.
Rows	Gets the rows in this table.
TableName	Gets/sets the name of the table.

Table 22.29   Noteworthy public methods of DataTable objects.

Method	Means
AcceptChanges	Accepts (commits) the changes made to the table.
BeginInit	Begins the initialization of a table.
BeginLoadData	Turns off table updating while loading data.
Clear	Clears the data in the table.
Compute	Computes an expression with rows that pass the filter criteria.
Copy	Copies the table.
EndInit	Ends the initialization of a data table.
EndLoadData	Ends the data loading operation.
GetChanges	Gets a copy of the table with all changes made to it since the **AcceptChanges** method was last called.
GetErrors	Gets the rows that contain errors.
ImportRow	Copies a row into a table.
LoadDataRow	Finds and updates a row; if the row can't be found, a new row is created.
NewRow	Creates a new row, using the table's schema.
RejectChanges	Rolls back the changes made to the table since it was created or since the **AcceptChanges** method was called.
Select	Gets an array of rows.

Table 22.30   Noteworthy public events of DataTable objects.

Event	Means
ColumnChanged	Occurs after a value in a column was changed.
ColumnChanging	Occurs when a column's value is being changed.
RowChanged	Occurs after a row has been changed.
RowChanging	Occurs when a row is being changed.
RowDeleted	Occurs after a row was deleted.
RowDeleting	Occurs when a row is about to be deleted.

Using the **DataRow** Class

The **DataRow** class represents a data row of data in a data table. Here is the inheritance hierarchy of this class:

```
Object
    DataRow
```

You can find the more notable public properties of **DataRow** objects in Table 22.31 and their more notable methods in Table 22.32. (This class has no non-inherited events.)

Table 22.31   Noteworthy public properties of DataRow objects.

Property	Means
HasErrors	Indicates if there are errors in the row.
Item	Gets/sets data in a specified column.
ItemArray	Gets/sets all the data in a row.
RowError	Gets/sets a row's error description.
RowState	Gets the current state of a row.
Table	Gets the table that contains this row.

Table 22.32 Noteworthy public methods of DataRow objects.

Method	Means
AcceptChanges	Accepts (commits) the changes made to the row.
BeginEdit	Begins an edit operation.
CancelEdit	Cancels the current edit operation.

(continued)

Table 22.32   Noteworthy public methods of DataRow objects *(continued).*

Method	Means
ClearErrors	Clears the errors in the row.
Delete	Deletes the row.
EndEdit	Ends the current edit operation.
GetChildRows	Gets the row's child rows.
GetColumnError	Gets a column's error description.
GetColumnsInError	Gets the columns that have errors.
GetParentRow	Gets the parent row of a row.
GetParentRows	Gets the parent rows of a row.
IsNull	Indicates if a column contains a **null** value.
RejectChanges	Rolls back the changes made to the table since it was created or since the **AcceptChanges** method was called.
SetColumnError	Sets a column's error description.
SetParentRow	Sets the parent row of a row.

Using the **DataColumn** Class

The **DataColumn** class represents a data column in a data table. Here is the inheritance hierarchy of this class:

```
Object
    MarshalByValueComponent
        DataColumn
```

You can find the more notable public properties of **DataColumn** objects in Table 22.33 and their more notable methods in Table 22.34. (This class has no non-inherited events.)

Table 22.33   Noteworthy public properties of DataColumn objects.

Property	Means
AllowDBNull	Gets/sets if **null** values are allowed.
AutoIncrement	Gets/sets if the column automatically increments the column's value when new rows are added to the table.
AutoIncrementSeed	Gets/sets the starting value for an **autoincrement** column.
AutoIncrementStep	Gets/sets the increment for an **autoincrement** column.
Caption	Gets/sets the caption for the column.

(continued)

Table 22.33   Noteworthy public properties of **DataColumn** objects *(continued)*.

Property	Means
ColumnMapping	Gets/sets the column's mapping type.
ColumnName	Gets/sets the name of the column.
DataType	Gets/sets the type of data in the column.
DefaultValue	Gets/sets the default value for the column (used in new rows).
Expression	Gets/sets an expression used to filter rows, calculate the values, create aggregate values, and so on.
MaxLength	Gets/sets the maximum length of a text column.
Namespace	Gets/sets the XML namespace of the column.
Ordinal	Gets the position of the column in the **Columns** collection.
ReadOnly	Gets/sets if the column is read-only.
Table	Gets the table the column belongs to.
Unique	Gets/sets if the values in this column must be unique.

Table 22.34   Noteworthy public methods of **DataColumn** objects.

Method	Means
ToString	Gets the **Expression** value for this column, if there is one.

Using the **DataRelation** Class

The **DataRelation** class supports data relations between data tables. Here is the inheritance hierarchy of this class:

```
Object
   DataRelation
```

You can find the more notable public properties of **DataRelation** objects in Table 22.35 and their more notable methods in Table 22.36. (This class has no non-inherited events.)

Table 22.35   Noteworthy public properties of **DataRelation** objects.

Property	Means
ChildColumns	Gets the child column objects for the relation.
ChildKeyConstraint	Gets the child key constraint for the relation.
ChildTable	Gets the child table of this relation.

(continued)

Table 22.35   Noteworthy public properties of DataRelation objects *(continued)*.

Property	Means
DataSet	Gets the dataset the relation is contained in.
Nested	Gets/sets if relations are nested.
ParentColumns	Gets the parent column objects for the relation.
ParentKeyConstraint	Gets the constraint that ensures values in the parent column of the relation are unique.
ParentTable	Gets the parent table for the relation.
RelationName	Gets/sets the name of the relation.

Table 22.36   Noteworthy public methods of DataRelation objects.

Method	Means
ToString	Gets the relation's name, if there is one.

Creating a Dataset in Code

How do you create a dataset in code, then bind it to a data grid? To see how this works, take a look at the DataSetCode example on the CD-ROM, which I'll cover in the next few topics in this chapter. This example creates a connection object, a command object, a data adapter, and a dataset corresponding to the **authors** table in the pubs sample database, and then binds and displays that table in a data grid, as you see in Figure 22.1.

To see how this example works, look at the next few topics.

Figure 22.1   Creating a dataset in code.

> **NOTE:** *This example uses a data connection and data adapter to retrieve data from a database. If you want to create a dataset entirely from scratch, no data connection needed, see "Creating a Data Table in Code" in this chapter.*

Related solution:	Found on page:
Creating a Dataset	861

Creating a Data Connection in Code

To create a dataset in code in the DataSetCode example on the CD-ROM, and to load the **authors** table from the pubs database into it, I start by creating a dataset object when the user clicks the "Load data" button in this example (see Figure 22.1):

```
Private Sub Button1_Click(ByVal sender As System.Object, _
    ByVal e As System.EventArgs) Handles Button1.Click
    Dim ds As New DataSet()
    ds = New DataSet("authors")
        .
        .
        .
```

Now we'll need a connection object to connect to the **authors** table, and I create that connection like this, using a connection string (for more on creating connection strings, see the In Depth section of this chapter):

```
Private Sub Button1_Click(ByVal sender As System.Object, _
    ByVal e As System.EventArgs) Handles Button1.Click
    Dim ds As New DataSet()
    ds = New DataSet("authors")

    Dim ConnectionString As String = "Provider=SQLOLEDB.1;Integrated " & _
        "Security=SSPI;Persist Security Info=False;Initial " & _
        "Catalog=pubs;Packet Size=4096;Workstation ID=STEVE;" & _
        "Use Encryption for Data=False"

    Dim Connection1 As OleDbConnection = New _
        OleDbConnection(ConnectionString)
        .
        .
        .
```

Next, we'll need a command object. See the next topic.

Creating a Command Object in Code

After creating a connection object to connect to the **authors** table in the pubs database in the DataSetCode example on the CD-ROM (see the previous two topics), we need a command object to load the **authors** table into our dataset. Here's how I create an **OleDbCommand** object, give it the SQL "**SELECT * FROM authors**" and set the command's type to **CommandType.Text** (which is the value you use for SQL, and is the default). Then, after opening the connection object we created in the previous topic, assign that connection object to the command object's **Connection** property:

```
Private Sub Button1_Click(ByVal sender As System.Object, _
    ByVal e As System.EventArgs) Handles Button1.Click
    Dim ds As New DataSet()
    ds = New DataSet("authors")

    Dim ConnectionString As String = "Provider=SQLOLEDB.1;Integrated " & _
        "Security=SSPI;Persist Security Info=False;Initial " & _
        "Catalog=pubs;Packet Size=4096;Workstation ID=STEVE;" & _
        "Use Encryption for Data=False"

    Dim Connection1 As OleDbConnection = New _
        OleDbConnection(ConnectionString)

    Dim Command1 As OleDbCommand = _
        New OleDbCommand("SELECT * FROM authors")
    Command1.CommandType = CommandType.Text

    Connection1.Open()
    Command1.Connection = Connection1
        .
        .
        .
```

Our command object is now ready to be used with a data adapter to get the **authors** table from the pubs database. See the next topic for the details.

Creating a Data Adapter in Code

In the previous topic, we created a command object that will get the **authors** table from the pubs database in the DataSetCode example on the CD-ROM. To actually get the **authors** table, I'll create an **OleDbDataAdapter** object, and assign our command object to that adapter's **SelectCommand** property, because the select command of a data adapter is used when you use the **Fill** method. I also add a default table mapping to the data adapter (see the discussion on table mappings in the In Depth section of this chapter for more information), and fill the dataset, **ds**, with data. Finally, I bind the filled dataset to the data grid you see in Figure 22.1:

```
Private Sub Button1_Click(ByVal sender As System.Object, _
    ByVal e As System.EventArgs) Handles Button1.Click
    Dim ds As New DataSet()
    ds = New DataSet("authors")

    Dim ConnectionString As String = "Provider=SQLOLEDB.1;Integrated " & _
        "Security=SSPI;Persist Security Info=False;Initial " & _
        "Catalog=pubs;Packet Size=4096;Workstation ID=STEVE;" & _
        "Use Encryption for Data=False"

    Dim Connection1 As OleDbConnection = New _
        OleDbConnection(ConnectionString)

    Dim Command1 As OleDbCommand = _
        New OleDbCommand("SELECT * FROM authors")
    Command1.CommandType = CommandType.Text

    Connection1.Open()
    Command1.Connection = Connection1

    Dim OleDbDataAdapter1 As OleDbDataAdapter = New OleDbDataAdapter()

    OleDbDataAdapter1.SelectCommand = Command1
    OleDbDataAdapter1.TableMappings.Add("Table", "authors")
    OleDbDataAdapter1.Fill(ds)

    DataGrid1.SetDataBinding(ds, "authors")
End Sub
```

And that's the complete code—all you need to create a dataset from a connection to a data table in a database. Actually, you don't need to connect to a database to access a data table—you can create your own tables in code. See the next topic for the details.

Related solution:	Found on page:
Data Access Using Data Adapter Controls	872

Creating a Data Table in Code

The DataTableCode example on the CD-ROM creates a data table from scratch, uses it to create a dataset, and then binds that dataset to a data grid, as you see in Figure 22.2. This example will show us how to create not only a data table from scratch, but also an entire dataset.

Let's see how this works in code. When the user clicks the "Create and bind new data table" button you see in Figure 22.2, the code starts by creating a data table named Employees, like this:

```
Private Sub Button1_Click(ByVal sender As System.Object, _
    ByVal e As System.EventArgs) Handles Button1.Click
    Dim Table1 As DataTable
    Table1 = New DataTable("Employees")
    .
    .
    .
```

The next step is to stock the data table with columns, and we'll do that in the next topic.

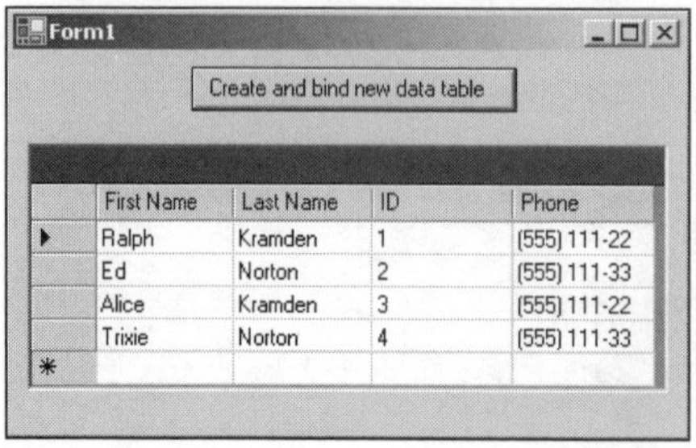

Figure 22.2   Creating a data table in code.

Creating Data Columns in Code

After creating a table in the DataTableCode example in the previous topic, it's time to create the columns in that table. The columns specify the structure of the table because they specify the type and name of each column; after the table has been so constructed, we can add data—that is, the rows.

I'll add three text string fields to the Employees table in this example: "First Name", "Last Name", and "Phone". I'll also add an **Int32** field to hold an ID value. To add a new column, you must specify a type in the column's **DataType** value. The data types you can use for columns in Visual Basic are **System.Boolean**, **System.Byte**, **System.Char**, **System.DateTime**, **System.Decimal**, **System.Double**, **System.Int16**, **System.Int32**, **System.Int64**, **System.SByte**, **System.Single**, and **System.String**. Here's how I create the new columns:

```
Private Sub Button1_Click(ByVal sender As System.Object, ByVal e As_
    System.EventArgs) Handles Button1.Click
    Dim Table1 As DataTable
    Table1 = New DataTable("Employees")

    Dim FirstName As DataColumn = New DataColumn("First Name")
    FirstName.DataType = System.Type.GetType("System.String")
    Table1.Columns.Add(FirstName)


    Dim LastName As DataColumn = New DataColumn("Last Name")
    LastName.DataType = System.Type.GetType("System.String")
    Table1.Columns.Add(LastName)


    Dim ID As DataColumn = New DataColumn("ID")
    ID.DataType = System.Type.GetType("System.Int32")
    Table1.Columns.Add(ID)


    Dim Phone As DataColumn = New DataColumn("Phone")
    Phone.DataType = System.Type.GetType("System.String")
    Table1.Columns.Add(Phone)
        .
        .
        .
```

Now we've added four columns to the Employees table. It's time to start adding some data to this table, and I'll do that in the next topic.

Creating Data Rows in Code

We've created a data table named Employees in the DataTableCode example on the CD-ROM in the previous two topics, and now it's time to stock that table with data, using **DataRow** objects. I'll add four rows of data to our table here.

To create a **DataRow** object for insertion in a particular table, you call the table's **NewRow** method, which returns a **DataRow** object configured with the columns you've already set up in the table. You can then reach the fields in the row with the **Item** property. For example, to set the "First Name" field to the value "Ralph", you can use this code: **Row1.Item("First Name") = "Ralph"**. In fact, you can abbreviate this as **Row1("First Name") = "Ralph"**. After you've filled the fields in the row you're working on, you can add it into the table with the table's **Rows** collection's **Add** method. Here's how I add the data you see in Figure 22.2 to the Employees table:

```
Private Sub Button1_Click(ByVal sender As System.Object, ByVal e As_
    System.EventArgs) Handles Button1.Click
    Dim Table1 As DataTable
    Dim Row1, Row2, Row3, Row4 As DataRow
    Table1 = New DataTable("Employees")

    Dim FirstName As DataColumn = New DataColumn("First Name")
    FirstName.DataType = System.Type.GetType("System.String")
    Table1.Columns.Add(FirstName)
        .
        .
        .
    Dim Phone As DataColumn = New DataColumn("Phone")
    Phone.DataType = System.Type.GetType("System.String")
    Table1.Columns.Add(Phone)

    Row1 = Table1.NewRow()

    Row1("First Name") = "Ralph"
    Row1("Last Name") = "Kramden"
    Row1("ID") = 1
    Row1("Phone") = "(555) 111-2222"

    Table1.Rows.Add(Row1)

    Row2 = Table1.NewRow()

    Row2("First Name") = "Ed"
    Row2("Last Name") = "Norton"
    Row2("ID") = 2
    Row2("Phone") = "(555) 111-3333"

    Table1.Rows.Add(Row2)

    Row3 = Table1.NewRow()

    Row3("First Name") = "Alice"
    Row3("Last Name") = "Kramden"
    Row3("ID") = 3
    Row3("Phone") = "(555) 111-2222"
```

```
    Table1.Rows.Add(Row3)

    Row4 = Table1.NewRow()

    Row4("First Name") = "Trixie"
    Row4("Last Name") = "Norton"
    Row4("ID") = 4
    Row4("Phone") = "(555) 111-3333"

    Table1.Rows.Add(Row4)

    Dim ds As New DataSet()
    ds = New DataSet()
    ds.Tables.Add(Table1)
    DataGrid1.SetDataBinding(ds, "Employees")
End Sub
```

And that's all it takes; note that at the end of the code, I add the new table to a dataset and bind that dataset to the data grid you see in Figure 22.2. In this way, we've created an entire dataset from scratch, no database connection needed.

Accessing Individual Data Items

How do you access the individual values in a database table? To see how this works, take a look at the ReadData example on the CD-ROM, which you can see at work in Figure 22.3. In this example, I'm reading data from the **authors** table in the pubs database directly, and displaying that data in a text box.

To make this example work, I've dragged a data adapter onto the main form, connected it to the **authors** table, and created a dataset, **DataSet11**, from that data adapter. The first step in using this dataset to create the display you see in Figure 22.3 is to determine the name of each column to create the headers you see in that figure. To do that, I'll loop over the **authors** table as **DataSet11.Tables("authors")** (you also can use **DataSet11.Tables(0)**, because the **authors** table is the only

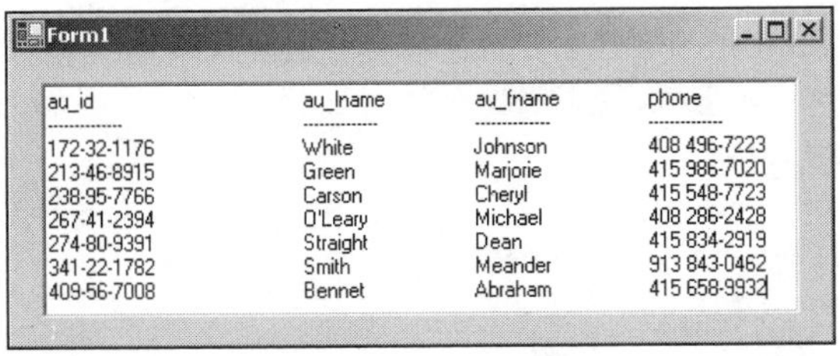

Figure 22.3   The ReadData example.

table in this collection), and access each column with the **Columns** collection of the table. Each column's name is stored in the **ColumnName** property, so here's how I create the header you see in Figure 22.3 (I'm using double tabs to make sure the data is displayed in straight columns):

```
Private Sub Form1_Load(ByVal sender As System.Object, _
        ByVal e As System.EventArgs) Handles MyBase.Load
    Dim RowLoopIndex, ColLoopIndex As Integer
    DataSet11.Clear()
    OleDbDataAdapter1.Fill(DataSet11)

    For ColLoopIndex = 0 To (DataSet11.Tables("authors").Columns.Count - 1)
        TextBox1.Text &= _
            DataSet11.Tables( _
            "authors").Columns(ColLoopIndex).ColumnName & _
            ControlChars.Tab & ControlChars.Tab
        If ColLoopIndex = 0 Then 'Handle wide au_id field
            TextBox1.Text &= ControlChars.Tab
        End If
    Next ColLoopIndex

    TextBox1.Text &= ControlChars.CrLf

    For ColLoopIndex = 0 To (DataSet11.Tables("authors").Columns.Count - 1)
        TextBox1.Text &= "————" _
            & ControlChars.Tab & ControlChars.Tab
        If ColLoopIndex = 0 Then 'Handle wide au_id field
            TextBox1.Text &= ControlChars.Tab
        End If
    Next ColLoopIndex

    TextBox1.Text &= ControlChars.CrLf
        .
        .
        .
```

Now I can get the actual data in each row of the table using the table's **Rows** collection, and the **Item** property of each **DataRow** object to get the data in each field. For example, to get the data in the first field of the first row in the **Rows** collection, I can use the expression **Rows(0).Item(0)**. Here's how I get all the data in the rows of the **authors** table:

```
Private Sub Form1_Load(ByVal sender As System.Object, _
        ByVal e As System.EventArgs) Handles MyBase.Load
    Dim RowLoopIndex, ColLoopIndex As Integer
```

```
DataSet11.Clear()
OleDbDataAdapter1.Fill(DataSet11)

For ColLoopIndex = 0 To (DataSet11.Tables("authors").Columns.Count - 1)
    .
    .
    .
Next ColLoopIndex

TextBox1.Text &= ControlChars.CrLf

For ColLoopIndex = 0 To (DataSet11.Tables("authors").Columns.Count - 1)
    .
    .
    .
Next ColLoopIndex

TextBox1.Text &= ControlChars.CrLf

For RowLoopIndex = 0 To (DataSet11.Tables("authors").Rows.Count - 1)
    For ColLoopIndex = 0 To _
        (DataSet11.Tables("authors").Columns.Count - 1)
        TextBox1.Text &= _
    DataSet11.Tables("authors").Rows(RowLoopIndex).Item(ColLoopIndex) _
    & ControlChars.Tab & ControlChars.Tab
    Next ColLoopIndex
    TextBox1.Text &= ControlChars.CrLf
Next RowLoopIndex
End Sub
```

If you prefer, you can loop over all data with **For Each** loops instead, which makes the code easier:

```
Dim CurrentRow As DataRow
Dim CurrentColumn As DataColumn

For Each CurrentRow In DataSet11.Tables("authors").Rows
    For Each CurrentColumn In DataSet11.Tables("authors").Columns
        TextBox1.Text &= CurrentRow(CurrentColumn) & ControlChars.Tab _
            & ControlChars.Tab
    Next CurrentColumn
    TextBox1.Text &= ControlChars.CrLf
Next CurrentRow
```

And that's all it takes to create the display you see in Figure 22.3.

Note that you can access the data in the various fields of a data row by numeric index or by name, and you can abbreviate expressions by eliminating the keyword **Item**. For example, if you're working with a row of data named **CurrentRow**, and the "First Name" field is the first field in the row, all these statements are equivalent:

```
FirstName = CurrentRow.Item("First Name")
FirstName = CurrentRow("First Name")
FirstName = CurrentRow.Item(0)
FirstName = CurrentRow(0)
```

Looping over all Tables in a Dataset

In the previous topic, we looped over all the rows and columns in the **authors** table in the pubs database. But what if you wanted to loop over all the tables in a dataset as well? You can access the tables in a dataset with its **Tables** property, so here's how to display all the data in an entire dataset, table-by-table, row-by-row, and column-by-column:

```
For Each CurrentTable in DataSet11.Tables
    For Each CurrentRow In CurrentTable.Rows
        For Each CurrentColumn In CurrentTable.Columns
            TextBox1.Text &= CurrentRow(CurrentColumn) & ControlChars.Tab _
                & ControlChars.Tab
            Next CurrentColumn
        TextBox1.Text &= ControlChars.CrLf
    Next CurrentRow
Next CurrentTable
```

Writing Datasets to XML and Reading Datasets from XML

As you know, the data in datasets is transported using XML. In this topic, I'll take a closer look at that XML, using the DataSetXML example on the CD-ROM. This example writes the **authors** table of the pubs database to an XML file, dataset.xml, using the **WriteXml** method, and then reads that file back into a second dataset using the **ReadXml** method, as you see in Figure 22.4.

Here's the code—when the user clicks the "Write existing dataset to XML file" button, the **authors** table in the **DataSet11** dataset is written to dataset.xml, and

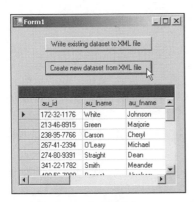

Figure 22.4   Writing a dataset's XML and reading that XML back in.

when the user clicks the "Create new dataset from XML file" button, a new dataset
is created and reads its data in from dataset.xml:

```
Private Sub Button1_Click(ByVal sender As System.Object, _
        ByVal e As System.EventArgs) Handles Button1.Click
    DataSet11.Clear()
    OleDbDataAdapter1.Fill(DataSet11)
    DataSet11.WriteXml("dataset.xml")
End Sub


Private Sub Button2_Click(ByVal sender As System.Object, _
        ByVal e As System.EventArgs) Handles Button2.Click
    Dim ds As New DataSet()
    ds.ReadXml("dataset.xml")
    DataGrid1.SetDataBinding(ds, "authors")
End Sub
```

You can see the dataset's data in the dataset.xml file (another file, DataSet1.xsd,
will hold the XML schema, because this is a typed dataset):

```
<?xml version="1.0" standalone="yes"?>
<DataSet1 xmlns="http://www.tempuri.org/DataSet1.xsd">
  <authors>
    <au_id>172-32-1176</au_id>
    <au_lname>White</au_lname>
    <au_fname>Johnson</au_fname>
    <phone>408 496-7223</phone>
    <address>10932 Bigge Rd.</address>
    <city>Menlo Park</city>
    <state>CA</state>
    <zip>94025</zip>
```

```
  <contract>true</contract>
</authors>
<authors>
  <au_id>213-46-8915</au_id>
  <au_lname>Green</au_lname>
  <au_fname>Marjorie</au_fname>
  <phone>415 986-7020</phone>
          .
          .
          .
```

Using a Data Reader

As discussed in the In Depth section of this chapter, you use data readers to get low-level access to the data in a database. Data readers let you read record after record (going forward in the database only) and retrieve individual values in each record. To see how to use data readers, take a look at the DataReader example on the CD-ROM. When the user clicks the button in that example, the program uses a data reader to read the data in the **authors** table in the pubs database, as you see in Figure 22.5.

There are no data reader controls in the Visual Basic toolbox—you have to create them in code. To create a data reader, you can use the **ExecuteReader** method of a command object. Here's how I create a data reader in the DataReader example, and load the **authors** table into it:

```
Private Sub Button1_Click(ByVal sender As System.Object, _
        ByVal e As System.EventArgs) Handles Button1.Click
    Dim Connection1String As New String(_
        "Provider=SQLOLEDB;Data Source=;User ID=sa;Initial Catalog=pubs;")
    Dim Connection1 As New OleDbConnection(Connection1String)

    Dim Command1 As New OleDbCommand("SELECT * FROM authors", Connection1)

    Connection1.Open()

    Dim Reader1 As OleDbDataReader = _
        Command1.ExecuteReader(CommandBehavior.CloseConnection)
        .
        .
        .
```

Note in Figure 22.5 that the program gives the names of each field in headers at the top of the display. To get the names of the columns in this table, I can get the

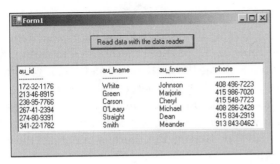

Figure 22.5   Using a data reader to read from a database.

XML schema of the table using the data reader **GetSchemaTable** method, and I
retrieve the names of the columns, like this:

```
Private Sub Button1_Click(ByVal sender As System.Object, _
        ByVal e As System.EventArgs) Handles Button1.Click
    Dim LoopIndex As Integer
    Dim Connection1String As New String(_
        "Provider=SQLOLEDB;Data Source=;User ID=sa;Initial Catalog=pubs;")
        .
        .
        .
    Dim schemaTable As DataTable = Reader1.GetSchemaTable()

    For LoopIndex = 0 To schemaTable.Rows.Count - 1
        TextBox1.Text &= schemaTable.Rows(LoopIndex).Item(0).ToString() & _
            ControlChars.Tab & ControlChars.Tab
        If LoopIndex = 0 Then    'Handle wide au_id field
            TextBox1.Text &= ControlChars.Tab
        End If
    Next

    TextBox1.Text &= ControlChars.CrLf

    For LoopIndex = 0 To (schemaTable.Rows.Count - 1)
        TextBox1.Text &= "———" & ControlChars.Tab & _
            ControlChars.Tab
        If LoopIndex = 0 Then 'Handle wide au_id field
            TextBox1.Text &= ControlChars.Tab
        End If
    Next LoopIndex

    TextBox1.Text &= ControlChars.CrLf
        .
        .
        .
```

To actually read a row of data from a data reader, you use the **Read** method. After the reader has read a row, you use **Get** methods to read the data in the fields in the row, one after the other (see Table 22.27 for these methods). For example, if you know the field holds string data, you use the **GetString** method. If you know it holds a **Double** value, use **GetDouble**. You can determine the data type of a field with the table's XML schema, as I do in this example, or with the data reader **GetFieldType**. Here's how I read in the data in the **authors** table, row by row; mostly, the fields in that table are of type **String**, but there is one field (the contract field) that is of type **Boolean**:

```
Private Sub Button1_Click(ByVal sender As System.Object, _
        ByVal e As System.EventArgs) Handles Button1.Click
    Dim LoopIndex As Integer
    Dim Connection1String As New String(_
        "Provider=SQLOLEDB;Data Source=;User ID=sa;Initial Catalog=pubs;")
    Dim Connection1 As New OleDbConnection(Connection1String)
        .
        .
        .
    TextBox1.Text &= ControlChars.CrLf

    While Reader1.Read()
        For LoopIndex = 0 To schemaTable.Rows.Count - 1
            If schemaTable.Rows(LoopIndex).Item(5).ToString() = _
                "System.String" Then
                TextBox1.Text &= Reader1.GetString(LoopIndex) & _
                ControlChars.Tab & ControlChars.Tab
            End If
            If schemaTable.Rows(LoopIndex).Item(5).ToString() = _
                "System.Boolean" Then
                TextBox1.Text &= Reader1.GetBoolean(LoopIndex).ToString() _
                    & ControlChars.Tab & ControlChars.Tab
            End If
        Next LoopIndex
        TextBox1.Text &= ControlChars.CrLf
    End While

    Reader1.Close()
    Connection1.Close()
End Sub
```

And that's it—now we've used a data reader to read data.

Creating a Data Relation Object in Code

In Chapter 21, the ParentChildData example used the publishers and titles tables in the pubs database and related them through the pub_id key. This example displayed the publishers.pub_name field in the combo box you see in Figure 21.12, and when the user selected a publisher, the program displayed all that publisher's books in the datagrid below. In that chapter, we created a data relation object visually, but now we'll see how to do the same thing by creating a **DataRelation** object in code, as shown in the ParentChildDataCode example on the CD-ROM.

To create the new **DataRelation** object, I just pass this object's constructor the name of the new object, the parent column, and the child column. Then I add the new relation object to a dataset's **Relations** collection, and bind a data grid to that object, like this:

```
Private Sub Form1_Load(ByVal sender As System.Object, _
        ByVal e As System.EventArgs) Handles MyBase.Load
    DataSet11.Clear()
    OleDbDataAdapter1.Fill(DataSet11)
    OleDbDataAdapter2.Fill(DataSet11)

    Dim PublishersColumn As DataColumn
    Dim TitlesColumn As DataColumn

    PublishersColumn = DataSet11.Tables("publishers").Columns("pub_id")
    TitlesColumn = DataSet11.Tables("titles").Columns("pub_id")

    Dim publisherstitles As DataRelation
    publisherstitles = New DataRelation("publisherstitles", _
        PublishersColumn, TitlesColumn)

    DataSet11.Relations.Add(publisherstitles)
    DataGrid1.SetDataBinding(DataSet11, "publishers.publisherstitles")
End Sub
```

This creates the same master/detail connection that the ParentChildData example gave us in Chapter 21. You can see this example, ParentChildDataCode, at work in Figure 22.6 (compare it to Figure 21.12).

Related solution:	Found on page:
Using Master/Detail Relationships and Data Relation Objects	919

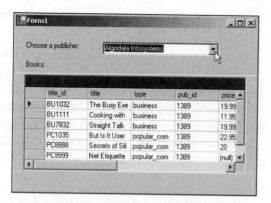

Figure 22.6   Using a data relation object.

Chapter 23

Database Access in Web Applications

In Depth

In this chapter, we'll take a look at using databases in Web applications. The actual work you do with databases in Web applications is back on the server in Visual Basic code, of course, even if the database is on another Web server somewhere, so you still use the data connection, data adapter, and dataset objects that we've been using up to now. This means that the behind-the-scenes code that works with databases is going to be the same here as in previous chapters. We'll still use data adapters to fill datasets, and use connection objects to connect to databases, for example.

However, we're dealing with a different user interface here—Web forms. Web forms are displayed in the browser, which means your application doesn't have direct access to Visual Basic without being sent back to the server, and that's going to affect the way we do things here. The difference between working with data in Windows forms and Web forms is largely a matter of differences in data binding and in the types of controls you can use, as we'll see here.

TIP: *Needing a server roundtrip to access your data can slow things down considerably. The Internet Explorer actually does have a number of data source objects that you can use to work with recordsets directly with scripting languages in the browser. For a complete discussion on how to use those objects to support direct database handling in the Internet Explorer and how to work with that data in JavaScript, see the Coriolis HTML Black Book. One of the data source objects built into the Internet Explorer, the Remote Data Service (RDS), even lets you use connection strings, SQL, and so on, to fill a recordset object. For an example that uses the Internet Explorer XML data source object, which lets you read database files written in XML, see "Using XML-Format Databases Directly in the Internet Explorer" in the Immediate Solutions section of this chapter.*

Because there's no direct connection maintained between a dataset and controls bound to that dataset, you're responsible for refreshing the data binding to controls in a Web form each time the page loads. In a Windows application, you don't need to do that; when the page loads, all you have to do is to clear the dataset and use a data adapter to fill a dataset, and the data bindings in the form are automatically updated:

```
Private Sub Form1_Load(ByVal sender As System.Object, _
    ByVal e As System.EventArgs) Handles MyBase.Load
    DataSet11.Clear()
    OleDbDataAdapter1.Fill(DataSet11)
End Sub
```

In Web applications, the process is similar, but now you also have to explicitly run the **DataBind** method of any controls bound to the dataset, like this:

```
Private Sub Page_Load(ByVal sender As System.Object, _
    ByVal e As System.EventArgs) Handles MyBase.Load
    DataSet11.Clear()
    OleDbDataAdapter1.Fill(DataSet11)
    TextBox1.DataBind()
End Sub
```

This refreshes the data in the bound control each time the page loads, which you don't have to do in Windows applications, because there, that connection is "live." Besides having to use **DataBind** to maintain data bindings, and aside from the obvious fact that Web server controls have fewer properties than Windows forms controls, working with databases in Web applications is remarkably similar to working with databases in Windows applications. Most of what we've done in the previous three chapters still applies here, because the actual work you do with a database is still done in Visual Basic code (this time on the server).

The biggest differences come when you're working with binding data to controls, but even here, the process is similar to what you'd do in Windows forms. For example, as with Windows database programming, there are two types of data binding—simple and complex.

Simple Data Binding

Say that I want to bind a text box in a Web form to a field in the authors table in the pubs database. Assuming that I have access to a server that can run Web applications and that I have a data connection to the pubs database using a data provider on that or another server, I can start the whole process just as I would in a Windows application. All I have to do is to drag a data adapter onto the Web form from the Data tab of the toolbox, use the Data Adapter Configuration Wizard to configure the data adapter to use the connection to the pubs database, and select all fields in the authors table in that database, as we have done before. Then I would use the Data|Generate Dataset menu item to create the dataset to use. That's all it takes to get a dataset ready for use in a Web form, and we haven't done anything we wouldn't have done in a Windows form.

NOTE: *To create data connections to databases on servers locally or on the Web, see "Creating a New Data Connection" in Chapter 20. You also can use the Server Explorer—which displays all your current data connections—for this purpose; see "Using the Server Explorer" in Chapter 20.*

And as in Windows applications, you can bind any property of any control in a Web application to a data source. To do that, you click the ellipsis ("...") button that appears when you select the control's **(DataBindings)** property. Doing so opens the DataBindings dialog box you see in Figure 23.1.

In Figure 23.1, I'm binding the **Text** property of a text box Web server control (all the controls in this chapter will be Web server controls) to the au_fname field in the pubs database's authors table—that is, to the author's first name. And that's all it takes to support simple data binding—you just use a control's **(DataBindings)** property as I have done here. You can bind any property of any control to a data source. Just bear in mind that you're responsible for maintaining that binding yourself, using the **DataBind** method, which you can call each time you want to refresh that data binding, as when the page loads.

Complex Data Binding

As with a number of Windows controls, some Web server controls support complex data binding, such as the Web server data grid control (other such controls include list boxes, checkbox lists, data lists, and so on). In complex binding, a control can display multiple fields at once, as in a data grid, which can display an entire table. Here are the properties you use to support complex data binding in Web applications (not all complex-bound controls will support all these properties):

- **DataSource**—Gets/sets the source of a list of data values.

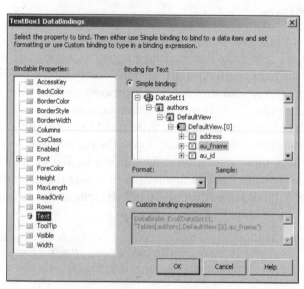

Figure 23.1   Simple binding in a Web application.

- **DataMember**—Gets/sets the data member in a data source to bind to.

- **DataKeyField**—Gets/sets the primary key field in the data source assigned to the **DataSource** property.

- **DataTextField**—Gets/sets the field name from a data source to bind to.

- **DataTextFormatString**—Gets/sets the string that specifies a data display format.

- **DataValue**—Gets/sets the data field to use for the value of each list item, much like the **ValueMember** property in Windows controls.

Note that you use the **DataTextFormatString** property to create a custom display format for data. The data format string consists of two parts, separated by a colon, in the form **{X:Ynn}**. The value before the colon (**X** here) specifies the parameter index in a zero-based list of parameters (currently, this should always be **0**), the character after the colon (**Y** here) specifies the format to display the value in, and **nn** specifies format options. Here are the possible formats for the **Y** parameter:

- **C**—Uses currency format.

- **D**—Uses decimal format.

- **E**—Uses scientific (exponential) format.

- **F**—Uses fixed format.

- **G**—Uses general format.

- **N**—Uses number format.

- **X**—Uses hexadecimal format.

For example, the formatting string **{0:D4}** formats a data item with four decimal places.

That's how things look in overview—now let's take a look at a full data-binding example to get us started.

TIP: *Even with complex-bound controls, you also can use the **(DataBindings)** property in addition to those listed here to bind every property of the control to a data source.*

Binding Data Grids

The quintessential data-bound control is the data grid, so let's see an example using a Web server data grid. This example will be called WebDataGrids on the CD-ROM. To create this example, just drag an **OleDbAdapter** object onto a Web form, and use the Data Adapter Configuration Wizard to make the adapter return the authors table from the pubs database. Next, create a dataset from that adapter, using the Data|Generate Dataset menu item. Finally, drag a data grid onto the Web form, and connect its **DataSource** property to the dataset you've created, and the **DataMember** property to the authors table in the dataset.

You'll also need to add some code in the **Page_Load** event handler (alternatively, you can add a Load button to the form) to fill the dataset with data from the adapter, and to bind the data grid to that data. Here's what that looks like:

```
Private Sub Page_Load(ByVal sender As System.Object, _
    ByVal e As System.EventArgs) Handles MyBase.Load
    DataSet11.Clear()
    OleDbDataAdapter1.Fill(DataSet11)
    DataGrid1.DataBind()
End Sub
```

That's all it takes—you can see the results in Figure 23.2, where the data grid is displaying the authors table.

The data grid you see in Figure 23.2 looks pretty plain, and it's obviously modeled on the HTML **<table>** element. You can customize a data grid easily—just right-click the data grid and select the Auto Format item, opening the Auto Format dialog you see in Figure 23.3. This dialog lets you select from a number of pre-built styles for the data grid, setting header color, border width, and so on.

You also can customize the data grid with the Property Builder tool—just right-click the data grid and select the Property Builder item, opening that tool as you see in Figure 23.4. For example, in the Property Builder, you can select which columns the data grid should display (for an example of this, see "Creating Master/Detail Web Forms" in the Immediate Solutions section of this chapter), what

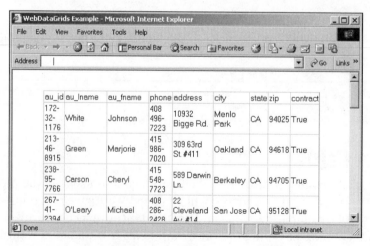

Figure 23.2   Displaying data in a data grid in a Web application.

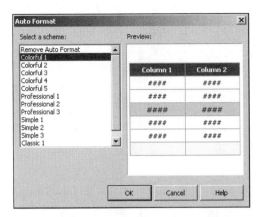

Figure 23.3   Customizing a data grid in a Web application.

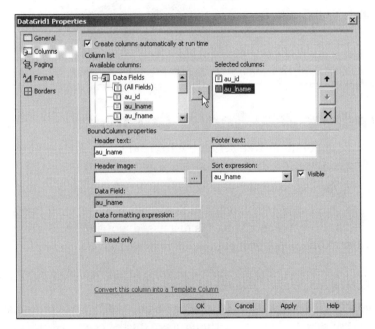

Figure 23.4   Using the Property Builder.

borders to use, and whether or not to use *paging*. Paging lets you display a table in pages, where only a few records are visible in a data grid one page at a time. The user clicks hyperlinks to see additional pages in which the data grid displays additional records.

As always, data grids are easy to use and are useful for displaying an entire table. But what if we want to bind list boxes or text boxes? I'll take a look at doing that next.

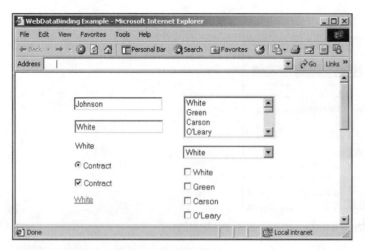

Figure 23.5   The WebDataBinding example.

TIP: *In fact, you can make a column of data in a data grid display hyperlinks, and the user can click those hyperlinks to make a **SelectedIndexChanged** event occur. See "Creating Master/Detail Web Forms" in this chapter for the details.*

Binding Standard Web Server Controls

You can see a number of common Web server controls bound to a data source in the WebDataBinding example on the CD-ROM, shown at work in Figure 23.5.

The controls at left in Figure 23.5 are all simple-bound controls. I've bound the **Text** property of the text boxes, the label, and the hyperlink, and the **Checked** property of the radio button and checkbox. As discussed, you implement simple binding with the **(DataBindings)** property, and I've done that here.

The controls on the right are complex-bound controls. At top, you can see a list box. I've set the **DataSource** property for this list box to the dataset in this example, and the **DataTextField** property to the au_lname field to display the authors' last names, as you see in Figure 23.5. Underneath the list box is a drop-down list, which also lists all the authors' last names. That's bound in the same way as the list box. And under the drop-down list you can see a bound checkbox list, also bound the same way. At run time, the checkbox list displays a checkbox for each record it's bound to, as you see in Figure 23.5. (Radio button lists act the same way.)

In addition, I use the **DataBind** method for each control when the page loads, like this:

```
Private Sub Page_Load(ByVal sender As System.Object, _
    ByVal e As System.EventArgs) Handles MyBase.Load
```

```
      DataSet11.Clear()
      OleDbDataAdapter1.Fill(DataSet11)
    TextBox1.DataBind()
    TextBox2.DataBind()
    ListBox1.DataBind()
    DropDownList1.DataBind()
    CheckBox1.DataBind()
    RadioButton1.DataBind()
    CheckBoxList1.DataBind()
    Label1.DataBind()
    HyperLink1.DataBind()
End Sub
```

The actual data binding takes place in the WebForm1.aspx file, using an object of
the **DataBinder** class. You don't have to use this class yourself—Visual Basic
handles all the details—but it's instructive to see how this works:

```
<%@ Page Language="vb" AutoEventWireup="false"
    Codebehind="WebForm1.aspx.vb" Inherits="WebDataBinding.WebForm1"%>
<!DOCTYPE HTML PUBLIC "-//W3C//DTD HTML 4.0 Transitional//EN">
<HTML>
  <HEAD>
    <title></title>
    <meta name="GENERATOR" content="Microsoft Visual Studio.NET 7.0">
    <meta name="CODE_LANGUAGE" content="Visual Basic 7.0">
    <meta name=vs_defaultClientScript content="JavaScript">
    <meta name=vs_targetSchema
        content="http://schemas.microsoft.com/intellisense/ie5">
  </HEAD>
  <body MS_POSITIONING="GridLayout">

    <form id="Form1" method="post" runat="server">
<asp:TextBox id=TextBox1 style="Z-INDEX: 101; LEFT: 100px; POSITION:
absolute; TOP: 41px" runat="server" Text=
'<%# DataBinder.Eval(DataSet11,
"Tables[authors].DefaultView.[0].au_fname") %>'>
</asp:TextBox>
<asp:CheckBoxList id=CheckBoxList1 style="Z-INDEX: 107; LEFT: 285px;
POSITION: absolute; TOP: 165px" runat="server" DataTextField="au_lname"
DataSource="<%# DataSet11 %>"></asp:CheckBoxList>
<asp:TextBox id=TextBox2 style="Z-INDEX: 102; LEFT: 101px; POSITION:
absolute; TOP: 79px" runat="server" Text=
'<%# DataBinder.Eval(DataSet11,
"Tables[authors].DefaultView.[0].au_lname") %>'></asp:TextBox>
<asp:ListBox id=ListBox1 style="Z-INDEX: 103; LEFT: 291px; POSITION:
absolute; TOP: 39px" runat="server" Height="70px" Width="156px"
```

```
DataSource="<%# DataSet11 %>" DataTextField="au_lname"></asp:ListBox>
<asp:DropDownList id=DropDownList1 style="Z-INDEX: 104; LEFT: 292px;
POSITION: absolute; TOP: 129px" runat="server" Height="22px" Width="156px"
DataTextField="au_lname" DataSource="<%# DataSet11 %>"></asp:DropDownList>
<asp:CheckBox id=CheckBox1 style="Z-INDEX: 105; LEFT: 97px; POSITION:
absolute; TOP: 173px" runat="server" Text="Contract" Checked=
'<%# DataBinder.Eval(DataSet11,
"Tables[authors].DefaultView.[0].contract") %>'></asp:CheckBox>
<asp:RadioButton id=RadioButton1 style="Z-INDEX: 106; LEFT: 96px;
POSITION: absolute; TOP: 144px" runat="server" Text="Contract"
Checked='<%# DataBinder.Eval(DataSet11,
"Tables[authors].DefaultView.[0].contract") %>'></asp:RadioButton>
<asp:Label id=Label1 style="Z-INDEX: 108; LEFT: 102px; POSITION:
absolute; TOP: 114px" runat="server" Text=
'<%# DataBinder.Eval(DataSet11,
"Tables[authors].DefaultView.[0].au_lname") %>'></asp:Label>
<asp:HyperLink id=HyperLink1 style="Z-INDEX: 109; LEFT: 100px; POSITION:
absolute; TOP: 203px" runat="server"
Text='<%# DataBinder.Eval(DataSet11,
"Tables[authors].DefaultView.[0].au_lname") %>' NavigateUrl="http://
www.microsoft.com"></asp:HyperLink>
    </form>
  </body>
</HTML>
```

Note, however, that the simple-bound controls in Figure 23.5 only bind to the first record in the dataset. What if you want to display the data from other records as well?

Navigating in Datasets

As you know, datasets do not maintain a "current record" that is displayed in bound controls. In Windows forms, that's handled with a **BindingContext** object, which lets you set the record bound controls display. But there is no **BindingContext** object available in Web forms. So how do you bind a particular record to the controls in a Web form?

To see how this works, take a look at the WebDataNavigation example on the CD-ROM. This example, shown in Figure 23.6, lets the user move through the records in a database with navigation buttons, displaying selected fields of those records. (This is *not* to say it's a good idea to use navigation buttons in Web data applications, because each time you click one, a server round trip is needed. This example is just to show you how to select the record that controls bind to.)

To single out a particular record to display in bound controls, I'm going to use not a dataset but a *data view* (see "Using Data Views" in Chapter 20). You can use the

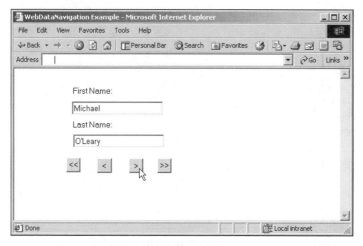

Figure 23.6   The WebDataNavigation example.

RowFilter property of a data view to select the record(s) to work with; I'll use that property to select the record to display in the bound controls, and bind those controls to the data view, not the dataset.

To follow along in this example, create a Web application now, drag a data adapter to the main form in that application, connect the data adapter to the authors table in the pubs database, and create a dataset, **DataSet11**, using that data adapter. In this example, we'll use a data view, so click the Data tab in the toolbox and drag a **DataView** object onto the main form. Next, set the **Table** property of the data view to **DataSet11.authors**.

Then add two text boxes, as you see in Figure 23.6, to display authors' first and last names. Bind them to the au_fname and au_lname fields using the data view, **DataView1** (not the dataset) and add this code to the **Page_Load** event:

```
Private Sub Page_Load(ByVal sender As System.Object, _
    ByVal e As System.EventArgs) Handles MyBase.Load
    DataSet11.Clear()
    OleDbDataAdapter1.Fill(DataSet11)
    TextBox1.DataBind()
    TextBox2.DataBind()
End Sub
```

That gets us started displaying data from the first record in the authors table. The next step is to display the other records as well when the user clicks the navigation buttons.

To keep our place in the dataset, we'll need an index value of some kind, so I'll create a new variable named **Index**, and save it across server round trips using the **ViewState** property (see "Saving Program Data across Server Round Trips" in Chapter 14). For example, when the user clicks the << button, we want to move to the beginning of the dataset, so I'll set **Index** to 0 for the first record:

```
Private Sub Button1_Click(ByVal sender As System.Object, _
    ByVal e As System.EventArgs) Handles Button1.Click
    Dim ID As String
    Dim Index As Integer
    Index = 0
    Me.ViewState("Index") = Index
        .
        .
        .
```

Now we have the numeric index of the record we want the bound text boxes to display, but how do we make them display that record? To select a record in a data view, I'll use the **RowFilter** property. You set this property to a string specifying the text value of a field, like "au_id = '222-33-555'", where I'm selecting the record whose au_id field is "222-33-555". That's easy enough to implement in code; here, I'm finding the author ID of the record corresponding to the value in **Index**:

```
Private Sub Button1_Click(ByVal sender As System.Object, _
    ByVal e As System.EventArgs) Handles Button1.Click
    Dim ID As String
    Dim Index As Integer
    Index = 0
    Me.ViewState("Index") = Index

    ID = DataSet11.Tables(0).Rows(Index).Item("au_id")
        .
        .
        .
```

Then, I use that ID value with the **RowFilter** property and bind the text boxes to the newly selected record, like this:

```
Private Sub Button1_Click(ByVal sender As System.Object, _
    ByVal e As System.EventArgs) Handles Button1.Click
    Dim ID As String
    Dim Index As Integer
    Index = 0
    Me.ViewState("Index") = Index

    ID = DataSet11.Tables(0).Rows(Index).Item("au_id")
```

```
    DataView1.RowFilter = "au_id = "" & ID & "'"
    TextBox1.DataBind()
    TextBox2.DataBind()
End Sub
```

That's all it takes—now the user can click the << button and move to the first record in the dataset. Because the text boxes are bound to the data view, they'll be updated with the new record's data. Here's how to implement the <, >, and >> buttons in similar fashion:

```
Private Sub Button2_Click(ByVal sender As System.Object, _
    ByVal e As System.EventArgs) Handles Button2.Click
    Dim ID As String
    Dim Index As Integer
    Index = Me.ViewState("Index")
    Index -= 1
    If Index < 0 Then
        Index = 0
    End If
    Me.ViewState("Index") = Index

    ID = DataSet11.Tables(0).Rows(Index).Item("au_id")
    DataView1.RowFilter = "au_id = '" & ID & "'"
    TextBox1.DataBind()
    TextBox2.DataBind()
End Sub

Private Sub Button3_Click(ByVal sender As System.Object, _
    ByVal e As System.EventArgs) Handles Button3.Click
    Dim ID As String
    Dim Index As Integer
    Index = Me.ViewState("Index")
    Index += 1
    If Index > DataSet11.Tables(0).Rows.Count - 1 Then
        Index = DataSet11.Tables(0).Rows.Count - 1
    End If
    Me.ViewState("Index") = Index

    ID = DataSet11.Tables(0).Rows(Index).Item("au_id")
    DataView1.RowFilter = "au_id = '" & ID & "'"
    TextBox1.DataBind()
    TextBox2.DataBind()
End Sub

Private Sub Button4_Click(ByVal sender As System.Object, _
    ByVal e As System.EventArgs) Handles Button4.Click
```

23. Database Access in
Web Applications

985

```
        Dim ID As String
        Dim Index As Integer
        Index = DataSet11.Tables(0).Rows.Count - 1
        Me.ViewState("Index") = Index

        ID = DataSet11.Tables(0).Rows(Index).Item("au_id")
        DataView1.RowFilter = "au_id = '" & ID & "'"
        TextBox1.DataBind()
        TextBox2.DataBind()
    End Sub
```

And we're set—that's all it takes. Now you can select which record the controls in a Web form are bound to.

Controls Designed for Use with Databases

There are three Web server controls that are specifically designed to be used with data sources. We've already seen one of them at work—data grids. The other two are data lists and repeaters. Here's an overview of these three controls:

- **DataGrid**—Creates a tabular display of an entire table or selected columns. You can auto-format this control. Data grids can support edit, update, and deletion operations as well as paged output, sorting, and single selection (see "Creating a Data Grid" in the Immediate Solutions in this chapter).

- **DataList**—Creates a (non-tabular) list display that you can customize. Data lists have an auto-format option and support single selection of items. You can edit the contents if you display text boxes in the list (see "Creating a Data List" in the Immediate Solutions in this chapter).

- **Repeater**—Creates simple, read-only output. In fact, repeaters only let you iterate over the records they're bound to; they have no default appearance at all. You're responsible for adding any HTML you want to use to display data (see "Creating Repeaters" in the Immediate Solutions in this chapter).

I'll take a look at these three controls in more detail now. You'll find them all used in code in the Immediate Solutions section of this chapter.

Using Data Grids in Web Applications

As you know, you use a data grid to display an entire table, or selected columns from a table. You can see a data grid at work in Figure 23.2. Web server data grids are much like Windows forms data grids, but there are differences. A Web server data grid uses an HTML table to display its data, for example. And different column types determine the behavior of the columns in the control. Here are the different column types that can be used:

- **BoundColumn**—Shows a column bound to a field in a data source (this is the default column type).

- **ButtonColumn**—Shows a button for each item in the column.

- **EditCommandColumn**—Shows a column with editing commands for each item.

- **HyperLinkColumn**—Shows a hyperlink for each item.

- **TemplateColumn**—Shows each item using a given template.

By default, the **AutoGenerateColumns** property is set to **True** in data grids, which means the control will create a column for each field in the data table; each field is displayed as a column in the data grid in the order that it appears in the table. You can customize which columns appear in the **DataGrid** control by setting the **AutoGenerateColumns** property to **False** and adding the columns you want to display to the data grid's **Columns** collection (for an example of this, see "Creating Master/Detail Web Forms" in the Immediate Solutions section of this chapter).

You also can customize the appearance of a data grid by setting various style properties:

- **AlternatingItemStyle**—Sets the style for alternating items.

- **EditItemStyle**—Sets the style for the item being edited.

- **FooterStyle**—Sets the style for the footer.

- **HeaderStyle**—Sets the style for the header.

- **ItemStyle**—Sets the style for the items.

- **PagerStyle**—Sets the style for page selections.

- **SelectedItemStyle**—Sets the style for selected items.

In fact, you can even customize the appearance of a data grid by adding HTML attributes to the **<td>** and **<tr>** elements used by this control in code. You can set those attributes by adding code to the event handler for the **OnItemCreated** or **OnItemDataBound** event. For example, to add an attribute to an **<td>** cell, you first need to get a **TableCell** object corresponding to that cell. You do that with the **Item** property of the event argument object passed to you in the event handler, and then using the **Controls** collection of the item. Then you use the **Add** method of the **Attributes** collection of the **TableCell** object to add attributes to the cell.

Using Data Lists in Web Applications

You use a data list to display a data-bound list of items. The formatting of each item is handled with templates, and we'll see how to create those templates in this chapter. To see how to use data lists, take a look at the WebDataList example

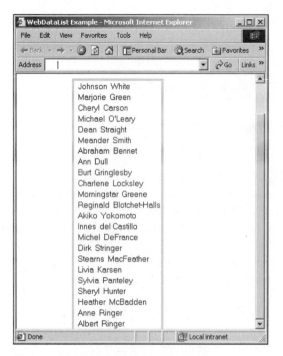

Figure 23.7   The WebDataList example.

on the CD-ROM, which you see in Figure 23.7. This example displays the first and last names of all the authors in the authors table in a data list, formatted with a simple border around the list. Each row in the list is created with a template, and in this case, that template is a label control bound to the first name of an author, followed by a space, and a second label control bound to the last name of an author. This is a very simple template; you can add all kinds of HTML to customize templates as you like.

To follow along in this example, create a Web application now and add a dataset corresponding to the authors table. How do you actually bind the controls in a template to a data source? You start by binding the data list to a data table. To do that, create a dataset and use the **(DataBindings)** property of the data list to bind the data list to the authors tables, shown in Figure 23.8.

Next, to create a template to display a data item, right-click the data list and select the Edit Templates|Item Template item. This displays the templates used to display data items, as you see in Figure 23.9. In the Item Template line, place a label control, **Label1**, followed by a space, and another label, **Label2**, as you see in the figure. That creates an item template, which is used to display data items. Now we have to bind the labels to the authors' first and last names.

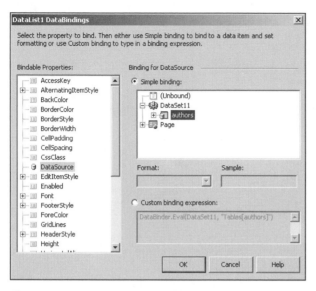

Figure 23.8   Binding a data list.

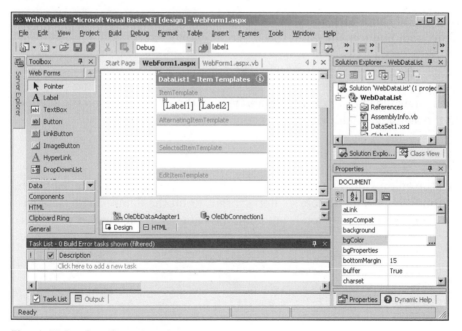

Figure 23.9   Creating a template.

To bind the labels to the au_fname and au_lname fields, start by selecting the first label's **(DataBindings)** property in the properties window, opening the DataBindings dialog you see in Figure 23.10.

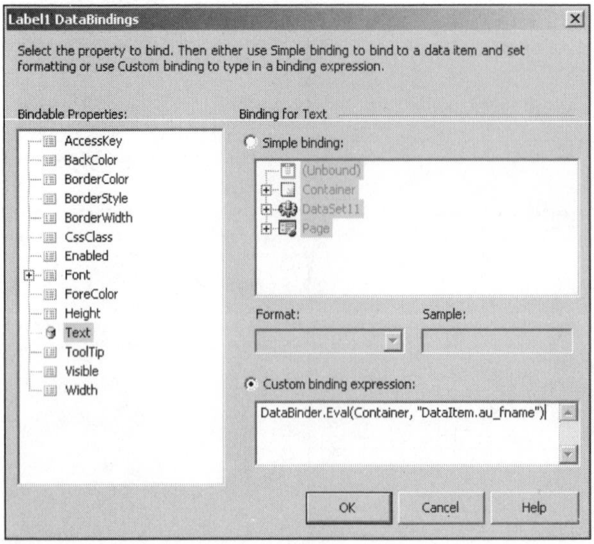

Figure 23.10   Binding a template item.

In the DataBindings dialog for the first label, click the "Custom binding expression:" radio button and enter this custom binding expression:

```
DataBinder.Eval(Container, "DataItem.au_fname")
```

This binds the label to the au_fname field. In the same way, bind the second label to the au_lname field with this custom binding expression:

```
DataBinder.Eval(Container, "DataItem.au_lname")
```

To stop editing the template, right-click the data list and select the "End Template Editing" item. And, of course, don't forget to fill the dataset with data from the adapter when the page loads and bind the data list to the dataset with this code:

```
Private Sub Page_Load(ByVal sender As System.Object, _
    ByVal e As System.EventArgs) Handles MyBase.Load
    DataSet11.Clear()
    OleDbDataAdapter1.Fill(DataSet11)
    DataList1.DataBind()
End Sub
```

And that's all you need—now when you run the program, you'll see the display in Figure 23.7.

We've seen the Item Template now, which is the only template that you're required to create in order to display a data list, but there are others. Here are all the supported templates for data lists:

- **AlternatingItemTemplate**—Specifies content and layout for alternating items.

- **EditItemTemplate**—Specifies content and layout for the item being edited.

- **FooterTemplate**—Specifies content and layout for the footer.

- **HeaderTemplate**—Specifies content and layout for the header.

- **ItemTemplate**—Required template that specifies content and layout for displayed items.

- **SelectedItemTemplate**—Specifies content and layout for selected items.

- **SeparatorTemplate**—Specifies content and layout for separators between items.

You also can customize the appearance of a data list with various style properties, and here they are:

- **AlternatingItemStyle**—Specifies the style for alternating items.

- **EditItemStyle**—Specifies the style for the item being edited.

- **FooterStyle**—Specifies the style for the footer.

- **HeaderStyle**—Specifies the style for the header.

- **ItemStyle**—Specifies the style for the displayed items.

- **RepeatDirection**—Specifies the display direction of a data list; can be vertical or horizontal.

- **RepeatLayout**—sets the layout of the data list; setting this property to **RepeatLayout.Table** will display data in a table format; **RepeatLayout.Flow** displays data without a table format.

- **SelectedItemStyle**—Specifies the style for selected items.

- **SeparatorStyle**—Specifies the style for separators between items.

In addition, data lists support several events:

- **ItemCreated**—Gives you a way to customize the item-creation process at runtime.

- **ItemDataBound**—Gives you the ability to customize the DataList control, but after the data is available for examination.

You can display buttons in items in a data list, as we've displayed labels in the WebDataList example, and certain events are connected to those buttons depending on the buttons' **CommandName** properties. For example, if the **Command**

Name of a button is "edit", clicking that button will cause an **EditCommand** event to occur; if the **CommandName** of a button is "delete", clicking that button will cause a **DeleteCommand** event to occur. Here are the possible events:

- **EditCommand**—Occurs when a button with the **CommandName** "edit" is clicked.

- **DeleteCommand**—Occurs when a button with the **CommandName** "delete" is clicked.

- **UpdateCommand**—Occurs when a button with the **CommandName** "update" is clicked.

- **CancelCommand**—Occurs when a button with the **CommandName** "cancel" is clicked.

There's also an **ItemCommand** event that occurs when a user clicks a button that doesn't have a predefined command.

Using Repeaters in Web Applications

Unlike data grids and data lists, repeaters have no intrinsic appearance at all; it's up to you to create that appearance, which is good if you want to write the HTML for a custom data display from scratch. A repeater is a template-driven control, but here, you must edit the template directly in HTML. In other words, you use a repeater when you want to fill your own HTML with data from a dataset or data view.

You can see this in the WebRepeaters example on the CD-ROM, shown at work in Figure 23.11. This example uses a fairly advanced template with a header, a footer, an item template, and an alternating item template. (The alternating item template is what gives the display in Figure 23.11 its striped appearance.)

To follow along in this example, add a dataset to a Web application, **DataSet11**, and add a Repeater control from the Web Forms tab of the toolbox to the main Web form of the application. Next, set the **DataSource** property of the Repeater, **Repeater1**, to **DataSet11**, and its **DataMember** property to authors.

To create the display you see in Figure 23.11, you have to edit the application's HTML directly; you can't create templates with a template editor here. When you switch to HTML view, you'll see this code for the repeater:

```
<form id="Form1" method="post" runat="server">

<asp:Repeater id=Repeater1 runat="server" DataSource="<%# DataSet11 %>"
    DataMember="authors">
</asp:Repeater>

</form>
```

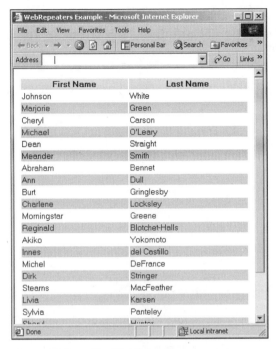

Figure 23.11   The WebRepeaters example.

I'll enclose the repeater in an HTML table, so I'll use the **<table>** element here. To create a header template with the text "First Name" and "Last Name" as you see in Figure 23.11, with a background of cyan, you can add this code, which also uses **<tr>** elements to create table rows and **<th>** elements to create table headers:

```
<form id="Form1" method="post" runat="server">

<table width="100%">
<asp:Repeater id=Repeater1 runat="server" DataSource="<%# DataSet11 %>"
   DataMember="authors">
  <HeaderTemplate>
  <tr style="background-color:cyan">
    <th>First Name</th>
    <th>Last Name</th>
  </tr>
  </HeaderTemplate>
        .
        .
        .

</asp:Repeater>
</table>
```

To create the item template, you can bind table cells to fields like au_fname with an expression like **<%# DataBinder.Eval(Container, "DataItem.au_fname") %>**. Here's how that looks in HTML:

```
<form id="Form1" method="post" runat="server">

<table width="100%">
<asp:Repeater id=Repeater1 runat="server" DataSource="<%# DataSet11 %>"
   DataMember="authors">
  <HeaderTemplate>
  <tr style="background-color:cyan">
    <th>First Name</th>
    <th>Last Name</th>
  </tr>
  </HeaderTemplate>
  <ItemTemplate>
  <tr>
    <td><%# DataBinder.Eval(Container, "DataItem.au_fname") %>
    </td>
    <td><%# DataBinder.Eval(Container,"DataItem.au_lname") %>
    </td>
  </tr>
  </ItemTemplate>
         .
         .
         .
</asp:Repeater>
</table>
```

That displays the data items themselves. To create the alternating appearance you see in Figure 23.11, you can use an alternating item template, which looks like this, where I'm giving alternate lines a pink background:

```
<form id="Form1" method="post" runat="server">

<table width="100%">
<asp:Repeater id=Repeater1 runat="server" DataSource="<%# DataSet11 %>"
   DataMember="authors">
  <HeaderTemplate>
  <tr style="background-color:cyan">
    <th>First Name</th>
    <th>Last Name</th>
  </tr>
  </HeaderTemplate>
  <ItemTemplate>
```

```
<tr>
    <td><%# DataBinder.Eval(Container, "DataItem.au_fname") %>
    </td>
    <td><%# DataBinder.Eval(Container,"DataItem.au_lname") %>
    </td>
</tr>
  </ItemTemplate>
  <AlternatingItemTemplate>
<tr>
    <td bgcolor="pink">
    <%# DataBinder.Eval(Container, "DataItem.au_fname") %> </td>
    <td bgcolor="pink">
    <%# DataBinder.Eval(Container,"DataItem.au_lname") %> </td>
</tr>
  </AlternatingItemTemplate>

       .
       .
       .

</asp:Repeater>
</table>
```

You also can add a footer template to this display, like this; the added footer looks just like the header:

```
<form id="Form1" method="post" runat="server">

<table width="100%">
<asp:Repeater id=Repeater1 runat="server" DataSource="<%# DataSet11 %>"
  DataMember="authors">
  <HeaderTemplate>
  <tr style="background-color:cyan">
    <th>First Name</th>
    <th>Last Name</th>
  </tr>
  </HeaderTemplate>
  <ItemTemplate>
<tr>
    <td><%# DataBinder.Eval(Container, "DataItem.au_fname") %>
    </td>
    <td><%# DataBinder.Eval(Container,"DataItem.au_lname") %>
    </td>
</tr>
  </ItemTemplate>
  <AlternatingItemTemplate>
<tr>
```

```
            <td bgcolor="pink">
            <%# DataBinder.Eval(Container, "DataItem.au_fname") %> </td>
            <td bgcolor="pink">
            <%# DataBinder.Eval(Container,"DataItem.au_lname") %> </td>
        </tr>
        </AlternatingItemTemplate>
        <FooterTemplate>
        <tr style="background-color:cyan">
            <th>First Name</th>
            <th>Last Name</th>
        </tr>
        </FooterTemplate>
</asp:Repeater>
</table>

</form>
```

And that's it—you can see the result in Figure 23.11.

A Repeater must have an Item Template, but any other templates are optional; here are the templates supported by this control:

- **ItemTemplate**—Required template that specifies content and layout of displayed items.

- **AlternatingItemTemplate**—Specifies content and layout of alternating items.

- **SeparatorTemplate**—Specifies the separator between items.

- **HeaderTemplate**—Specifies content and layout of the header.

- **FooterTemplate**—Specifies content and layout of the footer.

That completes the In Depth section of this chapter—we've gotten a good look at working with databases and Web applications here. For more details, it's time to turn to the Immediate Solutions section.

Immediate Solutions

Using the **BaseDataList** Class

The **BaseDataList** class acts as the abstract base class for the **DataList** and **DataGrid** classes. Here is the inheritance hierarchy of this class:

```
Object
    Control
        WebControl
            BaseDataList
```

You can find the notable public properties of **BaseDataList** objects in Table 23.1, their notable methods in Table 23.2, and their notable events in Table 23.3. Note that as with other Web server controls, I am not listing the notable properties, methods, and events this class inherits from the **Control** and **WebControl** classes—you can find them in Chapter 15, Tables 15.1 to 15.5.

Table 23.1 Noteworthy public properties of BaseDataList objects.

Property	Means
CellPadding	Gets/sets the cell padding used in the display.
CellSpacing	Gets/sets the cell spacing used in the display.
DataKeyField	Gets/sets the primary key field in the data source.
DataKeys	Gets the key fields in the data source.
DataMember	Gets/sets the data member to bind to.
DataSource	Gets/sets the source to a list of data to use.
GridLines	Gets/sets grid line styles.
HorizontalAlign	Gets/sets horizontal alignment of the control.

Table 23.2 Noteworthy public methods of BaseDataList objects.

Method	Means
DataBind	Binds the control to the data source.

23. Database Access in Web Applications

Table 23.3   Noteworthy public events of BaseDataList objects.

Event	Means
SelectedIndexChanged	Occurs when an item is selected.

Using the **DataGrid** Class

A data grid control that displays the items from data source in a table. Here is the inheritance hierarchy of the **DataGrid** class:

```
Object
    Control
        WebControl
            BaseDataList
                DataGrid
```

You can find the notable public properties of **DataGrid** objects in Table 23.4 and their notable methods in Table 23.5. (This class has no non-inherited events.) Note that as with other Web server controls, I am not listing the notable properties, methods, and events this class inherits from the **Control** and **WebControl** classes—you can find them in Chapter 15, Tables 15.1 to 15.5.

Table 23.4   Noteworthy public properties of DataGrid objects.

Property	Means
AllowCustomPaging	Gets/sets if custom paging is enabled.
AllowPaging	Gets/sets if paging is enabled.
AllowSorting	Gets/sets if sorting is enabled.
AlternatingItemStyle	Gets the style properties for alternating items.
AutoGenerateColumns	Gets/sets if columns are automatically created for every field.
BackImageUrl	Gets/sets the URL of an image for the data grid's background.
Columns	Gets the columns of the data grid.
CurrentPageIndex	Gets/sets the index of the current page.
EditItemIndex	Gets/sets the index of an item to be edited.
EditItemStyle	Gets the style properties of edited items.
FooterStyle	Gets the footer style properties.
HeaderStyle	Gets the header style properties.
Items	Gets the items in the data grid.

(continued)

Table 23.4   Noteworthy public properties of DataGrid objects *(continued)*.

Property	Means
ItemStyle	Gets the item style properties.
PageCount	Gets the number of pages in the data grid.
PagerStyle	Gets the paging section style properties.
PageSize	Gets/sets the number of items in a page.
SelectedIndex	Gets/sets the index of the selected item.
SelectedItem	Gets the currently selected item.
SelectedItemStyle	Gets the style of the currently selected item.
ShowFooter	Gets/sets if the footer should be displayed.
ShowHeader	Gets/sets if the header should be displayed.
VirtualItemCount	Gets/sets the number of items for custom paging.

Table 23.5   Noteworthy public methods of DataGrid objects.

Method	Means
CancelCommand	Occurs when **Cancel** is clicked.
DeleteCommand	Occurs when **Delete** is clicked.
EditCommand	Occurs when **Edit** is clicked.
ItemCommand	Occurs when any button is clicked.
ItemCreated	Occurs when an item is created.
ItemDataBound	Occurs when an item is data bound to the data grid.
PageIndexChanged	Occurs when a page selection element is clicked.
SortCommand	Occurs when a column is sorted.
UpdateCommand	Occurs when **Update** is clicked.

23. Database Access in Web Applications

Creating a Data Grid

We've seen how to create data grids and bind them to data sources in the In Depth section of this chapter. To see how this works, take a look at the discussion in the In Depth section, and the WebDataGrids example on the CD-ROM. All you have to do is to drag a data grid from the toolbox onto a Web form and bind it to a data source with the **DataSource** and **DataMember** properties.

TIP: You also can customize a data grid extensively; see the discussion in the In Depth section of this chapter for more details.

Binding Standard Controls

As discussed in the In Depth section of this chapter, there are two kinds of data binding in Web forms—simple and complex. To use simple binding, you use the **(DataBindings)** property of a control; with complex data binding, you use the **DataSource**, **DataMember**, **DataKeyField**, **DataTextField**, **DataTextFormat String**, and **DataValue** properties (not all complex-bound controls will support all these properties). For more on these topics, see the In Depth section of this chapter.

We saw an example in the In Depth section—the WebDataBinding example on the CD-ROM—which bound controls using both simple and complex data binding. You can see this example at work in Figure 23.5, with simple-bound controls on the left, and complex-bound controls on the right. The actual data binding is accomplished with the **DataBinder** object. For a discussion of this example, see the In Depth section of this chapter.

Navigating in Datasets

How do you navigate through the data in a dataset or select the current record bound to controls in a Web form? Datasets don't maintain a current record to bind to data controls, and bound controls in Web applications don't maintain an active connection to a dataset. However, one way of letting the user select which record should be displayed in bound controls is to create a data view, as we did in the In Depth section of this chapter, bind those controls to the data view, and use the **RowFilter** property of the data view to select the record you want the bound controls to display.

We did that in the WebDataNavigation example on the CD-ROM, as discussed in the In Depth section of this chapter. That example displayed some fields of the authors table in the pubs database in bound text boxes, and let the user select which record to look at with navigation buttons. To keep track of which record we're currently displaying, I set up a variable named **Index** and persisted it with the **ViewState** property. And to display the record with a specific numeric index, I used the **RowFilter** property of a data view object, and bound the text boxes to that data view. Here's the important code from this example—the navigation buttons—which set the **RowFilter** property as needed:

```
Private Sub Button1_Click(ByVal sender As System.Object, ByVal e As_
    System.EventArgs) Handles Button1.Click
    Dim ID As String
    Dim Index As Integer
    Index = 0
    Me.ViewState("Index") = Index
```

```
    ID = DataSet11.Tables(0).Rows(Index).Item("au_id")
    DataView1.RowFilter = "au_id = '" & ID & "'"
    TextBox1.DataBind()
    TextBox2.DataBind()
End Sub

Private Sub Button2_Click(ByVal sender As System.Object, ByVal e As_
    System.EventArgs) Handles Button2.Click
    Dim ID As String
    Dim Index As Integer
    Index = Me.ViewState("Index")
    Index -= 1
    If Index < 0 Then
        Index = 0
    End If
    Me.ViewState("Index") = Index

    ID = DataSet11.Tables(0).Rows(Index).Item("au_id")
    DataView1.RowFilter = "au_id = '" & ID & "'"
    TextBox1.DataBind()
    TextBox2.DataBind()
End Sub

Private Sub Button3_Click(ByVal sender As System.Object, ByVal e As_
    System.EventArgs) Handles Button3.Click
    Dim ID As String
    Dim Index As Integer
    Index = Me.ViewState("Index")
    Index += 1
    If Index > DataSet11.Tables(0).Rows.Count - 1 Then
        Index = DataSet11.Tables(0).Rows.Count - 1
    End If
    Me.ViewState("Index") = Index

    ID = DataSet11.Tables(0).Rows(Index).Item("au_id")
    DataView1.RowFilter = "au_id = '" & ID & "'"
    TextBox1.DataBind()
    TextBox2.DataBind()
End Sub

Private Sub Button4_Click(ByVal sender As System.Object, ByVal e As_
    System.EventArgs) Handles Button4.Click
    Dim ID As String
    Dim Index As Integer
    Index = DataSet11.Tables(0).Rows.Count - 1
    Me.ViewState("Index") = Index
```

```
            ID = DataSet11.Tables(0).Rows(Index).Item("au_id")
            DataView1.RowFilter = "au_id = '" & ID & "'"
            TextBox1.DataBind()
            TextBox2.DataBind()
        End Sub
```

You can see the results in Figure 23.6. For more details, see the In Depth section of this chapter.

Related solution:	Found on page:
Saving Program Data across Server Round Trips	654

Using the **DataList** Class

A data-bound list control displays items using templates. Data lists are supported with the **DataList** class; here is the inheritance hierarchy of that class:

```
Object
    Control
        WebControl
            BaseDataList
                DataList
```

You can find the notable public properties of **DataList** objects in Table 23.6 and their notable events in Table 23.7. (This class has no non-inherited methods.) Note that as with other Web server controls, I am not listing the notable properties, methods, and events this class inherits from the **Control** and **WebControl** classes—you can find them in Tables 15.1 to 15.5 in Chapter 15.

Table 23.6   Noteworthy public properties of DataList objects.

Property	Means
AlternatingItemStyle	Gets the style for alternating items.
AlternatingItemTemplate	Gets/sets the template for alternating items.
EditItemIndex	Gets/sets the index number of the selected item to edit.
EditItemStyle	Gets the style for the item selected for editing.
EditItemTemplate	Gets/sets the template for the item selected for editing.
FooterStyle	Gets the style for the footer.

(continued)

Table 23.6   Noteworthy public properties of DataList objects *(continued)*.

Property	Means
FooterTemplate	Gets/sets the template for the footer.
GridLines	Gets/sets the grid line style.
HeaderStyle	Gets the style of the header.
HeaderTemplate	Gets/sets the template for the header.
Items	Gets the items in the list.
ItemStyle	Gets the style for the items in the list.
ItemTemplate	Gets/sets the template for items.
RepeatColumns	Gets/sets the number of columns to display.
RepeatDirection	Gets/sets if data is displayed horizontally or vertically.
RepeatLayout	Gets/sets if the control is displayed as a table or with a flow layout.
SelectedIndex	Gets/sets the selected item's index.
SelectedItem	Gets the selected item.
SelectedItemStyle	Gets the style properties for selected items.
SelectedItemTemplate	Gets/sets the template for selected items.
SeparatorStyle	Gets the style of separators.
SeparatorTemplate	Gets/sets the template for separators.
ShowFooter	Gets/sets if the footer is displayed.
ShowHeader	Gets/sets if the header is displayed.

Table 23.7   Noteworthy public events of DataList objects.

Event	Means
CancelCommand	Occurs when **Cancel** is clicked.
DeleteCommand	Occurs when **Delete** is clicked.
EditCommand	Occurs when **Edit** is clicked.
ItemCommand	Occurs when any button is clicked.
ItemCreated	Occurs when an item is created.
ItemDataBound	Occurs when an item is data bound to a data list.
UpdateCommand	Occurs when **Update** is clicked.

Creating a Data List

In the In Depth section of this chapter, we created the WebDataList example, which is on the CD-ROM, and used a data list to display data from the authors table in the pubs database. In that example, we created an Item Template to display the authors' first and last names, using label controls. Here's what the actual HTML looks like for the data list in this example:

```
<asp:DataList id=DataList1 style="Z-INDEX: 101; LEFT: 95px; POSITION:
absolute; TOP: 69px" runat="server" DataSource=
'<%# DataBinder.Eval(DataSet11,
"Tables[authors]") %>' BorderStyle="Solid">
<ItemTemplate>
 
<asp:Label id=Label1 runat="server" Text=
'<%# DataBinder.Eval(Container, "DataItem.au_fname") %>'>
</asp:Label> 
<asp:Label id=Label2 runat="server" Text=
'<%# DataBinder.Eval(Container,
"DataItem.au_lname") %>'></asp:Label>
</ItemTemplate>
</asp:DataList>
```

You can see the results in Figure 23.7; for more details on this example, see the In Depth section of this chapter.

Using the **Repeater** Class

A repeater is a data-bound list control that allows custom layout by repeating a specified template for each item displayed in the list. Repeaters are supported with the **Repeater** class, and here is the inheritance hierarchy for that class:

```
Object
    Control
        Repeater
```

You can find the notable public properties of **Repeater** objects in Table 23.8 and their notable events in Table 23.9. (This class has no non-inherited methods.) Note that as with other Web server controls, I am not listing the notable properties, methods, and events this class inherits from the **Control** and **WebControl** classes—you can find them in Chapter 15, Tables 15.1 to 15.5.

Table 23.8   Noteworthy public properties of Repeater objects.

Property	Means
AlternatingItemTemplate	Gets/sets the template for alternating items.
DataMember	Gets/sets the specific table to bind to.
DataSource	Gets/sets the data source to bind to.
FooterTemplate	Gets/sets the template for the footer.
HeaderTemplate	Gets/sets the template for the header.
Items	Gets the items in the repeater.
ItemTemplate	Gets/sets the template for items.
SeparatorTemplate	Gets/sets the template for separators.

Table 23.9   Noteworthy public events of Repeater objects.

Event	Means
ItemCommand	Occurs when any button is clicked.
ItemCreated	Occurs when an item is created.
ItemDataBound	Occurs when an item is data bound to the repeater.

Creating Repeaters

When you use a repeater in a Web form, the HTML is up to you. You can create the various templates you need in HTML, using elements like **<HeaderTemplate>**, **<ItemTemplate>**, and so on.

We saw how to do this in the WebRepeaters example on the CD-ROM, as discussed in the In Depth section of this chapter. That example displays the authors table in the pubs database using alternating lines, as you see in Figure 23.11. Here's how to create the necessary templates by editing the HTML directly:

```
<form id="Form1" method="post" runat="server">
  <table width="100%">
<asp:Repeater id=Repeater1 runat="server" DataSource="<%# DataSet11 %>"
DataMember="authors">
    <HeaderTemplate>
    <tr style="background-color:cyan">
      <th>First Name</th>
      <th>Last Name</th>
    </tr>
    </HeaderTemplate>
    <ItemTemplate>
```

```
  <tr>
    <td><%# DataBinder.Eval(Container, "DataItem.au_fname") %>
    </td>
    <td><%# DataBinder.Eval(Container,"DataItem.au_lname") %>
    </td>
  </tr>
   </ItemTemplate>
   <AlternatingItemTemplate>
  <tr>
    <td bgcolor="pink">
    <%# DataBinder.Eval(Container, "DataItem.au_fname") %> </td>
    <td bgcolor="pink">
    <%# DataBinder.Eval(Container,"DataItem.au_lname") %> </td>
  </tr>
   </AlternatingItemTemplate>
   <FooterTemplate>
   </FooterTemplate>
</asp:Repeater>
   </table>

</form>
```

And, of course, you have to fill the data adapter and bind the repeater as well:

```
Private Sub Page_Load(ByVal sender As System.Object, _
    ByVal e As System.EventArgs) Handles MyBase.Load
    DataSet11.Clear()
    OleDbDataAdapter1.Fill(DataSet11)
    Repeater1.DataBind()
End Sub
```

The result appears in Figure 23.11. For more details on this example, see the In Depth section of this chapter.

Using Data Readers

As with Windows forms, you can use data readers to access data, not just datasets (see "Using a Data Reader" in Chapter 22 for more on data readers). To see how this works, see the WebDataReader example on the CD-ROM. In that example, I use an **OleDbCommand** object to retrieve the authors table and connect that table to a data grid. Here's the code—note that you use the **ExecuteReader** method of the command object to get the data reader:

```
Private Sub Page_Load(ByVal sender As System.Object, _
    ByVal e As System.EventArgs) Handles MyBase.Load
    OleDbConnection1.Open()
    Dim Reader1 As System.Data.OleDb.OleDbDataReader
    Reader1 = OleDbCommand1.ExecuteReader()
    DataGrid1.DataSource = Reader1
    DataGrid1.DataBind()
    Reader1.Close()
End Sub
```

You can see the results in Figure 23.12, where the data from the data reader is displayed in the data grid in this example.

Related solution:	Found on page:
Using a Data Reader	968

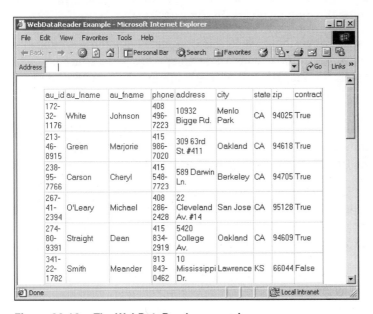

Figure 23.12   The WebDataReader example.

Creating Master/Detail Web Forms

We've seen how to create master/detail Windows forms (see "Using Master/Detail Relationships and Data Relation Objects" in Chapter 21, for example); you also can create master/detail Web forms. To see how this works, take a look at the

WebParentChildData example on the CD-ROM. You can see this example at work in Figure 23.13, where it's displaying data from the authors table of the pubs database.

Note in particular that the Last Name column in the data grid in Figure 23.13 holds hyperlinks. When the user clicks one of those hyperlinks, the corresponding author's data is displayed in the text boxes next to the data grid, as you see in the figure.

This example uses a data view, and uses the **RowFilter** property of the data view to select a single record to display in the bound text boxes. (The text boxes in this example are bound to that data view, as in the WebDataNavigation example in the In Depth section of this chapter.) The question here is—how do we let the user click a record in the data grid and set the data view's **RowFilter** property?

We can do that by using a *button column* in the data grid (see the In Depth section of this chapter for more on what kinds of columns you can use in a data grid). The button column in Figure 23.13 is the Last Name column that displays hyperlinks; to create this button column, right-click the data grid and select the Property Builder item, opening the dialog you see in Figure 23.14.

Click the Columns tab in this dialog box, and deselect the "Create columns automatically at run time" check box, which lets us specify what columns the data grid should display. Next, add the au_fname column, giving it the header text "First Name", and the au_id column, giving it the header text "ID". This creates the two standard columns you see in Figure 23.13. Now select the Button Column item in the Available Columns box, and add it to the columns of the data grid. Give this new button column the header text "Last Name", and select au_lname in the Text field drop-down box, as you see in Figure 23.14.

This creates the column of hyperlinks you see in Figure 23.13. When the user clicks one of these hyperlinks, a **SelectedIndexChanged** event occurs, and we can display the clicked record's fields in the bound text boxes by selecting that record in the data view's **RowFilter** property. Here's the code to do that:

```
Private Sub DataGrid1_SelectedIndexChanged(ByVal sender As System.Object, _
    ByVal e As System.EventArgs) Handles DataGrid1.SelectedIndexChanged
    DataView1.RowFilter = "au_id = '" & _
        DataGrid1.SelectedItem.Cells(1).Text & "'"
    TextBox1.DataBind()
    TextBox2.DataBind()
    TextBox3.DataBind()
    TextBox4.DataBind()
End Sub
```

And, of course, we have to load the dataset and bind it when the page loads:

```
Private Sub Page_Load(ByVal sender As System.Object, _
    ByVal e As System.EventArgs) Handles MyBase.Load
    DataSet11.Clear()
    OleDbDataAdapter1.Fill(DataSet11)
    DataGrid1.DataBind()
    TextBox1.DataBind()
    TextBox2.DataBind()
    TextBox3.DataBind()
    TextBox4.DataBind()
End Sub
```

And that's it—you can see the result in Figure 23.13. When the user clicks a hyperlink in the data grid's button column, the corresponding record's details are displayed in the text boxes.

Related solutions:	Found on page:
Using Relational Databases	878
Using Master/Detail Relationships and Data Relation Objects	919
Creating a Data Relation Object in Code	971

Using XML-Format Databases Directly in the Internet Explorer

As mentioned in the In Depth section of this chapter, you can waste a lot of time waiting for server round trips to handle your data. The Microsoft Internet Explorer has some built-in data source objects that can hold recordsets (note—here, I'm discussing ADO *recordsets*, not ADO.NET *datasets*) that you can access in scripting languages like JavaScript, which means you can work with records from a database directly in the browser. For a complete discussion on this topic, including examples, see the Coriolis *HTML Black Book*.

Here's an example using the XML data source object (DSO) in the Internet Explorer; this example is named ie.html in the IE folder on the CD-ROM. You can use the XML DSO to read in data in XML format and create an ADO recordset. For example, here's the authors table from the pubs database in XML format, in a file named dataset.xml (this file was created in the example in "Writing Datasets to XML and Reading Datasets from XML" in Chapter 22):

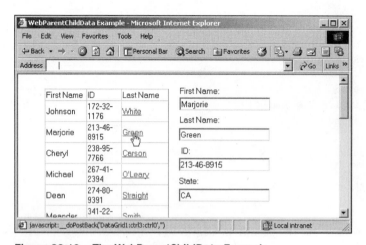

Figure 23.13   The WebParentChildData Example.

```xml
<?xml version="1.0" standalone="yes"?>
<DataSet1 xmlns="http://www.tempuri.org/DataSet1.xsd">
  <authors>
    <au_id>172-32-1176</au_id>
    <au_lname>White</au_lname>
    <au_fname>Johnson</au_fname>
    <phone>408 496-7223</phone>
    <address>10932 Bigge Rd.</address>
    <city>Menlo Park</city>
    <state>CA</state>
    <zip>94025</zip>
    <contract>true</contract>
  </authors>
  <authors>
    <au_id>213-46-8915</au_id>
    <au_lname>Green</au_lname>
    <au_fname>Marjorie</au_fname>
    <phone>415 986-7020</phone>
        .
        .
        .
```

Now I can read in dataset.xml and navigate through the data in it using navigation buttons in JavaScript like this in ie.html (the **com.ms.xml.dso.XMLDSO.class** applet used here comes built into Internet Explorer):

```html
<HTML>
    <HEAD>
        <TITLE>
            Using the XML Data Source Control
        </TITLE>
```

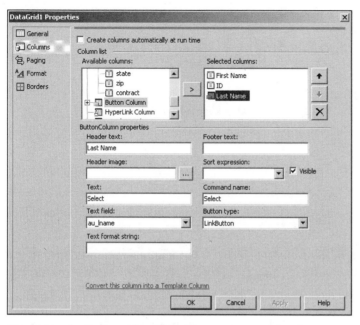

Figure 23.14   A data grid properties dialog.

```
    </HEAD>

<BODY>
    <CENTER>
        <H1>
            Using the XML Data Source Control
        </H1>

        <APPLET CODE="com.ms.xml.dso.XMLDSO.class"
            ID="dsoAuthors" WIDTH=0 HEIGHT=0 MAYSCRIPT=true>
            <PARAM NAME="URL" VALUE="dataset.xml">
        </APPLET>

        First Name: <INPUT TYPE="TEXT" DATASRC="#dsoAuthors"
            DATAFLD="au_fname" SIZE=10><P>
        Last Name: <INPUT TYPE="TEXT" DATASRC="#dsoAuthors"
            DATAFLD="au_lname" SIZE=10><P>
        ID: <INPUT TYPE="TEXT" DATASRC="#dsoAuthors"
            DATAFLD="au_id" SIZE=12><P>

        <BUTTON ONCLICK="dsoAuthors.recordset.MoveFirst()" >
            &lt;&lt;
        </BUTTON>
        <BUTTON ONCLICK="if (!dsoAuthors.recordset.BOF)
            dsoAuthors.recordset.MovePrevious()" >
```

```
                            &lt;
                </BUTTON>
                <BUTTON ONCLICK="if (!dsoAuthors.recordset.EOF)
                    dsoAuthors.recordset.MoveNext()" >
                    &gt;
                </BUTTON>
                <BUTTON ONCLICK="dsoAuthors.recordset.MoveLast()">
                    &gt;&gt;
                </BUTTON>

        </CENTER>

    </BODY>
</HTML>
```

You can see the results in Figure 23.15; this technique offers a simple way of viewing data and navigating through it in the Internet Explorer without any server round trips.

TIP: *For other ways of binding data in the Internet Explorer, including the Remote Data Service (RDS), which can connect directly to databases on servers using connection strings and SQL, see the Coriolis HTML Black Book.*

Related solution:	*Found on page:*
Writing Datasets to XML and Reading Datasets from XML	966

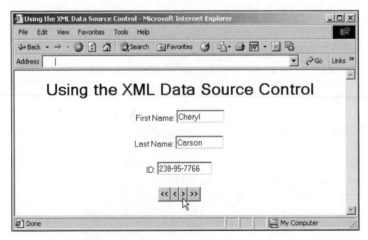

Figure 23.15   Using the XML Data Source Control in the Internet Explorer.

Chapter 24

Creating User Controls, Web User Controls, and Multithreading

In Depth

In this chapter, we'll work with user controls, Web user controls, and multithreading. User controls are those controls you can build yourself for use in Windows forms, if, for example, you want to create an alarm clock or a stock ticker. Web user controls are the same, but for Web forms. Multithreading gives your programs the ability to do several things at once; each stream of execution is called a *thread*. When you create new threads in a program, those threads can execute code you give them in the background, no matter what the user is doing with the user interface. Multithreading is often used for lengthy tasks that would otherwise make your program seem to hang. For example, your program may maintain a large database, and it can use a thread in the background to sort that database while the user can get on with other work. I'll take a look at the topics in this chapter—user controls, Web user controls, and multithreading—now, in more depth.

User Controls

Creating your own customized controls for use in Windows forms isn't hard—you just need to create a user control. A user control works much like any other Windows form—except that you can add it to other forms just like any other control. To see how this works, you can take a look at the UserControls example on the CD-ROM, which creates a user control and uses it in a Windows form.

To create the user control, you use the File|New Project menu item, opening the New Project dialog you see in Figure 24.1, and selecting the Windows Control Library item.

When you click the OK button in the New Project dialog, the new user control is created, as you see in Figure 24.2. The user control looks like a small Windows form; you can add your own controls to it or give it a custom appearance in code. I've added a label control to the user control, as you can see in Figure 24.2.

Like any other control, user controls can support properties, methods, and events. For example, to let the user set the background color of the label in our user control, I can add a property named **DisplayColor** to the user control. I do that by opening the code for the user control in a code designer—note that the user control is based on the **System.Windows.Forms.UserControl** class (see "Using the **System.Windows.Forms.UserControl** Class" in this chapter):

```
Public Class UserControl1
    Inherits System.Windows.Forms.UserControl

' Windows Form Designer generated code...
        .
        .
        .
```

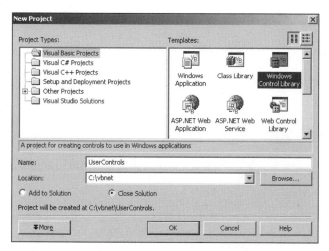

Figure 24.1 Creating a user control project.

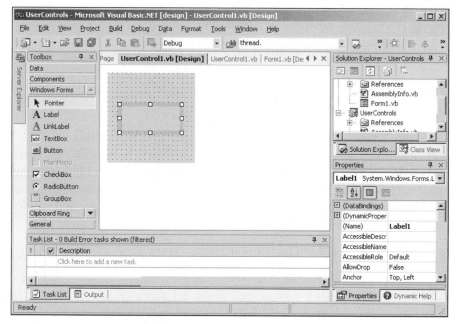

Figure 24.2 Creating a user control.

I can add the **DisplayColor** property to this code, like this (see "Creating Properties" in Chapter 11):

```
Public Class UserControl1
    Inherits System.Windows.Forms.UserControl

' Windows Form Designer generated code...

    Private LabelColor As Color

    Property DisplayColor() As Color
        Get
            Return LabelColor
        End Get

        Set(ByVal Value As Color)
            LabelColor = Value
            Label1.BackColor = LabelColor
        End Set
    End Property
```

TIP: *This code implements the **DisplayColor** property with a property get/set method pair, but any **Public** data member of the user control will be treated as a property of the control.*

I can add new methods to the user control as easily (see "Creating Methods" in Chapter 11). For example, to add a **SetText** method to set the text displayed by the label in this user control, just add a public method to the control's code, following the implementation of the **DisplayColor** property above:

```
Public Sub SetText(ByVal NewText As String)
    Label1.Text = NewText
End Sub
```

And I can add an event easily as well; all I have to do is to declare that event and the parameters sent to its event handlers. For example, we could implement a **TextModified** event in the control that happens when the text changes in the label in the control. Event handlers for this event should be passed the new text, so here's how I declare this event (see "Creating Events" in Chapter 11):

```
Public Class UserControl1
    Inherits System.Windows.Forms.UserControl

' Windows Form Designer generated code...
```

```
Private LabelColor As Color
Public Event TextModified(ByVal NewText As String)
        .
        .
        .
```

We can make the **TextModify** event happen when the **SetText** method is called to change the text displayed in the control. All we have to do is to use the **RaiseEvent** statement:

```
Public Sub SetText(ByVal NewText As String)
    Label1.Text = NewText
    RaiseEvent TextModified(NewText)
End Sub
```

And that completes the user control. To make this control available to other projects, it must be compiled into .dll (dynamic link library) form, so select the Build|Build Solution menu item now, which builds the .dll file we'll need.

To add this new user control to a Windows form, select the File|Add Project|New Project menu item to add a new Windows form project to the current solution; I've named this new project TestApplication in the UserControls example on the CD-ROM. Because you can't run user controls directly, you should make the new text application the startup project for the whole solution by selecting that project in the Solution Explorer, followed by the Project|Set as Startup Project menu item.

The next step is to add a new user control of the type we've created to the main form in the text application. To do that, we'll need a reference to the user control's project, so right-click the test application's References item in the Solution Explorer, and choose the Add Reference menu item, opening the Add Reference dialog you see in Figure 24.3. To add a reference to the UserControls project, click the Projects tab and double-click the UserControls item, adding that item to the Selected Components box at the bottom of the dialog, and click OK.

This adds the user control to the toolbox of the text application, as you see in Figure 24.4. You can now add a user control, **UserControl11**, to the test application's main form, as you would any other control. You can see this new user control in Figure 24.4, and you also can see our custom property, **Display Color**, in the Properties window. (In fact, because we've declared this property as type **Color**, Visual Basic will display a drop-down list of palette colors you can select from if you select this property in the properties window.) In this example, I've selected the color Aqua as the background color for use in our user control; you can see that color (in glorious black and white) in the user control in the test application's main form shown in Figure 24.4.

24. Creating User Controls, Web User Controls, and Multithreading

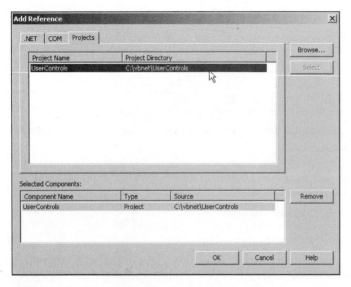

Figure 24.3   The UserControls example at work.

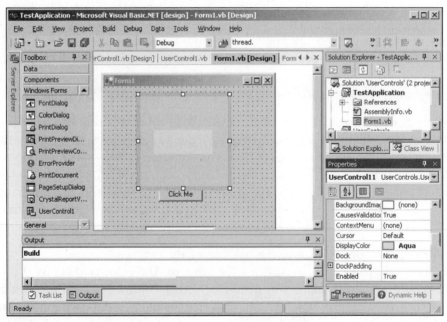

Figure 24.4   Adding a user control in the Visual Basic IDE.

Besides setting the **DisplayColor** property, I also can use the new control's **SetText** method. To do that, I've added the "Click Me" button you can see in Figure 24.4, and used that button's **Click** event handler to set the text "Hello!" in the user control, like this:

```
Private Sub Button1_Click(ByVal sender As System.Object, _
    ByVal e As System.EventArgs) Handles Button1.Click
    UserControl11.SetText("Hello!")
End Sub
```

When the text in the control changes, that control causes a **TextModified** event, and we can add code to that event's handler just as you would any other control's event (that is, by using the drop-down list boxes at the top of the code designer for the test application's main form). In this example, I'll display the new text in a text box when the **TextModified** event occurs:

```
Private Sub UserControl11_TextModified(ByVal NewText As String) _
    Handles UserControl11.TextModified
    TextBox1.Text = "New text: " & NewText
End Sub
```

Now I can run the test application, giving us the result you see in Figure 24.5. You can see the user control in that figure, and when I click the button, the text in the control is set to "Hello!", as it should be, the **TextModified** event occurs, and the text box in the example handles that event, displaying the new text.

And that's all we've needed to do to create a new user control, complete with a property, method, and event.

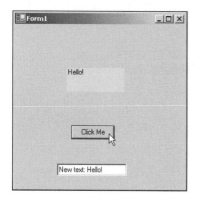

Figure 24.5   Using a user control.

Web User Controls

You also can create Web user controls, which are the Web equivalent of user controls. The process is much like creating and coding a user control; in fact, to show how similar these types of controls are to create, I'll duplicate the previous example now as a Web user control. This new example is WebUserControls on the CD-ROM.

This time, we'll start by creating a new Web application named WebUserControls. Then add a new Web user control to this application by selecting the Project|Add Web User Control menu item, opening the Add New Item dialog you see in Figure 24.6. To accept the default name, **WebUserControl1**, click OK.

This adds the new Web user control, as you see in Figure 24.7. The new Web user control's class is **WebUserControl1**, and at design time, it just looks like a standard Web page. I've added the label we'll use in this control to that page, as you also see in Figure 24.7.

In fact, I can apply the very same code to the Web user control that I used in the user control to support the **DisplayColor** property, **SetText** method, and **TextModified** event, so add this code to the Web user control's code designer now:

```
Public MustInherit Class WebUserControl1
    Inherits System.Web.UI.UserControl
    Protected WithEvents Label1 As System.Web.UI.WebControls.Label

' Web Form Designer Generated Code ...

    Private LabelColor As Color
    Public Event TextModified(ByVal NewText As String)

    Private Sub Page_Load(ByVal sender As System.Object, _
        ByVal e As System.EventArgs) Handles MyBase.Load
        'Put user code to initialize the page here
    End Sub

    Property DisplayColor() As Color
        Get
            Return LabelColor
        End Get

        Set(ByVal Value As Color)
            LabelColor = Value
            Label1.BackColor = LabelColor
        End Set
    End Property
```

```
    Public Sub SetText(ByVal NewText As String)
        Label1.Text = NewText
        RaiseEvent TextModified(NewText)
    End Sub
End Class
```

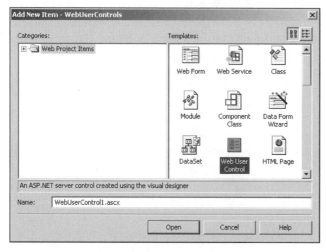

Figure 24.6   The Add New Item dialog.

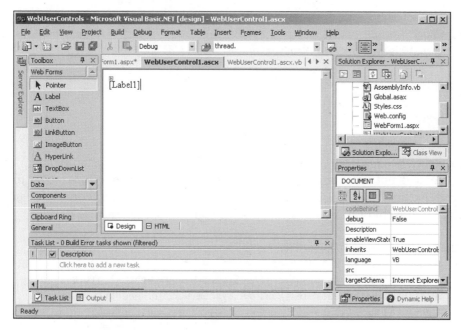

Figure 24.7   Working on a new Web control.

This is where the process for Web user controls differs from Windows user controls, however. You can't compile the Web user control as we could the user control earlier, so you can't add a reference to that control to the main Web application's form. Instead, here's what you do—open the Web application's main form in a form designer, then *drag* the WebUserControl1.ascx entry from the Solution Explorer onto that form, adding the Web user control, **WebUserControl11**, to the form as you see in Figure 24.8. Note that because the Web user control has not been compiled, Visual Basic doesn't know what it will look like at run time, so it gives it a generic appearance at design time.

This creates the new Web user control, **WebUserControl11**, in WebForm1.aspx, like this:

```
<%@ Page Language="vb" AutoEventWireup="false"
Codebehind="WebForm1.aspx.vb" Inherits="WebUserControls.WebForm1"%>
<%@ Register TagPrefix="uc1" TagName="WebUserControl1"
Src="WebUserControl1.ascx" %>
<!DOCTYPE HTML PUBLIC "-//W3C//DTD HTML 4.0 Transitional//EN">
<HTML>
  <HEAD>

      .
      .
      .

    <form id="Form1" method="post" runat="server">
<uc1:WebUserControl1 id=WebUserControl11
    runat="server"></uc1:WebUserControl1>

    </form>

  </body>
</HTML>
```

However, because this control will not actually be compiled until run time, Visual Basic does not automatically add the user control, **WebUserControl11**, to the "code-behind" file, WebForm1.aspx.vb. To use this control in code, we can declare it in WebForm1.aspx.vb, so add this code to that file now:

```
Public Class WebForm1
    Inherits System.Web.UI.Page
    Protected WithEvents Button1 As System.Web.UI.WebControls.Button
    Protected WithEvents TextBox1 As System.Web.UI.WebControls.TextBox
    Protected WithEvents WebUserControl11 As WebUserControl1
        .
        .
        .
```

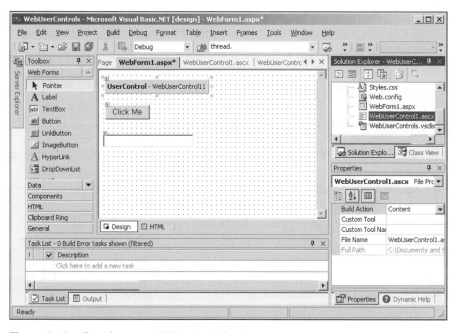

Figure 24.8   Creating a new Web control.

Now we're ready to use the new control's **DisplayColor** property, **SetText** method, and **TextModified** event. Because the control has not yet been compiled, we can't set properties at design time, so I'll set the **DisplayColor** property to Aqua when the test application's main Web form loads:

```
Private Sub Page_Load(ByVal sender As System.Object, _
    ByVal e As System.EventArgs) Handles MyBase.Load
    WebUserControl11.DisplayColor = Color.Aqua
End Sub
```

Next, as in the UserControls example we saw earlier, I'll add a button (caption: "Click Me") and a text box to the Web application, as you see in Figure 24.8. Now I can use the Web user control's **SetText** method and **TextModified** event, just as we did in the UserControls example:

```
Private Sub Button1_Click(ByVal sender As System.Object, _
    ByVal e As System.EventArgs) Handles Button1.Click
    WebUserControl11.SetText("Hello!")
End Sub

Private Sub WebUserControl11_TextModified(ByVal NewText As String) _
    Handles WebUserControl11.TextModified
    TextBox1.Text = "New text: " & NewText
End Sub
```

And that's all we need—in this way, we've been able to duplicate the work we did with the UserControls example earlier, but this time we're using a Web user control. You can see this example at work in Figure 24.9; when you click the "Click Me" button, the new text is displayed in the Web user control and the text box, as you see in that figure.

Multithreading

As mentioned earlier, threading lets your program seem as though it's executing several tasks at once. What's actually happening is that time is divided by the computer into *slices*, and when you start a new thread, that thread gets some time slices, which means that thread's code can execute. (The program itself is also running a thread, called the main thread, to execute its own code.)

> **TIP:** *Although you can use threads with user interface elements such as forms and controls in Visual Basic, that's risky. (Microsoft recommends you only execute methods of a form or control only in the thread in which the form or control was created, and that you don't use the **SyncLock** statement—see "Using **SyncLock** to Synchronize Threads" in this chapter—to lock threads that work with controls or forms.) Visual Basic threads are primarily designed to be used with code that executes but doesn't directly access user interface elements, and that's the way we'll use them in this chapter.*

Creating a Thread

To see threads in practice, take a look at the Threading example on the CD-ROM, which you see in Figure 24.10. This example demonstrates a lot of thread techniques; it creates a new thread and uses that thread to count to 1,000,000.

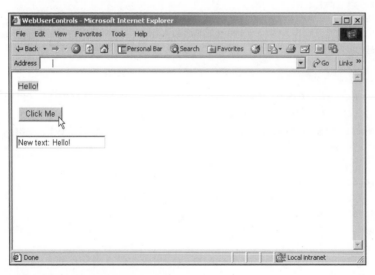

Figure 24.9   Using a Web user control.

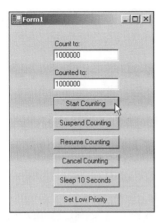

Figure 24.10   The Threading example.

After starting a new thread, you typically use events to let the thread communicate with the rest of your program. To follow along, create a new Windows application named Threading now, and add a new class to the application named **counter**, using the Project|Add Class menu item. This class will count from 1 to a value specified in a public data member named **CountTo** when you call the **Count** method. After the count has reached the value in **CountTo**, a **FinishedCounting** event will occur. Here's the code for the **counter** class; note the use of **RaiseEvent** to make the **FinishedCounting** event occur, and that I'm passing the total value we've counted to the **FinishedCounting** event handler:

```
Public Class counter
    Public CountTo As Integer
    Public Event FinishedCounting(ByVal NumberOfMatches As Integer)

    Sub Count()
        Dim LoopIndex, Total As Integer
        Total = 0

        For LoopIndex = 1 To CountTo
            Total += 1
        Next LoopIndex

        RaiseEvent FinishedCounting(Total)
    End Sub
End Class
```

How do we make use of this class with a new thread? In the main form of this example, I'll create both an object of this class, **counter1**, and a new thread, **Thread1**. The code for a new thread must be in a Sub procedure which takes no arguments. In this case, I'll call the **counter1** object's **Count** method, which will perform the counting operation:

```
Public Class Form1
    Inherits System.Windows.Forms.Form
    Dim counter1 As New counter()
    Dim Thread1 As New System.Threading.Thread(AddressOf counter1.Count)
        .
        .
        .
```

When the user clicks the "Start Counting" button in this example, the code will read the value it's supposed to count to from the top text box you see in Figure 24.10, **TextBox1**, and assign that value to **counter1.CountTo**. We'll also clear the text in the result text box, **TextBox2**, and connect an event handler to the **FinishedCounting** event using the **AddHandler** method (for more on **AddHandler**, see "Creating a **LinkLabel** in Code" in Chapter 5). Then we'll start the new thread with its **Start** method:

```
Public Class Form1
    Inherits System.Windows.Forms.Form
    Dim counter1 As New counter()
    Dim Thread1 As New System.Threading.Thread(AddressOf counter1.Count)

' Windows Form Designer generated code...

    Private Sub Button1_Click(ByVal sender As System.Object, _
        ByVal e As System.EventArgs) Handles Button1.Click
        TextBox2.Text = ""
        counter1.CountTo = TextBox1.Text
        AddHandler counter1.FinishedCounting, AddressOf _
            FinishedCountingEventHandler
        Thread1.Start()
    End Sub
        .
        .
        .
```

This starts the new thread, and when it's done counting, it'll cause a **FinishedCounting** event. We can handle that event in the **FinishedCounting EventHandler** Sub procedure, displaying the total count in the second text box in the example:

```
Public Class Form1
    Inherits System.Windows.Forms.Form
```

```
    Dim counter1 As New counter()
    Dim Thread1 As New System.Threading.Thread(AddressOf counter1.Count)

' Windows Form Designer generated code...

    Private Sub Button1_Click(ByVal sender As System.Object, _
        ByVal e As System.EventArgs) Handles Button1.Click
        TextBox2.Text = ""
        counter1.CountTo = TextBox1.Text
        AddHandler counter1.FinishedCounting, AddressOf _
            FinishedCountingEventHandler
        Thread1.Start()
    End Sub

    Sub FinishedCountingEventHandler(ByVal Count As Integer)
        TextBox2.Text = Count
    End Sub
        .
        .
        .
```

You can see the results in Figure 24.10; when you click the "Start Counting" button, the code uses the new thread to perform its counting operation and displays the total count in the second text box.

Suspending a Thread

You also can *suspend* a thread, which stops it temporarily until you resume its operation. You can suspend the new thread in the Threading example by clicking the "Suspend Counting" button, which uses this code:

```
    Private Sub Button5_Click(ByVal sender As System.Object, _
        ByVal e As System.EventArgs) Handles Button5.Click
        Thread1.Suspend()
    End Sub
```

Resuming a Thread

You also can resume thread operation by clicking the "Resume Counting" button in the Threading example, which uses this code:

```
    Private Sub Button6_Click(ByVal sender As System.Object, _
        ByVal e As System.EventArgs) Handles Button6.Click
        Thread1.Resume()
    End Sub
```

Stopping a Thread

And you can stop a thread altogether with its **Abort** method. Here's how that works when you click the "Cancel Counting" button in the Threading example on the CD-ROM:

```
Private Sub Button2_Click(ByVal sender As System.Object, _
    ByVal e As System.EventArgs) Handles Button2.Click
        Thread1.Abort()
End Sub
```

Putting a Thread to Sleep

You also can make a thread go to "sleep" when you want it to, suspending execution for a specified amount of time. You do this by passing the number of milliseconds (1/1000ths of a second) you want the thread to sleep to the thread's sleep method. Here's how that works in the Threading example on the CD-ROM when you click the "Sleep 10 Seconds" button:

```
Private Sub Button3_Click(ByVal sender As System.Object, _
    ByVal e As System.EventArgs) Handles Button3.Click
        Thread1.Sleep(10 * 1000)
End Sub
```

TIP: *Although the time you pass to **Sleep** is in milliseconds, in practice, the precision with which a Windows machine can measure time intervals is limited. In my tests, the smallest sleep interval I can get is a hundredth of a second, which means that calling **Sleep(1)** gives the same result as calling **Sleep(10)**.*

Setting a Thread's Priority

Threads are scheduled for execution based on their *priority*. You can get and set the priority of a thread by accessing its **Priority** property and setting it to a value from the **ThreadPriority** enumeration. Here are the possible values:

- **AboveNormal**—Gives a thread higher priority.
- **BelowNormal**—Gives a thread lower priority.
- **Highest**—Gives a thread highest priority.
- **Lowest**—Gives a thread lowest priority.
- **Normal**—Gives a thread average priority.

Here's what that looks like in the Threading example, where I set the thread's priority to **BelowNormal**:

```
Private Sub Button4_Click(ByVal sender As System.Object, _
    ByVal e As System.EventArgs) Handles Button4.Click
```

```
    Thread1.Priority = System.Threading.ThreadPriority.BelowNormal
End Sub
```

Determining Thread State

The **ThreadState** property gives you information about the status of a thread. Because threads can be in more than one state at any given time, the value stored in **ThreadState** can be a combination of the values in the **System.Threading. Threadstate** enumeration. Here are the values in that enumeration:

- **Initialized**—The thread was initialized, but it hasn't started.
- **Ready**—The thread is ready.
- **Running**—The thread is running.
- **Standby**—The thread is on standby.
- **Terminated**—The thread has terminated.
- **Transition**—The thread is in transition between two states.
- **Unknown**—The thread state is unknown.
- **Wait**—The thread is waiting.

Synchronizing Threads

Threads operate largely by themselves, which is why you have to give a little thought to how to coordinate them. For example, two threads may be working with the same data, and you might not want the second thread to work with that data until the first thread is finished with it.

One common practice is to synchronize threads using events. We've seen how to use events with threads already. You can use an event to signal a thread that another thread is finished working with some critical data, for example.

There are two additional ways to synchronize thread execution in Visual Basic—the **SyncLock** statement, and the **Join** method. We'll see both of them at work in the SynchronizeThreads example on the CD-ROM. This example uses two threads to increment a single value, and because both threads operate on a single data item, we'll get a chance to synchronize those threads here. This example uses a class named **counter** as the Threading example did, but this **counter** class is much simpler, containing a single data member named **Total**:

```
Public Class counter
    Public Total As Integer
End Class
```

Now, in the example's main form, I'll create an object of this class, **c**, and two threads, **Thread1** and **Thread2**:

```
Public Class Form1
    Inherits System.Windows.Forms.Form
    Dim c As New counter()
    Dim Thread1 As New System.Threading.Thread(AddressOf Counter1)
    Dim Thread2 As New System.Threading.Thread(AddressOf Counter2)
    .
    .
    .
```

When the user clicks a button, both these threads will be started; the code for **Thread1** is in a Sub procedure named **Counter1**, and the code for **Thread2** is in a Sub procedure named **Counter2**. And here's the important point, the code for both threads will increment the *same* value, **c.Total**:

```
Public Class Form1
    Inherits System.Windows.Forms.Form
    Dim c As New counter()
    Dim Thread1 As New System.Threading.Thread(AddressOf Counter1)
    Dim Thread2 As New System.Threading.Thread(AddressOf Counter2)

' Windows Form Designer generated code...

    Private Sub Button1_Click(ByVal sender As System.Object, _
        ByVal e As System.EventArgs) Handles Button1.Click
        Thread1.Start()
        Thread2.Start()
    End Sub

    Private Sub Counter1()
        Dim LoopIndex As Integer

        For LoopIndex = 1 To 100
            Dim temp = c.Total
            Thread1.Sleep(1)
            c.Total = temp + 1
        Next LoopIndex
    End Sub

    Private Sub Counter2()
        Dim LoopIndex As Integer

        For LoopIndex = 1 To 100
            Dim temp = c.Total
```

```
            Thread2.Sleep(1)
            c.Total = temp + 1
        Next LoopIndex
    End Sub
End Class
```

The code for each thread executes a loop 100 times, reading the value in **c.Total**, sleeping for a millisecond, then incrementing the value in **c.Total**. Because there are two threads, each incrementing this value 100 times, we should end up with a value of 200.

However, there's a problem here. When **Thread1** has copied the value in **c.Total** to a variable named **temp** and is sleeping, the other thread, **Thread2**, increments the actual value in **c.Total**. Then, when **Thread1** wakes up, it'll increment the value it has already stored a millisecond ago, **temp** (instead of using the new value in **c.Total**, which was just incremented by the other thread), and overwrite **c.Total** with its own, out-of-date value. In this way, it cancels out the new value stored in **c.Total** by the other thread, and the two threads will interfere with each other. If you run this code as it stands, the total count it will display will be 100, not 200 as it should be.

To fix the problem, we have to restrict access to **c.Total** by one thread when the other thread is using that value. We can do that with the **SyncLock** statement. To use that statement, you pass it an expression to use to lock access, such as an object. (The type of this expression must be a reference type, such as a class, a module, an array, or an interface.) For example, if you pass it an object, **SyncLock** will lock access to that object, giving access only the current thread and denying access to that object by any other thread. When an **End SyncLock** statement is reached, the lock is removed, and other threads get access to the object again. This means that we can fix the problem in this example by locking access to the **c** object when a thread is working with it like this:

```
Public Class Form1
    Inherits System.Windows.Forms.Form
    Dim c As New counter()
    Dim Thread1 As New System.Threading.Thread(AddressOf Counter1)
    Friend WithEvents Label1 As System.Windows.Forms.Label
    Dim Thread2 As New System.Threading.Thread(AddressOf Counter2)

' Windows Form Designer generated code...

    Private Sub Button1_Click(ByVal sender As System.Object, _
        ByVal e As System.EventArgs) Handles Button1.Click
        Thread1.Start()
        Thread2.Start()
```

```
            End Sub

            Private Sub Counter1()
                Dim LoopIndex As Integer

                For LoopIndex = 1 To 100
                    SyncLock c
                        Dim temp = c.Total
                        Thread1.Sleep(1)
                        c.Total = temp + 1
                    End SyncLock
                Next LoopIndex
            End Sub

            Private Sub Counter2()
                Dim LoopIndex As Integer

                For LoopIndex = 1 To 100
                    SyncLock c
                        Dim temp = c.Total
                        Thread2.Sleep(1)
                        c.Total = temp + 1
                    End SyncLock
                Next LoopIndex
            End Sub
        End Class
```

This synchronizes the two threads—now only one at a time has access to **c.Total**. However, we're not done yet—we still have to display the total count in a text box when the two threads are done. In the Threading example, we used an event—the **FinishedCounting** event—to determine when a thread had done its work, but there's another way to find out when a thread has finished; you can use the **Join** method. When you call this method, it'll return only when the thread has finished. After the two threads have finished, which we can determine using the **Join** method after we've started the threads when the user clicks a button, we can display the total count in a text box like this:

```
        Private Sub Button1_Click(ByVal sender As System.Object, _
            ByVal e As System.EventArgs) Handles Button1.Click
            Thread1.Start()
            Thread2.Start()
            Thread1.Join()
            Thread2.Join()
            TextBox1.Text = c.Total
        End Sub
```

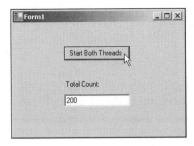

Figure 24.11   The SynchronizeThreads example.

And that's it. When you run this example, the total count ends up as 200, as you see in Figure 24.11. The two threads in this example are now synchronized, even though they work with the same data item.

There are other forms of the **Join** method; see "Joining Threads" in this chapter for more details. Now it's time to turn to the Immediate Solutions section to get to all the details on the topics we've been discussing in this chapter—user controls, Web user controls, and multithreading.

Immediate Solutions

Using the **ScrollableControl** Class

The **ScrollableControl** class is a base class for controls that support auto-scrolling behavior. This class is the base class for the **ContainerControl** class, which is the base class for the **System.Windows.Forms.UserControl** class. Here is the inheritance hierarchy for this class:

```
Object
    MarshalByRefObject
        Component
            Control
                ScrollableControl
```

You can find the more notable public properties of the **ScrollableControl** class in Table 24.1 and the more notable methods in Table 24.2. (This class has no non-inherited events.) Note that as with other Windows controls, I am not listing the notable properties, methods, and events **ScrollableControl** inherits from the **Control** class, such as the **Click** event—you can see all that in Chapter 5, Tables 5.1, 5.2, and 5.3.

Table 24.1   Noteworthy public properties of ScrollableControl objects.

Property	Means
AutoScroll	Gets/sets whether the user can scroll to controls outside of the control's boundaries.
AutoScrollMargin	Gets/sets the auto-scroll margin's size.
AutoScrollMinSize	Gets/sets the auto-scroll's minimum size.
AutoScrollPosition	Gets/sets the auto-scroll's position.
DockPadding	Gets the dock padding values.

Table 24.2   Noteworthy public methods of ScrollableControl objects.

Method	Means
SetAutoScrollMargin	Sets the margin size of the auto-scroll.

Using the **ContainerControl** Class

The **ContainerControl** class is the base class of the **System.Windows.Forms. UserControl** class. Here is the inheritance hierarchy for this class:

```
Object
   MarshalByRefObject
       Component
           Control
               ScrollableControl
                   ContainerControl
```

You can find the more notable public properties of the **ContainerControl** class in Table 24.3 and the more notable methods in Table 24.4. (This class has no non-inherited events.) Note that as with other Windows controls, I am not listing the notable properties, methods, and events **ContainerControl** inherits from the **Control** class, such as the **Click** event—you can see all that in Chapter 5, Tables 5.1, 5.2, and 5.3.

Table 24.3   Noteworthy public properties of ContainerControl objects.

Property	Means
ActiveControl	Gets/sets the active control in this container.
ParentForm	Gets/sets the parent form of this container control.

Table 24.4   Noteworthy public methods of ContainerControl objects.

Method	Means
Validate	Validates the last invalidated control.

Using the **System.Windows.Forms.UserControl** Class

The **System.Windows.Forms.UserControl** class (I'm listing its full namespace here to differentiate it from the **System.Web.UI.UserControl**, which we'll also see in this chapter) is the class that supports user controls. Here is the inheritance hierarchy for this class:

```
Object
   MarshalByRefObject
       Component
           Control
```

```
ScrollableControl
    ContainerControl
        UserControl
```

You can find the more notable public events of the **System.Windows.Forms. UserControl** class in Table 24.5. (This class has no non-inherited properties or methods.) Note that as with other Windows controls, I am not listing the notable properties, methods, and events **System.Windows.Forms.UserControl** inherits from the **Control** class, such as the **Click** event—you can see all that in Chapter 5, Tables 5.1, 5.2, and 5.3.

Table 24.5   Noteworthy public events of System.Windows.Forms.UserControl objects.

Event	Means
Load	Occurs when the control is loaded and before it becomes visible.

Creating User Controls

You can create a new user control with the Project|Add User Control menu item, or by creating a new project based on a user control by selecting the File|New|Project menu item, then selecting the Windows Control Library icon and clicking OK.

We saw an example showing how to create a new user control with properties, methods, and events in the UserControls example, as discussed in the In Depth section of this chapter. You can see this user control at work in Figure 24.5; here is the code for the user control in that example, UserControl1.vb (without the Windows Form Designer generated code):

```vb
Public Class UserControl1
    Inherits System.Windows.Forms.UserControl

' Windows Form Designer generated code...

    Private LabelColor As Color
    Public Event TextModified(ByVal NewText As String)

    Property DisplayColor() As Color
        Get
            Return LabelColor
        End Get
```

```
        Set(ByVal Value As Color)
            LabelColor = Value
            Label1.BackColor = LabelColor
        End Set
    End Property

    Public Sub SetText(ByVal NewText As String)
        Label1.Text = NewText
        RaiseEvent TextModified(NewText)
    End Sub
End Class
```

For more information, see the In Depth section of this chapter, and the next few sections.

Adding Properties to User Controls

Adding properties to user controls is no problem—you just use a **Property** statement with **Get** and **Set** methods. For more details on the **Property** statement, see "Creating Properties" in Chapter 11.

For example, here's how we added the **DisplayColor** property to the UserControls example discussed in the In Depth section of this chapter; this property set the background color of the label used in the user control, like this:

```
    Private LabelColor As Color

    Property DisplayColor() As Color
        Get
            Return LabelColor
        End Get

        Set(ByVal Value As Color)
            LabelColor = Value
            Label1.BackColor = LabelColor
        End Set
    End Property
```

See the In Depth section of this chapter for more details on the UserControls example.

Related solution:	Found on page:
Creating Properties	508

Sidebar (right margin): **24. Creating User Controls, Web User Controls, and Multithreading**

Adding Methods to User Controls

You can add a method to a user control as you would to any class; just place the implementation of that method into the user control's code. You can make the method public, protected, or private.

For example, here's how we added a method named **SetText** to the user control in the UserControls example discussed in the In Depth section of this chapter. This method displays text in the label control in the user control and sets the text displayed in the user control:

```
Public Sub SetText(ByVal NewText As String)
    Label1.Text = NewText
End Sub
```

That's all it takes. See the In Depth section of this chapter for more details on the UserControls example.

Related solution:	Found on page:
Creating Methods	506

Adding Events to User Controls

You can add an event to a user control as you would to any class; all you have to do is to declare the event and the parameters passed to the event's handler procedure.

Here's how that looked in the UserControls example discussed in the In Depth section of this chapter, where we declared an event named **TextModified**:

```
Public Event TextModified(ByVal NewText As String)
```

This event occurs when the text displayed in the user control in this example is modified. In the UserControls example, we made this event happen when the **SetText** method (see the previous topic) was called, using the **RaiseEvent** method:

```
Public Sub SetText(ByVal NewText As String)
    Label1.Text = NewText
    RaiseEvent TextModified(NewText)
End Sub
```

That's all it takes. See the In Depth section of this chapter for more details on the UserControls example.

Related solution:	Found on page:
Creating Events	510

Testing User Controls

To test a user control, you must first build the control to make it available to other projects, using the Build|Build Solution menu item. Then you can add a new Windows application to the solution to test the user control. To add the user control to the test application, right-click the References item of the test application in the Solution Explorer and select the Add Reference item. After adding a reference to the user control, drag the user control from the toolbox to the main form of the test application, set the properties of the user control as you like, and run the test application.

In the UserControls example discussed in the In Depth section of this chapter, we did that by creating a new application named TestApplication, which tested the user control's **DisplayColor** property, **SetText** method, and **TextModified** event. To see how to add a user control to that test application, take a look at the discussion of that example in the In Depth section of this chapter. Here is the code for the main form in TestApplication that does all the work:

```
Public Class Form1
    Inherits System.Windows.Forms.Form

' Windows Form Designer generated code...

    Private Sub Button1_Click(ByVal sender As System.Object, ByVal _
        e As System.EventArgs) Handles Button1.Click
        UserControl11.SetText("Hello!")
    End Sub

    Private Sub UserControl11_TextModified(ByVal NewText As String) _
        Handles UserControl11.TextModified
        TextBox1.Text = "New text: " & NewText
    End Sub
End Class
```

Using the **TemplateControl** Class

The **TemplateControl** class is the base class of the **System.Web.UI.UserControl** class. (I'm using this class's full namespace to distinguish this class from the **System.Windows.Forms.UserControl** we also saw in this chapter.) Here is the inheritance hierarchy of that class:

```
Object
    Control
        TemplateControl
```

You can find the notable public methods of **TemplateControl** objects in Table 24.6 and their notable public events in Table 24.7. (This class has no non-inherited properties.) Note that as with other Web server controls, I am not listing the notable properties, methods, and events this class inherits from the **Control** class—you can find them in Chapter 15, Tables 15.1 to 15.3.

Table 24.6 Noteworthy public methods of TemplateControl objects.

Method	Means
LoadControl	Loads the user control from a user control file.
LoadTemplate	Loads a template from a file.
ParseControl	Parses an input string.

Table 24.7 Noteworthy public events of TemplateControl objects.

Event	Means
AbortTransaction	Occurs when a transaction is aborted.
CommitTransaction	Occurs when a transaction is committed.
Error	Occurs when an exception is unhandled.

Using the **System.Web.UI.UserControl** Class

The **System.Web.UI.UserControl** class supports a Web user control. (I'm using this class's full namespace to distinguish this class from the **System.Windows. Forms.UserControl** we also saw in this chapter). Here is the inheritance hierarchy of this class:

```
Object
    Control
        TemplateControl
            UserControl
```

You can find the notable public properties of **System.Web.UI.UserControl** objects in Table 24.8 and their notable public methods in Table 24.9. (This class has no non-inherited events.) Note that as with other Web server controls, I am not listing the notable properties, methods, and events this class inherits from the **Control** class—you can find them in Chapter 15, Tables 15.1 to 15.3.

Table 24.8   Noteworthy public properties of System.Web.UI.UserControl objects.

Property	Means
Application	Gets the HTTP **Application** object.
Attributes	Gets all attribute name and value pairs.
IsPostBack	Indicates if the user control is used after a postback, or if it is being accessed for the first time.
Request	Gets the HTTP **Request** object.
Response	Gets the HTTP **Response** object.
Server	Gets the **Server** object.
Session	Gets the user session information.

Table 24.9   Noteworthy public methods of System.Web.UI.UserControl objects.

Method	Means
InitializeAsUserControl	Initializes the user control.

Creating Web User Controls

Creating a Web user control is not difficult; just select the File|New|Project and choose the Web Control Library item, or select the Project|Add Web User Control menu item.

For example, we created a new Web user control in the WebUserControls example on the CD-ROM, as discussed in the In Depth section of this chapter. The Web user control we created supports a **DisplayColor** property, a **SetText** method, and a **TextModified** event; here's the code in the WebUserControl1.ascx.vb file in that project that supports the new control:

```
Public MustInherit Class WebUserControl1
    Inherits System.Web.UI.UserControl
    Protected WithEvents Label1 As System.Web.UI.WebControls.Label

' Web Form Designer Generated Code...
```

```
        Private LabelColor As Color
        Public Event TextModified(ByVal NewText As String)

        Private Sub Page_Load(ByVal sender As System.Object, _
            ByVal e As System.EventArgs) Handles MyBase.Load
            'Put user code to initialize the page here
        End Sub

        Property DisplayColor() As Color
            Get
                Return LabelColor
            End Get

            Set(ByVal Value As Color)
                LabelColor = Value
                Label1.BackColor = LabelColor
            End Set
        End Property

        Public Sub SetText(ByVal NewText As String)
            Label1.Text = NewText
            RaiseEvent TextModified(NewText)
        End Sub
End Class
```

For the details on this example, see the In Depth section of this chapter, as well as the next few topics.

Adding Properties to Web User Controls

Adding a property to a Web user control is easy; just add a **Property** statement with **Get** and **Set** methods. For more details on the **Property** statement, see "Creating Properties" in Chapter 11.

For instance, in the WebUserControls example on the CD-ROM, as discussed in the In Depth section of this chapter, we added a property, **DisplayColor**, to a Web user control; here's the code that supports this property:

```
    Private LabelColor As Color

    Property DisplayColor() As Color
        Get
```

```
        Return LabelColor
    End Get

    Set(ByVal Value As Color)
        LabelColor = Value
        Label1.BackColor = LabelColor
    End Set
End Property
```

For more details on how this example works, take a look at the In Depth section of this chapter.

Adding Methods to Web User Controls

You can add a method to a Web user control as you would to any class; just place the implementation of that method into the user control's code. You can make the method public, protected, or private; see "Creating Methods" in Chapter 11 for more details.

For example, in the WebUserControls example discussed in the In Depth section of this chapter, we added a method named **SetText** that set the text displayed in the Web user control. Here's what that method looks like:

```
Public Sub SetText(ByVal NewText As String)
    Label1.Text = NewText
End Sub
```

For more details on how this example works, and the **SetText** method, take a look at the In Depth section of this chapter.

Adding Events to Web User Controls

Adding an event to a Web user control is not difficult; you just need to declare the event and the parameters you want passed to the event's handler procedures. For more information, see "Creating Events" in Chapter 11.

For example, in the WebUserControls example discussed in the In Depth section of this chapter, we added an event named **TextModified** to the control:

```
Public Event TextModified(ByVal NewText As String)
```

This event occurs when the text in the Web user control is modified, which happens in the **SetText** method (see the previous topic), so we can use the **RaiseEvent** method in the **SetText** method to make this event occur:

```
Public Sub SetText(ByVal NewText As String)
    Label1.Text = NewText
    RaiseEvent TextModified(NewText)
End Sub
```

For more on how this works, including how to handle this new event in code when it occurs, see the discussion of the WebUserControls example in the In Depth section of this chapter.

Testing Web User Controls

To test a Web user control, you need a Web application. Typically, you use a Web application that's part of the same solution as the Web user control itself, as we did in the WebUserControls example in the In Depth section of this chapter.

To add a Web user control to a form in the test Web application, you can drag the ASCX file that supports the Web user control onto the form. For example, dragging the file WebUserControl1.ascx file creates the Web user control **WebUserControl11**. You should also declare that control in the Web form you're using it in, like this:

```
Public Class WebForm1
    Inherits System.Web.UI.Page
    Protected WithEvents Button1 As System.Web.UI.WebControls.Button
    Protected WithEvents TextBox1 As System.Web.UI.WebControls.TextBox
    Protected WithEvents WebUserControl11 As WebUserControl1
    .
    .
    .
```

In the WebUserControls example discussed in the In Depth section of this chapter, we tested the Web user control's **DisplayColor** property, **SetText** method, and **TextModified** event in the test application. Here's how that was done in that example's WebForm1.aspx.vb file:

```
Public Class WebForm1
    Inherits System.Web.UI.Page
    Protected WithEvents Button1 As System.Web.UI.WebControls.Button
    Protected WithEvents TextBox1 As System.Web.UI.WebControls.TextBox
    Protected WithEvents WebUserControl11 As WebUserControl1

' Web Form Designer Generated Code...

    Private Sub Page_Load(ByVal sender As System.Object, _
        ByVal e As System.EventArgs) Handles MyBase.Load
        WebUserControl11.DisplayColor = Color.Aqua
    End Sub

    Private Sub Button1_Click(ByVal sender As System.Object, _
        ByVal e As System.EventArgs) Handles Button1.Click
        WebUserControl11.SetText("Hello!")
    End Sub

    Private Sub WebUserControl11_TextModified(ByVal NewText As String) _
        Handles WebUserControl11.TextModified
        TextBox1.Text = "New text: " & NewText
    End Sub
End Class
```

For more on this example and on how we set up the test Web application, see the In Depth section of this chapter.

Using the **Thread** Class

The **Thread** class supports threads in Visual Basic. Here is the inheritance hierarchy for this class:

```
Object
    Thread
```

You can find the notable public properties of **Thread** objects in Table 24.10 and their notable public methods in Table 24.11. (This class has no non-inherited events.)

Table 24.10   Noteworthy public properties of Thread objects.

Property	Means
IsAlive	Indicates if the thread has been started and is alive.
IsBackground	Gets/sets whether or not this is a background thread.
Name	Gets/sets the thread's name.
Priority	Gets/sets the thread's priority.
ThreadState	Gets the thread's state.

Table 24.11   Noteworthy public methods of Thread objects.

Method	Means
Abort	Aborts the thread.
Interrupt	Interrupts threads in the **WaitSleepJoin** state.
Join	Waits for a thread to complete.
Resume	Resumes thread execution for threads that have been suspended.
Start	Begins execution of the thread.
Suspend	Suspends thread execution.

Creating Threads

To create a new thread, you use the **Thread** class's constructor, passing that constructor the address of the Sub procedure that holds the thread's code, like this:

```
Dim NewThread As New System.Threading.Thread(AddressOf ThreadCodeProcedure)
```

We saw how this worked in the Threading example on the CD-ROM, as discussed in the In Depth section of this chapter (and you can see this example in Figure 24.10). There, we used a class named **counter** that had a procedure named **Count** we used as a thread procedure; this procedure counted from 1 to a value held in the class's **CountTo** data member and then raised a **FinishedCounting** event:

```
Public Class counter
    Public CountTo As Integer
    Public Event FinishedCounting(ByVal NumberOfMatches As Integer)


    Sub Count()
        Dim LoopIndex, Total As Integer
        Total = 0
```

```
        For LoopIndex = 1 To CountTo
            Total += 1
        Next LoopIndex

        RaiseEvent FinishedCounting(Total)
    End Sub
End Class
```

Then we created an object of the counter class and a new thread, **Thread1**, to run the code in the **Count** procedure:

```
Dim counter1 As New counter()
Dim Thread1 As New System.Threading.Thread(AddressOf counter1.Count)
```

And that creates the new thread. To see how to work with this thread, examine the next few topics. You can see the Threading example at work in Figure 24.10; here's the code for that example, Form1.vb:

```
Public Class Form1
    Inherits System.Windows.Forms.Form
    Friend WithEvents Button1 As System.Windows.Forms.Button
    Friend WithEvents Button2 As System.Windows.Forms.Button
    Friend WithEvents Label1 As System.Windows.Forms.Label
    Friend WithEvents Button3 As System.Windows.Forms.Button
    Friend WithEvents Button4 As System.Windows.Forms.Button
    Dim counter1 As New counter()
    Friend WithEvents Button5 As System.Windows.Forms.Button
    Friend WithEvents Button6 As System.Windows.Forms.Button
    Dim Thread1 As New System.Threading.Thread(AddressOf counter1.Count)

' Windows Form Designer generated code...

    Sub FinishedCountingEventHandler(ByVal Count As Integer)
        TextBox2.Text = Count
    End Sub

    Private Sub Button1_Click(ByVal sender As System.Object, _
        ByVal e As System.EventArgs) Handles Button1.Click
        TextBox2.Text = ""
        counter1.CountTo = TextBox1.Text
        AddHandler counter1.FinishedCounting, AddressOf _
            FinishedCountingEventHandler
        Thread1.Start()
    End Sub
```

```
        Private Sub Button2_Click(ByVal sender As System.Object, _
            ByVal e As System.EventArgs) Handles Button2.Click
            Thread1.Abort()
        End Sub

        Private Sub Button3_Click(ByVal sender As System.Object, _
            ByVal e As System.EventArgs) Handles Button3.Click
            Thread1.Sleep(10 * 1000)
        End Sub

        Private Sub Button4_Click(ByVal sender As System.Object, _
            ByVal e As System.EventArgs) Handles Button4.Click
            Thread1.Priority = System.Threading.ThreadPriority.BelowNormal
        End Sub

        Private Sub Button5_Click(ByVal sender As System.Object, _
            ByVal e As System.EventArgs) Handles Button5.Click
            Thread1.Suspend()
        End Sub

        Private Sub Button6_Click(ByVal sender As System.Object, _
            ByVal e As System.EventArgs) Handles Button6.Click
            Thread1.Resume()
        End Sub
    End Class
```

For more on how this example works, take a look at the discussion in the In Depth section of this chapter.

Starting Threads

To start a thread, you can use the thread's **Start** method:

```
NewThread.Start()
```

This makes the thread begin executing the code in the thread procedure you passed to its constructor (see the previous topic). Here's how we used the **Start** method in the Threading example on the CD-ROM, as discussed in the In Depth section of this chapter (you can see this example at work in Figure 24.10):

```
    Dim counter1 As New counter()
    Dim Thread1 As New System.Threading.Thread(AddressOf counter1.Count)
```

```
            .
            .
            .
    Private Sub Button1_Click(ByVal sender As System.Object, _
        ByVal e As System.EventArgs) Handles Button1.Click
        TextBox2.Text = ""
        counter1.CountTo = TextBox1.Text
        AddHandler counter1.FinishedCounting, AddressOf _
            FinishedCountingEventHandler
        Thread1.Start()
    End Sub
```

When the thread in this example finished counting, it created a **Finished CountingEvent** event, which we handled by displaying the total count in a text box:

```
    Sub FinishedCountingEventHandler(ByVal Count As Integer)
        TextBox2.Text = Count
    End Sub
```

For more on how this example works, take a look at the discussion in the In Depth section of this chapter.

Suspending Threads

To suspend a thread's execution, you can use the thread's **Suspend** method:

```
NewThread.Suspend()
```

This just stops the thread's execution until you use the **Resume** method (see "Resuming Threads" coming up next).

For example, we used the **Suspend** method in the Threading example discussed in the In Depth section of this chapter; this method was called when the user clicks the "Suspend Counting" button in that example (you can see this example at work in Figure 24.10):

```
    Dim Thread1 As New System.Threading.Thread(AddressOf counter1.Count)
            .
            .
            .
    Private Sub Button5_Click(ByVal sender As System.Object, _
        ByVal e As System.EventArgs) Handles Button5.Click
```

```
        Thread1.Suspend()
End Sub
```

For more on how this example works, take a look at the discussion in the In Depth section of this chapter.

Resuming Threads

After you've suspended thread execution using the **Thread** class's **Suspend** method (see the previous topic), you can resume execution with the **Resume** method, like this:

```
NewThread.Resume()
```

For example, we used the **Resume** method in the Threading example discussed in the In Depth section of this chapter to resume thread execution after the user clicked the "Suspend Counting" button. Here's how that example uses the **Resume** method when the user clicks the "Resume Counting" button (you can see it at work in Figure 24.10):

```
Dim Thread1 As New System.Threading.Thread(AddressOf counter1.Count)
    .
    .
    .
Private Sub Button6_Click(ByVal sender As System.Object, _
    ByVal e As System.EventArgs) Handles Button6.Click
        Thread1.Resume()
End Sub
```

For more on how this example works, take a look at the discussion in the In Depth section of this chapter.

Stopping Threads

You can stop a thread with the **Abort** method:

```
NewThread.Abort()
```

This brings a thread to a halt. Usually, it's far better to let the thread simply end (that is, return from the thread procedure) by itself, but if you really need to end a thread, you can do so with the **Abort** method.

We used the **Abort** method in the Threading example, as discussed in the In Depth section of this chapter; in that example, the user could stop a thread by clicking the "Cancel Counting" button, which executed the **Abort** method like this (you can see this example at work in Figure 24.10):

```
Dim Thread1 As New System.Threading.Thread(AddressOf counter1.Count)
    .
    .
    .
Private Sub Button2_Click(ByVal sender As System.Object, _
    ByVal e As System.EventArgs) Handles Button2.Click
    Thread1.Abort()
End Sub
```

For more on how this example operates, take a look at the discussion in the In Depth section of this chapter.

Sleeping Threads

You can put a thread to sleep for a number of milliseconds (1/100ths of a second) with the **Sleep** method:

```
NewThread.Sleep(NumberOfMilliseconds)
```

Putting a thread to sleep for a length of time simply makes it stop executing for that length of time. This is particularly useful if you want to give another thread access to a resource that a thread is using; you can just put the active thread to sleep for a while.

We saw how to use the **Sleep** method in the Threading example, as discussed in the In Depth section of this chapter. When the user clicks the "Sleep 10 Seconds" button, the code puts the thread it created to sleep for 10 seconds, like this (you can see this example at work in Figure 24.10):

```
Dim Thread1 As New System.Threading.Thread(AddressOf counter1.Count)
    .
    .
    .
Private Sub Button3_Click(ByVal sender As System.Object, _
    ByVal e As System.EventArgs) Handles Button3.Click
    Thread1.Sleep(10 * 1000)
End Sub
```

For more on how this example functions, take a look at the discussion in the In Depth section of this chapter.

TIP: *As mentioned earlier in the chapter, although the time you pass to **Sleep** is measured in milliseconds, Windows machines can only measure time intervals with limited precision. In my tests, the smallest sleep interval I can get is a hundredth of a second, which means that calling **Sleep(1)** is the same as calling **Sleep(10)**.*

Setting Thread Priority

You can set the *priority* of threads with the **Priority** property. The **ThreadPriority** enumeration lists the possible values (a thread with higher priority gets more time than one with lower priority):

- **AboveNormal**—Gives a thread higher priority.
- **BelowNormal**—Gives a thread lower priority.
- **Highest**—Gives a thread highest priority.
- **Lowest**—Gives a thread lowest priority.
- **Normal**—Gives a thread average priority.

Using the **Priority** property, you have some control over how much time a thread gets, compared to others. For example, here's how you give a thread the highest priority:

```
NewThread.Priority = System.Threading.ThreadPriority.Highest
```

For example, we set the priority of a thread in the Threading example discussed in the In Depth section of this chapter. When the user clicks the "Set Low Priority" button in that example, the new thread is assigned "below normal" priority. Here's how that looks in code (you can see this at work in Figure 24.10):

```
Private Sub Button4_Click(ByVal sender As System.Object, _
    ByVal e As System.EventArgs) Handles Button4.Click
        Thread1.Priority = System.Threading.ThreadPriority.BelowNormal
    End Sub
```

For more on how this example works, take a look at the discussion in the In Depth section of this chapter.

Synchronizing Threads

When you start multiple threads and need to coordinate their operation in some way—for instance, so that they can share the same resource in memory—you need to synchronize them. As mentioned in the In Depth section of this chapter, you can use events to communicate between threads. You also can use the **SyncLock** statement or the **Join** method—see the next two topics in this chapter.

For example, we took a look at all these techniques in the SynchronizeThreads example, discussed in the In Depth section of this chapter. In that example, we created a new class named **counter** with one data member, **Total**:

```
Public Class counter
    Public Total As Integer
End Class
```

The SynchronizeThreads example used two synchronized threads to increment the **Total** data member to a value of 200, as you see in Figure 24.11. Here's the code for the main form in that example, Form1.vb:

```
Public Class Form1
    Inherits System.Windows.Forms.Form
    Dim c As New counter()
    Dim Thread1 As New System.Threading.Thread(AddressOf Counter1)
    Friend WithEvents Label1 As System.Windows.Forms.Label
    Dim Thread2 As New System.Threading.Thread(AddressOf Counter2)

' Windows Form Designer generated code...

    Private Sub Button1_Click(ByVal sender As System.Object, _
        ByVal e As System.EventArgs) Handles Button1.Click
        Thread1.Start()
        Thread2.Start()
        Thread1.Join()
        Thread2.Join()
        TextBox1.Text = c.Total
    End Sub

    Private Sub Counter1()
        Dim LoopIndex As Integer
```

```
            For LoopIndex = 1 To 100
                SyncLock c.GetType
                    Dim temp = c.Total
                    Thread1.Sleep(1)
                    c.Total = temp + 1
                End SyncLock
            Next LoopIndex
        End Sub

        Private Sub Counter2()
            Dim LoopIndex As Integer

            For LoopIndex = 1 To 100
                SyncLock c.GetType
                    Dim temp = c.Total
                    Thread2.Sleep(1)
                    c.Total = temp + 1
                End SyncLock
            Next LoopIndex
        End Sub
End Class
```

For more details on this example, see the discussion in the In Depth section of this chapter, and the next two topics.

Using **SyncLock** to Synchronize Threads

To synchronize threads, you can use the **SyncLock** statement. This statement lets you block access to shared resources by other threads. Here's how you use this statement:

```
SyncLock Expression
    [sensitive code]
End SyncLock
```

To use that statement, you pass it an expression to use to lock access, such as an object. (The type of this expression must be a reference type, such as a class, a module, an array, or an interface.) For example, if you lock an object, no other thread can access the object until it's unlocked.

For example, we saw how to use **SyncLock** in the SynchronizeThreads example in the In Depth section of this chapter. In that example, we used two threads to increment a value. The two threads paused for a millisecond each before updating the incremented value, which meant that the threads interfered with each other, as discussed in the In Depth section of this chapter. By using **SyncLock**, we were able to lock the object being updated, which stopped the threads from interfering with each other:

```
Private Sub Button1_Click(ByVal sender As System.Object, _
    ByVal e As System.EventArgs) Handles Button1.Click
    Thread1.Start()
    Thread2.Start()
    .
    .
    .
End Sub

Private Sub Counter1()
    Dim LoopIndex As Integer

    For LoopIndex = 1 To 100
        SyncLock c
            Dim temp = c.Total
            Thread1.Sleep(1)
            c.Total = temp + 1
        End SyncLock
    Next LoopIndex
End Sub

Private Sub Counter2()
    Dim LoopIndex As Integer

    For LoopIndex = 1 To 100
        SyncLock c
            Dim temp = c.Total
            Thread2.Sleep(1)
            c.Total = temp + 1
        End SyncLock
    Next LoopIndex
End Sub
```

TIP: *Microsoft recommends that you don't use the* **SyncLock** *statement to lock threads that work with controls or forms.*

For more on this example, see the In Depth section of this chapter.

24. Creating User Controls, Web User Controls, and Multithreading

Joining Threads

You can use the **Join** method to wait until a thread finishes; this method will return when the thread is finished executing. Here are the various forms of this method:

- **Sub Join**—Waits for a thread to die.

- **Function Join(TimeOut As Integer) As Boolean**—Waits for the thread to die or for a specific timeout, given as a number of milliseconds, to elapse. Returns **True** if the thread died, **False** if the call timed out.

- **Function Join(TimeOut As TimeSpan) As Boolean**—Waits for the thread to die or for a specific timeout, given as a **TimeSpan** object, to elapse. Returns **True** if the thread died, **False** if the call timed out.

We used the **Join** method in the SynchronizeThreads example, discussed in the In Depth section, which was to wait until the two threads in that example were done executing before displaying the value those threads were incrementing. Here's how that looked in code:

```
Private Sub Button1_Click(ByVal sender As System.Object, _
    ByVal e As System.EventArgs) Handles Button1.Click
    Thread1.Start()
    Thread2.Start()
    Thread1.Join()
    Thread2.Join()
    TextBox1.Text = c.Total
End Sub
```

And that's all there is to it—for more information on this example, see the In Depth section of this chapter.

Chapter 25

Creating Windows Services, Web Services, and Deploying Applications

In Depth

In this chapter, we'll take a look at creating Windows services, creating Web services, and deploying Visual Basic applications. These are all powerful techniques, and they'll add a lot to your Visual Basic arsenal.

Windows services are programs that don't usually support a user interface (although you can display a notify icon in the Windows taskbar and handle events for that notify icon—see "Creating Notify Icons and Using Icon Designers" and "Handling Notify Icon Events" in Chapter 8). They run in the background, providing services, and are often tied to device drivers, such as those that handle printers, audio devices, CD creation, and so on.

Web services are Web components that can be called by other applications to perform a particular function and return data, from working with complex calculations to returning data from data sources. What makes these components useful is that they do their work on servers on the Web, which lets you create business objects to implement the custom logic—such as checking credit cards before accepting payment—on the Web. Web services can be used to provide a "middle-tier" business object to work with data from a Web server in three-tier database applications.

When you're done creating an application, the next step is to deploy it in the field. Visual Basic .NET applications (both Windows and Web applications) are designed to be installed with the Windows installer program, which use Microsoft Installer (.msi) files. We'll see how to create .msi files for applications in this chapter; to actually install an application, all you have to do is to copy the .msi file and double-click it, and the Microsoft Installer does the rest.

That's our agenda for this chapter. I'll start with Windows services.

Creating Windows Services

Windows services are much like other Windows applications, but there are a few differences. First, they usually don't have a user interface except for, perhaps, a control panel that can be opened by double-clicking a notify icon. Second, their life cycle is different from standard programs because they typically start automatically when you boot your computer and quit only when you shut down. Third, they usually provide support services rather than acting as a front-line application. Device drivers, such as those that control printers, displays, volume controls, and so on, often let the user configure how they work with Windows services that use notify icons to display control panels. However, Windows services don't need to have control panels, and, in fact, the example we'll see in this chapter won't.

In Visual Basic .NET, Windows services are based on the **ServiceBase** class; that class provides most of the support we'll need. To create a working Windows service, you should override the **OnStart** and **OnStop** event handlers, which are called when the service starts and stops, respectively. You can configure a service to start automatically when the computer boots, or start manually using a tool built into Windows: the Service Control Manager (SCM). And you might also want to override the **OnPause** and **OnContinue** event handlers as well to handle occasions where the service is paused and resumed.

TIP: *You can specify if a service can be paused and resumed using the **CanPauseAndContinue** property of the **ServiceBase** class; by default, this property is set to **False**.*

Usually, Windows services run under the System account in Windows (which is not the same as an Administrator account). However, when you install a Windows service, you can use a **ServiceProcessInstaller** object to set up the service to run in a specific user's account. A single executable file can contain multiple services, but you need an *installer* for each of them; we'll see how to create Windows services installers when we create a Windows service ourselves. In fact, the Windows services you write in Visual Basic .NET can't install themselves; you have to install them with the InstallUtil.exe tool that comes with Visual Basic.

Let's see how this works in practice. There's an example, WindowsService, on the CD-ROM, and I'll take a look at how that program works here.

To create a new Windows service project, select the File|New|Project menu item, and this time, select the Windows Service icon in the Templates box of the New Project dialog, giving this new service the name WindowsService. This creates a new Windows service project, as you see in Figure 25.1. The name for this new service, using the default Visual Basic has given it, is "Service1", as you can see in the Properties window in the figure.

As with any other Visual Basic project, you can design this one visually, at least up to a point. Our Windows service isn't going to do much—it'll just write entries to an event log, in fact, so click the Components tab in the toolbox now and drag an **EventLog** object to the Windows service, as you see in Figure 25.2. Set the event log's **Log** property to the name of the log; in this case, I'll use "NewLog1". Also make sure the Windows service's **AutoLog** property is set to **True** (which is the default).

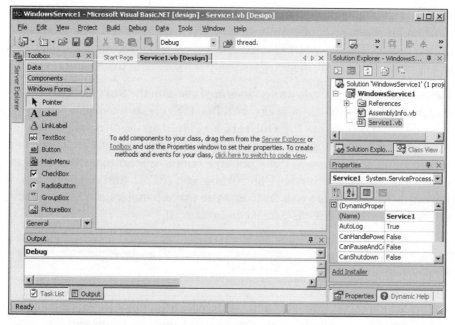

Figure 25.1   A new Windows service project.

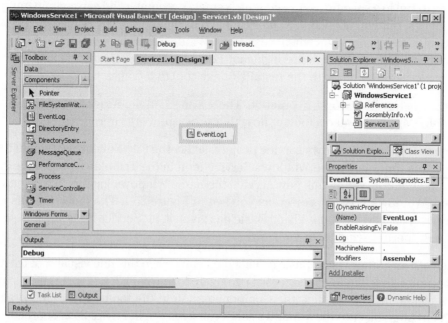

Figure 25.2   Adding an event log to a Windows service project.

EventLog objects let you access Windows 2000 event logs, which record information about software or hardware events. You can read from existing logs, write to logs, delete logs, and handle log entries. In this example, we'll write to our Windows service's event log in the **OnStart** and **OnStop** event handlers.

To use an event log, you must specify or create an event *source*. The source registers your application with the event log as a source of data; the source can be any random string, but the name must be distinct from any other source. I'll register our event log in the Windows service's constructor, which you can find in the "Component Designer generated code" region of the Windows service's code, Service1.vb, and which looks like this originally:

```
Public Sub New()
    MyBase.New()

    ' This call is required by the Component Designer.
    InitializeComponent()

    ' Add any initialization after the InitializeComponent() call
End Sub
```

In this example, I'll create a source named "Source1". After the new source is created, I'll assign its name to our **EventLog** object's **Source** property, like this:

```
Public Sub New()
    MyBase.New()
    InitializeComponent()

    If Not EventLog1.SourceExists("Source1") Then
        EventLog1.CreateEventSource("Source1", "NewLog1")
    End If
    EventLog1.Source = "Source1"
End Sub
```

Also, set the **Source** property of the event log to "Source1" in the Properties window. Now we're ready to write to our new event log when the service starts and stops. You can do that in the **OnStart** and **OnStop** event handlers, which currently look like this in Service1.vb:

```
Protected Overrides Sub OnStart(ByVal args() As String)
    ' Add code here to start your service. This method should set
    ' things in motion so your service can do its work.
End Sub
```

```
Protected Overrides Sub OnStop()
    ' Add code here to perform any tear-down necessary to stop your
    ' service.
End Sub
```

To write to an event log, you use the log's **WriteEntry** method, and I'll simply insert a message into the log appropriate to the event that's occurred, like this:

```
Protected Overrides Sub OnStart(ByVal args() As String)
    EventLog1.WriteEntry("Starting...")
End Sub

Protected Overrides Sub OnStop()
    EventLog1.WriteEntry("Stopping...")
End Sub
```

Now when the service starts, "Starting..." will be written to the event log NewLog1, and when the service stops, the code will write "Stopping..." to the log.

To actually install our Windows service, we'll need an installer, so click the "Add Installer" link in the description section of the Properties window. (This link is visible at bottom right in Figure 25.2.) This creates ProjectInstaller.vb with two objects in it, **ServiceProcessInstaller1** and **ServiceInstaller1**, as you see in Figure 25.3.

ServiceInstaller objects are used by installation utilities to write registry values for the service to a subkey in the **HKEY_LOCAL_MACHINE\System\Current ControlSet\Services** registry key. The service itself is identified with its **ServiceName** value in this subkey. **ServiceProcessInstaller** objects handle the individual processes launched by your service.

You should indicate the account the service is to run under; in this case, I'll click **ServiceProcessInstaller1** and set its **Account** property to **LocalSystem**. You also can set this property to **LocalService**, **NetworkService**, or **User**. To set up the service to run under a specific account, you set **Account** to **User.** (Be sure to set the **Username** and **Password** properties of the **ServiceProcessInstaller1** object in that case.)

Next, click the **ServiceInstaller1** object and make sure its **ServiceName** property is set to the name of this service, **Service1**. You also can use the **ServiceInstaller1** object's **StartType** property to specify how to start the service; here are the possibilities, from the **ServiceStartMode** enumeration:

- **Automatic**—Specifies that the service is to be started automatically at system startup.

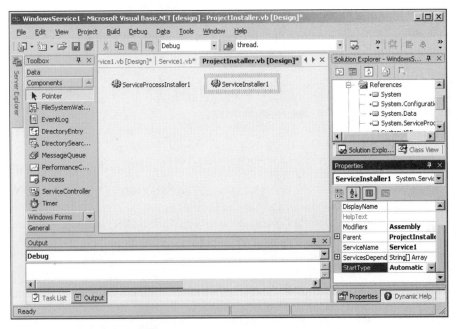

Figure 25.3   Creating a Windows service installer.

- **Disabled**—Specifies that the service is disabled, which means that it cannot be started.

- **Manual**—Specifies that the service can only be started manually, by either a user using the Service Control Manager, or by an application.

The safest of these while testing a new Windows service is **Manual**, so set the **StartType** property of the **ServiceInstaller1** object to **Manual** now.

And that's all it takes—now we'll build and install our new Windows service, Service1. To build the service, just select the Build|Build menu item, which creates WindowsService.exe. To install this service, you use the InstallUtil.exe tool that comes with Visual Basic. (You can also deploy Windows services with setup packages in Visual Basic—see "Deploying Applications" in the In Depth section of this chapter for more information on deploying application.) In Windows 2000 installations, you can usually find InstallUtil.exe in the C:\WINNT\Microsoft.NET\Framework\vxxxxxxxx directory, where xxxxxxxx is a version number. Here's how I install WindowsService.exe using InstallUtil.exe at the command prompt (the command line here in the text is split onto two lines only because it's too long for the page width), and what you see when you do:

```
C:\WINNT\Microsoft.NET\Framework\vxxxxxxxx>installutil
c:\vbnet\WindowsService\bin\WindowsService.exe
```

```
Microsoft (R) .NET Framework Installation utility
Copyright (C) Microsoft Corp 2001. All rights reserved.

Running a transacted installation.

Beginning the Install phase of the installation.
See the contents of the log file for the
c:\vbnet\WindowsService\bin\WindowsService.exe assembly's progress.
The file is located at
c:\vbnet\WindowsService\bin\WindowsService.InstallLog.
Call Installing. on the
c:\vbnet\WindowsService\bin\WindowsService.exe assembly.
Affected parameters are:
    assemblypath = c:\vbnet\WindowsService\bin\WindowsService.exe
    logfile = c:\vbnet\WindowsService\bin\WindowsService.InstallLog
Installing service Service1...
Service Service1 has been successfully installed.
Creating EventLog source Service1 in log Application...

The Install phase completed successfully,
and the Commit phase is beginning.
See the contents of the log file for the
c:\vbnet\WindowsService\bin\WindowsService.exe assembly's progress.
The file is located at
c:\vbnet\WindowsService\bin\WindowsService.InstallLog.
Call Committing. on the c:\vbnet\WindowsService\bin\WindowsService.exe
assembly.
Affected parameters are:
    assemblypath = c:\vbnet\WindowsService\bin\WindowsService.exe
    logfile = c:\vbnet\WindowsService\bin\WindowsService.InstallLog

The Commit phase completed successfully.

The transacted install has completed.
```

That installs the new Windows service. If the new service hadn't installed successfully, InstallUtil.exe would have rolled the installation back automatically, and removed the non-working service.

The next step is to use the Service Control Manager to start the service. Here's how you start the SCM in Windows 2000:

- In Windows 2000 Professional, right-click My Computer on the desktop, then select the Manage item. In the dialog box that appears, expand the Services and Applications node and find the Services entry.

- In Windows 2000 Server, click Start, select Programs, click Administrative Tools, and then click Services.

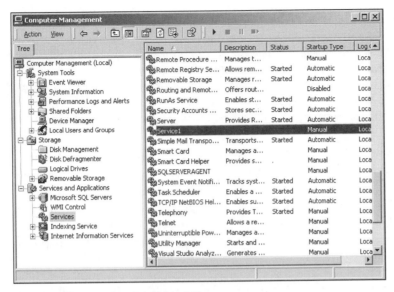

Figure 25.4   The Service Control Manager.

For example, you can see the SCM for Windows 2000 Professional in Figure 25.4. Note that you can already see our service, Service1, listed.

To start the service, right-click Service1 and select the Start item. This starts the service, as you see in Figure 25.5, where Service1 is listed as "Started".

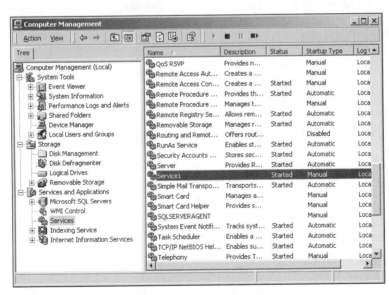

Figure 25.5   Our new Windows service at work.

TIP: *A problematic Windows service can make your computer unusable, so be careful when creating Windows services. Until you're sure a Windows service is working the way you want it to, it's a good idea to keep its start mode as **Manual** so it doesn't start again automatically if you need to reboot. And make sure that if there's a problem starting the service, the computer doesn't automatically reboot, at least until you're sure the service is working as it should be. To do that in the Service Control Manager, right-click the service, select the Properties item, click the Recovery tab, and make sure the "Take No Action" item is selected for the case where the service fails to start. It's also a good idea to make the service's logic code execute on a different thread than the main thread so the service can still react to **Start** and **Stop** events, even if hung.*

To stop the service, right-click Service1 in the SCM and select Stop. We've now started and stopped our new service, so it should have written to its event log, NewLog1. We can check that from inside Visual Basic—just open the Server Explorer's Event Logs node as you see in Figure 25.6, and check the entry for Source1 in NewLog1, as you see in that figure. You can indeed see the two entries our service has written to the event log, "Starting..." and "Stopping..." in the Server Explorer in Figure 25.6.

And that's it—our new Windows service is a success, and it did what it was supposed to; it's written to the event log. You can uninstall a service like this with InstallUtil.exe—just use the /u option. Here's what you see when you do:

```
C:\WINNT\Microsoft.NET\Framework\vxxxxxxxx>installutil
c:\vbnet\WindowsService\bin\WindowsService.exe /u

Microsoft (R) .NET Framework Installation utility
Copyright (C) Microsoft Corp 2001. All rights reserved.

The uninstall is beginning.
See the contents of the log file for the
c:\vbnet\WindowsService\bin\WindowsService.exe assembly's progress.
The file is located at
c:\vbnet\WindowsService\bin\WindowsService.InstallLog.
Call Uninstalling. on the
c:\vbnet\WindowsService\bin\WindowsService.exe assembly.
Affected parameters are:
    assemblypath = c:\vbnet\WindowsService\bin\WindowsService.exe
    logfile = c:\vbnet\WindowsService\bin\WindowsService.InstallLog
Removing EventLog source Service1.
Service Service1 is being removed from the system...
Service Service1 was successfully removed from the system.

The uninstall has completed.
```

That provides the framework you need to create Windows services; now you're able to write behind-the-scenes code for Windows, and keep that code available when it's needed. Next, I'll take a look at creating Web services.

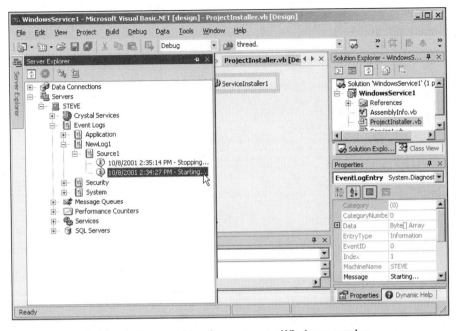

Figure 25.6 Entries in the event log from our new Windows service.

Creating Web Services

Web services are services that operate on the Web and can be used by other applications. For example, when you want to display data from a data source on the Web in a Windows application, a Web service is a perfect solution, because the Windows application can call methods in the Web service to get that data. Web services are often used to implement multitiered, distributed data applications; I'll create a Web service here to do exactly that.

This example is called WebServ on the CD-ROM, and it'll read the authors table from the pubs database using SQL Server on a Web server. This service will implement two methods, **GetAuthors** and **UpdateAuthors**, to return a dataset holding the authors table and update that table in the data source, respectively. I'll use a Windows application to call these methods and display data.

The Web service here is the middle tier of our distributed data application, and although it does nothing more in this case than read and update the authors table, you can implement all kinds of logic in this tier, creating a business object that implements business rules. For example, your Web service could check if particular items are in stock, and omit any records for items that are currently not available.

To follow along, create a new Web service project now by selecting the File|New|Project menu item. This time, make sure that you select the ASP.NET Web Service icon in the Templates box of the New Project dialog, and give this

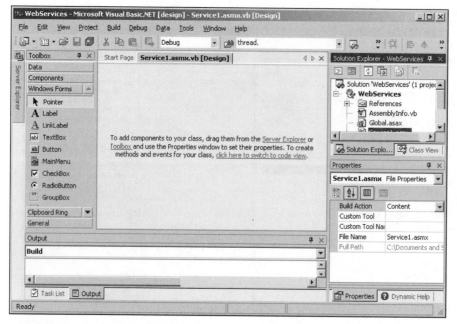

Figure 25.7   A new Web service project.

project the name WebServ. This creates the new Web service project that you see in Figure 25.7.

The support file for the new Web service is Service1.asmx.vb, and the name of the new service is Service1. If you open Service1.asmx.vb in Visual Basic, you'll see that this new service is derived from the **WebService** class:

```
Imports System.Web.Services

Public Class Service1
    Inherits System.Web.Services.WebService
        .
        .
        .
```

As with other Visual Basic projects, you can drag components into the new Web service at design time. To get access to the authors table, drag an **OleDbDataAdapter** object into the Web service, and use a data connection to connect the data adapter to the authors table on a server (see Chapter 20 for the details on how to do this; for example, see "Creating a New Data Connection" and "Data Access Using Data Adapter Controls" in that chapter). Next, use the Data|Generate Dataset menu item, which will create a new dataset class, **DataSet1**. This is the dataset class we'll use to access the authors table.

To expose methods from a Web service, you use the **<WebMethod()>** attribute. For example, to write the **GetAuthors** method, which returns a dataset filled with data from the authors table, add this code to Service1.asmx.vb now:

```
<WebMethod(Description:="Gets the authors")> _
   Public Function GetAuthors() As DataSet1
      Dim AuthorsTable As New DataSet1()
      OleDbDataAdapter1.Fill(AuthorsTable)
      Return AuthorsTable
End Function
```

This new method, **GetAuthors**, will be available for other applications to call once they add a reference to our Web service. Similarly, we can add another method, **UpdateAuthors**, to update the authors table when we pass a dataset of changes to this method. Here's what that method looks like—note that to be safe, this method always returns a value, even if that value is **Nothing**:

```
<WebMethod(Description:="Updates the authors")> _
   Public Function UpdateAuthors(ByVal _ _
   Changes As DataSet1) As DataSet1
      If (Changes Is Nothing) Then
         Return Nothing
      Else
         OleDbDataAdapter1.Update(Changes)
         Return Changes
      End If
End Function
```

That completes the Web service. To build this Web service and make it available to other applications, select the Build|Build menu item now.

The next step is to create an application that will act as a user interface for the Web service. Add a Windows application project to the solution now by selecting the File|Add Project|New Project menu item. When the Add New Project dialog opens, select the Windows Application icon in the Templates box, name this new project WebServWindowsApplication, and click OK to open this new Windows application, as you see in Figure 25.8. Make this application the startup project by selecting the Project|Set as StartUp Project menu item.

The next step is to add a reference to our Web service to make the **GetAuthors** and **UpdateAuthors** methods available to us. To add that reference, right-click WebServWindowsApplication in the Solution Explorer and select the Add Web Reference item. This opens the Add Web Reference dialog, listing the available Web service directories. To add a Web reference to a Web service, you navigate to that service's DISCO or VSDISCO file. You can do that by entering the URL for

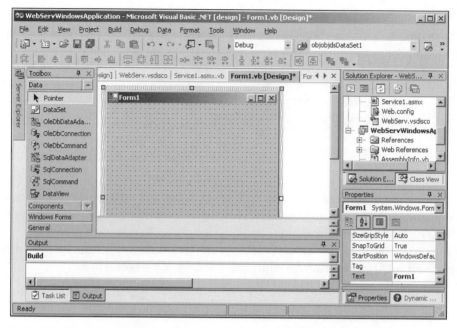

Figure 25.8   A new Windows application for using our Web service.

that file directly in the Address box at the top of the Add Web Reference dialog (such as **http://*ServerName*/WebServ/WebServ.vsdisco**). Or, you can browse for the file you want on the server by clicking the link in the Add Web Reference dialog for the server you want to use; then, in the Available References box in that dialog, clicking the WebServ/WebServ.vsdisco entry. Either technique opens our Web service's entry in the Add Web Reference dialog, as you see in Figure 25.9. To add a reference to this Web service to our Windows application, click the Add Reference button.

Now that we have a reference to our Web service, we can use types defined in that Web service, such as **DataSet1**, and call the methods of that Web service, **GetAuthors** and **UpdateAuthors**. Let's see this in action. Add a data grid, **DataGrid1**, to the main form in our Windows application, WebServWindowsApplication, and two buttons with the captions "Get Data" and "Update Data" respectively.

Now drag a **DataSet** object from the Data tab of the toolbox onto the main Windows form, which will open the Add Dataset dialog you see in Figure 25.10. Make sure the Typed dataset option is selected, and select **DataSet1** from the dropdown list. (In this example, I'm running the IIS Web server locally, so **DataSet1** is given as **WebServWindowsApplication.localhost.DataSet1** in Figure 25.10.) This creates a new dataset for us, **DataSet11**, which matches the type returned by our Web service, and which we can bind to the data grid.

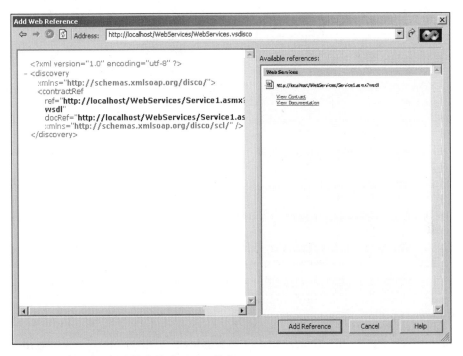

Figure 25.9   The Add Web Reference dialog.

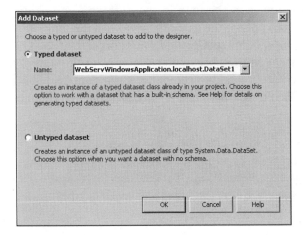

Figure 25.10   The Add Dataset dialog.

To bind the data grid to our new dataset, select the data grid now and set its **DataSource** property to **DataSet11**, and its **DataMember** property to **authors**. The data grid is now bound to **DataSet11**, so we can fill that dataset with the Web service's **GetAuthors** method, and we'll do that when the "Get Data" button is clicked. The **GetAuthors** method returns a dataset, and the easiest way to fill **DataSet11** with the data in that dataset is to use the **DataSet11** object's **Merge** method. First, when the user clicks the "Get Data" button, we create an instance of our Web service, **WebServ**, so we can call that instance's methods:

```
Private Sub Button1_Click(ByVal sender As System.Object, _
    ByVal e As System.EventArgs) Handles Button1.Click
    Dim WebServ As New WebServWindowsApplication.localhost.Service1()
        .
        .
        .

End Sub
```

Now we can use the methods in our Web service with the **WebServ** object. Here's how to fill the dataset **DataSet11** from the Web service:

```
Private Sub Button1_Click(ByVal sender As System.Object, _
    ByVal e As System.EventArgs) Handles Button1.Click
    Dim WebServ As New WebServWindowsApplication.localhost.Service1()
    DataSet11.Merge(WebServ.GetAuthors())
End Sub
```

Using a Web service like this is cool—the Windows application connects to the Web service and calls Web service methods just as if they were part of a local component.

Similarly, if the user makes changes in the data in the data grid and clicks the "Update Data" button, we want to update the authors table with the new changes. To find those changes, we can use the **GetChanges** method of **DataSet11** (as discussed in Chapter 21, as soon as the user makes changes in the bound data grid, those changes are immediately made to the dataset the data grid is bound to) to create a new dataset, **Changes**, which holds only the changed records:

```
Private Sub Button2_Click(ByVal sender As System.Object, _
    ByVal e As System.EventArgs) Handles Button2.Click
    If DataSet11.HasChanges() Then
        Dim WebServ As New WebServWindowsApplication.localhost.Service1()
        Dim Changes As New WebServWindowsApplication.localhost.DataSet1()
        Changes.Merge(DataSet11.GetChanges())
            .
            .
            .

    End If
End Sub
```

And we can use the **UpdateAuthors** Web method to update the data source on the Web server, like this:

```
Private Sub Button2_Click(ByVal sender As System.Object, _
    ByVal e As System.EventArgs) Handles Button2.Click
    If DataSet11.HasChanges() Then
        Dim WebServ As New WebServWindowsApplication.localhost.Service1()
        Dim Changes As New WebServWindowsApplication.localhost.DataSet1()
        Changes.Merge(DataSet11.GetChanges())
        DataSet11.Merge(WebServ.UpdateAuthors(Changes))
    End If
End Sub
```

Note that I also merge the dataset **UpdateAuthors** returns with **DataSet11** as we did when updating datasets in Chapter 23. (For example, the data provider may have added data to calculated fields, or updated primary key values, so it's a good idea to merge the returned dataset of changes with our main dataset.) And that's it—the example is ready to go. Run the example now and click the "Get Data" button, filling the data grid with data from the authors table via the Web service, as you see in Figure 25.11.

And that's it—our Web service works. Now we've created both Windows and Web services and put them to work. Next, it's time to take a look at how to deploy Visual Basic .NET applications.

Deploying Applications

After you've created an application, you can use Visual Basic to create a Windows Installer file—an .msi file—to install it. All you need to do is to transfer the .msi file to the target machine—a desktop, a notebook, or a Web server—and double-click it to install it, provided that the target machine supports the Windows Installer and the .NET framework so your application can function. You can create .msi installer files with Setup and Deployment projects in Visual Basic.

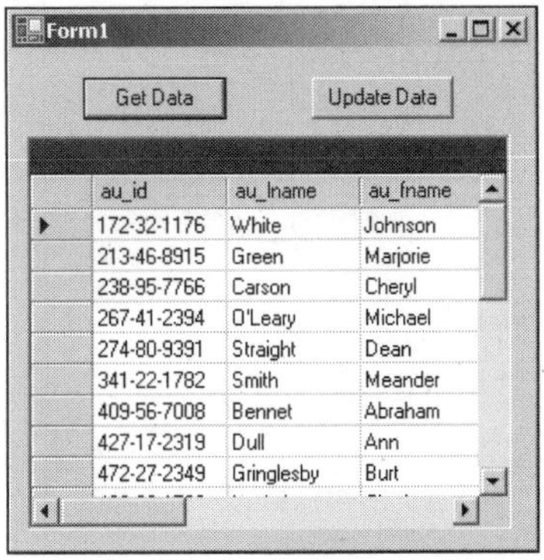

Figure 25.11   Using our Web service to get database data.

Let's see an example. In this case, I'll create an installer for an application named WonderApp, version 6.33, which you can see under design in Figure 25.12. When the user clicks the "Click Me" button, this application simply displays "Thank you for using WonderApp633!" in the text box, using this code:

```
Private Sub Button1_Click(ByVal sender As System.Object, _
    ByVal e As System.EventArgs) Handles Button1.Click
    TextBox1.Text = "Thank you for using WonderApp633!"
End Sub
```

That's all there is to the WonderApp application. To create the executable file to distribute, select the Build|Build menu item now, building WonderApp.exe, which is the executable file we'll actually deploy.

Now we're ready to create an installer file for WonderApp, which I'll call WonderApp633.msi. To do that, select the File|Add Project|New Project menu item, opening the Add New Project dialog you see in Figure 25.13. Select the "Setup and Deployment Projects" icon in the Project Types box, and the Setup Wizard icon in the Templates box, as you see in the figure. The Setup Wizard lets you create deployment projects in the easiest possible way (although you also can create deployment projects directly, using the deployment project templates you see in Figure 25.13).

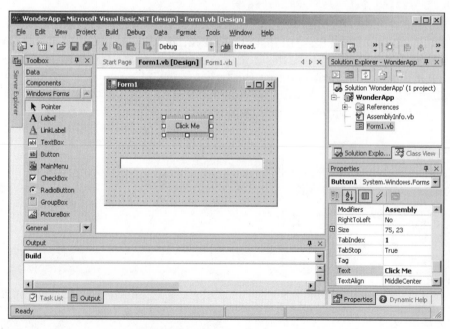

Figure 25.12   Designing WonderApp.

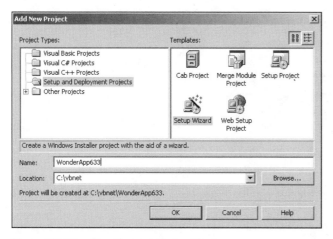

Figure 25.13   Creating a setup project.

Figure 25.14   The Setup Wizard, first pane.

Give the new project the name WonderApp633, as you see in Figure 25.13, and click OK to open the Setup Wizard, as you see in Figure 25.14.

Click Next to move to the second pane in the Wizard, as you see in Figure 25.15. As you can see in that figure, the Setup Wizard allows you to create different types of deployment projects, including those for Windows and Web applications.

In this case, select the "Create a setup for a Windows application" radio button, and click Next to open the third pane in the Setup Wizard, as you see in Figure 25.16. In this pane, you specify what you want to deploy. For example, you can deploy just the program itself, or the program and its source code, and so on. In

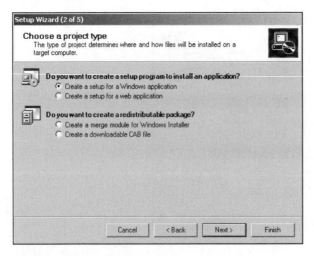

Figure 25.15   The Setup Wizard, second pane.

this case, let's deploy the works—everything in the WonderApp application—by selecting all items, as you see in Figure 25.16.

Then click Next to go on to the fourth pane of the Setup Wizard, as you see in Figure 25.17. In this pane, you can include other files to be deployed, such as readme.txt files, licensing agreements, and so on.

We won't include any other files with the deployment package here, so just click Next to bring up the fifth pane of the Setup Wizard, as you see in Figure 25.18. This is the last pane of the Setup Wizard, so to create the installer file we'll use, click Finish.

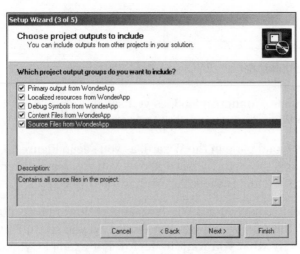

Figure 25.16   The Setup Wizard, third pane.

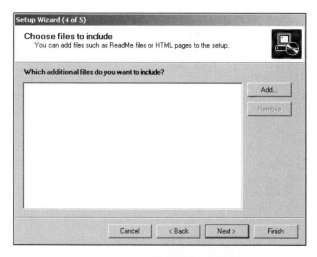

Figure 25.17   The Setup Wizard, fourth pane.

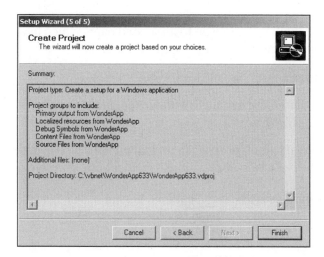

Figure 25.18   The Setup Wizard, fifth and final pane.

When the setup project is created, select the Build|Build Solution menu item; this creates WonderApp633.msi for us, and that's the file you use to deploy WonderApp. To deploy the application, you copy WonderApp633.msi to the target machine. Double-clicking that file opens the Windows installer, as you see in Figure 25.19.

TIP: *To set the name of the application that the Windows installer displays as it installs, select the setup project in the Solution Explorer and set its **ProductName** property. You also can set the **Manufacturer** property to the name of your company.*

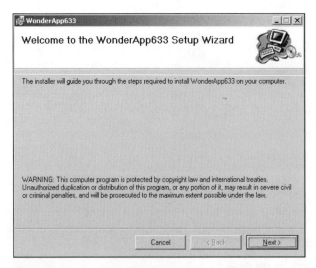

Figure 25.19   The Windows installer, first pane.

Click Next in the Windows installer to move on to its second pane, which lets you specify where to install the application, as you see in Figure 25.20.

Clicking Next installs the application, as you see in Figure 25.21.

Now you can double-click the newly installed WonderApp.exe to run it, as you see in Figure 25.22.

And that's it—we've created an installation package and installed it. The process is similar for creating .msi files for Web applications—in that case, you select the

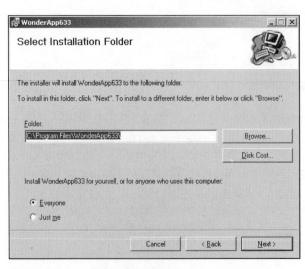

Figure 25.20   The Windows installer, second pane.

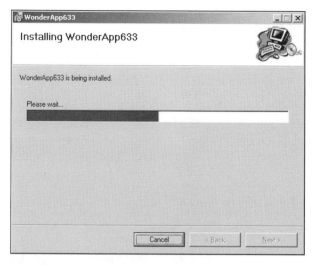

Figure 25.21   Installing an application.

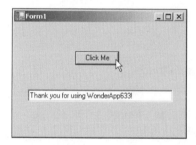

Figure 25.22   Running the newly installed application.

"Create a setup for a Web application" option in the second pane of the Setup Wizard instead of the "Create a setup for a Windows application" option.

And now I'll turn to the Immediate Solutions section of the chapter for more details.

Immediate Solutions

Using the **ServiceBase** Class

The **ServiceBase** class is the base class for a Windows service. Here is the inheritance hierarchy of this class:

```
Object
    MarshalByRefObject
        Component
            ServiceBase
```

You can find the more notable public properties of **ServiceBase** objects in Table 25.1 and their more notable protected methods in Table 25.2. (This class has no non-inherited events.)

Table 25.1   Noteworthy public properties of ServiceBase objects.

Property	Means
AutoLog	Specifies whether to record **Start**, **Stop**, **Pause**, and **Continue** commands in the event log.
CanPauseAndContinue	Gets/sets if you can pause and resume the service.
CanShutdown	Gets/sets if the service should be informed at system shutdown.
CanStop	Gets/sets if the service can be stopped.
EventLog	Gets an event log you can use to write to.
ServiceName	Gets/sets the name used to identify the service.

Table 25.2   Noteworthy protected methods of ServiceBase objects.

Method	Means
OnContinue	Executes when a service resumes after being paused.
OnPause	Executes when a service pauses.
OnPowerEvent	Executes when the computer's power status changes, as when notebooks go into suspended mode.
OnShutdown	Executes when the system is shutting down.
OnStart	Executes when the service starts.
OnStop	Executes when a service stops running.

Using the **EventLog** Class

The **EventLog** class supports access to Windows event logs from Windows services. Here is the inheritance hierarchy of this class:

```
Object
    MarshalByRefObject
        Component
            EventLog
```

You can find the more notable public class methods of **EventLog** in Table 25.3, the more notable public properties of **EventLog** objects in Table 25.4, their more notable methods in Table 25.5, and their more notable events in Table 25.6.

Table 25.3   Noteworthy public class (shared) methods of the EventLog class.

Method	Means
CreateEventSource	Enables an application to write event data to a log.
Delete	Removes a log.
DeleteEventSource	Removes an application's event source registration.
Exists	Indicates if a log exists.
GetEventLogs	Returns an array of event logs.
LogNameFromSourceName	Gets the name of the log a source is registered with.
SourceExists	Checks for a specific event source.
WriteEntry	Writes an entry in the log.

Table 25.4   Noteworthy public properties of EventLog objects.

Property	Means
EnableRaisingEvents	Gets/sets if the event log gets **EntryWritten** events.
Entries	Gets the contents of the log.
Log	Gets/sets the name of the log.
LogDisplayName	Gets the log's display name.
MachineName	Gets/sets the name of the log's computer.
Source	Gets/sets the source name to use when writing to the log.

Table 25.5   Noteworthy public methods of **EventLog** objects.

Method	Means
BeginInit	Begins the initialization operation of an event log.
Clear	Clears all entries from the log.
Close	Closes the log.
EndInit	Ends the initialization operation of an event log.
WriteEntry	Writes an entry in the event log.

Table 25.6   Noteworthy public events of **EventLog** objects.

Event	Means
EntryWritten	Occurs when data is written to an event log.

Using the **ServiceProcessInstaller** Class

ServiceProcessInstaller objects install the specific processes in a Windows service. Here is the inheritance hierarchy of this class:

```
Object
    MarshalByRefObject
        Component
            Installer
                ComponentInstaller
                    ServiceProcessInstaller
```

You can find the more notable public properties of objects of the **ServiceProcessInstaller** class in Table 25.7, their more notable methods in Table 25.8, and their more notable events in Table 25.9. Note that I'm including the properties, methods, and events inherited from the **Installer** and **ComponentInstaller** classes in these tables.

Table 25.7   Noteworthy public properties of **ServiceProcessInstaller** objects.

Property	Means
Account	Gets/sets the account type for this service.
Context	Gets/sets data about the installation.
HelpText	Gets help text for service options.
Installers	Gets the installers used.
Parent	Gets/sets the parent installer.
Password	Gets/sets the password for a user account.
Username	Gets/sets a user account.

Table 25.8   Noteworthy public methods of ServiceProcessInstaller objects.

Method	Means
Install	Writes service information to the registry.
Rollback	Rolls back service information written to the registry.
Uninstall	Overridden to remove an installation.

Table 25.9   Noteworthy public events of ServiceProcessInstaller objects.

Event	Means
AfterInstall	Occurs after the install.
AfterRollback	Occurs after the installations are rolled back.
AfterUninstall	Occurs after uninstallation operations.
BeforeInstall	Occurs before the **Install** method has run.
BeforeRollback	Occurs before the installers are rolled back.
BeforeUninstall	Occurs before uninstall operations.
Committed	Occurs after all the installers have committed their installations.
Committing	Occurs before the installers commit their installations.

Using the **ServiceInstaller** Class

ServiceInstaller objects install Windows services. Here is the inheritance hierarchy of this class:

```
Object
    MarshalByRefObject
        Component
            Installer
                ComponentInstaller
                    ServiceInstaller
```

You can find the more notable public properties of objects of the **Service Installer** class in Table 25.10, their more notable methods in Table 25.11, and their more notable events in Table 25.12. Note that I'm including the properties, methods, and events inherited from the **Installer** and **ComponentInstaller** classes in these tables.

Table 25.10   Noteworthy public properties of **ServiceInstaller** objects.

Property	Means
DisplayName	Holds the display name of the service.
HelpText	Gets the help text for the installers.
Installers	Gets the installers themselves.
Parent	Gets/sets the parent installer.
ServiceName	Holds the name used to identify this service.
ServicesDependedOn	Specifies the services that must be running to support this service.
StartType	Specifies when this service is started.

Table 25.11   Noteworthy public methods of **ServiceInstaller** objects.

Method	Means
Commit	When overridden, commits the **install** operation.
Install	Installs the service by writing service data to the registry.
Rollback	Rolls back data written to the registry.
Uninstall	Uninstalls the service.

Table 25.12   Noteworthy public events of **ServiceInstaller** objects.

Event	Means
AfterInstall	Occurs after the installers have run.
AfterRollback	Occurs after the installations are rolled back.
AfterUninstall	Occurs after all the installers finish their uninstallation operations.
BeforeInstall	Occurs before the each installer's **Install** method runs.
BeforeRollback	Occurs before the installers are rolled back.
BeforeUninstall	Occurs before the installers execute uninstall operations.
Committed	Occurs after all the installers commit installations.
Committing	Occurs before the installers commit installations.

Creating a Windows Service

You can create a new Windows service easily in Visual Basic—just use the File|New|Project menu item, select the Windows Service icon in the templates box, and click OK.

For example, we created a full working Windows service example, WindowsService, in the In Depth section of this chapter—see that section for the details. Here's the code for that Windows service, Service1.vb:

```vb
Imports System.ServiceProcess

Public Class Service1
    Inherits System.ServiceProcess.ServiceBase

#Region " Component Designer generated code "

    Public Sub New()
        MyBase.New()

        ' This call is required by the Component Designer.
        InitializeComponent()

        ' Add any initialization after the InitializeComponent() call
        If Not EventLog1.SourceExists("Source1") Then
            EventLog1.CreateEventSource("Source1", "NewLog1")
        End If
        EventLog1.Source = "Source1"

    End Sub

    'UserService overrides dispose to clean up the component list.
    Protected Overloads Overrides Sub Dispose(ByVal disposing As Boolean)
        If disposing Then
            If Not (components Is Nothing) Then
                components.Dispose()
            End If
        End If
        MyBase.Dispose(disposing)
    End Sub

    ' The main entry point for the process
    <MTAThread()> _
    Shared Sub Main()
        Dim ServicesToRun() As System.ServiceProcess.ServiceBase

        ' More than one NT Service may run within the same process. To add
        ' another service to this process, change the following line to
        ' create a second service object. For example,
        '
        '    ServicesToRun = New System.ServiceProcess.ServiceBase () {New
```

```vb
        ' Service1, New MySecondUserService}
        '
        ServicesToRun = New System.ServiceProcess.ServiceBase () _
            {New Service1}

        System.ServiceProcess.ServiceBase.Run(ServicesToRun)
    End Sub

    'Required by the Component Designer
    Private components As System.ComponentModel.IContainer

    ' NOTE: The following procedure is required by the Component Designer
    ' It can be modified using the Component Designer.
    ' Do not modify it using the code editor.
    Friend WithEvents EventLog1 As System.Diagnostics.EventLog
    <System.Diagnostics.DebuggerStepThrough()> Private Sub _
        InitializeComponent()
        Me.EventLog1 = New System.Diagnostics.EventLog()
        CType(Me.EventLog1, _
            System.ComponentModel.ISupportInitialize).BeginInit()
        '
        'EventLog1
        '
        Me.EventLog1.Log = "NewLog1"
        Me.EventLog1.Source = "Source1"
        '
        'Service1
        '
        Me.ServiceName = "Service1"
        CType(Me.EventLog1, _
            System.ComponentModel.ISupportInitialize).EndInit()

    End Sub

#End Region

    Protected Overrides Sub OnStart(ByVal args() As String)
        EventLog1.WriteEntry("Starting...")
    End Sub

    Protected Overrides Sub OnStop()
        EventLog1.WriteEntry("Stopping...")
    End Sub

End Class
```

TIP: *You also can add a notify icon for your Windows service to the taskbar in Windows—see "Creating Notify Icons and Using Icon Designers" in Chapter 8.*

Related solutions:	Found on page:
Using the **NotifyIcon** Class	368
Handling Notify Icon Events	370

Creating a Windows Service Installer

After you've created a Windows service, you need an installer. You can create one by clicking the "Add Installer" link, as we did in the WindowsService example in the In Depth section of this chapter. (This link is visible at bottom right in Figure 25.2.)

Here's the code for the installer in the WindowsService example, Project Installer.vb:

```
Imports System.ComponentModel
Imports System.Configuration.Install

<RunInstaller(True)> Public Class ProjectInstaller
    Inherits System.Configuration.Install.Installer

#Region " Component Designer generated code "

    Public Sub New()
        MyBase.New()

        'This call is required by the Component Designer.
        InitializeComponent()

        'Add any initialization after the InitializeComponent() call

    End Sub

    'Installer overrides dispose to clean up the component list.
    Protected Overloads Overrides Sub Dispose(ByVal _
        disposing As Boolean)
        If disposing Then
            If Not (components Is Nothing) Then
                components.Dispose()
            End If
```

```
          End If
          MyBase.Dispose(disposing)
      End Sub


      'Required by the Component Designer
      Private components As System.ComponentModel.IContainer

      'NOTE: The following procedure is required by the Component
      'Designer
      'It can be modified using the Component Designer.
      'Do not modify it using the code editor.
      Friend WithEvents ServiceProcessInstaller1 As _
          System.ServiceProcess.ServiceProcessInstaller
      Friend WithEvents ServiceInstaller1 As _
          System.ServiceProcess.ServiceInstaller
      <System.Diagnostics.DebuggerStepThrough()> Private Sub _
          InitializeComponent()
          Me.ServiceProcessInstaller1 = New _
              System.ServiceProcess.ServiceProcessInstaller()
          Me.ServiceInstaller1 = New _
              System.ServiceProcess.ServiceInstaller()
          '
          'ServiceProcessInstaller1
          '
          Me.ServiceProcessInstaller1.Account = _
              System.ServiceProcess.ServiceAccount.LocalSystem
          Me.ServiceProcessInstaller1.Password = Nothing
          Me.ServiceProcessInstaller1.Username = Nothing
          '
          'ServiceInstaller1
          '
          Me.ServiceInstaller1.ServiceName = "Service1"
          '
          'ProjectInstaller
          '
          Me.Installers.AddRange(New _
              System.Configuration.Install.Installer() _
              {Me.ServiceProcessInstaller1, Me.ServiceInstaller1})

      End Sub

  #End Region

  End Class
```

Using the **WebService** Class

The **WebService** class is the base class for Web services. Here is the inheritance hierarchy of this class:

```
Object
    MarshalByRefObject
        Component
            WebService
```

You can find the more notable public properties of objects of the **WebService** class in Table 25.13. (This class has no non-inherited methods or events.)

Table 25.13   Noteworthy public properties of *WebService* objects.

Property	Means
Application	Gets the HTTP application object for the current request.
Context	Gets the **HttpContext** object for the current request.
Server	Gets the **HttpServerUtility** object for the current request.
Session	Gets the **HttpSessionState** object for the current request.
User	Gets the current ASP.NET server user object.

Creating a Web Service

Creating a Web service is not difficult—just select the File|New|Project menu item, select the ASP.NET Web Service icon, and click OK. That creates a new Web service project, ready for use.

To illustrate, we created an entire Web service example operating as the middle tier of a distributed data application in the In Depth section of this chapter. For more details, see the discussion of that example, WebServices, in the In Depth section "Creating Web Services." Here's the code for the Web service we developed, Service1.asmx.vb:

```
Imports System.Web.Services

<WebService(Namespace := "http://tempuri.org/")> _
Public Class Service1
    Inherits System.Web.Services.WebService

#Region " Web Services Designer Generated Code "
```

```
Public Sub New()
    MyBase.New()

    'This call is required by the Web Services Designer.
    InitializeComponent()

    'Add your own initialization code after the
    'InitializeComponent() call

End Sub

'Required by the Web Services Designer
Private components As System.ComponentModel.IContainer

'NOTE: The following procedure is required by the Web Services Designer
'It can be modified using the Web Services Designer.
'Do not modify it using the code editor.
Friend WithEvents OleDbDataAdapter1 As _
    System.Data.OleDb.OleDbDataAdapter
Friend WithEvents OleDbSelectCommand1 As System.Data.OleDb.OleDbCommand
Friend WithEvents OleDbInsertCommand1 As System.Data.OleDb.OleDbCommand
Friend WithEvents OleDbUpdateCommand1 As System.Data.OleDb.OleDbCommand
Friend WithEvents OleDbDeleteCommand1 As System.Data.OleDb.OleDbCommand
Friend WithEvents OleDbConnection1 As System.Data.OleDb.OleDbConnection
<System.Diagnostics.DebuggerStepThrough()> Private Sub _
    InitializeComponent()
    Me.OleDbDataAdapter1 = New System.Data.OleDb.OleDbDataAdapter()
    Me.OleDbSelectCommand1 = New System.Data.OleDb.OleDbCommand()
    Me.OleDbInsertCommand1 = New System.Data.OleDb.OleDbCommand()
    Me.OleDbUpdateCommand1 = New System.Data.OleDb.OleDbCommand()
    Me.OleDbDeleteCommand1 = New System.Data.OleDb.OleDbCommand()
    Me.OleDbConnection1 = New System.Data.OleDb.OleDbConnection()
    '
    'OleDbDataAdapter1
    '
    Me.OleDbDataAdapter1.DeleteCommand = Me.OleDbDeleteCommand1
    Me.OleDbDataAdapter1.InsertCommand = Me.OleDbInsertCommand1
    Me.OleDbDataAdapter1.SelectCommand = Me.OleDbSelectCommand1
    Me.OleDbDataAdapter1.TableMappings.AddRange(New _
        System.Data.Common.DataTableMapping() {New _
        System.Data.Common.DataTableMapping("Table", "authors", New _
        System.Data.Common.DataColumnMapping() {New _
        System.Data.Common.DataColumnMapping("au_id", "au_id"), New _
        System.Data.Common.DataColumnMapping("au_lname", "au_lname"), _
        New System.Data.Common.DataColumnMapping("au_fname", _
```

```
        "au_fname"), _
        New System.Data.Common.DataColumnMapping("phone", _
        "phone"), New System.Data.Common.DataColumnMapping("address", _
        "address"), New System.Data.Common.DataColumnMapping("city", _
        "city"), New System.Data.Common.DataColumnMapping("state", _
        "state"), New System.Data.Common.DataColumnMapping("zip", _
        "zip"), New System.Data.Common.DataColumnMapping("contract", _
        "contract")})})
Me.OleDbDataAdapter1.UpdateCommand = Me.OleDbUpdateCommand1
'
'OleDbSelectCommand1
'
Me.OleDbSelectCommand1.CommandText = "SELECT au_id, au_lname, _
    au_fname, phone, address, city, state, zip, contract FROM" & _
" authors"
Me.OleDbSelectCommand1.Connection = Me.OleDbConnection1
'
'OleDbInsertCommand1
'
Me.OleDbInsertCommand1.CommandText = "INSERT INTO authors(au_id, _
    au_lname, au_fname, phone, address, city, state, zip, " & _
    "contract) VALUES (?, ?, ?, ?, ?, ?, ?, ?, ?); SELECT au_id, _
    au_lname, au_fname, " & _
    "phone, address, city, state, zip, contract FROM " & _
    authors WHERE (au_id = ?)"
Me.OleDbInsertCommand1.Connection = Me.OleDbConnection1
Me.OleDbInsertCommand1.Parameters.Add(New _
System.Data.OleDb.OleDbParameter("au_id", _
System.Data.OleDb.OleDbType.VarChar, 11, "au_id")) _
Me.OleDbInsertCommand1.Parameters.Add(New _
System.Data.OleDb.OleDbParameter("au_lname", _
System.Data.OleDb.OleDbType.VarChar, 40, "au_lname")) _
Me.OleDbInsertCommand1.Parameters.Add(New _
System.Data.OleDb.OleDbParameter("au_fname", _
System.Data.OleDb.OleDbType.VarChar, 20, "au_fname")) _
Me.OleDbInsertCommand1.Parameters.Add(New _
System.Data.OleDb.OleDbParameter("phone", _
System.Data.OleDb.OleDbType.VarChar, 12, "phone"))
Me.OleDbInsertCommand1.Parameters.Add(New _
System.Data.OleDb.OleDbParameter("address", _
System.Data.OleDb.OleDbType.VarChar, 40, "address"))
Me.OleDbInsertCommand1.Parameters.Add(New _
System.Data.OleDb.OleDbParameter("city", _
System.Data.OleDb.OleDbType.VarChar, 20, "city"))
Me.OleDbInsertCommand1.Parameters.Add(New _
```

```
        System.Data.OleDb.OleDbParameter("state", _
        System.Data.OleDb.OleDbType.VarChar, 2, "state"))
        Me.OleDbInsertCommand1.Parameters.Add(New _
        System.Data.OleDb.OleDbParameter("zip", _
        System.Data.OleDb.OleDbType.VarChar, 5, "zip"))
        Me.OleDbInsertCommand1.Parameters.Add(New _
        System.Data.OleDb.OleDbParameter("contract", _
        System.Data.OleDb.OleDbType.Boolean, 1, "contract"))
        Me.OleDbInsertCommand1.Parameters.Add(New _
        System.Data.OleDb.OleDbParameter("Select_au_id", _
        System.Data.OleDb.OleDbType.VarChar, 11, "au_id"))
        '
        'OleDbUpdateCommand1
        '
        Me.OleDbUpdateCommand1.CommandText = _
        "UPDATE authors SET au_id = ?, au_lname = ?, " & _
        "au_fname = ?, phone = ?, address = ?," & _
        " city = ?, state = ?, zip = ?, contract = ? " & _
        "WHERE (au_id = ?) AND (address = ? O" & _
        "R ? IS NULL AND address IS NULL) AND (au_fname = ?) " & _
        "AND (au_lname = ?) AND (city" & _
        " = ? OR ? IS NULL AND city IS NULL) AND (contract = ?) " & _
        "AND (phone = ?) AND (stat" & _
        "e = ? OR ? IS NULL AND state IS NULL) AND (zip = ? OR " & _
        "? IS NULL AND zip IS NULL)" & _
        "; SELECT au_id, au_lname, au_fname, phone, address, " & _
        "city, state, zip, contract F" & _
        "ROM authors WHERE (au_id = ?)"
        Me.OleDbUpdateCommand1.Connection = Me.OleDbConnection1
        Me.OleDbUpdateCommand1.Parameters.Add(New _
        System.Data.OleDb.OleDbParameter("au_id", _
        System.Data.OleDb.OleDbType.VarChar, 11, "au_id")) _
        Me.OleDbUpdateCommand1.Parameters.Add(New _
        System.Data.OleDb.OleDbParameter("au_lname", _
        System.Data.OleDb.OleDbType.VarChar, 40, "au_lname"))
        Me.OleDbUpdateCommand1.Parameters.Add(New _
        System.Data.OleDb.OleDbParameter("au_fname", _
        System.Data.OleDb.OleDbType.VarChar, 20, "au_fname"))
        Me.OleDbUpdateCommand1.Parameters.Add(New _
        System.Data.OleDb.OleDbParameter("phone", _
        System.Data.OleDb.OleDbType.VarChar, 12, "phone"))
        Me.OleDbUpdateCommand1.Parameters.Add(New _
        System.Data.OleDb.OleDbParameter("address", _
        System.Data.OleDb.OleDbType.VarChar, 40, "address"))
        Me.OleDbUpdateCommand1.Parameters.Add(New _
```

```
            System.Data.OleDb.OleDbParameter("city", _
            System.Data.OleDb.OleDbType.VarChar, 20, "city"))
        Me.OleDbUpdateCommand1.Parameters.Add(New _
            System.Data.OleDb.OleDbParameter("state", _
            System.Data.OleDb.OleDbType.VarChar, 2, "state"))
        Me.OleDbUpdateCommand1.Parameters.Add(New _
            System.Data.OleDb.OleDbParameter("zip", _
            System.Data.OleDb.OleDbType.VarChar, 5, "zip"))
        Me.OleDbUpdateCommand1.Parameters.Add(New _
            System.Data.OleDb.OleDbParameter("contract", _
            System.Data.OleDb.OleDbType.Boolean, 1, "contract"))
        Me.OleDbUpdateCommand1.Parameters.Add(New _
            System.Data.OleDb.OleDbParameter("Original_au_id", _
            System.Data.OleDb.OleDbType.VarChar, 11, _
            System.Data.ParameterDirection.Input, False, _
            CType(0, Byte), CType(0, Byte), "au_id", _
            System.Data.DataRowVersion.Original, Nothing))
        Me.OleDbUpdateCommand1.Parameters.Add(New _
            System.Data.OleDb.OleDbParameter("Original_address", _
            System.Data.OleDb.OleDbType.VarChar, 40, _
            System.Data.ParameterDirection.Input, False, _
            CType(0, Byte), CType(0, Byte), "address", _
            System.Data.DataRowVersion.Original, Nothing))
        Me.OleDbUpdateCommand1.Parameters.Add(New _
            System.Data.OleDb.OleDbParameter("Original_address1", _
            System.Data.OleDb.OleDbType.VarChar, 40, _
            System.Data.ParameterDirection.Input, False, _
            CType(0, Byte), CType(0, Byte), "address", _
            System.Data.DataRowVersion.Original, Nothing))
        Me.OleDbUpdateCommand1.Parameters.Add(New _
            System.Data.OleDb.OleDbParameter("Original_au_fname", _
            System.Data.OleDb.OleDbType.VarChar, 20, _
            System.Data.ParameterDirection.Input, False, _
            CType(0, Byte), CType(0, Byte), "au_fname", _
            System.Data.DataRowVersion.Original, Nothing))
        Me.OleDbUpdateCommand1.Parameters.Add(New _
            System.Data.OleDb.OleDbParameter("Original_au_lname", _
            System.Data.OleDb.OleDbType.VarChar, 40, _
            System.Data.ParameterDirection.Input, False, _
            CType(0, Byte), CType(0, Byte), "au_lname", _
            System.Data.DataRowVersion.Original, Nothing))
        Me.OleDbUpdateCommand1.Parameters.Add(New _
            System.Data.OleDb.OleDbParameter("Original_city", _
            System.Data.OleDb.OleDbType.VarChar, 20, _
            System.Data.ParameterDirection.Input, False, _
```

```
CType(0, Byte), CType(0, Byte), "city", _
System.Data.DataRowVersion.Original, Nothing))
Me.OleDbUpdateCommand1.Parameters.Add(New _
System.Data.OleDb.OleDbParameter("Original_city1", _
System.Data.OleDb.OleDbType.VarChar, 20, _
System.Data.ParameterDirection.Input, False, _
CType(0, Byte), CType(0, Byte), "city", _
System.Data.DataRowVersion.Original, Nothing))
Me.OleDbUpdateCommand1.Parameters.Add(New _
System.Data.OleDb.OleDbParameter("Original_contract", _
System.Data.OleDb.OleDbType.Boolean, 1, _
System.Data.ParameterDirection.Input, False, _
CType(0, Byte), CType(0, Byte), "contract", _
System.Data.DataRowVersion.Original, Nothing))
Me.OleDbUpdateCommand1.Parameters.Add(New _
System.Data.OleDb.OleDbParameter("Original_phone", _
System.Data.OleDb.OleDbType.VarChar, 12, _
System.Data.ParameterDirection.Input, False, _
CType(0, Byte), CType(0, Byte), "phone", _
System.Data.DataRowVersion.Original, Nothing))
Me.OleDbUpdateCommand1.Parameters.Add(New _
System.Data.OleDb.OleDbParameter("Original_state", _
System.Data.OleDb.OleDbType.VarChar, 2, _
System.Data.ParameterDirection.Input, False, _
CType(0, Byte), CType(0, Byte), "state", _
System.Data.DataRowVersion.Original, Nothing))
Me.OleDbUpdateCommand1.Parameters.Add(New _
System.Data.OleDb.OleDbParameter("Original_state1", _
System.Data.OleDb.OleDbType.VarChar, 2, _
System.Data.ParameterDirection.Input, False, _
CType(0, Byte), CType(0, Byte), "state", _
System.Data.DataRowVersion.Original, Nothing))
Me.OleDbUpdateCommand1.Parameters.Add(New _
System.Data.OleDb.OleDbParameter("Original_zip", _
System.Data.OleDb.OleDbType.VarChar, 5, _
System.Data.ParameterDirection.Input, False, _
CType(0, Byte), CType(0, Byte), "zip", _
System.Data.DataRowVersion.Original, Nothing))
Me.OleDbUpdateCommand1.Parameters.Add(New _
System.Data.OleDb.OleDbParameter("Original_zip1", _
System.Data.OleDb.OleDbType.VarChar, 5, _
System.Data.ParameterDirection.Input, False, _
CType(0, Byte), CType(0, Byte), "zip", _
System.Data.DataRowVersion.Original, Nothing))
Me.OleDbUpdateCommand1.Parameters.Add(New _
```

```
System.Data.OleDb.OleDbParameter("Select_au_id", _
System.Data.OleDb.OleDbType.VarChar, 11, "au_id"))
'
'OleDbDeleteCommand1
'
Me.OleDbDeleteCommand1.CommandText = _
"DELETE FROM authors WHERE (au_id = ?) AND _
(address = ? OR ? IS NULL AND address I" & _
"S NULL) AND (au_fname = ?) AND " & _
"(au_lname = ?) AND (city = ? OR ? IS NULL AND cit" & _
"y IS NULL) AND (contract = ?) AND " & _
"(phone = ?) AND (state = ? OR ? IS NULL AND st" & _
"ate IS NULL) AND (zip = ? OR ? IS NULL AND zip IS NULL)"
Me.OleDbDeleteCommand1.Connection = Me.OleDbConnection1
Me.OleDbDeleteCommand1.Parameters.Add(New _
System.Data.OleDb.OleDbParameter("Original_au_id", _
System.Data.OleDb.OleDbType.VarChar, 11, _
System.Data.ParameterDirection.Input, False, _
CType(0, Byte), CType(0, Byte), "au_id", _
System.Data.DataRowVersion.Original, Nothing))
Me.OleDbDeleteCommand1.Parameters.Add(New _
System.Data.OleDb.OleDbParameter("Original_address", _
System.Data.OleDb.OleDbType.VarChar, 40, _
System.Data.ParameterDirection.Input, False, _
CType(0, Byte), CType(0, Byte), "address", _
System.Data.DataRowVersion.Original, Nothing))
Me.OleDbDeleteCommand1.Parameters.Add(New _
System.Data.OleDb.OleDbParameter("Original_address1", _
System.Data.OleDb.OleDbType.VarChar, 40, _
System.Data.ParameterDirection.Input, False, _
CType(0, Byte), CType(0, Byte), "address", _
System.Data.DataRowVersion.Original, Nothing))
Me.OleDbDeleteCommand1.Parameters.Add(New _
System.Data.OleDb.OleDbParameter("Original_au_fname", _
System.Data.OleDb.OleDbType.VarChar, 20, _
System.Data.ParameterDirection.Input, False, _
CType(0, Byte), CType(0, Byte), "au_fname", _
System.Data.DataRowVersion.Original, Nothing))
Me.OleDbDeleteCommand1.Parameters.Add(New _
System.Data.OleDb.OleDbParameter("Original_au_lname", _
System.Data.OleDb.OleDbType.VarChar, 40, _
System.Data.ParameterDirection.Input, False, _
CType(0, Byte), CType(0, Byte), "au_lname", _
System.Data.DataRowVersion.Original, Nothing))
Me.OleDbDeleteCommand1.Parameters.Add(New _
System.Data.OleDb.OleDbParameter("Original_city", _
```

```
System.Data.OleDb.OleDbType.VarChar, 20, _
System.Data.ParameterDirection.Input, False, _
CType(0, Byte), CType(0, Byte), "city", _
System.Data.DataRowVersion.Original, Nothing))
Me.OleDbDeleteCommand1.Parameters.Add(New _
System.Data.OleDb.OleDbParameter("Original_city1", _
System.Data.OleDb.OleDbType.VarChar, 20, _
System.Data.ParameterDirection.Input, False, _
CType(0, Byte), CType(0, Byte), "city", _
System.Data.DataRowVersion.Original, Nothing))
Me.OleDbDeleteCommand1.Parameters.Add(New _
System.Data.OleDb.OleDbParameter("Original_contract", _
System.Data.OleDb.OleDbType.Boolean, 1, _
System.Data.ParameterDirection.Input, False, _
CType(0, Byte), CType(0, Byte), "contract", _
System.Data.DataRowVersion.Original, Nothing))
Me.OleDbDeleteCommand1.Parameters.Add(New _
System.Data.OleDb.OleDbParameter("Original_phone", _
System.Data.OleDb.OleDbType.VarChar, 12, _
System.Data.ParameterDirection.Input, False, _
CType(0, Byte), CType(0, Byte), "phone", _
System.Data.DataRowVersion.Original, Nothing))
Me.OleDbDeleteCommand1.Parameters.Add(New _
System.Data.OleDb.OleDbParameter("Original_state", _
System.Data.OleDb.OleDbType.VarChar, 2, _
System.Data.ParameterDirection.Input, False, _
CType(0, Byte), CType(0, Byte), "state", _
System.Data.DataRowVersion.Original, Nothing))
Me.OleDbDeleteCommand1.Parameters.Add(New _
System.Data.OleDb.OleDbParameter("Original_state1", _
System.Data.OleDb.OleDbType.VarChar, 2, _
System.Data.ParameterDirection.Input, False, _
CType(0, Byte), CType(0, Byte), "state", _
System.Data.DataRowVersion.Original, Nothing))
Me.OleDbDeleteCommand1.Parameters.Add(New _
System.Data.OleDb.OleDbParameter("Original_zip", _
System.Data.OleDb.OleDbType.VarChar, 5, _
System.Data.ParameterDirection.Input, False, _
CType(0, Byte), CType(0, Byte), "zip", _
System.Data.DataRowVersion.Original, Nothing))
Me.OleDbDeleteCommand1.Parameters.Add(New _
System.Data.OleDb.OleDbParameter("Original_zip1", _
System.Data.OleDb.OleDbType.VarChar, 5, _
System.Data.ParameterDirection.Input, _
False, CType(0, Byte), CType(0, Byte), "zip", _
```

```
            System.Data.DataRowVersion.Original, Nothing))
            '
            'OleDbConnection1
            '
            Me.OleDbConnection1.ConnectionString =
            "Provider=SQLOLEDB.1;Integrated Security=" & _
            "SSPI;Persist Security " & _
            "Info=False;Initial " & _
            "Catalog=pubs;Use Procedure for Prepare=1;Auto " & _
            "Translate=True;Packet Size=4096;Wo" & _
            "rkstation ID=STEVE;Use Encryption for Data=False;Tag " & _
            "with column collation when " & _
            "possible=False"


        End Sub

        Protected Overloads Overrides Sub Dispose(ByVal disposing As Boolean)
            'CODEGEN: This procedure is required by the Web Services Designer
            'Do not modify it using the code editor.
            If disposing Then
                If Not (components Is Nothing) Then
                    components.Dispose()
                End If
            End If
            MyBase.Dispose(disposing)
        End Sub

#End Region

        ' WEB SERVICE EXAMPLE
        ' The HelloWorld() example service returns the string Hello World.
        ' To build, uncomment the following lines then save and
        ' build the project.
        ' To test this web service, ensure that the .asmx file is
        ' the start page
        ' and press F5.
        '
        '<WebMethod()> Public Function HelloWorld() As String
        '       HelloWorld = "Hello World"
        ' End Function

        <WebMethod(Description:="Gets the authors")> Public _
        Function GetAuthors() As DataSet1
            Dim AuthorsTable As New DataSet1()
            OleDbDataAdapter1.Fill(AuthorsTable)
```

```
                    Return AuthorsTable
        End Function


        <WebMethod(Description:="Updates the authors")> Public _
        Function UpdateAuthors(ByVal _
        Changes As DataSet1) As DataSet1
            If (Changes Is Nothing) Then
                Return Nothing
            Else
                OleDbDataAdapter1.Update(Changes)
                Return Changes
            End If
        End Function


End Class
```

Using a Web Service

To make use of a Web service, you have to add a Web reference to your application. We did that in the WebServWindowsApplication project in the In Depth section of this chapter; see that discussion for all the details. Here is the code for the WebServWindowsApplication application, Form1.vb:

```
Public Class Form1
        Inherits System.Windows.Forms.Form

#Region " Windows Form Designer generated code "

        Public Sub New()
            MyBase.New()

            'This call is required by the Windows Form Designer.
            InitializeComponent()

            'Add any initialization after the InitializeComponent() call

        End Sub

        'Form overrides dispose to clean up the component list.
        Protected Overloads Overrides Sub Dispose(ByVal disposing As Boolean)
            If disposing Then
                If Not (components Is Nothing) Then
                    components.Dispose()
```

```
        End If
    End If
    MyBase.Dispose(disposing)
End Sub


'Required by the Windows Form Designer
Private components As System.ComponentModel.IContainer

'NOTE: The following procedure is required by the Windows Form Designer
'It can be modified using the Windows Form Designer.
'Do not modify it using the code editor.
Friend WithEvents DataGrid1 As System.Windows.Forms.DataGrid
Friend WithEvents DataSet11 _
    As WebServWindowsApplication.localhost.DataSet1
Friend WithEvents Button1 As System.Windows.Forms.Button
Friend WithEvents Button2 As System.Windows.Forms.Button
<System.Diagnostics.DebuggerStepThrough()> Private Sub _
    InitializeComponent()
    Me.DataGrid1 = New System.Windows.Forms.DataGrid()
    Me.DataSet11 = New WebServWindowsApplication.localhost.DataSet1()
    Me.Button1 = New System.Windows.Forms.Button()
    Me.Button2 = New System.Windows.Forms.Button()
    CType(Me.DataGrid1, _
        System.ComponentModel.ISupportInitialize).BeginInit()
    CType(Me.DataSet11, _
        System.ComponentModel.ISupportInitialize).BeginInit()
    Me.SuspendLayout()
    '
    'DataGrid1
    '
    Me.DataGrid1.DataMember = "authors"
    Me.DataGrid1.DataSource = Me.DataSet11
    Me.DataGrid1.HeaderForeColor = _
        System.Drawing.SystemColors.ControlText
    Me.DataGrid1.Location = New System.Drawing.Point(16, 56)
    Me.DataGrid1.Name = "DataGrid1"
    Me.DataGrid1.Size = New System.Drawing.Size(264, 176)
    Me.DataGrid1.TabIndex = 0
    '
    'DataSet11
    '
    Me.DataSet11.DataSetName = "DataSet1"
    Me.DataSet11.Locale = New System.Globalization.CultureInfo("en-US")
    Me.DataSet11.Namespace = "http://www.tempuri.org/DataSet1.xsd"
    '
    'Button1
    '
```

```
        Me.Button1.Location = New System.Drawing.Point(16, 16)
        Me.Button1.Name = "Button1"
        Me.Button1.Size = New System.Drawing.Size(96, 23)
        Me.Button1.TabIndex = 1
        Me.Button1.Text = "Get Data"
        '
        'Button2
        '
        Me.Button2.Location = New System.Drawing.Point(184, 16)
        Me.Button2.Name = "Button2"
        Me.Button2.Size = New System.Drawing.Size(96, 23)
        Me.Button2.TabIndex = 2
        Me.Button2.Text = "Update Data"
        '
        'Form1
        '
        Me.AutoScaleBaseSize = New System.Drawing.Size(5, 13)
        Me.ClientSize = New System.Drawing.Size(292, 253)
        Me.Controls.AddRange(New System.Windows.Forms.Control() _
            {Me.Button2, Me.Button1, Me.DataGrid1})
        Me.Name = "Form1"
        Me.Text = "Form1"
        CType(Me.DataGrid1, _
            System.ComponentModel.ISupportInitialize).EndInit()
        CType(Me.DataSet11, _
            System.ComponentModel.ISupportInitialize).EndInit()
        Me.ResumeLayout(False)

    End Sub

#End Region

    Private Sub Button1_Click(ByVal sender As System.Object, _
        ByVal e As System.EventArgs) Handles Button1.Click
        Dim WebServ As New WebServWindowsApplication.localhost.Service1()
        DataSet11.Merge(WebServ.GetAuthors())
    End Sub


    Private Sub Button2_Click(ByVal sender As System.Object, _
        ByVal e As System.EventArgs) Handles Button2.Click
        If DataSet11.HasChanges() Then
            Dim WebServ As New _
                WebServWindowsApplication.localhost.Service1()
            Dim Changes As New _
                WebServWindowsApplication.localhost.DataSet1()
```

```
            Changes.Merge(DataSet11.GetChanges())
            DataSet11.Merge(WebServ.UpdateAuthors(Changes))
        End If
    End Sub
End Class
```

Deploying Applications

To create a deployment package for Windows and Web applications, you can use a setup project. All you have to do is to add such a project to a solution to create a setup package. For example, in the In Depth section of this chapter, we used the Setup Wizard to create a Microsoft Windows Installer (.msi) file for an application named WonderApp.

To install this application, you just double-click the .msi file to start the Windows Installer, as we did in the example in this chapter. For all the details, see the discussion of this example in the In Depth section of this chapter.

And That's It!

We've come far in this book, covering Visual Basic .NET from the very beginning up to some advanced topics—Web user controls, distributed data applications, Windows services, and more. We've added hundreds of techniques and skills to our programming arsenal. We've seen many examples at work, showing us what Visual Basic .NET has to offer. I hope that you've enjoyed reading this book as much as I've enjoyed writing it; all that remains is to put all this to work for yourself. *Happy Programming!*

Index

S

What's On The CD-ROM

The *Visual Basic .NET Black Book*'s companion CD-ROM contains elements specifically selected to enhance the usefulness of this book, including:

- *The .NET SDK*—The SDK features:
  - The complete CLR class library
  - The most current version of the command-line C# compiler
  - Complete debugging libraries and symbol files
  - Documentation for the .NET class libraries
  - Complete example applications ready to compile and run
  - Up-to-date documentation for the .NET system

Note: This program was reproduced by The Coriolis Group under a special arrangement with Microsoft Corporation. For this reason, The Coriolis Group is responsible for the product warranty and for support. If your diskette is defective, please return it to The Coriolis Group, which will arrange for its replacement. PLEASE DO NOT RETURN IT TO MICROSOFT CORPORATION. Any product support will be provided, if at all, by The Coriolis Group. PLEASE DO NOT CONTACT MICROSOFT CORPORATION FOR PRODUCT SUPPORT. End users of this Microsoft program shall not be considered "registered owners" of a Microsoft product and therefore shall not be eligible for upgrades, promotions or other benefits available to "registered owners" of Microsoft products.

Please note that Coriolis is providing the .NET SDK under license from Microsoft Corporation. While we are happy to assist you with defective, damaged or unusable CDs, we are unable to address any technical or product support issues associated with the Microsoft SDK.

- *The sample code used throughout this book*
- *An entire HTML 4.01 reference, htmlref.html*

System Requirements

Software

- You must be running Visual Basic .NET.
- To run the database examples, you should have access to a version of SQL Server supported by Visual Basic .NET, such as SQL Server 2000.
- To run the Web application and service examples, you should have access to a Web server running Microsoft Internet Information Server (IIS) that has the .NET framework installed. IIS can be installed on the same machine on which you're running Visual Basic .NET, and comes with some operating systems, such as Windows 2000 Server and Windows 2000 Professional (although IIS must be installed from the Windows CDs if you have Windows 2000 Professional).
- Your operating system must be Windows ME, Windows NT 4, Windows 2000, or Windows XP.
- You must have Internet Explorer 5.5 or higher to view some of the newer documentation.

Hardware

- An Intel (or equivalent) Pentium 300MHz processor is the minimum platform required; an Intel (or equivalent) Pentium 500MHz processor is recommended.
- 64MB of RAM is the minimum requirement. 128MB is the minimum amount you should consider.
- The .NET CLR requires approximately 200MB of disk storage space.
- A color monitor (256 colors) is recommended.